# A GRAMMAR OF POLITICS

# A GRAMMAR OF POLITICS

HAROLD J. LASKI
PROFESSOR OF POLITICAL SCIENCE
IN THE UNIVERSITY OF LONDON

ANAMIKA PUBLISHERS & DISTRIBUTORS (P) LTD.
4697/3, 21A, Ansari Road, Daryaganj, New Delhi 110002
Phones: 011-23281655, 011-43708938
E-mail: anamikapublishers@yahoo.co.in

*Edition 2026*



ISBN 978-81-7975-361-3

PRINTED IN INDIA

Published by Anamika Publishers & Distributors (P) Ltd., 4697/3, 21A, Ansari Road, Daryaganj, New Delhi 110002. Typeset by Shivani Computers, Delhi 110093 and Printed at Vikas Computer & Printers, Tronica City, Ghaziabad

*To*

*The London School of Economics and Political Science*

*and to*

*Sidney and Beatrice Webb*

*Its Founders*

For freedom we know is a thing that we have to conquer afresh for ourselves every day like love; and we are always losing freedom just as we are always losing love because after each victory, we think we can now settle down and enjoy it without further struggle.... The battle of freedom is never done, and the field never quiet.

HENRY W. NEVINSON
*Essays in Freedom*, p. xvi

The great question is to discover, not what governments prescribe, but what they ought to prescribe; for no prescription is valid against the conscience of mankind.

LORD ACTON
*History of Freedom*, p. 24

# Contents

# Preface to the Fourth Edition

I have taken advantage of a reprint of this book to add a new introductory chapter which seeks to survey developments in doctrine since 1925. Otherwise the book remains unchanged.

November 1, 1937 H.J.L.

# Preface to the Third Edition

In the nine years that have passed since the publication of this book little has occurred which seems to me to call for any change in its essential doctrine. Indeed, time has, I think, reinforced rather than diminished the truth of the central principles it sought to lay down.

The necessarily federal character of society; the incompatibility of the sovereign State with that economic world-order so painfully struggling to be born; the antithesis between individual property rights in the essential means of production and the fulfilment of the democratic idea; the thesis that liberty is a concept devoid of real meaning except in the context of equality; the refusal to regard law as valid merely in terms of the formal authority from which it emanates; the argument that in any society, even when based on equal and universal suffrage, the existence of serious economic inequalities biases the incidence of government in favour of the rich; all these seem to me to have received explicit confirmation from the events of the last decade.

For the interpretation of this period is bound to proceed upon two assumptions.

1. It is clear that Fascism, in its various national forms, is simply the expedient adopted by capitalism in distress to defeat the democratic political foundation with which it could be successfully linked in its period of creative expansion. Democratic institutions are, as Tocqueville insisted a century ago, inseparably associated with the drive towards economic equality; and when, as now, that drive encounters an epoch of economic decline, the democratic institutions are attacked in order that the owners of property may be safeguarded against the consequences of their

operation. Only in this way can we explain the widespread attack on principles like freedom of speech, due process in political offences, (so remarkably illustrated by Hitlerite legislation and activities), and the grave attack on the right of labour to strike. Wherever the movement of democratic opinion seeks to revise the traditional foundations of economic individualism, the owners of property seek to change the system which makes that movement possible. The survival of political democracy today is, all over the world, definitely impossible unless it can conquer the central citadel of economic power. There cannot, in a word, be democracy unless there is socialism. That does not mean the necessary victory of democracy. Its expansion in the nineteenth century into a world-ideal now appears, in the perspective of post-war events, to have been simply a function of capitalism in prosperity; with the eclipse of capitalism it is not improbable that civilisation may have to pass through an age of dictatorships which, whatever their formal professions, will, in fact, simply seek to inhibit the emergence of egalitarian institutions for the benefit of the invested interests.

2. It is clear, also, that capitalism in distress makes impossible the effective operation of international institutions; it is, therefore, fatal to the creative functioning of the League of Nations. For capitalism (though in many aspects itself international) is organised on a national basis; and, since this is the case, the owners of capital in each national community utilise the framework of State power for their protection. Since capitalism forces them to press ever more strongly to the capture of foreign markets the State largely becomes for them a means of protecting and extending their investments abroad. The outcome of this tendency is the clash of competing economic imperialisms which arm themselves to the teeth to secure their gains. Fear, suspicion and hatred are born of this atmosphere; the sovereign State will not, in these terms, be persuaded to submit its will to a power outside itself. That is what is meant by failures like that of the World Economic Conference in 1933 and the Disarmament Conference in 1934. The interest of the world community has to give way before the interests of powerful States protecting their national capitalists in some special advantage they propose either to maintain or secure. This is the history, for example, of the Japanese adventure in Manchuria; Japan has preferred to sacrifice the hope of peace and international security to the imperial ambitions of her governing class. Capitalism, in a word, is rooted in a system which makes power the criterion of right and war the ultimate expression of power.

> No reconciliation is possible between its necessary policies and the idea of a world-community founded upon the sovereign State's surrender of its right to be judge in its own cause.

A considerable literature upon these themes has appeared since the first edition of this book. Here I would like only to draw attention to a few works which seem to me of special significance. Mr. H.N. Brailsford's *Property or Peace* (London, 1934), Dr. H. Lauterpacht's *The Function of Law in an International Community* (London, 1933), Professor R.H. Tawney's *Equality* (1931) have all cast a brilliant light upon fundamental political questions. They do not stand alone. The work of Gurvitch in France; of Kelsen, Verdross and Kunz in Vienna; of the late Herman Heller in Germany, have been of profound significance. Nor is it unimportant to emphasise the changing temper in English juristic thinking which seems to portend the coming of a new epoch of legal reform. In this context the work of my friend and colleague Dr. W.I. Jennings, and especially his *Law and the Constitution* (London, 1933), marks a decisive change in the legal approach to fundamental problems.

HAROLD J. LASKI

London
May 18, 1934

# Preface to the Second Edition

It is four years since this book was first printed; and the time has not, I think, yet come when I dare venture upon any drastic revision. But I have added some notes, chiefly of a bibliographical character, where they seemed likely to be helpful.

On two definite points I have changed my mind. In 1925 I thought that liberty could most usefully be regarded as more than a negative thing. I am now convinced that this was a mistake, and that the old view of it as an absence of restraint can alone safeguard the personality of the citizen. I have taken advantage of an invitation from Brown University to deliver the Colver Lectures, there to work out afresh and in greater detail than is here possible the whole problem, in a book entitled *Liberty in the Democratic State,* to be published in the spring of 1930.

The last chapter, in earlier impressions, spoke of the League of Nations as a superstate (p. 588). This was, of course, an error; and I have accordingly excised it. Further experience of the League at work, and especially, discussion with my friends Professor W.E. Rappard, Dr. H. Lauterpacht, and Mr. K. Zilliacus, have convinced me that the grave problems involved can only be thoroughly understood by a reconstruction of the philosophy of international law. I have been working at this problem for the last few years; and I hope within a reasonable time to be able to publish the results. Meanwhile, I may perhaps venture the remark that the reader who seeks to grasp the implications of Dr. Lauterpacht's brilliant *Private Law Analogies in International Law* (1927) and Dr. A. Verdross's *Die Einheit des Rechtlichen Weltbildes* (1923) will see in what direction the debate is tending.

Despite the demand of the Mond-Turner Conference (1929) for a National Industrial Council I remain unconvinced, especially in the light of further German evidence, that it would serve any useful purpose. I have accordingly left unchanged the argument at pp. 72 f. and 83 f. which deals with the matter.

The kindness with which this book has been received, not merely in England, but also in Germany and America, has been far greater than I could ever have dared to hope; I only wish it were more worthy of the friends it has been fortunate enough to make. His death impels me to add how much it owes to the friendship of Lord Haldane; there are few of the outstanding problems of which it treats of which the discussion does not bear the impress of his kindly wisdom and affectionate generosity.

London H.J.L.
October 15, 1929

## Preface to the First Edition

This volume completes an effort, begun in 1915, to construct a theory of the place of the State in the great society. Earlier volumes (*The Problem of Sovereignty*, 1917; *Authority in the Modern State*, 1919; *The Foundations of Sovereignty*, 1921) were either mainly critical or intended to discuss somewhat technical issues in political philosophy. The present book is more positive and general, since it attempts to outline the institutions which my researches have suggested as desirable. I have sought, so far as I could, to discuss the objections of those who criticised the earlier volumes; and I am anxious to note my obligations to the generosity with which they have been received. I am particularly indebted, in America to Professors M.R. Cohen, W.J. Shephered and F.W. Coker, and in England to Mr. L.S. Woolf, Mr. Bertrand Russell and an (to me) unknown writer in *The Times Literary Supplement,* for indicating difficulties I ought to analyse. If I have not always accepted their views, they will not, I am sure, attribute differences to obstinacy, but to genuine disagreement. I have done my best to learn better ways.

Of one great gap in the volume I ought to warn the reader at the outset. I have said nothing in this book about agriculture and the land problems. That is because I know nothing directly of either; and it has seemed to me better frankly to confess ignorance than to construct, out of books, a paper scheme inevitably unrelated to experience.

My book owes an immense debt to friends. Among my colleagues, Professors L.T. Hobhouse and Graham Wallas, Mr. M. Ginsberg and Mr. R. H. Tawney, both by their books and in conversation, have been endlessly helpful; and, of others, I should like especially to thank Lord Haldane, Mr. Justice Holmes, Dr. Josef Redlich, Professor Felix Frankfurter and Dean Pound.

Chapter Eight was originally delivered as lectures at Magdalene College, Cambridge; and it is a special pleasure to an Oxford man to place on record his sense of the gracious hospitality dispensed there by the Master and Fellows.

My wife has helped me at every state of the book; and she will, I hope, accept it as an apology for long hours of silence.

The London School of Economics
and Political Science

H.J.L.

## Preface to the Second Impression

In the few months that have passed since this book was published, there has been neither time nor opportunity to make any substantial alterations. But I may note that the Committee on Civil Research, created by Mr. Baldwin while the book was in the press, follows almost precisely the model here (p. 373) suggested; while the Food Council, under the able chairmanship of Lord Bradbury, has already shown the value of the advisory committees the creation of which was here (p. 377) strongly urged. I have corrected obvious misprints and one or two trifling errors the existence of which was kindly pointed out by various friends.

A book which covers so wide and so controversial a field as this offers many temptations to critics of different views. Perhaps I may therefore emphasise my sense of the uniform kindness with which it has been received.

November, 1925 H.J.L.

# Introduction
# The Crisis in the Theory of the State

## I

No theory of the state is ever intelligible save in the context of its time. What men think about the state is the outcome always of the experience in which they are immersed. The massacre of Saint Bartholomew produces Whiggism in the author of the *Vindicicae*; the Puritan Rebellion sets Hobbes searching for the formula of social peace; the "Glorious Revolution" of 1688 enables Locke to affirm that the power of the Crown is built upon the consent of its subjects. Rousseau, Hegel, T.H. Green, all sought to give the mental climate of their time the rank of universal validity. And the more critical the epoch in which we live the more profound is the emphasis upon universality. Men fight grimly for the status of ideologies lest the experience they seek to validate be denied by their opponents.

Our age, in this regard, is no different from its predecessors. It is an age of critical transition in which, as at the end of the fifteenth and the eighteenth centuries, a new social order is struggling grimly to be born. Our scheme of values is in the melting pot, and the principles of its refashioning have not yet been determined. As always, in such a time, men have gone back to the foundations of politics; and they seek anew to explain the nature and functions of the state. There is a confusion in the atmosphere of discussion which betokens the advent of a revolutionary age. War, and a peace that it is not easy to distinguish from war, an economic crisis of unparalleled intensity, in Russia the foundation of a socialist society, in the Far East the birth of a new and aggressive imperialism—these have compelled new approaches to problems which, hardly a generation ago, seemed to men settled beyond dispute. What is in issue now is not the minor matter of the state's form; what is in issue is the nature of the state itself. We cannot, as I conceive, understand the profundity of the debate unless we realise that it is a crisis which involves the ultimate substance of society's constitution.

There is no avenue of politics into which it does not enter. The limits of state intervention, the validity of the democratic hypothesis, the place of the executive in the scheme of government, the relation of expert to amateur in the processes of administration and legislation, the nature of law in general, and of international law in particular, the claims of reason in politics, the function of leadership—all these, to take only some outstanding examples, have been found to require re-assessment and re-definition. In all of them, we are at the beginning only of what will unquestionably prove an epoch of decisive importance in the history of political philosophy; and it is too early, as yet, to predict with any confidence what stability will be attained. It took nearly three hundred years for the idea of the liberal state to grow to a mature expression. Its supremacy lasted for less than a century. All that, as yet, we can say of our own time is our certainty that the challenge to the liberal doctrine is clearly a decisive one. There is no evidence to indicate with clarity on what side the victory will rest.

Ours, as I say, is an epoch in which the characteristic confusion of a transitional time is the main feature of speculation. The call is loud for a new social philosophy; the prophets are many. I cannot attempt within a brief compass even to set out, much less to estimate, the chaos of competing doctrines. All that this chapter will seek to do is to state, as plainly as I can, what seems to me the fundamental issue as it is beginning to emerge; and I shall then attempt to illustrate its character by reference to four essential fields of enquiry. These are (1) the nature of law; (2) pluralism; (3) the attack on the democratic state; and, finally, (4) the special problems to which the emergence of an international order in whose fate, for good or ill, we are all involved, has given rise.

## II

The fundamental issue, at least, is straightforward; what is challenged is the liberal theory of the state. This, as it was fashioned by three centuries of discussion, assumed that in every political society where anarchy was to be avoided there must be a supreme authority which gives orders to all and receives orders from none. This authority was the sovereign power; and it was exercised in the name of the state by the government to whom its operation was entrusted. The justification of this power was variously conceived. Broadly, we may say, as a liberal democracy based upon universal suffrage became, before the war, the main objective of Western civilisation, it was argued that the title of the state to obedience lay in its performance of three functions: (1) it secured order, (2) it provided a technique of peaceful change, and (3) it enabled demand to be satisfied on the widest possible scale.

There was, of course, dissent from this view, both in detail and in principle. But, predominantly, this was the view which commanded assent. This, also, is the view which has been fundamentally attacked in the last twenty years, and so widely that its title to predominance may now be regarded as doubtful. The main ground for the attack does not lie in a denial that the state-power secures order; this is universally admitted.

What is argued is that what the order maintained by the state secures does not provide a technique of peaceful change and does not permit demand to be satisfied on the largest possible scale.

The state, it is urged, is, in fact, the supreme coercive power in any given political society; but it is, in fact, used to protect and promote in that society the interest of those who own its instruments of production. The state expresses a will to maintain a given system of class-relations. It does so by the use of its supreme coercive power to that end. In the last analysis, this power consists of the defence forces of the state. These are used, in ultimate challenge, to impose the will of the owners of the instruments of production upon those excluded from such ownership. Whatever the philosophic purposes attributed to the state-power these, it is said, are the naked facts. There may be more or less of coercion at any given moment, according as the economic condition of society enables more or less concessions of material well-being to be made to those excluded from the privileges of ownership. But any state in which the instruments of production are privately owned cannot, by its inherent nature, achieve either the second or the third of the objectives I have listed above.

It does not provide a technique of peaceful change. For men who have the privileges of ownership seek to maintain them, the more vehemently as they contract; and they are certain to be resisted by those excluded from them as these find their expectation of increasing material welfare disappointed. The only way open to the latter if they wish to avoid this disappointment is to capture the state-power in order to use it for a re-definition of class-relations. Theoretically, no doubt, this can be done peacefully in a constitutional system based on universal suffrage. In fact, historically, whenever an attempt at such re-definition has been made, it has always been resisted by the owners of property who, thereby, have been possessed of the state-power. The result of the incompatibility of the views of the use to which the state-power should be put is revolution. This, in its nature, is essentially a battle for the maintenance or change of the objectives to which the state-power is devoted. The battle is inescapable (whatever its result) so long as the state-power is used to confirm a body of legal postulates which stereotype any given system of class-relations in a condition where their economic and psychological results are regarded as unjust by those who do not conceive themselves to profit from the privileges it maintains.

The state, further, cannot in this context achieve its end of satisfying demand on the largest possible scale. For the demand satisfied in terms of its legal postulates is effective demand; and the nature of this depends upon the system of property in the given society. Where, as in the capitalist state, the essential incentive to production is the making of profit, it follows that in the process of distribution there will not be either (a) an equal claim upon what there is of common welfare or (b) such a rational justification of differences in reward as will relate them to a good in which the welfare of those discriminated against is involved; in a word in such a society the distributive process has no inherent connection with the end of justice. But this is to say that in such a society the coercive power of the state is used to promote differences in relation to the satisfaction of demand which may be (and in fact often are) unjust. Only the capture of the state, followed by the re-definition of its legal postulates, could remedy this condition.

This, as I understand it, is the challenge issued to the classic theories of the state in recent years. In its general outline, it was first formulated by Marx and Engels, and it received its classic re-statement by Lenin in his *State and Revolution*. I am not aware of any adequate answer to it from opponents of the challenge. The idealist theory of the state (as, for example) in its famous formulation by Bosanquet remains a formulation of a conceptual state *in posse* rather than of the states we know. The liberal and anti-idealist view, as expressed by L.T. Hobhouse, assumes, but does not prove, that, given time, reason will always be victorious in matters of social conflict. Neither Bosanquet's view, nor that of Hobhouse, fulfils the scientific canon of prediction. Broadly speaking, the Marxian theory of the state has so defined its nature and functioning as to enable us to predict with assurance the course its operations will follow. As an index to the problems of our age it decisively, in my judgment, holds the field.

On this basis, it follows that those who defend the classic theories of the state must be able to show not that an ideal state which exists only in their own construction, but the actual states, England, France, Germany, the United States of America, that we know, are inherently capable, granted the class-relations they maintain, of fulfilling demand on the largest possible scale, and that, therefore, they have a moral claim to the allegiance of their members on this ground. I do not myself see how this could be argued logically for, say, a few in Hitlerite Germany, or a socialist in Fascist Italy; each refuses to take the announced purposes of the state as embodying intentions related to his actual good. For the individual member of any political society is bound to infer its ends not from its proclamation of purpose, but from his judgment, based on his own experience, of that purpose in action. From this angle, we are in a psychological condition comparable, as I have said, to the end of the feudal period, or to the epoch of the French Revolution, when men seek to reconstitute the foundations of society. This they are now, as then, unable to do unless they redefine its class-relations. They cannot re-define them without possession of the state-power since it is in the use of its coercive authority that the means of re-definition are to be found.

## III

This, as I see it, is the general problem that we confront. I propose now to apply the result of my argument to the problem of the nature of law. The lawyer approaches the law as a body of rules binding upon those who come within its jurisdiction. The explanation of its binding force is, of course, of a varying character. To Hobbes and Austin it was the power behind the rules, the coercive sanctions which could, in the last resort, be brought into operation against those who infringed it. They sought to make, as, in our own day, Kelsen has sought to make, a self-consistent theory of pure law into which neither ethical nor sociological considerations could penetrate. Law, on this view, was completely separated from justice on the ground that this latter concept introduces non-juristic postulates foreign to the nature of law. On this view, the authority of law ultimately derives from the final norm in a series—the state—and this norm, in its turn, is a postulate incapable of examination since, as the supreme source of authority, it cannot be called into question.

Granted its postulates, I believe the pure theory of law to be unanswerable, but I believe also that its substance is an exercise in logic and not in life. For we know in fact that the law of any given society is the expression of the push of social forces in that society; and we cannot explain its substance or its operation without regard to those forces. That is why, in the last forty years, there has been a growing movement towards a less formal, and more realistic, jurisprudence. The relation between sociology and law has grown ever more intimate; and a jurisprudence of formal concepts now satisfies few save the veterans of an earlier age.

What is to replace it? Law is regarded as binding because it is useful, or because it embodies reason, or because it expresses the general ends of society in particular rules, or because it is a search for those canons of behaviour the observance of which will maximise the satisfaction of demand. From the angle of this chapter, none of these answers is satisfactory. To say that law is useful is to ask at once to whom it is useful; and that is always a question to which the most various answers can be given. To say that it embodies reason is merely to raise the enquiry of whose reason it embodies. To say that it expresses the general ends of society is to ask as conceived by whom? At every point, in short, the ideal purpose of law is not necessarily identical with the actual purposes of law as these are experienced by those who receive the law.

But the law is, normally, obeyed. What explains the fact of normal obedience? Is it fear, or habit, consent or utility? No doubt, in some degree, it is all of these. Yet to offer them as explanations does not explain the nature of law. To understand it we must grasp the nature of the authority upon which it rests. In the last analysis, this is always the supreme coercive power of the state; for it is this power which is called into operation to prevent or to punish infractions of the law. But since, again in last analysis, the object of the state is to maintain some given system of class-relations in society, the laws behind which it puts its supreme coercive power will have this end also. Law, ultimately, therefore is a body of rules which seek to fulfil the object of the state. The rules are maintained because, normally, those who dissent from the rules are not in a position to challenge the authority which lies behind them.

From this standpoint, we can answer the questions I have already put. Law in a feudal state is made as law because it is useful to the owners of land; the reason it embodies is their reason; the general end of society it seeks to fulfil is their conception of what that general end should be; the canons of behaviour it will seek to enforce will derive from their conception of how demand may best be maximised. In a capitalist society, like Great Britain, for instance, the substance of law will, similarly, be predominantly determined by the owners of capital. In a socialist society, like Soviet Russia, the substance of law will be determined by the fact that the common ownership of the means of production subordinates the interest of a class to the interest of the society as a whole.

Recent work in jurisprudence gives this view a status with which the last generation was unfamiliar. The proceedings of the American courts, to take a notable instance, in the use of the injunction, in the interpretation of the Fourteenth Amendment, in their reading of industrial conspiracy into the category of tort, in their attitude to free speech and free assembly, are all pervaded by the notion, often hardly conscious in the individual judge, that the purpose of the law in fact is, whatever its ideal professions, to maintain existing class-relations. It represents the use of the state's supreme coercive power for this end and for no other end. American constitutional law is, no doubt, elastic enough as a broad statement of principles. When it falls to be applied by the judges it is, in general, permeated by a philosophy which prevents a change in class-relations being introduced through the interstices of law.

The same is true of Great Britain. The interpretation of trade union law, of much of the jurisprudence surrounding workmen's compensation, the law of search, the law relating to freedom of speech and assembly (especially in these last critical years) derives its meaning from judicial belief that the existing social order (that is, the existing system of class-relations) must be maintained. At bottom, only the Marxian interpretation of law can explain the substance of law. There cannot, that is, be equality before the law, except in a narrowly formal sense, unless there is a classless society. For the unstated assumption of all law in any society in which the instruments of production are privately owned is the inherent necessity of maintaining the system of class-relations through which the privileges of private ownership are secured to their possessors.

This conclusion, it should be added, is not invalidated by either of two considerations. The lawyer's search for consistency seeks always to build a legal system that is internally logical; the history of the law of torts is an interesting example of this effort. But the essential shape of his effort, is, despite the reaction of the search for consistency upon the material, inescapably set by the relations of production in any society at any given time. Nor is it invalidated by the fact that lawyers, like most other men, search for the good of society in the rules they evolve. They search for the good of society as they see it; and they see the good, broadly speaking, in terms of an experience in which they are placed by the relations of production in which they are involved. The economic philosophy of those who made the Napoleonic Code, of Chief Justice Marshall, of Baron Bramwell, and Lord Farwell is stamped unmistakably on the whole fabric of their work. Each of them was serving the law to the best of his great ability, but each brought to that service a body of class-prepossessions of which he was definitely the prisoner. Here and there, a remarkable individual, like Mr. Justice Holmes, may show a noteworthy power to transcend those limitations. But such remarkable individuals are rarely lawyers successful enough, granted our technique of judicial appointment and promotion, to reach the Bench.

Just, therefore, as there is a crisis in the theory of the state, so, also, there is a crisis in the theory of law. None of its characteristic landmarks has gone unchallenged. It is especially notable that liberal theories of the law, which seek to utilise the new sociological relationships of law, are not less helpless than the older theories to grapple with the central problem. Dean Pound, for example, has, with great learning and energy, proposed an "engineering" theory of law. This he defines as "thinking not of an abstract harmonising of human wills, but of a concrete securing or realising of human interests"?[1] But Dean Pound nowhere discusses the relation of this "concrete securing or realising" to the inescapable consequences of a society whose class-structure predominantly confines the "human interests" realised or secured to those who have effective demands to make—i.e., the owners of property. At bottom his whole philosophy, like that of Kohler, is really an Hegelian plea that the law should be penetrated by that mystic entity the spirit of a new time. He wants law, as it were, kept up to date; but he has wholly failed to see that this is, in fact, like all Hegelian philosophy, merely a beatification of the *status quo* of any given society at any given time. By refusing to see, with Marx, that legal relations are rooted in class relations, Dean Pound has thrown away the essential answer to the problem of what "human interests" will be "secured or realised" in a society of given class-relations or one in which the power of class over class has been abolished.

The new approach has, necessarily, a different technique of analysis. It conceives of law always in the context of a state supporting a given system of class-relations and it is in this context, always, that it finds the clue to its necessary substance. Law, in this view, is those rules of behaviour which secure the purposes of the society's class-structure and will be, if necessary, enforced by the coercive power of the state. They are obeyed so long as the relations of production enable the full potentialities of the society to be exploited; they will be challenged when the forces of production are in conflict with the relations of production and this exploitation is no longer possible. Whenever this conflict occurs, the foundations of law are called into question. A struggle for their reconstruction takes place; and, if those who challenge the law are successful in their effort, they move to the use of the state-power to redefine the legal postulates of society. It is upon the basis of this conception alone that the movement of juristic thought can, in its fundamental outlines, be explained.

## IV

During the war, and its immediate aftermath, an attack was made by a group of thinkers usually called the pluralists upon the sovereignty of the state. As I was myself perhaps as much concerned as anyone in the formulation of the doctrine, it will perhaps not be wholly out of place for me to explain the nature and purpose of the attack.

It was born essentially of two things. The state claimed legal omnicompetence; and it claimed the allegiance of its citizens on the ground that it represented the total interest of the society within its territorial jurisdiction. The pluralists pointed out that legal omnicompetence was a purely formal concept often invalid in fact; and they argued that the claim to allegiance could not be *a priori* valid since the allegiance of men was, in fact, plural and not single; that they were frequently presented with choices in which they made their decision without regard to the formal, pre-eminence of the state. The pluralists therefore argued that, however majestic and powerful, the state in fact was only one of many associations in society, that, in experience, there were always limits to its powers, and that these were set by the relation between the purpose the state sought to fulfil and the judgment made by men of that purpose. They insisted that the state's title to obedience lay, not in the fact of its willing, but in the substance of what it chose to will as this met the experience of men seeking to satisfy the demands born of their experience.

In part, as a matter of history, it is clear enough that this pluralism was born of reaction from the Moloch-like demands of the state in wartime. In part, also, it derived from the realisation that the state's claim to pre-eminence always means, in fact, the sovereignty of a government composed of fallible men whose intentions alone are not a sufficient justification for so vast a claim. There went into the making of pluralism an historic analysis derived from the conflict between churches and the state, between trade unions and the state, between, as in the case of the conscientious objector to military service, the individual and the state.

What, as I think now, was right in the pluralist doctrine, were its perceptions (1) that a purely legal theory of the state can never form the basis of an adequate philosophy of the state; (2) that the state is, in fact, no more entitled to allegiance than any other association on grounds of ethical right or political wisdom; and (3) that its sovereignty is, at bottom, a concept of power made valid by the use of a coercion which, in itself, is morally neutral. Society as a complex whole is pluralistic; the unified power of the state which we call sovereignty, that legal right, as Bodin put it, to give orders to all and to receive orders from none, is made monistic (as in the classical legal theory) by the fact that it has behind its will, on all normal occasions, the coercive power to get its will obeyed.

The weakness, as I now see it, of pluralism is clear enough. It did not sufficiently realise the nature of the state as an expression of class-relations. It did not sufficiently emphasise the fact that it was bound to claim an indivisible and irresponsible sovereignty because there was no other way in which it could define and control the legal postulates of society. It was through their definition and control that the purposes of any given system of class-relations was realised. If the state ceased to be sovereign, it ceased to be in a position to give effect to those purposes. Its pre-eminence was, therefore, inevitably claimed on that ground. The ethical characteristics attributed to it by philosophers like Hegel were nothing more than a protective colouration for the end the state was bound to fulfil as the expression of the relations of production in any given time and place.

That realised, I submit, the purpose of pluralism merges into a larger purpose. If it be the fact, as I have here argued, that the state is inevitably the instrument of that class which owns the instruments of production, the objective of the pluralist must be the classless society. In that event there is no room for, because there is no need of, its supreme coercive power. It then becomes possible to conceive of a society in which (a) men have an equal claim on the common good and (b) differentiation in response to that equal claim can be so made that the good of those differentiated against is involved in the good of those in whose favour differentiation is made. In such a society we remove those conflicts based on property which, as James Madison saw and said, are "the only true source of faction". It is these conflicts which render normally necessary the vast apparatus of state-coercion. If the main ground of conflict is thus removed, it becomes possible to conceive of a social organisation in which the truly federal nature of society receives institutional expression. And in such a social organisation, authority can be pluralistic both in form and expression. The prospect of immense institutional changes comes at once into view.

This is not the place for me to venture upon any full treatment of the problems to which this outlook gives rise. It is, perhaps, sufficient for me to say here that I now recognise (so far at least as I am concerned) that the pluralist attitude to the state and law was a stage on the road to an acceptance of the Marxian attitude to them. Only by means of Marxism can I explain phenomena like the state as it appears in Fascist countries. That state seeks the total absorption of the individual within the framework of its coercive apparatus precisely because it is there, nakedly and without shame, what the state, covertly and apologetically is, in capitalist democracies like Great Britain or the United States. To limit its power, as the pluralist sought to limit its power, we must destroy the class-structure of society; for the state is simply the executive instrument of the class in society which owns the means of production. When a class-society in this sense is destroyed, the need for the state, as a sovereign instrument of coercion, disappears; in Marx's phrase, it "withers away". As that is achieved, both the nature of authority and the law it ordains undergo a fundamental transformation.

## V

In the war period it was widely assumed that the universal attainment of democracy was the highest political objective before mankind; since the war it has had a decreasing empire over the minds of men. Not a little of the present confusion in political theory is the outcome of a failure to state the problems to which this change in the mental climate of our time has given rise in anything like adequate terms. Men have been asked to accept a formal political democracy as good in itself without taking regard to the complex of economic relationships in which that formal political democracy is involved.

For in every state in the modern world save Soviet Russia the essential fact which must be the starting-point of political analysis is that the capitalist mode of production there prevails. The ownership of the means of production is in a comparatively small number of hands; and this narrow basis of economic power is in wide contrast to the broad basis of a political power which, as in England and the United States, is usually based upon universal suffrage. The contrast is important since it means that the motives to production in a capitalist society are in contrast with the theoretical end a democracy seeks to serve. In a capitalist society the motive to production is profit for the owner of the instruments of production. In a democracy the citizen seeks, by the use of his political power, to use the authority of the state to increase the material well-being at his disposal.

This union of economic oligarchy and political democracy worked well enough so long as capitalism was in its phase of expansion. Its triumphs, in Great Britain and the United States, are too well known to need description here. But generally in the last thirty years, and particularly since the war, capitalism has entered into a period of contraction from which it seems neither able nor likely to emerge. Its power to produce increases indefinitely; its power to distribute is continually less effective. The system of ownership which gives rise to the relations of production is in contradiction with the forces of production. As at the end of the feudal period a re-definition of class-relations has become necessary if we are to secure a full exploitation of the resources at our disposal.

But here the difficulties of capitalist democracy come into the foreground. The concern of the capitalist is profit; the concern of the masses is material well-being. When the contraction of the economic system limits profit-making, the results are unemployment and a lowered standard of life. This can be met for a period. But since the masses use their political power to insist, at some stage, in an increase of material welfare, they are driven to attack the class-relations in which they are involved to secure it. Their political power then becomes a challenge to the economic power of the owning-class. The latter has then the alternatives of co-operating peacefully in the re-definition of the legal postulates of the state or of suppressing a democratic system in which their privileges are threatened by the voting power of the masses.

The coming of Fascism, as in Italy and Germany, is an example of what is meant by the suppression of a democratic system. The right of the majority to decide how it wants to be ruled is destroyed. The characteristic institutions of the working-classes, the trade unions, the co-operative societies, the socialist party, are overthrown. The Fascist Party, invariably in union with big business and the defence forces of the state, is then in a position to alter the constitution of the state in the interests of the owners of economic power. Dictatorship is established; and while it is, of course, announced that this has been done in the interest of the society as a whole, what is notable is that its results are always built (1) upon the forcible suppression of recalcitrant elements and (2) a lower standard of life for the masses. Fascist dictatorship enables the uneasy marriage between capitalism and democracy to be dissolved by the simple expedient of forcing the masses, by terror, to renounce their claim to increased material welfare. It is vital to the understanding of this process to recognise that, under it, the class-relations typical of capitalism remain unchanged.

From this angle, the problem of democracy in our time is, relatively, a simple one. There is no effective evidence to suggest that, as a method of government, it is any less efficient than in the past. What has happened is that the entrance of capitalism into the phase of contraction has brought into vivid perspective the contradiction between the ends of an economic oligarchy on one plane and those of a political democracy on another. This contradiction threatens the security of the owning class. They begin to see the democratic system in the light of the threat to their security. They insist that democracy must conform to the end capitalism seeks to serve. They ask for sacrifices in the belief that these will be temporary; when their temporary character is thrown into doubt they begin to use the state-power to repress the criticism or attack they fear. If these actions are not enough to restore the security the challenge to which they fear, as in Italy and Germany, they frankly abandon their belief in political democracy.

This is, of course, to state starkly a situation that is far more complex, especially in its psychological aspects, than I have here attempted to set forth. But in its large outlines it is, I believe, the essential key to the problem of democracy at the present time. It alone explains such legislation as the British Trade Union Law Amendment Act of 1927, or the use of the Supreme Court to declare unconstitutional so much of President Roosevelt's legislation. When Mr. Justice Roberts can declare the Railroad Retirement Act of 1934 unconstitutional on the ground that, under the Fifth Amendment, the "means adopted" do not bear "any reasonable relation to the ostensible exertion of the power",[2] he substitutes, in fact, his conception of what "reasonable" and "ostensible" mean for those of Congress; the words are taken to narrow the authority of Congress while they widen the latitude of judicial interpretation. Put in another way, Mr. Justice Roberts is arguing that the Fifth Amendment, read as he proposes to read it, protects railway shareholders from any legal obligation to give pensions to their employees even when Congress believes that they should assume this legal obligation. The function of the Supreme Court, from this angle, becomes that of safeguarding the owners of capital from the results of a legislative effort to increase the material well-being of the masses. Taking President Roosevelt's legislation as a whole, the attitude of the Courts to it may be broadly described as an insistence that political democracy shall not seriously interfere with the habits of a capitalist society. This attitude is the more important since President Roosevelt has not attempted to undermine those habits, but only to make such concessions to mass well-being as will, in his judgment, preserve the stability of capitalist society. The Supreme Court, in essence, is saying that its conception of what is "reasonable" may be substituted for that of the President and Congress whenever it thinks fit. It becomes, in short, the protective rampart of capitalism against any attempt it dislikes of democratic invasion.

The British situation is different in form, though not in substance. The problem of the Labour Party there is to maintain the validity of democratic rule if and when it attains a majority in the House of Commons even though it attempt socialist legislation. Its opponents seem willing to mobilise against any such effort the powers of the Crown, the House of Lords, and the investing class. It remains a grave question whether the Labour Party could, as a government, successfully challenge the combination of these forces. A parallel position, again different in detail, exists in France; and, though socialist governments exist in Scandinavia, it is important that none of them has ventured to introduce socialist measures. What appears to emerge from the post-war experience is that capitalism is willing to suppress democracy rather than forego the privileges which accrue to ownership under the system of class-relations that it involves. No state in modern history in fact, has been able, so far, to change its class-basis without revolution. The crisis in democracy is due to the fact that in the present phase of capitalist contraction its alliance with democracy is dangerous to the owners of property who, as in the past, prefer to fight for their privileges rather than give way. The history of Soviet Russia since 1917 lends additional weight to this interpretation.[3]

## VI

The central problems of post-war international law lie in the economic relations in which they are involved. Scientific advance, especially in the means of communication, has produced a world-market; and in that situation no state can live a life in which it affects itself alone. American silver policy may determine the economic position of China; the Canadian monopoly of tungsten may determine the effectiveness of German re-armament; Great Britain's departure from the gold standard, or her tariff-policy may shape the economic life of the Scandinavian countries. We have reached so intense a degree of international interdependence that the theory of sovereignty has consequences, in foreign relations, of an entirely different character from those of the period when Grotius and his successors laid the fundamental bases of international law.

The world is divided into sovereign states, each of which is, in formal fact, the sole arbiter of the policy it will pursue. The making of peace and war, the scale of its armaments, its financial and economic policies, its attitude to colonial expansion, all these, to take examples only, are matters upon which it recognises no will superior to its own. What, then, is international law, and how far is it binding upon states? International law may be defined as the body of rules which govern the relations between states; and its binding force depends upon their consent to observe the rules it imposes. If it is objected here that this attitude to the nature of international law fails to take account of the existence of a well-settled body of rules by which all states conceive themselves as bound, the answer is that, in any final analysis, states regard themselves as free to break the obligations to which they are committed whenever they choose to do so. The existence of a body of juristic rules which, in minor matters, states accept because it is convenient for them to do so is not sufficient to give international law a status independent of their wills. For in matters of major concern, as Japan has shown over Manchuria, and Italy over Abyssinia, they are not prepared to sacrifice what they conceive to be their sovereign interests to the claims of international law. They do not recognise its validity as superior to the will they make for themselves. There is no organic community with a law of its own to which their own law is subordinate. The validity of international law depends upon their consent to its operation.

This view is not, I think, destroyed either by the existence of the League of Nations, or by the fact that an adequate international life is now impossible unless at least the major wars are definitely outlawed. For what the experience of the last sixteen years has surely shown is the incompatibility of the League with the co-existence of sovereign states; and the latter display no sign of a serious willingness to abandon their sovereignty. They need it, in fact, for the protection of interests which cannot be promoted or maintained save by the technique of war. The ambitions of Japan and Germany, of Italy and Hungary, to take some obvious instances, assume a period when they will make demands upon other states which only the arbitrament of the sword can enforce; and recent experience seems decisive that they are willing to break legal obligations, however morally profound, in order to realise them. The answer of the League should be opposition in terms of collective security; but both the Manchurian and the Abyssinian incidents make it plain that collective security assumes the existence of an international community able and willing to act as an effective unit against an aggressor. No such possibility appears to exist within the framework of the present system. And while it does not exist, the binding force of international law is as great, or as small, as the strength of the aggressor who breaks it. It is a function of the power-politics which express the modern relationships of states; and power-politics cannot give rise to a social order in which international law has a status independent of the states that assent to it.

It is, in fact, inherent in the idea of law that those who live under it should be bound to obey its orders independently of their own will; and that their infractions of its principles should be punished by the infliction of penalties. For international law no such situation exists save as individual states choose to assume, and to be bound by, obligations of this kind. International law, therefore, is built upon postulates that are rather metajuridical than truly legal, in their nature. Granted the postulates, all the results that follow are of a truly legal kind; but the sovereign nature of the state, in relation to the postulates, strikes them with impotence as soon as in crucial instances they seek to assume the full character of law.

Why is this? The answer, I suggest, lies in the understanding of the nature of the state. Since it exists to protect a given system of class-relations, it cannot escape from the implications contained in them. Once a society lives by the profit-motive, and depends upon access to foreign markets for its satisfaction, it is bound, as the condition of its own well-being, to protect and promote that access. It then becomes involved in that complex web of imperialism which means the acquisition of colonies and spheres of influence with military and naval force to protect the acquisition. As the undeveloped territories of the world shrink, the rivalries between states for access to markets becomes ever more acute. Its purpose seizes hold of, and colours, the whole psychological contact between peoples. Almost independently of the wills of statesmen, as, most notably, in the war of 1914, the clash of objectives cannot be settled in terms of peaceful negotiation. The necessary outcome of the system, at some stage, is war; and war, it must be remembered, is the highest expression of the state's sovereignty.

To deprive the state of sovereignty, in a word, is to deprive it of the power to enforce the logic that is inherent in its economic system. Great Britain in India and Egypt, France in Morocco and Indo-China, Japan in Korea and Manchuria, become impossible save in that context. For sovereignty means supreme coercive power; and, without this, the state cannot enforce a will to which it is compelled by the class-relations it exists to maintain. No doubt each state wants peace. But, given the consequences of its class-relations, it wants, also, objectives which it cannot obtain or safeguard without the power to make war on their behalf; and it must retain its sovereignty in order to retain the right to make war. But once it retains its sovereignty it cannot be bound by any rule of international law save by its own consent. For, were it so bound, it would cease by definition to be sovereign.

The inference from this view is twofold. On the one hand, it implies that, given the class-relations of the modern state, it is impossible to realise the ideal of an effective international community. A body like the League of Nations is bound to remain partial and incomplete, both as to structure and function, simply because, in order to achieve its aims, it must be able to transcend the sovereignty of its individual members.

This it cannot do since, if they were to surrender their sovereignty, they would cease to be able to maintain those class-relations for which they exercise supreme coercive power. On the other hand, it implies that the sanctions of international law are bound to remain, also, partial and incomplete since their ability to get themselves applied depends upon the consent of those who infringe that law to their application; the alternative, when the transgressor refuses such consent, is the use of a force against him from which, as the cases of Manchuria and Abyssinia have made evident, other states will shrink. There is no way of making international law more than what Austin called a species of positive morality save by the abrogation of state-sovereignty; and this involves a revolution in the economic structure of the modern world.

This conclusion is not weakened by the effort of the Austrian school of international lawyers to remake the foundations of international law by postulating its primacy over municipal law. Their effort, which, given its postulates, is logically sound, is nevertheless unrealistic. It is, for practical purposes, an essay in the optative mood. So long as the individual state remains sovereign the question of primacy remains a matter upon which it is itself, in each individual instance, free to decide; and post-war experience is surely decisive that such primacy will be disregarded by any state (if it can afford to do so) once it considers that such recognition will jeopardise interests it regards as fundamental. It is, no doubt, true that, among modern states, Spain has actually written into its constitution the recognition that international law has primacy over municipal law. But it is important to realise, first, that Spain has a lonely pre-eminence in this regard, and, second, that states which have signed either the Kellogg-Briand Pact or the Optional Clause have, for the most part, done so with significant reservations which amount, in sober fact, to the retention of that right to make war, or to refuse arbitration, in such instances as they think fit. They have agreed, that is, to abrogate their sovereignty in those matters upon which they do not think it worth while to fight; but, for all fundamental matters, they remain not less distinctively sovereign than before.

We may agree that, granted the fact of international economic interdependence, this is an unsatisfactory position. It is unsatisfactory because we are living in a world in which the relations of production are in contradiction with the forces of production. A sovereignty which, in its origins, served the important purpose of freeing bourgeois society from the trammels of medieval canons of conduct, now operates to prevent the transcendence of the contradictions of bourgeois society. The sovereignty of the great state today is a technique for the protection of its imperialism. That imperialism is the outcome of its own internal relations which, given the distribution of effective demand within its boundaries, is driven to the competitive search for markets abroad in order to realise profit. Its sovereignty is the protective armament of that adventure. The international law it can recognise is, therefore, always hampered and frustrated by the logical requirements of imperialism. It cannot part with the control of any vital function, the scale of its armament, the right to make war, its hold on colonies and spheres of influence, its power over tariffs, currency, migration, labour conditions, because to do so is to threaten, internally, the relations of production its sovereignty exists to maintain. But an international community, and therefore the law of such a community, cannot be real or effective unless it can control these functions independently of the wills of the states which are its constituent parts. To achieve the necessary consequences, that is, of the world-market, we have to go beyond the power of the individual state to veto international action. We cannot, in fact, go beyond that power while the state remains sovereign; and we cannot deprive it of its sovereignty so long as, outside of Soviet Russia, the present class-structure of society remains undisturbed.

The development of international law in modern times, and, especially, in the post-war period, is an admirable example of the lawyer's effort to reconcile consistency with postulates which deny the possibility of its full attainment. The best examples of this effort in recent years have been those of Lauterpacht in England, and of the Austrian school.[4] Each has striven to make of international law a truly legal system by discovering for it a power to bind its subjects indifferently to their will. Each has been able to find a mass of illustrative material—the existence of international servitudes is a notable illustration—which appears to bear out his case. But each effort has broken down before the crucial fact that the postulates from which it has to start are not broad enough to bear the weight of the superstructure founded upon them. At some point, the state may choose not to accept the obligations it has assumed; and, at that point, it always emerges that the validity of the obligation is self-determined. Once that is the case, the incompleteness of the sanctions behind international law emerge with momentous clarity. They are operative only so far as states choose to make them operative; and this willingness depends upon factors so powerful as to prevent international law from being, like municipal law, a complete and self-sufficient system.

The reason for this inadequacy is, of course, a simple one. Law cannot transcend the relations it is intended to enforce. Its ultimate postulates are never self-determined, but given to it by the economic system of which it is the expression. Once the driving-power of an economic system depends upon the profit derived from the private ownership of the means of production within a state, the sovereignty of that state must organise the relations of production within the framework born of that purpose. To its consequences, all the habits of the society dominated by the state will be necessarily adjusted, as well in the international, as in the municipal sphere. To alter those habits, there must be an alteration, also, in the relations of production upon which they depend. So far, at least, that alteration has not been attempted, outside of Soviet Russia, in the modern world. The result is to confine the international lawyer to a medium in which his work is inevitably incomplete simply because the postulates from which he starts do not themselves constitute a complete system. To achieve that completeness, he would have to deal with states which accepted the findings of law as fully as the citizen in a municipal community. The starting-point of his adventure is the fact that this is not, and, within the present relations of production, cannot be, the case. The international law he operates is, no doubt, inadequate to the purposes it now seeks to fulfil; but it will require a complete change in the foundations of our economic system to adjust its postulates to the new needs it encounters.

## VII

The crisis in *staatslehre* that I have here described will not be solved in terms of discussion alone; ideas must wait upon the events which give them birth. The Liberal ideology which, both in the old world and the new, is now challenged, becomes, in the perspective of history the expression of a particular economic system upon whose fate it is dependent. That system made the individual ownership of the means of production the pivot of its way of life; and to the realisation of that end it shaped, first the culture, and then the political institutions, of the medieval world it displaced. By reason of its emphasis upon such individual ownership, it shaped all the foundations of law, both public and private, to that end. Its validity, as an ideology, depended upon its power so to exploit the forces of production as to satisfy, on the largest possible scale, the demands that it encountered. So long as it seemed to fulfil that condition it was able, though in fact a theory limited by a specific environment, to represent itself, and to be accepted, as a universal. But as soon as its power of satisfaction diminished—which, roughly, has synchronised with the contradiction, between its power to produce and its power to distribute—its adequacy as an ideology became doubtful to all whose expectations of material benefit from its operations was disappointed.

No doubt its achievements were great; the increase in the standard of life that it has universally affected is beyond discussion. But, once it ran into the period of its material contradiction, what was revealed was the narrow and formal character of the institutional system by which it lived. Its political democracy, even on the basis of universal suffrage, did not mean, hardly, indeed, pretended to mean, a recognition of an equal claim to a share in the common good; what political democracy could secure was always limited by the power of an economic oligarchy to exact privileges prior in status to the claim of the masses to benefit. Its equality before the law was, again, almost always more substantial in form than in practice; for the simple reason that the principles of the law were always, if rarely consciously, anchored in the assumption that the protection of private ownership was the fundamental purpose of the law. The ideology, in a word, of the liberal state favoured reason and toleration only on the implicit condition that these, as they worked, did not threaten the economic foundations of the regime itself.

But reason and toleration are attitudes of mind in human beings. They depend upon an environment about which men feel passionately. Their empire functions only as legitimate expectations are fulfilled by those who have formed them. When those expectations are insecure, men are no more capable of service to reason and toleration than they have been in past ages. Their ideas of right and wrong are largely born of their position in society; and when this, with its profound habituations, is challenged, now, as in the past, they go forth to do battle in behalf of their ideas of right and wrong. Liberalism is challenged in our own day for the same reason that feudalism was challenged at the end of the fifteenth century; within the framework of the class-relations it imposes, it is unable adequately to exploit the forces of production. So challenged, it defends itself; and the conflict between the forces it represents and those by which it is attacked has led to the crisis in state-theory which has been here analysed.

What the outcome of that crisis will be, it is as yet too early to say. Much, clearly, depends on whether the capitalist system has latent powers of recovery more profound than have yet been made apparent; much, also, upon whether the experiment of Soviet Russia is able, within a measurable period, to develop for its citizens a standard of life which compares favourably with that of capitalism. Certain it is, also, that the capitalist system, in its imperialist phase, must avoid the danger of war if it is to preserve any vestige of liberal ideas. For war means an organisation of social life so rigorous that the conception of individual rights cannot hope to survive its onset. Were it to come, the private ownership of the means of production could be maintained only by a Fascist dictatorship so stark as to resemble in its intensity the worst forms of Oriental despotism. Even then, it may be argued, it is doubtful enough if such a dictatorship could, over any considerable period, attain stability. For its relations of production would continue to exhibit that contradiction with the forces of production that is the cause of the present crisis. It would be a government of naked coercion; and, thereby, it would fail to meet that essential test of all governments which is the transformation, at some stage, of the processes of coercion into the processes of consent. But, historically, this transformation is only achieved in those epochs where the relations of production correspond to the forces of production; this correspondence, inherently, a Fascist state is unable to attain. Its emergence, therefore, offers no more to the owners of economic power than a temporary and hazardous breathing-space before they encounter a new challenge. For power is always held upon the condition that its possessors are able to confer increasing material well-being upon the masses. This no Fascist system is able to do for the simple reason that it starts from a premiss incompatible with the achievement of that increase. It is, by its nature, an attempt only to arrest in the interest of privilege the decay of that capitalist enterprise which has now passed into its phase of final contraction.

This position need cause us no surprise. All the characteristics of our age have always marked the last phases of an economic system in decay. Scepticism of accepted values, lack of self-confidence in the ruling class, increasing hostility to traditional authority, the making of new social principles to fit new needs, the attack, in a word, upon the foundations of the old order, these were symptomatic of the Reformation and the French Revolution as they are symptomatic of our own time. Then, as now, the traditional social discipline—which is another phrase for the system of class relations—inhibited the full exploitation of scientific discovery. Then, as now, this incompatibility produced profound social antagonisms which issued in widespread conflict. Then, as now, a rising social class assumed the offensive by denying the right of those who lived by the traditional ways to the privileges inherent in their position. Then, as now, also, those whose right was denied were so convinced of the legitimacy of their claim that they preferred, as they have always preferred, rather to fight than to give way. In essence, the historic movement from the Reformation to the French Revolution is the history of the advance of the middle class to full political status. As it advanced, it transformed political and legal philosophy to satisfy the claims it had formulated. Once it had captured the state, it sought, as all classes seek, to make rigid and unassailable the boundaries of its empire. For something like sixty years it was successful in that effort because it was able to confer increasing material benefit upon the workers; hence, in that period, its feelings of security and self-confidence. But, for something like the last generation, and, with immense rapidity since the war, its ability at once to satisfy its own claims and those of the workers has declined. With real decline has come doubt, increasing in volume, of the system by which it lived. An alternative social hypothesis has come into the field which, as in Soviet Russia, has assumed the significant panoply of an armed state. Russia represents a new way of life, built upon foundations which threaten the supremacy of the traditional order. Its challenge awakens in that order the sense of insecurity and danger which has always made a privileged class arm itself for defence. The crisis in the theory of the state is no more than the ideological expression of this conflict between tradition and experiment.

It shows itself as a crisis in the theory of the state simply because when a new class is advancing to power, it is bound to capture the state for the achievement of its ends. Thereby it becomes possessed of the ultimate authority in society; thereby, that is, it can give orders to all, and receive orders from none. To capture the state-power is to have authority to re-define, for new purposes, the legal postulates of society. These, at bottom, are always no more than principles which determine in what way the social product shall be distributed. They attach to the claims men make the sanctions supreme coercive power in society is able to enforce. Our age is watching a debate in legal philosophy, the intensity of which measures with some precision the degree to which the traditional conception of the state-power is in jeopardy. As always in the past, a challenge to legal ideas is the harbinger of a revolutionary time. The supreme problem for the jurists of this epoch is the need to awaken to the responsibilities of the issue they confront. For only a realistic awareness of what that issue fully implies can save us from the grim rigours of a new dark age.

London School of Economics
and Political Science

HAROLD J. LASKI

## REFERENCES

1. *Spirit of the Common Law*, p. 195.
2. *Railroad Retirement Board* v. *Alton R.R.* (1935) 295 U.S. 330, 347-8. On this see the pungent comments of Professor T.R. Powell in the *Harvard Law Review* for November, 1935, p. 1 f.
3. I have dealt at length with the problems here summarised briefly in my *Democracy in Crisis* (1933) and my *State in Theory and Practice* (1935).
4. Cf. his *Private Law Analogies in International Law* (1924) and *The Function of Law in the International Community* (1935); for the Austrian school cf. especially A. Verdross, *Die Einheit des rechtlichen Weltbildes*, 1923. On the whole problem cf. my *State in Theory and Practice* (1935), ch. iii.

# Part 1

## 1. The Purpose of Social Organisation

### (i) The Change of Scale

A new political philosophy is necessary to a new world. The perspective of social thought has shifted in a direction different from the horizon set for it by Bentham and Hegel in the last century. If the large aims we have in view are not dissimilar to theirs, the materials at our command and the scale upon which we live are both, for good or ill, vaster than at any previous time. We have, above all, lost confidence in the simplicity of the earlier thinkers. We are even coming to recognise that any theory of society which avoids complexity will be untrue to the facts it seeks to summarise. Bentham was a philosopher living in retirement from the world; it was easy for him to lay down a universal code of conduct so long as he drew his assumptions from observation of the handful of eager rationalists who regarded him as their master. It was easy, even, for Hegel to universalise the Prussian monarchy into the ultimate expression of the time-spirit when we remember how relatively small was the number of wills regarded in his age as significant. So, too, with Rousseau and Karl Marx. The one had grasped the importance of making the State find place for the personalities of ordinary men; but when he was confronted with the problem of an institutional expression for that insight, his solution was, in fact, an evasion of it. Marx in his turn showed with indomitable energy the weakness of a State, built upon the sandy foundation of a division into rich and poor. But the reconstruction he suggested was largely a prophecy of inevitable conflict, and the prospect he envisaged was less a remedy than an unexplored formula.

Our task is at once more various and less straightforward. We deal with a world in which many of the assumptions which the nineteenth century fought for seem so obvious that men can scarcely realise either the novelty they represent or the anger to which they gave rise. For Western Europe, at least, democratic government has become a commonplace beyond discussion. Political power is, as a matter of theory, built, not upon birth or property, but upon the personality of men. That does not mean that birth has ceased to count or that property is not still certain of a predominant influence in the State. It means only that we have no longer to battle for the assumption that the ordinary man is instinct with civic quality. That is, doubtless, gain of an unquestionable kind. No statesman of our own day would dare, whatever his thought, to speak of the "swinish multitude". In the theory of politics the "swinish multitude" is enthroned in the seat of power. But the problem still remains of making the possession of power a fruitful thing by determining the ends to which it should be devoted; and the question of ends is simple compared to the further problem of the methods by which those ends may be attained.

Clearly, we must abandon the optimism with which the Benthamites approached the issue. They did not doubt that the possession of the franchise would, in combination with the natural reason of mankind, build a State in which effort would secure the reward of liberty and equality. We have no such assurance now. We have been taught by long experience that the part played by reason in politics is smaller than we have been content to suppose. Nor is the facile equation by Hegel between social status and governmental capacity likely to carry conviction even to his avowed disciples; the political art is unrelated to the social structure of the time. Our task, assuredly, is to give to reason the largest possible place in the conduct of affairs; either we must plan our civilisation or we must perish. But the result of reflection, even on the largest scale, is not to bring within the ambit of political activity the mass of men and women who, at the electoral period, give the ultimate direction to the event. They are scarcely articulate about their wants; and even when they are articulate, they are not trained to judge whether the solutions suggested are in fact an adequate response to their desires.

Democratic government is doubtless a final form of political organisation in the sense that men who have once tasted power will not, without conflict, surrender it. But not the less certainly democratic government is less a matter for eulogy than for exploration. We still need to know what working hypothesis it involves and what institutions can effectively embody their purpose. We need to know these things in the perspective of a realisation that the administration of the modern State is a technical matter, and that those who can penetrate its secrets are relatively few in number. The problem of democratic government is not less a problem of finding men apt to the use of its machinery than the problem of a monarchy is to find a race of kings fitted by their endowments to benefit the State. Any system of government, upon the modern scale, involves a body of experts working to satisfy vast populations who judge by the result and are careless of, even uninterested in, the processes by which those results are attained. If, therefore, we want a plan of political organisation to meet the basic condition that ultimate power must be confided to those who have neither time nor desire to grasp the details of its working, it is clear that we are driven back to the foundations of the State.

### (ii) The Necessity of Government

Man finds himself, in the modern world, living under the authority of governments; and the obligation to obey their orders arises from the facts of his nature. For he is a community-building animal, driven by inherited instinct to live with his fellows. Crusoe on his desert island, or St. Simon Stylites upon his pillar, may defy the normal impulses which make them men; but, for the vast majority, to live with others is the condition of a rational existence.

Therein, at the outset, is implied the necessity of government. If the habits of peaceful fellowship are to be maintained, there are certain uniformities of conduct which must be observed. The activities of a civilised community are too complex and too manifold to be left to the blind regulation of impulse; and even if each man could be relied upon to act consistently in terms of intelligence there would be need for a customary standards by which the society in its organised form agreed to differentiate right from wrong. The theory of philosophic anarchy is impossible, in fact, so long as men move differently to the attainment of opposed desires. The effort involved in the peaceful maintenance of a common life does not permit the making of private decisions upon what the society deems essential to its existence. At some point, that is, spontaneity ceases to be practical, and the enforced acceptance of a common way of action becomes the necessary condition of a corporate civilisation.

Nor is the absence of such spontaneity a limitation upon freedom; it is rather its primary safeguard. For once it is admitted that no man is sufficient unto himself, there must be rules to govern the habits of his intercourse. His freedom is largely born from the maintenance of those rules. They define the conditions of his personal security. That maintain his health and the standards, spiritual not less than material, of his life. Without them he is the prey of uncertainties far more terrible than the uniformities by which the sea of his experience is charted. No society is known in which the individual can, in any final way, mould the tradition to his desires. Everywhere the historic environment shapes its substance and limits its possibilities. It is only on the moon that men can cry for the moon.

Man is not, in fact, born free, and it is the price he pays for his past that he should be everywhere in chains. The illusion of an assured release from captivity will decide few who have the patience to examine his situation. He comes into a society the institutions of which are in large part beyond his individual control. He learns that they will inevitably shape at least the general outlines of what fortune he may encounter. The organised effort of a determined group of men may, with patience, change the character of those institutions; but the individual who stands apart from his fellows is unlikely to be their master. The capacity, indeed, of most men will be exhausted by the mere effort to live; and the search to understand life will lead them into complexities they have rarely the energy, and seldom the leisure, to penetrate. For it is a grave error to assume that men in general are, at least actively and continuously, political creatures. The context of their lives which is, for the majority, the most important is a private context. They are conscious of their neighbours; they rarely grasp the essential fact that their neighbours are, in truth, the whole world. They set their wills by the wills of institutions they rarely explore. They do not examine those wills to give their own a rational relationship to them. They obey the orders of government from inertia; and even their resistance is too often a blinds resentment rather than a reasoned desire to secure an alternative. No faculty, indeed, is more rare than that sense of the State which enables a few thinkers—Hobbes, Locke, Rousseau, Marx—to move their fellows to the measure of their thought. With most, even the interest to grasp the expression is uncommon. The characteristic of social life is the unthinking obedience of the many to the will of the few. It is the sudden invasion of our lives by unwonted experience that drives most of us to realise the vast discipline in which we are involved.

In a sense, that unawareness will appear human enough to anyone who recognises the complexity of civilisation. A civil war in America may cause starvation in the cotton towns of Lancashire. The labours of a physicist who investigates the nature of the ether may span the distance between London and New York. An injury to the credit-structure of Germany may involve a panic on the Bourse of Pairs. Not less significant is the pace at which change proceeds. Feudal Japan may become, as it were overnight, the modern State. Men are still living to whom the railway was an incredible innovation; nor are they yet dead to whom compulsory education seems a grave attack upon personal responsibility.

Science, in brief, has changed the whole scale upon which we live. In less than a century we have entered upon a world different in final texture from that upon which our ancestors gazed after Waterloo. We no longer live in those placid villages where the visitor from London seemed a stranger from another planet. Where prayer and incantation were the weapons of the last age against disease, we may, if we are wise, use the microscope and the sanitary engineer. Nor can we depend any longer for the necessaries of life upon our own productive system. The inhabitant of the great society is accustomed to have at his call commodities fashioned by every nation of the earth. He thinks less of a voyage from London to Peru than, a century ago, his ancestor thought of a visit to Paris or Rome. The whole world has been reduced at least to the unity of interdependence; and the politicians of Tokyo make social decisions not less momentous for New York than those of Chicago or Washington. And this physical mutuality is supported by an economic system the mere description of which is so intricate that specialists hardly agree either upon its character or the results of its working.

It is a big world, about which, at our peril, we have to find our way. For the theory upon which the government to which we give our obedience acts is that its will somehow embodies the wills of us all. It professes, if not in detail, then at least in large outline, to embody within its general purpose the individual purpose we believe ourselves to embody at moments of clearest consciousness. The faith of civilisation is built upon the assumption that by reason of its mechanisms an increasing number of human beings realise at their best their highest faculties. To the extent that those mechanisms fail, so do our faculties, at their best, remain unrealised. In such a background, it is clear that the prospects of civilisation depend, in large degree, upon our ability to work its institutions. Our awareness of their nature will be, also, the degree in which we perceive their fragility. For we can have none of the comfortable assurance of a century ago that, whatever our errors, we may rest confident in the knowledge of progress. Our civilisation is held together by fear rather than by goodwill. The rivalry of States, the war of classes, the clash of colour—these haunt its margins as prospects instinct with disaster. It is not uncommon for men to sacrifice the welfare of their fellows to a private end. It is not infrequently that from the analysis of their relationships, honourable and selfless men have judged that modern civilisation is vicious at its foundations. Science may have given us the weapons of a creative life; but those weapons are, as we have become aware, the instruments of destruction. It does not seem likely that society will, in any coherent form, survive their devotion to ends of conflict.

In such an analysis, the study of modern politics can hardly avoid becoming an inquiry into the dynamics of peace. We seek to know what will bind men's allegiance, not inertly, but with passion, to its preservation and enlargement. We seek to find the ways in which their impulses as men may be satisfied at a level which secures the enrichment of the common life. We begin with the State because the context of men's lives is set most firmly in the background of its institutions. For there is no area of activity that is not, at least in theory, within the ambit of its control. The modern State is a territorial society divided into government and subject claiming, within its allotted physical area, a supremacy over all other institutions. It is, in fact, the final legal depository of the social will. It sets the perspective of all other organisations. It brings within its power all forms of human activity the control of which it deems desirable. It is, moreover, the implied logic of this supremacy that whatever remains free of its control does so by its permission. The State does not permit that men should marry their sisters; it is by its graciousness that they are allowed to marry their cousins. The State is the keystone of the social arch. It moulds the form and substance of the myriad human lives with whose destinies it is charged.

This does not mean that the State is an unchanging organisation. It has been subject at every point to the laws of an unceasing evolution. New forms of property, an alteration in the character of religious belief, physical conditions at the moment of their coming beyond the control of men—these and things like these have shaped its substance. Nor are its forms unmoving. It has been monarchic, aristocratic, democratic; it has been in the control of the rich and of the poor. Men have ruled it by reason of their birth or by their position in a religious fellowship.

What, as a matter of history, can alone be predicted of the State is that it has always presented the striking phenomenon of a vast multitude owing allegiance to a comparatively small number of men. Thinkers since the time of Socrates have sought to explain that curiosity. To some it has seemed that men obey their masters because, at least ultimately, the will of the few is sufficiently the will of the many to secure obedience. Consent, it is said, is the basis of the State. But if by consent be meant anything more than an inert acceptance of orders obeyed without scrutiny, it is clear that there has not yet been an epoch in the history of the State in which this is true. Nor can we accept as obvious the view of Hobbes that men obey the State through fear. Something if this, indeed, may colour the attitude of men to particular laws. I may refrain from murder upon a nice balance of consequences. But I send my children to school from motives far more complex than that of self-interest built upon fear. It is far nearer the truth to urge, as Sir Henry Maine would have us admit, that the State is built upon habit; but this still leaves unexplored the dispositions which enter into habit; and the point at which their infraction, as in the France of the Revolution, becomes possible. And if, as with Bentham and the Utilitarians, we ground the whole upon utility, the difficulty arises of explaining to whom the particular State is useful, and why (as in pre-Revolutionary Russia) the character of its utility should not provoke dissent instead of obedience.

The answer to the problem of obedience is, of course, that all theories which strive to explain it in purely rational terms are beside the mark; for no man is a purely rational animal. The State as it was and is finds the roots of allegiance in all the complex facts of human nature; and a theory of obedience would have to weight them differently for each epoch in the history of the State if it were to approximate to the truth. In a social situation which made thought itself a danger, it was natural for Hobbes to seek in fear the ultimate source of men's acts; just as the eighteenth-century moralist tended to make of benevolence the basic spring of action. In fact, nothing is gained by the postulation of separate forces of this kind as socially predominant. Distinct impulses, of whatever sort, operating to lead men to obey the State are as unreal as an explanation of the facts they resume as a fire-principle is worthless as an explanation of the character of fire. We meet man as a bundle of impulses which act together as a total personality. He will want to live with his fellows. He will build churches that he may worship with them, and clubs that he may enjoy the peace of silence. He will fall in love and marry and have children; and he will fiercely protect what he deems their interests against the demands the world will make upon them. He will be curious in the face of nature, and that curiosity will lead in most to a constructiveness which, as William James said, is "a genuine and irresistible instinct in man, as in the bee and the beaver". He will seek to acquire things, and that collector's zest will, for the majority, translate itself into whatever forms the society holds of greatest worth. A hatred of insecurity, a desire to build a home, a yearning to move into unknown regions from the place where he was born, a hunter's impulse which may take him to the African desert, or, less romantically, satisfy him by saturation in detective stories—all these are yearnings written into the fabric of our institutions. Man is a pugnacious animal; and the task of finding an outlet for that fruitful source of destruction is omnipresent. He desires to master his environment, to be the leader in his platoon; yet, under fitting conditions, he finds pleasure also in submission which, as in military organisation, can be turned to effective ends. He is a vain creature, seeking, as Veblen has shown, to waste his substance conspicuously, anxious, often enough, to be judged by the transient display rather than the solid achievement; so the workman will buy the piano he cannot play as an index to respectability, and the society leader will offer to the Moloch of fashion the income which might educate her children to social usefulness.

Hunger, drink, sex, and the need of shelter and clothing seem the irreducible minimum of human wants. All else is capable of transmutation into forms as various as the history of society. All that we know with certainty is that the wants are there. Some, as hunger, we cannot deny in general measure if the society is to live; others we can meet with response so complex as almost to conceal the true desire beneath. But what, above all, is urgent is that we should realise that our institutions are the response to the totality of these impulses. They are inexplicable save in terms of their formidable complexity.

It is, of course, vital to the structure of political philosophy that man should be not merely a creature of impulse, but also the possessor of reason. He can reflect upon his conduct. He can observe disharmonies, correlate means and ends. He can, that is to say, so observe the results of his activity as to rectify the ills from which he suffers by directing into them a principle of conduct that increases his chance of self-fulfilment. Where the tiger and the cuckoo hit upon that principle by accident, men can achieve its discovery by deliberate thought. It is here there enters the concept of a social good. For good, it must be emphasised, is either social, or it is not good at all. If man is to live in community with his fellows it is a necessary condition of his life that what he attains should, at least in the long run, involve benefit also to others. Social good, therefore, seems to consist in the unity our nature attains when the working of our impulses results in a satisfied activity. It is a full response to the forces of human nature as these work in the lives of the myriad men about us. The substance of that good may vary; a changing tradition implies a difference from age to age. As the body of our knowledge grows we become, at least as a matter of doctrine, the better able intelligently to organise the method and degree of response. The unification that is achieved demands, of course, close scrutiny lest falsehood he mistaken for truth. In the long run, for example, the desire to acquire property is hardly satisfied by the consistent flotation of fraudulent companies. What is rather wanted is a certain balance of forces within our nature that, when achieved, relieves the pressure of gnawing want and, more positively, makes possible the continuous satisfaction of initiative. It is not a question of attaining a static environment in which immobile habits may be satisfied. All situations that we confront are ultimately unique; and experiment is the condition of survival. Since the same good never occurs twice, immobility in a changing world must spell disaster, and the unification we must seek is one that intelligently anticipates the future as it reasonably interprets the past.

All this, it may be noted, is a special adaptation of the Benthamite theory to the special needs of our time. It follows Bentham in its insistence that social good is the product of co-ordinated intelligence; that, though the difficulties be admittedly great, we must plan our way to the end in view. It follows Bentham, also, though from a different basis, in urging that social good means the avoidance of misery and the attainment of happiness. It applies reason, that is, to the task of discovering ways in which wants can be satisfied; and it evaluates the quality of wants according to the degree in which, when satisfied, they minister to the permanent happiness of the whole community. Where it differs from the Utilitarian outlook is in its rejection of the egoistic nature of impulse and the elaborate calculus of pains and pleasures which, though couched in the terminology of the Industrial Revolution, was in fact derived from evangelistic assumptions. Our view is rather, first, that individual good cannot, over a long period, be usefully abstracted from the good of other men and, second, that the value of reason is to be found in the degree to which it makes possible the future, not less than the immediate, harmony of impulses. For, otherwise, these war within us to frustrate the realisation of what is best both for ourselves and others. Social good is thus such an ordering of our personality that we are driven to search for things it is worth while to obtain that, thereby, we may enrich the great fellowship we serve.

## (iii) The End of the State

From such an outlook we may derive a sense of the purpose embodied in the State. In this aspect it becomes an organisation for enabling the mass of men to realise social good on the largest possible scale. Necessarily, it is clear, its functions are confined to promoting certain uniformities of conduct; and the area it seeks to control will shrink or enlarge as experiment seems to warrant. There are obvious regions of life into which it has no thought of entry. It will promote a minimum of courtesy between neighbours as that minimum is set by the observance of order; but it will not compel Jones of Belgravia to invite Robinson of Brixton to dinner, whatever may be the social ambitions of Mrs. Robinson. It is less and less likely, as time proceeds, to set special store by the religious opinions of its citizens; it has discovered by painful experience that social welfare is unthinkable in terms of religious intolerance. It seems to be driven more and more to control, in some shape or form, those obvious commodities, water, power, transport, on which the welfare of its members so intimately depends; but it is equally driven to assume that the manufacture, say, of perfumes and cosmetics may be left, within certain limits, to the play of private enterprise. What it is and does will be determined by the history it encounters.

The State, therefore, does not set out to compass the whole range of human activity. There is a difference between the State and society. The State may set the keynote of the social order, but it is not identical with it. And it is fundamental to the understanding of the State that we should realise the existence of this distinction. That is apparent from an analysis of the way in which the State acts; as a source of reference the will of the State is the will of government. The teeming millions it seeks to organise cannot be deliberately articulate about the mass of decisions that are required; for the most part, they can do no more than indicate in a vague fashion the general direction in which they wish to see events move. They desire to see houses built; but the policy which brings houses into being cannot be formulated by twenty million people. Granted that, in any ultimate analysis, the real rulers of a State are undiscoverable, the legal source of daily power is resident in those who legislate. A State is, of course, conceivable in which the whole citizen-body takes part in the making of decisions, as ancient Athens gathered the members of the State into the market-place. But to the modern State of forty, seventy, or even one hundred millions, that experience is impossible in any continuous way. In practical life, therefore, the effective source of State-action is the small number of men whose decisions are legally binding upon the community. They are at once the trustees and governors of the whole. It is their business to glean the needs of the society and to translate those needs into terms of effective statutes. The purpose of the State finds its personification in them.

But there is a difference between the purpose they embody and the substance they give to that purpose. There was a difference between the philosophic theory which sought to justify the institutions of the *Ancien Régime* in France and the realisation of that theory in the facts. Our obligation to obey the State is, law apart, an obligation dependent upon the degree to which the State achieves its purpose. We are the judges of that achievement. What it is, and the difference therein from what it has the actual power to become, is written into the innermost fabric of our lives. We must obey the State, not because its theoretic purpose is a splendid one, but because of our conviction that it is genuinely seeking to make that purpose valid in events. Power is thus in itself morally neutral; what gives it colour is the performance it can demonstrate. Our ultimate allegiance is always to the ideal; and to the legal power that seeks to bind us our loyalty is conditioned by the purpose and substance we can discover in its effort.

The performance of the State, moreover, is significant for each one of us. It seems clear, therefore, that unless we can assume an *a priori* knowledge of the social value of each citizen, the State must be democratic. We shall, of course, differ as to what is implied in the notion of democracy. What, at the moment, is here alone intended is the argument that every man and woman is entitled to act upon what experience of the State is theirs. The final case against the government of one or a few is that either will, in the end, identify their private good with the good of the community. No class less than the adult population is entitled to consider its experience final. The judgment of Poplar is as urgent and imperative as the judgment of Mayfair. The purpose of the State affects each like in its working, and its performance is therefore of equal interest to each. This has been the obvious lesson of history. Classes excluded from a share in power have always been classes excluded from a share in benefits. The limitation in the number of those upon whom social good is conferred, whose personality, that is to say, finds satisfaction in the working of political institutions, has always meant, in the end, an assault upon the foundations of the State by those excluded from its direction. For the identity of men's nature makes them need a common minimum of satisfaction for their wants. The implication of that common minimum is a share in power that they may protect the fulfilment of their desires.

The equal interest of men in the results of its working thus implies a responsible State. It does not possess power without conditions. It possesses power because it has duties. It exists to enable men, at least potentially, to realise the best that is in themselves. It is judged, not by what it is in theory, but by what it does in practice. The State, accordingly, is subject to a moral test of adequacy. There is no *a priori* rightness about its decisions. It issues orders in the background of seeking consistently to make possible the expression of those impulses by which the common life is enriched. It is dangerous, of course, to exaggerate its powers in this regard. No State will directly lead its members to appreciate the best in life. But it is at least equally dangerous to underestimate the influence it can contribute. A State which builds, for example, an educational system which regards its citizens, not as helots, but as men, in which, as Plato desired, the Minister of Education is more important than the Minister of War, can at least mould conclusively an environment in which an appreciation of the best lies open to its members. Its orders, therefore, must be scrutinised in terms of its powers. Its true purpose is that which lies implicit in the achievement it encompasses by its actions.

To discuss the actions of the State involves, in the first place, knowing precisely what the State is. And here we must avoid the elementary confusion of identifying the State with the whole hierarchy of social institutions. Any true theory of political action must be a theory which visualises the men who operate the daily administration of its machinery. A theory of State, that is to say, is essentially a theory of the governmental act. To understand the latter we must doubtless consider all the influences which play upon it. The will it expresses may be the largest will we normally encounter. But it is not the will of society as a whole. The interests, social, artistic, religious, personal, political, which make up the substance of civilisation cannot be reduced to a single category. The will of the State is a particular aspect of the whole. It is an urgent aspect, in the same sense that the skeleton is a vital aspect of the body. But it is not one with the will of society any more than the life of the body is in its supporting skeleton.

Nor, in fact, can the State claim such universality as its identification with society would imply. For churches have always asserted their right not merely to transcend national limits, but to go beyond a given social order to the expression of a world-ideal. An English Roman Catholic does not find his religious allegiance enfolded within the margins of his political loyalty. So, too, with organisations like the Labour International. Its members would admit a measure of allegiance to the State; but they would insist that they owe allegiance also to the theory of right embodied in an organisation which reaches outside the boundaries of the State. They might agree with the State-will. But the chance of disagreement does not involve an ultimate moral right in the State to exact obedience from them. Their ultimate obedience is to a conception of right which the State may seek to attain but which, also, it may fail in serious measure to express.

The will of the State, therefore, seems to mean the will of government as the orders of that will are accepted by the citizen-body. Clearly, such a will, however important, has no special moral claims. It is doubtless a will to which is attached force of a peculiarly majestic kind. But the exercise of that force is always a moral issue, and the judgment passed upon it is a judgment made by each one of us. Citizenship, that is to say, means the contribution of our instructed judgment to the public good. It may lead us to support the State; but it may lead us also to oppose it. The will of the State is only my will in so far as I freely lend my judgment to its enforcement. I make my own obligations from scrutiny of its demands, or they are not, in any real sense, obligations at all. My support must be freely given, for, obviously, if I am penalised in weighing right and wrong. I become, sooner or later, a merely vacant recipient of decisions and lose the qualities which make me distinctively a person. I am a part of the State, but I am not one with it. An adequate theory of social organisation must always begin by recognising that the individual is finite. If he is a member of the herd, he is also outside it and passing judgment upon its actions.

## (iv) State and Society

This is, of course, a purely realistic view of the State; and it is worth while to inquire what is involved in the opposite view. Broadly speaking, this view goes back to the Greek equation between State and society, and it has been redefined in successive generations by Rousseau, Hegel and Bosanquet. It seeks in the individual that real will of which, did he know all the facts, he would without doubt be the expression. For could each of us count the cost of wrong, and reason out in detail its meaning and consequence, it is obvious that we should choose the right. We are, it is urged, most truly ourselves when this real will finds embodiment in our actions. This will, moreover, is the same in every member of society; and this identity exists because, at bottom, the real will in each of us is part of a common will which finds its highest form in the State. In such an aspect, therefore, the State is the highest part of ourselves. What it is and does represents the thing we would strive to be if the temporary, the immediate, and the irrational were stripped from the wills we desire. It is, so to say, the long and permanent end that, in the long run, we come individually to will after a private experience of wrong direction and erroneous desire.

From such a standpoint, the problem of political obligation can, of course, be easily resolved. We obey the State because in the end it most truly represents ourselves. We discover the identity of our will and its own the more clearly we grasp the nature of social relationships. What it does, it is doing always in the expression of that good which we ourselves would seek if all the facts were open to us. When we obey it we are, in truth, obeying ourselves; or, rather, we are obeying that best self which makes us one with and of our fellows. The State is thus the universal in which each of us, as particulars, finds our meaning. Where our knowledge and the will we build upon it are limited in range and purpose, it is compounded of the myriad intelligences from the interplay of which social organisation derives its ultimate form Liberty, in such a context, is a kind of permanent tutelage to the real self embodied in the State; and I may, in fact, be free even when I am suffused with the sense of compulsion.

The argument is an attractive one; and in the form given to it by Rousseau particularly it has had an immense influence upon the substance of State-action. But it is important at the outset to insist that a true theory of politics depends above all things upon its rejection. For what, at least ultimately, is involved in its acceptance is essentially the paralysis of will. If the citizen is not to find the source of his judgments in the contact between the outer world and himself, in the experience, that is, which is the one unique thing that separates him from the rest of the herd, he ceases to have meaning as an individual in any creative sense. He is what he is not merely by reason of the contacts with the world that he shares with others, but, above all, because those contacts are reached through a channel which he alone can know. His true self, that is, is the self that is isolated from his fellows, and contributes the fruit of isolated meditation to the common good which, collectively, they seek to bring into being.

Let us take separately each assumption of this theory. My true self, it is argued, is the self that I would be if I were consistently so rational in my conduct that means and ends were always perfectly correlated for good. But, in fact, no such self exists in me, and, if it did, it is unlikely that I should recognise it. My true self is the total impression I produce upon the fellowship of which I am part. It is an impression produced by a bewildering variety of acts, good and bad and indifferent. For the memory of some I am grateful; others come from a mood, a sudden fit of anger, perhaps, which is a permanent source of regret. But they are all of them the self which relates me to my neighbours; and even those which seem outside the normal experience of what I am are so only because an expectation uniform enough to be recognised has, on some occasion, failed to secure the wonted realisation.

Nor is it true to say that the will that is willed by this real self is identical in every member of society. For the starting-point of every political philosophy is the inexpugnable variety of human wills. There is no continuity between them. There are common objects of desire. City aldermen may will with equal intensity a low municipal rate. Chancellors of the Exchequer may will the boon of an unexpected surplus. But each alderman and each Chancellor is distinct from every other. The objects they encounter may affect them similarly. The wills those objects may arouse may be kindred in each. But kindred sensation and kindred will do not unite to produce a single will in any sense that is not purely metaphorical. The wills converge to a common purpose; but they are separate in everything save the substance of the thing willed.

If the will itself is separate in each member of society, it is still more clear that it does not form a single and common will. Anyone, indeed, who looks at the character of modern life would find its most distinguishing feature in the existence of a multiplicity of wills which have no common purposes which drive them to identity. The will of a good Roman Catholic to whom membership of his Church is the condition of salvation is for him the most real part of himself; and it has nothing in common with the will of a South Wales Communist engaged in promoting the objects of the Third International. These wills, doubtless, act upon one another. Their conflict produces restatement of the substance to be detected in the purpose of each. But they are not at any point part of a common general purpose which lies, somehow, at the back of the myriad purposes to be discovered in the general flow of action. It is true that, in classifying the wills we encounter in politics, we describe them in terms of unity. We speak of the will of the Conservative Party, the will of England, the will of the Anglican Church. But that predication of unity is a predication of wills so united as to give a predominant appearance, not of some will over and above the separate wills of which it is compounded. The unity is the recognition by me of the way in which the wills I shall encounter are related to each other. It is, to use technical terms, a unity, not of object, but of subject. It is not a unity in the sense that my personality, or that of Brown or Jones, is unified. Corporate personality, and the will that it embodies, is real in the sense that it makes those upon whom it acts different from what they were before. But it remains different from the uniqueness which makes me separate from the rest of the universe. The unity of England is in the historic tradition which orientates a vast number of wills in a similar direction; it is not in some mystic super-will built from their fusion.

The rejection of this notion of a common will has an important bearing upon the problem of freedom. If my real will is not the will that appears, but the common will that is embodied in the State, I many legitimately, as in Rousseau's famous phrase, be forced to be free. For to express what I truly desire is to be most truly myself; and to be most truly myself is of the essence of freedom. Yet if there is one thing fundamental to the life of the spirit it is the absence of force. In the view here combated, there is ultimately no real constraint when the prisoner in the dock is sentenced to penal servitude. He would, in fact, will his own imprisonment were he in full possession of the facts upon which his will is based. Yet the truth surely is that there is all the difference in the world between a restraint I put upon myself and a restraint put upon me by others. If I voluntarily refrain from the use of tobacco for twenty-four hours, the force I put upon myself does not seem to me a violation of my freedom. I have myself willed a certain harmony of impulses; and if that harmony does not work, I can alter the substance of my will, can, in other words, alter the balance of impulses at which I am seeking to arrive. But that is not the same thing as to be restrained from the use of tobacco by a will I do not recognise as my own. Force, that is, means imposition from without in a sense entirely antithetic to freedom because it is not welcomed as self-desired. It is the compulsory subjection of the individual to an experience he would not voluntarily share.

That does not mean, of course, that the use of force is wrong. There are rules, the law of school attendance for example, which I ought to obey even if I disapprove: for, obviously, if each man is to follow his every impulse wherever it leads, an organised social life would be impossible. It means that force must be used in those directions only where the common sense of society is on the side of the type of conduct it seeks to compel. But it means also that, in extreme cases, I may decide that I shall disobey the law and accept whatever punishment it inflicts. That is the only way, at least ultimately, in which I can make the unique contribution of my personality to the life of the community. Luther is Luther because he defied the Roman Church at Worms; Nevil Beauchamp was not less truly a citizen when he fought against his country because he loved it. My freedom, in fact, consists in emphasising my differences from the rest of society, and in acting upon the basis of those differences. Some of them may be, most will be, too trivial to be the cause of conflict; but the surrender of those I deem to be fundamental to a will in which my own discovers no apparent identity is the frustration of personality and not its fulfilment.

Still less than the notion of a common will can we accept the doctrine that if finds embodiment within the State. It is argued, to use a phrase of Dr. Bosanquet, that all State-action is, at bottom, the exercise of the real will of society. But if this means that social life is ultimately the product of a single and rational mind organising its activities in terms of a logical process, it is contrary to every fact we encounter in daily experience. The things about us, customs, institutions, beliefs, grow up in haphazard, semi-conscious fashion. Deliberation there often is, but it does not inform the whole. He would be an optimist indeed who could discover any system of governing principles applied to civilisation. The paths we tread are too often the result of accidental experience for us to dignify them as rational searches for the right direction.

Nor are they based upon the effort of some unified will. What, rather, exists is an amazing welter of wills which press upon each other. What, in fact, we call the State is simply a source of ultimate references which makes a decision upon grounds that it deems adequate. It is not a will unified in the sense that my will is unified when, for example, I send for a book I have seen in a bookseller's catalogue. There I have weighed cost of purchase against desirability of acquisition and counted the balance as advantage. But the decision of a State to act has no such simple environment. When England declared war in 1914, a majority of the Cabinet decided first that they must repel the invasion of France and Belgium, and second that they could carry their fellow-citizens with them in so doing. But in fact the decision was not a unified act, but the coherence in varying degrees of separate wills so to act as to achieve a single end. The unity was in the objective purpose at which they aimed. And, as a rule, the decision to make war is a simple one because the emotional penumbra it implies is hostile to difference of outlook. If we take domestic legislation—an Insurance Act, for instance—it is clear that there goes to the making of the will it embodies influences, compromises, amendments, pressure, which clearly reveal how chaotic and indeterminate are the sources of its origin. The will of the State, in short, is the will which is adopted out of the conflict of myriad wills which contend with each other for the mastery of social forces. It is never deliberate in the sense that it is always determined by rational considerations. It is never single, in the sense that it derives from a unanimous agreement of those to whom it applies. Often enough, as in the *Ancien Régime* in France, it is not even instinct with good will. And if this is the case we have not the right to attach any special moral attribute to the will of the State until we have estimated the results of that will at work. It is a good will when it combines good intention with beneficent consequence. But it is to be judged not by the purpose it embodies in theory so much as by the effort that it makes in practice.

## (v) The Nature of Political Power

A working theory of the State must, in fact, be conceived in administrative terms. Its will is the decision arrived at by a small number of men to whom is confided the legal power of making decisions. How that power is organised is rather a matter of form than of substance. It may, of course, be organised in such a way that it cannot, as in Czarist Russia, attain the end which theory postulates for it. Power, that is to say, is always a trust, and it is always held upon conditions. The will of the State is subject to the scrutiny of all who come within the ambit of its decisions. Because it moulds the substance of their lives, they have the right to pass judgment upon the quality of its effort. They have, indeed, the duty so to pass judgment; for it is the plain lesson of the historic record that the wants of men will only secure recognition to the point that they are forcibly articulate. The State is not ourselves save where we identify ourselves with what it does. It becomes ourselves as it seeks to give expression to our wants and desires. It exerts power over us that it may establish uniformities of behaviour which make possible the enrichment of our personality. It is the body of men whose acts are directed to that end. Broadly, that is to say, when we know the sources from which governmental acts derive we know the sources of the State's will.

But as those sources are not in themselves either good or bad, so the will of the State is in its nature morally neutral. It secures recognition from its members from a wide variety of causes. Some obey from conviction that the particular act is right. To others, the act arouses so feeble an emotion that indifference does not create the sense either of support or opposition. Others, as with the Education Act of 1902, actively oppose because they believe that the given act represents an abuse of power. What we are always given is a series of actions about which we have to make up our minds. The wills of those persons who form a government coalesce to make a decision; and that in its turn becomes the will of the State as it is translated into terms of daily administration.

A view such as this has at least the supreme merit of realism. It admits that acts emanate from persons, and it insists that those persons are subject to the scrutiny of their fellow-citizens. It does not postulate the rightness of their acts. It does not even postulate that the duty of inquiry and acceptance will be undertaken by the mass of men. It argues only that the acts of a government are built upon their obligation to labour that the citizens of the State may have full opportunity to realise the best in themselves. That is what gives a moral support to government policy. But it is an hypothesis that can be proved true only by historic experience. The power of government is the right of government in the degree to which it is exercised for the end of social life. There is a note of interrogation at the end of every governmental pronouncement. It is for the citizen to decide in what manner the question shall be answered.

The great advantage of this attitude lies in the importance it attaches to individual personality. For since the State is seeking to realise the fruits of social experience, it must clearly act upon the largest interpretation of experience that is open to it. It can neglect no source that, even potentially, has hints and ideas to contribute. That is the real case for democratic government. Once every adult member of the community finds unbarred the access to self-expression, there is at least the avenue open to its attainment. That implies two things. It means that the quality of any State will depend upon the degree to which men consciously seek to give the State the import of the meaning they find in their lives. It means, secondly, that the first effort of the State must be to place its members in that situation where the analysis of their experience is creatively possible. Men whose whole lives, for instance, are passed in the daily struggle for bread will not, on any large scale, know how to explain why that bread is for them ground from a bitter corn. Every State lives upon the character of its citizens; and it can use that character only as it is informed by articulate knowledge.

The State is thus a fellowship of men aiming at the enrichment of the common life. It is an association like others: churches, trade unions, and the rest. It differs from them in that membership is compulsory upon all that live within its territorial ambit, and that it can, in the last resort, enforce its obligations upon its subjects. But its moral character is no different from that of any other association. It exacts loyalty upon the same grim condition that a man exacts loyalty from his friends. It is judged by what it offers to its members in terms of the things they deem to be good. Its roots are laid in their minds and hearts. In the long run, it will win support, not by the theoretic programme it announces, but by the perception of ordinary citizens that allegiance to its will is a necessary condition of their own well-being. It must offer them assurances that it seeks to protect that well-being. It has no moral claim upon their loyalty save in so far as they are offered proof of its realisation.

There is even a sense in which the judgement of State-effort ought to be more radical in its nature than the judgment upon other associations. The width of the functions that it exercises, the extent of the power it brings to their control, the difference it can make in the happiness of men—all of these give to its acts a penumbra of significance more vital than that of any other body. If I do not obey the injunctions of the Church, I can always leave it. I may suffer social ostracism from those whose friendship I cherish. I may be threatened with anathemas at which I tremble. But so far, at least, as earthly and perceptible consequences are concerned, I shall be protected in my normal source of conduct by all the resources of law and order. So, too, with any other fellowship to which I choose to belong. It cannot compel me to accept its jurisdiction. I can even, at certain points, invoke the resources of society against its interference with my actions. With the State, the case is different. I can dissent from its conclusions only at the cost of penalty. I cannot, in any fundamental way, withdraw from its jurisdiction. I cannot, as the world is now organised, appeal from the tribunals it has created. It is the ultimate source of decision within the normal environment about which my life is lived. Clearly, that attaches to its will an importance for me greater than that which belongs elsewhere. It may choose to tax me out of existence. It may refuse to allow me to practice my religion. It may compel me to sacrifice my life in a war that I believe to be morally wrong. It may refuse me those means of intellectual training without which, in the modern world, I can hardly hope to realise myself. In such a background, the price of power ought obviously to be a special vigilance about its exercise.

It is also, surely, obvious that such a vigilance is to-day worthless unless it is organised. If the modern State were no larger than ancient Athens, the individual citizen might hope to make his voice penetrate to the seat of power. He cannot do so with ourselves. He may, in concert with others, exercise a pressure to which, in the end, adjustment will be offered. But it is still more urgent that the forms of the State assume such a shape that the power of government can, at every point, be made responsible. Here the experience of history must in large part be the guide of our methods. Certain ways of governmental life are excluded from the area of acceptance because they have proved incompatible with responsibility. That was the case, for example, with States in which the franchise was bestowed upon a limited class alone. It is the nature of men to identify, over a short period, their private good with the welfare of others. Unless their conception of the commonweal is subject to external check, its misuse is probable. Power, in other words, is in its nature dangerous to those who exert it; and whatever may be the reasons for its extent, they are reasons also for the creation of safeguards against its misuse.

There is in such a doctrine as this at least a hint of anarchy. It is, in the first place, an individualistic doctrine. It makes the reasonable satisfaction of my impulses the test of institutional adequacy. It insists that if the State exists to protect the interests of other persons, it exists also to protect my interests; and if it fails to do so, it assumes on my part a moral duty to inquire into the grounds of failure. Further, it urges that the results of my inquiry oblige me to take action. Contingently, that is, analysis of the State may ethically compel me to seek its overthrow. If I hold that its power is being in fact exercised, not for the ends implied in its nature, but for the ends incompatible therewith, the civic outcome of such perception is the duty of resistance. For I am a member of the State in order that, in common with my fellows, I may be myself at my best. I ought not to resist if I am convinced that the State is seeking, as best it may, to play its part; and for most that perception will doubtless result from what inquiry they undertake. I ought not, further, to resist unless I have reasonable ground for the belief that the changes I advocate are likely to result in the end I have in view; I must, moreover, be certain that the methods I propose to realise my end will not, in their realisation, change its essential character: men have often enough sought power for good and ended by exercising it for its own sake. But my citizenship is, within the ambit of these precautions, either a moral adventure or it is nothing. It gives me my perceptions of right and wrong. I most truly serve its purpose when I act by the moral certainties it conveys.

This view may be stated in another way. I have, as a citizen, a claim upon society to realise my best self in common with others. That claim involves that I be secured those things without which I cannot, in Green's phrase, realise myself as a moral being. I have, that is, rights which are inherent in me as a member of society; and I judge the State, as the fundamental instrument of society, by the manner in which it seeks to secure for me the substance of those rights. They are, of course, counterbalanced by the duties I owe in return. I am given rights that I may enrich the common life. But if those rights fail of realisation, I am entitled to examine the State upon the hypothesis that its will is directed to ends other than the common good. I regard its power as force exercised in order to secure those rights. Its moral character is known to me by the rights that it maintains. If I see it make possible a full and rich existence for others, I am justified in seeking to know whether that rich and full existence is open to myself. I have, in a word, rights against the State because I am a citizen. I am entitled at any given moment to the fullest potentialities it can offer my moral self, the most satisfactory harmony of impulses I can attain. As I have no meaning, save as a slave, without those rights, so the State which fails to secure them for me is devoid of meaning for myself.

Rights, in this sense, are the groundwork of the State. They are the quality which gives to the exercise of its power a moral character. And they are natural rights in the sense that they are essential to the good life. As they remain unfulfilled, so am I, socially not less than personally, deprived of the chance to serve the fellowship of men. A State which neglects them fails to build its foundations in the hearts of its citizens. It becomes known to them by the rights it maintains; and, over any long period, it wins their allegiance by the effort it makes to give those rights increasing substance. They are objective as well as natural, in the sense that scientific investigation may be able to demonstrate their necessity for right living, and the view that social action may reasonably seek to secure their attainment.

It follows from the conception here outlined that this view of rights is a functional one. We do not possess them as avenues of personal enjoyment. We do not realise them because we are only and merely ends in and for ourselves. We possess them because each part of us is suffused with social implications. Whatever we do affects the life about us. Our joys and sorrows are in a real sense historic events which, minute as they may be in the record of the political fabric, are collectively urgent in the test of its future. By a functional theory of rights is meant that we are given powers that we may so act as to add to the richness of our social heritage. We have rights, not that we may receive, but that we may do. Granted that we shall contribute unequally to the store of social well-being, it is yet imperative that the means of contribution shall be there. Some, doubtless, whatever the barriers in their path, will hew their way to achievement. Others, whatever the powers that are offered them, will remain historically unrecognisable from the mass of their fellow-men. But any society is ultimately tested by the manner in which it offers avenues of creative service to any who are willing to utilise them. That, broadly speaking, was the test which France failed to meet in 1789 and Russia in 1917. The rights they recognised were unrelated to the lives of most of their citizens. When the State was challenged, it could not rely upon them to defend a fabric unconnected with the organisation of their interests.

This theory of rights sets the perspective of the powers attributed to the State. It claims to be a sovereign organisation; it has, that is to say, the right ultimately to demarcate the boundaries of its action. The test of such a claim is, in the view here set out, a purely pragmatic one. We have to decide what powers the State should enjoy, and how it should organise those powers, if it is to serve the end implied in its philosophy. The test of any social organisation is not an absolute logic to which is accorded *a priori* rightness, but the experience by its members of the logic it maintains. It will, in that aspect, be important to remember that every claim has an historic environment which, more than any other consideration, will explain its substance. It will be important, also, to remember that if the State is in fact that small body of men to whom the actual operation of its will is confided, the analysis of such an ultimate power as sovereignty implies is a far more serious task than when, for reasons here rejected, we assume it to be, in some mystic fashion, the best part of ourselves. That organisation of society is best which is most likely to produce a race of erect-minded men. There may be involved in such an effort a single ultimate centre of control. It may be also that the ethical limitation upon the use of power involves an administrative limitation also. That view, certainly, must be maintained by anyone who regards power as in its nature a trust subject to continuous scrutiny because it is subject to continuous abuse. If the State is known by the rights that it maintains, clearly it needs the power to maintain those rights. But there is always present the danger that a power which exists to secure good may, from its very strength, be used to frustrate it. Certainly the assurance of good intent is no longer adequate. Those who sit in the seat of government must be judged by their elevation of humble and ordinary men.

One other remark must be made. A thesis such as this depends upon the assumption that the average man is, in fact, a political animal. It involves the argument that he can be made to show interest in affairs of State and that such interest may be made to coincide with understanding adequate to the democratic conduct of affairs. It ought, at the outset of any political discussion, to be admitted that these are large assumptions. Any view of modern society reveals how large is the number of men from whom a sense of the State is absent. They remain obstinately enfolded in a narrow sphere of private interest. They make no effort not merely to grasp the general stream of social tendency, but even the way in which that stream flows through the particular position they occupy. They view the political conflict as a drama in which they have no part. They show no interest in its actors or its scenes. They ask only that their private affairs remain unfettered by public interruption.

Such a situation might mean one of two things. It might mean that we can discover a body of persons to whom the guardianship of the State might, as a matter of nature, be entrusted. The relationship between master and slave, which Aristotle commanded, might, in that view, be the ideal solution of this difficulty. But in fact we cannot discover "natural" masters and "natural" slaves save by the method of trial and error; and that involves a democratic system of government. It is, in the second place, clear that the private affairs of men have in fact a consistent public connotation; they can be kept unfettered only by attention to politics and not by indifference to them. More urgent, perhaps, is the question of understanding. The complexity of the modern State does not yield its secrets without long study. But if we regard citizenship as a discipline in which men can be trained, at least its large outlines are intelligible to all who are interested in life itself. Our error in the past has been to oppose an abstract man to an abstract community, to the common injury of both. The truth is that our immersion in political affairs extends, whether we recognise it or no, to the intimate substance of our lives. The only privacy man can hope to enjoy is that of judgment; and even judgment entails consequences of social import.

Men, in fact, are, in their every context, making political decisions; and the real question for them is simply to what authority the decision is referable. The complexity, doubtless, means that their judgment can be asked for only on the larger issues; and, very certainly, that those issues, to be decided, must be consistently reduced to the simplest terms. A democracy, in other words, must, if it is to work, be an aristocracy by delegation. But the fact of delegation is vital. Men grow to their full stature only in the environment of responsibility. Their character, as Goethe said, is formed upon the billows of the world. To realise life, they must control life; to control it, they must make articulate to their fellow-citizens what intuition they have of the experience they have enjoyed. It is the largest task before civilisation to train men to the coherent statement of what their experience implies.

[*Note:* On all this see the remarkable last essay in Mr. A.E. Zimmern's *The Prospects of Democracy* (1929).

# 2. Sovereignty

## (i) The General Nature of Sovereignty

The modern State is a sovereign State. It is, therefore, independent in the face of other communities. It may infuse its will towards them with a substance which need not be affected by the will of any external power. It is, moreover, internally supreme over the territory that it controls. It issues orders to all men and all associations within that area; it receives orders from none of them. Its will is subject to no legal limitation of any kind. What it purposes is right by the mere announcement of intention.

But such a theory of sovereignty has at least three aspects from which it demands a careful scrutiny. It needs, in the first place, historical analysis. The State as it now is has not escaped the categories of time. It has become what it is by virtue of an historical evolution. That development both explains the character of its present power and, at the last, offers hints as to its possible future. It is, secondly, a theory of law. It makes of right merely the expression of a particular will, without reference to what that will contains. Such a definition, as will be seen, has about it an unquestionable logic; but the assumptions upon which it is compelled to build make it valueless for political philosophy.

The modern theory of sovereignty is, thirdly, a theory of political organisation. It insists that there must be in every social order some single centre of ultimate reference, some power that is able to resolve disputes by saying a last word that will be obeyed. From the political angle, such a view, as will be argued, is of dubious correctness in fact; and it is at least probable that it has dangerous moral consequences. It will be here argued that it would be of lasting benefit to political science if the whole concept of sovereignty were surrendered. That, in fact, with which we are dealing is power; and what is important in the nature of power is the end it seeks to serve and the way in which it serves that end. These are both questions of evidence which are related to, but independent of, the rights that are born of legal structure. For there is, historically, no limit to the variety of ways in which the use of power may be organised. The sovereign State, historically, is merely one of those ways, an incident in its evolution the utility of which has now reached its apogee. The problem before us has become, because of the unified interests of mankind, that of bending the modern State to the interests of humanity. The dogmas we use to that end are relatively of little import, so long as we are assured that the end is truly served.

The territorial and omnipotent State is the offspring of the religious struggles of the sixteenth century. Before that time Western civilisation was regarded as a single Commonwealth in which sovereignty, in the modern sense, had no existence. Ultimate power was, at least in theory, the possession of a view of right which found embodiment in Pope and Emperor. The two powers clashed; and the imminent victory of Rome was frustrated by a moral degeneration coincident with the growth of nationality. The appeal against a Church which remained obstinately deaf to demands for reform involved the creation of the national State. For when Luther appealed against the divine Church, he was driven to assert the divinity of States, that the right of a secular body to interfere might be made manifest. There were European princes ready to accept his views; and when they met the challenge of a reviving Church, insistence upon their sovereignty and the unified allegiance it implied was the simplest theoretic justification they could discover. The State became incarnate in the prince. What he willed was right because it was his will. Right ceases to mean, as in the Middle Ages, a particular aspect of universal justice; it comes to mean that which emanates from a single centre in the body politic and by its predominating unity gives strength and decisiveness to the striking power of the community. The *Republic* of Bodin, in which the theory of sovereignty is first treated in modern terms, shows clearly the urgency of this perspective to his generation. For Bodin was making a plea for peace in an age of war. *Jus est quod jussum est* is the direst high road to the goal. If men can be persuaded to accept the will of the sovereign organ as pre-eminent, opposition is deprived of its main pretensions, and Henry IV, for example, may restore to France the prosperity religious conflict has endangered.

The sovereign State thus emerges to vindicate the supremacy of the secular order against religious claims; and it forces the clerisy into the position of subordinate authority from which, after the Dark Ages, it had itself so painfully emerged. It is argued by Bodin, as later by Hobbes in a period of similar disintegration, that if the State is to live there must be in every organised political community some definite authority not only itself obeyed, but also itself beyond the reach of authority. This was the root of Hobbes' argument. The will of the State must be all or nothing. If it can be challenged, the prospect of anarchy is obvious. So, too, in their different ways, with the views of Rousseau and Chief Justice Marshall. A sovereign people, they argued, cannot suffer derogation from the effective power of its instruments. Its will must be unimpeachable if it is to direct the destinies with which it is charged. We must not forget the atmosphere, not merely in which the theory of sovereignty was born, but also in which, at the hands of each of its great exponents, it has secured new emphasis. That has been always, from Bodin to Hegel, a period of crisis in which the State seemed likely to perish unless it could secure the unified allegiance of its members. That allegiance might be secured if legal superiority were vested in the sovereign organ. So long as religious intolerance was a European habit, it was difficult for the suppressed minority to accept the view that legal superiority implied moral authority. With the coming of toleration, however, that difficulty was removed. The fact that religious difference was now permanently recognised left the State the sole association with an identical claim upon those who dwelt within its boundaries. It provided a ground where, as it seemed, all who possessed citizenship might meet in common. There, at least, there seemed to be neither Jew nor Greek, neither bond nor free. The social bond seemed to find, particularly as the forms of democratic government made their way, its ultimate expression in a State which, differently from all other associations, had no partial character about it. The State embraced all men because it was the one compulsory form of association. It was easy to identify its sovereignty with pre-eminence.

Another cause contributed to this elevation. Driven by the Reformation from a position of universal competence, the papacy sought the compensation of an international position. As the French King was to Frenchmen abroad, so, the Jesuits argued, was the papal relationship to Roman Catholics. Behind that claim, indeed, there lurked certain shadowy vestiges of supremacy which disappeared only with the regretful recognition of permanence in the secular State. What was important was the notion that rules were necessary for the regulation of affairs between the organs of sovereign powers. The hinterland between nations could, so Grotius magistrally declared, become the subject of agreements not less morally binding than the will of States was binding upon their subjects. It was agreed that the State was, through its governmental organ, the natural unit through which such agreement might be made. When States became, in the course of the seventeenth century, the natural and ultimate channels of diplomatic intercourse, the final safeguard of the rights of their subjects abroad, the last link in the chain of their predominance was complete. Thenceforth, their will knew, legally at least, no external check of any kind. The sanction of international law was their assent to it; and the implication of assent was a withdrawal as free as the original assent. What was called, in brief, the comity of nations did not imply, except as metaphor, the redintegration of the mediaeval *Respublica Christiana*. The acknowledged rights of humanity became simply those rules which States agreed to observe, rules which, as in the case of Belgium in 1914, States were legally free to break if they so pleased. The chain was then complete. The individual could then read the details of his rights and duties in the list of orders and prohibitions enforced by the government under which he lived. At home he could have those powers implied in the fabric of its statutes. Abroad he could use those privileges its dexterity had wrung from the courtesy of other States.

Yet what in all this is most striking to the observer is the fact that it represents, not an absolute but an historical logic. Internationally, it is not difficult to conceive the organisation of an allegiance which reaches beyond the limits of the State. To leave with a handful of men, for instance, the power to make war may well seem anachronistic to those who envisage the consequences of war. When State sovereignty in international affairs was recognised, there was no authority existent to which that type of control might be entrusted. It is at least arguable now that an authority predominant over States may be conceived to which is entrusted the regulation of those affairs of more than national interest. That is clear in the case of war. It is, for most, clear also in the case, for example, of those native races who cannot pit their skill in exploitation against the genius of the modern trader. Wherever, in short, the interests of a unified and interdependent world seem to demand an international standard of conduct, the corporate organisation of that standard, and its corporate application, are at least conceivable. We shall discuss later what is implied in such a notion. Here it is sufficient to insist that it involves, at any rate on the international side, the abolition of State sovereignty. It sees the State simply as a unit in a society of States, the will of which would then be set by a process in which it would have no final say. It even implies, as the acceptance of this doctrine grows, a duty on the part of the individual citizen of a recalcitrant State to look beyond the emotional penumbra of patriotism to the issue of conflict. He might then, perhaps, choose to declare that obedience to the will of the society of States is, in the given instance, the highest duty that he knows.

The logic of this evolution is not dissimilar on the internal side. Any study of the working of the State will be compelled largely to concern itself with the history of the limitations upon the exercise of power. Those who practise are theoretic substance of sovereignty find themselves sooner or later deprived of it. For the State must work through persons. The government which acts as its sovereign organ never, as a matter of history, has the prospect of permanence if it consistently seeks to be absolute. Civil war and revolution in the England of the seventeenth century, 1789 in France, 1917 in Russia, are all of them footnotes to the problem of sovereignty. What they seem to mean is the fact that power has always to be organised for action in accordance with rules, and that the obedience of the community has been proffered to the government only when it abides by those rules. Power, that is to say, when vested in a number of persons, is not only limited as to method, but also as to the objects to which it can be directed. Sovereignty, that is to say, is historically conditioned always by the environment it encounters. It is secure only when it is so exercised with responsibility. But the definition of sovereignty is that it is unlimited and irresponsible; and the logic of its hypothesis is thus directly antithetic to the experience it has encountered.

Another point of interest may here be made. Those who have most powerfully shaped the theory of sovereignty—Bodin, Hobbes, Rousseau, Bentham and Austin—were, with the exception of Austin, all of them writing before the nature of a federal State had been at all fully explored. Either, like Bodin, they thought in terms of the unlimited power of the prince, or, like Bentham, in terms of the unlimited power of the legislature; and they might, like Rousseau, deny legitimacy to any act which emanated merely from a representative organ. The difficulty of fitting their assumptions to a State like the United States is obvious. The congress is a limited body the powers of which are carefully defined; the separate States are similarly cabined within the four corners of the Constitution; and even the amendment of the Constitution is limited by the exception that no State shall, without its own consent, be deprived of its equal suffrage in the Senate. In the theoretic sense, therefore, the United States has no sovereign organ; for the Judges of the Supreme Court, being overridden by Constitutional Amendment, are clearly only a penultimate court of reference. A peculiar historical experience has therefore devised the means of building a State from which the conception of sovereignty is absent. We may, of course, as certain German theorists have done, prize so highly the theory of sovereignty as to urge that a society which does not possess it is not a State at all. But a political philosophy which rejects the title of the United States to Statehood is unlikely to apply to a world of realities.

## (ii) Legal Sovereignty

The legal aspect of sovereignty is best examined by a statement of the form given to it by John Austin. In every legal analysis of the State, he argued, it is first of all necessary to discover in the given society that definite superior to which habitual obedience is rendered by the mass of men. That superior must not itself obey any higher authority. When we discover the authority which gives commands habitually obeyed, itself not receiving them, we have the sovereign power in the State. In an independent political community that sovereign is determinate and absolute. Its will is illimitable because, if it could be constrained to act, it would cease to be supreme, since it would then be subject to the constraining power. Its will is indivisible because, if power over certain functions or persons is absolutely and irrevocably entrusted to a given body, the sovereign then ceases to enjoy universal supremacy and therefore ceases by definition to be sovereign. Its will is also clearly inalienable for the obvious reason that if a sovereign authority parts with its sovereignty it cannot of its own will resume it. Law, therefore, is simply the will of the sovereign. It is a command obliging the subject to do, or to refrain from doing, certain acts, failure to obey being visited by a penalty. The sovereign itself is unlimited by positive law because it is its creator. Within the sphere of law, there is therefore, as Hobbes bluntly said, no such thing as an unjust command. The sovereign being unlimited, he has the legal right to will whatever he may happen to desire.

It may be useful to emphasise the threefold implication of this view. The State for Austin is a legal order in which there is a determinate authority acting as the ultimate source of power. Its authority, secondly, is unlimited. It may act unwisely, or dishonestly, or, in an ethical sense, unjustly. For the purpose of legal theory the character of its actions is unimportant. If they emanate from the authority competent to issue the particular command, they are the law. Command thirdly, is of the essence of law. You must do certain things; you must not do other things. Failure to fulfil in either direction your obligation is punished by a penalty.

Within the narrow field that it covers, the Austinian view is a correct analysis of what flows from certain definite assumptions. If the lawyer regards sovereignty as important only as a form of command. He is obviously entitled to discuss it in that aspect. He may, further, assume that the force which lies at the disposal of the sovereign is unlimited, and that force need be considered only as it is applied by the courts of modern and relatively orderly States. But these assumptions make it worthless as an explanation of the modern State for political purposes. There it is clear that the sovereign power is engaged in work which cannot at all reasonably be reduced to the form of a command. It is, obvious, further, that no organisation disposes in actual fact of unlimited force; and we shall fail completely to understand the character of society, unless we seek to grasp exactly how the sovereign is compelled to will things desired by bodies in law inferior to itself.

On the historical side, of course, it was sufficiently shown by Sir Henry Maine that the Austinian theory is artificial to the point of absurdity. There is nothing genuinely comparable between the sovereignty of the King in Parliament, of an Eastern theocracy, and the people of ancient Athens. Nor, as we saw in the case of America, can a determinate sovereign body always be found. No sovereign has anywhere possessed unlimited power; and the attempt to exert it has always resulted in the establishment of safeguards. Even the Sultan of Turkey in the height of his power was himself bound down by a code of traditional observance, obedience to which was practically compulsory upon him. In law there was no part of the field of social fact he could not alter; in practice he survived only by willing not to will those changes which might have proved him the sovereign of Austinian jurisprudence.

To think, moreover, of law as simply a command is, even for the jurist, to strain definition to the verge of decency. For there is a character of uniformity in law in which the element of command is, practically speaking, pushed out of sight. This is true, for instance, of all enabling statutes. When the Lord Chancellor is directed, if he so decide, to sell the presentation to benefices of which he has the advowson according to 26 and 27 Vic. c. 120, the statute is undoubtedly a law, but the element of command is very indirectly present. The Lord Chancellor is not directed to do anything; unless he takes certain action, there is no obligation of any kind; and if he acted contrary to the terms of the Act, its only sanction is that the courts would treat his sale of the advowson as void. When a Franchise Act conferred the vote on women, it is an exceedingly circuitous way of explaining its nature to resolve it into terms of command. No obligation is imposed, unless we regard the duty of the registration officer to accept women as voters as an obligation. No law has probably aroused so much discussion as the Rule in Shelley's case. That rule simply lays it down that when an analogous case occurs certain words shall be construed in an particular way. The notion of command is contingent and indirect; and the idea of penalty is, again save in the most circuitous way, notably absent. And it is very difficult to see how the exercise of delegated authority can be brought within the ambit of the Austinian definition. A royal warrant regulates the pensions and pay of the army. It is a command emanating from a qualified authority; but the Secretary of State for War cannot be compelled to obey it.

The most perfect example of the Austinian view is, of course, the position held by the King in Parliament. Any command which issues therefrom will, as Dicey pointed out in a classic analysis, be obeyed by enforcement through the courts. But everyone knows that to regard the King in Parliament as a sovereign body in the Austinian sense is absurd. No Parliament would dare to disfranchise the Roman Catholics or to prohibit the existence of trade unions. If it made the attempt, it would cease to be a Parliament. That is to say that in practice legally unlimited power turns out to be power exercised under conditions fairly well known to each generation. There is probably a larger degree of obedience from the sovereign Parliament to its constituents than there is the other way round; a series of by-elections, for instance, produce with amazing rapidity a change in the will and temper of the sovereign. Behind, that is, the legally omnipotent authority it is not very difficult to discern an electorate to whose opinions and desires increasing deference must be shown. That notion of an increasing deference is important. As the community becomes organised into associations with the end of bringing pressure to bear on government, the sovereign organ becomes, as a general process, little more than a machine for registering decisions arrived at elsewhere. All the forms of an Austinian arrangement are preserved; but it is upon their saving condition that their substance is surrendered.

It has been pointed out that the discovery of sovereignty in a federal State is, practically, an impossible adventure; but that difficulty is not confined to federal States. It is doubtful, for example, whether, in the Austinian sense, Belgium may be termed a sovereign State at all. The Constitution guarantees certain rights to every Belgian citizen. He may exercise his religion as he thinks fit; his property may not be taken without due compensation; he has the right freely to assemble so long as he does not carry arms and does not meet in the open air. Now it is quite true that these and similar rights are all of them alterable by the Belgian Assembly. But before the Constitution can be altered the decision of one Assembly must be ratified by a new one rechosen by the electorate for that purpose. There is no guarantee not merely that the new Chambers will in a sitting at which two-thirds of the members are present and two-thirds of these vote for the change, ratify the constitutional alteration; even more, there is no guarantee that the new Assembly will have the same complexion as the old, and, it might, as a matter of theory, prove impossible to alter the Constitution. In that background either Belgium is not a sovereign State in its internal affairs (though it is a sovereign State for the purpose of international law) or its sovereignty resides in the electorate. But any electorate is an indeterminate body which is legally bound to act through organs and agents; and it is, according to Austin, the characteristic of sovereignty to be determinate and illimitable.

Difficulties such as these Professor Dicey attempted to meet by dividing the notion of sovereignty into two parts. The King in Parliament, he suggested, might be regarded as the legal, the electorate as the political, sovereign. But this is at once to imply that the notion of sovereignty is divisible, which is entirely contradictory of the original definition. Nor is the case improved by accepting Austin's own suggestion that the sovereign in England is the electorate which exercises its powers through representatives. For, in the first place, the Crown and the House of Lords are not representative of the Commons in any sense to which precision can be attached, and when Austin goes on to argue that the sovereign electorate may delegate its powers either "subject to a trust or trusts" or "absolutely and unconditionally", he fails to remember the logical meaning of a definition which implies the impossibility of alienation. If the electorate merely created a trust, the latter would not be a sovereign body. If it created a sovereign body, in the sense Austin gave that term, it would itself cease to be sovereign.

The maze, in fact, to which Austinianism ultimately leads, implies in the modern State the theory of popular sovereignty. It is well to urge at the outset that it is impossible to give precision to this view. The people cannot govern in the sense of acting continually as a unit; for the business of the modern State is far too complex to be conducted by perpetual referenda. If popular sovereignty simply means the paramountcy of public opinion, this is an abstraction of the most vicious kind. For we need to know when public opinion is public and when it is opinion. The elicitation of a popular will is always a delicate task to the result of which grave uncertainty attaches. If we attempt to enshrine it within institutional forms, as when the American Constitution sought to make certain notions fundamental, we may end, not by enthroning public opinion, but what five out of nine judges consider to be reasonable, which is a very different thing. And if, as with the French Constitution of 1791, we say that the nation is the source of all powers which are to be exercised by the legislative body and the King, we are reducing popular sovereignty to a metaphor. We should then encounter on the one hand the argument of Rousseau that to part with paramount power is to betray it, and, on the other, the view of Burke and Mill that a restricted mandate is fatal to the moral character of the representative. All, in fact, that the theory of popular sovereignty seems to mean is that the interests which prevail must be the interests of the mass of men rather than of any special portion of the community; and it is further an implicit insistence that the prevalence of this general interest is the criterion of political good. But this is to raise debate, not to settle it; for the real problem is not the announcement, but the realisation, of the substance of this creed.

In the background of difficulties such as these it is impossible to make the legal theory of sovereignty valid for political philosophy. We are given the State and, from the fact of its existence, we can proceed to discuss what are its organs, and in what fashion they work for the purpose it has in view. Any attempt, as with Austin, to discover the sovereign is a difficult, and often an impossible, adventure. It postulates for the sovereign the possession of qualities which cannot in fact be exercised. It narrows down the meaning of vital terms to a content which, if maintained, would be fatal to the existence of the society. Political philosophy must, doubtless, consider law as an important factor in the life of the State. But it must also bear ceaselessly in mind that the method of approach to the nature of law is, for itself, either akin to that suggested by Montesquieu, or else more likely to deceive than to assist. Law, for the student of politics, is built upon the general social environment. It expresses what are held to be the necessary social relations of a State at some given period. The organ by which it is declared to be law is, for politics, incomparably less important than the forces which made that organ act in the particular way.

## (iii) Political Sovereignty

We here verge upon the political nature of sovereignty. What, fundamentally, is involved is the question of whether there ought to be, in any State, a power subject to no limits of any kind. But it is first necessary to remember that unlimited power is nowhere existent. Attention has always to be paid to the thousand varying influences which go to shape the nature of the sovereign will. Here we are in the realm rather of fact than of theory; and the attempt to trace out the sources of any single decision would lead most to declare, as John Chipman Gray insisted, that the real rulers of society are undiscoverable. A realistic analysis would probably content itself with saying that the will of the State is, for practical purposes, the will which determines the boundaries within which other wills must live. The will of the State, in fact, is the will of government as that will is accepted by the citizens over whom it rules.

Clearly, in such a background, the will of the State cannot be an irresponsible will. It is no more than the judgment of a small body of men to whom, in an organised way, have been entrusted the reins of power. What they conceive to be right may clash with the community's notion of right. It may be built upon assumptions controverted by historic experience. It may be a deliberate perversion of the end of the State. That is why it has been the judgment of most modern communities that the term of power enjoyed by any government must be subject to periodical renewal. The community over which they preside must be given the chance to decide that it prefers a different body of men as governors. There is, that is to say, no permanent right to power. Every government must submit itself to the judgment of those who feel the consequences of its acts. The reason for such submission is the simple historical fact that unconditional power has always proved, at least ultimately, disastrous to those over whom it is exercised.

The notion of such periodical submission implies two things. It involves, firstly, a measureless importance in the method of submission. The way in which the popular judgment is elicited must be such as to secure a valid expression of public opinion. It involves, in the second place, the certainty that, in the period of office, a normal government will seek so to act that it keeps, so far as it can, the balance of the popular judgment in its favour. But that is in fact to say that its will is largely determined from outside itself. Government, for example, might in Great Britain confer a peerage on every butcher in the community; but it would not do so, because it would be overwhelmed in the ridicule certain to be heaped upon it by its opponents. As soon, therefore, as we know that any government is largely controlled by the need to defer to wills outside itself, we have to ask two questions. We have to know what wills direct the will of government in any actual State. We have to know, further, what environment is urgent to the will of government if the end of the State is, in any large degree, to be attained.

It is better to take the second question first. Each individual, it has here been argued, is entitled to expect from the performance of the State an environment in which, at least potentially, he can hope to realise the best of himself. If power is exercised in any given State so as to differentiate, for this purpose, between its members, we have a denial of the condition which legitimises governments. It thus becomes necessary that the conditions of legitimacy be postulated as the primary limitation upon governmental power. We postulate them by translating them into a system of rights: by which is meant a set of demands which, if unrealised, prevent the fulfilment of the State-purpose. We shall have, later, to discuss the substance of those demands. Here, it is enough, for the moment, to say that every government in its working must seek to translate them into the daily substance of men's lives. Every government is thus built upon a contingent moral obligation. Its actions are right to the degree that they maintain rights. When it is either indifferent about them, or wedded to their limitation, it forfeits its claim to the allegiance of its members.

When, of course, we turn from such a conception to the actual character of States, this notion may seem hardly less abstract than the legal theory of sovereignty itself. For a given right may be refused recognition. A government may, either honestly or dishonestly, doubt its wisdom and refuse to it statutory form; and since any normal government is likely to dispose of the greatest amount of available force, it will probably be able, except in the event of successful revolution, to maintain its refusal. That does not give its action validity. It means only that the preponderating material force of the community refuses to exercise its proper functions. The reasons for that refusal are usually of the most complex nature; but, almost always, they are derived from a view of right which denies to all save a section of the State the opportunity of equal participation in its benefits. If the refusal is persisted in over any length of time, it results in the organisation of an opposition which may grow until it is itself powerful enough to become the government. It is the historic nature of ideal right to gather power unto itself that, in the end, it may cease to be merely ideal.

But a right, in the sense defined above, which is seeking realisation is not the bare and empty thing such a refusal would seem to imply. Rights admit of organisation in two ways; and each of them is a limitation upon the acts of the government. They may, in the first place, be written into the constitution of the State. The sovereign power, that is to say, may be compelled to act in certain ways. It may, as in Belgium, be unable to limit religious freedom; or, as in England by convention, it may be unable to place its officials in a category different from that occupied by ordinary citizens. Every government may, in this fashion, be placed under the rule of laws which it is in actual fact powerless to change. And the more such laws lie at the root of social cohesion, the more powerless will be the government to alter them. Whether that ought to imply, as in the United States, a difference legally recognised, between constitutional and ordinary statutes, the government being hampered in its ability to alter the former, is a nice point of historical interpretation. Certainly freedom of speech has been more amply protected in England, where no such difference obtains, than in the United States, where it does. What seems to be the fruit of historical experience is that the more directly a government is related to a public opinion accustomed to self-expression in political terms, the more difficult it will be to avoid observance of the standard of conduct expected by the citizen-body. Legally, for example, the King in Parliament may outrage public opinion; practically, it can do so only on the implied condition that it ceases, as a consequence, to be the King in Parliament. Wherever legislation, therefore, is defining the sphere which other wills than that of the government may occupy, it is doing so upon the terms that it wins sufficiently the assent of those wills as not to provoke them to rebellion.

But, in the second place, to think of the attitude of a government to rights in terms of their acceptance is to imagine that it is in fact more free than is, as a rule, the case. Men are members of the State; but they are members also of innumerable other associations which not only exercise power over their adherents, but seek also to influence the conduct of government itself. All voluntary societies are seeking to make solutions peculiar to themselves general solutions accepted by the State. They are minority-wills seeking, through the channels of legislation, to become the legally declared will of the majority. Things like the Trades Disputes Act of 1906 stand out as examples of what they can achieve; or, in another sphere, the way in which a small body like the Workers' Educational Association has won from the State the recognition of its principles, is an extraordinary example of the power of opinion to organise its way to success. That is not true of England alone. The National Consumers' League of America has driven State after State into the acceptance of the limitation of the hours of labour and the establishment of a minimum wage for women. These are instances in which the will of government has been altered by direct action upon it. But not less important as a limitation upon its power to determine itself is the control exercised over their own sphere of activity by different associations.

For it is integral to the proper understanding of any given society that it should be regarded as essentially federal in its nature. It has activities of which the nature interests every member of the society; it has activities also that are primarily specific in their incidence. General activities of the first kind belong to the State, though that does not imply an identical form of organisation. Activities of the second kind interest the State only in so far as their results bear upon the rest of the community. No State, in such a background, has the right to interfere with the dogmas of churches. The Roman Catholic Church, for example, may deny that all outside of its communion are deprived of their title to external salvation, but unless it acts, as with the Inquisition, upon the thesis that they are damned also in an earthly existence, that belief is outside the power of the State to alter. It is, in short, outside the competence of the State to interfere with any conduct from which general consequences do not flow. If the Quakers preach the moral wrong of military service in a society where conscription is the rule, the State has the right to punish the individual recusant, but it has not the right to punish the Society of Friends. If foreign Jews resident in England seek to live by the divorce law of the Bible, the State has the right to punish individual offenders against its marriage laws, but it has not the right to punish the Jewish synagogue. Associations of this kind are as natural to their members as the State itself. What, of course, they lack, and wherein their difference from the State consists, is the power to inflict corporal punishment upon their members. They may assess them for fines; they may inflict spiritual penalties; they may expel from the given society. Herein their power is, and ought to be, as original and complete as that of the State itself. Interference with them by the State almost always fails to win either the right consequences or the consequences that are expected. For these associations are, in their sphere, not less sovereign than the State itself; with, of course, the implication that their sovereignty is similarly limited by the refusal or willingness of the individual member to accept their decisions.

Nor must we forget that when we speak of "the will" of the government we are postulating, especially in a democratic State, an artificial unity which has no existence. For no government attempts to take into the hands of a single group of men the whole direction of affairs. Centralisation may vary as with the two extremes of France and America; but it is becoming generally recognised that efficient administration is impossible unless the diffusion of power creates a wide sense of responsibility. Men who do no more than carry out the will of others soon cease to be interested in the process of which they are part. It is only when they can themselves shape the will that is to be applied that it becomes in any real measure creative. A local authority that has the power to make mistakes is more likely to do useful work than a local authority which merely carries out the will of a central body. It is necessary, indeed, to pick out the subjects in which mistakes can be made. It is, for example, legitimate to allow a town to decide whether or not it desires municipal electricity; it is illegitimate to allow it to decide whether it desires an educational system. In services, that is to say, of which the incidence of interest is almost entirely local, the right of the central government to intervene is the better exercised the less it exists. What is required is rather advice and comment and investigation than actual direction. In concrete terms, the question of whether the tramway service of Manchester is adequate ought never to engage the attention of the King in Parliament. The interest of its proper functioning touches a specific, and not a general, sphere. Practically, that is to say, we can lay down a system of territorial functions in which a final devolution of powers by the central government upon the authorities of local areas is the best method known of securing responsible government.

That is true not merely of territorial areas. It is possible to entrust to functions of a non-territorial kind the control of their internal life. That is true in England of such professions as the Bar and medicine. They are allowed to regulate their own qualifications and, thereby, the rule of admission to the trade. They create their own standards of professional conduct. They elect, along predetermined lines, those by whom their rules are to be administered over a given period. And it is fundamental to this method of organisation that there should be no way of appeal from decisions at which they have arrived. If, for instance, a candidate for the Bar has failed in one of his examinations, the courts of the State will not lie open to him save for inquiry into some abnormal circumstance. The area covered by such functional self-government is constantly increasing. Every trade has come to have its customs worked out by those engaged therein. It is even possible to conceive of industries to which would be confided the power to legislate for themselves over a vast variety of subjects, the State accepting as final the results of such legislation. Functional devolution, in fact, has exactly the same case for itself as territorial decentralisation. It creates a corporate sense of responsibility. It is a training in self-government. It confides the administration of powers to those who will feel most directly the consequences of those powers.

It is, of course, both true and important that at the back of this delegated authority there should be the ultimate reserve power of the State. But it is not less urgent to realise the circumstances under which that reserve power is brought into play. It is not a will exercised against an inferior will, merely as an exhibition of legal competence. It is a will exercised because those who urge the need for reform in the control of some delegated authority have been able to persuade the government either to undertake inquiry or to attempt deliberate change. But here, again, the will of government is very largely a compromise between opposing views; and that compromise rarely involves the direct control of the given function by the government. It rather means that the social interests of the community are not held by those upon whose counsel the government relies to be adequately protected under some existing scheme; and the direction of change is towards a new experiment in which, as it is thought, that social interest may be more fully realised.

In such a perspective as this, the theory of sovereignty in its political aspect begins to assume a very different shape from what its orthodox claims imply. It becomes clear that if the State is to be a moral entity, it must be built upon the organised acquiescence of its members. But this demands from them the scrutiny of government orders; and that, in its turn, implies a right to disobedience. Such a right is, of course, reasonably to be exercised only at the margins of political conduct. No community could hope to fulfil its purpose if rebellion became a settled habit of the population. But, at least equally, no community could hope to fulfil its purpose unless the will of its government were limited in a variety of ways. It must answer at started periods to those from whom it derives its powers. It must be powerless to touch certain fundamentals (of which freedom of speech is the supreme example) without which the benefits of social life will not, as a matter of history, be widely shared among the mass of men. It must be legally responsible for its mistakes. Its officers, that is to say, must be personally suable in the courts; and where they have clearly acted as agents the party whom they have unduly injured ought to be able to secure compensation from public funds.

It has been here insisted that no man can be a good citizen unless he personally interest himself in the affairs of the State. That conception is important if we are to realise, in any organised way, the notion of an equal interest in the results of the political process. While it is too much to say that minority-action is always selfish action, it is beyond doubt that unhampered enjoyment or power by a minority will always result in a selfish use of power. That is why the conception that authority not merely is, but ought to be, limited, is fundamental to political philosophy. For if we once admit that a body of men can enjoy unlimited power, we are, in geographical fact, exalting the local divisions of mankind above all other aspects of the human fellowship. That is an illegitimate exaltation. Logically, there is no reason to suppose that any one set of men is likely to be right as against any other. The real constraining force upon ourselves is not the legal obligation to obey government, but the moral obligation to follow what we regard as justice. There is no *a priori* conduct implied by such a moral obligation. All that can be said is that the individual is, ultimately, the supreme arbiter of his behaviour; and that he most fully realises the purpose of the State when he offers to it the substance, whatever that may be, of his judgment.

This, it may be said, is to push rationality to an impossible point. No Englishman will ever think that France is right as against England; and no Frenchman will fail to surrender his dislike, say, of France's diplomatic policy to her call for aid in the hour of supreme need. It would, of course, be folly to deny the emotional penumbra which surrounds allegiance to the national State. Men will die on the battle-field for England to whom the justice or injustice of its cause is hardly matter even for understanding. We must not evade the fact of such loyalty. Rather we must seek a method of organisation which can direct the power of sacrifice to an ideal into channels of use to society as a whole. For action built upon uninformed impulse is always, at bottom, anti-social action; and policy which uses uninformed impulse for its purposes is always hostile to the well-being of society. That is why those who, for example, obey their government because it has declared war, cease to be moral beings. The Germans who marched through Belgium, the Hungarians who have watched the deliberate butchery of their liberal fellow-citizens, have betrayed that which makes them men. Nor is it an answer to say that protest will involve severe penalties. To perish, as Royer Collard said, is also a solution; and those who, especially in a crisis, respond with passion to the Athanasius-element in their nature are likely to be the truest servants of civilisation.

Externally, surely, the concept of an absolute and independent sovereign State which demands an unqualified allegiance to government from its members, and enforces that allegiance by the power at its command, is incompatible with the interests of humanity. If we are to have a morally adequate theory of political obligation, we must approach the problem from a different angle. In a creative civilisation what is important is not the historical accident of separate States, but the scientific fact of world-interdependence. The real unit of allegiance is the world. The real obligation of obedience is to the total interest of our fellow-men. And granted that the discovery of where that interest lies is difficult, granted also that it is obscured by complex passions of every kind, that only makes the obligation more real and urgent. Our problem is not to reconcile the interest of humanity with the interest of England; our problem is so to act that the policy of England naturally implies the well-being of humanity. If we are to achieve that end, we must regard society as a complex of functions none of which is, for its government, limited by the concept of final allegiance to a given State. We may, indeed, assume that the larger the degree of self-government we can confide to a specific area within some given function, the better it is likely to be administered. But we have to assume also that no function can, in any final way, be entrusted with ultimate powers. At some point, co-ordination in the interests of those who live by the results, as against the interests of those who live by making the results, of the function is essential. We cannot, to take a simple instance, leave the government of a Church solely to its priests, or the government of coal-mines solely to the miners. Nor can we, in the sphere of international facts, leave England or France to decide in an absolute fashion upon the way in which each should live. There are problems of which the impact upon humanity is too vital for any State to be left to determine by itself what solution it will adopt. The notion of independent sovereignty, for example, leaves France free to invade Germany when and how she pleases; and the only retort that can be made is either a dissent which does not alter the fact, or a war which destroys civilisation. Once we realise that the well-being of the world is, in all large issues, one and indivisible, the co-ordinate determination of them is the primary condition of social peace.

### (iv) Sovereignty in International Affairs

In such an aspect the notion of an independent sovereign State is, on the international side, fatal to the well-being of humanity. The way in which a State should live its life in relation to other States is clearly not a matter in which that State is entitled to be the sole judge. That way lies the long avenue of disastrous warfare of which the rape of Belgium is the supreme moral result in modern times. The common life of States is a matter for common agreement between States. International government is, therefore, axiomatic in any plan for international well-being. "But international government implies the organised subordination of States to an authority in which each may have a voice, but in which, also, that voice is never the self-determined source of decision". How best to translate this conception into institutional terms is a matter to be discussed latter. "It is enough, for the moment, to postulate the disappearance of State-sovereignty as the conditions without which the life of reason is impossible to States. England ought not to settle what armaments she needs, the tariffs she will erect, the immigrants she will permit to enter. These matters affect the common life of peoples; and they imply a unified world organised to administer them".

The argument against such a view as this is ultimately the argument of despair. It assumes that men will always love blindly the little platoon into which they are born; and it forgets that irrational passion now plays with instruments too dangerous to be called into use. No one doubts that it is a difficult task to fit the interests of the world into institutions which can express its needs. But no one can read the history of States which have regarded their private welfare as the supreme end without the sense that the outlawry of the power of exclusive decision is the most urgent need before us. If men are to live in the great society, they must learn the habits of co-operative intercourse. They must learn to think of their platoon as a part of the great regiment of mankind. They must grow accustomed to sinking immediate and temporary good for the lasting benefit which comes from space. For, at least over a long period, the victories won in international intercourse by violence are rarely of permanent vague. Germany did not gain by the annexation of Alsace-Lorraine in 1871; Austria did not profit by her sovereignty over Bosnia and Herzegovina. The traditions established by conduct of this kind are, ultimately, as materially fatal as they are morally disastrous. They are built upon the notion that the State is sovereign as against other States. They assume, as Hobbes said, that the hinterland between organised peoples is a *bellum omnium contra omnes*. That assumption is a betrayal of the reason which distinguishes man from his animal kindred; or, rather, it is to devote that reason to ends which would destroy the distinction between man and the brute. The fact that in the great society actions ramify until Tokyo and Paris become cities of a single community implies the organisation of Statehood for that community. In a world-State, however it be built, and whatever the measure of decentralisation that obtains, there is no room for separate sovereignties. Those functions which influence the life of the great society must be subject to the common and concerted decision of men.

## (v) State and Association

When we turn from the external to the internal sovereignty of States, we meet a more complex situation. The problem of the power of a State over its own members is, very largely, a problem of representing wills. If social institutions permit me so to express myself that my life acquires a satisfactory balance of impulses. I am, in a creative sense, free. But it is obvious that, taken merely as an individual, my will is lost amid the myriad competing wills which strive with my own for expression. That is why men build associations that, from the collective strength of the wills fused there, they may secure the chance of self-determination. Associations exist to fulfil purposes which a group of men have in common. They support and imply functions. Will, therefore, as they secure expression in the State, are essentially of two kinds. There is the will of the individual as himself a final unit, a universal of which each act and each intention is a particular. There is the will, also of the individual as the member of some special association seeking, through its means, to fulfil some definite purpose.

Here it is important to realise two things. To exhaust the associations to which a man belongs is not to exhaust the man himself. You do not state the total nature of Jones by saying that he is a Wesleyan barrister who belongs to the Reform Club and the Ancient Order of Oddfellows. You have to take account, also, of the Jones who builds from out those varying aspects of his life a self which effects, or seeks to effect a harmony between them. The Jones who realises that some part of himself lives in each of these associations, who seeks by means of them to shape the lines of his wants and hopes, is the ultimate Jones who belongs only to himself. That intimate, unabsorbed personality is the thing he seeks to satisfy by the system of relationships into which he enters. Its will is compounded, doubtless, of the innumerable single acts he performs. It yet stands over and above them and judges not merely the acts, but the society they influence, by the degree to which they produce a satisfied and co-ordinated life as the result.

Nor, in the second place, can the will of any single association be made a final will. To leave to the Bar, for instance, the ultimate control of itself is to leave a single aspect of man the power to mould his total aspect. Man is not merely a barrister. A given function is always a narrow purpose, alongside the full end of realisation as a complete human being. We have, therefore, to find a plane in which the wills of men are given powers of expression in their aspect of centres of universal decision as against the particular decisions from which these centres are compounded.

So stated, of course, the issue is unduly simplified. The Jones who is to will upon a universal plane may, in fact, be unable to free himself from a sense of overwhelming import implicit in some special aspect of himself. No ability is so rare as the power to look into one's own mind and judge the totality of one's effort as an ordered whole in which, as a matter of social logic, good can only come when the parts are related to the well-being of one's fellow-men. That ability is made the rarer by the complexity of motives which reside in the purpose of any association as it works. Associations which seem purely acquisitive in nature will often acquire a view of social welfare which modifies their ministration to appetite. There is no such thing as a purely political association if by that we mean a body dealing with functions which arise solely from the personal relationships of men. For those relationships are affected and coloured at every stage by the push of the total order in society. Economic and social facts, intellectual and religious considerations, influence them, consciously and unconsciously, at every stage. The universal plane of which we have spoken is, therefore, simply mythical so far as its existence in a pure form is concerned. The will which receives expression there cannot, in the nature of things, be directed solely to the interests over and above the private decisions from which its motives take their final shape. A general will, in Rousseau's sense, is, therefore, an impossibility.

But because we reject a general will in this ideal form, we are not driven to rely upon a system of associations as the method in and through which the end of society can be best achieved. Each association, we may agree, ought to have its chance to influence the conduct of the social order. But where orders are issued which, until their revocation, determine the character of that social order as a whole, we have to receive them for scrutiny upon a plane of equality. Each person, that is to say, must be taken by society as of equal value with every other person. If the will that effects the harmony between associations were merely compounded of them, that equality would be impossible. A diamond cutter cannot, as a diamond cutter, influence society in the same degree as a miner can influence society as a miner. The problem of so weighting associations that each receives not merely an equal, but, more, its due place in an institution which congeals them into unity is an insoluble one. Nor does Jones secure the thing at which his will aims by taking fragments of the will and giving to each a power of influencing decisions in the sphere to which it belongs. For what is important for him is the way in which those fragments are co-ordinated. It is their relationship, not their isolation, which determines the degree to which his nature is satisfied.

Social organisation, therefore, does not present a single problem in relation to its government. On the one hand, it is fairly simple to construct a government for each function in society in terms of the particular purpose each embodies. But no man's activities are confined to a single function. It is necessary to safeguard his interests as a user of services he has no part in producing. It is essential, in other words, to protect him as a consumer. The co-ordination of functions is the sphere in which, to that end, the State must operate. It has so to organise the conditions of their lives that the individual members of the State are assured of reasonable access to those goods without which they cannot fulfil their vocations as men. Where their needs are identical as undifferentiated persons, at least at some minimum level, it is essential to have a single centre of control to achieve them. That does not mean that the State itself will, as the controlling body, provide directly the response to such needs. It means only, that it will so direct the functions which produce the required services as to secure effective conditions of response.

In an aspect of this kind, the State is obviously a public service corporation. It differs from every other association in that it is, in the first place, an association in which membership is compulsory. It is, in the second place, essentially territorial in nature. The interests of men as consumers are largely neighbourhood interests; they require satisfaction, for the most part in a given place. And, at a given level, the interests of its members are identical interests. They all need food and clothing, education and shelter. The State is the body which seeks so to organise the interests of consumers that they obtain the commodities of which they have need. Within the State, they meet as persons. Their claims are equal claims. They are not barristers or miners, Catholics or Protestants, employers or workers. They are, as a matter of social theory, simply persons who need certain services they cannot themselves produce if they are to realise themselves. Clearly, a function of this kind, however it is organised, involves a pre-eminence over other functions. The State controls the level at which men are to live as men. It is, in administrative terms, a government whose activities are shaped by the common needs of its members. To satisfy those common needs, it must control other associations to the degree that secures from them the service such needs require. The more closely a given function—education, for example, or the provision of coal—lies to the heart of the society, the more closely it will require to be controlled. Each function, that is to say, must be so organised in the interest of the consumer that it permits him access to a full civic life. There is a limit to the number of hours of labour a man can work and yet remain a human being. There is an income below which no man can be allowed to fall if he is to maintain himself as a decent citizen. The State is regulating, directly and indirectly, to secure common needs at the level which the society as a whole deems essential to the fulfilment of its general end.

That is the function of the State in society. It is the association to protect the interests of men as citizens, not in the detail of their productive effort, but in the large outline within which that productive effort is made. But we must differentiate sharply between State and government. To define the function of the State is not to define the powers of government; it is to define only the purpose it is the end of government to secure. Here we meet the problem of internal sovereignty in its sharpest form. It is possible to argue that because the State implicates, in James' phrase, the universal aspect of men, the fiat of its against is by itself adequate. It is possible to argue also that since every action taken by those agents in the name of the State is ultimately a question between the State and some given function, the fiat of those agents is inadequate, since to make it final is ultimately to make them judges in their own cause. This, without question, is the central issue in the organisation of internal power. If, as has been argued here, the nature of the State makes it akin to other associations, even if different and greater in the range it covers, to leave to its agents the final discretion in what action they may choose to take is as impossible as to leave to the legal profession the complete control over its destinies. For it is to imply that judgments made by the agents of the State differ from the judgments of agents of other associations in uniquely regarding the welfare of the members of the State. It is to suggest that their will is, *a priori,* a general will in a sense that cannot be predicated of any other will that we encounter in social life. That is not, in fact, the case. The agents of any State are not different in character from the rest of its members. They are liable to the same temptations. They are fallible for the same reasons. Their outlook, like that of any other person, is limited by the experience they encounter. They exert power for purposes always limited by a system of assumptions derived from the environment about them. The squirearchy in office protects the country gentleman from a whole-hearted belief that his interest is identical with the public welfare. John Bright remained unable to the end of his life to see grounds for the limitation of the hours of labour. William Windham could not understand that the working-classes had the right to educational facilities The danger of leaving to the State a sovereign position among other associations lies in the fact that it must always act through agents and that those agents are drawn from a body of experience which is not necessarily coincident with the general interest of the community. They will even tend, as a rule, to identify their own experience of good with the common needs of mankind; for it is, as Rousseau said, the natural tendency of all governments to deteriorate. Power has the habit of corrupting even the noblest of those who exercise it; and it follows that to leave to the State the final control of all other wills in the community is, in fact, to leave to a small number of men an authority it is difficult not to abuse.

Any State must therefore be, internally, a responsible State. The problem of making such responsibility creative may be approached in two ways. We may seek so to organise the various functions other than the State that they may join with it in a co-ordinate body for the making of final decisions. This, broadly speaking, is the view that has been urged by guild socialist theory. Its difficulties, however, are insurmountable. There is, first, the question of whether functional units can be built up which, proportionately to other units, will enable an adequate representative body to be created. It is possible to construct a representative body which will fairly contain the needs of any given class of producers; but the problem here is the very different one of weighting functions one against the other in order to secure a just numerical relationship. It seems very doubtful whether this can be done. Anyone who has followed, for example, the difficulties which attended the composition of the German Economic Council will be driven to the belief that the rough adjustment reached prevents it from functioning as anything more than an advisory body. It seems to be useful as a vehicle of advice upon particular industrial issues; it does not possess moral authority as an organ entitled to speak for the vocational world as a whole.

The same, it may be pointed out, is true of the Trade Union world in England. No one doubts the authority of the Miners' Federation to speak for its members on all issues which concern coal; but it is legitimate to doubt whether the resolutions of the Trade Union Congress possess, outside a narrow industrial area, any binding force over its individual constituents. It is, similarly, difficult to see how exactly a body in which businessmen and trade unionists were combined would usefully construct general industrial legislation; especially if, as seems inevitable under a capitalist regime, they were combined in equal proportions. And this, it must be noted, is to omit the grave problem of finding how to combine the reality of the industrial unit with the due emphasis of fairness to the vocations within some given unit of this kind. A medical guild, for example, would undoubtedly be dominated by general practitioners; but they are hardly entitled to make their voice the final statement of expert knowledge upon issues which concern as well the interests of nurses, of dentists, of bonesetters and medical masseuses.

The value, in other words, of vocational organisation lies in the contribution it can make to the particular problems of the craft, not in the help it has to offer upon general social questions. Immediately these are in issue, the members of some particular vocation either approach them in the spirit of their craft, in which case no special validity attaches to their judgment, or they approach them from a larger standpoint, in which case they are no longer speaking as members of their craft. Vocational bodies, therefore, have value for the resolution of functional problems; but they are not, by their very nature, built to deal with the general issues which must be faced by society as a whole.

The second problem involved in this question is not less complex than that of structure. Even if we suppose that a satisfactory functional representation could be secured, the question remains of developing its relations with the political State. There is first the question of deciding how the general boundaries of subject-matter are to be fixed between them. That is, clearly, a judicial matter which some such body as the Supreme Court of the United States is best fitted to settle. In such a background, final decisions belong, not to the competence of elected assemblies, but to that of an appointed body which decides whether some given statute is *ultra vires* or no. For we know too much of the electoral process to trust to its hazards the choice of men who are to decide the most delicate of all social tasks. Mr. Cole, indeed, proposes to surmount this difficulty by leaving the processes of law and police to the control of a joint body composed of "essential" functional organisations. That, in fact, only increases the complexity of the issue. What functional organisations are "essential"? What are to be the numbers of such a joint body? Are they to choose the members of a Supreme Court by voting? Where is the initiative of nomination to be? Immediately, it is clear, we seek to make the political State a body on the same footing as the Miners' Federation, we destroy the chance of that direct intelligibility in social organisation which is of decisive importance if it is to remain democratic. For any governmental system not capable of being grasped by the ordinary elector is certain sooner or later to be perverted by those who have the secret of its manipulation.

Any such view as this of the place of functions in social organisation must take account of the vital fact of capitalism. If all industries were socialised, their government would, so far as structure is concerned, be, at least relatively, a straight-forward matter. But in fact we are faced by a division into employers and employed in almost every industry of importance; and, short of revolutionary catastrophe, it is unlikely that the majority will pass from the sphere of private enterprise in any period it is now necessary to contemplate. If this be the case, the government of every industry not publicly administered requires at once the twofold representation of employers and employed; and the complexity of the functional assembly built from all industries which would result would probably be fatal to its effective working.

When, in other words, men vote as men, and the postulate of the franchise is identity of need, a working simplicity results. As a matter of influence, the great employer is, of course, more powerful than the individual worker; as a unit of governmental reference, they meet upon the same plane. But when the postulate of the franchise is difference, and not identity, the shades of variation are so manifold that the body which results is too intricate and too unwieldy to be useful. It falls, like the Trade Union Congress, into the hands of a small number of large bodies who dominate its policy, or into those of a group of men who, like the "bosses" of an American party, are skilful at the art of electoral manipulation.

### (vi) The State as Responsible

If this argument be valid, we must seek the institutions of a responsible State in other directions. It is, in the first place, essential to note that to divide responsibility as a method of limiting power may result in its total destruction. To divide it as, for example, it is divided by the separation of powers in the United States, may be to evade it altogether. In any effective administration it is urgent that the orders issued may be ultimately traced to a small group of persons. Its responsibility is secured in three ways. It is made effective, in the first place, by adequate methods of dismissing it from power. It is made effective, in the second place, by the sources of organised consultation with which it is surrounded. It is, thirdly, fundamental that those who are to pass ultimate judgment upon the acts of the State should be in a full position to make that judgment intelligent and articulate. A State, that is to say, must be composed of citizens between whom there are no vast disparities of education and economic power.

The will of the State cannot, in this view, be made legally co-ordinate with wills that in fact over a lesser area than its own. Moral co-ordination may be achieved; legal co-ordination is impossible because the State, through its agents, defines the manner of vocational life. And however much we may reduce the direct administrative capacity of the political State, the fact remains that once it is charged with the provision of services of which men stand in common need, it has their interests in trust to a degree with which no other body can, at least in a temporal sense, compete. Even if we abstract from the modern State the final control of international affairs, the civic area of internal matters that is left seems, in any casual glance, overwhelming. Education, public health, housing, the preservation of order, the regulation of vocations at that point below which their operation is detrimental to the public interest, merely, it is obvious, to state these functions in a broad way is to make the voice of government important in a very special manner. Practically speaking, what it surveys is the interest of man as citizen, the point at which he ceases to be a producer of services that he may live, and seeks from the result of that production to give meaning to his life.

It is here argued that production and consumption cannot be placed upon an equal footing so long as the division of labour makes no man sufficient unto himself. Put in a broad way, the protection of the interests of the consumer as citizen are paramount. However far decentralisation may go in leaving producing functions to govern themselves, at some point their will becomes subject to the will of those who, in the leisure-period, are seeking to make of life an art and not the fulfilment of a special task.

To grasp this point of view, it is most useful to take the individual citizen and build, so to speak, the community from his relationships. He lives upon the services of other men. For him, they exist that his leisure may be rich and fruitful. Only as they provide in a full degree the commodities of which he has need can be realise the impulses of his nature. For him, that is to say, the aspect of consumer is the predominant aspect. It is what he will enjoy, not what he can produce, that is important for the fulfilment of himself. It is true, and it must be emphasised, that there are those to whom the aspect of producer is fundamental. The artist, the statesman, the man born to write, to administer, to teach, find all of their best in the daily task from which they derive the means of life. No theory of social organisation would be complete that did not endeavour to find ample room for the expression of that creative faculty.

It is yet only a minority to whom the effort of production contains the die upon which their personality is imprinted. In a civilisation which, like our own, is built upon large-scale production, most are inevitably destined to find their best selves outside the categories from which they secure their livelihood. The clerk who copies entries in a ledger, the printer who sets the type for a journal, the waiter who carries plates from kitchen to table and table to kitchen, the stoker who feeds the engines of a great ship—these are most themselves, not in the hours of productive toil, but when the day's work is done. And for them, accordingly, the thing that is supremely important is the opportunity their leisure affords. What they desire is that the productive effort should use as little as may be of their energy, and that it should result in as much as possible of the means to use that energy in the fashion that pleases them best. Society, for them, is essentially judged by what it does towards that end. Government becomes the arbiter between the parties to production, not as an end in itself, but as a means to the end for which men produce.

This does not, of course, imply that men can, or should, in their daily labour be regarded as the mere tenders of machines. But it does mean that, if we are to continue our civilisation upon the present scale, it is important to realise that, whatever the form of industrial organisation, the number of those who will find a creative channel of activity in their daily work is inevitably small. Even if one grant the satisfaction that comes to the craftsman in his effort, machine-technology destroys for most the prospect of any work that is not the mere repetition of a routine. There are, of course, those to whom the conduct of industrial direction is, at one point or another, confided; and there will always, doubtless, be the masterless craftsman who lives by satisfying the personal taste of a few. Yet when we measure these numbers against the serried masses of the general population, they remain pitifully small. They are the source of much discontent; and social change is, on the side of productive reorganisation, mainly an effort to satisfy impulses of leadership for which there is inadequate room in the present system. For the rest, the interest lies, not in the process itself, but in the results of the process. They watch, so to say, not the details of the strategy, but the fruits of the victory. By them, accordingly, the State is judged as it makes that victory meagre or ample.

The State, then, serves its members by organising the avenues of consumption on their behalf. It effects that end in part by direct expenditure of the proceeds of taxation, in part by regulating the conditions under which commodities are produced. It is made responsible to its members in a variety of ways. Its government is, firstly, subject to dismissal by its constituents. That dismissal may be secured by different methods. The period of office may be limited; and the legislature itself may, through the pressure of public opinion, compel the resignation of the executive by which it is itself directed. The limitation of the period of office means that at a fixed term all who are legally to direct the affairs of State are subject to the choice of an electorate which has now come, generally speaking, to include the adult population of most communities which live under the aegis of modern civilisation; and in States where orderly government is a general habit, that test can hardly be evaded save under penalty of revolution. Governments are therefore driven, within limits of real importance, to defer to popular desires if they wish to remain in power.

Deference to popular desire is, of course, a vague term; and the degree to which it is effective depends naturally upon the degree to which public opinion is organised and, through its organisation, can make its will known. We shall discuss later the problem of satisfying that opinion in a legislative assembly; obviously the methods by which it is elected are of extreme importance. It suffices to say here that election does not mean that I choose Jones to represent me in the sense of feeling that my will is embodied in his; it means only that I believe Jones likely, over a period after which I can judge his activities, to vote for a policy I can broadly approve.

But, clearly enough, if I am to pass judgment upon him, I must be so instructed that my judgment may be adequate and articulate. The education of the citizen, in other words, is the heart of the modern State. Most of the disgust which even the adherents of democratic government have felt with its working is due to the fact that it has never been trained to the understanding of its functions; most, also, of the difficulties which social theorists have sought to meet by changes in the machinery are largely due, less to defects in the machinery itself, than to the fact that it is seeking to cope with a population which often passes through life without even the knowledge of its existence. Children who are herded into industry at the age of fourteen, when the problem of knowledge has scarcely begun to exert its fascination, can hardly be expected, under the conditions of modern industrial life, to understand, much less to work, the complicated technique upon which their well-being depends. The defects of democracy are most largely due to the ignorance of democracy; and to strike at that ignorance is to attack the foundation upon which those defects are built. In the presence of that ignorance, it is inevitable that those who can afford the luxury of knowledge will alone by likely, or even able, to make their desires effective. A State which fails to offer an equal level of educational opportunity to its citizens is penalising the poor for the benefit of the rich. There cannot be a responsible State until there is an educated electorate.

But even an educated electorate will not secure the essential conditions of responsibility. The individual in the modern State is, after all, a voice crying in the wilderness unless he acts with those whose interests are kindred to his own. The individual worker, for example, cannot, as a normal rule, bargain with the individual employer for reasonable terms; equality of bargaining power is the necessary prelude to freedom of contract. And equality of bargaining power can only be secured by means of association. The individual who seeks an economic master and yet strives to stand alone destroys the standard of satisfaction that his fellows can hope to secure. He acts as a reservoir from which power may be drawn to compete against some standard urged as a necessary minimum; and that is still more true in a system which, like that of private enterprise, compels the maintenance of a reserve of unemployed. The compulsory recognition of trade unionism is essential if decent working conditions are to be maintained; and this, in its turn, means the disappearance of that unassociated worker who has been supposed, by an unamiable fiction, free to sell his labour in the dearest market. The worker who does not stand by his fellows is in fact destroying their access to proper standards of life.

On the other side, the anarchy of modern trades is fatal to any attempt properly to cope with their conditions. The variations in the sanitary quality of factories, of book-keeping, of estimation of cost, of methods of sale, of research into the technique of production, of engagement and promotion, of access by the workers to some share in the direction of the enterprise, are all of them fatal to the proper conduct of the industry. We have combinations to diminish the share the worker may hope to obtain from his part in production. We have combinations to wring the highest possible price from the consumer. We have not yet had a combination to build some given industry into what can be recognised as a public service. It seems clear that if the relations between the State and industry are to be upon an equitable footing, each trade must have its associations for organised and coherent consultation with the government. Anything less than a body to which, on either side, each worker and each employer must belong, leaves the opinion inadequately explored through the expression of which a government finds its policy. It leaves, also, influential men with access to the sources of power that is consistently liable to abuse.

We can imagine such an organisation of industry in modern society as gives to its working the character and responsibility of constitutional government. It will have standards, statutory and traditional, to maintain; it will have channels through which those standards may be enforced. It cannot be too emphatically insisted that the maintenance of those standards is, as to their ultimate definition, always a matter for the State. For whatever may be the vehicles of their administration, those standards are maintained to protect the interest of the consumer. They mean, of course, that no man, to use the current phrase, can be left to conduct his own business in his own way; the context of citizenship always determines the methods by which it is administered. And that context is defined by the State. The problem, therefore, is to find channels through which the relationship of the State to industrial functions may make consistently explicit the civic interests of men.

## (vii) Government as Consultation

There are three clear avenues towards that end. The first great need of the modern State is adequately to organise institutions of consultation. The weakness of the present system, and one of the real roots of its irresponsibility, is that a government is compelled to consult, not an association which represents the interests affected by some statute, but those only whose protest against its action it chooses to deem important. If industry were given such a constitutional form as that here outlined, it would be possible to compel the prior consultation of authoritative bodies before any policy was given statutory form.

The advantages of such a method are obvious. It secures, in the first place, effective access to the government by the interests involved. Their wills, that is to say, at the least receive authoritative exposition. They are placed in a position where they can learn, in detail and in principle, the purpose a government has in view. They are thereby enabled the more effectively to oppose or support such measures. They can appeal with the confidence of knowledge to opinion outside. They can seek from an assured basis to influence the supporters and opponents of the government in the legislature. They can supply to the minister information of real value in the construction of the details of his measure. They can offer him suggestions as to its probable working. They form, in brief, a deposit of *expertise* upon the different aspects of policy which, effectively used, create an atmosphere of responsibility about governmental acts. If the minister acts upon their opinion, he is at least building upon a foundation of experience; if he rejects them, the creation of an opposition and, as a consequence, of the discussion that is the life-blood of democratic governance, is adequately assured.

The issue here at stake may perhaps be usefully stated in another way. The responsibility of modern governments is largely a subjective responsibility. The interpretation that prevails is not controlled in any organised way by the interests it directly affects. Such control can only be introduced if those interests are given immediate institutional access to the seat of decision. A government which must summon advisory committees, which must place before those committees the policy it proposes to enforce, which listens to the criticism of men who are entitled to speak on behalf of organised associations, is in a very different position from a government which, as in the United States, remains in power for a fixed term, or, as in England, can threaten its supporters into acquiescence by the fear of a general election. It is not necessary to divide power in order to make it responsible; what is essential is to make coherent the organs of reference to which that power must defer.

For no government can have contact with bodies of men entitled to speak with authority and remain uninfluenced by their views. No member of a legislative assembly could learn that a government decision had awakened widespread expert dissent without feeling that an unconsidered vote was out of place. If informed public opinion is to surround the activities of the State, that opinion must be given channels through which it flows to the seat of power. A letter to a journal, the publication of a pamphlet, the holding of a public meeting, are all, doubtless, useful methods of ventilating some special view, but they do not directly reach the will of government. They do not necessarily evoke that official duty to respond, that moral need to explain, which are the root of responsible action. And the atmosphere of such advisory bodies is very different from that, for example, of a modern cabinet. There the minister must think of issues not necessarily connected with the public good. He must say, for instance, that he cannot adopt conscription because to do so is political suicide; where the inference is not that the advisability of conscription is the basic issue, but that the life of the government is itself the highest good. In the cabinet the minister is driven to think of interests not necessarily coincident with the public welfare. He must keep in mind the need to preserve party unity, the knowledge that the resignation of a powerful colleague must be prevented, the hundred queer shades of distracting occurrence which develop in personal relations. In an advisory committee of experts which has the character of a permanent institution these disturbing influences are absent. The discussion is rooted in the principles of its subject; personal considerations are, *a priori*, out of place. The minister is dealing directly with minds and only indirectly with votes. He is being driven to counter reason with reason. He is being trained in responsibility to those whose desires must shape his will.

We shall later analyse the forms that such advisory institutions might reasonably assume. But it will be useful here to explain why the notion of leaving the government of the State to decide, and compelling it only to consult, seems preferable to the system either, as in guild socialism, of attaching power to a functional body, or, as in the German Economic Council, retaining the theory of advice, but building that theory into a single institution instead, as here urged, of attaching separate advisory organs to the different units of the government. The difficulties of the guild theory are fourfold. There is, in the first place, the fact that while it is practically possible to discover adequate units of consultation, it is practically impossible to discover practical units of government. And there is no reason to suppose, secondly, that a union of all guilds into a single functional body charged with the ultimate control of production would be superior in character to, for example, the House of Commons. Guild officials would tend, just as ministers tend, to become bureaucratic and conservative. They would lose touch with their constituents in much the same way as now. There would be the same risks attaching to majority-rule. Nor, as Mr. Cole seems to think, would any of this be remedied by the device of the recall.[1] It is the plain lesson we have of the experience of its working that it decreases the sense of responsibility in elected persons. It makes them more subordinate to interests that they believe to be powerful. It sways their decisions through motives at least as inadequate as those upon which their present judgment is based. It produces, as in the United States, a race of men who subordinate care for principle to the desire for place. Nor, in the third place, is there any way in which a distinction can be drawn between the area of the guild congress and the area of the territorial assembly. The one which taxes persons will, sooner or later, dominate the other. If the division, fourthly, be made through the channels of judicial interpretation, on the one hand, the two bodies are a clumsy source of appointment, and, on the other, the judges become the ultimate repository of social power. It is surely the clearest inference from the history of the American Supreme Court that while judges are invaluable for saying what statutes mean, they do more harm than good when they determine whether statutes ought to be made. The latter office, in fact, is the replacement of the communal will by their own notions of social justice.

The objections to the German system rest upon considerations of a different kind. The Economic Council is a purely consultative body. It is barely three years old. It is yet already clear that its best work is done not on general, but on particular subjects, and, further, not in plenary session but in the intimate discussion of its various committees. Its weaknesses lie in a variety of directions. Its initiatory power tends to lead it to multiply suggestions for legislation without having the responsibility to carry them into effect. It entails upon ministers a serious burden of extra labour. The need to appear and speak before it, the knowledge that its activity is always encroaching upon the margins of the Reichstag's competence, the satisfaction of its immeasurable appetite for documents and information, are rather a hindrance than a help to the channels of administration proper. It seems clear that when a measure is sent to the Economic Council, the proper committee can help the minister concerned by its special knowledge. It does not equally appear that the Council as a whole performs this function. Its independent authority makes it appear, both to the ministers and their officials, a source of competition rather than an avenue of aid. It does not, through the absence of parties, secure that consolidated unity of decision which is vital to the success of representative assemblies. It may be true, as Rathenau declared, that we need to emancipate ourselves from the principle of popular choice and move towards the principle of ability. But it is necessary to remember that in a democracy the ultimate principle is, after all, self-government; and that means, in the last resort, that final decisions must be made by elected persons. Where ability is required is in giving advice to the persons elected; and in nine cases out of ten that advice needs to be special rather than general. It needs, that is, to be ability connected with a sphere of narrow competence; it does not gain by being congealed, with other *expertise*, into a unity that has no driving power. It is, moreover, notable that the debates in the plenary Economic Council tend to become eloquent expositions of class-ideology rather than careful explorations of the formulae in dispute. Nor should we omit the immense opportunity such a body opens to the growth of what the French call *paperasserie*. If the German Economic Council continues to increase the subjects of its attention at the present rate, a period will soon arrive when every department of the State will be driven to erect a special bureau merely to supply the information demanded by the different committees. There is yet a limit to the number of officials any State can hope to afford; and the area of investigation must surely have as its reasonable boundary direct contact with a policy related to the will of government. The present system multiplies projects most of which, like the bills in an American legislature, simply exist in a vacuum. What we require to make government responsibility real is the clarification of projects that are, or may immediately be, in legislative debate.

The territorial assembly built upon universal suffrage seems, therefore, the best method of making final decisions in the conflict of wills within the community. That assembly, it should be noted, could not, at least in theory, act in an irresponsible fashion. It would, in the first place, be the creature of electoral will; and the more fully that electorate was informed, the more fully the legislature would respond to its desires. It would, in the second, be subject to the need to consult the organised wills of the community before it acted upon them. Its executive would be responsible before the courts in exactly the same manner as any other citizens. If there is added to these controls decentralisation both of area and of function there is secured as much as may legally be secured, of limitation upon political power.

### (viii) Certain Limiting Factors

Underlying this argument is the assumption that no body which represents the community as a whole whether, as in guild socialism, it represents the producers or, as in a territorial assembly, it seeks to represent the consumers, will ever, by itself, adequately safeguard the right of the individual to realise himself. That can only be done by organising those who seek to secure some special interest into an association which is prepared, in the last instance, to resist the will of government. In any State where there is an absence of the critical spirit in the attitude of the citizens to their rulers, the preservation of rights is a difficult matter. An attitude of contingent attack involves, it may be, the possibility of disorder, but it makes government itself vigilant to the opinion about it; and men who prefer, in the internal life of a State, the path of perpetual peace to that of organised protest will, sooner or later, lose the habit of freedom. For, in the end, governments are made responsible less by the laws they must obey than by the character they will encounter. A public opinion that is informed and organised is worth, for this purpose, all the checks and balances that have ever been described by political philosophers. For as governments degenerate unless they are forced to live at a high level, so, also, they improve where they meet the alert and erect intelligence of men.

It is integral to this conception of the mechanism of political responsibility that every State should possess a vigorous and independent judiciary. The government must be suable in the courts for tort and breach of contract in the same fashion as the most humble member of the community. The judges themselves, if they are appointed by, must also be irremovable by, the executive. Nor can there be any administrative law which permits the final interpretation of statutes to be made by government officials. Their powers, especially in a period which has seen the vast growth of administrative discretion, must always be powers directly traceable to statute. They must be so exercised that they fulfil, in their operation, the obvious canons of reasonableness. Whether this involves the writing of a Bill of Rights into the Constitution, those rights being accessible only by special procedure, is a delicate question. Certainly Bills of Rights have served this purpose in the United States that they have reminded men of things for which, because they were precious, they had to fight and may yet again be driven to do battle for. They create a tradition of conduct the habits of which are valuable. Here it is enough to say that the principle that no man shall be judge in his own cause applies as well to government as to any other institution in the community. Only when the judiciary is accorded a special pre-eminence can it act as the guardian of a freedom which the least measure of dependence will at once cause to suffer encroachment.

Two other considerations are here of the first importance. The avenue to responsibility lies along the road of critical publicity. The freedom of a people depends, to a degree we are only beginning to realise, upon the quality of the news with which it is supplied. Its press must be free to attack authority in whatever manner it thinks fit, to publish what it please, to defend what programme it desires, the only limitation being the law of libel. How best to secure the supply of adequate and truthful news is a question to be discussed later. But anyone who has watched, for instance, the way in which newspapers can turn the public mind to the direction their proprietors desire will realise that an alliance between the government and the press might be fatal to the very heart of democratic government.

The other consideration is equally urgent. We have justified the concept of a territorial State on the ground that it provides the most direct method available of organising that plane of life where the interests of men, as the users of services, are relatively identical. The territorial State, that is to argue, can in theory protect the interests of consumers better than any other association. But it can only do so on the essential condition that there is, broadly speaking, approximate economic equality in the community. For, ultimately, the possession of wealth means the power to determine what is produced for consumption; and if society is divided, as it is now divided, into a small number of rich and a struggling mass who exist upon the very margins of adequacy, it is obvious that the State, whatever its theoretic purpose, will always be weighted against the interests of the poorer citizens. They fail to secure access to all which makes life worth living. Their houses will be mean, their education of low quality. The conditions of their existence will never afford them that resiliency of mind which comes from the possession of material comfort. Any State which hopes for permanency must at least abrogate the struggle for bread.

This seems to involve either some form of communism or else such a control of private enterprise as mitigates in every direction the harsh results of its operation. The experience of Russia has shown us that the establishment of communism is not likely to come rapidly; men will sooner part with their souls than with their possessions. Social change in the direction of equality is more likely to be the result of slow and even painful experiment. We are not faced by the prospect, at least over a long period, of the communal ownership of the means to wealth. But if government is to be morally legitimate, we are certainly faced by the need so to control the production and distribution of wealth that the general interest of the community is not regarded as the happy result of a mere sum of private interests, but is a recognised minimum in which each citizen has an equal share.

We shall inquire later into the institutional implications of this view of equality. What mainly follows from it, so far as the State is concerned, is the doctrine that all systems of property are justified only to the degree that they secure, in their working, the minimum needs of each citizen as a citizen. No legal rights, therefore, are ethically valid which do not arise from a contribution made to that need. I ought to have what I enjoy only as the result of the services I perform. My property is, from the standpoint of political justice, the measure of economic worth placed by the State upon my personal effort towards the realisation of its end. Obviously, therefore, there can be no property-rights without functions. I can possess only because I serve; I cannot, morally, possess because someone else has served. There is no justice in a State which exacts labour from some of its members as the price of their life, and allows others to live upon labour in which they have had no share. Property is therefore never justified, as Burke believed, in a special representation in the State. The only representation there entitled to find place is the representation of persons; and these are entitled, for common needs, to be considered as of equal worth. This does not mean that the bricklayer will win the same reward or the same esteem as the great artist; but it does mean that the human impulses we can hope to satisfy by social organisation are of equal importance, whether we meet them in bricklayer or in artist. The degree of success that any State can win is measured by its power to realise that equality in the event.

One last remark may be made. That the State is, in some form or another, an inevitable organisation will be apparent to anyone who examines the human nature that we encounter in daily life. But to admit that it is inevitable is not to admit that it is entitled to moral pre-eminence of any kind. For, after all, the State is not itself an end, but merely the means to an end, which is realised only in the enrichment of human lives. Its power and the allegiance it can win depend always upon what it achieves for that enrichment. We are, that is to say, subjects of the State, not for its purpose, but for our own. Realisable good means always some happiness won for the lives of persons, or it means nothing. Power, therefore, must seek the widest possible distribution of such happiness. We are entitled to suspect the State save as we see under its aegis the unfettered growth of human personality. We are entitled to condemn it save as its powers are used deliberately to defeat the forces which stand in the way of that growth. Ultimately, at least, the minds of men can give service to no end less than the realisation of what is best in themselves. They can give allegiance to no lesser ideal. They exercise most truly their citizenship when they seek with wisdom a release from the servitude, alike material and spiritual, that is born of the perversion of power.

## REFERENCE

1. Except in the limited sense suggested below. See Chapter 8.

# 3. Rights

## (i) The Nature of Rights

Every State is known by the rights that it maintains. Our method of judging its character lies, above all, in the contribution that it makes to the substance of man's happiness. The State, therefore, is not, at least for political philosophy, simply a sovereign organisation with the power to get its will obeyed. It cannot, save in a narrowly legal sense, demand allegiance from its subjects save in terms of what that allegiance is to serve. The citizen, that is to say, just because he is a citizen, has the duty of scrutinising both the motive and the character of governmental acts. They are not right merely by reason of the authority from which they emanate. There is a standard by which they are to be tried. There is a purpose with which they must be invested. The State, briefly, does not create, but recognises, rights, and its character will be apparent from the rights that, at any given period, secure recognition.

The theory of rights is the avenue to a creative view of politics, and it is therefore essential to define with some care the meaning they embody. We do not mean by rights the grant of some historic conditions possessed in the childhood of the race, but lost in the process of time. Few theories have done greater harm to philosophy, or more violence to the facts they seek to summarise, than the notion that they represent the recovery of a lost inheritance. There is no golden age to which we may seek to return. The protection afforded to men by the modern State is, at least in Western civilisation, at all points more ample and more adequate than it has been at any previous time.

Nor do we imply by rights the reflection of a natural order which lies behind the shifting appearance of contemporary society. For such an order cannot be permanent in a world which science changes at a pace so rapid as we have come to expect. The natural order of what was a swamp in the Illinois of the eighteenth century cannot be the natural order of the Chicago of our own day. The idea of a natural order is, of course, intended to convey some quality of the imperative to rights. But these, in fact, must always change with the facts of time and place. It is absurd to emphasise their supposed identity in Anglo-Saxon England and the England of the twentieth century. It is not less absurd to suppose that the natural order of a generation of Englishmen implies the same rights as that which distinguishes the primitive races of Melanesia. Our natural order is, at any moment, a problem for pragmatic analysis. Its only permanence lies in the certainty that it will change.

Nor do we mean by rights the power, as Hobbes urged, to satisfy desire. For there are desires, as to murder, for example, which cannot be grounded in rights. All of society is dependent upon the desires which, as we recognise, have a claim to satisfaction. They are never equally valid; and the effort made by the State for their satisfaction must depend in large degree upon the results that effort involved. For obviously, no State would long survive in which the law sought room to respond to the homicidal impulse of its members. The first condition of adequate living is security of life; and the first term, therefore, in a definition of rights is the limitation of desires.

It is easy, in such a background, to take the step urged upon as by Hobbes and Bentham and to define rights as claims recognised by the State. My right is then that claim which the force of the State will, upon order of its courts, be used to substantiate. Here, at the least, is certainty; for the body of statutes and legal rules will give to the observer a means of laying down with some precision exactly the rights each citizen of each State may expect to enjoy. Changes in the law then produce changes in the substance of rights, and an annual scrutiny of statutes and decisions gives us the rule of judgment.

It is an attractive theory; for since the courts enforce the will of the State as they discover that will, we know what claims are immediately entitled to recognition. But so purely legalistic a view has nothing to contribute to an adequate political philosophy. A legal theory of rights will tell us what in fact the character of a State is; it will not tell us, save by the judgment we express upon some particular State, whether the rights there recognised are the rights which need recognition. A legal theory of rights, say in the England of 1923, needs, for its understanding, a test in terms of a criterion external to itself. When we say that a man has the right to bestow his possessions as he will, we state a fact; but we do not thereby determine whether he ought to have that right. When we say that a deaf-mute has the right to marry, we mean that no church and no registrar can refuse, in proper circumstances, the performance of the necessary ceremonial; but we do not mean that we think he ought to have the right. At the back of any legal theory there is a system of presumptions each one of which requires a careful examination before it can be admitted as valid for politics. Laws, in fact, are not, as Montesquieu said, the necessary relations of society. They become those relations as they reflect something beyond the merely barren will of an authority competent to enact them.

Rights, in fact, are those conditions of social life without which no man can seek, in general, to be himself at his best. For since the State exists to make possible that achievement, it is only by maintaining rights that its end may be secured. Rights, therefore, are prior to the State in the sense that, recognised or no, they are that from which its validity derives. They are not historical in the sense that they have at sometime won their recognition. They are not natural, in the sense that a permanent and unchanging catalogue of them can be compiled. They are historical in the sense that, at some given period and place, they are demanded by the character of its civilisation; and they are natural in the sense that, under those same limitations, the facts demand their recognition. That does not mean they will be recognised. A revolution, as in eighteenth-century France, may be necessary to wring their recognition from the existing legal order. But a legal system is surrounded by the penumbra of an attainable ideal which it must reach as the price of its preservation. Rights are asserted in new form as the rights which have gained the cognisance of law become inadequate or outworn. They have a content which changes with time and place. They win their way the more securely they can justify themselves in the facts about them.

They are rights because they are useful to the end the State seeks to serve. They may, indeed, controvert existing legal rights; for it well may be that an order preserves privileges which cannot be defended upon the existing facts. So, for example, the demand for the right to vote contravened the outworn political system before the Reform Act of 1832; and it was the pressure of the facts behind the demand which secured the recognition of a new claim. The same thing is true of the Ten Hours Act of 1844. The same thing, upon a wider scale, is true of the right claimed by the American colonies in 1776 to determine of themselves the character of their taxation. Any given State is set between rights that have been recognised and rights which demand recognition. There is no better historic test of its adequacy than the temper in which it confronts the new demands.

We are making the test of rights utility; and that, it is clear, involves the question of those to whom the rights are to be useful. There is only one possible answer. In any State the demands of each citizen for the fulfilment of his best self must be taken as of equal worth; and the utility of a right is therefore its value to all the members of the State. The right, for instance, of freedom of speech does not mean for those in authority, or for members of some special church or class. Freedom of speech is a right either equally applicable to all citizens without distinction or not applicable at all. For the plane upon which men meet with identical claims upon the common good is that of which the State fixes the horizon. It cannot set bounds to those upon whom the enjoyment of the right is to be conferred. It must assume, at some point in its policy, a sufficient identity of nature in men to secure identity of response. Where it differentiates between them, whether in terms of the kind of property they hold, as in feudal society, or in terms of the religion they profess, as in the France of the *Ancien Régime*, it is, to the degree of differentiation, denying its claim upon the allegiance of those excluded from the enjoyment of rights. For in any adequate view of citizenship a State which refuses to me the thing it declares essential to the well-being of another is making me less than a citizen. It is denying that which invests its power with moral authority. It is admitting that its claim upon me is built, not upon its ethics, but its strength.

It is clear, in such a view, that the citizen has claims upon the State. It must observe his rights. It must give him those conditions without which he cannot be that best self that he may be. This does not mean the guarantee that his best self will be attained. It means only that the hindrances to its attainment are removed so far as the action of the State can remove them. Here, obviously enough, the clue to the interpretation of rights becomes an historical one. The claims that we must recognise are those which, in the light of history, involve disaster when they are unfulfilled. That is the case, for example, upon which a democratic polity is most securely founded. For it has been the obvious lesson of history that when the experience associated with power is less than that of the adult population, the welfare secured almost always is less than that of the citizen-body. My personality, in other words, cannot be adequately protected when others, but not myself, have access to the sources of power. I cannot secure for myself a harmony of impulses unless the balance that is struck in the ultimate rules of political conduct is one that builds upon my experience not less than upon the experience of others. History, in this sense, is assuredly a philosophy of rights built upon example. We do not gain from its survey the power to predict the exact effort men will make. We do at least gain the knowledge that, over a period, certain uniformities of conduct in the rulers of a State will be followed by certain uniformities of conduct in those over whom they rule. We can, from the record we obtain, draw up a code of rights. Its general outline will alone possess validity; and the method and level of its application will depend upon the special conditions of each State. But for Western civilisation, at least, the outlines of such a code begin to formulate themselves with some distinctness.

But the possession of rights, in the sense here used, does not mean the possession of claims that are empty of all duties. We have rights to protect and to express our personality. We have rights to safeguard our uniqueness in the vast pressure of social forces. But our rights are not independent of society. We have them because we are members of the State. We have them by reason of an organisation through which, in the world as it is, the contribution of that uniqueness can alone be made. Our rights are not independent of society, but inherent in it. We have them, that is to say, for its protection as well as for our own. To provide for me the conditions which enable me to be my best self is to oblige me, at the same time, to seek to be my best self. To protect me against attack from others is to imply that I myself will desist from attacking others. To give me the benefit of education is to imply that I will so use the advantages education confers as to add to the common stock. I do not exist solely for the State; but neither does the State exist solely for me. My claim comes from the fact that I share with others in the pursuit of a common end. My rights are powers conferred that I may, with others, strive for the attainment of that common end. My personality, so to speak, bounds and limits the law of the State. But that boundary and that limitation are imposed upon the condition that in seeking to be the best self of which I am capable I seek, in virtue of the common end I share with others, their well-being in my own.

Rights, therefore, are correlative with functions. I have them that I may make my contribution to the social end. I have no right to act unsocially. I have no claim to receive without the attempt, at least, to pay for what I receive. Function is thus implicit in right. In return for the conditions with which I am provided, I seek to make possible a contribution that enriches the common stock. And that contribution must be personal, or it is not a contribution at all. I do not contribute by being the child of my parents. I do not contribute by withdrawal from my fellow-men. I have to do something that is worth doing in order to enjoy that which the experience of history has proved to be worth enjoying. I may pay my debt to the State by being a bricklayer or an artist, or a mathematician. Whatever form my payment takes, it is essential that I should realise that the rights I have are given to me because I am performing some given duties. He that will not perform functions cannot enjoy rights any more than he who will not work ought to enjoy bread. The usefulness of my personality to the social order the State can recognise only in terms of what I do on its behalf. I must recognise the civic equation of which I am part, or forfeit my citizenship.

I have, therefore, no right to do as I like. My rights are built always upon the relation my function has to the well-being of society; and the claims I make must, clearly enough, be claims that are necessary to the proper performance of my function. My demands upon society, in this view, are demands which ought to receive recognition because a recognisable public interest is involved in their recognition. That does not mean that I must, in Mr. Bradley's phrase, accept without repining the duties of my allotted station. It is the primary fact in personality as such that it has no allotted station. It wins, or ought to win, the station in which it may best fulfil itself. It can do so by experiment alone. It must be trained that it may be able to interpret the meaning of experiment. For in any system of rights the ultimate uniqueness, and, therefore, isolation of the individual, is the basic starting-point. Any attempt at the division of society into "natural" classes with "natural" functions is bound to break down. We discover what we naturally are in terms only of what we seek to become. And the discovery is intimately our own. Others may glimpse our sense of failure and success. But the real meaning of our experience is known only to ourselves. That is what makes essential in the modern State a minimum basis at which rights are realised. Whatever I am, whether the statesmen who directs the commonwealth or some humble hewer of wood, I must realise my rights at the level which makes possible the interpretation of my experience to myself. I must be trained, that is, at least to the point at which I can make my desires articulate as life unfolds them. And if that is true for me, it holds equally for all. Rights, therefore, regardless of the exact function to which they relate, are at a minimum basis, identical. The State, at that level, must secure them for each of its citizens. Differentiation arises only when the elementary needs of each individual have been satisfied.

We build rights upon individual personality because, ultimately, the welfare of the community is built upon the happiness of the individual. I cannot have rights against the public welfare, for that, ultimately, is to give me rights against a welfare which is intimately and inseparably associated with my own. But that is not to say that I cannot have rights against the State. For the State, at any given moment, means a body of men and women in possession of actual power; and their judgment of the rights that ought to be recognised may be mistaken. It was judged, for example, that Galileo had no right to suggest hypotheses contrary to accepted Catholic doctrine; but it is Galileo's right that we now admit. The situation is, of course, reciprocal. The State has rights against me. It has the right to exact from me that conduct which secures to others the enjoyment of the rights it secures to myself. For the community, the interest of each citizen is of equal importance. No claim of mine, at least at the minimum level of rights, can be recognised by the State which involves the surrender by some other person of rights without which he, also, cannot be his best self. The mutual claims of the State and of its citizens must be claims clearly justifiable by reference to a common good which includes the goods of all.

In a sense, indeed, it does not matter whether that common good is recognised by an existing State. My duty is to act as though it ought to be recognised. My citizenship implies conduct on my part which attempts the enforcement of that recognition where it is denied. I may, of course, in such action encounter the hostile forces of the State. I may—I probably shall—provoke hopeless defeat, or a victory which is purchased only at a terrible price. I must yet make the choice, in and of myself, of the conduct that citizenship implies. To act otherwise is to subordinate truth to authority; and it is historically evident that this habit of subordination ultimately makes men indifferently accept the orders of authority without regard to their substance.

My duty, therefore, to the State, is, above all, my duty to the ideal the actual State must seek to serve. There are, then, circumstances in which resistance to the State becomes an obligation if claims to right are to be given validity. We can lay down no general rules, either of time or situation. Anyone who studies at all carefully the history of revolution will be convinced that the element of chance is too large to admit the entrance of prediction. We can only say that a general order becomes moral only in the degree to which it is built in the conscience of its citizens. Antagonism to the demands of authority will always be the exception in history; but those demands will win their way from inert acceptance rather than active consent unless, over a period of time, they offer service to the theoretic purpose of the State. For any social order which fails consistently to recognise the claims of personality is built upon a foundation of sand. Sooner or later it will provoke the dissent of those whose nature is frustrated by its policy. Its disasters will become their opportunity. For to deny the claims of right is to sacrifice the claim to allegiance. The State can exercise moral authority upon no other basis.

## (ii) Rights and the State

Rights so discussed seem to imply a State and an individual which strike a balance between their mutual claims. This is, in fact, to state, the problem of rights in a fashion too narrow to express with accuracy the environment we encounter. For it is not merely as a member of the State that the individual has rights. His personality express itself in a hundred other forms of association. Wherever men are banded together to perform a task that is part of the common welfare the body so formed has rights as real, and as compelling, as the rights of the State. The community, so to say, is a federal process; and the division of power is achieved by the natural expression taken by man's gregarious impulse. To limit his rights to the single category which membership of the State involves is to destroy his personality and not to preserve it. The Roman Catholic Church must live its life unhindered by the State because invasion of its sphere means the destruction of the quality it brings into the life of its members. And nothing is gained by urging that the rights of the State as such are superior to those of other associations. Any such decision is a pragmatic one; it must be made in terms of the particular conflict that has arisen. It must be made, further, in the background of the knowledge that when, and if conflict comes the individual will, whatever the law, choose his own course of action; Throgmorton will decide one way and Howard of Effingham another. The sphere of rights to be enjoyed by any corporate body cannot be determined in *a priori* fashion. Their powers must be set in the light of our knowledge of how those powers will be used.

This is not to dethrone the State from the position it now occupies of the co-ordinating factor in the community. But it is at least to indicate the way in which its power of co-ordination should be used. The State cannot, for instance, allow a religious association to determine the belief of those who do not belong to its communion; but it has no moral, and therefore at least ideally, no legal right to determine what the members of a given association are to believe. The spectacle, for example, of the House of Lords settling the religious doctrine of the Free Church of Scotland is a ludicrous one; it is an invasion of rights for which no justification can be attempted. It is a survival of the period when the Church had ceased to be a State, but when men had not yet seen that a State cannot at once realise itself and retain the character of a church. So, too, with a trade union. If the members of such a body decide that political representation is a function they should seek to support, the remedy for those of their members who dissent from that policy is not in the courts of the State but in resignation. Within the ambit that it seeks to cover, any fellowship is, to the degree that it is real, as original and as compelling as the State itself. To make the powers of the State supreme over all other bodies is possible only when we have the certainty that the rights through which alone the individual can realise his best self are amply secured to each member of the community.

This is to suggest, of course, that there is differentiation in the manner in which rights are now secured. It is to imply that men do not share equally in the gain as well as in the toil of living. If we may say broadly that the personality of men can now hope for a larger expression that at any previous time, it still remains true that the number of those to whom happiness is open in a creative sense is still pitiably small. The State, in other words, is biased in the emphasis it places upon the attainment of rights. It does not adjudicate impartially between its members. Its decision is weighted on behalf of the actual holders of power. It tends to identify the thing that is right with the thing to which it has grown accustomed. It does not distribute equally the means—especially knowledge and economic power—to influence the policy that is adopted. The older views both of liberty and of order can hardly be said to benefit the masses of men. The wealth of the community increases, but it does not in a critical way relieve their wants. Our knowledge increases by leaps and bounds; but those who have genuine access to the intellectual heritage of the race are still but a fragment of the people. Religion, doubtless, has brought to its devotees immeasurable comfort; but it has not, in a vital sense, affected the substance of the social order. The rule of the rich, whether of landed men or of those who owned industrial capital, has been devoted firstly to the accumulation of wealth, and secondly to preventing its diffusion. The whole character of social life and, therefore, the whole character of the State, is above all determined by its division into a small number of wealthy persons and a large number who dwell upon the margins of subsistence. We enjoy security and order. But the security we enjoy means the protection of most in their impotence, and the order is, very largely, the safeguarding of the few against the demands of the many for a richer and a fuller life.

The prescriptions of the State are never, therefore, final prescriptions. The guide to our conduct is not the voice of authority, save in so far as the results of authority go to the realisation of ideal right. A State must give to men their due as men before it can demand, at least with justice, their loyalty. And it may be urged that in a period when active citizenship is coincident, broadly speaking, with the adult population, the test to which the State is submitted becomes more serious than at any previous time. Men who are granted political power sooner or later become insistent that the result of power be rights. They will seek the institutions through which the substance of rights can be best secured. They will either universalise privilege, or else abolish it. They will insist that liberty and equality are inevitable corollaries of a democratic system. They will seek the diffusion of those notions through the whole fabric of the community, at least to the point where the power of the State is placed with approximate fairness at the disposal of all. In the end, resistance to such demands is difficult; for, as Acton pointed out, there is a reserve of latent power in the people which few minorities have either the strength or the cohesion to overcome. The State, therefore, which seeks to survive must continually transform itself to the demands of men who have an equal claim upon that common welfare it is its ideal purpose to promote.

We are concerned here, not with the defence of anarchy, but with the conditions of its avoidance. Men must learn to subordinate their self-interest to the common welfare. The privileges of some must give way before the rights of all. Indeed, it may be urged that the interest of the few is in fact the attainment of those rights, since in no other environment is stability to be assured. Russian aristocrats who earn a precarious livelihood after being the spoiled children of fortune have learned, like the *émigrés* of 1789, the penalty that is ultimately paid when the mass of mankind is deprived of access to its inheritance. The guarantee of a stable civilisation is that men in general should have at least that minimum without which they cease to be men. Rights are ideas more strongly armed than the most efficient despotism; and they are, above all, most powerful in a democracy where the universal character of their application is the assumption upon which they are built. It is possible—

it is perhaps even desirable—to maintain degrees of freedom and equality in a democratic civilisation. But it is certainly necessary that the minimum amount of freedom and equality shall be such as to ensure to each citizen the full opportunity of personal development. There is too rarely that opportunity now. Mean environments beget mean children, and the fruit rottens as it ripens. The protest evoked by modern conditions is the natural challenge of men who are deprived of the things that make life worth living; and nothing is really gained, as Burke pointed out, by the ascription of popular violence to agitation or conspiracy. Man is in general too little of a public creature, the force at the disposal of any government is, as a rule, too powerful, for either agitation or conspiracy to make its way unless there existed an atmosphere of frustrated impulse which made for their reception. The demand for the realisation of rights only secures a hearing when the absence of those rights is felt as injustice. The demand may be postponed; it may suffer temporary defeat; but any demand that is genuinely related to the basic impulses of men must, sooner or later, be given response. To reform if we would preserve is, as Macaulay said, the voice of great events.

This contention is not answered by the argument that in a democracy the people have power and that whatever legal rights obtain the people wills their existence. There is all the difference in the world between a power informed and conscious of its strength and a power so latent and suppressed that its holders are hardly aware that they may exercise it. People as ignorant as the modern citizen body is left by our social system make of it a picture for themselves which deludes them in their search for the causes of their misfortune. They are not trained in the relation of cause and effect. They are not educated to see that institutions are historic ideas the utility of which dies with the cessation of the circumstances which gave them birth. They are, for the most part, brought up in an atmosphere of inferiority. Subordination to their lot is the one creed in which they are trained to believe. Myth and legend surround them on every side; and it is no part, as yet, of modern educational effort to wonder the ability to be sceptical upon those who are born within its ambit. The disparity of influence between those who defend and those who attack an existing system is, therefore, immense. The one can appeal to solid and tangible reality; the others ask for a leap into a dark hinterland which requires effort and imagination to be understood. The members of a democracy cannot be truly said to possess their power until they have been deliberately trained to use it. We are still far from such a time.

That is why the formidable centralisation of the modern State is so great an enemy to an ideal system of rights. For only where power is distributed widely is there any effective restraint upon those who wield it. To multiply the centres of authority is to multiply the channels of discussion and so promote the diffusion of healthy and independent opinion. But, to this end, it is necessary to regard the social order as a whole. We cannot attempt the democratisation of political authority and leave it there. Adequately to work the instrument we have created, we must democratise whatever auxiliary powers affect that instrument in any important way. Anything, that is to say, which is directly related to that minimum basis of rights we have been discussing can never be left to the control of a few. A man clearly must have the opportunity to share in the disposition of whatever makes him, at least in an intimate way, a member of the citizen body; liberty and equality, therefore, are at the very base of the political system.

We shall discuss in detail later the implications of liberty and equality. Here it is enough to emphasise two things. Neither of them is an unchanging notion. Each has a special perspective which relates it to the special environment of any given time and place. Liberty in the France of the later sixteenth century meant, above all, the power of a citizen to worship God in his own way, as liberty in the seventeenth century in England meant, above all, the absence of arbitrary taxation by the monarch. What seems to be of the permanent essence of freedom is that the personality of each individual should be so unhampered in its development, whether by authority or by custom, that it can make for itself a satisfactory harmonisation of its impulses. In this perspective the thing of importance is that the harmonisation should be self-effected. The rules laid down by the State should not bar the way to any individual as distinct from another. They should leave room for trial and error. They should not, as now, unduly penalise the individual because he has not been careful in the selection of his parents. Equality, in other words, seems to mean the minimisation of the handicaps our present social order imposes. We cannot offer identity of opportunity. On the average, the son of Charles Darwin will have a better chance of displaying an interest in science than the son of a stock-broker or a tailor. But at least we can seek to make it generally possible that the son of a stockbroker with scientific leanings should not be driven to sell bonds. We can make it possible for each member of the State to try out what he believes to be his special faculties. Most, doubtless, will be more than content with security and a routine. Our task is to assure what pioneers we have the avenue to inventiveness.

### (iii) Particular Rights

Yet all this, it may be said, is to dwell upon the heights of theory. It is one thing to show the notions a State must recognise if it is to move the achievement of its purpose; it is a very different thing to show how that purpose is in fact to be achieved. It is even easy to insist that States which fall consistently below the standard of ideals men think at some definite period to be attainable will, sooner or later, be challenged at their foundations. Such a declaration of right provides neither a catalogue of actual rights which demand recognition, nor the institutions through which their conquest is made possible. The argument, though important, is less formidable than it appears. Though we can never determine with exactitude the level at which the demand for rights ought to be satisfied, we can, at least, infer from the historic record the rights which will claim recognition. Though we can never say that any definite institutions are bound to result in their recognition, we can at least postulate that, without certain institutions the rights which seek fulfilment will never gain it. We cannot, that is, ever positively assure the fulfilment of the State-purpose; but, at least negatively, we can point out the conditions which destroy the chance of such fulfilment.

What, at the very outset, needs to be emphasised is that rights are not merely, or even greatly, a matter of the written record. Musty parchments will doubtless give them greater sanctity; they will not ensure their realisation. The first amendment to the American Constitution legally secures freedom of speech and of peaceable assembly; the fourth amendment legally secures the citizen that his house shall not be searched except upon a warrant of probable cause; the eighth amendment legally secures the citizen against excessive bail. Yet in one hysterical week the action of the executive power rendered all these amendments worthless;[1] and the fifteenth amendment, which sought political equality for the coloured citizens of the South, has never been applied either by the executive or by the courts. A case like *Ex Parte O'Brien*[2] in England, and the *Pluchard Case*[3] in France, both go to show that the maintenance of rights is much more a question of habit and tradition than of the formality of written enactment. This does not imply the worthlessness of the latter. It is always valuable to be able to attack the executive in terms of a law it has clearly offended; and the written enactment always serves to remind a people that it has had to fight for its rights. But, at least ultimately, only deliberate challenge will be successful in breaking the purpose of a government determined upon unlawful conduct. It is the proud spirit of citizens, less than the letter of the law, that is their most real safeguard.

Nor is the necessary protection to be found in that separation of powers which both Locke and Montesquieu thought to be the secret of freedom.[4] That classic doctrine enshrines the vital truth that the more independent a judiciary, the more adequate are the safeguards of rights; but since any judiciary is ultimately appointed by the executive, its independence is rarely final. The separation of powers acts as a check upon the undue expansion of each authority's allotted sphere; but it does not determine the quality and extent of the powers that are allotted. Nor, moreover, is it possible to define with any precision the boundaries between the three divisions into which it is customary to divide the power of the State. Judges are compelled to make the law;[5] when legislatures confirm nomination to office they are acting within the executive sphere; and the ordinance power of the modern executive is not only genuinely legislative, but has reached dimensions more formidable than that of Parliament itself.[6] To separate powers with the theoretic nicety of the American Constitution may well be rather to confound them than to make them clear. At best, such separation is merely an index to competence; but the use made of the index will depend upon the prevailing atmosphere of the given State. It is the legislature of modern Italy which has made of Mussolini an executive and legislature in one.

The problem, in short, of the realisation of rights is best approached by discussing particular rights. We can, then, build from their sum a system of limitations upon the power of the State. Such a method serves several purposes. It indicates, in the first place, the position occupied by the individual in the community. It shows what he must possess if he is, in any creative way, to contribute his share to the common stock of welfare. It is the approach, secondly, to the meaning of liberty and equality. When we know the rights we desire to maintain, we are in a better position to judge the positive institutions those concepts involve. And, thirdly, to define in outline particular rights is to indicate, at least in a general way, the necessary character of political structure. From such an outline we can begin to fashion the way in which the co-ordinating power of the State should be executed. We shall perceive that the State, in such a background, is essentially, a *communitas communitatum,* and not the crowning-point of a hierarchical structure. It is not the body from which other bodies derive; its relationship to them is pre-eminent only as it is so judged by citizens upon grounds of moral rights. Its authority, accordingly, becomes dependent upon the way in which it maintains such a system of rights as is here outlined. These, therefore, are not born of the State, but with it. They are the primary condition upon which, if not its existence, at least its quality, depends. Not, we say, its existence; for a State may well, like Czarist Russia, go to work against all decent justice and yet have power over a long period to maintain itself without serious challenge.

Let us first remind ourselves of what will be involved in a theory of rights to which we now seek to give concrete expression. A State, it has been argued, is a territorial society divided into government and subjects. It exists, it exerts authority, it claims allegiance, in order that those citizens may realise in their lives the best of which they are capable. To that end they have rights. These are defined as the conditions without which no citizen can hope to achieve the best that is in him. Obviously, therefore, rights are not the creatures of law, but its condition precedent. They are that which law is seeking to realise. Institutions are, then, bad or good in proportion as they fail or succeed in the promotion of the purpose of rights. At the back of those conceptions there is a view of society as a system of finite selves, each unique and precious by reason of its uniqueness. That self seeks embodiment in a society the cohesiveness of which endangers the preservation of its special individuality save as the maintenance of its rights enables it to carve out its own channel of expression. It does not possess its rights as an empty and formal claim. It possesses them that the fulfilment of diversity may maximise the richness of social effort. It has rights because it has duties. Our society is a functional society in which the test of structure is the service it can render. And service is personal service. It is the deliberate and conscious striving of each self in each generation that makes possible the increase of our social heritage. We are justified, not by what we are, but by what we can become. We experiment with our powers. We mould an environment in which those powers secure always an ampler field of play. The citizen has a right to work. He is born into a world where, if rationally organised, he can live only by the sweat of his brow. Society owes him the occasion to perform his function. To leave him without access to the means of existence is to deprive him of that which makes possible the realisation of personality. This does not mean the right to some particular work. A prime minister who has been overthrown has not the right to be provided with labour of an identical character. Society cannot afford each man the choice of the effort he will make. It cannot, in any ultimate way, afford undue emphasis upon occupations which carry with them special dignity of recompense. It needs a supply of goods and services to maintain its life. The right to work can mean no more than the right to be occupied in producing some share of those goods and services. Alternatively, therefore, the man who is deprived of the opportunity actively so to share is entitled to the equivalent reward of that opportunity. And since it is clear that no society could, over any long period, bear the cost of paying that equivalent to any large proportion of its members, it follows that the principle of insurance against unemployment is integral to the conception of the State. We must year by year abstain from consuming some due proportion of what we produce, that, in the lean years, those who, either temporarily or permanently, are deprived of the opportunity to labour may not, also, be deprived of the means to live. How such a system of insurance is most wisely organised is, with all its importance, rather a question of detail than of principle. What is fundamental is the recognition that to be his best self a man must work, and that the absence of work must mean provision until employment again offers the opportunity of work. What is here urged is not a defence of parasitism, but a recognition that the performance of service is implicit in the nature of social life.

A man has not only the right to work. He has the right also to be paid an adequate wage for his labour. By the work that he performs he must be able to secure a return capable of purchasing the standard of living without which creative citizenship is impossible. In such a notion there can be no fixity of amount. He needs the food which keeps him physically fit, the clothing and shelter which make him begin life at least at that level where his energies are not wholly engaged in attention to purely physical wants. He needs the little comforts that make of life something more than a mean satisfaction of ugly wants. The right to an adequate wage does not imply equality of income; but it does, it may be urged, imply that there must be a sufficiency for all before there is a superfluity for some. The contrast in the modern world between men and women who have never known a decent house, a decent meal, and clothing that barely protects them against the elements, and those who have never known what it is to have unsatiated a want that the possession of property can supply is an intolerable one.

Ethically, at least, it is no answer to this demand to argue that the productivity of the world makes impossible the realisation of this right. The statistical proof that an equal division of the product of industry would hardly better the condition of the worker[7] only means the condemnation of the present system of production. It only means that the method we require for our end is different from the method we now use. It means that we must reorganise the instruments of production that they may satisfy the human demands made upon them. Obviously, also, there is involved in the realisation of this right the grave problem of population. We must chain the "devil" of Malthus if we are to satisfy our needs. We must make the increase of our numbers proportionate to our ability to satisfy the right of those numbers to an adequate standard of living. Here it is important to realise how closely the problem of population is related to the standard of life. Where the presence of numbers is most apparent, there, also, the human wants are most appealing.[8] Immediately the standard of life is sufficient to cover the purely material appetite, the number of children ceases to act as a source of economic depression. It would seem the logical inference that the more rapidly we recognise the right to this adequacy the more rapidly we shall realise the most effective condition of its maintenance.

But, it may be said, even supposing that we can grapple with the problem of population, it is still dubious whether industrial productivity is sufficient to meet the problem of this adequate standard. The answer to that scepticism is, at the least, a twofold answer. Our industrial organisation has not, thus far, been devised to meet a demand of this kind. It has been devised to satisfy the owner of capital; it has sought to fulfil not the function of service, but the function of acquisition. We do not know of what our industrial system is capable until we organise it for use and not for profit. Anyone who studies, for example, the facts of the coal industry in Great Britain will be appalled at the wastage the present technique of ownership involves. Anyone, to generalise, who regards the casual and haphazard character of the modern businessman will realise how rarely he is competent for the proper performance of his task. We demand proof of competence from the lawyer and the doctor; from the businessman there is demanded nothing save the ownership of property or the power to obtain credit. We do not allow a doctor to hand over his practice to his son unless the son has obtained the necessary qualifications; but the son of a businessman may succeed to his father's enterprise without regard to the quality of his mind or his knowledge of its processes. We take no steps to direct the flow of capital into socially necessary production. We rarely—there are honourable exceptions—seek to enlist an interest in production from those concerned with manual effort. We are only beginning to realise that research into the processes of manufacture may improve them as surely as science has increased the power of modern warfare to destroy. Until, in brief, experiment with the character and constitution of industry has proceed upon a far vaster scale than we have so far known, the function we must seek that it fulfil is still the realisation of adequate standards for those who live by its results.

Nor is that all. If it were true that the productivity of industry offers no hope of an adequate standard of life for all citizens we should be faced by a dilemma which perhaps Hobbes only in the history of political philosophy would have had the courage to confront. For in that event, either the social process must be a blind struggle to acquire, uninformed by moral purpose, or else those upon whom adequacy was conferred would have to be selected upon some rational principle. In the first case all political philosophy would be superfluous. We might, indeed, have an art of politics akin in character to the maxims of Machiavelli, but it would be totally devoid of ethical content. In the second case, the present system would stand self-condemned. For no one would seriously claim that the rewards of the modern State are distributed upon any recognisably organised basis. They are not, in the mass, a return to character or ability or service. Men succeed because they have chosen their parents with foresight, or because some product they manufacture happens to satisfy the public want. The incommensurable difference of the reward to a great artist like Meredith and a great pill-maker like Sir Joseph Beecham is at least evidence that the method of valuation does not now proceed by ordered reason.

The fact surely is that we have so little attempted the conscious control of social organisation that we have hardly sought to inquire into the principles it involves. If we start from the assumption that we must either, over a period, satisfy the basic impulses of men, or court disaster, it becomes obvious that we must organise the processes of production with the purpose of satisfying those basic impulses. To that end we must end the anarchy of the modern scheme. From the mere competition of private and selfish interests we cannot secure a well-ordered society. From combination effected, as we have recently learned in detail,[9] to levy financial blackmail from the wants of society, we shall never secure a service conceived in terms of justice. Either the State must control industrial power in the interest of its citizens, or industrial power will control the State in the interests of if possessors. The first need of the masses is to realise the right to adequate payment for their effort. The first principle, therefore, of industrial organisation is a system of institutions directed to that end.

We shall discuss later the forms such institutions might take. Here it will be sufficient to indicate certain obvious possibilities involved. The State must be regarded as the protector of the standards of industrial adventure. It must control the operations of capital at least to the point of making the rate of profit contingent upon the payment of an adequate rate of wages. Just as stringent legislation prevents the sale of impure food, so must stringent legislation prevent the payment of wages below a reasonable standard of living. Already in the Trade Board system in Great Britain[10] and the minimum wage legislation of the United States,[11] we have the dawn, at least, of the recognition of this principle. What it means in theory is the restriction of the field covered by freedom of contract to a definite area. Industry, in Sir Frederic Pollock's phrase, is regarded as a dangerous trade which can only be entered upon conditions. Men may agree to work, or to pay for work, only above that level of reward which the State deems necessary to the performance of its functions. Obviously the minimum so fixed will vary with time and place; though it may be hoped that the growth of international control will tend to make the highest State average the general average of civilisation. But no State will permit businessmen to conduct an enterprise where the cost of that effort can be paid for only by the sacrifice of the essential conditions of citizenship. The labourer is worthy of his hire because he is a human being. He must receive the reward which makes possible the realisation of his humanity.

Nothing in this, it should be added, involves either uniformity in the method or similarity in the technique of payment; it involves only the establishment of an adequate wage as the basis of the industrial adventure. It may well be that inequality of payment, above that level, is demanded if the incentive to effort is to be sufficient. Certainly the persistence of habit will probably make it necessary to give differential rates to the rare ability of the few for a long period of time. What we seem to require, wherever it is practicable, is the payment, at least in manual labour, of a basic wage which offers adequacy and of a piece-rate in return for effort above some average standard. In that event what is clearly of the first importance is to secure an impartial authority to fix that standard. It cannot be left to the employer, since it is too greatly to his interest to fix the standard unduly high. It cannot be left to the worker who, similarly, would tend to fix it unduly low. We require an external body which can by research discover a basis from which an effort may be made to render a return to each man according to his powers. But those powers, where they are especially remarkable, can only be satisfied after the general wants of all have been supplied.

The obvious corollary of the right to an adequate wage is the right to reasonable hours of labour. The thing that makes a man a citizen is thought. He must, therefore, so distribute the period of labour that he may have leisure for creative tasks. Obviously there is a physiological limit to the energy a man can afford to expend. But there is a civic limit to the amount the State can, for its own sake, permit him to expend. Those who devote their energies to attendance upon a machine become, as Aristotle saw, disqualified for the nobler tasks of life unless they have ample leisure to be other than the tenders of a machine. Certainly the frustration of personality involved, in the long hours of toil characteristic, for instance, of the first part of the nineteenth century has been made obvious by inquiry into its results. Men and women came home from their daily toil incapable of thought and even of feeling. Their machines were their masters. There was no leisure in which they could find themselves. They knew only a life of endless toil. The right to reasonable hours of labour is the right to discover the land of the mind. It is the key to the intellectual heritage of the race.

The interpretation of "reasonable" in the analysis of this right has no fixity about it; its content will depend upon the technique of production at any given time. Certainly in a world so complex as this, the eight-hour day has become the maximum a man dare work at manual labour and still hope to understand the life about him. It will be possible, almost certainly, to decrease that maximum as mechanical invention progress; the application of science to industry is, after all, only a hundred and fifty years old. But whatever be the improvements we can here expect, the notion of such a maximum is essential. A man may hope to write or paint, to administer or to teach, even to be employed in the handicrafts where the personal factor is important, and still remain conscious of creative powers; wherever he has to plan of himself the deadening effect of toil is mitigated, with a consequent gain to his contingent social utility.

But as soon as his sphere of effort is mainly the repetition of a mechanical routine, the evidence is decisive that such labour is a barrier to happiness. He ceases to be able to experiment with himself. The world outside does not appear a mystery he would explore. What he desires is simply to deaden the senses, to find, rarely in the realm of beauty, the means of forgetting the pain of toil. Anyone who reads the description[12] of the factory worker in the early period of the Industrial Revolution will realise how fatigue expressed itself in terms of a brutal coarseness fatal to that fine and free perceptiveness which comes to men whose creative faculties are given room for expansion.

But it is not enough, on the industrial side, to limit the hours of labour and to make the reward of effort adequate to the basic needs of life. A man might posses both these rights and yet remain fettered by the conditions of his service. Any theory of rights in the modern State must take account of the implications of large-scale industrialism. It must realise that the institution of private property, of which we shall later examine the consequences, leaves the control of the industrial machine to the owners of capital, and that individual freedom, as when the single handicrafts-man worked for a master, is no longer possible. Obviously, in such a background, we must prevent that ownership of capital from degenerating into dictatorship. Exactly as the evolution of political authority has been concerned with the erection of limitations upon the exercise of power, so also with economic authority. There is a right, that is to say, to be concerned in the government of industry as there is a right to be concerned in the government of politics. In a sense not less urgent than that in which Lincoln used it, no State can survive that is half-bond and half-free. The citizen as an industrial unit must somehow be given the power to share in the making of those decisions which affect him as a producer if he is to be in a position to maximise his freedom.

We must not unduly maximise the power he will have. The work of the world has to be done; and the number of people who will be able to hope for genuine significance in their daily toil is probably smaller than some are eager to imagine. What, certainly, we can mitigate is the unlimited power which the ownership of capital has conferred. We can compel discussion before action is taken where, for instance, it is proposed to dismiss a worker. We can compel discussion before changes are made in the technique of production. We can erect institutions upon which the workers are represented for the governance of industry, and compel reference to them for the settlement of industrial method. We can universalise the standards exacted from industrial direction, and give to the workers such share as we choose in the fixation of those standards. We can transform the power of industrial capital from that in which it becomes the residuary legatee of the industrial process to one in which it receives a fixed remuneration determined by agreement for the service it contributes. Just as the holder of government bonds has no control, as such, over government policy, so it is possible to prevent interference with the direction of an industrial enterprise by the loaners thereto of capital. What is here being urged is that the present system of private property does not in the least involve the present technique of industrial direction; while that technique, above all with the largely unqualified right to hire and fire that it involves, is simply a mitigated form of slavery. The right to a representative government in industry is the right to channels through which, in the necessary toil of life, the personality of the worker may find expression. In a democratic system it is impossible to maintain political freedom with industrial autocracy; and that the more clearly when the system of ownership so largely controls the substance of State-policy.

Citizenship has been defined as the contribution of one's instructed judgment to the public good. It follows therefore that the citizen has the right to such education as will fit him for the tasks of citizenship. He must be provided with the instruments which make possible the understanding of life. He must be able to give articulate expression to the wants he has, the meaning of the experience he has encountered. There is no more fundamental division in the modern State than that between those who have the control of knowledge and those who lack such control. In the long run, power belongs to those who can formulate and grasp ideas. Granted that such ability exists in a wide range of inequality, there is yet, once more, a minimum basis of education below which no one of average intelligence can be permitted to fall. For unless I can follow with understanding the processes of politics those things which effect my life will be effected without my having the opportunity to make my will enter in to the result. "First of all things", said Antiphon the Sophist, "I place education"; certainly in the modern world the citizen who lacks it is bound to be the slave of others. He will not be able to convince his fellows. He will not be able to restrain his nature into those paths along which it is best fitted to travel. He will not rise to the full height of his personality. He will go through life a stunted being whose impulses have never been ordered by reason into creative experiment.

The right to education does not mean the right to an identical intellectual training for all citizens. It involves the discovery of capacity and the fitting of the discipline conferred to the type of capacity made known. Obviously, it would be foolish waste to give an identical training to Meredith and Clerk-Maxwell. But obviously, also, there is a minimum level below which no citizen can fall if he is to use the necessary intellectual instruments of our civilisation. He must be trained to make judgments. He must learn to weigh evidence. He must learn to choose between the alternatives between which he is called to decide. He must be made to feel that this is a world in which he can by the use of his mind and will shape at once outline and substance.

And it may be said here that any examination of the standards attained by modern States will reveal their inadequacy. The child who is turned at fourteen into an industry the organisation of which rarely admits of mental creativeness in any save those few who direct it is unlikely, as a general rule, to have been provided with the equipment necessary to the proper use of his native intelligence. A first-class mind may well fail to realise its powers simply because it has never been trained to the point where it is conscious of them. Genius, it may well be, will always make its way whatever, or in spite of, the training afforded; but the talent of the average man demands the most careful cultivation if it is to bear its due fruit.

A democratic system, it has been argued, is one in which the will of the average citizen has channels of direct access to the sources of authority. There is, therefore, a right to political power. This right may be said to contain three derivative rights. There is, in the first place, the right to the franchise, however that be organised. Every adult citizen has the right to indicate what persons he desires should undertake the task of government. That right will clearly involve a choice of institutions. The basis of the franchise may be industrial or geographical; citizens may even be grouped, as Hare desired, by their voluntary choice. I shall argue later that for the purpose of ultimate political decisions, the geographical method has the maximum advantage; in this connection it is sufficient to establish the existence of the universal claim. Neither sex nor property, neither race nor creed, ought to prevent the citizen from aiding in the choice of his rulers. If it be argued that his choice is often wrong, the answer is that democracy lives by the method of trial and error. If it be said that he rarely has the knowledge necessary to give a reasoned choice, the answer is that the State must then organise on his behalf access to that knowledge. For, as has already been pointed out, whenever the body of voters is limited, the welfare realised usually excludes that of the persons excluded. No test has been devised which enables us to limit the franchise in such fashion as to equate civic virtue with its possession. Its limitation to property-owners was disastrous to those who did not own property. Its limitation to a creed or caste meant always special privilege for that creed or caste. Even Mill's test of education,[13] is, beyond simple literacy, unrelated to the qualities we require. An historian, for example, whose expertness in the dissection of an early charter may be exquisite, may lack completely a sense of evidence when it is a question of deciding the merits of tariff reform. A scientist whose discoveries make possible the development of oceanic telegraphy may be utterly useless when it comes to the practical expression of his ideas.[14] Certainly in the present state of our knowledge of human nature we have no warrant for limitations of any general kind.

But it is not enough to admit a general and unlimited right to the franchise. I vote in order that I may choose my governors. I decide between points of view the qualities of which I am trained at some level to appreciate. But just as those who choose cannot be drawn from any special class in the community, so, also, those who are chosen cannot be members of a limited section only. We have need, in the first place, of governors who represent the widest possible experience. No class can ever successfully give the law to another class; no class, indeed, is ever good enough to legislate for another class. The absence of limitation is more urgent than in previous periods .for the simple reason that the entrustment of power to the mass of people means, inevitably, a more stringent scrutiny of the results of legislation than in the past. And it is, moreover, clear that to limit the right to share in the exercise of power is always, at least ultimately, to limit the numbers of those who share in the benefits of power. The exclusion, for instance, of the Nonconformists from the franchise has left its definite impression upon the character of the older universities of Great Britain. The political habits of the land-owning class in England have profoundly affected the methods of its taxation. The right to represent becomes, in the background of historic experience, the logical result of the right to choose.

That does not mean that any person may, whatever qualifications he may lack, submit himself for choice without conditions. Rights, as has been insisted, are always relative to functions; and there is no evident reason why the implications of the representative function should not define the conditions of assuming it. So long as the limits made do not press unequally upon different sections of the population, they are capable of defence if they aim at the improvement of the function concerned. An example will make this clear. It has been the custom of the English aristocracy to send their sons into the House of Commons at an early age. Training has often been absent; little has been known of aptitude; but the power of family has usually been sufficient to discover a means of access to Parliament. Obviously there have been real advantages in the system; cases like those of Fox and the younger Pitt show that it has not been devoid of benefit. But it would be no invasion of the right to be elected to the House of Commons to make it contingent, for example, upon three years' service in a local public authority. It would be perfectly legitimate to hold that service in the central legislative assembly is so important in its results that proof of aptitude and experience must be offered before the claim to represent can be admitted. A limitation of this kind would press equally upon all members of the community; it would benefit no special section. If the use of a right can be improved in this faction there is no need to regard it as thereby weakened or destroyed. No democracy can afford to neglect the proved sources of efficient service. That is the basis of its life. Therein it differs from either monarchy or aristocracy, since these bring to their maintenance a certain quality of the mysterious a democracy does not contain. A monarchy, for instance, may, as in the France of the eighteenth century, win affection for its institutions, even when they are in fact obsolete, simply because the facts about them are unknown. It removes its foundation from the field of popular choice, where the bases of a democracy are, in the nature of things, revealed by the necessity of public analysis. Inevitably, therefore, the rights of a citizen are circumscribed by the needs of the community of which he is a part. What he is entitled to demand is that such circumscription bears equally upon all other citizens.

The right to be chosen as a governor implies as well the right to be chosen for political office. We do not, it will be noticed, argue that the right to vote implies the right to choose more than the representatives of a political assembly. So chosen, there cannot be limitations against the right to be chosen as a member of an administration. But the experience of democratic systems does not lend weight to the belief in a multiplied electoral power. Direct government of this kind, whether in the choice of men or of measures, may have worked with some success in the restricted area of the city-state. There a man might hope to be genuinely known to his neighbours, and a judgment based upon sufficient intimacy to be real became possible. That is not the case with States of the modern size. Even the plebiscite of the American Commonwealth results in the selection of a ruler distinguished rather by negative than by positive virtues; the system may produce a Lincoln, but it is by accident rather than by design. The ruler of the modern State needs to be chosen by men who have familiarity with his mind, who have tested him in the intimate fellowship of daily politics. They also, as the case of Lord Goderich testifies, will make mistakes. But there is larger room in the indirect method for the recognition of quality than in the direct method. That has been made fully evident in those American States where the judiciary is elected by the people. And since they are the choosers of those from whom the leaders will be taken, restriction is not a limitation which involves privilege for a few. The equality is there, though the road to it ascends more steeply.

A political system in which the pivot is the right of the citizen to be articulate about his wants clearly requires to safeguard his articulateness. There must be, that is to say, freedom of speech with all that makes freedom of speech effective. What is the substance of the right to such a freedom? It cannot merely mean the protection of a man in what he says, for thought is too closely interwoven with action to be dissociated from it. It cannot merely mean, either, the protection of a man as an individual, for much of what he says that is most urgent comes from his speech in concert with others. Freedom of speech is a right that, clearly, needs definition in terms of the function it seeks to serve. A man's citizenship, as I have argued, is the duty to contribute his instructed judgment to the public good. He cannot make that contribution if a penalty is attached to the expression of his thought. The case against persecution for opinion deemed wrong at some given time is perhaps the clearest issue in the whole course of history. The impalpable barriers of custom and convention will almost always be sufficient to deter men from originally unless they possess qualities of an extraordinary kind. To allow a man to say what he thinks is to give his personality the only ultimate channel of full expression and his citizenship the only means of moral adequacy. To act otherwise is to favour those who support the *status quo,* and thus either to drive the activities of men into underground and, therefore, dangerous channels, or to suppress experience not less entitled than any other to interpret publicly its meaning.

In general, the Western world, outside of politics, has grown to the acceptance of freedom of speech. A man may now be an atheist or a vorticist without fear of legal penalty. It does not seem, however, to be realised that religious toleration cannot be fully attained so long as a State maintains special relations with a given Church. For, in that case, whatever the law, there is bound to be a special prestige for those who belong to the official connection. For the State to stamp with its approval some special religious doctrine is to offer privilege to that doctrine even if the privilege does not assume institutional form. If the Church of England were separated from the State, Anglican theology could not maintain itself at Oxford and Cambridge against scientific theology. If the Church of England were separated from the State, a single form of religious belief would not hold a privileged position in the educational system of the community. A State Church is bound to receive privileges in some shape or form; and no citizen enjoys genuine freedom of religious conviction until the State is indifferent to every form of religious outlook from Atheism to Zoroastrianism.

The real source of conflict in the recognition of this right lies in the field of politics. The position of the modern State seems to be that opinions which strike at the existing order are illegal and must be suppressed. The grounds for that suppression assume very varied forms. Sometimes the opinion is penalised because it is held in itself to be evil; sometimes the opinion is attacked because it is held to threaten the structure of the State; sometimes it is penalised because it is held to involve disorder. We must distinguish here with sharpness between the expression of these opinions, whether by a citizen, or by a group of citizens, and the doing of overt acts to give effect to their substance. We must, further, consider separately the important issue of the power to control the expression of opinion in time of war or similar crisis. The relation of action to opinion is a separate question from the nature of opinion itself. The needs of an abnormal period have, in our own day, been so strikingly illustrated that their discussion serves to throw special light upon the general problem.

The view I am concerned to urge is that from the standpoint of the State the citizen must be left unfettered to express either individually, or in concert with others, any opinions he happens to hold. He may preach the complete inadequacy of the social order. He may demand its overthrow by armed revolution. He may insist that the political system is the apotheosis of perfection. He may argue that all opinions which differ from his own ought to be subject to the severest suppression. He may himself as an individual urge these views or join with others in their announcement. Whatever the form taken by their expression he is entitled to speak without hindrance of any kind. He is entitled, further, to use all the ordinary means of publication to make his views known. He may publish them as a book or pamphlet or in a newspaper; he may give them in the form of a lecture; he may announce them at a public meeting. To be able to do any or all of these things, with the full protection of the State in so doing, is a right that lies at the basis of freedom.

For consider the alternatives. All criticism of social institutions is a matter of degree. If I prohibit X from preaching violent revolution, I shall ultimately prohibit X from suggesting that the given social order is not of divine origin. If I begin by assuming that Russian communism is politically obnoxious, I shall end by assuming that language-classes to teach English to Russians are a form of communist propaganda.[15] There is never sufficient certitude in social matters to make it desirable for any government to denounce it in the name of the State. American experience of the last few years has made it painfully clear that there will never be present in constituted authority a sufficient nicety of discrimination to make it certain that the opinion attacked is one reasonably certain to give rise to present disorder. Men who are prevented from thinking as their experience teaches them will soon cease to think at all. Men who cease to think cease also to be in any genuine sense citizens. The instrument which makes them able to make effective their experience rusts into obsolescence by disuse.

It is no answer to this view to urge that it is the coronation of disorder. If views which imply violence have a sufficient hold upon the State to disturb its foundations, there is something radically wrong with the habits of that State. Men cling so persistently to their accustomed ways that the departure from them implied in violence is almost always evidence of deep-seated disease. For the common man has no interest in disorder; where he either embraces it, as in revolutionary Russia, or is indifferent to its occurrence, as in Sinn Fein Ireland, it is because the government of the State has lost its hold upon his affections; and no government loses the affection of its subjects save from a moral cause. The degree, in fact, to which a State permits criticism of its authority is the surest index to its hold upon the allegiance of the community. Almost always—there are rare cases in which persecution has proved successful—the result of free expression is such a mitigation of the condition attacked as to justify its use; almost always, also, to prohibit free speech is to drive the agitation underground. What made Voltaire dangerous to France was not his election to the Academy, but his voyage to England. Lenin was infinitely more dangerous to Czarist Russia in Switzerland than he would have been in the Duma. Freedom of speech, in fact, with the freedom of assembly therein implied, is at once the katharsis of discontent and the condition of necessary reform. A government can always learn more from the criticism of its opponents than from the eulogy of its supporters. To stifle that criticism is—at least ultimately—to prepare its own destruction.

Two related questions demand a note of explanation. Freedom of speech means freedom to express one's view of general subjects. It means the absence of all powers of censorship in the government of the State. It does not mean any right to insinuate that Jones murdered his mother-in-law, or that Robinson, if justice were done, would be charged with embezzlement. The statements for which I have the right to demand the absence of control are either general statements or personal statements of which the public import is immediate and direct. The right of free speech does not include the right to free scandalmongering. The only pain I have the right to inflict on individuals is a pain which the public welfare demands. Obviously, if the use of that power is abused by me in the case of some individual, he ought to be able to seek his remedy in the courts. He is as entitled to protect the interest of his personality in privacy[16] as I am to invade it; and the common sense of an average jury ought, in such a case, to decide between us. This limitation, it should be added, does not extend to general questions such as the publication of blasphemies or of obscene literature. These are too much matters of dubiety to make it possible to erect criteria of satisfactory judgment. A dramatic censorship prohibits *Mrs. Warren's Profession* and a literary control excludes Boccacio from the public library. It is wiser to trust the free exercise of the mind than to seek, *ex cathedra,* to put it in swaddling clothes.

I have argued that the right to freedom of speech carries with it the right to freedom of association and of public meeting. Each of these aspects deserves a separate word. In the modern world the individual cannot impress his views save by acting with his fellows. In the vast majority of cases, so to act entails no harm of any kind. What of the cases where, as with the communists, the object of the association is the violent overthrow of established order, or, as with the Salvation Army in its early days, freedom of assembly almost always involved a breach of the peace? Neither of these rights is as secure to-day as it seemed a decade ago. The American Statute-book, for instance, is littered with statutes against a variety of political groups; and there are even more political bodies which are forbidden to meet in public places. I submit that all such restrictions have no warrant in an adequate theory of the State. Legally to prevent men from associating as communists does not prevent them from so associating; it serves only to make the forms of communist activity more difficult to discover. To prohibit a meeting on the ground that the peace may be disturbed is, in fact, to enthrone intimidation in the seat of power; and it is noteworthy that the English law has sanctioned the notion that a peaceful demonstration does not become illegal because other people are incited to disorder thereby.[17]

The situation is, of course, different when an association aims at, and proposes to act towards, the overthrow of the State. The problems raised by this issue belong rather to the art than to the theory of politics. Every government must assume that its continued orderly existence is, within the ambit of such a system of rights as that here outlined, a desirable thing; every government is, within that ambit, entitled as a consequence, to take steps to protect itself. It is, therefore, entitled to destroy any group which seeks definitely and presently to usurp its authority. But no government ought, in its purely executive aspect, to be the sole judge of whether its action is right. It ought always to be compelled to the submission of proof; and it ought always to be compelled to the submission of proof under the fullest judicial safeguards. There is no more reason to suppose that the judgment of an executive will, in this aspect of the issue, be right than there is to suppose rightness in the judgment of any body of thoughtful citizens. The test ought to be the ability of the executive to convince a court of law that there is the imminent danger of unlawful acts inherent in the continued existence of the association. There ought, that is to say, to be the provable danger of conduct and not merely the influence of conduct from opinion. Anyone who studies the treason trials of 1794, or, even more decisively, the trials under the Espionage Act of 1917 in America, will be convinced of the danger of allowing the executive an undue latitude in this regard.[18] At a time of crisis judicial protection is a fairly slender safeguard, but it is at least a protection. We do not want a clumsy minister to assume that a society of Tolstoyan anarchists is likely to attempt a new gunpowder plot. We do not desire to give license to those amazing citizens who see in every movement of unconventional thought a cover for the unscrupulous assassin. The State, clearly, has a right to self-protection, but it should be in obvious danger before it is given leave to act.

These hypotheses, it is argued, are untenable in time of war or such similar crisis. It is obvious that they are untenable in a period of civil war, when armed forces contend internally for the possession of the State. They are untenable for the sufficient reason that no one will observe them. Violence always makes the play of reason impossible; and political philosophy cannot contribute hypotheses to a period of unreason. Revolution, in fact, means the suspension of any existing system of rights. Whatever authority comes to the exercise of power will, until it permits the renewed choice of governors by the citizens, build its acts upon the force it exerts, and not upon the rights it seeks to represent. That has been evident in the history of every revolution in the modern time. It is, indeed, the hypothesis of revolution that confidence in the persuasive power of reason is misplaced.[19] It would, then, be absurd to expect respect for rights under such circumstances. But an unsuccessful revolution raises the problems, than which none are more difficult or delicate, of the treatment of rebels by the government and of the acts of those who destroy the revolution.

Here, surely, different considerations emerge. The hypothesis of any government which successfully defends the State against attack is the desirability of its system of rights. If, then, that system contain such elements of judicial protection as are contained, for example, in the English insistence upon the rule of law, it immediately becomes obvious that the character of governmental acts becomes subject to the control of that principle. Laws that have been broken then demand either punishment or indemnity; and there are occasions on which an indemnity ought to be refused. It is, above all, urgent that the superiority of the civil courts over the naked force of military law be emphasised; in that aspect the *Wolfe Tone* case[20] and the dicta of *ex parte* O'Brien[21] are of the essence of a State built upon the notion of right. For, otherwise, the citizen is powerless against the authority of the executive, unless the unlikely event occurs of the executive being overridden by the legislature; and in the vast majority of cases any such attempt at control will come too late. An executive that is liable to continuous scrutiny by an independent-minded judiciary is far more likely to observe the substance of rights than an executive which can, as under the Defence of the Realm Act in England during the European War, practically suspend the guarantees of the constitution. The experience of Hungary in the years since 1919 is evidence of the danger implicit in the absence of those guarantees.

The problem of freedom of speech in wartime raises quite different considerations. But it is first of all important to urge that the scale of operations makes no difference to the issue. The rights and duties of an

English citizen in a period of struggle with a minor nation like the Boers in South Africa remain the same as his rights and duties in a struggle with a first-class power like Germany. His business, as I have insisted, is to contribute his instructed judgment to the public good. He must, that is to say, support the war if he think it right and oppose it if he think it wrong. That the executive has embarked upon an adventure in which unity of opinion is a condition of strategic success does not alter the moral position that he occupies. No executive has a right to move on its way, whatever the opinion of its citizens. Those opinions must be made known in order to affect its activities. To penalise them at a time when it is above all urgent to perform the task of citizenship is fatal to the moral foundations of the State. If a man think, like James Russell Lowell, that war is but an alias for murder, it is his duty to say so, however inconvenient be the time of his pronouncement. Indeed, there is ground for the view that an inconvenient time is not unlikely to secure a closer attention to the substance of such opinions. And what can be urged on the other side? It is said that the utterance of hostile opinion hinders the successful prosecution of the war. But this, in fact, is to raise not one, but several, issues.

Does "hostile opinion" mean hostility to the inception of war, to the methods of its prosecution, to the end at which it aims? In the last European struggle the opponents of the war were divided into camps of each of those views. Is criticism of military or naval commanders an attack upon the prosecution of the war? If a statesman not in office thinks, for example, that the diplomatic policy of the executive will be attended with fatal results, must be confine himself to private representations, lest public avowal of his opinion hinder the national unity? If a man believes that peace by negotiation is preferable to victory in the field because of the human cost that victory entails, has he no obligation to his fellow-citizens who are paying that cost? It is, surely, evident that to limit opinion in periods of war to opinion which does not hinder its prosecution is first to give the executive a completely free hand, whatever the policy it pursues, and, second, to assume that while the armies are in the field an absolute moral moratorium is operative. That is an impossible position. No one who has watched at all carefully the process of government in time of war can doubt that criticism was never more necessary. And to limit criticism is to stifle criticism. An executive that has a free hand will commit all the natural follies of dictatorship. It will assume the semi-divine character of its acts. It will deprive the people of information upon which it can be judged. It will misrepresent the situation it confronts by that art of propaganda which enables it, as Mr. Cornford has said, to deceive its friends without deceiving its enemies. It will be obtuse to suggestion. It will regard inquiry as menace. It will be careless of truth. An executive in wartime is, in fact, moralised only to the degree to which it is subject to critical examination in every aspect of its policy. And to penalise the critic is, if the struggle be severe, to poison the moral foundations of the State.

Freedom of speech in wartime involves, therefore, the same rights as freedom of speech in peace. It involves them the more fully because a period of national trial is above all the period when it is the duty of citizens to bear their witness. Their activity will doubtless be unpopular; the answer is, of course, that it is easy to be a martyr when authority refuses crucifixion. If the policy of a State in making war does not command the assent of its citizens in general, it has no right to make war. If those hostile to it are a considerable proportion of its citizens, the policy is, at the least, a dubious one. If the number is small, there is no need to attempt suppression in the interest of success. The one way, in other words, to attain the right is by free discussion; and a period of crisis, when the perception of right is difficult, only makes more fundamental the emphasis upon freedom.

The view here taken may perhaps be illustrated by reference to one of the decisive factors in the Peace of Versailles. It is usually agreed that its worst elements were the result of the Secret Treaties by which the Allies, exclusive of America, bound themselves before the latter's entrance into the conflict.[22] Nowhere, moreover, amongst them was the desire for a just peace more widespread than in America; nowhere also was the discussion of peace-aims more rigorously curtailed as a hindrance to the full prosecution of the war. Had discussion of the peace been full and effective in those critical years, the liberal instincts of President Wilson might, when reinforced by the weight of informed opinion, have compelled at least their mitigation. The Secret Treaties were published in the American press after their issue in Petrograd in the second Revolution of 1917; full discussion would have revealed their inadequacies and enabled the President to counteract what of evil there was in their substance. But the destruction of free opinion acted as a smoke-screen to conceal them, and Mr. Wilson did not know of their existence until he reached Paris.[23] It was then too late to undo their consequences. Uncontrolled power, in other words, acts like a miasma to conceal that atmosphere in which truth is made manifest. Governments cannot do their duty because the means are wanting to inform them of their duty.

I have argued that freedom of speech is a right that war does not mitigate. It is important, however, to discuss a special case of this aspect of that right. If Belgium is invaded by a foreign army, the maintenance of free speech may be fatal to the continued existence of the State. Is, therefore, an invasion an exception to the general rule? This, first, must be said, that, ultimately, war and democratic government are incompatible. The emotions to which conflict gives rise do not tolerate the presence of reason; and the more urgent the danger, the greater will be the demand for its suppression. Invasion is the supreme example of this situation. To discuss the origins of the war of 1914 while the German siege-guns hammered at the defences of Liége would have been, in any case, an academic exercise. But Belgium in 1914 was blameless. France in 1870 was hardly less to blame than Bismarck himself. It was morally open to any Frenchman, if he conceived it to be his duty, to denounce the Chauvinism of Napoleon III. He had the right to press for a rapid peace. He had the right, if he so wished, to denounce the premature negotiations of Jules Favre. He had the right to urge, like Gambetta, the duty of France to fight to exhaustion. In each case he was entitled to the full protection of the law in his effort. In each case he was contributing, according to his lights, his instructed judgment to the public good. The more acute the danger to be confronted, the more urgent is it to build the view of government upon the largest available structure of opinion. The greater the heed that opinion is given, the more likely is a government of civic support. For, ultimately, the most sure resource against foreign oppression is the zeal for the State of erect-minded men and women.

I have spoken of the protection of the law. It is integral to the notion of a State built upon right that the citizen should be surrounded by full judicial safeguards. If he is accused, he should be entitled so to be tried that his innocence, if he be guiltless, has the full chance to emerge; he cannot, therefore, be imprisoned without trial.[24] If he disputes with another, he should have reasonable access to his judicial remedy. No State can be free unless its courts are accessible and swift and certain. I shall discuss later certain forms that are essential to these conditions. Here I can only say that there is rarely a better index to the quality of the State-life than the justice it offers to its citizens. It must be a justice without discrimination. It must not be harder upon the poor than upon the rich. It should not denominate as mental disease in a resident of Kensington what it calls petty theft in a resident of Whitechapel. It must organise the fullest means of defence for those charged with the commission of crime. It must not set apart the acts of its officials into a category different from that of other men. It must itself answer in its own courts. The sovereignty of the State must never mean that it is not amenable to law. A tort is none the less a tort because it is committed in the name of the sovereign. The judiciary must be able to deal with every complaint of offence without distinction of persons. The rule of law, in brief, is fundamental; and the rule of law means that no person, and no office, however exalted, are exceptions to the rule of law.

There are two obvious corollaries to this doctrine. The first is the genuine independence of the judiciary. For what they do in the process of making and applying the law, they must be answerable to no one except their own consciences. They must not be removable because the executive dislikes their decisions. They must not be changeable because some judgment has offended the whim of the public. In no other fashion is it possible to secure the impartial administration of law. I shall show later that attempts, as in America, to make judges responsive to popular opinion by short-term appointments is a fatal error. Election, in any case, is not a sovereign specific for all members of a government; and when rights are to be protected, the first thing essential is to multiply the safeguards of those who are to protect the assurance of rights.

The second corollary is that the union of the executive and the judicial function is inadmissible. Every citizen needs the amplest protection against the danger that the administrator will himself interpret the meaning of the law that he applies. The concentration of the power to interpret in the same hands as the power to administer has always, historically, been associated with tyranny. It was the characteristic hall-mark of Oriental despotism. Even with a bureaucracy so generally impartial as that of British India it has not been free from grave objection.[25] Where the subject to be administered is in its nature so complex—as when, for example, an attempt is made to fix a "fair" gas-rate in a municipality—those who adjudge fairness ought never, even if they are not the ordinary courts, to be those who usually administer the service. It may be necessary, given the intricate nature of the modern State, to create special courts for special subjects. Whatever the solution, the separation and supremacy of the judicial power is integral to the maintenance of rights. For, otherwise, those who serve the State are governed by rules different from those under which their fellow-citizens must live. They are made judges in their own cause; and however hard they may strive to do justice they cannot hold squarely the balance between themselves and other men.

It remains to be discussed whether there is such a thing as a right to property. If property must be possessed in order that a man may be his best self, the existence of such a right is clear. But it is also obvious that such a right is immediately susceptible of stringent limitations. Rights, as I have argued, are the correlative of functions. I have the right to property if what I own is, broadly speaking, important for the service I perform. I have the right to own if what I owe can be shown to be related to the common welfare as a condition of its maintenance. I can never justly own directly as a result of the effort of others. I can never justly own if the result of my ownership is a power over the life of others. For if the personality of other men is directly subject to changes of my will, if their rights as citizens, in other words, become the creatures of this single right of mine, obviously they will soon cease to have any personality at all. No man, in such a background, has the right to own property beyond that extent which enables the decent satisfaction of impulse. After that point, it is not his personality that he contributes to the community, but the personality of his property. He will be guided not by his interests, but by its interests. He will act not to be his best self, but to win through his possessions the influence which maximises their safety. Exceptions, of course, there are; and the value of that munificence which Aristotle commanded[26] deserves more scrutiny than it has received. But in a general system of rights the response to the acquisitive impulse is a response that, of necessity, does not require a level of which zest to acquire is the only limit. It is set in the background of the function served by the person of whom it is part.

## (iv) The Realisation of Rights

So armed, the citizen might hope to confront the State with at least the prospect of self-realisation. But it is, of course, one thing to postulate these rights as essential; it is another thing to ensure their realisation. And that raises the central issue of the position of the State in the community. Legally, it is inescapable that there must be in every organisation of men some body which enforces the acceptance of the common rules. Those rules, as the previous discussion has sought to show, are concerned with the erection of a minimum basis of civilisation for the members of the community. They seek to make them conscious of the art of life. But it is one thing to urge that there must be a body enforcing the acceptance of the common rules; it is another thing to urge that this body is the State. For the State is, for the purposes of practical administration, the government; in England, that is, the State in its daily appearance is the King in Parliament. If it is legitimately to exercise its functions, it must be upon the basis that it moves consistently to the realisation of rights. It sets the conditions within which other associations move only because its mission is to enable the citizen, through those associations, to be that best self of which he is capable. It is not exercising unlimited power. It is exercising a power conceived within the terms of a definite function. It is protecting the plane upon which the interests of men, and therefore their rights, are, broadly speaking, identical. It co-ordinates the activities of other groups with a view to that end.

In this aspect there clearly comes into view a State, for instance, is not identical with the community. It is a State, for instance, which can prevent the Roman Catholic Church putting a man to death for heresy; but it cannot force the Roman Catholic Church to surrender the dogma of papal infallibility. It could prevent Jones from practising in the education of his children the belief that ignorance is bliss; but it could not refuse education, say on the ground of expenses, to any class or section of its members. It could not pass legislation which relieved itself of the obligation to provide, either directly or indirectly, work or maintenance for its members. It could not invade the activities of any other association unless it could show in a court of law that such activities were directly hostile to the system of rights it was its own business to maintain. The State fulfils a function in the community just like every other association; its powers are set by the nature of that function. It is not, therefore, the reserve-power in society. Its will (which means in effect the will of the central legislature) is not a will charged with special or pre-eminent authority. To release, therefore, any system of rights such as I have outlined, it is necessary to work out with care the conditions under which the authority of the State is exercised.

These conditions are, generally, three in number. The State must be a decentralised State. The organs which exercise power must not be concentrated at a single point in the body politic. Local questions must imply local control. There may be the duty of central inspection; but the problems of which the decision predominantly concerns Lancashire—whether, for instance, it shall have art-galleries—must be settled in Lancashire and not in Whitehall. It is, moreover, urgent that the local authority shall exert a power which is general in nature and not limited by specified delegation from the central government. If the London Country Council, for instance, desires to spend money on taking the children in its schools to see Shakespeare's plays, its own resolution to do so should be sufficient legal warrant. Obviously, the exercise of local originality must not involve invasion of a sphere that is obviously central; the list of legal poisons must, for example, be unified in Whitehall and not drawn differently in Aberdeen or Aberyswyth. But it is the outstanding virtue of decentralisation that not only does it prevent the application of uniform solutions to different things; it also, by multiplying the centres of the administrative act, ensures a fuller participation in the responsible business of government. Responsibility, in other words, is born of a definite share in the exercise of power. To concentrate power at any point where it can, without danger to the system of rights, be diffused, is to open the door to the abuse of authority. And it must be remembered that it is the nature of authority to abuse its power unless it is consistently surrounded by the mechanisms of control.

It is necessary, in the second place, to surround the central government in particular with bodies it is compelled to consult. That does not mean merely the consultation of the legislative assembly by the executive. It means the organised and prior consultation of all interests which are affected by a decision it is proposed to take. It means, for example, that a government which proposes to alter the pay of teachers must first submit its proposals for scrutiny to the bodies which represent those teachers. It is important, also, to insist that consultation ought not to mean selective consultation. An executive can always secure a biased expression of opinion by the careful choice of biased representatives. Consultation means eliciting opinions from representatives nominated by the bodies concerned. If a government, for instance, wishes to appoint a commission to inquire into the advisability of a protective tariff, the representative of the cotton industry ought to be chosen by the cotton industry and not nominated therefrom because he is a tariff reformer. If a Labour government desires to examine a proposal for a capital levy, it ought not to select a banker already in its favour, but to ask the Institute of Bankers to name its representative. And the corollary of consultation is, at some stage of action, publicity. A government which embarks upon a policy must offer the means of judging that policy. The opinions it has elicited by organised inquiry are fundamental to that end. The evidence it has collected, the facts at its disposal, can never be refused to its subjects if it is to build its opinion in the reasoned judgment of its citizens.

Not less integral to the proper control of its powers is the limitation upon its authority to intervene in the internal life of other associations. That power must be circumscribed by the principle that intervention is built upon the infraction by the association of a right that is essential to citizenship. The best field from which illustrations of illegitimate intervention may be taken is that of the relationship between Church and State. It ought never to be competent for the State to intervene in the settlement of ecclesiastical doctrine. It ought never to be competent for the interpretation of ecclesiastical trusts to be left to the secular courts. That has always involved an attempt by the lawyers to reduce a church to a body of associated beneficiaries[27] and to refuse to its members the power to change their opinions. A church is never a body of men bound by an unalterable contract to the worship of certain doctrines; its purposes have a life embodied in the wills and opinions of its members. If the latter change, the purpose changes also; and the disposal of the property which supports the doctrine is clearly and unmistakably a matter for the constituted authorities of the Church. That, at least, is clear so far as property derived from the dead is concerned; to rule as the English courts have ruled is to refuse to a church the right to move outside the four corners of its original title-deeds. Similarly, too, with industrial bodies. If trade unions choose to devote their funds to maintaining their members in the political legislature, the State has no right to intervene. Associations, in brief, do not act *ultra vires* so long as what they do is demonstrably the act of the association and leaves untouched the rights the State is to protect; and the question of what is an act of the association is a question to be answered, not by the scrutiny of doctrinal purposes, but by examination of the organ that is competent to act in its name.[28]

### (v) Rights and Power

We reach here a problem perhaps as difficult as any in the realm of political science. A government, I have argued, is limited by the purposes that it serves. It has no moral authority to act *ultra vires* those purposes. It has no authority, for instance, to invade the right to freedom of speech, to protect the employer who enforces impossibly long hours upon his workers. But how can its acts, whether of omission or of commission, be adequately scrutinised? Is the remedy, as in the United States, to postulate fundamental rules in a written constitution, and to make them difficult to change by the temporary holders of power? Is it necessary, as in Australia and the United States, to make the judiciary the guardian of constitutional right, and to confer upon it, as in those countries, the power to declare void such acts of the legislature as seem to infringe it? Or is the answer that of Mr. Cole, who would, as it seems, construct a special organ for the exercise of coercive jurisdiction, and find, somehow, a place therein for the representatives of functions other than the State?

The attempt to weigh the respective advantages of what Lord Bryce has called "flexible" and "rigid" constitutions is an impossible one. The balance of merit depends always upon factors in the State-tradition which are inapplicable elsewhere. The advantages of rigid constructions are very great. They enable us to define with some exactness the limits of legislative power. They prevent some sudden gust of public opinion from overturning what it is, on a long view, important to maintain. They enable the nature of institutions to be more easily apprehended by the mass of men. They emphasise in a striking manner the things that are deemed of fundamental import;[29] and even when, as with the First Amendment to the American Constitution, the thing of decisive import suffers serious invasion, the fact that it is postulated as urgent both mitigates the attack it might otherwise suffer, and allows its supporters a valuable basis in tradition for their plea of sanctity.

Yet in actual historic experience the safeguards afforded by a written constitution are not so straightforward as they might appear. Things that appear fundamental to one age appear unnecessary to another; yet the fact of their appearance in the framework of the constitution acts as a serious lever against what may well be desirable change. The constitution, secondly, will need interpretation. If that is left, as in France and Belgium, to the legislature, it is in fact, merely confided to the holders of power. If it is left, as in the United States, to the judiciary, five out of nine judges have actual control of the constitution; and the death of a single judge may well shift the whole balance of interpretation. Certainly the Supreme Court of the United States has been amazingly divided on what is meant by the first and the fourteenth amendments; and the use of the latter to prevent the enactment of a minimum wage suggests that there is a stage at which judicial interpretation means in fact political pronouncement.[30] The American system means, in short, that the ethos of legislation depends on the character of those appointed to the Supreme Court. It does not seem that this safeguard of rights is necessarily less frail than that of a legislative assembly which is checked by the action of an alert public opinion outside.

Not, indeed, that a flexible system is not open to serious criticism. If we take the British Constitution as the chief—today almost the sole—example of flexibility, some obvious considerations emerge. The English constitution is built upon the unlimited sovereignty of Parliament. It knows no such thing as fundamental laws; the statutes which govern the succession to the throne are changed in the same way as statutes which regulate the sale of intoxicating liquors. The system of limitations upon the power of government, inferentially, therefore, of the State, cannot be gleaned at a single view. Sometimes, as in the Habeas Corpus Act, they are embodied in a statute; sometimes, as in *Entick* v. *Carrington,* they are embodied in a judicial decision. The absence, that is to say, of a single centre of reference makes the grasp of the meaning of authority a difficult task in flexible constitution. The maintenance there of an ideal system of rights will depend—supposing that the State in fact embodies such a system—upon the existence in the community of one of two conditions.[31] Political power must rest with a minority that is both upright and educated; citizens must be able, while retaining supreme power, to choose rulers who are anxious to observe the theoretic end of the State. In fact, for the most part, the second only of these conditions is immediately practicable in Great Britain.

But it is at once obvious that such a power as it implies is a matter beyond positive institutions altogether, though positive institutions may be important. The quality of rulers is always a function of the general social character of a people, and, whatever the checks and balances we may invent, it is the pressure of the total forces in a community which will determine that character. The State, in other words, reflects the complete environment it encounters, and not merely a section of that environment. It is easy to invent ways and means of limiting authority; it is even easy—as in the new constitution of the German commonwealth—to postulate magnificent ideals as the purpose at which it aims. But no amount of institution-making will accomplish the achievement of that purpose unless the general mass of the people is educated to appreciate, and therefore to enforce, its meaning; unless, also, there is in the community approximate equality of economic power. If those conditions generally obtain, the system of rights is likely to be realised. Short of them, no rights of a positive nature can find security of an institutional kind. We cannot, for instance, so frame the nature of self-government in industry as to make it a right capable of being used as the test of statutes. Nor can that be achieved with a right like the right to work. The mechanisms of their protection must be sought, not in the State itself, but, as I shall show later, in the pressure brought to bear upon the State by other institutions.

That is not, however, the case with rights of which the essence is a matter of outline rather than of detail. We can safeguard things like the right to the franchise and the right to freedom of speech at least to the point where revolution supervenes to make all rights temporarily cease. Take, for example, the Habeas Corpus Act of 1679. Everyone agrees that its presence upon the statute-book is the chief protection against, for instance, such an access of terror as Pitt displayed in the French Revolution. It is possible to make especially important statutes of that kind capable of suspension by special procedure. They might be a matter for such a majority as the Senate of the United States now demands for treaties. There might be a period of compulsory delay between their passage and their application. If they are passed, a special administrative court might be created to deal with the problems to which they give rise. The penalties for the invasion of such rights might be so framed as to make the habit of Acts of Indemnity rigorously difficult of access by the executive. I do not think it likely that a referendum would be of much assistance on this issue. With the weapons at the disposal of the interests which control a State, the average population is only too likely to be stampeded into panic by executive pronouncements. The real needs are two. There must be an interval in which criticism of authority can make itself heard. There must be a certainty that the mere possession of a majority in the legislative assembly is not the basis of an abuse of power. Beyond these checks, the main safeguards against abuse lie in the temper induced by the standard of popular education and the power of organised groups other than the State effectively to protest against unwarranted invasion of rights.

The view urged by Mr. Cole is not without a real attractiveness. To postulate a unified interest in the State as an attainable ideal is one thing; to postulate modern States as representing that unified interest is not only another, but also without basis in fact. So long as men share with such vast inequality in the gain of living, it is obvious that there is a basic disharmony of interest; and the legal institutions of the modern State, especially its laws of property, might well seem devised to maximise that disharmony. It is natural, therefore, to seek, as Mr. Cole seeks, an organ for the exercise of the coercive power of the community which prevents its legal concentration in political institutions. I agree with Mr. Cole that, in the present phase of social development, the concentration of coercive power is bound to act as a hindrance to the transformation of the State. I agree also that in the State as it now is we have an institution which cannot make good its claim equally to represent the interests of its members. It is, frankly, weighted against the poor in favour of the rich.

But I do not think that a joint "Congress of the supreme bodies representing each of the main functions in Society"[32] will really solve the problem we confront. For the real issue is not the paper-construction of such an organ, but weighting the functions which compose it. Mining is an essential function; so also is medicine. How are we to decide on the number of members each is to have in such a Congress? How are we to weigh the interests of men as members of a given neighbourhood-men, for instance, in search of an efficient system of main drainage—against men as members of the different professions they practise in and out of their neighbourhood life? The adventure, as I argued earlier, is an impossible one. It means that the aspect of man in which his needs as consumer are broadly identical with his fellow's must be selected as the ground upon which co-ordination takes place. That does not mean the pre-eminence of that aspect in the sense that it is entitled to a special allegiance. It does not mean that it is, so to say, invested with the power compulsorily to arbitrate between the various functions of men. It means only that, for the purpose of convenience, the administration of the general rules of the community are probably better managed by a simple than by a complex institution, granted the necessary safeguards.

The thing, in fact, at which Mr. Cole aims—the wide dispersion of authority—can be achieved in simpler fashion than he is prepared to admit. The organ of registration may remain a legislative assembly. Its power may be mitigated, as I have suggested, (1) by decentralisation at once functional and territorial; (2) by building about it organs of prior and compulsory consultation; (3) by making the invasion of such rights as freedom of speech an adventure of the highest difficulty. These, in the background of an adequate educational system and a revised property system, afford as full a guarantee of natural rights as it is likely that positive institutions can affect. It is not necessary, in our anxiety to prevent the present perversion of the territorial principle, to sacrifice the obvious administrative convenience it contains. What is necessary is that territorial unity shall not destroy functional independence and individual freedom. A State is not made responsible merely by the subtraction from it of coercive power. That still leaves the problem open of the principle upon which coercive power shall be exercised. That principle will, in fact, be variously interpreted; and parties will arise to support and maintain the most antithetic views. It is, I think, significant that none of Mr. Cole's discussions of this issue contain a reference to the problem of party; and the reason, I think, will be found to lie in the fact that his edifice is inaccessible to an electoral scheme with the two vital merits of simplicity and intelligibility. A State is made responsible by informing its co-ordinating power with notions of justice. It is made to play its due part in the communal synthesis by making it directly accessible to the interests which compose that synthesis. It then becomes a one which partakes of the nature of a many because the many enter into it and transform it.

All this, of course, is only to assert, as Alexander Hamilton insisted, that the raw materials of an adequate theory must be found in human nature. We ought probably to assume that our best-devised schemes will only produce a small portion of the beneficent results we expect. We ought certainly to insist that in seeking to transform the present system we shall bring into play factors which make possible adjustments we cannot now foresee. But, at least, for the immediate future it seems clear that we must surround the administrative self-determination of functional units with the territorial control of the State. It is, of course, true that territorial propinquity is no longer coincident with community of interest. A Bolton weaver has more in common with a weaver in Oldham than he has with a doctor in Bolton. But it is as a weaver that he has more in common. As a person to whom the drains and schools of Bolton are important he has more in common with the doctor than with his fellow weaver. We must supply the territorial function with its means of response no less than the vocational function. That means, put briefly, rights conceived in territorial, as well as rights conceived in vocational terms; it means that Bolton must be a basis of representation as well as the weaver's union. Nor must we forget that the doctor has an interest in good weaving, as the weaver has an interest in the existence of a competent medical profession. While each naturally desires a dominant administrative control over the interests of his special vocation, it is obvious that there is also a mutual interest which requires an institution to maintain it. That mutual interest is the sphere within which the large outlines of a system of rights must be defined. I have argued here that the territorial State is the unit within which, under adequate safeguards, they are most likely to receive effective definition.

Any system of rights, therefore, has three essential aspects from which it must be regarded. There is the interest of the individual, always, at least ultimately, finally isolated from his fellow men. There is the interest of the various groups in and through which his personality finds channels of expression. There is the interest of the community which is the total result of the whole pressure of social forces. We cannot leave the groups within the community to define their rights by conflict, any more than we can permit individuals so to determine their rights. We must live by common rules. We must build an organ which enforces and interprets those common rules. We must so build it that both group and individual are safeguarded in their freedom and their equality so far as institutions can provide a safeguard. For it is well to realise at once that no system will ever fail to be weighted in some special interest. There will always be either powerful individuals or powerful groups who make their way against others less apt to assertiveness. Our effort must be a search to the compromise which allows to the largest possible number a life that is worthy of our resources.

## REFERENCES

1. Cf. L. Post, *The Deportations Delirium.*
2. (1923) 2 K.B. 13, 361.
3. *Sirey*, 1910, p. 1029.
4. On this general question see Artur, *Separation des Pouvoirs*, and Fairlie, *The Separation of Powers* in the *Michigan Law Review* for 1922.
5. Cf. J. Holmes, in *Jensen* v. *Southern Pacific*, and B. Cardozo, *The Nature of the Judicial Process*, lect. iii.
6. Cf. Carr., *Delegated Legislation*, lect. i.
7. A.L. Bowley, *The Division of the Product of Industry*.
8. As shown clearly by investigations like those of Booth and Rowntree.
9. Cf. *Report of the Committee on Trusts* (Great Britain), 1918.
10. Dorothy Sells, *The British Trade Boards System*.
11. Cf. the evidence collected in Professor Frankfurter's brief in *Stetteler* v. *O'Hara*, published separately by the National Consumers' League in New York.
12. Cf. J.L. and Barbara Hammond, *The Town Labourer and the Skilled Labourer.*
13. *Representative Government*, chap. viii.
14. E. St. J. Hankin, *The Mental Limitations of the Expert*.
15. Post, *op. cit.*, p. 31.
16. Cf. Braindeis, *The Right to Privacy* in 4 *Harvard Law Review*, 193.
17. Cf. *Beatty* v. *Gillbanks*, 9 Q.B.D. 308, and the classic comment of Professor Dicey, *Law of the Constitution* (8th edition), pp. 270 ff.
18. Cf. Brown, *The French Revolution in English History*, especially chap. vi; and J.H. Rose, *William Pitt*. On the Espionage Act see Chafee and Post, *op. cit.* During 1917-19 there were 1900 cases relative to freedom of speech. The climax of war-mentality was the Sacco-Vanzetti Tragedy, on which Prof. Frankfurter's book is the final word.
19. Cf. L. Trotsky, *The Defence of Terrorism*, passim. And see my *Communism* (1927), chaps. iv and v.
20. Robertson, *Select Constitutional Documents*, p. 354.
21. *Ut supra*.
22. Cf. Gooch, *History of Modern Europe*, p. 661, and the references cited throughout the chapter.
23. See Chafee, *op. cit.*, p. 37.
24. A *Habeas Corpus* Act is, therefore, of the essence of rights.
25. See Joseph Chailley, *Administrative Problems of British India*, pp. 442 f. For another view of R.N. Gilchrist, *The Separation of Powers* (1925).

26. *Politics*, ii.5; and cf. *N. Ethics*, IV, i.1.
27. See *Free Church of Scotland Case Report* (ed. Orr), p. 223; and on the whole question, my paper on the strict interpretation of ecclesiastical trusts in *Canadian Law Times*, vol. 36, pp. 190 ff.
28. Churches could, I think, easily safeguard the problem of minority rights to which this theory gives rise by a provision in their constitution that secession on doctrine shall involve the right to a proportionate share in the church property.
29. See the admirable remarks of Bryce, *Studies in History and Jurisprudence*, pp. 200 f.
30. Cf. Cardozo, *ut supra*; Brooks Adams, in *Centralisation and the Law*.
31. Bryce, *op. cit.*, p. 160.
32. *Social Theory*, p. 135.

# 4. Liberty and Equality

## (i) The Nature of Liberty

By liberty I mean the eager maintenance of that atmosphere in which men have the opportunity to be their best selves. Liberty, therefore, is a product of rights. A State built upon the conditions essential to the full development of our faculties will confer freedom upon its citizens. It will release their individuality. It will enable them to contribute their peculiar and intimate experience to the common stock. It will offer security that the decisions of the government are built upon the widest knowledge open to its members. It will prevent that frustration of creative impulse which destroys the special character of men. Without rights there cannot be liberty, because, without rights, men are the subjects of law unrelated to the needs of personality.

Liberty means absence of restraint; it is essentially a negative thing. But regulation, obviously enough, is the consequence of gregariousness; for we cannot live together without common rules. What is important is that the rules made should embody an experience I can follow and, in general, accept. I shall not feel that my liberty is endangered when I am prohibited from committing murder. My creative impulses do not suffer frustration when I am bidden to drive on a given side of the road. I am reasonably restrained when the law ordains that I must educate my children. Historic experience has evolved for us rules of convenience which promote right living; and to compel obedience to them is a justifiable limitation of freedom. To permit such compulsion is to invade liberty; but it is not necessarily to destroy the end liberty seeks to serve.

That is not, of course, to argue that every such prohibition is justified merely because it is made by an authority legally competent to issue it. Governments may in fact invade liberty even while they claim to be acting in the common interest. The exclusion of Nonconformists from full political privilege was an invasion of liberty. The restriction of the franchise to the owners of property was an invasion of liberty. The Combination Acts of 1799-1800 destroyed the liberty of working men. They could not realise their best selves because they could not unite in the effort to translate their experience into terms of statute. It is, in other words, essential to freedom that the prohibitions issued should be built upon the wills of those whom they affect. I must be able to feel that my will has access to avenues through which it can impress itself upon the holders of power. If I have the sense that the orders issued are beyond my scrutiny or criticism, I shall be, in a vital sense, unfree.

Liberty, therefore, is not merely obedience to a rule. My self is too distinct from other selves to accept a given order as good unless I feel that my will is embodied in its substance. I shall, of course, be compelled to endure irksome restraints. I must fill up income-tax returns; I must light the lamps upon my own motor-car at a set time. But no normal person will regard restrictions of this kind as so unrelated to his will as to constitute coercion of it. Where restraint becomes an invasion of liberty is where the given prohibition acts so as to destroy that harmony of impulses which comes when a man knows that he is doing something it is worth while to do. Restraint is felt as evil when it frustrates the life of spiritual enrichment. What each of us desires in life is room for our personal initiative in the things that add to our moral stature. What is destructive of our freedom is a system of prohibitions which limits the initiative there implied. And it is important that the initiative be a continuous one. The minds of citizens must be active minds. They must be given the habit of thought. They must be given the avenues through which thought can act. They must be accustomed to the exercise of will and conscience if they are to be alert to the duties implied in their function as citizens. Liberty consists in nothing so much as the encouragement of the will based on the instructed conscience of humble men.

In such a background, we cannot accept Mill's famous attempt to define the limits of State interference. All conduct is social conduct in the sense that whatever I do has results upon me as a member of society. There are certain freedoms I must have in order to be more than an inert recipient of orders; there is an atmosphere about those freedoms of quick vigilance without which they cannot be maintained. Liberty thus involves in its nature restraints, because the separate freedoms I use are not freedoms to destroy the freedoms of those with whom I live. My freedoms are avenues of choice through which I may, as I deem fit, construct for myself my own course of conduct. And the freedoms I must possess to enjoy a general liberty are those which, in their sum, will constitute the path through which my best self is capable of attainment. That is not to say it will be attained. It is to say only that I alone can make that best self, and that without those freedoms I have not the means of manufacture at my disposal.

Freedoms are therefore opportunities which history has shown to be essential to the development of personality. And freedoms are inseparable from rights because, otherwise, their realisation is hedged about with an uncertainty which destroys their quality. If, for example, my utterance of opinion is followed by persecution, I shall, in general, cease to express my mind. I shall cease, in fact, to be a citizen; and the state for me ceases to have meaning. For if I cannot embody my experience in its will, it ceases, sooner or later, to assume that I have a will at all. Nothing, therefore, is so likely to maintain a condition of liberty as the knowledge that the invasion of rights will result in protest, and, if need be, resistance. Liberty is nothing if it is not the organised and conscious power to resist in the last resort. The implied threat of contingent anarchy is a safeguard against the abuse of government.

I have set liberty here in the context of opportunity, and, in its turn, opportunity in the context of the State. That is the only atmosphere in which it admits of organisation. We can create channels; we cannot force men to take advantage of those channels. We can, further, create channels only in limited number. A man may feel that all that he cares for in life depends upon success in love; we can remove the barriers of caste or race or religion which, in the past, have barred his access to that love. But we cannot guarantee to him that his plea will be successful. The avenues which organisation can create are always limited by the fact that the most intimate realisation of oneself is personal and built upon isolations which evade social control.

Yet the social control is important. If, in the last resort, the State cannot make me happy, certainly it can, if it so will, compel unhappiness. It can invade any private life in wanton fashion. It can degrade me as a political unit in a fashion which distinguishes me from other citizens. It can protect an economic order which "implicates", in William James' phrase, unfreedom. None of these things is, of course, a genuinely separate category; at most the distinction is one of convenience. For liberty is a definite whole, because the life I lead is a totality in which I strive to realise a whole personality as harmonious. Yet each of these aspects is sufficiently clear to warrant a separate word.

But it must first be urged that in this context State-action is action by government. It means the maintenance of rules which affect my liberty. Those rules will be issued by persons, and, normally, those persons will be the government. Theories which seek to differentiate between State and government almost always ignore the substance of the administrative act. Rights withheld mean rights which the holders of power withhold. To say that in a democratic theory the mass of citizens are the holders of power is to miss the vital fact that the people, in the pressure of daily affairs, cannot exercise that power in detail in States of the modern size. They may have influence and opinion; but these are not the power of government. It is the cumulative force of administrative acts which are the heart of the modern State. The principles behind these acts are, of course, of prime importance. But principles may be invalidated by the method of their application; and it is governments which have the actual administration of them.

Liberty, therefore, is never real unless the government can be called to account; and it should always be called to account when it invades rights. It will always invade them unless its organisation prevents it from being weighted in some special interest. The three aspects of liberty I have noted are always relative to this situation. By private liberty, for example, I mean the opportunity to exercise freedom of choice in those areas of life where the results of my effort mainly affect me in that isolation by which, at least ultimately, I am always surrounded. Religion is a good instance of this aspect. I am not truly free to decide without hindrance upon my creed unless there is not merely no penalty on any form of religious faith, but, also, no advantage of a political kind attached to one form rather than another. When the government of England denied public employment to Dissenters it invaded private liberty. It did not directly punish; but, at least, it offered special benefit to an alternative faith. When France repealed the Edict of Nantes it invaded private liberty; for the honourable profession of religious conviction involved political outlawry.

These are simple instances. In the complex modern State invasions of private liberty may be more subtle. Private liberty may be denied when the poor citizen is unable to secure adequate legal protection in the Courts of Justice. A divorce law, for example, which gives the rich access to its facilities but, broadly, makes them difficult, if not impossible, for the poor, invades their private freedom. So does the demand for excessive bail; so, too, when the poor prisoner, with inadequate counsel, confronts the legal ability at the command of government. Private liberty is thus that aspect of which the substance is mainly personal to a man's self. It is the opportunity to be fully himself in the private relations of life. It is the chance practically to avail himself of the safeguards evolved for the maintenance of those relations.

Political liberty means the power to be active in affairs of State. It means that I can let my mind play freely about the substance of public business. I must be able without hindrance to add my special experience to the general sum of experience. I must find no barriers that are not general barriers in the way of access to positions of authority. I must be able to announce my opinion and to concert with others in the announcement of opinion. For political liberty to be real, two conditions are essential. I must be educated to the point where I can express what I want in a way that is intelligible to others. Anyone who has seen the dumb inarticulateness of the poor will realise the urgency of education in this regard. Nothing is more striking than the way in which our educational systems train the children of rich or well-born men to habits of authority while the children of the poor are trained to habits of deference. Such a division of attitude can never produce political freedom, because a class trained to govern will exert its power because it is conscious of it, while a class trained to deference will not fulfil its wants because it does not know how to formulate its demands. Combination in the period of experience will, of course, as with trade unions, do something to restore the balance; but it will never fully compensate for the defect of early training. For the inculcation of deferential habits will never produce a free people. It is only when men have learned that they themselves make and work institutions that they can learn to adjust them to their needs.

The second condition of political liberty is the provision of an honest and straightforward supply of news. Those who are to decide must have truthful material upon which to decide. Their judgment must not be thwarted by the presentation of a biased case. We have learned, especially of late years, that this is no easy matter. A statesman can sometimes be made what the press chooses to make him. A policy may be represented as entirely good or bad by the skilful omission of relevant facts. Our civilisation has stimulated the creation of agencies which live deliberately on the falsification of news. It would, indeed, not be very wide of the mark to argue that much of what had been achieved by the art of education in the nineteenth century had been frustrated by the art of propaganda in the twentieth. The problem is made more complex than in the past by the area over which our judgment must pass. We have no leisure to survey that area with comprehensive accuracy. We must, very largely, take our facts on trust. But if the facts are deliberately perverted, our judgment will be unrelated to the truth. A people without reliable news is, sooner or later, a people without the basis of freedom. For to exercise one's judgment in a miasma of distortion is, ultimately, to go disastrously astray.

By economic liberty I mean security and the opportunity to find reasonable significance in the earning of one's daily bread. I must, that is, be free from the constant fear of unemployment and insufficiency which, perhaps more than any other inadequacies, sap the whole strength of personality. I must be safeguarded against the wants of tomorrow. I must know that I can build a home, and make that home a means of self-expression. I must be able to make my personality flow through my effort as a producer of services, and find in that effort the capacity of enrichment. For, otherwise, I become a stunted and shrunken being in that aspect of myself which lends colour and texture to all that I am. Either I must, in this sense, be free, or I become one of those half-souls who are found in the slums and prisons as the casualties of civilisation. Nor is this all. I must be more than the recipient of orders which I must obey unthinkingly because my labour is only a commodity bought and sold in the market, like coal and boots and chairs. Without these freedoms, or, at least, an access to them, men are hardly less truly slaves than when they were exposed for purchase and sale.

Economic liberty, therefore, implies democracy in industry. That means two things. It means that industrial government is subject to the system of rights which obtain for men as citizens, and it means that industrial direction must be of a character that makes it the rule of laws made by co-operation and not by compulsion. Obviously, the character of those laws must depend upon the needs of production. Those needs leave less room for spontaneity than is true either of private or of political liberty. A man is entitled to be original about his politics or his religion; he is not entitled to be original when he is working with others, say, in a nitro-glycerine factory. But he is entitled to co-operate in the setting of the standards by which he is judged industrially and in the application of those standards. Otherwise, he lives at the behest of other men. His initiative becomes not the free expression of his own individuality, but a routine made from without and enforced upon him by fear of starvation. A system built upon fear is always fatal to the release of the creative faculties, and it is therefore incompatible with liberty.

### (ii) The Safeguards of Liberty

Freedom, therefore, will not be achieved for the mass of men save under special guarantees. It can never, firstly, exist in the presence of special privilege. Unless I enjoy the same access to power as others, I live in an atmosphere of contingent frustration. It does not matter that I shall probably not desire to take full advantage of that access. Its denial will mean that I accept an allotted station as a permanent condition of my life; and that, in its turn, is fatal to the spontaneity that is of the essence of freedom. Anyone who has seen the political inertia of English rural life will have realised how slow to mature is the plant of initiative. The English agricultural labourer lived for so long in an atmosphere of frustrated impulse that, when he was raised to the status of citizenship, he rarely, in general, knew how to take advantage of his opportunities. The genius of a Joseph Arch might stir him into angry and sudden revolt against intolerable conditions, but he was too habituated to uncritical inertia to persist when opposition came. So, too, the endurance of oppression by Negro slaves was the outcome of their wonted subjection to a régime of privilege. They lost the habit of creativeness. They became, in fact, those "animate tools" which Aristotle described as the characteristic of the natural slave. Men who see others selected to govern by a principle other than their own choice tend, over a period, to believe that these have come to govern by nature. They will lose both the will and the power to act for themselves. They will learn to think that institutions made by their ancestors are the necessary foundations of the State. They will think it their duty to accept where, in truth, it is their duty to inquire. Whenever men accept, their habits, sooner or later, come to be formed at the will of others. They lose the ability to realise their own good. Their personality lies at the disposal of others whose action is not instinct, at least inherently, with a desire for the good of all; for those who desire the good of all begin by the abolition of special privilege.

Nor must we omit here the influence of such privilege upon those who possess it. They are free in the sense that they can build their own system of restraints. But their restraints will be manipulated for their own advantage. They will come to regard those outside their own circle as inferior beings. They will insist that their subordination is part of a natural order. They will even argue, like the slave-owners of the South, that exclusion from privilege is a benefit to those so excluded. They will discover special virtues in themselves, as when Macaulay argued that the middle class is "the natural representative of the human race". They will tend to identify demands for the admission to power of the unemancipated as the very definition of evil. They will part with their power, too often, only at the point of the sword; for voluntary abdication from special privilege has been the exception, and not the rule, in history. They will therefore seek at all costs to maintain their authority; and that will mean, most often, the further depression of the unfree. So Lord Sidmouth passed the Six Acts lest inconvenient criticism be made of an effete political regime. And the reaction from such policy will, as in France and Russia, tend to be proportionately violent to the degree of repression it has encountered. Special privilege is incompatible with freedom because the latter quality belongs to all alike in their character as human beings. We cannot differentiate between men until we have shown those excluded from a share in power that their exclusion is in their own interest. There seems no reason to suppose that the demonstration can be made.

Nor, secondly, can there be liberty where the rights of some depend upon the pleasure of others. Our common rules must bind those who exercise power as well as those who are the subjects of power. No groups of men must be in a position to encroach upon my enjoyment of the rights which attach to me as a citizen. That is not the case to-day. My livelihood may be destroyed by the whim of an employer. The meaning of my wage-standard may be injured by the cornering of the market in some essential commodity. The whole quality of my citizenship may be impaired by the manner in which the wealth of the community is distributed; and while I seem to enjoy political freedom, the absence of economic freedom may, in fact, render illusory my hope of a harmony of impulses. At every point, therefore, where the action of a man or group of men may impinge upon the exercise of rights a control is wanted which will frustrate their power so to impinge. That control, I submit, is, above all, a matter for the State, because it is upon the plane of citizenship that the undifferentiated interests of men come most clearly into view. State control means, in daily fact, control by government. It therefore follows that the action of all men who, by what they do, have the fate of others in their hands, is set in the perspective of limitation by the power of authority.

This, it should be added, does not necessarily mean intervention by the government at every turn and twist of individual life. It means the planning of the principles of social action. It means the absence from social organisation of those uncertainties which result in social loss and are deliberately planned by individuals. We cannot abolish the uncertainties due to such natural phenomena as earthquakes; but we can at least destroy the uncertainty that comes when, say, the Standard Oil Trust drives competitors out of the field by making an agreement for differential rates with the Pennsylvania Railroad.[1] We can at least prevent the dismissal of teachers from their posts because some utterance has proved displeasing to the trustees they serve.[2] Our principles of control are general principles; but because their application will need to be as various as the problems they indicate, they will, as a rule, require decentralised administration.

All this is to assume, thirdly, that the incidence of State action is unbiased. In a full sense, doubtless, we cannot achieve that ideal. In any society the varied personalities of which it is composed, the weight of the different interests involved, the degrees of effort men will make, the amount of knowledge they will possess, are certain to bend its authority in the support of some special interest. The most we can do for the maintenance of freedom is to seek that system which will minimise the bias involved. That is why rights assume so vast an importance; they are the guarantee of a minimum bias. They give us what assurance we may have that the State power will not be perverted to the use of some few. But it is important to insist that it is bound to suffer perversion unless men are unceasingly vigilant about its exercise. Those who consented to the passage in 1917 of the American Espionage Act did not realise that it would become the parent of similar legislation destined to protect the most powerful industrial autocracy in the world from criticism of its foundations. Those who voted in the House of Commons for the Restoration of Order in Ireland, October 1920, can hardly have expected that it would be used to deprive British citizens of the ordinary resource of justice.[3] Obviously, few things are more urgent than the scrutiny of the problem of liberty in the terms that are most likely to prevent the operation of that bias. A citizen-body that is quick to resent its presence, and willing, in the last resort, to compel its repudiation, has the most obvious guarantee that it will be minimised. But even such a body of citizens as that of ancient Athens, to whom, as Pericles said in the great Funeral Speech, "the secret of liberty is courage", will have need of the channels through which courage may flow to its appointed purpose.

## (iii) Liberty and Equality

Those channels converge towards the concept of equality. No idea is more difficult in the whole realm of political science. To minds so ardent for liberty as Tocqueville and Lord Acton liberty and equality were antithetic things. It is a drastic conclusion. But it turns, in the case of both men, upon a misunderstanding of what equality implies. Equality does not mean identity of treatment. There can be no ultimate identity of treatment so long as men are different in want and capacity and need. The purpose of society would be frustrated at the outset if the nature of a mathematician met an identical response with that to the nature of a bricklayer. Equality does not even imply identity of reward for effort so long as the difference in reward does not enable me, by its magnitude, to invade the rights of others.

Equality, broadly, is a coherence of ideas each one of which needs special examination. Undoubtedly, it implies fundamentally a certain levelling process. It means that no man shall be so placed in society that he can overreach his neighbour to the extent which constitutes a denial of the latter's citizenship. It means that my realisation of my best self must involve as its logical result the realisation by others of their best selves. It means such an ordering of social forces as will balance a share in the toil of living with a share in its gain also. It means that my share in that gain must be adequate for the purposes of citizenship. It implies that even if my voice be weighed as less weighty than that of another, it must yet receive consideration in the decisions that are made. The meaning, ultimately, of equality surely lies in the fact that the very differences in the nature of men require mechanisms for the expression of their wills that give to each its due hearing. The power, in fact, of the ideal of equality lies in the historical evidence that so far in the record of the State the wills of men have been unequally answered. Their freedom, where it has been gained, has accordingly been built upon the unfreedom of others. Inequality, in a word, means the rule of limited numbers because it secures freedom only to those whose will is secure of respect. They will dominate the State and use its power for their own purposes. They will make the fulfilment of their private desires the criterion of public good.

Equality, therefore, means first of all the absence of special privilege. I have already discussed the general meaning of that phrase. In the penumbra of equality, it means, in the political sphere, that my will, as a factor in the counting of heads, is equal to the will of any other. It means that I can move forward to any office in the State for which men are prepared to choose me. It means that I am not to find that there are persons in the State whose authority is qualitatively different from my own. Whatever rights inhere in another by virtue of his being a citizen must inhere, and to the same extent, in me also. There is no justification in such a view for the existence of an hereditary second chamber. For, obviously, in the second generation of such an assembly men exercise political authority not in virtue of their own qualities, but by reason of parental accident. So, also, no office that carries with it power can ever be rightly regarded as an incorporeal hereditament, for that is to associate important functions with qualities other than fitness for their performance. The exclusion of any man, or body of men, from access to the avenues of authority is always, that is to say, a denial of their freedom.

Equality means, in the second place, that adequate opportunities are laid open to all. By adequate opportunities we cannot imply equal opportunities in a sense that implies identity of original chance. The native endowments of men are by no means equal. Children who are brought up in an atmosphere where things of the mind are accounted highly are bound to start the race of life with advantages no legislation can secure. Parental character will inevitably affect profoundly the quality of the children whom it touches. So long, therefore, as the family endures—and there seems little reason to anticipate or to desire its disappearance—the varying environments it will create make the notion of equal opportunities a fantastic one.

But that is not to say that the opportunities created may not be adequate. We can at least see first that all men are given such training as seems, in the light of experience, most likely to develop their faculties to the full. We can at least surround those circumstances with the physical media without which the training of the mind can hardly be successful. We can, where we discover talent, at least make it certain that it does not perish for want of encouragement. These conditions do not exist to-day. Children who come hungry to school cannot, on the average, profit by education in like degree to those who are well fed. The student who is trying to do his work in a room which serves for the various tasks of life cannot find that essential isolation without which the habit of thought can rarely be cultivated. The boy or girl who has to assume that at fourteen they are bound to pass into the industrial world rarely acquires that frame of mind which searches with eagerness for the cultivation of intelligence. In the modern world, broadly speaking, opportunity is a matter of parental circumstance. Boys of a certain social status may assume that they will pass from the secondary school to the university. Boys whose parents are, broadly, manual workers will in the vast majority of cases be inevitably destined to manual work also. There is no reason to decry either the value or the dignity of manual work; but there is every reason to examine the social adequacy of a system which does not at every point associate the best training available with those whose qualities most fit them to benefit by that training. We do not want—possibly we cannot afford—to prolong the period of education unduly. But no State has established conditions of reasonable adequacy until the period of education is sufficiently long, first, to ensure that the citizen knows how to use his mind, and second, that those of special capacity are given that further training which prevents the wastage of their talent.

No one can deny that this wastage to-day is enormous. Any student of the results of adult education in Europe will have realised how great is the reservoir of talent we leave unused until it is too late. The sacrifices to-day involved when the average manual worker seeks the adequate education of his children are sacrifices we have no right to demand. Often enough, the training of one child is built upon the conviction of others to a life of unremitting toil. The circumstances which those who live by intellectual work know to be essential to its performance are, as a matter of definition almost, denied to the vast majority of the population. And since citizenship is largely a matter of the use of trained intelligence, it is obvious, accordingly, that its substance is denied to all save a fraction of the community. Our business, therefore, is to assure such an education to all as will make every vocation, however humble, one that does not debar those who follow it from the life of intelligence. That certainly means an extension of the period within which the earning of one's living is impossible. It means also that even after the earning period has commenced there are full opportunities for the devotion of leisure to intellectual ends. It means, thirdly, that those who devote themselves to the business of teaching represent the best minds at the service of the community. In the modern State the teacher has a responsibility far greater than that which devolves upon any other citizens; and unless he teaches from a full mind and a full heart he cannot release the forces which education has in leash.

Nothing in all this denies the probability that mental qualities are inherited and that, other things being equal, the children of able parents will be abler than the children of average parents. But it does deny the equation, characteristic of the modern State, between ability and material position. The average trade-union leader cannot afford to send his sons to the university; but the ability of the average trade-union leader is probably not inferior to that of the average banker or the average bishop. Where, that is to say, the inequalities of our system are not due to natural causes, there is a clear case for their remedy. Nor can we hope to discover the existence of capacity unless our system provides for its discovery. It may do so to-day in the case of the rich; assuredly it does not do so in the case of the poor. And it is urgent to remember that, important as nature may be, it requires an adequate nurture if it is to function satisfactorily. The present inequalities are not referable to principle. We have therefore to define the outlines of such a system as build the inequalities we admit upon the needs of society. At present they most largely arise from the impact of the property system upon the structure of the State. But what is reflected by the property system is less ability to serve the community than ability to gain economic power without reference to the quality of wants supplied.

The provision of adequate opportunity is, therefore, one of the basic conditions of equality, and it is mainly founded upon the training we offer to citizens. For the power that ultimately counts in society is the power to utilise knowledge; and disparities of education result, above all, in disparities in the ability to use that power. I am not pleading for equality of function. I am pleading only for the obvious truth that without education a man is not so circumstanced that he knows how to make the best of himself and that therefore, for him, the purpose of society is, *ab initio,* frustrated. Once men are in that situation where they can know themselves; the use they make of their opportunities becomes subject to principles of which equality is only one.

But if we agree, as I have argued earlier, that a democratic State regards its members as equally entitled to happiness, it follows that such differences as exist must not be differences inexplicable in terms of reason. Distinctions of wealth or status must be distinctions to which all men can attain and they must be required by the common welfare. If a State permits the existence of an hereditary aristocracy it must be because it is capable of proof that an hereditary aristocracy multiplies the chances of each man's realising his best self. If we are to have an economic system in which the luxury of a few is paralleled by the misery of the many, it must be because the common welfare requires that luxury. In each case the proposition is open to historical disproof. An hereditary aristocracy is bound, sooner or later, to use its political power to general disadvantage, unless, like the peerage of France, it has ceased to be anything but a faded memory. A State divided into a small number of rich and a large number of poor will always develop a government manipulated by the rich to protect the amenities represented by their property. It therefore follows that the inequalities of any social system are justified only as it can be demonstrated that the level of service they procure are obviously higher because of their existence. It is obvious that a general must have larger powers than a private because, thereby, the purpose of an army is more likely to be fulfilled. It is obvious that a statesman in office must be so remunerated that he is not oppressed by narrow material cares; and that might well involve placing him in a higher financial rank than a bootmaker or a shop assistant. In each case the measure of difference is conceived in social terms. It is set in a principle which is demonstrably rational. It is fitting the circumstances of function to the environment of which it has need.

Such a view admits, at least as a matter of theory, of fairly simple statement in institutional terms. The urgent claims of all must be met before we can meet the particular claims of some. The differences in the social or economic position of men can only be admitted after a minimum basis of civilisation is attained by the community as a whole. That minimum basis must admit of my realising the implications of personality. Above that level, the advantages of the situation I occupy must be advantages necessary to the performance of a social function. The advantages I enjoy must be the result of my own effort, because they are the return to me for my own services, and I am clearly not entitled to enjoy them as the result of someone else's services. One man is not entitled to a house of twenty rooms until all people are adequately housed; and one man, even in that environment, is not entitled to a house of twenty rooms because his father was a great advocate or a large industrialist. The things that are due to me are the rights I must enjoy in order to be a citizen, and the differential advantages which society adjudges inherent in the particular occupation I follow. We may, in other words, have Belgravias, if their existence is a necessary condition of social welfare; but we are not entitled to have Belgravias until we have secured the impossibility of Poplar's existence.

If all this is true, equality is most largely a problem in proportions. There is an aspect in which the things without which life is meaningless must be accessible to all without distinction in degree or kind. All men must eat and drink and obtain shelter. But those needs are, in their turn, proportionate to what they do. My wants are my claims to find a harmony of impulses. I do not want the same harmony if I am a miner as I shall want if I am a surgeon. But the system which obtains must not satisfy the claims of the surgeon at the expense of the miner's claims. My urgent needs are not less urgent than the needs of any other person, and they are entitled to equal satisfaction. Once urgency is satisfied superfluity becomes a problem of so fixing the return to service that each man can perform his function with the maximum return to society as a whole.

In this aspect, the problem of proportions is largely an economic problem. It is a question of the methods we use to determine the claim of each citizen upon the social dividend, and of the environment which surrounds the application of those methods. There have been famous answers to this problem. We have been told that response should be made in terms of need, or in terms of contribution; it has been insisted that identity of response is alone adequate. Of these solutions that which would reward me by what I do for society is certainly the least satisfactory. For it is impossible in any genuine way to measure service. We cannot say what Newton or Lister, Shakespeare or Robert Owen were "worth" to their fellow-citizens. We cannot measure the contribution of a banker against the contribution of a bricklayer. Often enough, as in the case of Galileo, for example, we may not be able to see how vast in truth the contribution is. Nor, it may be argued, is the communistic solution adequate. For, in the first place, there is no total identity of needs between men; nor is their effort so equal as to merit an identical return. The communistic principle is adequate up to the point where human urgencies are in question; it is not adequate after that point. And it is adequate only so far as its application wins the result of a deliberate effort on the part of those whose needs are satisfied to do work of civic quality. And since to do work of civic quality involves differentiation of function, it is, I think, clear that when the primary needs of all men are met, the differences they encounter must be differences their function requires; requirement involving always the context of social benefit.

But this, it will be argued, is to assume sufficiency. It implies that there is in fact enough to go round, whereas we know that the productivity of men does not suffice for their wants. What we ought rather to do is to allow the free play of capacity to win response to its need and let those prosper who show the power to triumph in the race. The answer involved in this attitude is far less simple than it seems. If the State exists for social good, "capacity", can only mean capacity to add to social good. It is not in the least certain that the exercise of talent in a society like our own does in fact result in social benefit. Capacity, in short, must run in the leading-strings of principle. It must be excited to the end our institutions have in view. And since that end is the achievement of happiness for each individual, it seems obvious that we must, if the margin be insufficient, suffer equally by its insufficiencies. We can never, therefore, as a matter of principle, justify the existence of differences until the point is reached when the primary claims of men win a full response. I have no right to cake if my neighbour, because of that right, is compelled to go without bread. Any social organisation from which this basis is absent by denying equality denies all that gives meaning to the personality of men.

Equality, therefore, involves up to the margin of sufficiency identity of response to primary needs. And that is what is meant by justice. We are rendering to each man his own by giving him what enables him to be a man. We are, of course, therein protecting the weak and limiting the power of the strong. We so act because the common welfare includes the welfare of the weak as well as of the strong. Grant, as we may well grant, that this involves a payment by society to men and women who limp after its vanguard, the quality of the State depends on its regarding their lives as worth preserving. To act otherwise is to regard them not as persons, but as instruments. It is to deny that their personality constitutes a claim. It is deliberately to weight institutions against a section of the community.

If they are to harmonise their impulses in the effort after happiness, such bias is inadmissible. For it is utilising their service not for their own well-being, but for the well-being of others. That is essentially the definition of slavery.

It is no answer to this view to urge that it bases social organisation upon a principle hitherto inoperative in history. The decay of previous systems has been most largely based on the fact that it was inoperative. Men have seen institutions pass, or have co-operated to destroy institutions, precisely because they did not see in them the forces which sought response to what made them men. Nor are we seeking to compel all citizens to win from life an identical response. We seek identity only up to the level where the facts insist upon identity. We argue that some will not starve quietly if others have abundance. We urge that the conference of knowledge upon some while others are excluded from its benefits is, in fact, their exclusion from the purpose of the State. And no other principle, as a working system, will effect the results the State has in view. For immediately we admit privilege within the area of equal need, it will use every weapon at its disposal to multiply its access to special benefits. The history of privileges is not a history of voluntary abdication in terms of social welfare; it is rather the history of a careful limitation of the idea of social welfare to those who enjoy the opportunity it offers. It is only, as a consequence, by making identity the basis of our institutions, and differences an answer to the necessities of social functions that we can make our society call into play the individuality of men.

I shall inquire later into the principles upon which those differences may be organised. Here it is immediately important to insist on certain conditions upon which alone that basis of identity may be maintained. A first essential is approximate equality of wealth. I do not mean by that the absence of varying rates of payment for effort. I mean only that the rates of payment shall not so differ that merely, in virtue of those differences men can exert an unequal pressure upon the fabric of institutions.

That unequal pressure obviously exists to-day. There are men in every community whose power is built not upon what they are or do, but upon the possessions they embody. The influence they exercise is not a tribute to themselves but an offering to their wealth. They act by owning. They command the service of others to the performance of functions built upon a private will not necessarily relevant to the social welfare. They can direct the flow of production into channels notable only for their wastefulness. They can dominate the supply of news, and so influence to their own ends the working of political institutions. They can adjust the economic power of the community to purposes fatal to the welfare of those who have nothing but their labour to sell. The desire, for instance, of the great iron masters of France to dominate the heavy industries of

Europe may well send the next generation to die on the battlefield. Where there are great inequalities of fortune, there is always inequality of treatment. It is only when no man merely by virtue of his possessions can influence the course of affairs that the equal interest of men in the results of the political process can secure validation. The surest way to that end is to prevent those disparities of wealth which permit the owners of fortune to manipulate unfairly the mechanisms of power.

Broadly, I am urging that great inequalities of wealth make impossible the attainment of freedom. It means the dictation of the physical and mental circumstances which surround the less fortunate. It means the control of the engines of government to their detriment. The influence of the great corporations upon the legislative system of the United States is only a supreme example of that control. Hardly less deleterious is the way in which it controls the intellectual environment it encounters. It is able to weight the educational system in its interest. It is able, by the rewards it offers, to affect the propertyless brain-worker to its service. Since the judiciary will be largely selected from its paid advocates, legal decisions will largely reflect the lessons of its experience. Even the Churches will preach a gospel which is permeated by their dependence upon the support of the wealthy.

Political equality, therefore, is never real unless it is accompanied by virtual economic equality; political power, otherwise, is bound to be the handmaid of economic power. The recognition of this dependence is in the main due to the explanation of historic evolution, and it is, indeed, almost as old as the birth of scientific politics. Aristotle pointed out the equation between democracy and the rule of the poor, between oligarchy and the rule of the rich. The struggle to remedy economic disparity is the key to Roman history; it is at the root of English agrarian discontent. It underlies the sermons of John Ball, the *Utopia* of More, the *Oceana* of Harrington. The early history of socialism is most largely the record of a perception that the concentration of property other than labour-power in a few hands is fatal to the purpose of the State. It was that perception which Marx, in the *Communist Manifesto*, made the foundation of the most formidable political philosophy in the modern world. For though the materialistic interpretation of history is an over-emphasis of one link in the chain of causation, it is the link most intimately related to the experience of ordinary men. It is overwhelmingly right in its insistence that either the State must dominate property, or property will dominate the State.

For, as Madison wrote,[4] "the only durable source of faction is property". But it is obvious that to base the differences between men on a contest for economic wealth is to destroy the possibility of a well-ordered commonwealth. It is to excite all the qualities in men—envy, arrogance, hatred, vanity—which prevent the emergence of social unity. It is to emphasise a competition based on their separation, instead of a competition based upon their mutual interest. As soon as we postulate approximate equality of wealth, our methods of social organisation enable us to respond to men's needs in terms of the substance of those needs. We are the more bound to this effort immediately we admit the logic of universal suffrage. For to confide to the mass of men the control of ultimate political power is broadly to admit that the agencies of the State must be utilised to respond to their needs. They involve, if they are to be satisfied, such a distribution of influence over authority as will balance fairly the incidence of its results among the members of society. It means, that is, that I must adjust my scale of wants to social welfare as that is organised in terms of a valuation which equally weights the primary needs of citizens; and that valuation remains ineffective if my power is a function not of my personality, but of my property.

But virtual equality in economic power means more than approximate equality of wealth. It means that the authority which exerts that power must be subject to the rules of democratic governance. It means the abrogation of unfettered and irresponsible will in the industrial world. It involves building decisions on principles which can be explained, and the relation of those principles to the service any given industry is seeking to render. The authority of a medical officer who orders the isolation of an infected house is intelligible; he is relating his powers to the preservation of public health. But the authority of an employer is not intelligible except in terms of self-interested motives. His demands cannot be scrutinised. They are not referable to his capacity for his post. They are not relevant to the well being of his servants. If a worker refuses to adulterate the product made by an employer, he may suffer dismissal. He may be penalised if he refuses to falsify his accounts, even when the sufferer by that falsification is the public revenue the burden of which he himself partially bears. There is, that is to say, all the difference in the world between an authority which grows naturally out of functions which are set consistently in a public context, and an authority which, equally consistently, is the outcome of private and irresponsible will.

The existence of this latter type is fatal to the civic implications of equality. It poisons industrial relations. It makes the position of master and servant one of waiting upon the threshold of war. Above all, it is intolerable wherever the function involved is one where continuity of service is essential to the life of the community. That industries like coal and electric power, transport and banking, the supply of meat and the provision of houses, should be left to the hazards of private enterprise will appear as unthinkable to a future generation as it is unthinkable to our own that the army of the State should be left to private hands. They must be subject to rules as rigorous as those which govern medicine, simply because they are not less vital to the national life. That does not mean direct operation by government as the inevitable alternative. It means the planning of constitutions for essential industries; and the possible types of constitutions are as various in industry as elsewhere.

I shall discuss in a later chapter the forms such constitutions may usefully take. Here it is enough to emphasise the urgency to freedom of making the relationship between men in industry one in which no will affected by decisions is regarded as insignificant. That does not mean that all wills are to be weighed equally; all men, obviously, are not equally entitled to give orders. But it does imply that those who exercise authority can, like the minister in office, or the trade union official, be called to account for the orders they issue. My freedom is not hampered if I have the sense that I have access to the source of authority. The members of a trade union feel "free" because they are governed by men made by, and responsible to, themselves. That cannot be the case where authority, as in modern industry, is unconstitutional in its nature. The inequalities of status, the power which results from status, are unrelated to the interests of personality. The worker is involved in a hierarchy in which he has no spiritual recognition. The university teacher, the doctor, the lawyer, are all of them involved in hierarchies; but these breed equality because they are established by co-operation. Their members feel that they contribute to the definition of their working lives. We cannot secure professional standards in industry until room is found there also for principles which destroy the present irresponsible autocracy.

## (iv) The International Aspect

So far, I have discussed conceptions of liberty and equality as though they raised problems soluble within the confines of a single State. But in fact the issues go far beyond that territorial limitation. World co-operation, as I argued earlier, has advanced to the point where we must legislate for civilisation as a whole. We have, therefore, in matters of common world concern, to apply methods which affect the Bantu in Africa and the Melanesian in the Pacific as well as the Englishman and the Frenchman. What do liberty and equality mean in the presence of such complexities? The Dutchman in Java finds his freedom in the application of all his powers to an intense labour for wealth built upon a supply of native workers. The Javanese means by freedom such spasmodic effort as will give him the food he wants, and, otherwise, leave him to lie out in the enjoyment of the sun. How are these different wants to be reconciled? How are we to assure, for instance, equality of treatment between black and white in tropical Africa, when the fact from which we start is that of unequal power? How are we to ensure in a conference of European States that the interests of Switzerland will be considered equally with the interests of England, or Russia, or France?

Until the Peace of Versailles, the common method was to assume the equality of States in international law, and to leave each State free to discover, by what means it would, its own salvation; and force resided in the background as the sanction most likely to secure the ultimate solution. But it is obvious that, for example, Nicaragua and the United States, Venezuela and England, cannot really, in vital matters, bargain on equal terms. Even the most genial fictions of law cannot make a small State equal to a great one.

The possibility of equal consideration and, consequently, of freedom, depends upon two things. It depends first upon the outlawry of war. Concepts like freedom are devoid of meaning so long as a State is free to force its solution upon its neighbour. But the outlawry of war depends, in its turn, upon the building of international institutions which are capable of mobilising the authority of the world against any belligerent. That will be the outcome only of a proof that international institutions can be built which take the problems which give rise to war on to a plane of discussion where they can be analysed in terms of reason. Such institutions will not, I think, be discovered by counting each State as equal in voting power to every other State. It will be impossible to make a league of States effective by the maintenance of that fiction. The solution rather lies in choosing the subjects of international control and finding a method of proportional representation for their governance. There will emerge, for instance, the view that only Englishmen can choose the Prime Minister of England, but that the size of the British Navy is a matter for international determination. France may settle the foreign languages to be taught in her schools, but the character of her foreign loans will be settled by international consent. Each State will be entitled to bargain, to criticise, to object; but when the decision is given against her, she will be compelled to give way. Equality, then, will mean (1) that the method of discussion gives full weight to the facts each State puts forward, (2) that the use of force is ruled out from consideration. Freedom will mean that without the ambit of international control each State is entitled to decide its own life. Just as, that is, no individual can find freedom outside the common rules of his society, so, also, no State can find freedom save by accepting limitation of its sovereignty by the will formed by the common decision of a society of States.

That this habit of rational settlement will be slow in growth needs no emphasis. At the moment I am concerned only to argue that the solution lies in conceiving of the world as a federal State, the members of which do not possess equal voting power. The problem, I suggest, is one of starting a tradition of inquiry and judgment, and finding the appropriate institutions for the range of questions such a federal State will have to administer. When once a great State accepts a verdict given against her we shall at least have begun the exploration of such a tradition. When once a great subject—the protection of the native races, for example—is administered with competence by an international authority we shall have begun the building of a belief in its possibilities. Freedom will come to mean only self-determination in the things peculiar to a given State; outside that sphere it will mean freedom to state a case and not the right to begin war. Equality will mean that the solutions adopted—say in access to raw materials—seek the statistical measurement of need in one range of problems with assurance of response to it; in another it will mean the protection afforded by the presence in an international organisation of other States whose representatives assist in the making of decisions.

The more these issues are brought before international authorities, the more they will be found susceptible of such treatment. The responsibility of Serbia for the assassinations of Serajevo was a subject obviously capable of intellectual inquiry. The action of Austria settled nothing about the facts; she used her power and her prestige to make judgment impossible. Had Serbia, upon investigation, been found guilty, punishment could have been assessed in a way which would have made equality real, in that both States, though unequal in power, would have been equally bound by a body external to them both. If she was innocent, a world-war, which involved the destruction of Austria-Hungary, was a heavy price to pay for a mistaken notion of prestige.

Those, in truth, who talk of non-justiciable disputes do sorry service to civilisation. They speak in terms of a historic condition which no longer fits the facts of the world. To suggest that a nation is humiliated by being proved in error is as wise as to suggest that trial by battle is likely to result in justice. A power, indeed, which urges its prestige as a means of evading international jurisdiction is fairly certain to be wrong. The prestige of England was not diminished when she submitted the *Alabama* incident to arbitration; what lowered her prestige was the administrative carelessness in permitting the incident to occur. States, like men, never protest their honour loudly unless they have a bad case to argue. And if it be said that this is to over-rationalise a problem in which the exercise of reason is inadmissible, the answer is that our choice is between the deliberate adoption of reason and an anarchy which, by the weapons at its disposal, is like to make civilisation itself a legend buried beneath the ruins of its discoveries.

The situation is somewhat different in the case of subject-peoples. No institutions can give genuine equality to a discussion between a European race and, say, the Bushmen of Australia. The problem here is rather the discovery of principles which, when applied, will enable the backward races to draw from life such means of happiness as they desire; adding thereto the benefits that scientific discovery will enable us to confer upon them. We must, it seems clear, prohibit slavery, and human sacrifice and tribal warfare. We must reserve for them the lands of which they have need. We must prohibit all forced labour save where it is devoted to such public matters as the making of roads. We must utilise the tribal organisation for all the purposes to which it seems obviously suited. We must prevent such traffic—that, for instance, in drink—as we know to be destructive of native morale. We must allow no traders to make contracts with the native save under supervision of officials, and that the more particularly when natural resources are in question. Above all, it is essential that those who enter the public service among these subject-peoples should be fully trained in that knowledge which can only be real when the results of anthropological science are behind it. It is no use sending out a man to Africa who has not already learned the true method of approach to its problems. He will not learn it from the European society there. He will only learn it adequately from the native himself if he has been given beforehand that point of view which is the clue to its sympathetic interpretation. Most native customs, weird as they are to the European mind, have their roots deep in the tribal consciousness. To adjust them forcibly to a point of view the native finds inexplicable is to destroy for him all that gives his life its meaning. The result is a psychological *malaise* which ruins his happiness.

Nor can we allow any State the full control of territory mandated to it. What it does there, the method and the results of its administration, it must answer for to an international organisation. That involves, I think, something more than the issue of a report by the mandatory power. It means some such institution as the presence of an international minister at the capital of the territory who will watch the interests of the natives in the same way, for example, as the French Ambassador watches the interests of Frenchmen in London. He will be entitled to inspect and to report. His word will carry weight against the pronouncement of the mandatory power. He will be able to suspend projected action, to warn, and to encourage. He ought, it is clear, only in rare cases to be of the same nationality as the power in actual control. Only when, for example, South Africa knows that there is independent authority to report upon its activities will the suppression of an *émeute* like that of the Bondelwarts rebellion become definitively impossible.

This is, of course, frankly to abandon the meaning of freedom and equality in the sense those terms possess in the context of Western civilisation. On any realistic analysis, it is necessary to abandon them. The formulation by the native of his wants deserves all the response we can give; but it must be admitted that the clash of backward and advanced civilisations means that the wants formulated must be met by special considerations. There is, I think, more likelihood that the Zulu or the Hottentot will achieve what he will regard as a full life under such conditions of protection as those outlined than if we proceed upon the basis that he is being made ready for Western institutions. What Graham Wallas has called "the optimistic ethnology of Exeter Hall" is the most fatal attitude in which to approach these questions. It destroys all that has meaning for the native by denying, at the outset, all that gives colour and substance to the life he knows. It seeks to prepare him for another life in which, in general, it is unlikely that he will find meaning. His freedom, therefore, must be relative to his peculiar situation. It must mean all that he can be given without the destruction of the basic Western ideal. It means, above all, his protection against what has too often been the result of those ideals in operation.

[*Note:* On the material of this section see L.S. Woolf, *Imperialism and Civilisation* (1928), and E.D. Dickinson, *The Equality of States* (1924)].

### (v) Liberty and Government

This view of liberty and equality lays cardinal importance upon the powers of government and the mechanisms by which they may be made to respond to the wills of those affected. I do not argue that the action of legislation can make men free and equal; but unless some such conditions exist as those here urged, it is certain enough that the effect of legislation will be to keep the majority unfree and unequal. To make the personality of the ordinary man creative, it is necessary to build the conditions within which creativeness is possible. That can only happen when ordinary men are made to feel significant, and this, in the absence of liberty and equality, we cannot hope to achieve. Where there is in a community the absence of those factors which make the interests of men so differently considered, there is likely to be the means at hand for the development of personality. The enforcement of equality by the State has the great merit of promoting freedom by preventing the private person from the exercise of force for his own ends. By force I do not necessarily mean physical violence, but the use of a differential advantage to hinder another from the opportunity to be the best he can.

But it is also important to remember that whatever adds to the power of government is always attended by contingent danger. The individual in the modern State tends to feel impotent before the vast administrative machine by which he is confronted. It seems to have absorbed all initiative towards a single centre and to have deprived him of the power to make, or to share in making, responsible decisions. That is a real difficulty. In relieving the individual from the power of his fellow, we may well seem to subject him to a collective power under which he seems hardly more free than before. That was the danger which made Rousseau insistent that liberty is the product of the small State only, and to find in a modern Athens the area within which alone democratic initiative is possible.

We cannot adopt that view because the nature of modern economic organisation makes it impossible to return to the city-State. But in States of the modern size the mere achievement of equality would be harmful without the maximum decentralisation. That is the solution to the paradox by which Rousseau was haunted. It solves the dread of constraint by making men in wider numbers the authors of the power to which they are subjected, and, through that authority, the utilisation of power to liberate the creative energy which is in them. Ultimately, at least, any laws save those which men make for themselves are devoid of meaning. But to make laws for themselves at all adequately, they must have the instruction to judge what laws they ought to make and the character to operate those laws. Someone, doubtless, they will have to trust; the artist will have no desire to scrutinise each act of the policeman. But they must be so intimately a part of the system as to know that they can trust with safety or, if there is abuse of confidence, to be able to apply pressure to its correction. In that sense, liberty is the organisation of resistance to abuse; and the chief safeguard against the emergence of abuse is such a wide distribution of power as makes certain and effective the onset of refusal to obey.

But the utmost that the action of government can achieve will be worthless save in so far its action is paralleled by effort on the part of individual men. Ultimately, each one of us has sufficient of the Athanasius in him to make it certain that the true liberty we build for ourselves. The State is built so certainly upon the character of men that they can only mould it to their desire by consistent devotion to its activities. If men are indifferent or careless, if they are satisfied to withdraw from the arena, not the most ingenious mechanisms can ultimately prevent abuse of power. That was the meaning of Thoreau's great sentence that "under a government which imprisons any unjustly, the true place for a just man is also prison".[5] Men must learn that the actions of the State are their own. They must learn that they will realise justice only to the degree that they bend their efforts to the making of justice. Every man is essential to the State if he has a mind and will. Every man can make that State responsive to the things he needs only by making his knowledge of life accessible as a basis for its actions. He can be free, ultimately, only by willing to be free. No State will be governed by that reason which alone guarantees him significance save as he makes his mind a part of its possessions.

But if the individual is thus, in concert with his fellows, the author of his own freedom, he cannot exert himself to build it save as he is prepared for that constructiveness. He must know what it means to find himself before he seeks the adventure. That is no easy task in a world encumbered by its traditions. There is never likely to be an enlightened State until there is respect for individuality; but, also, there will not be respect for individuality until there is an enlightened State. It is only the emphasis upon equality which will break this vicious circle. When the source of power is found outside of property, authority is balanced upon a principle which bases prestige on service. At that stage, the effort of statesmanship is the elevation of the common man. A society which seeks to protect acquisition is replaced by a society which seeks to protect the spiritual heritage of the race. We cannot assure ourselves of an entrance to that heritage, but at least we can discover the pathway to the goal.

## REFERENCES

1. Cf. H.D. Lloyd, *Wealth against Commonwealth*, pp. 87 ff.
2. Cf. Lightner Witmer, *The Nearing Case*, and, in general, Upton Sinclair, *The Goose Step*.
3. Though, of course, *Rex*. v. *O'Brien* fortunately prevented the fulfilment of the Home Secretary's desire.
4. *The Federalist*, No. X.
5. Thoreau, *On the Duty of Civil Disobedience*.

# 5. Property

## (i) The Present System

The root instinct of man is self-preservation. Because he must guard himself from danger he has developed an acquisitive faculty which now forms the basis of all Western institutions. The world over, States are divisible into those who, out of that impulse to acquire, possess property which is a safeguard against the wants of the morrow, and those who, lacking that property, are uncertain whether the morrow will give them the means of life.

For from the possession of property there comes that which, above all, man seeks as the means to harmony in the shape of security. The man of property has a stake in the country. He is protected from the fear of starvation. He need not accept the work he does not desire. He can take the leisure in which most men must now find the opportunity of significance. He can, if he so will, surround himself with that environment which makes of life an artistic thing. He can avoid the grim routine, and become an explorer in that intellectual hinterland where the creative faculties most readily discover their channels of self-expression. He can protect his children against the dread of want. He can develop in them the tastes which give them also joy in the life creative. He has direct and immediate access—should he desire it—to the social heritage of Western civilisation.

I do not mean to imply that a man with property will necessarily possess these things, or that the propertyless man is necessarily deprived of them. Those who have security often luxuriate in a life devoid of meaning; and those who are poor can sometimes know the rarest things that life can offer. But the latter are exceptional men; poverty for most—and most are condemned to poverty—means a life passed amid mean things with but a fleeting moment, like the first hour of love, when the creative impulse receives a full response. Those who have security may, in fact, live a life as solid and as pointless as the ugly mahogany with which they are surrounded. But at least their existence is freed from the spectre of fear.

If they sought, in any general way, to understand the civilisation about them, they would be impressed by certain obvious facts. They would discover that the number of those in any community who own property enough to be significant is always small. They would find that such ownership is not necessarily related to the performance of duties or the possession of virtues. The owner might be the fortunate descendant of a mistress of Charles II, to whom was given a royalty on all coal exported from the Tyne; or he might be an outrageous moneylender who lived by extortion upon the unfortunate. He would find that the ownership of property involves the control of capital, and that in a régime of free enterprise the control of capital involves the power to direct the lives of those who depend upon the application of capital to production. He would discover that the development of industry in the scientific period has made the power of capital greater than in any previous age, in part because of the greater unit of production, in part because of the more integrated character of social life. He would discover, in short, that a régime of private property makes the State very largely an institution dominated by the owners of private property, and that it protects the will and purpose of those owners. In the absence of other considerations, a political system in which rights are built upon property is one in which the propertyless man will have no rights.

There are, of course, mitigating circumstances which have prevented the owners from realising their rights to the full. The power of combination has enabled the worker to establish certain minimum standards of wages and hours of labour which, however inadequate, do represent a real gain. Humanitarian sentiment has wrung from the owners of property such safeguards as Factory Acts, the prohibition of dangerous materials, and, in a limited way, adulteration. Education has enabled a few in each generation either to escape from the category of poverty or to utilise their knowledge to press for further concessions. But, fundamentally, the régime of private property, in the background of industrialism, perpetuates the division into rich and poor, and separates the poor from the conditions which make possible their effective citizenship.

The results of the system may be summarised briefly. Production is carried on wastefully and without adequate plan. The commodities and services necessary to the life of the community are never so distributed as to relate to need or to produce a result which maximises their social utility. We build picture palaces when we need houses. We spend on battleships what is wanted for schools. The rich can spend the weekly wage of a workman on a single dinner, while the workman cannot send his children adequately fed to school. A rich débutante will spend on an evening frock more than the annual income of the workers who have made it. We have, in fact, both the wrong commodities produced, and those produced distributed without regard to social urgency. We have a large class maintained in parasitic idleness, whose tastes demand the application of capital and labour to the satisfaction of wants unrelated to human need. Nor is that class set apart from the rest of the community. Because it has the power to make demand effective it stimulates the slavish imitation of those who seek to join its ranks. To be rich becomes the measure of merit; and the reward of wealth is the ability to set the standards of those who seek to acquire wealth. But those standards are set, not by the satisfaction of moral purpose, but by the satisfaction of the desire to be rich. Men may begin to acquire property to safeguard their lives from want, but they continue to acquire it because of the distinction which comes from its possession. It satisfies their vanity and their lust for power; it enables them to attune the will of society to their own.

The result is what might be logically expected from such an atmosphere. They produce goods and services, not for use, but to acquire property from their production. They produce not to satisfy useful demands, but demands which can be made to pay. They will ruin natural resources. They will adulterate commodities. They will float dishonest enterprises. They will corrupt legislatures. They will pervert the sources of knowledge. They will artificially combine to increase the cost of their commodities to the public. They will exploit, sometimes with hideous cruelty, the backward races of mankind. They infect with their poison those who work for the wages they offer. They induce sabotage in its varied forms. They compel strikes which result in serious damage to the community. And it is the grim irony of the system that the vaster part of those engaged in its promotion have little or no hope of enduring gain from the process they support. They may destroy the quality of political life. They may possess themselves, as in America, of the educational instruments of the community. They may even pervert religious institutions to the protection of their ideas. They do not, nevertheless, secure a well-ordered State. It remains historically obvious that a community divided into rich and poor is, when the latter are numerous, built upon foundations of sand.

For the basis of the State is envy, and envy is the nurse of faction. A State so divided is compelled to use its instruments to protect the property of the rich from invasion by the poor. It comes to think of order as the final virtue. It neglects its larger aims. It perverts the equal aid it owes to all in the effort to afford the special advantage required by some. That advantage—in the law, for example—may take the form of the fellow-servant doctrine, as in England, or, as in the United States, of the use of the injunction in labour disputes. It may limit the right to a share in political power to those only possessed of a certain property qualification. It may model its constitution so as to limit the power to criticise the existing regime or to prevent the passage of statutes which limit the power of property. It may keep the non-possessing class deliberately ignorant, as William Windham urged, in 1810, that they be kept ignorant. It may, as in Czarist Russia, so fiercely stifle protest that the mass of men is, over a long period, stricken into dumb inertia. It may even confer political power on the masses, and then, by the control of opinion, frustrate the full use of that power to its own needs. It may, as with Napoleon, seek by military adventure to divert attention from domestic concerns. Yet the State remains divided into rich and poor; and men, after a period, refuse to suffer quietly. Then revolution supervenes to alter the balance in the State.

The system, indeed, is prolific in self-justification. Sometimes the defence is psychological in character. Men in general, it is said, need an incentive to labour. The power to acquire property is such an incentive. It makes them work, and, in their working, the good of the community is involved. But there are two primary difficulties here. Labour only involves the good of the community if what is produced is related to that good and secures good in being distributed. Those who traffic in harmful drugs may work and acquire large fortunes, but what they produce is not for the good of the community. If, moreover, I am pre-eminently successful in my business, the fortune I acquire may actually inhibit my descendants from working at all; and the power to acquire property may defeat more incentives than it creates. The mere fact that there is a property-instinct does not go to prove that the present method of response to its demands is anything more than one of the ways in which it may be answered. The present method is a problem for analysis, not a solution of the problem.

Sometimes the justification has been ethical. Property, it has been argued, is the return made to the individual for effort. The builder of a railway, the inventor of a safety-razor, the discoverer of a patent medicine, have all worked hard, and their fortune is the result. But, obviously, certain additional factors must be considered. The fortunes of many who labour unceasingly never become other than insignificant. Property then becomes the reward for ability; the argument that it is the reward for abstinence has long been abandoned as too shameless for any save the ignorant. But, obviously again, it is the reward only for that particular kind of ability which consists in the capacity to make profit; and that altogether evades the problem of the value of such ability to society, and the type of effort in which it is desirable that profit should be made.

Or, it is urged, property is the nurse of virtues essential to society—love of one's family, generosity, inventiveness, energy. But if this is true it argues that the majority of mankind is unable to satisfy the impulses essential to social well-being. That is untrue, for these virtues have been present in persons who have never amassed property at all. No one can be generous in the way that Mr. Rockefeller has been generous unless he has the property of Mr. Rockefeller; but society has to weigh against the ability so to be generous the cost of arriving at the point where the generosity is possible. Professor Huxley never amassed a fortune, but his energy was outstanding even in a vigorous age. The inventiveness of men like Newton and Clerk-Maxwell and Laplace was not the outcome of an attempt to satisfy their property-instinct. Love of one's family cannot be the basis of the yearning for property in the mind of any who know the lives of the poor.

Sometimes, as with Lord Hugh Cecil, any attempt at an ethical basis is abandoned altogether, and property becomes simply the result of supplying effective demand.[1] That is a view without utility for social theory. For we must obviously consider whether the demand ought to have been effective, and the results which occur when it is supplied. There is a demand for slaves in Abyssinia; but most men will, I think, agree that response to the demand ought never to be allowed. There is a demand for obscene literature; but few would respect those who trafficked in it. There is a demand for prostitutes; but the law has a definite answer to those who live by satisfying it. Lord Hugh Cecil's theory merely identifies good with the existing order by the simple process of admitting that in no other way can it be proved morally adequate.

A historical argument is also put forward. The progressive societies, it is said, are those built upon the régime of private property; the backward societies are, in general, those founded upon a collectivist basis of some kind. There is, I think, an important truth in this view. Societies built on private property have gone farther towards the control of their environment than societies of a collectivist type; and they have been able to achieve a greater margin of freedom for individual personality than collectivist forms of social organisation. This does not mean, at least necessarily, that individualist societies attain a greater degree of happiness than is possible under alternative forms; we know too little of the mentality of backward peoples to generalise so far. But it does mean that Western civilisation is far less subject to the tyranny of Nature than is true, say, in Melanesia, or India before the British conquest.

But the historical argument is fallacious if it regards the régime of private property as a simple and unchanging thing. The history of private property is, above all, the record of the most varied limitations upon the use of the powers it implies. Property in slaves was valid in Greece and Rome; it is no longer valid to-day. In England there is great freedom of testamentary disposition; in France inheritance is regulated with much stringency. Until the Married Woman's Property Act, the unity of person between husband and wife gave the former complete control of his wife possessions; to-day that control is dependent upon her pleasure. The power of eminent domain may offer a not ungenerous compensation to the owner of private property, but its essence is that the State may annex Naboth's Vineyard on reasonable terms. The Public Health Acts do not allow me to build as I like on my own land; I must satisfy a local authority and conform to regulations centrally controlled. The régime of private property, indeed, means that a man may do as he wills with his own only to the point that the civil law permits him to will; and though the ambit of that will is, in all conscience, vast enough, the history of the rights of property is most largely the record of its circumscription.

It would not, indeed, be untrue to say that the historical argument means no more than that each man, adequately placed, is the best judge of his own interest, and that the society is most likely to prosper in which he finds room for the expression of his interest. But this is to shift the debate to the problem of adequacy, and that, in its turn, raises the whole issue of the rights which should inhere in property. At no period have those rights been generally absolute. Political and religious philosophy is most largely the attempt to evolve maxims of control which will at least minimise the dangers which arise from the distinction between mine and thine. It was the sense of those dangers which led Plato to reject the notion of private property. A similar perception underlies the insistence in the New Testament and the Fathers of the early Church upon the idea of Stewardship. That idea, indeed, was never fully applied; and its reinterpretation in the course of mediaeval history left it but little more than an emphasis upon responsibility which was never given the substance of active control. For the Church compromised with the world. It accepted charity as the substitute for right. It assuaged symptoms instead of attacking causes. The explanation, doubtless, is obvious enough. Granted its delicate beginnings, a Church which sought to attack the economic system of the time would have perished ignominiously; and by the time it had itself become a source of strength, it had discovered enough persons eager to purchase salvation at the expense of their possessions, to make it rooted in the implications of private property. The central test is the persecution of the Spiritual Franciscans. By that act the Church made it obvious that, beyond charity, it had no message to the disinherited.

The avenue to the modern attitude lay through Puritanism. The decay of corporate authority in the Roman Church, the emphasis upon the internal life a man leads, made the problem of his possessions relatively insignificant. Puritanism taught men to rely upon themselves. It implied, especially in the perspective of religious persecution, a distrust of all regulation made by the State. It provided a facile transition to an attitude which could argue that the ownership of wealth was a sign of grace, and poverty an index to God's disfavour. Puritanism, doubtless, had a keen sense of the dangers of property. Its rigorous attack on wasteful expenditure, its urgency, as with Richard Baxter, that wealth be not used to oppress the poor, are evidence that it was not uncritically individualist. But individualist it could not help being by its essential nature, and it tended to conceive of a State as a body of men moved by self-interest to whom, in the absence of barriers, success came as the reward of effort. Their views met the new philosophy of politics of which Hobbes was the most striking exponent. From him down to Adam Smith, however various the institutional expression it received, self-interest became the key to social organisation. The object of the State became the attainment of liberty in the sense of a clear path for the exertion of individual will. The commonwealth, said Locke, exists to promote civil interest, and "civil interest I call life, liberty, inviolability of Body, and the possession of such outward things as Money, Lands, Houses, Furniture, and the like".[2] There is no sense here of the individual sharing in the benefits of a moral order made by him in co-operation with his fellows. The common good is identified with the individual good, and whatever promotes the latter promotes the former also. But individual good depends upon each man for its achievement; the State has no function save to secure to the victors their spoils of conquest. This view was reinforced by the hedonistic psychology which lay at the root of utilitarianism. The Industrial Revolution, in brief, arrived at a period when, predominantly, a simple teleological optimism made the rights of property—and they were broadly unlimited rights—the cornerstone of social security.[3]

Protests against this doctrine there had, of course, been. At the height of Puritan power Winstanley and the agrarian communists had come to urge their belief in the iniquity of private property. Mably and Morelly had, under the influence of Rousseau's early views, insisted on the moral necessity of a communistic scheme. But the gradations of society were too firmly fixed for their argument to be taken seriously. It needed the combined power of the revolution in industry and the revolution in France to make the thesis of individualism untenable. The one gave birth to economic socialism, the other to a view of rights conceived in terms of personality. Their conjuncture meant the erosion of any view of rights which made property the foundation of the State. That is the meaning of views like those of Saint Simon and Fourier in France, of Hall and Thompson, of Bray and Owen in England. Property became conceived as a product less of individual exertion than of the total forces in society. The collapse of feudalism and the accession of the middle classes to power deprived the governing classes of the sanctity they had seemed to possess. For the French Revolution, perhaps only half-consciously, added to the desire for liberty the demand for equality; and however equality be interpreted, it involves a revision of the individualist theory of property. The preservation of the existing order, as that was beatified in the work of the classical economists, became impossible when to preserve it meant to crown the existing inequalities. The stage began to be cleared for novel conceptions.

That, in truth, is the real meaning of the *annus mirabilis* of 1848. Marx and Engels, Proudhon and Louis Blanc, were, in their various ways, demanding that organisation replace the anarchy of their time. Organisation involved readjustment, and readjustment meant a recognition of rights. The social order of Western Europe began slowly to adjust itself to new claims. The State which had begun the nineteenth century in the terms of *laissez-faire* began, as the twentieth century came into view, to search for a basis upon which it could compromise with socialism. And by socialism was meant the devotion of the productivity of the State to the fulfilment of the natural rights of men. So the taxation of the modern State was built upon the assumption that assessment must be graduated by ability to pay. Its franchise was well-nigh universal. It offered free education—if of a low standard—to the people. It began to insure against the hazards of sickness and unemployment. It made things like the provision of houses and pensions in old age a matter of corporate concern. It is difficult to interpret these changes except upon the view that the concept of property was undergoing a change. Men could still be rich, but the State was admitting its obligation to mitigate the inequalities of social opportunity.

That effort was proceeding when the war of 1914 threw all social systems into confusion. What has everywhere emerged from its results is an immense increase in the operations of the State. To sustain the injured fabric of society was an enterprise far vaster than in 1914, and far more costly; it involved, as in the protection of the householder against the landlord, great inroads upon what had previously been regarded as the normal rights of property. But the perspective of those operations was above all set by the changed scale of social conceptions. Men who had been asked to die for the State demanded also that they be able to live in it. Men who were told that they were important in war insisted that they were significant in peace. Private enterprise was challenged on the ground that it involved a preponderating share in the results of industry to those who did not labour for their production. Private ownership was asked to explain what contribution is made relative to the return it secured. Property as a basis of rights, it was argued, was obviously unsatisfactory. For all property depends upon the sustenance of society, and its rights are therefore socially created. But rights socially created are relative to social needs. These are the needs of individual persons, and, in the modern State, the majority do not satisfy their needs. The wider, moreover, the rights of property, the less equal is the incidence of legislative benefit, and the less close is the relation between property and service. Property as a right to control things to the exclusion of other persons raised in acute form the problems (1) of what things ought to be left to individual control especially in such matters, like electric power, as are vital to the life of the community; and (2) what amount of things a man can be permitted to control without, by the power such control involves, injuring the chance of equal access to the needs of citizenship. Beyond all, there was the demand for a philosophic theory of property which made the defence of private ownership morally possible. The need was the more urgent because the rapid growth of revolutionary communism had challenged at its root the whole structure of existing civilisation. Russia in the twentieth century was, it was immediately seen, likely to be as significant as France in the nineteenth. As the latter had implied the equalisation of political privilege, so the first foreshadowed the equalisation of economic privilege. The central issue of the generation was to discover a concept of property which satisfied the moral sense of men.

### (ii) The Moral Basis of Property

Such a concept of property is conceivable if we seek to view man as a subject of rights. He has then the right to control things in the degree that such control enables him to be his best self. He can claim, that is, such a share of the national dividend as permits him at least to satisfy those primary material wants, hunger, thirst, the demand for shelter, which, when unsatisfied, prevent the realisation of personality. The claim to such a share, the right to such property as that share implies, is, I believe, most usefully regarded as an individual and exclusive claim. It is not merely the right, as in a Platonic State, to a seat at a communal board. If we have learned anything from the evolution of institutions, it is the lesson that an enforced communism of habits is always dangerous. To share in a common life ought not to mean that the common life is built to a uniform measure. It does not mean the eating of identical meals, the wearing of identical clothes, the living in houses distinguishable from each other only by their position in the street. The life we lead must leave room to us for choice or else it ceases to be life at all. We must find ourselves; and we can find ourselves only by decision between varied possibilities. Our claim to a minimum property must be, therefore, a claim to choose, at that minimum, the things we desire to satisfy the claim.

That minimum claim is universal. It is the guarantee to the individual that the pressure of social forces will not leave him helpless and stranded. It is the assurance that he can find a place within its ambit, and that his personality is significant at least in the degree which gives it the chance of substance. But the right is relative to a duty. If I receive it must be in order that I return. Society cannot maintain me for the privilege of my existence. I must pay my way by what I do. I must perform such functions as will produce the amount required for my maintenance. No man, that is to say, has a moral right to property except as a return for functions performed. He has no right to live unless he pays for his living. He has no right to live because another has earned what suffices for his maintenance. That alone is morally his which he gains by his personal effort.

There is therefore moral legitimacy in the modern distinction between owning and earning. Those whose property is the result of other men's effort are parasitic upon society. They enjoy what they have not assisted to produce. They are given the means of avoiding a contribution to the total productivity of society. They have legal rights; but because those legal rights are not born of their personal effort, they lack the moral penumbra which entitle them to respect. It is possible to admire the architect of a great fortune; it is not possible to admire those who live by his achievement. Society literally cannot afford to pay tribute to the degree that inherited wealth exacts it. Even if the owners of such wealth are imbued, like Fox or Pitt or Shaftesbury, with a high sense of social obligation, the virtues of a few do not compensate for the social inertia of the many. Hereditary wealth involves two things: (1) There is a class freed from the legal obligation to labour. (2) So freed, it is able to utilise its leisure in a way that taxes the productive effort of the remaining members of society. Almost always, as Veblen has shown, it will, in the mass, misuse that leisure. That it may produce a Henry Cavendish does not destroy the fact that society pays extravagantly for his production. It will, in general, be idle and wasteful. It will devote itself to aimless pleasure. It will make politics a pastime and religion an aesthetic sensation. It may patronise art, but its patronage will destroy the soul of the artist. It may cultivate letters, but the literature it applauds will be deaf to the real needs of its time. A society which maintains a class which lives by owning can never adequately respect the claims of its humbler members. For the former will dominate its institutions. They will have the privileges which come from the possession of the spending-power. They will set the standards of taste. They will provide the employment for that legal class which, in any State, are almost necessarily dependent upon the rich. They will have immediate access to the sources of political power. They form the habits and ideals of the class which attains wealth by its own effort. Their economic position involves a definite social predominance. They are able, by their prestige, to set the perspective of the State.

Anyone can verify this account by the study of contemporary social structure. Our Parliament, for instance, is still predominantly aristocratic in texture because a political career involves difficulties for almost all who do not live by owning. Education is still largely determined by the position of one's parents; to go to Eton and Christ Church is a kind of family habit. Many of the best regiments in the army are practically a private reserve for the sons of ancient families. All of them show courage in the face of danger; but it is not all of them who develop a grasp of military science. Even the diplomatic service is a career access to which lies open only with difficulty to those not born within a fairly narrow circle. They give to charity the perfume of their presence. Their bazaars and their bridge-parties, beatified by the occasional presence of some member of the Royal House, serve to remind them that they have a duty to the poor. They maintain their interest in intelligence by a winter in Luxor; they keep alive the national character by their devotion to the fox and the partridge. They live in London only six months of the year. When they leave for the "shires", or the warmth of the Riviera, London is empty, save for the six million odd Londoners who work to keep them alive. And a vast journalistic organisation is maintained to gratify the populace with pictures of this incredible procession.

No one, I think, could seriously maintain that such a class is of measurable utility to the community, any more than the French *noblesse* of the eighteenth century could be defended because some few of their members were devoted to high ends. They live lives which are indefensible in ethical terms. And their social cost is the greater because their power to spend makes society devote no small part of its effort to satisfying their aimless pleasures. Nor does their cost stop there. About them is the charm of tradition; and those who have by their own effort won a sufficient income are driven by the force of imitation to seek a life similar in substance and aim. The aristocracy recruits itself by alliance with the city. The grocer of one generation is the peer of the next. The summit of the pyramid is a plutocracy in the mass without function and, in the mass again, with little or no sense of social obligations. There have been, of course, families whose zeal for the well-being of their tenants has been as honourable as it is rare. But the character of society is built upon the rules and not upon the exceptions. If all men are to have equal access to the social heritage, one class cannot, in the nature of things, be specially placed to secure a double share. That is what occurs when a class is permitted to live by owning. It means not only the denial for them of the need to contribute to society, but also the insistence that society must contribute to their needs. Their position is an accident of parenthood; and parenthood, however distinguished, is not entitled to levy a permanent tax on social effort. We do not recognise an obligation permanently to maintain the descendants of Milton; it is difficult to realise why, on any arguable principle, we should be obliged permanently to maintain the descendants of Nell Gwynn. The result of our system of property is, in this regard, unrelated to any principle of justice. It cannot, therefore, be part of any theory .of property which seeks to win the moral assent of men.

That is not, of course, to argue that a man is not entitled to provide for his immediate descendants. Obviously enough, no small part of his effort derives from a desire to win security for his children. It seems, therefore, to follow that his children should receive such training and such support as will enable them to enter the battle of life equipped to endure it. But that does not mean that they should receive such support as enables them to avoid altogether the fact of battle. They, like the average man, must earn their living by the sweat of their brow. They must be given security. He must be able to feel that his death before they are mature does not reduce them to circumstances so narrow that their life is mean and intolerable. That is, of course, the position of most men who die before their children are adult. Its cruelty does not entitle us to enlarge the numbers of those to whom it applies. Inheritance is always justified where it means the provision of an income for widowhood, on the one hand, and the education of children on the other. But the retention of property beyond that period cannot be justified in moral terms.

Nor, I imagine, would most object to property in those intimate, personal things of which the value is, in the main, a value of sentiment. A man's books and pictures, the things which by their possession bear the impress of his personality, are living memorials too precious to dissipate; it is only where they are utilised to form a fund that they become subject to State-scrutiny.

In this aspect, the justification of property begins to emerge. It is entitled to exist where it results from personal effort. It is rational when it is the outcome of function. The property of a doctor, a sailor, an inventor, a judge, all represent a definite return for definite service. Such property is legitimately the embodiment of rights because it is accompanied by the performance of duties. It comes from the fact that its possessor has fulfilled a station in society. He has endeavoured to pay his way. He has sought to return to society the cost of his maintenance before the years of maturity. He has not been parasitic upon the body politic. He has sought to be a citizen in the sense of pooling his effort in the enrichment of the social whole. He represents a definite addition to the productivity of those who live by what is produced. He is not a mere tax upon the effort of others.

But to argue that property is justified where it is the result of function is, of course, too wide a statement. It involves the analysis of property from two angles. Property, so conceived, implies, first of all, a theory of reward and, secondly, a theory of industrial organisation. It implies, that is to say, a method whereby we can fix the limits of the rights of property and a means of determining the kind of structure the utilisation of property may involve. Is a man, for instance, to obtain by effort that octopus-grasp over the economic life of Germany which the late Herr Stinnes secured? Does effort mean effort in terms of exertion, of effort in terms of capacity? Can we discover means whereby to differentiate the price we pay, say, for the effort of a bricklayer and the effort of a great surgeon? Can we distinguish between rights of property as such, the possessions, that is to say, which, when translated into money-terms, are available for investment, and the rights of property as the expression of personality? If I earn one thousand pounds a year and live, as I think adequately on seven hundred and fifty pounds, what rights attach to me as the owner of two hundred and fifty pounds which I annually invest? Am I entitled to a definite and fixed return for the use of a commodity of which I hire out the disposal? Ought my return to vary with the amount of risk I take in making the type of investment on which I decide? Am I entitled to embark with my capital upon adventures which, like that of the Mannesmann brothers in Morocco, may involve the destinies of a whole people which cannot hope for profit from my gain? Obviously, the rights of property do not admit of being fixed in simple terms. The statement of the problem is by its nature complex; and a reply which aimed at simplicity would be false to the issue it raised.

## (iii) Property and Effort

Practically speaking, theories of reward have divided themselves into four main classes. There is the general communist case for equality of income. The argument on its behalf is a much stronger argument than is generally admitted. A man's "pull" upon society is very largely what his purchasing power is; if, therefore, we are to equalise his access to society with that of his neighbour, it is advisable to make his income equal to his neighbour's. Once, moreover, we introduce distinctions, they are bound to rest upon an arbitrary foundation. The difference between the income of a judge and the income of a bricklayer is nothing more than a very rough-and-ready estimate of the price at which the services of each can be obtained. In fact, good judges are obtained at a much lower salary in the United States than in Great Britain; and the salary of a successful bricklayer, is, proportionately, much higher than in this country. Nor must we neglect the eugenic argument which Mr. Bernard Shaw has adduced with so much point.[4] Practically, as he insists, the main distinctions between classes are economic distinctions; and even if the Duke can on occasion marry the factory girl, his sister does not dream of marrying the factory "hand". If a royal princess marries a commoner, it is always a well-endowed commoner. Choice in marriage is, outside one's class, very largely determined by considerations of wealth. The English peerage has even established a kind of commodity-price on the American market. Equality of income would, as Mr. Shaw points out, have the excellent result of making the whole community inter-marriageable. There can be little doubt of the benefit that would accrue therefrom to the quality of the race.

But equality of reward meets certain difficulties to which, in our situation, there is at present no adequate reply. When effort is demanded of all if we are to live at all amply, there seems no justice in an equal reward for unequal effort. Nor does it seem just to reward equally where needs are unequal. The miserly bachelor, the church-devoted spinster, ought not, surely, to receive the same remuneration as the parents who have five or six children to maintain. Nor can we neglect the psychological argument that, granted the mental habits of Western civilisation, equality of income could only be secured by a revolution; and, probably, one of the chief features of the revolution would be the award of a special rate of pay to the soldiery in order to persuade them to be loyal to the government. It seems clear, moreover, in the experience of Russia that at least in the early stages of a new social order habits of differentiation must be given concessions. There seems no reason to suppose that there is an atom of logic about the present disparities. But, however greatly we bridge them, we cannot as yet travel the whole road to equality. The communist doctrine insists upon the vital truth that a society which mainly judges men in the terms of their economic possessions is morally unsound; but, for a long time ahead, the means to a better judgment must be found along different paths.

Not less inadequate is the antithesis of the communist scheme which urges that remuneration should be fixed by the haggling of the market. Supply and demand, we are told, are an index to the social appreciation of the labour a man has to sell. Their operation offers to his service a "natural" reward. No other index has the same merit of obvious charity. All this would be admirable if it were (1) in the least true and (2) if it were morally adequate. But, in the first place, before supply and demand can genuinely operate all countervailing factors must be withdrawn. The remuneration for medical officers of health is not fixed at what will attract competent medical men, but at the figure at which the British Medical Association will allow competent medical men to be attracted. The incomes paid in trustified industries are often specially fixed not by the demand and supply of services there, but by the special position a monopoly entails. A judge's salary is largely a customary figure; many men would accept the position, as many do, at great financial loss for the honour it implies. Supply and demand would only be a true index to income if there was an equal opportunity to apply for the post involved. In fact, most posts involve a kind of customary standard of living, and the incomes of the given profession are probably a Gaussian curve about the mean of that standard.

Nor, I have said, is the higgling of the market a morally adequate test of worth. It leaves one-third of the average industrial community on the verge of starvation. For them it means poor health, undeveloped intelligence, miserable homes, and work in which, broadly speaking, the majority can find no source of human interest.[5] Because the determination of wages has been left to the higgling of the market we have had, by

Trade Boards and Minimum Wage Legislation, to redress the balance due to the taking of an undue advantage of weakness. The higgling of the market is the apotheosis of inequality. It emphasises all the advantages the employer of labour has in the fact that the average worker cannot afford to wait. The competition involved is not a fair competition because its essence is that freedom of contract is absent. For freedom of contract, as I argued earlier, is present only where there is equality of bargaining power. It is of the heart of modern industrialism that equality of bargaining power should be non-existent as between master and man. There are, it is true, pivotal trades in which the relationship is, in the mass, more nearly equal. But this is the exception and not the rule.

Nor can supply and demand in any way indicate a genuine social value in the reward secured. Great fortunes are made in advertising enterprise; but, broadly speaking, advertising enterprise indicates the pathology of modern industrialism. The art of salesmanship, if it is an art, represents, in the mass, the ability to suggest that a commodity is what in truth it is not, and, in the individual instance, the capacity to sell a purchaser something that in fact he does not need. The incomes made by skilful special pleaders in the days before the reform of judicial procedure largely represented wealth secured in an effort to defeat the ends of justice. Great fortunes have been made in slum houses; but society has paid over and over again a bill many times greater than those fortunes in repairing the damage they wrought. The lady who invented the "Kewpie" doll is said to have made a large sum from her patent; but the social value of the source from which her wealth was derived is, at the best, not immediately obvious. The creator of a famous pill compounded soap and water in fixed proportions; but the social value of his mixture was considerably less than the millions he amassed. The theory that the price system fixes the "value" of service rendered omits the fact that the "value" considered has merely the connotation of effective demand. That value bears no necessary relation to the values which are socially important. If it did, our houses, the food we eat, the clothes we wear the schools (other than the public schools) we provide, would be very different from what they now are. The present distribution of rewards is an interesting index to the demands that are in fact effective; but we can only discover whether each demand and, therefore, each reward ought to be effective by a scrutiny of it. And, even then, we should have to determine whether the demand supplied, even when desirable, ought to give rise to the reward it involves. The merit of the present system is that by making entire abstraction of moral considerations it presents a facade of simplicity. But no system can hope to endure which in its nature makes abstractions of those elements which give permanence to social systems.

And, in fact, at least by implication, we condemn it ourselves. For there are ranges of service where we think reward in terms of income morally inappropriate; and we distinguish with an interesting sharpness between industry and the professions. No man would have respected Pasteur if he had demanded the market-price for his discoveries. The fame of Sir Ronald Ross is not in small part due to unending travail in a cause where there was no hope of financial gain. We realise that the great discoverer, the great artist, the great statesman, can only be paid in moral coin; and we do not even attempt the measure of their services in money-terms. The whole ethos of a profession, as distinct from industry, is that it measures the value of its effort by the service it renders to the public. It has standards to preserve, of competence, of method, of motive. It involves, at least at a certain level the element of disinterestedness. A man can be expelled from industry only by bankruptcy or the commission of crime; but the professions have types of conduct they will not permit even though the courts will not take cognisance of them. The very essence of these things is that the well-being of society demands therein the abrogation of the motives with which a theory of reward in terms of supply and demand would rest contented.

Nor is it, I think, unworthy of remark that the nations which went to war in 1914 were compelled to limit the operation of commercial motives. The very name of profiteer connoted dishonour to those who made fortunes from the misery of their country. A minister of the Crown who explained in defence of the businessman that it was his nature to sell in the dearest and buy in the cheapest market was felt thereby to have lowered his reputation.[6] The idea was widespread that the operations of trusts and combines must be limited on behalf of the consumer. The ideas of priority and price-fixing were significant admissions that the higgling of the market, so far from being a measure of social value, was like to destroy all social value. Those who gained esteem were those whose services could be measured by their contribution to the end of the State. The atmosphere, of course, was surrounded by the dramatic penumbra of war. Yet there emerged from the conflict great numbers of men who believed that such theses as these were not less applicable to peace. The strength, for instance, behind the demand for a capital levy (whatever may be its economic validity) came most largely from the perception that a State which holds the lives of its citizens at its disposal is entitled, in far higher degree, to hold their property at its disposal also. We have returned to the pre-war mood. Yet the exposure in those feverish years of the assumptions of a commercial civilisation are of high importance. What Mr. Tawney called the acquisitive society revealed itself as unfounded in the moral allegiance of men. It would win the acceptance of fear; it could not win the loyalty of faith. But no society is likely to endure in which men cannot believe with passionate conviction. That is why we require a principle of remuneration, and, therefore, an economic order, different from the one we have inherited.

A third theory of reward is more attractive, and it has, at least, foundations in moral principle. It rejects alike the theory of equality, and the view that supply and demand can regulate adequately. It demands that each contribute to society according to his powers, and be rewarded by society according to his needs. The claim is an historic one, and it has attracted distinguished men. But it is its transparent vice that it bears the appearance of a simplicity which, upon examination, will be found unrelated to reality. Let us take needs first. Obviously, we cannot take the idea of needs at their face value. We could not proffer a clerk a reward which enabled him to purchase the quartos of Shakespeare, however urgently he demanded their possession. The only needs we can recognise are the needs that are common to all men. And, even here, there must be a maximum beyond which we do not go. A clerk who decided to have thirteen children would have greater needs than a clerk with a family of four; but response to those needs is an undiscriminating endowment of stupidity. Needs can only mean average needs. We have to assume some mean of citizenship and make our principle of reward hinge upon that mean. We must therefore fix our standard remuneration at a level which does not take account of individual idiosyncrasy. Our effort can apply to the general only; the particular, beyond that effort, must look to itself.

Nor is the notion of powers much more helpful. If it means that each man must perform his function as best he may, the statement is a truism which no one would deny. Does it mean the duty to experiment with one's powers, until one finds the function which makes possible the maximum return? Does it mean the fixing of a minimum product to which each man, in his particular sphere, will be held? Are we to penalise those who fall below that minimum? Are we to expect greater productivity from those whose powers are obviously greater? What is to be the test of one's powers in the incommensurable sphere of intellectual work? If a judge gives a decision as he hears the case, while another delays the courts by reserving judgment, are we to hold that the latter does not act as his powers would warrant? What, in brief, is to be the best of a man's powers, especially in mental work? Are we to judge him by his own standards, or some common standard? Even, it may be noted, in manual labour, the task of measurement is difficult enough. The miner, for instance, may have a difficult place, he may not be in good condition; the tubs for his coal may not arrive as he wants them. So, too, in a textile factory. Light, temperature, humidity, period of work, existence of rest periods, proper methods of supplying the material, good supervision of machinery, may make all the difference to a worker's output. He may be blamed for "slacking", when, in fact, the blame rests on conditions over which he has no control. Obviously the only sense in which a man's powers are genuinely measurable is when he affirms honestly that he is doing his best. But no social system will rest satisfied with a purely subjective test of this kind, and that the more certainly when we know that the machine-technology of large-scale industry fails to secure the interest of the worker. For it is obvious that no man will work his best unless his heart is given to the task that he performs.

We are therefore driven back to a more complex view. Any principle of reward must satisfy the two complex conditions, that it enables the individual to reach out towards his best self, while, simultaneously, it preserves and develops the necessary functions of society. We have somehow to reconcile the interest of the individual with that of the community. We have therefore to meet the needs of citizens in the degree of their importance, while we do not, in meeting those needs, impair the general productive fabric. We have also, of course, to meet the demands of classes, children, old people, disabled and defective persons, who cannot pay their way. We have to make provision for the wastrel and the criminal in such fashion as will, at the worst, prevent their further degradation. Our basic condition must obviously be that every need related to the civic minimum, every need, that is, which, when unsatisfied, prevents the attainment of effective citizenship, must be satisfied before we deal with needs above that civic minimum. There is, therefore, as a primary level in remuneration a point below which no person can be permitted to fall who is capable of acting as a citizen.

But, secondly, no person can be permitted to secure remuneration except on the condition of performing work recognised as useful. He earns wages as a return for personal effort. What he does must be labour that adds to the national wealth. He can have no means of life at his disposal save on the condition that he has a useful function to perform. Once he performs work recognised as necessary he must be entitled to a reward which gives him the means of civic completeness. It must keep him in good health. It must give him room for the development of his faculties. It must enable him to build a home and pay such family-costs as the community does not provide. Such a reward is inherent in his quality as a human being.

It is said, of course, that such an ideal is illusory. Many workers would simply not pay their way at such increased labour-costs, and at that rate there would be an increase in the number of the unemployed.[7] But the history of wages in the nineteenth century has been the history of a very substantial rise in real wages without any correlated rise in unemployment. The higher the wage, indeed, the greater is the personal quality of the worker's life. His demands grow in width and depth, and the economic organisation of society shifts to meet those new demands. Mr. Hobson has shown that the inadequate and unequal distribution of purchasing power is, indeed, one of the main causes of unemployment.[8] In general, an increase in the rate of wages is attended by more good than an increase in the rate either of profit or of interest. And further, it is one of the valuable results of this levelling up of the standards of consumption that it tends to shift the emphasis of business enterprise over to those aspects of organisation in which the great defects can be mainly observed. No one can read evidence like the inquiries into the coal industry, both in England and America, or the railways of the United States, without seeing that the percentage of preventable waste is enormous. The scientific study of fatigue along is likely to result in greatly reduced costs. What is called labour turnover is, again, an obvious source of improvement.[9] There are vast possibilities of saving in the marketing of products, of which recent experience in coal is only an obvious example.[10] There is the possibility that the stabilisation of currency and credit contains the seed of great hopes.[11] We are not entitled, in short, to predicate the danger of high wages until we have experimented adequately with the reduction of cost in other directions. The standards of reward, doubtless, will always be lower in a poor community like Norway than in a rich community like the United States. But, in general, a society which aims at preserving its institutions will seek a level of reward at the highest rate compatible with its industrial existence. And it will, if it is wise, make the maintenance of that level the first charge upon the productivity of the society.

I have spoken of a common civic minimum. But I do not conceive that this civic minimum is the same for all members of the community. While there is an irreducible minimum of human want which each citizen must be able to satisfy, those wants are not identical in all. An agricultural worker, a miner, a stevedore need, for example, a more costly dietary than a clerk or an architect's draughtsman. The minimum we settle for each occupation will clearly involve differences built upon the costs that occupation involves. And here it is worth while to point out that difficult as intellectual work is, it is at best dubious whether it involves greater costs, training apart, than work mainly of a physical kind. Certainly if effort is the test of pay, it is not improbable that the present scale of wage-values will have to be almost nearly inverted.

But there here enters the second element in the fixing of a just principle of remuneration. It is one thing—and it is a great thing—to pay to the worker a wage that covers the cost of his effort. But we must also pay wages in such a fashion that we attract into each social necessary occupation a sufficiency of talent to run them adequately. We need enough miners; but we need also enough judges and enough doctors. Probably no judge works harder, even if he works differently, than a miner in the sea-pits of Durham. If we base our remuneration on effort alone, we should pay miner and judge at equal rates. Any deviation from this conclusion must be justified with some care. The true method of approach is, I think, to analyse the position from the standpoint of the social result we require. We must, I think, admit that the value to society of a great judge or a great doctor is greater than the value of a miner whose output stirs the imagination. The effort may be equal. For us, then, the justification for any difference in reward must lie in the probability that such difference will provide us with the service we require in greater numbers than would be true were equality of reward to obtain.

Here, I submit, we must begin by insisting that far too much emphasis has been laid on the importance of economic reward.[12] The great artist, whatever his *genre,* pursues his end for its own sake, independently of financial gain. Men like Leonardo, Newton, Pasteur, Darwin, are not seeking monetary wealth. The great soldier finds his reward not in the income he receives, but in the public esteem that is the measure of his repute. The average high civil servant could earn far more than his salary in the business world; but the consciousness that he has his hands on a great machine more than compensates for a comparatively modest income. Even with the average man, the desire for gain in itself is probably far more rare than we are content to imagine. Those who seem to pursue wealth for its own sake are, more frequently in fact, seeking those standards which, in a commercial civilisation, bring standing and power.

Yet, also, it is beyond doubt true that wealth can bring to life inducements which men of ability find attractive. Every society contains men who will endure the difficulties and irksomeness of a long training for the position and contingent affluence which lie at their end. Others there are who will take the adventurer's risk in the hope that some bold tempting of fate may land them in the harbour of ease. In cases such as these, payment by achievement as distinct from payment by effort seems, therefore, to have a real place in an imperfect world. In this aspect, we should then have a reward for most men based upon their output, and so calculated that the least skilled worker necessary to the industry would be able to earn his civic minimum. When we pass from manual work that is quantitatively measurable, we come to different considerations. We cannot, I think, really establish any satisfactory criterion of comparison between the work, say, of a Permanent Secretary of the Treasury and a judge of the High Court. All we can do is to set our rewards at the figure which gives us a full supply of the necessary services. That figure would, upon considerations I discussed earlier in this book, not involve anything like the present disparities between rich and poor. A great lawyer, one imagines, is not, save in an acquisitive society, only to be purchased at seven or eight times the price of a great university teacher. And it would, upon the same considerations, be urgent so to organise our society that no person capable of the highest effort was excluded from the chance to practise it by lack of opportunity. So far as organisation permitted, men would start equal in the race. So far as legislation could effect it, wealth, where it came, would be based upon function alone. There would be paid to all a reward that enabled them to give of their best and to be, so far as they knew, the best that they desired. Differences in reward would be built either upon effort or ability. But the difference would never permit the accumulation of reward so as to benefit other men. No one would be paid save for personal achievement. No one would earn save by the contribution he made to social good. And since each aspect of social life would lie open to him who would take advantage of it, we should, at the least, abolish that hereditary poverty that is the main feature of the present order.

Two other remarks may be made here. The reward each citizen earns must be his own to do with as he will. He may choose, as is so typical of America, to sacrifice the creature-comforts of his home to the possession of a motor-car; or he may wish, as in the case of many Londoners, to endure the discomfort of a long railway journey for the pleasure of cultivating a garden. The more a man is tempted to experiment with his own standards of consumption, the better it is for society. The one thing we want to avoid are those long rows of villas with identical wall-paper, identical books, and identical standards of pleasure. Life is an art which we can know only by experience. And the experience must be fully our own, shot through with the texture of our unique personality, if we are to realise the things within us that make us different from our fellows. If this be true, a society is well advised which avoids controlling the standards of consumption which exist. If the worker chooses to buy a piano upon which he cannot play, it is his business. If the businessman desires a house with endless bedrooms he can never occupy, equally it is his business and his alone. The sphere of social control lies in the realm of production. If it desires, as it may desire, to prohibit the consumption of alcoholic liquor, it is by the prevention of manufacture that it should proceed. What it must seek to avoid is the creation of class-standards in consumption. The prohibitions therein that it enacts must be enforceable on all alike, or they are without validity. Things like the mediaeval sumptuary laws are inapplicable because they assume a society in which the hypotheses of democracy do not apply. If we have abandoned such effort in strict fact, we have not abandoned them completely in actual life. "To know one's place" in the standards of consumption is still a demand tacitly applied to the weaker classes of society. It is inapplicable because no member of society has any place save that which he gains by the exercise of his powers.

This view of reward, moreover, applies equally to a collectivist and a non-collectivist society. It is a general principle of justice which arises from the fact that men live together, without taking special account of how they ought to organise their common life. It assumes (1) that all alike are entitled to find the means of full life, and that (2) beyond those means differences must be required by the common good of society. It attempts, that is to say, to found a theory of wages in the common consent of men. It removes from all that haunting dread of insecurity and inadequacy which now poisons the lives of most. It offers to some access to comforts which are paid for by the greater value they contribute to society in a realm where, admittedly, only the roughest estimate of value can be made. Ideally, doubtless, men should give of their best to their fellows for the sheer joy of giving. But, ideally also, Nature would have fashioned a world from which pain and danger were absent. We are not yet confronted by those conditions. We can only win what we have by the sweat of our brow. We can only maintain the scale of our civilisation by a division of labour which, unless we are careful, diminishes the moral stature of most. We must set our ideals by the facts we discover. Other solutions will, in the end, serve not to assist our progress but to betray our hopes.

### (iv) Property as a Theory of Industrial Organisation

A society might pay a just reward to its members and still remain essentially unfree. Nothing is easier than to persuade men to exchange power for material comfort. The rights of property must, therefore, to be well founded involve a theory of industrial organisation not less than a theory of reward. It must be a theory which aims at the release of personality in the industrial sphere as release for it has been sought in the sphere of politics. That does not mean the abrogation of discipline. But it does mean that industry shall be informed by a purpose relevant to the general well-being, and that the issue of orders shall be informed by that purpose. Well-being involves not merely the product itself, but also the methods by which that product is attained.

Property in industry means capital to be hired, and a discussion of its rights is a discussion of the powers which should belong to those who loan it on hire. Here, at the outset, we are met by a limit involved by our view of remuneration. No man, it has been argued, is entitled to wealth he has not earned. No man, therefore, will have capital to hire that is not the result of his personal effort. Hereditary business enterprise, in which the son takes over when the father feels ripe for retirement, and that without a nice scrutiny of competence, has no relation to a concept of justice.

Industry, in fact, must be made a profession. It needs to be informed by a principle of public service. It must not be merely a body of persons who are turning out goods for profit. It must be a body of persons who perform certain functions at some standard of competent performance even while, in that performance, they protect their members from undue competition from outside. They may be successful, and success will possibly imply riches; but their success, like that of the good lawyer or the skilful doctor, must be built upon an ability to enrich the public in enriching themselves. That element of service is integral to the idea of a profession, it is not yet integral to the idea of business enterprise. We do not hold a boot-manufacturer to the use of such qualities of leather as will make good boots. We do not inquire if a clothier has used shoddy material in the suits he sells. We allow the establishment of rings and monopolies of which the purpose is to cheat the public without regard to its need. But we do not allow the judge to debase the coinage of justice. We exact from the medical man certain standards of professional conduct. Their criterion of right is not the financial gain which may accrue, but the end their profession is to serve. And we ask that they subordinate their personal interest to the achievement of that end.

Let us freely grant that our success is, at best, very relative. Let us grant, also, that the line between the worst aspects of a profession and the best aspects of an industry cannot be easily drawn. Schoolmastering, for instance, is a profession, but there are teachers who would degrade any occupation. The law is a profession, and there are lawyers whose conduct is a perpetual denial of their vocation. So, also, there are businessmen whose ideal is to make their profit only by service to the public. It yet remains in general true that monetary gain is the object of an industry, while it is only a partial object with the professional man. For with the latter, monetary gain is subordinate to rules conceived in terms of function, and the purpose of function is social service.

If industry is to be professionalised, certain changes immediately become necessary. Broadly, these are divisible into three large categories. (1) There must be an alteration of the character of the owner of wealth into a person to whom a fixed dividend is paid for the use of his wealth. He must cease, that is, to control the business in which the property he owns is invested. Exactly as the owner of government stock is not given, as such, the advantage of a budget surplus, and does not, as the owner of government stock, influence the policy of the ministry in office, so, similarly, the owner of industrial capital would be paid the market price, and no more, for the service rendered by the loan of his capital. He would not be, as he now generally is, the residuary legatee of industry, profiting by the special ability of management, or a rise in price, or the special privilege a monopoly can enforce. (2) There must be an alteration in the character of the control exercised in industry. Just as the rules of a profession are made, subject to the will of society, by those engaged therein, so must the rules of industry be made by the working-force of industry. Those rules, doubtless, cannot be made in quite the same way. Industry will, inevitably, remain more hierarchical in structure than a profession, say, like the law. But once the functionless owner of capital is removed, an industry becomes an intelligible entity, and rules can be drawn up for its governance upon the basis of the functions performed by each element therein. We can, that is to say, make the relationship between a manager and a machine-tender an intelligible one, because each has a function to perform; but once the element of ownership is introduced the possibility of harmony is absent. And, surely, there is no more reason for offering industrial capital more than its fair market-price than there is for offering a wage to labour that is more than the industry can bear. We can only make industrial relationships creative by making the exercise of authority arise naturally out of function. If we strive, as we now strive, to introduce an element deprived of exactly that meaning which gives purpose to function, we are striving, as it were, to persuade the French peasant of the *Ancien Régime* that a nobility which has privileges without duties is really essential to his well-being and should receive the major part of his produce. But the peasant, slow as he is, soon ceases to believe us.

We must also (3) give larger room than we have done in the past for the social element in the industrial equation. That means, I take it, three things. It means, in the first place, the socialised production of those elements in the common welfare which are integral to the well-being of the community. By socialisation I do not necessarily mean nationalisation, though that is, of course, one of its forms. I mean the production of certain essential commodities, of which electric power is a fair example, by methods which do not leave them at the disposal of private profit. The technique may involve co-operative production, or consumer's co-operation, or such a form of control as that suggested by the Coal Commission of 1919 for the mining industry. Whatever the method, the chief point in it is that the profits therein earned will benefit the community and not the private undertaker. It means, in the second place, both in socialised industries and in industries retained under private management the introduction of a constitution. There must be standard hours and standard rates of pay. There must be the replacement of autocratic managerial control (as in the hiring and dismissal of employés) by methods of a more democratic character. The introduction of changes in machine-technology and piece-rates must be removed from the sphere of arbitrary will to the sphere of representative government. Promotion, the selection of a foreman, for instance, must be built not upon the whim of manager, but upon some approved combination of competence, with the approval of those the particular foreman is to control. It means, thirdly, throughout the field of industry insistence upon qualification and publicity. Exactly, that is to say, as a man must offer proofs of competence before he is admitted to the bar or to medical practice, before he can become the manager of a mine, or the master of a ship, so must he offer similar proofs before he becomes head of a factory or a department store. We must make an end of chance and nepotism in business enterprise if it is to attain the dignity of a profession.

Nor is publicity less urgent. What we are gradually learning in the present economic order is that secrecy in matters like costs of production and rates of profit is a fatal bar to a public spirit in industry. The claim of the businessman to manage his own enterprise in his own way is a claim to disregard new knowledge and public opinion. Exactly as we are driven to demand of colliery companies and coal merchants, of cotton-sewing companies and building-rings, the publication of their costs, so, if we are to professionalise industry, we must have means of measuring the efficiency of those who are practitioners in it. That is not only necessary for the public. It is necessary also for the workers whose livelihood may be jeopardised by the futility of their employer. It is necessary also to prevent those skilful manipulations by which industrial enterprises are floated at values where the bearing of a fair rate of profit is impossible in just terms. The enforcement of that publicity, and the utilisation of its results, will mean the construction of new industrial institutions. But only the scientific organisation of new industrial institutions. But only the scientific organisation of production, and its judgment upon a scientific basis, will enable us to make industry answer the purpose of social life.

It should be noted that so to regard industry, from the angle at which the rights of property cease to become rights of control, involves a transformation that will be accomplished in very various ways. There are industries, of which the building trade is a notable example, in which the owner is a manager as well as the proprietor of capital. To limit his rights in that first capacity is not to dispossess him in the second. He can, as the builders themselves saw, in their memorable report of 1919,[13] he utilised in the direction of his industry as transformed just because he has retained the capacity of a direct worker in it. That is not, however, the position in other industries. There, as in coal, for instance, and iron and shipbuilding, organisation, particularly in recent years, has taken a very different form. The categories of owner and manager rarely fuse. The owner is a financial figure not concerned with technical operations, but either passively receiving a dividend, or arranging for the receipt of a dividend for himself and other persons. He is there for profit and for no other purpose. He cannot help to manage the operations of the industry because, like the average coal-owner to-day, he has devolved those operations upon a certificated manager and knows nothing about them. He cannot share his power with the workers, from operative to director, in the industry because there is, in fact, nothing to share. The others can combine to provide service. He is there not to give but to receive. There cannot be joint control with him because he is morally unrelated to the conduct of the enterprise. All that he is entitled to ask for is the payment of that interest that is his due. If his practical intervention in the conduct of the enterprise is necessary to the provision of the product, he is then, like the mine-manager, a technician who can be absorbed in its transformation. If he is merely a profit-maker, so long as he receives his profit, his presence and control are, in point of fact, otiose.

Here, perhaps, it is worth while to point out that the classical defence of the capitalist undertaker rests upon an important confusion between theory and practice. The pivot of that defence was the fact that the division of labour becomes anarchy unless, somewhere in the scale, there was a factor which secured the integration of economic forces to some particular ends. The world is a chaos of wants, and every sort of enterprise is competing for the resources to satisfy those wants. The function of the entrepreneur is to control the distribution of those resources. He co-ordinates the mechanism of production. He measures his response by the delicate movements of market-demand. Without him, there would be unutterable confusion, since the more highly differentiated the society, the more urgent is his activity. What he earns is therefore a necessary cost of production, since it is implied in the nature of economic organisation. To dismiss him as functionless is, therefore, it is argued, to mistake altogether the world in which we live.

But even the most hardened defender of the present order does not present this defence as more than a rough approximation to the ideal. He admits that response is only made adequate to wants when the conditions provide for adequate response. In an ideal world of price-relations profit and social value would be proportionate. In an ideal world all resources, including labour, would be infinitely mobile. If they are not so proportionate and so mobile, that is not his fault. He is doing his best against difficult obstacles. To impede his operations is to prevent the performance of a task which must be provided for in some way.

That is indubitable. The point of the criticism I have here made is that if provided for as now industry must remain the instrument of gain instead of service. For what is of the essence of the present system is the fact of the unequal position in the struggle to secure response to want. Mainly, that unequal position is the result of the class-structure of society. It is due to the fact that most people are not in a position to make their wants a source of effective demand. Where, therefore, rich and poor strive for satisfaction, the superior economic power of the former compels the entrepreneur to adjust the system to the needs of the rich. The price-system responds, therefore, not to true utilities, but to the utilities represented by the power of money income. And since each additional "dose" of money income is a differential advantage in securing satisfaction, the entrepreneur is not supplying an economy conceived in terms of welfare, but an economy conceived in terms of the power of classes to press for response to their wants. And the inadequacy of this system is intensified by its individualism. For the presence of competition, and the secrecy which surrounds competition, leads to constant miscalculation through the risks and doubts of the market. Practically, the theses of this defence would be valid only in a society without classes, in which the demands of consumers were effectively equal. This is not the case. And the result of inequality is to intensify the special power of the class with property as against the class upon the margins of subsistence. For the "pull" upon the economic system by the former continually weights its effectiveness against the poor. Property becomes the more secure because the more its demands are supplied the wider are the avenues of profit. There is a growth of the investing class as distinct from the owner of capital who is a manager as well. The centre of industrial operations becomes financial. The object is simply the maximum profit, since that is the purpose of financial control. The entrepreneur then becomes more and more the salaried official of a company. The notion of function disappears from the direction of industrial enterprise. That, ultimately, is the real root of the disharmony between capital and labour. The divorce between ownership and work directly related to the purpose of a given industry means that there is then no basis upon which adequate relations between capital and labour admit of organisation.[14]

Wherever, therefore, functionless property is the controlling factor in industrial production, the abolition of its rights is the necessary path to justice. The abolition will be no easy matter, and there is no direct highroad to its accomplishment. Those who have suggested action by the proletariat to that end, a refusal, for instance, any longer to maintain the system, forget that men must live, and that only a peasantry growing its own food is in a position to continue its abstention for any length of time. It might, of course, come from political revolution which would destroy overnight the rights of ownership as feudal rights were abolished at a stroke by the States-General in 1789. It would be futile to suggest that political revolution is impossible. We can only say that it is, at best, a costly and dubious adventure which may end only in fixing the fetters of the present system more firmly upon those who suffer by it; that it may even, by its magnitude, destroy the whole fabric of civilisation. For the weapons at the disposal of a modern jacquerie are more destructive, above all, more permanently destructive than at any previous time. We are only entitled to employ revolutionary instruments when methods of persuasion are challenged by violence. For the resources of civilisation should only be abandoned in the last resort.

The alternative is a slower process, but in all probability a more fruitful one. It is to transform the structure of such industries in buying out, by legislative enactment, the rights of owners. They would then have the right to a dividend; but they would surrender alike profits and control. These would then pass, in part to the workers, from manual labourer to research scientist, in the industry, in part, as is essential, to the community. It is not necessary here to discuss how those rights would, when transformed, be distributed. There is not, I think, any one form of industrial organisation suited to all industries alike. Nor need we discuss here the order in which such transformation should take place. A wise community will proceed piecemeal and by stages, in order that it may learn by experience. The outstanding points of need are simple enough, however complex be their application. We must, first, buy out the existing owners of property rights. These must then be institutionalised into some system which represents the needs of each particular industry. By these means we can infuse the process of production with that sense of responsibility it now lacks. We can make the community as a whole a partner in that process. We can erect machinery which not only leaves the workers free to produce, but also permits the users of services to criticise and to have their criticisms translated into the working of the process. These things are impossible under the present system because its subordination to the motive of financial gain does not leave room for the ideal of service to express itself.

Three further remarks may be made. Extinction of rights by the payment of compensation seems to leave in full vigour a class of functionless owners. That is true; and in strict logic it is unjustifiable. But the life of a community must be adjusted to its experience and not to a strict logic. The sudden extinction of these legal rights would, if unaccompanied by compensation, probably result in an assault upon the government making the attempt. Men will sooner, as Machiavelli said, forgive the death of their relatives than the confiscation of their property. Nothing is so likely to poison the spirit of the body politic than the sudden disappointment of financial expectation. And, after all, the community has its compensations. In the system here outlined, payments to the existing owner would not pass to his descendants; he would, at the most, be the recipient of an annuity terminable at death. Nor, secondly, need it be supposed that the charges for such extinction are an unduly heavy burden. If Great Britain had bought out its coal-owners in 1913, it would have earned the purchase-price for the mines of 1920.[15] No investment is ever lost that maintains good-will; and in the transference to a new system, the more good-will we have, the greater is the augury of its success.

Nor, secondly, does what has been here outlined involve the rigorous formulae of control by a government department. The arguments usually laid down against the post office or the telephone service are entirely inapplicable, for the simple reason that the structure proposed is not built to that, or any other, uniform pattern. What is proposed is the making of a constitution for industries in which the autocracy built upon rights of functionless ownership prevents the expression of social purpose. Government control may be a necessary stage through which industries must pass to a more flexible form of operation. But, as will be seen later, the possibilities of variety are larger than the opponents of collectivism are prepared to imagine. Experiment is here as likely and as legitimate as it is in the realm of political organisation. It will, of course, make endless mistakes. It will, inevitably, require a higher degree of efficiency and public spirit than has been characteristic of the present order. But there is no birth without pain; and those who would confront the prospect of a better life must not turn aside because there are dangers on the road.

Above all, thirdly, it is important to remember that the present system is breaking down. It has ceased to attract the allegiance of the workers. They find no happiness in it. They give to their effort neither their mind nor their energy. Their inability to share in control makes them feel that the conduct of industry is a thing in which they have no part. Their sense is deep that the product is unjustly distributed between themselves and their masters. They resent, as in the coal industry, what they regard as the inefficiency with which the management is conducted. None of the proposed remedies—scientific management, a bonus-system on output, co-partnership, profit-sharing—has anything but an infinitesimal success. The roots of loyalty are gone. The system has ceased to act as a source of moral possibility, and not the most ingenious devices which thinker with its appearances can re-create its inspiration. The profit-making motive has lost the old magic which still glows in the pages of men like McCulloch and Nassau Senior. The growth of education has completed the disillusion of experience. The modern worker is outraged by the inhumanity and the hypocrisy of the existing order. He does not believe in its professions. He notes its declining success. He sees how the growth of trade-unionism has resulted in an advance towards the inner fortress of the capitalist citadel. He has become concerned with the overthrow of foundations.

## (v) The Problem of Incentive

If this be true, the main problem of property is a psychological one. The old system has passed because the spread of education made it impossible to utilise the motives which were sufficient for its functioning a half-century ago. Largely it was built upon fear, and systems built upon fear bear the marks of impermanence upon their face. Pioneers like Owen and Marx called what Mr. Shaw has termed the "moral bluff" of capitalism in the heyday of its success; in the passage of years there are few men conscious of themselves to whom their lesson has not been brought home. Is it likely that an order founded upon the principles here discussed will be more adequate than its predecessor? That depends, for the most part, on the degree to which it can secure the happiness of the average worker. It frankly abandons the profit-making motive as an incentive to the best work. It makes difficult, and, for all save a tiny fraction, even impossible, the accumulation of a large fortune. It was the operation of both those incentives that made for the success of the capitalism of the nineteenth century. That and a certain relentlessness were the chief characteristics of its zenith. For there were few who felt, as William Morris said, "ashamed when I have thought of the contrast between my happy working hours and the unpraised, unrewarded, monotonous drudgery which most men are condemned to".[16] Protests like those of Carlyle and Ruskin, pictures like that in Disraeli's *Sybil,* the unforgettable bitterness of the working-class autobiographies in the hungry 'forties, did not avail to arrest what seemed the irresistible tide of capitalist prosperity. Is a change so vast as that here implied simply a frank acceptance of impossibilist idealism?

Broadly speaking, the answer depends on fewer considerations than it has been customary to call into account. Much, I think, will result from the fact that a source of poison has been removed from the body economic. To make the worker feel that those who are paid must work that they may be paid is already to make it plain that industry is not the slave of unearned increment. The abolition of a parasitic class cannot but be attended by good. It is more likely than any single source of invention to secure that full-hearted co-operation on the part of the rank and file which is the real road to an increase in productivity. For, after all, the sense of injustice acts as an inhibition fatal to the doing of one's best. It corrodes both the mind and the heart. It secures imitation that is the more deadly because it is so often unconscious. Men not seldom begin to work badly from anger, and continue to work badly because anger freezes into indifference. The most fertile source of anger we can at least avoid by the permeation of industry with a just and discernible purpose.

But we have not merely to win the worker's moral consent. We have also to secure his continuous interest. We cannot do that in the way William Morris desired, by the surrender of large-scale industry and its replacement by the individual craftsman who is an artist vindicating his personality. But there is still much that we can do. The education of the worker will contribute a meaning to his performance. In knowing the life about him, he will cease to be transcended by his machine. We can discover by research into the fatigue of monotony ways of removing the main causes which deaden interest in work. We can, by the decentralisation of the factory-group find that number with which a man should work from which there develops ease of intercourse.[17] That quality is often seen in the "chapels" of the printing trade; it is the basis of the regimental platoon; it is the reason why the small common-room of a college at Oxford or Cambridge is so much more successful as a stimulus to effort than the vast faculty of a modern, especially an American, university. Team-work, in such a way, becomes real, and develops the pride and self-sacrifice and initiative which are so obviously lacking in the present order. What we call corporate personality is born, and a man merges himself in its spirit as the sailor becomes intimate with the qualities of his ship. By the creation in industry of self-government we shall build institutions through which the worker can feel that he is directly related to the centre of control. He will have the means of that "freedom" at hand which the Stoics understood so well—the provision of avenues through which internal spontaneity may find expression and, where it seems fruitful, response. Just as respect for law among the poor comes so largely from the knowledge that even the humblest may have his day in court, so will willingness to work come from the knowledge that the worker may penetrate to the seat of power. That has been, also, one of the great sources of trade-union authority: the knowledge that the vast organ at the centre is instinct with his own will and his own purpose. He is offered, further, a wage that permits of self-respect because it is built on needs that have been measured in the terms of his citizenship. Above all, perhaps, he will have a leisure that his education, on the one hand, and the new atmosphere of equality, upon the other, will translate, if he so will, into a new dignity and a new creativeness. He has had few of these things in the old order; he has had none of them richly; yet all of them are intimately related to the things which build his humanity. It does not seem excessive to have faith that, as they come to function, they will make of industry a branch of true citizenship.

It is not, as Mr. Tawney has said,[18] a change of human nature that is required so much as the emphasis of elements in human nature that are now ignored. Will this new motivation appeal to the brain-worker in industry, as I have argued that it is likely to appeal to the manual worker? I see no reason why that should not be the case. Nothing is involved in such a transformation as would be likely to degrade his position. And, often enough, his position is degrading now. The clerk, the commercial traveller, the insurance agent, are not only, in the mass, paid salaries which hardly, if at all, distinguish them from the skilled artisan, but their life is a harassing struggle to keep up pathetic appearances on inadequate means. They are continually called upon for tasks which an honourable or humane man would shrink from performing; and they must, for their livelihood's sake, obey the crack of the whip. They see the ambitions they have cherished realised by others, not seldom by uncritical favour or simple nepotism. Because, as a rule, gentility has prevented them from organising, they have been unable, like the mine-managers until these last days, to develop either corporate feeling or adequate self-protection. They have been judged, not by the values they can create, but by the profits they can earn. They have been subordinates to their employers, while they have been task-masters to their subordinates. They have been, in the mass, a proletariat in all but name.

Their tendency is more and more to recognise their common interest with the manual workers, and, as a result, to make common cause with them; and, as notably with the engineering profession in America, they have begun to protest against the waste and degradation of the present system.[19] What is their probable position in a functional society? They will exercise the power that is relevant to the function they perform. They will exercise their special technique as that is discovered to have purposive relationship to the end in view. They would give orders, as now; but their orders would be born of principle. They would submit, as now, to their superiors; but their superiors would be men co-operating with them in a common task and exercising authority by virtue of rational qualification. They would improve their positions by a performance related to a social value which benefited the community of which they were a part, instead of a pecuniary profit which is not necessarily related to any save private good. They would not be paid vast incomes, like the handful of rich brain-workers in modern industry, but their remuneration would be built upon their ability and their function, and they would enjoy security of tenure. And they, like the manual worker, would have the means at their disposal to make their views heard where they desire them to count and to prevail.

There is, I think, ample reason to believe that these motives would be adequate to call from the brain-worker the best of which he is capable. The professionalisation of industry is likely to make an instinctive appeal to his sense of his craft. It has proved adequate for the army and navy, adequate for teachers and doctors, adequate for the public services in their varied forms. "The desire to distinguish himself in the service of the State" is, as Lord Haldane has said,[20] "as potent a motive" with the brain-worker as the desire to make a fortune. "If he thinks he will be recognised", Lord Haldane adds, "because of his public spirit and his devotion to his duty, that public spirit and devotion to duty will make him do anything; there is no sacrifice of himself he will not make." That will always be true of the man who feels that he has important work to perform. There will, doubtless, remain many who will work only for the satisfaction of material appetite, as there will be many manual workers to whose best side these motives will not appeal. Any system of organisation is fortunate that secures half the result it desires. But those who have seen the devotion and energy of the best elementary teachers, and have realised the difficulties against which they have been contending, will have a sense of the possibilities involved in this experiment. We cannot abolish selfishness or slackness in any society merely by reorganising these institutions by which it is dominated, but we can at least so reorganise them that the minds of men are turned towards the qualities we need. We can offer the prospect of service to great ends in the faith that the higher the ideal, the more lofty will be the performance. Those who saw the armies on the battlefield will believe that our faith is reasonable.

## (vi) The Movement Towards a New Order

No effort is more suspect in our time than the criticism of the existing rights of property. It is wrong because it is subversive. It is futile because it is Utopian. It is erroneous because it runs counter to the eternal laws of human nature. But the existing rights of property represent, after all, but a moment in historic time. They are not to-day what they were yesterday, and to-morrow they will again be different. It cannot be affirmed that, whatever the changes in social institutions, the rights of property are to remain permanently inviolate. Property is a social fact, like any another; and it is the character of social facts to alter. It has assumed the most varied aspects, and it is capable of yet further changes.[21]

The present system is inadequate from whatever angle it is regarded. It is psychologically inadequate because, for most, by appealing mainly to the emotion of fear, it inhibits the exercise of those qualities which would enable them to live a full life. It is morally inadequate, in part because it confers rights upon those who have done nothing to earn them, in part because where such rights are related to effort, this in its turn has no proportionate relevancy to social value. It makes a part of the community parasitic upon the remainder; it deprives the rest of the opportunity to live ample lives. It is economically inadequate because it fails so to distribute the wealth it creates as to offer the necessary conditions of health and security to those who live by its processes. In the result, it has lost the allegiance of the vast majority of the people. Some regard it with hate; the majority regard it with indifference. It no longer infuses the State with the idea of purpose through which alone a State can prosper.

There is nothing inherently wrong in the notion of private prosperity. There is a sense in which it may be so held as genuinely to express personality and to contribute to its enrichment. But, so to be held, it must be derived from personal effort organised in such a way as to involve an addition to the common welfare. It must never be so large in amount that its owner exercise power by reason of its sheer magnitude; it must never be so small that its possessor cannot be himself at his best. The more equal its distribution, the more likely is the contribution of the citizen to be judged in terms of its social value, to become implicit with purpose as the way to recognition. Regarded as the result of function, it falls naturally into its proper place in society. It ceases to dominate our minds. The excess of it no longer produces idleness and waste; the failure to win a living wage will no longer breed in men that sense of outlawry, as in some, or that feverish envy, as with others. Men are no longer set over against society, either snatching from it some chance opportunity of advantage, or seeking to exploit it to some end which their conscience tells them to be mean and dishonourable. It does not exclude variety, though it transfers the emphasis of variety from material to spiritual things. It does not prevent the necessary basis of unified action, since co-ordination for function creates a plane where men can meet in common. It does not weave the pattern of organisation on any uniform scheme. There can exist every diversity of method, from a bureaucratic treasury official to a masterless craftsman, whose hand-woven fabrics some few persons may choose to wear. It will have, doubtless, a different scale of moral values from the present order. So large a change cannot but alter our judgment of good and bad. We shall think more of the creative artist because there will be more people with the energy of soul to appreciate him; we shall think less, one imagines, of the man who asks to be judged by the size of what he can accumulate. It may even, in its early days, appear a materially poorer society. For it will take time to train men to the habits born of new principles, and some, refusing to be trained, will doubtless withdraw from their effort the spirit that invigorates it. It may become a society in which there will be few wealthy men. Their disappearance will involve the absence of that conspicuous display which has made so much of our social life seem crude and tawdry. But it will be a society of deeper spiritual values, from which the worst tyranny, that of man over man, will have been banished. For fellowship is possible where men are won to a common service, and they can join together when that by which they live is born in justice.

[*Note:* On the effect of inheritance on the distribution of property see Mr. J. Wedgewood's very interesting volume, *The Economics of Inheritance* (1929)].

## REFERENCES

1. *Conservatism*, chap. v.
2. *A Letter Concerning Toleration* (Works, ed. of 1727, vol. ii, p. 239).

3. Cf. Hammond, *The Town Labourer*, chap. x.
4. *The Case of Equality*. Publications of the National Liberal Club, 1913.
5. See P. Sargant Florence, *Economics of Fatigue and Unrest* (1924), p. 374, and Wallas, *The Great Society*, pp. 363 f.
6. Cf. Zimmern, *Nationality and Government*, p. 282 n.
7. See A.C. Pigon, *Economics of Welfare*, III, XI-XVII, for a discussion on this point.
8. J.A. Hobson, *The Economics of Unemployment*.
9. S.H. Slichter, *The Turnover of Factory Labour* (1901).
10. See the correspondence between the Ministry of Mines and the Coal distributing merchants. *The Times*, April 19, 1914.
11. See E.H.M. Lloyd, *Stabilisation* (1923), and J.M. Keynes, *Monetary Reform* (1924).
12. See Lord Haldane's evidence before the Coal Commission of 1919, reprinted in*The Problem of Nationalisation*, for some striking testimony on this point.
13. See *The Industrial Council for the Building Industry*, Garton Foundation, 1919.
14. For an able defence of the opposite view see Mr. H.D. Henderson's *Supply and Demand* (1921). But Mr. Henderson fixes his attention upon the ideal conditions, and hardly deals with the divergence from them in practice.
15. And this apart from the advantages obtained by unification of ownership.
16. Quoted in *William Morris*, by Mrs. Townshend (1912), p. 12.—(Fabian Tract No. 167.)
17. Cf. Wallas, *The Great Society* (1914), p. 354.
18. *The Sickness of an Acquisitive Society* (1920), p. 74.
19. See the report of the Federated Engineering Societies, entitled *Waste in Industry* (1919).
20. *The Problem of Nationalisation* (1921), p. 20.
21. It is interesting to compare the remarks on the idea of evolution in property in the famous *Doctrine de Saint-Simon* (1829), p. 179.

# 6. Nationalism and Civilisation

## (i) The Nature of Nationalism

If the modern world could settle its organisation in economic terms only, the transition to an international order would not be a matter of overwhelming difficulty. The mechanisms of the credit system have already established an interdependence sufficient to overleap all physical boundaries; and modern scientific development, especially in the means of communication, is completing what economic discovery began. For practical purposes, we have already a world-market, with its corollary of a world-price, for the main essential commodities; and it is possible to infer therefrom an organised system in which each area would exchange the commodities it can produce under circumstances of special advantage against those similarly made by other areas. That was the order visualised by the free traders of the early nineteenth century. "Free Trade", wrote Cobden in 1842,[1] "by perfecting the intercourse and securing the dependence of countries one upon another must inevitably snatch the power from the governments to plunge their people into wars".

That has not, in fact, been the direction of events. The nineteenth century was, above all else, the epoch of nationalist development; and the events of our own time have made it clear that the end of its influence is not even remotely within view. Modern nationalism is, broadly speaking, hardly older than the first partition of Poland; and it differs from all previous forms into which its ideology has been cast because it seeks the organs of a sovereign State through which to express itself. It has required, therefore, the obvious indicia of self-sufficiency. It has demanded for each nationality an autonomous and independent government; the Italian will not serve the Austrian, as the Bulgar will not serve the Turk. It has sought frontiers that imply strategic security; France must have the Rhine as a barrier against German invasion. It has revived and developed the theories of Colbertism, and has sought, by means of the tariff, to make each nation a complete economic unit. And, having come to be, it has insisted that growth is the concomitant of life. Colonies, protectorates, spheres of influence, hinterlands of legitimate aspiration—all of these are the expression of that luxuriance of spirit which implies that a nation is mature. It is not insignificant that there is no powerful nation in modern Europe which has not won or lost a colonial dominion. In every case that has involved either temporary or lasting tutelage for the area concerned. Not seldom, also, the inhabitants of that area have themselves, like America, sought release from the swaddling-clothes of colonialism; and they have emerged, or sought to emerge, into the full panoply of a national State.

The idea of nationality is not easy to define, for there is no measurable factor to which it can be traced. The fervid nationalism of America has made it clear that race is of dubious importance, and, indeed, none of the older European nations can seriously lay claim to racial purity. Language is a factor of unquestionable significance; yet Switzerland has been able to transcend the difficulties presented by a variety of tongues. Nor does political allegiance explain anything. The history of the nineteenth century is very largely the history of changes in allegiance effected in nationalist terms. The possession of a homeland is of high value in making a nation conscious of its separation. Yet, as the Jews bear witness, it may be rather the aspiration towards recovery than possession itself that is essential to the concept of nationhood.

Broadly speaking, in fact, the idea of nationality is, as Renan insisted in a famous essay,[2] essentially spiritual in character. It implies the sense of a special unity which marks off those who share in it from the rest of mankind. That unit is the outcome of a common history, of victories won and traditions created by a corporate effort. There grows up a sense of kinship which binds men into oneness. They recognise their likenesses, and emphasise their difference from other men. Their social heritage becomes distinctively their own, as a man lends his own peculiar character to his house. They come to have an art, a literature, recognisably distinct from that of other nations. So England only could have produced Shakespeare and Dickens; so we admit that there are qualities in Voltaire and Kant from which they typify the nationalism of France and Germany.

Nationalism as a quality making for this separateness is builded, doubtless, upon the basis of gregariousness. The solidarity it implies must have had high survival-value when wandering nomads hunted for suitable feeding-grounds. The groups with a strong herd-instinct triumphed in the struggle for existence. They came to have territories they could call their own. They fought against those who would invade them. Victory intensified the value of their homeland, and gave them traditions which reacted upon their descendants to enhance the value of what had been dearly purchased. War, indeed, seems to have been the chief factor in building the modern nation. There are, of course, obscurities and to spare. We cannot fully explain how the indigenous tribes of England so mingled with the invaders from France as to form an English nation, or why the English invader of Ireland should have been so largely absorbed by those over whom his suzerainty was extended. What emerges, and what for us is significant, is the fact of nationality as urgently separatist in character. It is not a simple economic phenomenon, though it may be utilised for economic purposes. The break-up of Austria-Hungary was economically an obvious waste; but each of its parts demanded autonomy as the expression of separateness. Egypt, it is probable, will be the poorer for the disappearance of British administrative ability; but Egypt prefers autonomy to profit. Canada would probably gain, on the economic side, by incorporation with the United States; but she steadily prefers the maintenance of her connection with Great Britain. The disappearance of England from India will almost certainly, if it comes within some near period, result in anarchy for a time; yet there are thousands of Indians to whom the idea of an Indian-created anarchy is preferable to a British-created peace. Patriotism, the love of one's nation, may stray into devious paths; but, at bottom, it seems a genuinely instinctive expression of kinship with a chosen group that is deliberately exclusive in temper. And because it is exclusive, it seeks autonomy, even if autonomy involves economic sacrifice.

It is at the point where nationalism invokes autonomy as its right that the needs of civilisation begin to emerge. For to demand autonomy in the modern world is, in effect, to demand the whole panoply of the sovereign State. It means, to take some vital examples, that, in its allotted area, the nation-State will demand complete control of all the instruments of life. It will not be answerable, save in the arbitrament of war, to others outside itself. It will claim to settle its own frontiers, its own tariffs, the privileges it will accord to such minorities as dwell within its boundaries, the strangers it will admit, the beliefs it will exclude, the form of government it desires. Not must we fail to notice the way in which the solidarity, and therefore the exclusiveness, of a nation may be consciously fostered. That may be done by education. In America, very notably, emphasis upon the national tradition has welded the most diverse elements into a proudly self-conscious unity. It may be done by the sense of external danger. The presence of powerful and alien nations upon the frontiers of France and Germany has been powerful in making each of those peoples acutely aware of their difference from their neighbours. The press, of course, operates to a similar end. It feeds the herd-instinct of each nation. It praises those who are supposed to be the national allies, and belabours those who are supposed to be hostile. And that sense of exclusiveness promotes a loyalty which may often, like family affection, live its life independent of right to truth. Nations, for example, may be divided upon the issue of making war; but once war has been declared the instinct of the herd operates to banish dissent. Those who continue to emphasise disagreement are certain to be stigmatised as traitors; even, as in the South African War, when the nation-State is not seriously threatened, hostility to the official policy will be commonly equated with incapacity for the obligations of citizenship.

So regarded, nationalism is comparatively a new force in history, for in its aspiration to Statehood it can hardly be dated earlier than the first partition of Poland. The suppression of a national State almost synchronised with the assertion of national independence in America and national sovereignty in France. Each of those ideas proved a kind of political dynamite. At first, indeed, the forces of the French Revolution seemed to imply rather a European than a national movement; but the opposition of the reactionary forces of Europe gave birth in the French to a consciousness of special destiny, to which the strength of nationality gave peculiar emphasis. It was victorious in the person of Napoleon; but, in its victory, the latter kindled the flames of nationalism in the defeated forces. Thenceforth a new gospel was proclaimed. It might, as in Italy, move forward in the name of democracy, or, as in the subject-peoples of Turkey, colour its nationalism in a religious garb. What was the result in every case was the insistence that the dominion of one nation over another was politically inexpedient and morally wrong. It became the thesis of the nineteenth century that States composed of various nationalities were monstrous hybrids for which no excuse could be offered; hence, for example, the passionate sympathy of Victorian England with the Italian crusade against Austria. It was implied in the democratic theory of government, for it was difficult, as Mill said, to know "what any division of the human race should be free to do if not to determine with which of the various collective bodies of human beings they choose to associate themselves.... It is in general a necessary condition of free institutions that the boundaries of governments should coincide in the main with those of nationalities".[3] Unity and independence were the inevitable corollaries of this view; and it could be inferred, as thinkers so different as Hegel and Mazzini inferred, that the nation-State was the ultimate unit in human organisation and, accordingly, the ultimate unit in human allegiance.

I shall discuss below the moral difficulties involved in this view. But it is important first to discuss the two great counter tendencies of the period, which have united both to strengthen and to dissolve the force of nationalism. The one is the form taken by modern warfare, the other the inherent character of the industrial order. The second is, in some sort, the parent of the first, and it is convenient to discuss it as the main factor in the complex synthesis at which we have arrived.

That factor is the character of modern industrialism. It has created a world-market, and a world-market implies foreign competition. The Englishman who manufactures motor-cars must compete against the American engaged in a similar effort; the Lancashire cotton-mill spins against India and France, America, Germany and Japan. No nation can now consume all that it produces. It is compelled to find markets for its surplus good; and, in any given trade, it is worth while for a particular group of manufacturers to minimise the competition of their rivals in that trade. Domestically, the form taken by that minimisation is a protective tariff; abroad, it takes the form of colonisation, of concessions in undeveloped countries, of favoured-nation clauses in commercial treaties, and the like. Freedom of international trade, in other words, becomes limited by the demands of nationalism. It is found, in the classic phrase, that trade follows the flag. The power of the nation-State may be exerted to obtain a market dominated by some special national group. That has been our history in India and Egypt; that is largely, the history of Franco-German complications in Morocco. The trade may take the form of investment; a debtor-country may be forced to accept tutelage in the interest of bondholders. It may take the form of an exclusive or semi-exclusive market. As power extends, nationalism becomes transformed into imperialism. The latter is most generally an economic phenomenon. The romantic penumbra of patriotism is exploited, as in the South African War, to consolidate the interests of some special group. The notion that the material resources of a given area are a matter in which the whole world has a concern disappears. They belong to that given area. They may be used wisely or wasted as the nation-State thinks fit. To interfere is to attack national prestige. The problem then becomes one of honour, and, unless compromise, as with the Bagdad Railway, is arranged, it is discovered that problems of national honour are non-justiciable. In that event the only arbiter is war.

These conclusions, I am urging, are irresistible so long as the authority of the nation-State is held at the disposal of commercial interests. The instincts of the herd become inevitably manipulated to serve the special needs of a few. Ideals of self-sufficiency, the special protection of an infant industry, the privileged position of manufactures vital to the national safety, are all involved in the contact between political authority and commerce. The emigration of America is regulated to serve the interests of businessmen who need cheap labour; when the working-man organises, his voting power is then satisfied by restriction upon its entrance. English manufacturers of motor-cars obtain special duties against the foreign manufacturer. Armament-firms are given battleships to build as a subsidy for the maintenance of their works. India demands a special protection that she may develop industries which would not grow easily in the stern conditions of an open market. In the special conditions produced by the war of 1914, this atmosphere has been greatly intensified. For the discovery of the significance of the blockade has meant that the necessaries of life involve a self-subsisting people; and, in the absence of other considerations, that involves the building of trade upon a basis calculated to maximise protection against the dangers of war.

Nor is this all. The character of modern warfare implies further difficulties for civilisation. Its destructiveness is so great that nation-State must direct the organisation of its resources to safeguarding itself from the dangers involved in war. It must build its frontiers so as to make attack as difficult as possible. It must, if it can, so distribute their boundaries as to have access to the commodities, especially wheat and coal and iron, the supply of which is essential to war. It must maintain armies beyond the expenditure justified by its resources; and, to that extent, deliberately impoverish itself in the interest of its security. But each of its neighbours will do the same; and there is engendered a competition in the armament of power which acts so as to jeopardise the maintenance of peace, to provoke an atmosphere of nervous hostility, and to induce the smaller States into alliance with powerful neighbours that they may win security by that multiplied strength. So organised, the distribution of nation-States resembles nothing so much as a powder-magazine which, as in 1914, a single chance spark may suffice to provoke into conflagration.

Nor, I would add, is there reason to suppose that the control of natural resources by the State in the interests of security would diminish the explosiveness of the atmosphere. It is, I think, probable that a large measure of social control over the basic raw materials will develop to prevent their exploitation. That social control may even, as with Russia, assume the form of a communist State. But so long as it remains persistently nationalist in temper, and works through the mechanisms of exclusive sovereignty, it will simply be more powerful for the purpose it has in view. Russian communism was at least imperialist enough to overrun Georgia. Socialist England would still need cotton and oil, and would fight, if need be, for access to them. It may even be suggested that such socialist States would be able with peculiar facility to conduct their wars, since no one in them could claim that they were waged for private interests. Socialism is only international as such because capitalism is international. A world of socialist States, independent of, and sovereign to, each other, might easily become as mutually hostile as the States of the present epoch.

A nationalism that implies the sovereign right of self-determination is, therefore, a principle of which the consequences are far different from those envisaged by men like Mazzini and Mill. It involves the politics of prestige; and these, in their turn, involve a world so ordered that relationships between nations cannot become matters to be determined by justice. It is not necessary to deny the reality, even the validity, of national feeling to realise that it is built on emotions which are, in the atmosphere of contemporary civilisation, fraught with grave danger. No one need doubt that it is good to be an Englishmen; but it is also necessary to inquire for whom it is good and for what end. When the nationalism of

Englishmen, or of any other people, produces a State which demands allegiance whatever the cause it professes, considerations are involved which go to the root of political philosophy. A nation is entitled to live. But because it cannot live to itself alone, the question of how it is to live is not a question it is entitled to determine alone. For, in the political order of which it is a part, moral purposes are realised to which national interests, even, it may be, national existence, are secondary. Patriotism in a citizen is not the blind following of his nation-State wherever it may lead; and the rights of a nation-State do not consist in safeguarding its own interests at the expense of others. That is a politics of power which denies the idea of right in the relation between States; and it is elementary, as Burke insisted in his indictment of Warren Hastings, that the denial of right abroad means, sooner or later, the denial of right at home. Men cannot discipline themselves in injustice to strangers without, ultimately, denying the duty of justice to their brothers.

### (ii) Nationalism and Right

The problem, then, is the equation of nationalism, with right. I do not mean by "right" some mystic concept of transcendental ethics: I mean only that the interests sought to be realised are measured in terms common to all people affected by the habit of living together. I am arguing that since my neighbour is the whole world I must so conceive my "interest" that it implies the interest of those with whom I have to live. It is the old truth that no man can live to himself set in the new terms enforced by scientific discovery. It means that however we may recognise the separateness of those spiritual systems we call nations, there is a "togetherness" in their functioning which involves building the institutions of "togetherness". Those institutions can be built only upon the basis of joint decision upon matters of common interest. As soon, for example, as what England does directly affects France, the area of intersecting activity must give rise to a solution jointly planned by England and France. And, obviously enough, once the problem is so stated, the unit of reference cannot be confined to the two nations. Logically, the foundation of an approach to the common problems of civilisation is either international or it is worthless.

For, ultimately, effective decisions cannot be made if they implicate myself unless I co-operate in making them. That is not less true of the relationship of nation-States than it is true of individuals. I may be coerced into the performance of functions I dislike; but my service then becomes uncreative because it is unfree. So, too, with nations. They can work with another; they cannot be themselves at their best if they work against each other. The power they exert must be the power born of activity with others, not the power born of coercion over others. They must convince their neighbours that the relationship they have is one it is mutually worth while to maintain. Each must gain from it the sense of satisfied harmony which comes of service built upon self-respect. For an order based upon compulsion can never permanently maintain itself. That, at least, is the lesson of Ireland and India, of Austro-Hungary, and the Germany distorted by the Treaty of Versailles. Orders issued and relationships established must carry with them the assent of the interests they affect. They cannot, otherwise, grow into validity.

That means the disappearance of the sovereign nation-State. It means that no unit of civilisation can claim the right to dictate to the world-order in which it finds to-day its only meaning. For no unit is any longer self-sufficient; over a vast area of functions the decisions it takes involve that world-order in their incidence. Such decisions involve what Mr. Leonard Woolf has called "cosmopolitan law-making", if they are to be sure of a fruitful application. This is not, of course, an easy matter. It involves (a) the discovery of the functions that are universal in their incidence; (b) the building of institutions suitable to the operation of those functions; (c) a method of suitable representation for the nation-States which are to share in the government of such institutions. The implication, in a word, of modern conditions is world-government. The process, naturally enough, is immensely more complicated than the government of a single State. The spiritual tradition of co-operation has still to be created; the difficulty of language has to be overcome; the application of decisions has to be agreed upon in terms of a technique that is still largely unexplored. The only source of comfort we possess is the increasing recognition that modern warfare is literally a form of suicide, and that, as a consequence, the choice before us is between co-operation and disaster. That was the sense which, in 1919, led the makers of the Peace of Versailles to strive for the mitigation of its inequities by the acceptance of the League of Nations. The latter, indeed, is the facade of a structure which has not yet been called into being. But it has at least this great importance, that it constitutes an organ of reference which goes beyond the fiat of a given State. It is, in fact, either nothing, or else a denial of national sovereignty in world-affairs. It is upon the basis of that denial that we have to build.

The discovery of functions that are universal in their incidence is not a matter to be settled on *a priori* grounds. Scientific discovery would make such an effort out of date even before the ink in which the principles were written had grown dry. What rather it is wise to attempt is a vision of the kind of problem which has ceased to be merely national in character. Certain obvious categories immediately suggest themselves:

(a) Problems of communication.
(b) Problems of territorial limits.
(c) Problems of racial or national minorities.
(d) Problems of public health.
(e) Problems of industry and commerce.
(f) Problems of international migration.
(g) Problems concerning the direct prevention of war.

In each of these categories, we have already not merely a certain experience upon which to go, but also, with the exception of the control of migration, certain institutions which have already been tested by their actual operation. What mainly emerges from that experience and that operation? Above all, I suggest two things. It is, first of all, possible to administer and to legislate internationally. That has been shown in things like International Maritime legislation and such a complicated system as the International Postal Union; it is clear from the volume of achievement which already stands to the credit of the International Labour Office; it is clear from the very striking work of the Sugar Commission which arose out of the Convention of 1902. In these, and in innumerable similar instances, what we have secured is the imposition of international standards upon national interests which, often enough, sought to evade or to transcend those standards. It is clear, in the second place, that from the habit of international co-operation men of the most alien and, often enough, antithetic experience, can pool that experience to make a common solution. They can learn, in a word, to think internationally. They do not cease to be English or French or German; but they learn to adjust their nationalism to a richer perspective.

The second point of importance is the growing unification of law. We are compelled by the facts of civilisation to find common rules of conduct which can be observed in Paris as well as Tokyo, in London as well as New York. We can seek the universal establishment of a forty-eight hour week; we can see the universal abolition of the use of white lead in paint. We are driven, in a word, at least to a common minimum of civilised life for all nation-States whose behaviour at all seriously affects the world-order. What we must realise is the need for driving this process of unification much further than it has so far gone. We must use it to distribute the raw materials of industry. We must use it for the settlement of tariff-barriers. We must prevent, say, America making, single-handed, the decision that the Philippines are unfit for self-government; we must permit India to appeal beyond the decision of Parliament to the common will of a world unified into the League of Nations. Above all, we must prevent one nation-State making war upon another by insisting that their disputes are referable to, and must be decided by, an international tribunal, and we must define as an aggressor to be punished the State which refuses to submit its disputes to the tribunal and to abide by the award that is issued. When we realise the implications of this unifying process, we begin to get a vision of the world at every point different from that which sees it as a system of isolated and independent communities. We reject this latter system in part because it is the root of conflict, and in part because its implications are out of harmony with the facts to which our institutions now need to be adjusted.

But can suitable institutions be discovered through which this unifying process can be administered? There seems no reason to doubt that they can. I shall discuss in detail later in this book what seems an institutional pattern of which at least the large outlines are reasonable. What we need to know is whether the characteristic organs of democratic government—a legislature, an executive with a civil service, and a judiciary—can be made flexible enough to apply to the complicated structure of world-affairs. Here, certainly, there is room both for optimism and experiment. It is clear that we have reason to suppose that, as the work of the International Labour Office makes manifest, a considerable body of agreement is attainable on the most difficult of problems. It is clear that blindly to follow the classical structure of parliamentary government is to mistake altogether the nature of the problem. We cannot, at least in any practicable future, visualise the Prime Minister of a World-State unfolding his policy to a popularly elected Parliament at Geneva. What rather we have to envisage is continuous conference of governments in which mechanisms exist for effective compromise on the one hand, and for binding dissentients on the other. That does not mean the simple formula of majority-rule; but it does, I think, mean the abandonment of that principle of unanimity upon which the existing structure of the League of Nations is based. Our situation calls for government, and the very notion of government involves the binding of a minority to the acceptance of decisions made after free and full discussion. The major part of those decisions will, in the nature of the case, be nationally, and not internationally, administered. The civil service of an international authority will be a body of registration and information rather than a body applying solutions. An international judiciary will remit its decisions to national courts through which they will be made to work rather than maintain a police force to carry them out. The view to be taken at the international legislature by the government of any State will depend upon its power to get that view accepted beforehand in a national legislature. If it fails in its emphasis, it may lose its authority and be driven to resign; but the will of the international authority will be binding on its successor. The distinction drawn by Washington between influence and government is as urgent in international as it is in domestic affairs.

Nor is the problem of representation on an international authority at all straightforward. At a time when the dogma of State-sovereignty was at its apogee, it seemed logical to infer therefrom the notion of the equality of States and, consequently, to insist upon equal representation. But we know from bitter experience that equality of States does not produce workable solutions. We cannot make, say, Jugo-Slavia the equal of the United States by giving it equal membership of an international body. We cannot win results that can be applied if, for example, the votes of the South American republics are to outweigh those of the great powers. Our problem is not the discovery of equal electoral districts as in a democracy where personalities are, on a given plane, to be equally weighed. What rather we have to do is to assure to each State qualified for membership a voice that can speak with freedom and to States like England, America, Russia, that special authority which comes from their special incidence upon world-affairs. The solution, I suggest, will be found in making the legislature of the international authority accessible equally to all States, while reserving permanent places upon its executive to some only. The remainder may elect their representatives to sit with the delegates of the great powers, but they will be subject to the chances of elective fate. And it will, one imagines, be necessary to make the executive body a kind of upper chamber with a suspensive veto which can only be overridden in peculiar circumstances. Urgent as these details are, they are still, it must be insisted, details. Once the principle of unequal representation is admitted, it does not become impossible to find a framework into which even the intricate network of modern communities may be fitted. For to insist on unequal representation is ultimately to abandon the thesis of State-sovereignty; and it is from its abandonment that the chance of creative experiment emerges.

### (iii) Difficulties of Internationalism

But all this, it will be said, neglects the great fact of patriotism, and the root of patriotism is expressed in the determination to preserve national independence at all costs. With those who desire to maintain the *status quo,* patriotism is made an instinct, and the attempt, accordingly, to infuse the social order with rational purpose is made *a priori* superfluous. The argument is, of course, important, but it is, at bottom, much less formidable than it seems. For were it true in its full rigour, it would make impossible any discussion of international arrangements, and it would render absurdly illogical the whole and vast structure of international agreement that has so far emerged. Nor must it be forgotten that even the instincts of men can be made the subjects of rational control. Few more defend Calvin for his treatment of Servetus; yet it is hardly two hundred years since that action would have commended itself to the majority of average men. No one now defends man-traps and spring-guns; yet less than a century has elapsed since they were defended in the House of Commons almost as part of the eternal order of nature. We do not know what we can do with human instincts until we experiment with them; and there is, as I shall show, ground for the belief that patriotism can be sublimated into forms less dangerous to social welfare.

Patriotism is built in part from the gregarious instinct of man, and in part from the rational desire for self-government. The structure I have urged as essential outrages neither of these aspects. It does not propose that an Englishmen shall cease to love or cherish his fellow-Englishman, to live with them, to work with, even, it may be, to die for them. It does not even ask him to surrender his belief in his effortless superiority as an Englishman over other nations. It agrees that he should manage his own affairs. It would leave to him the unimpaired right to decide that he prefers a monarchy to a republic, parliamentary government to the Soviet System, the private ownership of the liquor traffic rather than prohibition. He could maintain, if he so desired, the present religious compromise in education without a single Frenchman or American or Japanese having the right to criticise his solution. He might continue to refuse State-recognition to the arts. He might insist on the retention of a divorce law which opens the floodgates of hypocrisy. Wherever the incidence of his decision palpably lay in the sphere of internal affairs it would leave his present position entirely unaffected.

But the right to manage his own affairs does not mean the right to manage other people's affairs. The development of international law and convention was due to the realisation that we cannot separate the two; that, because some of our decisions affect other people, it is well that other people should be consulted when they are being made. It did not insult English patriotism in 1832, that the middle class should be consulted in the choice of its governors. It was not even an insult that the working-class should be finally admitted to similar consultation in 1918. It was the perception that what touches all should be decided by all—an historic principle in English government—which broke down the narrow confines of the earlier system. Nor, though in a more meagre way, has the history of international arrangements in the last century been very different. The experiments that have been made arose from the realisation that where common interests are affected there should be common organs of government. That was the purpose, for example, of the Danube Commission; it has also, in a much vaster sphere, been the purpose, even if but half-achieved, of the Imperial Conference. And the solid result that has emerged from the working of these arrangements is the knowledge that, granted good-will, they can be extended into an efficient organisation of the world-order which makes provision for necessary unities even while it leaves room for the wise diversities of the human pattern of association. It is a one in a many; but the emphasis of that oneness is not a denial of its indestructible pluralism. Nor is this all. It is a supreme virtue of international government that it enables a truer emphasis to be placed on the well-being of the masses than is possible under the geographic limitations of the modern State-system. That is implicit, for example, in the conventions of the International Labour Office; they force upon a backward State those standards of industrial behaviour which are demanded by the public opinion of the world. It brings out the true national interest against that private interest masking as public welfare through the peculiar incidence of power in a given geographical area. No one, for instance, can seriously say that the protection of the Mannesmann brothers in Morocco was so vitally an interest of sixty million Germans that a war with France over Morocco would have been justified. Whether they were protected or no, would have made no difference to any but a small number of investors in the concessions they had obtained. What, indeed, is called "national interest" in these cases is rarely other than the protection of a band of financial adventurers who are risking their capital under the protective armour of the national Foreign Office. Skilful propaganda symbolises them as "England" or "France" or "America"; but the symbol is a tribute to the ignorance of the masses and not an offering upon the altar of their need.

When, that is to say, we are told that international government, by attacking national prestige, breaks down upon the rock of patriotism, we need, first of all, to know what national prestige in the given instance involves. Englishmen in general would hesitate to protect their prestige by war with Russia if they learned that in fact their prestige meant the protection of bondholders who had lent money to the Czarist despotism. Americans who are eager to rearrange the government of Mexico would have a different attitude to intervention if they knew that what is called an "intolerable insult to the United States" is, in fact, a refusal on the part of some Mexicans to be the subjects of an American oil company. One can understand the emergence of a sense of prestige if, for example, all Englishmen were refused access to American courts of justice or if all Germans were refused the right, not denied to other nationals, to travel in Italy. But, in the majority of cases to-day the patriotism that is called into being, however noble—and it often is noble—is largely misplaced. What it protects is, not the total interest of the geographical community, but the power of a small group within that community to exploit some undertaking in which they believe undue profit is to be found. The youth of the nation pays the price; and the youth of the nation is too precious to be made the victim of so sinister a misinterpretation.

I have argued that the emphatically territorial character of the sovereign-nation State enables a small section of its members to utilise its power for their own ends, even against the interests of their fellow-citizens. Against such a danger international government represents the most solid protection we have. But there is another aspect of importance to which attention must be directed. The assumption of Statehood by the nation obscures the urgent fact that the State is only one, however important, of the various groups into which society is divided. I argued earlier (1) that the State is, in daily administration, the government and that the government may lie at the disposal of a special interest, and (2) that to enforce upon it organised consultation with other groups is essential if the will realised is to represent a just compromise between competing wills. We balance, in fact, the territorial supremacy of government by making it work through functional organs. International government has advantages of a similar kind. It enables us to make its will responsive not merely to the political State, but also to group-interests which, if the political State stood alone, might well receive inadequate recognition.

The advantage of this possibility has already been made apparent in the operation of the International Labour Office. The tripartite composition of national delegations—government, employers and workers—gives a flexibility to the expression of group-interests that has been notably absent from ordinary diplomatic relations; and it is further reinforced by the possibility of substituting for the ordinary delegate from any group persons of special competence upon some particular problem. But the system admits of further extension. It is possible by sub-conferences of the national delegations to express a united view at the Assembly of the Labour Office. It is possible to transform the delegations into permanent commissions connected in an advisory capacity with the national government of the day. We could create, through the International Labour Office, permanent administrative commissions on special functions to which might be confided powers of the kind now possessed by such bodies as the Sugar Union.

Nor, of course, are such possibilities limited to the area covered by the International Labour Office. In the League of Nations itself it is clear that questions like the migration of peoples, the treatment of subject-races, the repression of the traffic in noxious drugs, all lend themselves to similar treatment. There is, surely, nothing to be lost, and much to be gained, by making the decisions of States based not merely upon the widest practicable induction open to them, but also an induction which is, *a priori*, assured of reasonable competence. All bodies which seek influence in the modern world, the co-operators, the trade unionists, the chambers of commerce, are driven to organise themselves internationally in the search to make their influence felt. More and more they are winning positions in which the State finds itself compelled to take account of their power. What is here urged is that to make that power direct instead of obscure is to ensure that the world-order is built upon an experience compounded of all the interests that are seeking expression of their purpose. It affords an opportunity for integration of resources instead of antagonism of resources. It provides channels of connection for those interests which transcend the boundaries of a single State and are yet limited, by the technique of geographical organisation, to adjustments which are wasteful and unreal. I may add that these international solutions rarely lend support to the plea that the interests of the national State are sacrificed in their making. For, in the long run, the only solutions that work are the solutions which mutually benefit the parties making them. That means, inevitably, compromise; and it means compromise beaten out by corporate discussion. We are unlikely to obtain such corporate discussion, at least in a permanently effective way, unless we have the institutions to compel it. And we cannot balance the interests of the parties concerned unless, above the impact of their power to enforce their will, considerations of right are given the opportunity of expression.

All this, it may be said, does not touch the ultimate question of national independence. For the international authority thus created might will, not merely territorial changes in some given State, but, possibly, the actual disappearance of the State itself. In the old order, Austria-Hungary was able to annex Bosnia and Herzegovina; what, in the new, is to prevent the League of Nations deciding that they shall be transferred against their will? Why should not a new Russia submit to membership of the League in return, for instance, for the restoration of her authority over Finland and Latvia, Lithuania and Esthonia? There is a variety of ways in which, it may be suggested, considerations of this kind can easily be met. Exactly as in the American Constitution, no State can be deprived of its equal suffrage in the Senate without its own consent, so would it be possible to prevent an attack on territorial integrity by making the consent of the State involved necessary to any proposal of change. To suppress the will to independence of any State, moreover, is not a mere matter of bargaining in the council chamber. It can only be done by making the State freely assent to that suppression. Just as the Treaty of Sevres involved the Treaty of Lausanne, so the neglect of justified nationalism would bring with it its own penalty. The statesmen who make the international solutions of the next age are not less likely to realise that fact than the statesmen of the last generation. They are being driven by the logic of experience to depend more and more upon the assent of the communities for which they legislate. They have either to find organs through which that assent may be made articulate or find their solutions wrecked by facts they were unwilling to consider. The history of Italy and Austria, of Alsace-Lorraine, of the Balkan Peninsula, is the kind of evidence which makes it likely that an international authority will be more careful to find genuinely corporate solutions than was possible when the issue was left to the arbitrament of force.

And, at least, the alternative is clear. Either national States must learn to co-operate instead of to compete, or, it is likely, the small national State will cease to possess effective independence. Even the brief but feverish interval since the Peace of Versailles has shown that the new States of Europe are driven to become the satellites of the greater Powers in their hurried search for avenues of survival. They are driven to barter what truly constitutes their freedom for military protection. Their armaments, their alliances, even the internal substance of their economic life, become not the expression of their own needs, but of the will of their superior neighbour. If this process proceeds unchecked, we shall see the world peopled, perhaps, by some half-dozen great empires each of which, in seeking its safety, will destroy the whole fabric of civilisation.

We cannot permit that process to go on if we have any regard for the riches of our heritage. And we can only prevent its development by the surrender of the fiction that, in the life of society, there is no word beyond the will of the individual State. We have to find middle terms between complete dependence and complete independence. Inquiry shows clearly that the invention is a possible one. Canada and South Africa have both found a full national life possible without the pursuit of the mirage of State-sovereignty; their citizens can assume a stature not less tall, a posture not less dignified, than those of Poland or Roumania. Their ambitions can be as fully satisfied in any sense in which the organisation of the modern world makes national ambition justifiable. Nor must we fail to realise the urgency of the issue. The day of the Laodicean passed when scientific-discovery made possible the steel ship and the aeroplane. There are no longer lotus-fields where men may linger careless of the life about them. The world is one and indivisible in a sense so compelling that the only question before us is the method by which we represent its unity.

Two other remarks may perhaps be made. The nation-State will act towards other nation-States as it acts towards its own citizens; external policy is always, in the end, a reflection of, and an adjustment to, internal policy. Where there is slavery within a State, the wars of that State are wars for the enslavement of its rivals. Where there is bitter class-conflict, the dominant class is always seeking to limit and to hinder the trade of dominant classes abroad. We seem, in the play of world-forces, to become to others that which we have been content to be to each other. The Ulster which was blind to the fact that behind the insurgency of nineteenth-century Ireland there lay an urgent protest of the Irish soul, adopted, when remedy of that condition was at last attempted, exactly that contempt for law of which it had earlier complained. Unless we can find the institutions which make possible the abrogation of conflict in the domestic life of the State, we shall not find them in the sphere of international affairs.

For hate is of all qualities the most cancer-like to its possessor. It leads us to develop in ourselves the character we condemn in others. Burke's great warning that freedom suppressed by Englishmen in India would lead them, sooner or later, to destroy English freedom, is a particular of which the universal lies at the heart of our social life. That is why the realisation of what is implied in democracy is the necessary prelude to the achievement of an ordered civilisation. We cannot, of course, achieve it separately, State by State; for each State has become so entangled in the world outside itself that the two are aspects of a relation that is unified. But it is clear that whatever makes for the betterment of relations between citizens of the same State develops also the prospect of friendship between citizens of different communities. Ultimately, that is, the purity of that corporate soul we call a nation is only maintained when the forces of the spirit are the masters of its life. It is only debased when it lends itself to other forms of power; and debasement is always easier than elevation.

It may be said that the big battalions triumph, and that a nation which neglects physical force is like a man who throws away his sword in a battle. But this, after all, is to beg the prior question of whether a battle was essential and whether other means of arbitrament could not have been found. Might, in the modern world, needs to be clothed with right if it is to be sure that it will achieve permanence. The spiritual life of Europe belongs not to Caesar and Napoleon, but to Christ; the civilisation of the East has been more influenced by Buddha than by Ghengis Khan or Akbar. It is that truth we have to learn, if we are to survive. We overcome hate by love, and evil by good; baseness begets only a progeny like to itself. We must set our own houses in order if we are to realise the vaster dream.

Nor are we, secondly, called upon to believe that the prevention of conflict by international government deprives life of its colour or its romance. The glamour of war is as unreal as the bought affection of the prostitute; it exists only in the inexperience of those who have not known its deadly furies. For the few to whom there comes the occasion of chivalrous exploit, there are the millions to whom it means death and disease and maimed lives. Its agonies do not touch, in any realistic way, those who direct its operations; and for the actual combatants, it is the organised and deliberate destruction of all that makes humanity a precious and lovely thing. Nor does the civilian population escape its impact. Death by starvation, by poison-gas, by aeroplane steals on some like a thief in the night; others are made moral lepers by either the avoidance of duty or the clutching at illegitimate gain. We must not, either, forget its mental legacies, fear and hate, envy and revenge. For that which, above all, has destroyed our belief in the tradition that war strengthens men's souls is the knowledge that in its modern form it transforms peace into its own grim image.

That is not the least reason why no man can give an unexpected allegiance to the nation-State. The true loyalty he owes is to the ideals he can build from his experience. The true battle in which he is a soldier is the battle to make those ideals ample and generous and compelling. At that point there comes into view the true romance of modern civilisation, the most genuinely co-operative effort in which we can lose consciousness of self. It is the conquest of knowledge that is the real source of our hopes, its conquest and its extension to the common man. For the real root of conflict is ignorance. It is the ill-informed mind and the narrow mind which are the servants of national hate. It is they which are exploited by the evil forces of an age. What is wanted, if we are to break down the barriers between knowledge and ignorance, is education. We can only surmount our problems by enlisting the service of every citizen in that task; and we can only make men citizens by training their minds to grasp the world about them. When the masses can understand they will have the courage to act upon their understanding. For intellect, as Carlyle said, is like light; from a chaos it makes a world.

## REFERENCES

1. Morley, *Life of Cobden* (Eversley edition), i, 248.
2. Renan, *Qu'est ce qu' une nation?* in *Discours et Conferences*, especially pp. 306-7.
3. Mill, *Representative Government* (1861), pp. 296, 298.

# 7. Authority as Federal

## (i) The Place of Consent in Politics

The view of the State discussed in the previous chapters involves a new attitude to the problem of authority. It involves, of course, the exercise of power by persons; and it admits that the number of persons legally entrusted with power is likely to remain small. But its centre of interest is less in the question of those who constitute the ultimate source of legal reference in society than in the relations established by them in order to make their decisions the result of the largest empirical induction it is open to them to obtain. It is emphatic that their power must be built from the experience of all persons affected by its exercise. Their authority is limited to the degree that it succeeds in integrating that experience.

This argument involves a re-interpretation of the doctrine of consent in politics. It involves, therefore, also a re-interpretation of the theory of representation upon which we at present depend. The modern doctrine of consent is largely a specious intellectualism. We do not choose our governors in the sense of actively making certain persons govern by our deliberate choice. We do not accept their legislation in the sense of our needs. Between us and our rulers there lies a vast abyss which is filled by the devices that power and its varied mechanisms bring into being. We are told that public opinion wills this and desires the other. But we have no satisfying channels either for the garnering of public opinion or for placing before it the materials upon which it may build an edifice of demand which represents its wants. Consent may in practice mean any of a score of things from blank ignorance through dumb inertia to deliberate coercion. It may mean, not the fusion of wills to achieve some purpose warranted by the facts, but the overcoming of wills which feel, sometimes actively, sometimes passively, that the thing proposed is wrong or mistaken or inadequate. Or there may be assent to a proposal which is, in fact, untrue because the administration of the things announced as realised renders impossible the achievement of the idea which seeks translation into the event.

Our doctrine of consent must therefore take account of certain uncomfortable situations which surround the existing system. We base our legislation on the expert interpretation of our environment. But the interpretation even by the expert is coloured by his own response to it, and the nature of that response alters the environment by the fact that it has been interpreted. No environment, in short, is ever a static thing.

We live in it and make it. It becomes ours by our experience of it, and it becomes different because it is ours. Our view of what the environment means is always intensely individual. It cannot be felt by others as we feel it. It does not convey to them the impact it makes on ourselves. There are no objective situations to be seized by a body of passionless experts who can present objective conclusions to the legislator. The solutions proposed make their way successfully only as they represent an interpretation of experience sufficiently akin to our own to be valid for us. That is why, for instance, the making of law can never be safely confined to a single class in the community. For its view of need is bound to be coloured by its special interest, and because it has never been made to integrate that interest with those of other classes, it will be unable to realise, if not their existence, at least their validity. That has been strikingly seen in the disputes in the coal-industry in recent years. Where the miners have seen the low standard of life to which they have been condemned, the owners have been impressed by their low rate of profit. It is seen, also, in the post-war relations of Germany and France. Where the former has seen mainly the savage humiliations of the period since 1918, France has been troubled in part by her own humiliation in the period of war, in part by the need for security against the anger to which German humiliation has given rise. The outsider who asks that each shall consider the position of its neighbour mistakes the nature of the problem. Each can only see the problem of the other when they participate in making a solution. But their present relation does not provide for the mutual creation of authority. So, too, the miner and the mineowner can only have interests in common by creating common interests. The interpretation each makes of his experience must have equal validity in the solution reached before consent to that solution is real. At present, when the parties to the State-relation, even more, to international affairs, demand justice, they mean in fact simply justice for themselves. We can only move beyond that exclusiveness when all can protect their interests by participating in the process which secures them.

That is the real case for self-government. It permits due attention being given to the interest affected, by making the consent to be secured the consent of those persons who alone know what the interest effectively is. Authority, therefore, is a function of relations; and it derives its validity from the way in which those relations are organised. It is important, moreover, that we should regard those relations are dynamic. They are changed by working, and they, in turn, change by their operation. The process is an interweaving one. The impact of interests alters the character of interests. Solutions become workable because they are able to garner the experience of those who make them. Authority imposed from without can never achieve that effect over a period. Its values are personal to those who make the decisions. It fails eventually to co-ordinate the experiences affected by its decisions. That is why, moreover, there is a point at which the administration of decisions must be decentralised if it is to be creative. For the incidence of their application weights differently for each area involved the substance of the decision made. That substance, indeed, actually becomes different as it meets the environment that is influenced; and, in its turn, it directly influences the environment it encounters. Few things are more interesting on a municipal body than the way in which membership of a committee persuades the elected councillor who is adamant about expenditure on other matters to feel that the subject he is concerned to administer is not receiving adequate attention. Will that is made by activity as distinct from constant that is inferred from reception is the foundation upon which authority must be based.

Authority, therefore, co-ordinates the experiences of men into solutions that harmonise the needs they infer from those experiences. I shall discuss later how those experiences are encountered in social organisation. What, for the moment, I am concerned to urge is that no authority is truly respected, wins, that is, a consent of substance save in those terms. I do not mean that, even in those terms, its co-ordination will be final, for even when it is made the environment has begun to change its character. Respect for law can never be guaranteed; all that we can do is to reduce the area of disrespect it will encounter. We can do so by the degree to which we build our decisions, not upon the fear we can inspire or the habits of deference they meet, but by the range of experience that they span. But because men interpret that experience differently, the possibility of conflict, though it can be minimised, is never finally absent. We can be certain that most orders will be obeyed. Yet history, we must also remember, is quite largely the record of disobedience to orders which have seemed to men a denial of what was most certain in their experience.

The clearest and most direct way to minimise conflict is to organise better information upon which to base decisions. Not seldom our difficulties have arisen from the fact that the parties to some given issue have not merely a different view of the result of the conflict, but also a different view of what the conflict is about. Here, the expert determination of facts is a fundamental matter; and the *expertise,* to be acceptable, must be drawn from a point outside the persons directly involved in the struggle. Miners, for instance, will rarely accept mineowners' views of overhead charges; and mineowners usually deny with fierceness the miners' statistics of wage-rates. The expert from outside who investigates and presents the available information is here the essential term in the equation: he determines, as no one else can adequately determine, the material upon which judgment is to be delivered. But he ought not to determine the judgment. That external imposition of a view not made by the persons involved is usually a compromise acceptable to neither side, or else a settlement denounced as biased by the side to which it is adverse. The expert ought always to provide the materials for a finding, but never the finding itself. For the latter at once becomes subjective in a way destructive of the character that makes its basis acceptable. It loses its quality of *expertise*. It becomes something to be impugned in order that the decision may be rejected.

That was shrewdly pointed out by Sir William Harcourt in a remark that goes to the root of the matter. "The value", he said,[1] "of political heads of departments is to tell the officials what the public will not stand". But so stated, the thesis is incomplete. What is not less important is to know from what sources the political head of a department derives his view. A Chancellor of the Exchequer who merely consulted property-owners upon the incidence of taxation would have but a poor clue to the mind of the public; a Viceroy who questioned the wives of Anglo-Indians would hardly be well-informed upon the state of native opinion. We have, therefore, to go beyond the statesman and to organise the experience he is seeking to interpret. We have to make known to him the wills embodied in that experience. We have to construct definite channels through which they can have access to him. And not merely access. For in the process of building such relationships we have, as nearly as we can, to weight those wills equally that they may be estimated with fairness.

There are involved in this view certain limits to the rightness of authority as such which need careful exploration. It is clear, first of all, that the experience of each member of the State, both by himself and in concert with others, must be made capable of expression. It must have, not merely awareness of itself, but the means of stating the things of which it is aware. That involves, I think, the systems of rights I discussed above; for, without them, the citizen has not the means of adequate statement at his disposal. And it would follow therefrom that no authority is legitimate which does not recognise and operate those rights. What it is and does derives its significance from them. To the degree that it denies them it is limiting not merely the body of knowledge at its disposal, but also its capacity to satisfy the wants of citizens. Limitation of that kind, even when originally unconscious, becomes, again perhaps unconsciously, systematic. For where men are silent because they have not been given the means of speech, it is always ultimately assumed that they are silent because they have nothing to say.

The power to state experience implies the right to be consulted about wants. My experience is pointless unless it leads me to demand satisfaction. And it must here again be insisted that the wants required are a private system of experience into which, at the best, others can only penetrate in small part. The consultation of experience therefore means the right to participate in the making of decisions. For any order that is issued without my sharing in its building will be an order that speaks for those who make it, and not for me. Anyone who analyses, for instance, the history of the landed system in this country will see that whatever experience it summarises, the peasant is not a participant therein. The law of sedition in India is, similarly, built upon the will of a conquering race to preserve its dominion from the danger of destructive criticism. It is so clear that power is limited by the experience which exercises it that it hardly needs argument to prove that its legitimacy is similarly limited to those who have shared in that exercise. The foundation of democratic government is therefore in the active sharing by citizens in its processes. The will of the State must be compounded of the separate and varying consciousnesses that are affected by its willing.

Here, of course, a complex problem emerges in the effort to discover how much participation is necessary in order that its results may be adequate. It is easy to make the idea of consultation absurd by thinking of it in terms of our present political structure and trying to visualise each statute and each administrative order being scrutinised by a helpless and muddled electorate. Participation certainly involves voting on a variety of matters; I have already argued that the people must periodically choose their governors. But the reality of participation will, I think, be found on a different plane from that of electoral machinery. To elect our officials and then to wait until we can cashier them will never give substance to our citizenship. It is not so much on the purely political plane as in the field of economic and administrative activity that participation is important. These can, as fields of activity, be related back in their turn to the political process. But what we need is inventiveness in the organisation of functions, and, within those functions, the attempt to avoid making authority purely hierarchical in its categories. For every separation of human beings by exclusion is a potential source of conflict. Every body in which the source of power is separated from the persons influenced by the exercise of power tends to acquire a life of its own, a self-interest, therefore, of its own, distinct from the purpose it seeks to fulfil. That separateness, indeed, changes the purpose; for it interacts with its environment to build a new atmosphere in which it drifts towards a new orientation.

This raises the problem of the way in which the individual is, in modern social organisation, related to the State; and, in particular, it raises the question of what I should like to call—the terms are not merely reiterative—the legality of law. Every citizen has, from the standpoint of politics, three aspects of primary importance. There is, first of all, the man himself, an ultimately unassimilable human being, to whom isolation from the rest of his kind, the privacy which he will die to protect, is at all costs important. A man's religion is a typical section of this aspect, though it has not, of course, been so typical save in very recent times. But in relation to the modern State each man is, in this department or elsewhere, ultimately an Athanasius. He will be broken by the world rather than yield to the world. In the decisions the State makes for these intimate aspects of man's self it must leave him room to move as he thinks fit; there is nothing it can do which will deflect his conscience without, by destroying it, making the whole of his experience invalid for him. For that experience, I suggest, makes law for him; and the decisions of an external authority have no hold on his respect save as they coincide with that experience in its results. There is, secondly, the man who is an associative animal, who belongs to this church, and that trade union, this international body and that employers' association. All these are functions of himself. They are corporate personalities through which his own personality is breaking into expression. Their decisions carry weight with him, even when they trench upon that civic aspect which is, as I argued above, most intimately the State's own sphere. In the last aspect, the State is seeking to lay down the general principles by which the life of the society as a whole may be directed. It is building, not an ultimate unity, but necessary unities, of conduct; it is finding minimal adjustments in behaviour. Most largely, in the modern world, it is seeking a harmony between the second and third aspects here outlined.

## (ii) Authority and Allegiance

Here is the head and centre of the problem of authority. That problem, as I conceive it, is twofold in nature. It is the problem (1) of making the solutions of the ultimately unifying authority able to command the willing allegiance of citizens, and (2) of discovering a process through which the likelihood of its making that ability pre-eminent is maximised.

So to state the problem is, it must be admitted, to depart from the classic path of political science. For it is the assumption of the classic theory that the ultimately unifying authority must be supreme just because it unifies. That was why Hobbes, in his own vigorous phrase, refused to permit the existence of associations in society on the ground that they were "like worms in the entrails of a natural man";[2] they detracted from allegiance to the State and thus endangered the acceptance of its decisions. So, too, with Rousseau, to whom corporations meant the interposition of a private will before that general will upon which the well-being of the State depended. So, too, it is argued that a strike in the public services stands upon a different ground from a strike in private employment. The State is conceived as the ultimate law-making body which gives their character to all other bodies and institutions. From the State, if not their existence, at least the rationale of their existence is derived. To deny its law, even if it seems unjust, is to loosen the cement which holds society together. It is not merely, we are told, to risk anarchy, but also, what is worse, it is to leave the settlement of social arrangements to a decision based on the might of the conflicting parties concerned.[3] We must therefore postulate the supremacy of the State's will over all other wills in society. Its authority then, I take it, has not merely a legal pre-eminence but also a moral pre-eminence, as the fountain of social peace. For no purely legal order can be maintained without persuading those who support it that they do so on moral grounds exclusively theirs. So stated, the first aspect of the problem of authority permits of an *a priori* solution. Because the State is the ultimately unifying organ, I must accept its orders and give my allegiance to it against the demands of any other body. The second aspect becomes then of merely minor importance.

I do not myself consider that the problem is so simple as this view world assume. For we are compelled, first of all, to analyse the State-will as a function not less than a purpose. We must infer, that is, the nature of the State, not from what it announces itself to be, but from what it does to the daily substance of men's lives. I have already argued that in general the State is the government, that the decisions of the latter body are the decisions which get enforced. The problem is then an inquiry into the authority of government which, in its turn, becomes an inquiry not merely into what a government is, but also what, in the modern social equation, a government is likely to be. I have suggested that the inference must be drawn in the main from the property-system in the given State, that this system will suggest the actual incidence of power (whatever be its theoretic distribution) and that, in general, the holders of power will divert its opportunities to their own use. I argued that only the operation of certain rights as the basis upon which authority rests can prevent that perversion, and that the existing system apotheosises inequality of power. I am driven, accordingly, to two conclusions. The claim of authority upon myself is, firstly, legitimate proportionately to the moral urgency of its appeal; and it is, secondly, important to make its decisions as closely woven from and into my own experience in order that its claim may be at a maximum.

Law is, of course, the origin of social peace, and I do not mean to deny for a moment the value of social peace. But I am arguing that I shall not feel it to be a condition inherently superior to any other until I know what it implies; and I shall judge its implications by experience of their result in terms of my own life. I have to see, that is, what body of experience its maintenance is protecting, and what other experience is excluded from its protection. Law will, in general, only appeal as legal to the citizen according as it seems to him genuinely, and not merely on *a priori* grounds, the reflection of a moral order. He will mean by that an order in which the rights he recognises as valid find place and sanction. Where they are absent he will feel entitled to rebel against the demands of law. The experience of citizens, in other words, is the true maker of law. What they find true to that experience will have authority for them. It is useless to ask them to yield to decisions which come to them without the reality they appreciate. They may yield to force or to fear. They may accept because they do not understand. They may feel that resistance, on some given occasion, is not worth the penalty contingently involved. But they will not, on any other conditions, give to the State the only allegiance worth having, the obedience of a free and convinced understanding.

Admittedly this involves the thesis that the exercise of authority is surrounded by a penumbra of anarchy. Is it worth while to deny that truth? Law for men is not the voice of an authority related permanently to some given organ, but the voice of the authority they are prepared to accept. That was what Ulster meant when it declared the Home Rule Act unconstitutional. That, also, was the motive force behind Passive Resistance to the Education Act of 1902. That is why Churchmen refuse to accept as valid the decisions of the Judicial Committee of the Privy Council. It explains the resistance of South Wales miners to the Munitions Act of 1915 and of Communists to the whole social order under which we live. Law, for them, has the authority of its substance and not the authority of the legal organ that is its source of reference. There are, therefore, as many organs of authority in society as there are bodies which command the assent of men. I shall be with my Church and against the State, with my trade union and against the State, if the impact of the State upon my experience seems inadequate compared to the impact of the Church or the trade union. It is my activity which gives legality to the law.

Law, therefore, has to make its way to acceptance through the channels of the mind. And it will convey a different meaning to each mind it encounters because the experience of each mind, the system, therefore, of its wants, are different. The sanctions of authority are thus never ultimately single, because those wants, though general in character, are never ultimately the same. We can therefore never guarantee respect for law. We can never say, for instance, that because the King in Parliament has spoken, therefore its will is bound to prevail. Normally, of course, we have assurance that the decision announced will be accepted. The real problems occur at the margin and not at the centre of law-making. But those margins are the urgent and controlling fact in any political philosophy which seeks to be true to its total environment. Legal right has no meaning for the individual save as he himself makes it have meaning. It has no sanctions save the authority he lends to it by articulating it with his own experience. We are loyal to the demands of the State just to the degree that the articulation accomplished results for us in a satisfied activity.

I am not, it should be noted, denying the need of obedience. Rather, I am arguing that it should be insisted that obedience is not a relation between an active source of decision and a passive receiver, but that, where it is to be creative, each is a participant in the environment built by their relationship. We have, if our loyalty is to be at all genuine, to contribute to the State, not a self that is an inert recipient of orders, but a self which contributes to those orders and colours them with its own personality. The State, that is to say, must make its law valid, must discover what I have called the legality of law, by compounding it from the experience of its citizens. It can only do so by associating them with the process of law-making. For when we say that the State makes law, we tend to forget that the State must act through agents who are also men. Their wants and purposes are built from their own experience of life, and, naturally, are valid for themselves as they satisfy the implications of that experience. But they are inadequate for others save as they include others. They lack, save in that way, the authority which makes their wants and purposes compelling because recognisable as our own. And that recognition can only come when we know that their authority is not merely made by us at some definite moment of origin, but continues to be so made by being interwoven, at each stage of the process of government with our own activities. These represent the wants we know as we only can know them. Authority, otherwise, has no profound roots in the soil of our own existence.

Certain contemporary examples will perhaps make this attitude clear. The most striking of all is the manner in which the Treaty of Versailles was made. It is generally agreed that, after the German Revolution of 1918, the desire for a reasonable peace in Germany was widespread. But a reasonable peace meant one in which the interests of the vanquished, not less than those of the victors, found a place. In the Treaty actually made, not only did the vanquished receive no consideration, but they were even prohibited from expressing the view of what the Treaty meant to them. They were driven into acceptance of the Treaty by the fear of what might follow if they repudiated it. The result is what might have been expected. The average German does not feel that maintenance of the Treaty is an obligation of honour. He does not find that his relationship to it is built out of any experience that has validity for himself. He accepts the Treaty to the point that force, actual or contingent, prevents his evasion of it. But what, in fact, is continually in his mind is the remaking of the Treaty. What, in fact, he is continually seeking is such a body of readjustments as will create obligations he can respect as reasonable. And no such adjustments will be found save as he participates in the search for them. The process of making them must give him a creative part in their finding. It may even, I think, be legitimately urged that the attitude of those politicians to whom the Treaty is a sacred document verbally inspired is largely derived from the recognition that its authority is inadequate. They were searching not for a solution, but for power over Germany. They were insisting not on an instrument which should join into harmony experiences previously antagonistic, but an instrument which embodied their own experience. The lesson they are being taught is the simple one that while the instrument they have forged has authority for themselves, it has no authority for Germans. They attribute this, of course, to inherent immorality in the nature of Germans; but it is, in fact, a simple psychological consequence verifiable from the everyday relationships of ordinary men.

Hardly less striking has been the post-war relation between Capital and Labour, especially in Great Britain. "Employers", a great capitalist told the House of Lords recently,[4] "have never been more anxious for the welfare of their workers than they are to-day; and never has there been less response". But good-will is inadequate as a means of creating response unless the objects to which it is directed are determined by co-operation. There is no such co-operation between Capital and Labour to-day, nor do there exist the institutions through which it might flow. The industrial world is organised not for peace but for conflict. Each party, as strategic advantage presents itself, imposes terms upon the other. Neither has real access to the other's mind. Neither has agreed upon common objects of endeavour. The employer who demands a larger output from his men has never set himself to discover the terms upon which a larger output can be secured. He has never tried to realise that it is a complex function of many variables. He is too often content to assume that if additional output is followed by an addition to wages, the worker's concern about the matter is over. He has never seen that what is important for the worker is not an aspect of his behaviour, but his integrated behaviour. Additional output raises the question not merely of increased wages, but of proper piece-rates, of continuity and volume of employment, of fatigue in industry, of the relation, through fatigue, of sickness to security, and so forth. None of these is a question that can be settled by the employer alone. Each of them, if it is to be settled in an adequate way, must be built upon the attachment of an equal weight to the worker's experience with that of the employer. At present the content of the phrase "welfare" in Lord Emmott's remark is utterly different for each party. And the fatal flaw in the whole relationship is that he assumes, as so many employers assume, that the lack of response on the worker's part is either a war-neurosis, or else a slackness due to irresponsibility. The fact, of course, is that the war has merely sharpened the worker's sense that he is not willing any longer to be ruled from without, even if the autocracy is a benevolent one. For the most benevolent autocrat cannot penetrate an experience he does not share; its joys and its pains are equally unknown to him. What we are witnessing in industry is the birth-pangs of a new order. It may well be that conflict will stifle it before it emerges. Certainly it cannot be quick with healthy life unless the environment it is to encounter is reshaped to fit its wants.

And here a particular argument is of interest because it illustrates, more vividly than any other, the approach to the problem of authority I am seeking to emphasise. Men say they can understand strikes in industries which do not seriously affect the society as a whole. If the makers of perfume choose to cease work, that is a matter of indifference; society will not die for lack of perfume. But on the railways or in the police force a strike, it is urged, is a very different thing. For these functions are clothed with a directly public purpose; where they cease to operate, a direct blow is aimed at the very heart of social organisation. It is, therefore, so it is said,[5] impossible to permit dislocation in enterprise of this kind. The State owes it to society to see that there is continuity of service. Either, then, it must make strikes in these functions definitely illegal, or it must have the means at its disposal of operating alternatively the dislocated service.

I do not deny the seriousness of dislocation in these functions. But it follows from what I have urged above that the legal prohibition of strikes will not add one jot or tittle to the authority which seeks to prevent them. To say that the purpose of these functions is continuity of service and that, therefore, a strike is a denial of their rationale, seems to me an entirely useless approach to the problem. For the purpose of a function is not a static form of words. The purpose is the meaning of the function in the daily life of those who are related to it. The way to prevent dislocation is not to prohibit it, but to enable those so related to participate in its working. For their control is then an expression of their experience. The discipline they adopt grows naturally out of the needs they know. Men are not less likely to strike, say on the railways, because strikes are illegal; that is only more likely to exacerbate their temper when they have struck. Nor, I suggest, does the provision of a temporary alternative really help the problem. For either it drives towards a settlement which, like the Treaty of Versailles, fails to carry with it a sense of obligation, or else, by using power on one side of the conflict, it turns the issue away from a consideration of the real facts involved to questions of method in truth irrelevant to them. The secret of avoiding dislocation in industries of this kind is to make the necessary institutions of agreement lie at their foundation instead of creating them spontaneously as each temporary difference arises. For then the agreement is cloaked in the authority derived from continuous knowledge; and that knowledge, in its turn, is a function of the total experience available to us. We can then evaluate the factors of solution before the differences are precipitated. We can examine before the request becomes a demand, and the demand a threat. Above all, we can examine in common. In our present arrangements, what is emphasised is always the line of partition instead of the territory of agreement; and, granted those arrangements, it is inevitable that it should be so.

I do not say that this method will prevent strikes; I only urge that it will minimise their number as no other method can do. But a new problem here arises upon which something must be said. So far I have mainly spoken of the individual as though he and the State were the only factors in the social process. Clearly, of course, the issue is more complex than this; for the State, as I argued earlier, does not exhaust the associative impulse in men. They build themselves groups as the expression of felt needs which cannot be satisfied by individual activity. The group is an attempt to advance some interest in which its members feel an answer to the wants of their experience. They are original functions of the environment. They are an effort so to adjust it that the individual can by its means feed impulses which, otherwise, are either starved or inadequately nourished. The group is real in the same sense as the State is real. It has, that is to say, an interest to promote, a function to serve. The State does not call it into being. It is not, outside the categories of law, dependent upon the State. It grows in the whole environment as a natural response to factors in that environment. It lives and moves as its surrounding circumstances seem to warrant.

The group, we say, is real. What is it real as? Is it real in the sense that Jones is real, or Smith, or Robinson, a complete finite entity to be immediately and recognisably differentiated from other complete and finite entities? The group is real, I suggest, as a relation or a process. It is a binding together of its individual parts to certain modes of behaviour deemed by them likely to promote the interests with which they are concerned. In that sense it possesses personality. It results in integrated behaviour. It enables its members to find channels of satisfied activity which, otherwise, would be absent. It has life only through that behaviour. It lives, not as a thing apart from its members, but in and through what they do. It enables them to form habits which satisfy, in greater or less degree, the needs their experience seems to warrant. It moulds the background of their lives and, simultaneously, serves as an instrument through which they themselves contribute to the moulding. It gathers together strands of conduct into a unification of behaviour for that area of experience it seeks to control. Its absence would be felt by them as the deprivation of a linkage between themselves and the outer world.

The variety of this group-life is almost bewildering in its profusion. Political parties, churches, trade unions, employers' associations, friendly societies, golf-clubs, research bodies like the Institute of France, dramatic societies, are only instances of their place in social organisation. They do not, of course, exhaust the allegiance of the individual. He is a centre from which there radiate outward lines of contact with the groups to which his experience calls him. They determine, quite largely, his choice of friends, of opportunities, of a career. They drive roads through life along which, a little timidly and dubiously, he makes his way to his goal. They represent, for the vast majority, a necessary economy of effort. They plan his activities and give him room in their planning for the expression of his desire. They fail or succeed as they are sensitive to his groupings for satisfaction, by the degree to which they realise in him the energy which is seeking to find a meaning that satisfies in the vast social forces before him. They seek to give him mastery of the event, to enable him, in concert with like-minded men, to control the environment to a destiny he wants. They have, often enough, a special validity for him because they are the channel of his deliberate preference. They mould a tradition about which he feels urgently, where he is recognisably at home. They evoke, accordingly, a loyalty which, not seldom, goes down to the very roots of his being. They give him a feeling that he has found himself, a power of self-recognition that is an invaluable factor in the achievement of personal harmony. What, without them, is a chaotic world, becomes a world ordered by the opportunity to do something he believes it worth while it do with others who share an experience akin to his own.

To urge in this way that the group is necessary to the individual is not necessarily to be blind to its possible defects. Like the nation-State, it tends to exclusiveness as a means of self-protection. It grows willing to sacrifice the tradition of other bodies to its own tradition. It asks of its members a surrender of their personality to its prevailing tone and atmosphere. It asks him to be loud about its merits and either complacent or silent about its defects. In the absence of keen criticism from within, it will become rigid and arrogant, unable to realise the possibility that it is not infallible. It will substitute for a healthy *esprit de corps* an idolatrous fanaticism which destroys what there is of plasticity in its members. It will persecute dissent and eulogise obedience with little regard to the substance they contain. It will insist that its partial good is good itself, and its glimpse of truth the whole truth. It will be impatient, particularly at moments of conflict with other groups, of a willingness in its members to consider solutions alternative to its own. Its leaders, like the governors of a State, will tend to develop purposes and interests different from, often in antagonism to, the purposes and interests of the general body of its members. "However faithfully", says Mr. Cole,[6] "the members of a committee may try to fulfil their whole duty to their members, an element of committee loyalty will almost inevitably enter into their actions". A cabinet that is in fact alien in temper from its party will seek to emphasise a non-existent unity with it. Its very sense of disharmony will make it insist on mechanical obedience even more than if it were satisfactory to its constituents. Absorption in any group tends to mean narrowness instead of breadth, rigour instead of plasticity, unquestioning acceptance instead of enlightened agreement.

Yet all this, after all, is only to say that groups are built from human beings and that they act as the State in its own turn acts. Everyone prefers the routine to the novelty. Everyone is more comfortable in obedience than in dispute. Everyone desires that his particular solution be accepted as universal truth. And with all groups save the State there is one saving condition of basic importance. They are voluntary bodies. They lack the instruments of ultimate coercion. If I do not like my club, I can resign. If I disagree with my Church, I can leave it. Even industrial bodies cannot coerce their members beyond the point of insisting on what may be termed mental conformity. The group, in other words, is largely driven by the circumstances of its situation to respond more vividly than the State responds to the wants of its members. It is compelled to lean much more heavily upon their conscious willingness to act together, must less upon the inert and almost automatic habit of indifferent acceptance. It is, if it is to be successful, much more dependent upon the assent which arises from deliberate mental activity. It has to readjust itself more continuously to new conditions. It has to revise its dogmas, to allow a broader interpretation of purpose, than the State. Its penalty is more costly to itself, and its failure to readjust entails a heavier penalty. For while its members are linked with it because they place value upon the interests it promotes, they do not all place the same value upon those interests; and those interests have for them a marginal utility which exists in the perspective of knowledge that loyalty may be transferred elsewhere. A Church of England that is unduly subservient to the State loses members to the Church of Rome; a Liberal Party which is vague about its industrial policy finds an apparent drift among its members to the forces of Labour. Even the proud boast of *semper eadem* does not persuade the Roman Catholic Church to forces upon its members an attempt to apply the Syllabus of 1864; and the development of a specifically Catholic Socialism is evidence that Popes are infallible rather as a matter of courtesy than of administration. A Republican Party which calls attention rather to its past than to its future finds that its own members search for the symbols of rebellion against it. Groups, in short, are forced in the end to the conviction that what gives them life is what their members think about them. No allegiance is permanent that does not prove itself to them as it works. Their obligations become sterilised save as they grow spontaneously from an experience that proves their worth.

This has been put by Father Tyrrell in an admirable phrase. "It is not their red robes", he said,[7] "but my own judgment about them that gives the pack of cardinals any title to distinction. Like Elizabeth, it has frocked them and can unfrock them. It is they who are in peril, not we". The authority of any group is based, in fact, upon the living and spontaneous trust it can command. If it betrays or stultifies itself it ceases to win the loyalty that is its life. Here, as elsewhere, it is plain that the real field of social action is the individual human mind. Its experience forces it to judge, and all judgment, ultimately is a choice, It is, of course, a choice with penalties. The soldier who comes to believe in the moral error of coercion has no alternative save to lay down his sword; but he will suffer from his decision. The Churchman who comes to doubt the validity of his faith has, equally, no alternative save resignation. There comes a point in individual experience when, again in Tyrrell's words,[8] one is driven on "to follow the dominant influence of one's life even if it should break the heart of all the world". That is the ultimate fact by which all authority, voluntary or otherwise, is conditioned. Loyalty is won from us, it cannot be imposed upon us. It must grow spontaneously out of our experience; and the body which seeks to retain it must be able continuously to adapt itself to an experience that is ever-changing. It will never quite succeed. Men will never be content to be syllables in the mouth of Allah. Their difference from their fellows will always prevent their absorption. Our sense is that we experience ourselves not in unity but in division. We are conscious of separateness from others, as well as an enfolding with others. We prove that separateness to be real by the disharmonies of which it makes us aware. We cannot act without the sense that we are only partially with our fellows, and with them partially only in parts which refuse reduction to an ultimate unity. Our isolation, however uncomfortable, is ultimately so inescapable and so immense that it makes us see the universe not as an alphabet in which we are the letters, but as a discrete series of symbols only part of which convey to us a meaning we can accept.

If this be true, it follows that there is no necessary unity in society. There are, at points within its structure, unities of which the transience varies in degree. But these unities are always external, and they unite at points only upon their boundaries. They are means through which men realise themselves, never ends in which they find themselves. We are never, as human beings, wholly included in any relation. About us is always an environment which separates us from others, or, at the best, makes our union with them but a partial one. For our minds, at least so far as social theory is concerned, are finite minds. We know some things, but not all things, and what we know we know differently from one another. We have to take the world of sense as we meet it, its losses and gains, its struggles and its victories, and assume that, as we meet it, it is a real world in space and time. We have to treat what seems to us evil as genuine and not merely as an appearance capable, otherwhere, of being harmonised into good. The unity we encounter in the world of social fact is never complete. For while we may all seek an end which can be described as identical, the end is one only in the description. The good life for me is not the same as the good life for you. It has, of course, resemblances. In a well-ordered society it has sufficient resemblance to make social peace effective. But resemblance does not involve identity. The things we want do not flow together with each other. What we meet is pluralistic and not monistic. There is no plane on which the differences can somehow be coerced into unity.

If this be true, it follows that what there is of unity in our relations is not *a priori* there. Our groups do not grow together into a vast monistic whole. We build them together as and how we can. We find the means of connection by the discovery of kindred purpose, of sameness in difference, of like origin. The oneness we achieve is a contribution we ourselves make. But we make it only in a partial way. I may co-operate with X in industry while I try to deprive him of his religious rights. I may be an earnest propagandist for the study of Czecho-Slovak literature even while I wish to restore Czecho-Slovakia to its old place in a re-made Austria-Hungary. I may, that is to say, relate myself to parts without, simultaneously, involving wholes. We are in, so to say, not a universe but a multiverse. We recognise as valid the claims not of some final synthesised unity, but of unities to which we feel ourselves sympathetic. We respond to those claims. But we do not feel them part of some great system which moves by logical sequence from its pieces to a whole. Our relations are not like chords in a great symphony in which what is important is the ultimate impression conveyed. Each piece of our experience is real for us; and, therefore, the attachments of each piece guide our personalities into a system of loyalties. How that system maintains its equilibrium, where, at any moment, the emphasis is to be thrown is a matter that each of us must decide. For that system is ours and ours only. Its impact is decisive for ourselves. Its authority for us is the fact that it has grown within our own conscience and our own mind, is, so to speak, ultimately a part of each. To accept another system is to make our own experience the slave of another. It is to yield my personality, all that makes me most distinctively myself, to the desires of another and to the will another bases upon those desires. But there is never enough oneness of desire between me and another to make a real solution of this kind. The co-operation I discover myself to need is, in James' phrase,[9] federal and not, imperial, in character. What I search for is not a centre of active willing in which I myself am lost, but a centre to the will of which I can myself contribute the thing that is distinctively myself.

If this be true, the implications, as I think, are of importance for political philosophy. The centre of significance is no longer the search for unity, but, rather, what that unity makes. And what it makes must, if it is to win my allegiance, include results I recognise as expressive of my need, results, even more, that I realise I have helped to make. For my needs will go unexpressed save as I make them articulate. I must build myself into the decisions which bind my behaviour. For, otherwise, the coherence that is effected is only accidentally relevant not only for myself, but also for those groups through which I seek self-expression. A unity achieved without my contribution may adjust me to the new environment it creates, but it will not be a creative adjustment. Once it is realised, that the structure made is intended to contain my activities, it is obvious that I must put my own hand to its construction. The edifice, whatever it emerges as, will not be perfect. Something of myself will be omitted in whatever synthesis is made. But, clearly, that synthesis will seem to me less an evasion or a betrayal if it is a process compounded in part from me not less than from others. It is the difference between occupying one's own house and living in a prison-cell. To the former I can add myself. It becomes a thing through which and in which I can add my peculiar grasp of life. In the latter I inherit uniformities which I am powerless to alter. The routine of form and activity is there for me to accept. No increment of myself can colour or change it. It remains consistently external to my personality. It separates me from the world instead of giving me a place in the world. It ensures dislocation instead of promoting union.

The political inference is, I think, clear. The structure of social organisation must be federal if it is to be adequate. Its pattern involves, not myself and the State, my groups and the State, but all these and their interrelationships. For when I respond to the demands of the State, there grows up between us a process which alters both response and demand. That process is compounded not merely from my State-context, but from the total environment in which I find myself. The State which seeks my loyalty by seeking it is altering my relation to Church and trade union, to all the multiplicity of fellowships to which I belong. It has to validate that alteration. It has to prove to me that the adjustment it asks me to make adds to my satisfaction. It can do so only by the demonstration that the change to be effected is not an imposition upon those fellowship but a growth from their experience. It has to show that its demand represents a genuine reciprocal increase of good. And good means good for me as well as others; it must be a co-operative creation in which I feel myself to share. It must be a good which elicits not merely an apathetic acceptance on my part, but a response which enables me to experiment with the growing realisation of my best self. That realisation, above all, must be my own. For it is when I am guided by self-knowledge to the sense of what I may become that I begin most genuinely to enter my inheritance.

## (iii) Representation for Authority

This is at least the path to a solution of the two issues in the problem of authority that I outlined earlier in this chapter. It does not, as in the classic theory of politics, begin by postulating the necessary unity of society and continue by insisting on the supremacy of the State as the organ of that unity. It admits that the varying factors in the equation of life impel the admission of diversity. It agrees that unity is not there, but has to be made. It does not demand a unity of Procrustes, in which individual personality is abridged to fit the formula of those who, at some given moment, dominate the State. That is, of course, a unity; but it is the unity of the cannibal and his victim. Rather it insists on unification made through a process of so associating interests that each, in the solution effected, finds sufficient concession to itself to experiment with the result. It does not even argue that the solution will succeed, or that it ought to be accepted because it happens to be a solution. Right, as it recognises, is not a static thing, but made and remade in the crucible of experience. It follows therefore that, in its view, the claim of authority is worth just as much as it proves itself to be worth as men in their various relationships make trial of the result of its claim. It admits the desirability of obedience, because it realises the superiority, in general, of order over conflict. But it argues that obedience is only creative when it arises from a self-imposed discipline. It sees the imperative element in law as something derived not from the persons proclaiming it as law, but from the impact of its content upon the persons affected by the command. Orders as such are, therefore, morally neutral in this view, they become right or wrong as they work in the substance of men's lives. And they are, it argues, the more likely to work as what they contain in their administration is wrought from and operated by the persons to whom the orders are issued. For building upon the basis that all experience is finite, that what I want and do is, ultimately, an induction limited by the narrow field I know, it seeks to expand my experience until it is shared with, and becomes a part-function of, the largest available volume of knowledge.

At this point, clearly, it becomes a theory of representation. It admits the necessity for co-ordination, though it urges that all co-ordination achieved is at best a partial thing. But it denies that simple view of the co-ordination effected by the legislature of a State which underlies, for instance, John Stuart Mill's *Representative Government*. "The theory is", says Mr. Lippmann,[10] applying it to the American position, "that the best man of each district brings the best wisdom of his constituents to a central place, and that all these wisdoms combined are all the wisdom that Congress needs". Obviously, nothing of the sort occurs. The wisdom of most men is simply never made available to their representatives in a central legislature. Those who choose are, often enough, unable to say what that wisdom is; those who are chosen are not seldom unable to interpret, sometimes from self-interest, sometimes from stupidity, the wisdom that does express itself. The idea that my will and my experience are, in some mystic fashion, embodied in the will and experience of my representative is contradicted by all the facts at our disposal. My will cannot, as Rousseau saw, ever be represented at all, and my experience is, for its intimate substance, essentially private to myself. I can recognise, in any average legislative assembly, men whose actions reveal a purpose sufficiently akin to my own to enlist my support. I can infer from those actions interests which go along with my interests, experiences which are relevant to my experiences. The problem of representation is the problem of enabling me to have contact with those men.

It should be realised that my contact will rarely be at all direct and intimate. There is not time for more than partial glimpses of one another in the shifting scene of politics. There are too many people in the State, and too much to do in the State, for the co-ordinations effected by a central legislature to be more than very rough first approximations. The views which find their expression there will be the powerful and the clamant views. They will not mirror the total volume of interests in society simply because that is, frankly, sheer impossibility. The size of the modern State makes it necessary for the people to surrender direct control of principles and direct control of administration. They can, broadly, say yes or no to large general solutions, they can be for free trade and against child labour. But they must, in general, express their will by choosing persons to say yes and no on their behalf. They must recognise that the persons so chosen cannot be made delegates in the sense either (a) of making all their views known beforehand, or (b) submitting their proposed views on new problems back to their constituents for scrutiny and approval. The rush of business does not permit the leisurely survey that method would involve. All the direct power the average citizen can hope for is, first the opportunity periodically to seek a change in the co-ordinating authority, and, in the intervals, to use the groups of which he is a part to bring pressure to bear upon that body.

It is the sense of the helplessness in which this seems to leave him that has led many to suggest a different basis for the task of co-ordination. Mr. Cole, for instance, sees society as a mass of functions, and he would make the ultimate co-ordinating authority an indirect organ to which those functions contribute representatives.[11] I have already rejected this view.[12] It seems to me clear that the basis of choice in a co-ordinating body must be personal, simply because the individual is not merely a system of affiliations to different functions, nor do I believe that the general thesis of social life permit statement in terms of some given functional view. The case for the magnicompetent and directly elected body driving a stream of tendency through affairs seems to me overwhelming. It is true that I cannot be fully represented as a citizen, but it is also true that I cannot be fully represented as an engineer or a doctor or a carpenter. And the simplicity which makes me choose as a person is too important to be discarded for a view which makes the co-ordinating body much more remote from me as a person than, say, the House of Commons now is. The success of the latter in affording satisfaction does not depend upon the rejection of its territorial basis. It is built rather upon other and more complex factors.

These are, I think, broadly contained within three categories. The character and ability of the members of the central legislature are important. The body which nominates them as candidates, the conditions on which men are admitted as candidates, obviously here count for much. The work of men like Ostrogorski and Graham Wallas has thrown a vivid light upon what may be termed the pathology of parliamentarianism. This, as I believe, is most largely due to the fact that our civilisation is organised, not for service, but for acquisition. It is dominated by the view that success means wealth, and the general stream of tendency in society is, accordingly, poisoned at its source. Here, once more, emerges the importance of that system of rights already outlined. It constitutes the second great factor in the building of an adequate method of representation. It acts as a check upon what a co-ordinating body can do, it defines the limits within which it can work. It means, for example, that there is outside it an alert-minded, because educated electorate, and that the power of property to sway its decisions is consciously limited. It means that it cannot interfere with the expression of opinion. It ensures, I think, the existence of parties the aims of which are more realistic, the terms of conflict between which are less, likely to involve the defeat of the general purposes of the State.

The third category is that of the information at the disposal of the co-ordinating authority. Its significance, I think, can hardly be over-estimated. Anyone who reads the speeches in an average debate of Congress or the House of Commons, and compares those speeches with the criticism, say, of a physical theory by physicists, will be appalled at the quality of the evidence upon which we rely for social decisions. It is defective in three primary ways. It is inadequate, first, in the range that it covers. Anyone, for example, who analyses the housing problem in England will find that we have no exact information upon any one of the constituent factors upon which that problem depends. The coal industry, again, is the only one whose organisation has been at all systematically surveyed. The most elementary statistics are lacking upon which successful educational policy depends. "Social processes", says Mr. Lippmann,[13] "are recorded spasmodically, quite often as accidents of administration. Though it (the material) deals with the conscious life of his fellow-citizens, it is all too often distressingly opaque, because the man who is trying to generalise has practically no supervision of the way his data are collected". We need immensely to develop the business of expert fact-finding if we are to possess the body of information out of which sound conclusions can emerge, and this, it should be added, is one of the most urgent ways in which the opinion formed by the public press may be invested with the atmosphere of myth.

But the finding of facts is one thing; their interpretation is another. Facts have to be evaluated by those to whom their import is directly relevant. What is here important is the way in which the co-ordinating authority is linked to the body of experience it is seeking to serve. At present, that linkage is largely a chaotic group of relationships, without even attempt at system. The opinion that filters through, the emphasis, accordingly, the co-ordinating body receives, is at every point spasmodic and haphazard. The validity of co-ordination depends upon two things. It depends, first, upon the way in which it is built from the experience it is seeking to co-ordinate, and the way, secondly, that the solution it reaches is later administered. I have already discussed these questions in part, and I shall later indicate in detail the institutions they seem to me to involve. Here it is enough to point out the grounds upon which I am emphasising the importance of this linkage, if representation is to be effective.

I am arguing that the only way to do things for people is to make them do things for themselves, that men who stand outside a situation can only be made responsible about it by being driven to make their minds march along with those who are inside. But they must not choose those whom they think inside, as, for instance, modern governments choose trade unionists who have long lost touch with the mind of labour to "represent" labour on inquiries they initiate. Those so chosen must be the nominated choices of the interests organised for consultation. We need, in short, permanent and continuous organs which are consulted before decisions are reached. If legislation is introduced about the mines, we need to know that the Minister of Mines has had to weigh the facts and opinions of every interest directly involved in mining. We need a system, to take an obvious example, which does for public bills, and in a coherently systematic way, what is now done for private bills in the House of Commons. We need, that is, to interweave the relationship of the co-ordinating authority to the group affected by it. For we then make that group share in the decision we reach. We make it interpenetrate with that decision so as to ensure the infusion of its experience into the will given effectiveness. We prevent the crystallisation of that will before it has sought the necessary foundations upon which it is to be built. We mould the purposes of each social function into a unity where they may so recognise their purpose as to admit the rightness of that unity. We maximise inventiveness by making our social decisions grow from the largest range we can hope to encompass.

I do not mean to imply that this method of making solutions will enable us to avoid all disagreement. The interests in society are too diverse to make it probable that men can always pool their differences by conferring upon them. A co-ordinating authority determined upon secular education could not, obviously, persuade the representatives of the Roman Catholic Church to accept its views. But I think it probable that their joint search into their differences would find a meeting-ground where each felt that its purpose found a just realisation, and it is not unlikely that this will be true of many of the problems we now state in the form of mutually exclusive alternatives. I think it possible that those who desire, and those who oppose, the nationalisation of banks might by conference reach a plan of organisation that would satisfy the fears of bureaucracy on the one hand and the dread of irresponsible finance on the other. Problems will, of course, arise in which the interests participating will feel that they have been unjustly treated; and they will fight rather than give way. There will even be occasions in which that injustice is real, and their pugnacity intelligible. But we can at least minimise that danger.

But when the solution has been made, it has to be applied. Here, I suggest, is the largest area of future inventiveness. The less there is of complex detail in the decisions of a co-ordinating authority, the more of flexibility that enables creative adjustment to the special case, the more are those decisions likely to be fruitful. We have recognised something of this in the principle of the grant in aid. We have admitted even more in the abrogation of Parliamentary Sovereignty where the will of the Dominions is concerned. What we need is to multiply the channels through which the general civic standards may be translated at the circumference into locally applied statutes. We need to let the cotton industry legislate for itself within the ambit of the general level at which the society broadly aims. We need to allow it to grow organs which can take initiative in detail on its behalf. War experience has thrown much light on possibilities of this kind. The Cotton Control Board, for example, was an instance where the solutions made were effective because they were administered by those who lived directly by the results; and its success is the more striking when the generally antithetic nature of the interests to be organised is borne in mind.[14] The plain lesson of the record of Works Committees during the war is that solutions which are the result of self-imposed authority operate far better that those imposed from without.[15] The power of the Shop-Steward Movement was largely derived from the fact that their connection with the rank and file looked outwards from within instead of looking inwards from without.[16] They were able to integrate their relationship with their constituents in a way impossible to other persons. They spoke much more nearly the mind of the workshop than others could hope to do, because they were in and of it. Their demands met the support they did because they grew recognisably out of a similar experience. What we need is to plan our industrial organisation as it relates to the State so that the voice which speaks to the State may have a character as genuine and veracious.

### (iv) Co-ordination and Federalism

My point may perhaps be made by saying that since society is essentially federal in nature, the body which seeks to impose the necessary unities must be so built that the diversities have a place therein. If it is true, as I have argued, that no association included the whole of myself, no association can legislate successfully for the whole of myself. No body, therefore, that builds directly from me can co-ordinate the various relationships which radiate outwards from any individual save as those relationships have an organised connection with it. It is not, I think, practicable to make that body a function of functions in the sense of building it from representatives elected by the various associations in society. Such a body would be unwieldy and remote. It would settle questions that are not, in fact, germane to the spheres within which its members had worked prior to their choice as members. An engineering guild as such, for example, cannot have general views upon foreign policy, it can have views only upon engineering and such decisions in foreign policy as affect engineers as engineers. The case for the territorial State is the final case that it moves beyond the partial glimpse to the wholeness into which those partial glimpses must be fitted. That wholeness is never perfect, never even adequate. But it is more likely, under conditions here outlined, to be effective than in an *ad hoc* body made from categories that are ultimately not less artificial than the territorial entities upon which we now depend, and it provides the one plane upon which men may meet under the conditions of an equality which alone gives validity to such ultimate solutions as we adopt.

But because society is federal, authority must be federal also. That involves, I have argued, the making of decisions out of the interests which will be effected by them, and, in turn, their application by those interests. It means making the mining industry a unit of administration in the same sense as Lancashire. It means surrounding the Ministry of Education with bodies entitled to speak on behalf of the parties to the educational process, and entitled to be consulted because they are entitled to speak. It means the abandonment of the sovereign State in the sense which equates the latter with society and gives it, thereby, the right to dictate to associations within society. Because it abandons the principle of sovereignty, it abandons the principle of hierarchy also. It does not envisage the allegiance of man as a series of concentric circles of which the great and all-embracing circle is the State. It sees him as bound now here, now there, as his experience seems to warrant in each problem that arises. It insists that his ultimate allegiance is not to some collective entity outside himself, but to the ideals his experience has taught him in his conscience to accept. It makes decision his business and his choice. It does so because, otherwise, human values are largely lost, and we lose the sense of personal good which is, in the end, the most precious of all. For our achievements, to be real, must take place in the additions they make to the happiness of individual men and women, if they are to be lasting and substantial. It is no use adding to the glory of a Church save by securing the salvation of its members. It is no use enriching a society unless the citizens of that society share as individuals in the gain that is won.

It need not be denied that the organisation which here emerges is immensely more complex than that which we have inherited. The grounds of complexity lie in the facts. Our civilisation is for the most part built upon the assumption that power belongs to a few, and our institutions have been constructed to make those few retain their power. Largely, they are not democratic institutions, because they do not attempt to take account of the mass of experience affected by their working. Their philosophy, in so far as they have a philosophy, is fringed about with these derived from an earlier stage of history when the common man could be disregarded by its processes. We are seeking different ends. By liberty we mean initiative for all men and not for some men, by equality we mean that each personality shall win such significance as it is entitled to, and not live as the servant of other personalities. We cannot so widen the horizon of the State purpose without great changes. We are living in a world the processes of which are, in general, set by the experience of the French Revolution. Its validity is largely exhausted for ourselves, or, rather, its validity has been found applicable to a much wider experience than it was, at its apogee, able to survey. We have to make provision for that extension.

The principle which underlies the organisation here envisaged is simple, even if its application is intricate. Postulating that ethical values are personal, and that each individual is entitled to act as his instructed conscience warrants him in acting, it finds the principle of social systems in the idea of function. By function it means the purpose aimed at by a body of men and women acting in concert. It argues that a function has validity, needs, therefore, recognition, because it grows naturally out of an experience they have proved for themselves. It represents a want, the response to which means happiness. It does not argue that all functions can be reconciled into a synthesis which embraces them all. It admits that many are conflicting, sometimes through ignorance, sometimes through genuine and permanent incompatibility. It admits, also, the necessity of a scheme of co-ordination that will enable the uniformities to be administered which are necessary because men live together in large societies. But it insists that the co-ordination shall grow from within, and not be imposed from without. It argues that the experience of no group of men is ever wide enough or true enough to make it possible for them to be entrusted, in any other way, with final powers. It agrees that a coercive authority is necessary, but it is distrustful of a coercive authority. It is distrustful because the psychological penumbra which surrounds coercion deadens those who exert it to the needs and wants of others. It limits the experience which enters into the decision made. It is exercised for the advantage of the few who possess its instruments, or have access to those possessors. It narrows the validity of wants by equating the welfare of a few with the happiness of the community.

To attempt a creative co-ordination it erects the authority which coordinates a system of guarantees or limitations. That system, admittedly, is intricate. Its framework is a system of rights postulated as natural because experience has shown them to be the necessary conditions of a good life. A man, we argue, cannot be his best self if he is involved in a perpetual struggle to satisfy the barest minimum of physical appetites. He must, therefore, win by his effort a sufficient wage, reasonable hours of labour, and such conditions of shelter as elevate his mind beyond wants otherwise sordid. But because his best self lives essentially in a spiritual world, his rights stretch beyond material necessity. He must interpret of and for himself what life seems to him to mean. His view of it is his own, and his isolation from his fellows means that no one can express it on his behalf. He must, therefore, have freedom of speech that he may make that view heard, and freedom of association that he may join with others to give substance to it. He must have the right to share in the government of the society in which he is involved. To that end, first of all, the right to education, is essential, for without it no man can formulate the meaning embodied in his experience of life. He must also have the right to vote for those by whom he is to be governed, and, as a corollary thereto, the right to be chosen, if he can, as a governor by his fellows. But self-government is not merely a matter of settling the character of the political fabric. Our lives are too must involved in the industrial vocation by which we live to admit of its nature being determined independently of our experience. Industrial democracy is, therefore, the necessary complement of political democracy. Self-government in the one completes the process of self-government in the other. It will, from its nature, involve a different type of organisation. The ascent in it to power will be graded more steeply in terms of technical competence. It will leave less room for the popular virtues, more opportunity for *expertise.* But the purpose to be served by the .rights maintained in each is in substance identical.

These rights, it must be added, do not maintain themselves. It is the clear result of history that they cannot be maintained in a society of which the chief motive is a love of monetary gain. Unless there is approximate equality of property as between its different members, their rights will in the mass be merely relative to the property they possess. The chief social motive must, therefore, be service, and property must be the result of service in personal terms. I must myself serve; I must not live by owning what arises from the service of another. While this excludes, at any rate over any period it is necessary to discuss, a rigorous communism, it certainly involves a large transformation of the legal rights now annexed to property. It assumes that the production of those goods and services without which the society cannot live must be directly organised by the society. It assumes that all other production must be carried out in terms of standards created and enforced as part of the minimum basis of civilised life. Where it leaves private enterprise in control of some allotted field, it defines with some vigour the conditions within which that private enterprise may work. For it insists that in all productive effort the public is an unseen partner whose wishes must be respected in the deed of partnership. It will not, for instance, allow the private employer to hire or discharge his workers as he pleases. It will not allow him to preserve that secrecy in finance which now so perverts the character of industry. Where capital is private, it argues that it has no more right to determine industrial policy, or to be the residuary legatee of industry, than the holders of the National Debt can justly determine foreign policy, or absorb some unwonted surplus in the Exchequer. It limits rigidly the rights of inheritance on the ground that no man is entitled to evade his contribution to the sum of social production. It believes that such a transvaluation of values, so far from destroying initiative and vigour, gives them opportunities of which, thus far in history, they have been rarely able to take advantage. It is confident that no other method gives the due weight to personality to which by its peculiar qualities it shows itself to be entitled.

Such a view as this involves a somewhat different attitude to liberty than that of the classical writers. It does not regard freedom merely as absence of restraint. It agrees that once men live together in the great society, there develop necessary uniformities of conduct which limit the habits possible of expression. But it does not, either, find the meaning of liberty in obedience to a rule laid down by a few in the interest of an order which protects mainly those few. Liberty in the social theory here urged means the exercise of initiative by each man in the attempt to secure the fulfilment of his best self. It means the guarantee of avenues through which that initiative may find its way to its appointed end. Obviously, therefore, liberty is inseparable from equality, since the *a priori* distinctions which announce differences of access restrict the chance of liberty to a few fortunately situated persons in the State. A society in which men are given an equal opportunity of self-realisation is, also, a society in which there is justice. For by justice we mean, as in the famous definition, the rendering to each man of his own. It is such an ordering of social arrangements as will give the maximum guarantee available that the wants of each individual receive their due recognition in the totality of wants supplied. It is not suggested that such recognition is, or can be, perfect. The magnitude of our scale of life makes certain the presence of confusion and error. But at least we can advance beyond the inherent possibilities of the existing system.

Justice implies law, but the view of law here outlined involves an unconventional approach to its definition. Law is, as Vinogradoff has said,[17] "a set of rules directing the relation and conduct of their (the State's) members". The important problem here is why the particular rules chosen are adopted, and how they work in the life of the society. Laws as such we discern to be morally neutral; they are merely decisions which get accepted in the presence of social forces. We reject, that is to say, the view of law which regards it as just merely because of its source of origin. We even refuse to take as urgent in the estimate of its claim the fact that it proceeds from good intent. For good intent may be ignorant or mistaken. It may come from a view of the facts too narrow to hope for adequacy. It may be blind to the extent of the forces it is its business to satisfy. For the end of law is the satisfaction of human wants. That means not the wants of a few, not the wants deemed right by those applying the law, but the totality of wants encountered by law. Law, therefore, to be justice, must be the expression of relations found adequate in the experience of men.

Who, it will be asked, are to act as judges of that adequacy? There can, I think, be only one answer to that question. The judges are all of those who desire that their desires should be fulfilled, the body of members, that is, in the given society Law, therefore, to be found adequate must be built upon an induction from the widest possible experience it can know. It must attempt, in Miss Follett's happy phrase,[18] "the reciprocal fitting of needs one to the other". Once we begin that process of reciprocal adjustment, we move from the earlier sphere of contract to the sphere of status or relation. The movement of societies is then no longer one, as in Maine's view, from status to contract, but a movement from contract to relation. It is an endeavour to make rights and duties flow from the functions involved. It makes, for instance, the liability of an employer dependent, not upon the thing he wills, but the will which experience deems to be involved in the relations occupied by an employer in the general social fabric.[19] In agency we interpret, not a contract of mandate, but a system of rights and duties which arise in the relation of principal and agent. This is a return to the basis of feudalism in distinction to the central notion of Roman law which seeks to give effect to the wills of the actors in the particular incident involved.[20] What, of course, is important for us in this doctrine of relation is the proportionate power of the parties to it. We have, that is to say, in judging law not merely to regard the fact that interests are united, but also the way in which they are united. For that way, in fact, determines the relation reached. If one party is at an advantage over another, the substance of law is affected in its favour. That is clear, for instance, in the game laws; it is clear in the general foundations of the law of master and servant. If law is to represent a "reciprocal fitting of needs", it cannot be right, as Acton said,[21] that one party should have retained "the making of the laws, the management of the conditions, the keeping of the peace, the administration of justice, the distribution of taxes, the control of expenditure, in its own hands exclusively". Reciprocal fitting only takes place where there is equality of power between the parties to the adjustment.

If law, therefore, is to order human relationships rightly, it must be built upon a right induction from human experience. But no such experience can be rightly interpreted unless it is systematically organised and systematically recorded. For to co-ordinate the innumerable and often conflicting social interests into a sufficient wholeness for the purpose of order is the most subtle and delicate of all tasks. We may premise that neither one man nor one class of men can hope to be sufficiently acquainted with their range and meaning, and that even less than in the past because of the high specialisation involved in the division of labour. I would even suggest that no class is less fitted for this co-ordination than the industrial class which, since the beginning of the nineteenth century, has mainly performed it or controlled its performance. It is composed of men whose genius has been specialised to the acquisition of fortune under the intricate conditions of a world-market. They tend, quite naturally, to look upon life merely or mainly as a conflict for wealth under terms which they only can fully understand because they have in fact framed them. What they mean by those terms has been well set out in the judgement of the court in *Mogul Steamship Co.* v. *McGregor*.[22] What, in fact, it broadly implies is the absence of a social context in the business relation. The industrial class will sell their service as they can and for what they can, and if public difficulty is involved in their activities, that is no concern of theirs. If legislation attempts restraint upon those activities, there is no limit, as American experience plainly shows, to the effort they will make either to annul or evade it. Nothing in all this precludes the view that they are admirable husbands and model parents, or that they act as I have suggested on other than the highest ground. But because they are involved in a narrow circle of special interest, they are too limited in their view to grasp the multiform relation of which law must be the expression. They are unsuited, that is, to dominate the State. For their power to equate their partial experience with the total social need inevitably results, not in the making of effective adjustments, but in the undue precipitation of conflict.

That is why, as I have argued, only approximate equality of property will enable the individual to make his experience duly felt. That is why, also, his experience, as it associates itself with that of his fellows, needs organised relation to the State if the law is to be suffused with justice. For law is not found, but made. It is written out of the experience brought home to those who have its ultimate definition in their hands. They permeate it with the wants and desires which make themselves felt in the total push of social action. It is not the abstract outcome of judicial or legislative momentum. Someone's urgency has shaped it one way rather than another way. Its life, as Mr. Justice Holmes has finely said, is in its experience and not its logic, and its "inarticulate major premise" has always been the will that has been powerful enough to inform that life. In the feudal period those so powerful were, mainly, the owners of land; in our own day they are, mainly again, the holders of industrial capital. And because their wills represent only a part of the needs struggling for satisfaction, the law becomes biased against those whose speech, as law is formulated, goes unheard. It loses authority because they do not recognise it as implicit with the substance also of their own desires. It fails to bind them to allegiance because what it ordains benefits, not themselves, but others. Only when it is based upon an induction to which each interest in the community has contributed does it truly co-ordinate, by creating a genuine, because general, satisfaction.

I say, therefore, that all men have an equal right to share in the making of law, and that only as our social arrangements make provision for that sharing will they win the loyalty of citizens. Otherwise, the rules accepted as law will be derived, not from the co-ordinating authority we call the State, but from that group whose rules seem to one or more citizens a truer response to their needs. For the sharing is important to the sanction needed by the process of making law. It enables us to find the methods by which we can interweave desires. It makes us in a position to grow our law out of the needs we totally confront, instead of dominating those needs by some special solution of which the substance is narrow and partisan. It makes the concepts of jurisprudence grow out of the facts of life, and thereby enables it the better to adjust itself to the changes in itself those facts will bring. It enables us to supplement the special perspective of the jurist by bringing him into contact with experiences and ideals from which his own environment is alien. I am arguing, broadly, that law has no moral appeal in any other terms. The legal order only makes itself valid by being the expression of the social order; and the social order means not one only but the whole of the myriad forces in our midst which are striving to fulfil their wants.

Here I may, perhaps, interpolate one remark. It is sometimes said that while the legal order is, as a rule, morally inferior to the ideals of a given period, it is always striving to make up its lost ground. The humanitarian temper, the power of equity, the compelling force of new facts, drive, so it is said, the legislature and the judge to adjust themselves to the growth of new needs. There is a real truth in this. We have Factory Acts at the height of the *laissez-faire* period; and the Lord Eldon who opposed every measure of social amelioration in Parliament was a great reforming judge, albeit but half-consciously, upon the Bench.[23] So, too, the pressure of business need has mitigated the irresponsibility of the State in the sphere of contract; and the *Conseil d'Etat* has ceased to protect the French government from its own blunders in those administrative courts which were held to transcend the rule of law.[24] But this is still inadequate. It is, as a continuous process, too accidental and haphazard to make certain that the adjustments effected are as nearly various as the needs encountered. Mr. Justice Holmes, for example, may be able to see that new ideas involve constitutional experiment, but the majority of his colleagues upon the Supreme Court of the United States will remain limited by an experience inherently alien from the new ideas.[25] The London County Council may admit that it is a valuable experiment in education to make school-children witness performances of Shakespeare's plays; but the absence of that novelty from the statutory definition of its powers will make the courts limit the concept of education to the earlier and more formalistic view.

That is why I have insisted on the systematic record and organisation of experience. The co-ordinating authority may still be chosen by persons who are not differentiated as they choose by the vocations into which they enter. That absence of differentiation is, I think, essential because it is simple, and involves the territorial basis of government. But the groups we encounter in social and industrial life need to be federally related to the government if the decisions of the latter body are to be wise. That means, I have urged, giving to those groups the means of prior and organic influence with government before it pronounces upon the problems of co-ordination. It means weighing their opinions, seeking their criticisms, meeting their special needs. It means, further, allowing them responsibility in their own life, the responsibility which comes from power over their intimate affairs. It means that Manchester can have a municipal theatre without Parliamentary sanction. It means, also, that (I use for the moment, a neutral term) the governing body of the mining industry can force upon its constituents, if it so desire, a pension scheme for miners over and above the national old-age pension. It means, broadly speaking, less direct administration by the State and a more flexible application of its statutes in terms of the varying situations to which they apply. It conceives, accordingly, of State-statutes as minimum solutions, and leaves to the interests they affect, as these are organised, the power and, not seldom, the duty of adding to them. The result will be a more intricate world; but it will be the better because its activities will have the chance of creative adventure.

Above all, it may be suggested, it will make, and for the first time, the co-ordinating work of the State a matter of principle. It will not say, as now, that somehow order must be preserved, and that the State is simply the body to which the keeping of order is entrusted. For the keeping of order, important as it is, may subordinate to itself all that is worth while in the purposes of society; and a State which is informed mainly or wholly by that desire will use its power to dwarf the moral stature of its citizens. For it cannot be too often insisted that power is poisonous to those who exercise it unless their authority is checked always by urgent criticism, and, if need be, in the end by resistance. That power, granted the weapons now at its disposal, is so vast that it can easily, in the effort after certainty, destroy all that there is of individuality in men. It tends, unless we are vigilant, to assume that silence means contentment, and that disturbance implies, not research into the grievance that it indicates, but punishment for the excess its form has assumed. It keeps men uninspired and uniform, inert and ignorant. It can, as in pre-revolutionary Russia, literally make a desert and call it peace. So used, power is the more disastrous because it merely postpones the day of reckoning. The absence from it of a larger purpose makes its organs the subjects of a conflict for the spoils they promise. They are then attacked from within; and alike their defenders and their opponents will seek the support of those outside the ranks of authority by appealing to them in the name of principles until then forgotten. Because the minds of men are responsive to noble desires, such appeal will not be made in vain.

The State here outlined is not, I think, so liable to these defects. It can claim that it performs a natural function. It is built to defend the civic minimum of rights without which, as I argued earlier, no man can hope to be his best self. It has no exact boundaries to the area it occupies, for life cannot be contained within categories of mathematical precision. It cannot even define itself those boundaries at any given moment of action in *a priori* terms. That does not mean that its function is any the less real, for any given purpose has to grow into, to make adjustments with, other purposes, in order to fulfil its end. The State protects the wholeness of men over and above those parts which express themselves through groups more specific in character. It does not do so by being something over and above them. It co-ordinates with them by associating itself with them, by becoming a means through which they reach a general medium of expression. To that end, it seeks to embody the largest induction open to it. It speaks, not for some, but for all. It decides, not for a few, but for the whole. It includes experience and does not exile experience. It is, for instance, legitimate for the Roman Catholic Church to deny salvation to all outside its membership: that is the condition of its being. But a State must secure temporal salvation for all who own its citizenship. It can do so only by counting as equal in worth the personalities of its citizens. For it, on this plane, there must be neither Jew nor Greek, neither bond nor free. It must compound its notions of general well-being from the total environment it encounters.

In such fashion the State might become a genuine search for social integration. It might cease to be the organ of a few because its will would become instinct with the desires of the many. It would be responsive, not to the purposes of those whose power makes their demands immediately urgent, but to all who have an individuality they would preserve and enlarge. They would be able to make their desires articulate. They would be able to feel that their desires were weighed, not in terms of the economic pressure they represent, but the social value they embody. Their experience of life, their sense of the meaning it has for themselves, would be taken into account. Such a State might be the true organ of a community, the meeting-ground on which its varied purposes found the means of a unity adequate for its general enrichment. It would not impose a uniform rule. It would recognise that the material is too diverse to permit of such simplicity. It could be taken as suffused with good faith in a sense in which the State in our own day is void of such virtue.[26] It will be less safe, doubtless, in the sense that its pronouncements of right will be more hardly won, and less inertly accepted, than is now the case. But that is likely to make it more careful in the making of its rules, at once more scrupulous in building their foundations, and more elastic in fitting them to the forces they seek to control.

But all this will hold only on two conditions. The State that is to achieve an ambition so high must begin by organising criticism of itself. It must posit fallibility as its foundation. It must realise that what it does is not right because it has willed to do it, but right because it works. And it can know that its will works justly only by the estimation of its results in the lives of those affected by them. Such knowledge means two things. It means, first of all, a citizen-body alert to the errors of government. Its members must be so disciplined in mind that they can appreciate the synthesis made, can also directly contribute themselves to its making. A State in which the art of politics is, in its general terms, apprehended only by a few can never enrich the lives of the many. For it can never genuinely know the wants of the many. It can only roughly imagine those wants by assuming their identity with the wants of its own directors. That identity is an unproven hypothesis, unproven because, predominantly, it is untrue. And the degree of its ignorance is the measure of the misinterpretation it will make. Because, therefore, that knowledge is so precious to it, the life-blood of the State is freedom of speech. To set boundaries to the effort of the mind is always, at least ultimately, to frustrate that effort. To stigmatise inconvenient thought as sedition, or blasphemy, or evil is, sooner or later, to stifle thought itself. Inconvenient thought rarely means other than unconventional thought, and unconventional thought is the parent of social discovery.

The second condition is that we take increasing opportunity to improve the quality of the information upon which we act. Our decisions are not taken in a vacuum. Whatever we do has its outcome in actions which may affect myriads of human lives. The picture in a statesman's head, say, of the intentions of Japan, may be the little increment which tips the beam towards peace or war. We have to analyse our environment, to measure the results of that environment. We have to transcend our self-centred experience, and the prejudices to which it gives rise, by externalising, by making as objective as we can, the pictures of the world about us. We want, for instance, statistics of miners' wages, not statistics of the mine-owners' view of miners' wages, and statistics of the miners' view; all that we derive from these are arguments to strengthen a decision we had already decided to make without them. Self-interest can only be persuaded from its subjectivity as it meets that audit by record which reveals its patent selfhood. We are deceived by press and party, by Church and State, because we lack the machinery of co-ordinated knowledge. We do not know the meaning of our activities because we do not in any serious way attempt to record them. Yet without that record the conflicts of modern social life are but a blind grouping in a darkened room.

I neither suggest nor believe that such a political system as this is likely to resolve our doubts and difficulties in a final way. Life is a kinetic thing, and the solutions we make only give rise to new problems. We create desires by satisfying desires. But I believe that such a State might hope, as it has not now the right to hope, to get its decisions accepted. It might claim to have gathered to itself a larger volume of experience deeply felt and carefully measured than in any previous time. It would have left a larger room for individual action and corporate action than the highly unified State of which we are now seeing the slow erosion. It would have bound to itself that passionate loyalty which comes to a great leader when men find in his words the echo of the song in their own hearts.

Yet it will not always get its decisions accepted. Man is nature's rebel, and it is his habit to protest against the will that seeks to bind his will. Where there is refusal of consent, we must not assume, whatever the character of government, that such refusal is wrong. Grievance never proceeds to rebellion unless it is deeply grounded in a sense of wrong. Grievance is never adequately met by suppression of its symptoms. Whatever the form and substance of the State, the judgment upon its policy, the resolution of conflict where it meets antagonism, remain a matter for the individual mind. It is there only that effective choices can be made. It is there only that allegiance arises from conviction. Athanasius is not reconciled by the issue of a command; he makes his peace by finding that the legal order can be so adjusted as to embody what he desires. The possibility, in every situation, that Athanasius may be right can only be overlooked when we prefer authority to truth, and the habit of such preference is, ultimately, to prefer ourselves to authority. That is the certain highroad to anarchy. For the real destruction of a social order arises, not from the existence of passionate dissent, but from the determination to refuse to dissent the opportunity of satisfaction; and that refusal is, as a rule, ground for the suspicion that dissent has right upon its side.

Whatever has here been said of the internal relations of a State holds also, with no less emphasis, of its external context. The nation-State is not the final unit of social organisation. Its power as a sovereign body represents a phase only of historic experience, and the pressure of world-forces has already made its sovereignty obsolete for any creative purpose. The nation-State is entitled to autonomy in all concerns of which the incidence is obviously local, but immediately what it wants and does impinges upon the interests of the larger world outside, its will is only one of many factors which must go to the making of a decision. It may choose its own Prime Minister; it is not entitled to settle the scale of its armament. It may dig its own coal; but it is not entitled so to pick and choose in the marketing of its coal that it deliberately prejudices the interests of other nation-States. The conditions, particularly economic, of modern civilisation demand the habit of organised international co-operation. We can only secure that habit by building institutions through which it may grow to its appointed purpose. Such institutions are incompatible with the existence of States which assert their will independently of the will of others. The incompatibility is the greater because, too often, the range of experience upon which that will is based is so narrow as in fact to traverse the needs therein implied. We can only remedy the danger that State power suffers perversion in the sphere of international affairs by making that State the subject of a control beyond itself. We need not postulate, for that end, the obsolete fiction of State equality. But we must at least assure to States, whatever their size, that their claims are met in terms of right and not in terms of force. War, therefore, must be outlawed; and the whole effort of civilisation must be directed against those States which trust to war as the instruments of their purpose. That implies a federal organisation of States, a will built from the integrating of interests in conference. It means, doubtless, the subordination of the great State to ends outside itself, and it will be difficult to win the surrender of their prestige. Yet no other way lies open to us if we are to prevent war on the one hand, and, on the other, to secure economic justice between peoples.

### (v) Law as a Source of Authority

To those for whom law is a simple command, legal by virtue of the source from which it comes, it is not likely that such complexities as these will be popular. We are urging that law is, in truth, not the will of the State, but that from which the will of the State derives whatever moral authority it may possess. That is, admittedly, the abandonment of simplicity. It assumes that the rationale of obedience is in all the intricate facts of social organisation and in no one group of facts. It denies at once the sovereignty of the State, and that more subtle doctrine by which the State is at once the master and the servant of law by willing to limit itself to certain tested rules of conduct. It insists that what is important in law is not the fact of command but the end at which that command aims and the way it achieves the end. It sees society, not as a pyramid in which the State sits crowned upon the summit, but as a system of co-operating interests through which, and in which, the individual finds his scheme of values. It argues that each individual scheme so found gives to the law whatever of moral rightness it contains. Law, that is to say, is made valid by my experience of it, and not by the fact that it is presented to me as law. Such experience, indeed, is rarely separate in kind (though it is always unique in degree) because it is shared with others in the effort to make an impact upon society. It appears as an interest which seeks the objectivity of realisation. It strives to suffuse the law with its sense of need. It judges the law by what it recognises therein of that sense as satisfied. It therefore demands a system of social conditions in which the end capable of being achieved is both worthy of achievement and relevant to itself. Therein appears the importance of the idea of rights. For these make the path of law a road which leads to the fulfilment of desire; and those who seek fulfilment are entitled to consider their needs equal in significance to the needs of others. Law then emerges as the evaluation of the interests by the interweaving of interests. It is a function of the whole social structure and not of some given aspect of it. Its power is determined by the degree to which it aids what that whole social structure reports as its desires.[27]

From the conception of law as the evaluation of interests we reach the most fruitful view available of the place of the individual in society. We can admit that some interests are so personal to a man's self that they can gain fulfilment only in isolation. We can thereby avoid the falsity of that philosophy which sees each man as meaningless save as a part of some social whole. We can admit, further, that interests may be incompatible and that even where harmony is possible the effort of adjustment is long and subtle. All the co-ordination achieved represents some sacrifice; and it is important to realise that the judgment of whether the sacrifice achieved is worth its cost can be made by individuals alone.

Their judgment, doubtless, will be different because their relations are never identical. The perspective is made through the shifting kaleidoscope of innumerable personalities. The rightness of that judgment will depend upon the care and knowledge with which men seek to make an integration of their wants with those of others. The judgment will never be complete or perfect because it is part of a process rooted in the past and stretching out towards an unknown horizon. The synthesis each man achieves creates, of course, a system of habits, and these, as they seek articulation with the habits of others, are bound to cause stress and pain. It is necessary, accordingly, to minimise the conflict which ensues as interests jostle one another in the struggle for survival. No adjustment effected is ever worth while save as it is reported as adequate by the largest number of minds influenced by its results.

That adequacy, of course, does not mean something merely personal or selfish. It means that whatever the individual judges as of value is recorded as valuable in the push of events. It means that his sense of right is that alone which validates for him the meaning of social organisation, and that there is no other way securing validation from him. I deny, therefore, that submission is ever a moral obligation unless, as an act, it carries with it the individual conviction of rightness which makes it moral. No *jus est quod jussum est* from a State will ever do more than compel upon a plane outside the field of ethics unless it carries with it a satisfying moral appeal. We cannot be certain that it will. We can only hope that decisions prepared for acceptance will be scrutinised with responsibility and with a due regard for what they totally imply.

Any other view has little relevance to the facts about us. Any other view is seeking to invest coercive authority with ethical content on grounds which analysis shows to be simply the fact of the power to coerce. That power may hew its way to success, but it does not, by the fact of victory, become a moral agent. We argue, rather, that our rules of conduct are justified only as what they are in working induces our allegiance to them. No such result can be known until those affected report that they accept the rules precisely on that ground. And those affected will not be in a position so to report until they have the power to make themselves respected. They can do so only when they win their due place in the negotiations which precede decision. That place can be assigned them if we conceive it as won, not by force, but by a give and take in which the unequal pressure of interests is mitigated by our knowledge of what, as property, for instance, ensures disharmony. It does not mean that we must take each man, as in the Benthamite view, to be the best judge of his own interests; but it does involve, I think, our willingness to recognise that each man's sense of his own interests is a fact we may not disregard. We have, therefore, to allow his personality full access to the organs which register our ultimate decisions. We have to maximise the responsiveness of those organs to the will he seeks to express. Out main effort must be to discipline his mind to the expression of his wants and to make possible such an enrichment of that mind that the satisfaction of those wants achieves a good something more than purely personal. We shall, of course, succeed but partially, for it is difficult in the pressure and scale of modern administration to have more than a partial glimpse of his need. Obviously, therefore, the more firmly we can make his sense of need available for us, the more likely are we to make possible for him the full realisation of his powers. And nothing else can justify the process of government.

Two other remarks may be made. It follows from what has been said that men are entitled to disobey a State which ceases to secure their self-realisation. Rebellion, therefore, is, as T.H. Green insisted, a contingent duty on the part of the citizen. To many this has seemed a doctrine of anarchy, and they have therefore sought to avoid its implications either by arguing that I cannot realise myself save through the State, or, as with Green himself, that I ought not to resist unless at least a considerable body of persons share my view and are willing to act with me. Neither of these views is, I think, well founded. The only State to which I owe allegiance is the State in which I discover moral adequacy; and if a given State fails to satisfy that condition I must, to be consistent with my own moral nature, attempt experiment. It is, of course, true that I can only realise myself in the ideal State; but we are not entitled to assume that any given State is seeking to achieve the ideal save as it proves that assumption by its use of power. Green's view is a wiser one; but what he urges is rather he higher expediency than a rigorous logic. Most action of this kind is inevitably minority action. Most minority action will fail unless it enlists upon its side at least the inertia of the multitude. Our first duty is to be true to our conscience, and we are the more likely to press the State into the service of right the more we fulfil that duty. We may have to pay the penalty. We may find ourselves involved in an effort far vaster than we intended to provoke. But unless we do that which it lies in us to do, our citizenship is nullified just at the moment where it becomes an urgent thing. We act, always, at our peril; but the peril involved in obedience may in the end be greater than the penalty of rebellion.

It has been said, also, that the individual for whose best self the State exists has little to contribute that we are entitled to regard as significant. What he is and does leaves little impress upon the record of mankind. To adjust the temper of social effort to average men is to crown mediocrity as king. Rather we must recognise that quality is the possession of a few, and we must equate function with the possession of that quality. For, otherwise, we deny differences of value in activity, and, in particular, we fail to value things not easily apprehended, like art and science, save as they minister to measurable utilitarian advantage. To build upon the rule of number is to sacrifice all that gives to the best of life the peculiar virtue for which it searches. What, rather, we require is to limit the possession of power to the few who are fit to exert it. These, by their inherent worth, would act as the trustees of mankind.

Ever since Plato drew the first great pattern of an aristocracy that ideal has proved attractive. Yet, on examination, its virtue are less self-evident than a cursory glance would surmise. It is the record of all history that no class of men can retain over a period sufficient moral integrity to direct the lives of others. Sooner or later they pervert those lives to their own ends. And even if, in a rapid survey, the majority of men seem indistinguishable from their fellows, to themselves the fact of distinction is of the first importance. They cannot achieve happiness vicariously. They must know it with their own minds and their own hearts. They must themselves make their own lives, because it is in the art of creation that they can best hope to realise whatever there is in them of fineness and nobility. Nor have we the means at our disposal to measure the qualities we should wish to find in those who rule us before they appear in the opportunity we provide for their emergence. They confine themselves to no given class or race. We recognise them as they prove themselves; and by offering them the largest room for proof we ensure their richest provision. So regarded, men may strive to make themselves the masters of the event because they have the chance to meet the challenge of life. The world outside them may remain mysterious, but within them is the call to penetrate the mystery. It is a call not less to sacrifice than to fulfilment. Or, rather, it is a call to fulfilment through sacrifice. It is the demand that we treasure things of the spirit; that we suffuse pedestrian habit with creative purpose; that we quarrel not over the petty differences of possession, but over the great issues of the mind. It will require all the imagination and thought at our disposal if we are to meet the challenge like free men. It is the most difficult and arduous of adventures. Yet, as Spinoza said, all things excellent are as difficult as they are rare. We can reach the summit in the end if we but seek the courage to go forward.

## REFERENCES

1. A.G. Gardiner, *Sir William Harcourt*, ii. 587.
2. *Leviathan*, ii. 29.
3. Mr. W.Y. Elliott's *The Pragmatic Revolt in Politics* (1928) is an interesting attack on these views, and a fairly complete guide to the relevant contemporary literature.
4. Lord Emmott in the House of Lords, July 7, 1924.
5. Cf. Leon Duguit, *Le Droit Social, Le Droit Individual et L'Etat* (1908), pp. 134 f.
6. *Social Theory*, p. 120.
7. *Life of George Tyrrell*, by M.D. Petre, ii. 196.
8. *Ibid.*, ii. 142.
9. *A Pluralistic Universe*, p. 321.
10. *Public Opinion*, p. 288.
11. *Social Theory*, chap. viii; *Guild Socialism Restated*, chap. vii-viii.
12. Chapter II.
13. *Public Opinion*, p. 374.
14. See H.D. Henderson, *The Cotton Control Board* (1922); and, more generally E.H.M. Lloyd, *Experiments in Certain State Controls* (1924).
15. Cf. the Report of the Ministry of Labour on Works Committees (1919), especially pp. 32, 117.
16. Cf. G.D.H. Cole, *Workshop Organisation* (1923), especially chaps. iv, v, x, xi.
17. *Historical Jurisprudence*, i. 52.
18. *Creative Experience*, p. 264.
19. Cf. my *Foundations of Sovereignty*, chap. viii.
20. Cf. Pound, *The Spirit of the Common Law*, especially lecture i., where this view is fully discussed.

21. *Letters to Mary Gladstone*, pp. 194-5.
22. (1892) A.C. 25.
23. It was Eldon who, by his decision in *Lloyd* v. *Learing* 6, *Vesey* 773, made possible the development of corporation law in the nineteenth century. Cf. my *Foundations of Sovereignty*, chap. iv.
24. *Ibid.*, chap. iii, especially pp. 130 ff.
25. Cf. Frankfurter, *The Constitutional Opinion of Mr. Justice Holmes, Harvard Law Review*, June 1916.
26. That is why, I think, Mr. Elliott's view of the modern State as essentially an umpire in the social conflict is inadequate. It assumes the impartiality of its agents, *op. cit.*
27. See this well put in the translator's introduction to Krabbe, *The Modern Idea of the State* (1922), especially pp. xlv f.; and cf. my paper on *The State and Law* in *Economica* for Nov. 1929.

**Part 2**

# 8. Political Institutions

## (i) The Forms of Political Power

The modern State, for practical purposes, consists of a relatively small number of persons who issue and execute orders which affect a larger number in whom they are themselves included; and it is of the essence of its character that, within its allotted territory, all citizens are legally bound by those orders.

What are the forms through which they should move to their appointed end? Since the time of Aristotle, it has been generally agreed that political power is divisible into three broad categories. There is, first, the legislative power. It enacts the general rules of the society. It lays down the principles by which the members of the society must set their course. There is, secondly, the executive power. It seeks to apply those rules to particular situations; where, for instance, an Old Age Pension Law has been enacted, it pays out the specified sum to those entitled to receive it. There is, thirdly, the judicial power. This determines the manner in which the work of the executive has been fulfilled. It sees to it that the exercise of executive authority conforms to the general rules laid down by the legislature; it may, as in *Ex parte O'Brien*,[1] declare that the particular order issued is, in fact, *ultra vires*. It settles also the relationship between private citizens, on the one hand, and between citizens and the government upon the other, where these give rise to problems which do not admit of solution by agreement.

It may be admitted at the outset that these categories are of art and not of nature. It is perfectly possible to conceive of all these functions being performed by a single body, or even in the name of a single person; and in the modern democratic state the distinction between them cannot, in fact, be consistently maintained. Legislatures often perform executive acts, as when the Senate of the United States confirms the nominations of the President. They perform judicial duties also; the House of Lords is a Court to pass upon impeachments authorised by the House of Commons. Executive bodies, especially in recent times, perform acts it is difficult to distinguish from legislation, on the one hand, and judicial functions on the other; of which the provisional order system in England, and the power of the Ministry of Health in *Arlidge* v. *Local* Government Board[2] are sufficient examples. The judiciary, moreover, is constantly acting as an executive. The English judges issue rules under the Judicature Acts. They act also as a legislature when they give expression to that part of the law not formally enacted by statute;[3] and it is a striking fact that the responsibility of the French State has been largely created by the jurisprudence of the *Conseil d'Etat*.[4] There exist, moreover, in every State powers like that of declaring war and making treaties, of recognising governments already *de facto* as *de jure,* of the veto of legislation by an executive authority, which it is no easy matter to classify with any precision. Little, indeed, is gained by the formal attempt—the effort, for instance, to make the judicial power merely a species of executive authority—to distinguish between the different types of function here outlined. For rules formulated to govern particular cases become, if they work satisfactorily, general rules; and general rules, in their turn, are made obsolete by the manner, or the result, of their application.

It may yet be fairly argued that, in every State, some distinction between the three powers is essential to the maintenance of freedom. Since the work of Locke and Montesquieu, we have come generally to admit the truth of Madison's remark that "the accumulation of all powers ... in the same hands ... may justly be pronounced the very definition of tyranny."[5] Nor is the reason for this insistence far to seek. Power that is not in some fashion divided is bound to be absolute; and power being, by its very nature, dangerous to those who exercise it, it needs to be limited before it can be exercised with safety. This was put concisely by Montesquieu in some famous sentences. "When the legislative and executive powers", he said,[6] "are united in the same persons or body, there can be no liberty, because apprehensions may arise lest the same monarch or senate should enact tyrannical laws, to enforce them in a tyrannical manner.... Were the power of judging joined with the legislature, the life and liberty of the subject would be exposed to arbitrary control, for the judge would then be the legislator. Were it joined to the executive power, the judge might behave with all the violence of an oppressor".

It is not, I think, possible so to define the area of each of these three authorities that each remains independent and supreme in its allotted territory. The separation of powers does not mean the equal balance of powers. If it is, broadly speaking, the business of the executive to carry out those principles of general policy enacted by the legislature, it must retain the confidence of the latter body; and such confidence implies the power to compel subordination of the executive to its will. The legislature, that is to say, can directly secure, as a matter of right, that the substance of executive acts is suffused with what it deems to be its purposes. So, too, though more indirectly, with the judiciary. The legislature ought not to dictate to any judiciary the nature of the results it should attain in a particular case; but it is entitled, within the limits hereafter discussed, to provide by statute against the recurrence of a decision of which it is in disagreement with the principles. So, also, when a particular decision, as in the *Free Church of Scotland* case,[7] is likely to result in injustice, a legislative compromise is not an unfair solution of the problems raised. In general, therefore, the powers both of executive and judiciary find their limits in the declared will of the legislative organ.

The case is different in the relationship of executive and judiciary. It is the business of the judge to be the task-master of the executive. He has to see that its interpretation of its powers is never so elastic that it either arrogates novelty to itself or bears unequally upon the body of citizens. To such ends as these, it follows that every executive act should be open to scrutiny in the courts; and the decision of the judiciary would always be binding upon the executive unless the legislature otherwise resolves. There should never be the power in an executive body which enables it to escape the scrutiny of men less tempted than itself to identify will with authority. What Professor Dicey has called the rule of law is, with all its implications, fundamental. It means that the State must be put on an equality with all other bodies, that it must answer for its acts; it means, also, that no mysterious prerogative should intervene to prevent the attainment of justice. The power of the judiciary over the executive is, therefore, if contingent, nevertheless essential. The one limitation of substance is that the courts cannot act *propriis motibus*. There must be complaint before decision, and the complaint must come from the citizen body. But when the complaint is proved, the executive should have no authority to transcend the judicial will. Remedy, if remedy be required, is the business of the legislature.

This separation of functions need not imply, though it has been taken to imply, a complete separation of personnel. Montesquieu's mistaken view of the relation between executive and legislature in England, consecrated as it was by Blackstone, led to the theory that no bridges ought to be built between the organs which represent these various powers. But, as Duguit has pointed out,[8] the execution of any order involves the assistance of all ultimate authorities in the State; and the attempt, as in the American Constitution, rigidly to separate the three powers, has only meant the building of an extra-constitutional relationship between them. The use of the patronage, on the one hand, and the peculiar structure of parties, on the other, has effected by means open to serious question a conjunction between executive and legislature which needs, in any case, to be made. Much the best method of obtaining it is to make the executive, as in England and France, a committee of the legislature. Thereby a variety of ends are served. The executive can only stay in office so long as it retains the confidence of the legislature. A flexibility in its policy is thus assured which prevents that deadlock in action which occurs whenever the American President is at odds with Congress, and that even when his own party is in power. The presence of the executive in the legislature enables it to explain its policy in the one way that ensures adequate attention and organised criticism. It is not attention and criticism in a vacuum. It is attention from, and criticism by, those who are eager to replace the executive if it proves unconvincing. It thus makes for responsibility. It prevents a legislature which has no direct interest in administration from drifting into capricious statutes. It arrests that executive degeneration which is bound to set in when the policy of a ministry is not its own. It secures an essential co-ordination between bodies whose creative interplay is the condition of effective government.

Nor is that all. The executive as a committee of the legislature has an opportunity to drive a stream of tendency through affairs. That is an urgent task. The modern legislature is, of necessity, too large to be left to direct itself; either it loses its centre of equipoise in a mass of statutes unrelated to the posture of affairs, or it gives rise to an interest as against the executive which sets one striving against the other in an effort to win credit from the electorate. The value of an executive which forces the legislature either to accept or to reject its measures is that the latter's efforts are then canalised into something like an organised policy. The play of ideas is not prohibited, but it is limited to the measures upon which men are prepared to risk their political existence. The executive is not made to administer measures it believes mistaken; the policy adopted is one for which it is prepared to make itself responsible. Or, alternatively, a different executive comes into view.

This relationship, moreover, presents a simple means whereby persons fitted to be members of an executive may make known their ability. Certainly whatever may have been the defects of the House of Commons, what has been called its selective function has been amazingly well done. It has proved character as well as talent. It has measured the hinterland between oratorical quality and administrative insight with much shrewdness. I know of no alternative method that in any degree approaches it. Certainly the choice of men for high executive office, as during the war, on the ground of great business capacity, or position in the trade union world, was, generally, a sorry failure. The average American President represents, at the best, a leap in the dark; his average cabinet rarely represents anything at all. But the average member of an English cabinet has been tried and tested over a long period in the public view. He has the "feel" of his task long before he comes to that task. He has spent his earlier career in contact with the operations he is now to direct. To give the executive, by this means, the initiative in law-making, and to build its life upon the successful use of that initiative in the legislature, is an elementary induction from historic experience.

Nothing in this implies the mastery of the legislature by the executive. Under the system, indeed, there have developed experiences so different as those of Great Britain and France. What, rather, is involved is the co-ordination of knowledge, so that each aspect of the governmental adventure is used to enrich the other. The position of the judiciary is different. Its whole purpose is impartiality. It is deliberately set aside from the normal process of conflict out of which law emerges. For its object is, above all, to protect the body of citizens from executive encroachment. To make it in any sense subordinate to the executive is to make impossible the performance of the most urgent function within its province. That is why most political systems have set themselves to protect the independence of judges. The federal judiciary in America, the bench in England, can only be removed by a special and difficult procedure; and it is noteworthy that in the American States, where election of judges usually prevails, a much less high standard of competence prevails. It is, I think, clear that the proper performance of the judicial function implies, first of all, that no judge shall be removed except for physical reasons or for corruption. The executive may dislike his pronouncements. His decisions may be unpopular with the people. Unless he is in a position to know that no penalty follows from doing the right as he sees the right, he is bound to be the creature of the passing phases of public opinion. It implies, secondly, the rule of law. That rule may be enforced through special tribunals, where technical problems, as in the fixation of gas-rates in America, are in issue; but there must be no organ of the executive exempt from judicial inspection. And, clearly, where the executive itself exercises quasi-judicial functions the judiciary should have such power of scrutiny as will enable it to see that the rules adopted by the executive are such as are likely to result in justice. Executives discretion is an impossible rule unless it is conceived in terms of judicial standards.

I do not think, as has sometimes been suggested, that judicial independence of the executive is attacked in the prerogative of pardon which inheres in the executive.[9] There are three clear reasons for its existence in practically its present form. In the first place, judicial errors do occur. They are, possibly, infrequent, but cases like the Beck case make it imperative that, where they are detected, there should be immediate means of remedy. There is, secondly, the possibility of a wrong assessment of penalty. Judges notoriously vary in the severity of punishment inflicted; it is necessary to have the means of balancing justice by mercy in the necessary cases. There is, thirdly, the fact that cases occur in which the penalty inflicted ought not to be operative for reasons made evident only after it has been assessed. The power to review in cases like these is obviously essential. It may be admitted that, under the first head, judicial pardon would not raise immense difficulties. But judicial action under the second and third would undoubtedly lead to public criticism, and that, in its turn, would bring the judiciary into an atmosphere peculiarly unfavourable to its functioning. When the power is, on the other hand, given to the executive, public criticism has its definite place. The *locale* of the power to pardon (or to mitigate) is simply a matter of convenience of which the utility hardly needs discussion.

The method of appointing judges raises questions which I shall discuss in detail later. Here I would urge only that either popular election, as in America, or legislative election as in Switzerland is neither of them adequate. Appointment by the executive has, on the whole, produced the best results. But it is, I think, urgent to prevent judicial office being made the reward for political services. To that end it is a matter of elementary wisdom to ordain that no member of a legislature, or of the political executive, should be eligible for judicial office. The English tradition, for instance, of giving the law officers of the Crown the refusal of such judicial vacancies as occur is a serious error. The qualities which make a man fit for the judicial function are not necessarily those which make a man a successful attorney-general; and it brings to the bench men accustomed to consider problems from the special angle of executive need, instead of men accustomed to the jealous scrutiny of the effort to satisfy that need. It follows, also, that such a fusion of executive and judiciary as is represented by the office of Lord Chancellor is similarly mistaken. The more complete the separation of the judiciary from politics the better for its quality and independence. The reverse logically follows. A man who serves in a judicial capacity ought not to be eligible for political office. To make it possible, for instance, for a judge of the Supreme Court of the United States to look forward to the Presidency is inevitably to introduce elements into his decisions of a peculiarly undesirable kind.

I have assumed, in this discussion, that while the judiciary may control the acts of the executive, it ought not to control legislative acts. This raises certain complex considerations which need some further analysis. It is obvious that there are two cases in which the work of a legislature is inevitably subject to the scrutiny of the courts. (1) Where the Constitution is written and the powers of the legislature are defined by it, the authority of the legislature is confined to what the courts hold to be within the competence of its powers. (2) In any federal State, even when the central legislature is left unhampered by such restrictions as those represented by the Fourteenth Amendment to the American Constitution, the question of the area of competence of the different elements of the Federation, is also a judicial matter.

Outside of Great Britain, it has been usual in most States to define with some exactitude the powers of a legislative assembly and, as in the United States, so attach to the definition of those powers a system of limitations embodied in a Bill of Rights. We have had experience of a written constitution in England under the Commonwealth; but no attempt has been made since that time to differentiate between constitutional and ordinary legislation. As a result, Parliament can, as a matter of strict law, abolish the Habeas Corpus Act as easily as it changes the laws relating to the liquor traffic. What prevents such an attempt is the tradition which gives to statutes like Habeas Corpus a majesty of a peculiarly impressive kind. Certainly the absence of this differentiation makes for a flexibility that has enormous advantages in a period of great social change. It means that new ideas can make their way without being compelled to pass through the complicated sieve devised to protect ideas deemed fundamental by an earlier period. If England wishes to abolish child labour, that change can be directly effected; but the will of the American Congress is thwarted by the Supreme Court. The English system clearly prevents the judiciary from deciding upon the desirability of legislation the principles of which were unknown, naturally enough, to the generation by which the Constitution was made. And it is obvious that the more the courts can be saved from passing upon such desirability, the more likely they are to retain the respect of citizens.

For it must not be forgotten that much legislation held unconstitutional by the Supreme Court is, in fact, so held not upon principles of strict legal theory, but upon a view of what is reasonable. The substance of reasonableness does not dwell in the clouds, but is built almost entirely upon the habits and contacts of those estimating it. A few men may be detached enough to project themselves beyond the special circle of their limited experience; most, certainly, will be content to be imprisoned therein without any sense of that captivity. Mr. Justice Braxfield has never a shadow of doubt that the Scottish radicals were criminal, not because of overt acts logically construable as crime, but because men in his own environment did not hold those opinions. Mr. Justice Grantham tried election petitions in the simple belief that a decision in favour of the Tory candidate fulfilled the requirements of justice.[10] The remarks of American judges in the political trials of the last ten years have been more frequently like those of counsel determined to secure a conviction than of men anxious to arrive at an impartial verdict on the facts.[11] To entrust the judge with the power to override the will of the legislature is broadly to make him the decisive factor in the State.

In that sense, a written constitution in which the legislature is so vigorously controlled seems to me a great mistake. For the constitution will always reflect the spirit of the time at which it was made. The judge will, on the average, be better acquainted with that spirit, more bound to the ideas it reflects, than he will be with a later and more novel, ideology. His views on the advisability, say, of economic legislation are no more likely to be right than those of the legislature, and there seems, therefore, no common sense in allowing his views to prevail.

But, equally, there seems no good reason why a legislature should be able to enforce its will on subjects of great magnitude without control of some kind. There are notions so fundamental that it is necessary in every State to give them special protection. Freedom of speech ought not to be interfered with as easily as the licensing laws. *Ex post facto* laws and bills of attainder rare, I think without exception, vicious both in principle and result. Acts of indemnity ought not to be available by the simple process of majority rule. Martial law ought not, as in the Punjab rising of 1919, to be antedated in order to include cases in which, under normal circumstances, it might be difficult to secure a prosecution.[12] Legislation which aims at the disfranchisement of a special class or creed is an outrage upon the whole thesis of citizenship. Powers such as these ought never to be within the compass of a legislature except under severe restrictions as to their exercise.

So also, I would urge, in matters like the period in which a legislature is to retain power, it ought not to be able to prolong its own existence. It ought not to be able to pass financial measures which provide the executive with funds for more than a year at a time. It ought not to be able to ally itself to a particular Church. It ought not, in a word, to be able to alter the basic framework of the State except under special conditions, direct access to which is rendered difficult.

This implies, I think, a written constitution. Ideas so fundamental as these cannot be left to the hazards of a chance majority in the legislature. The action of the Supreme Court in cases concerned with freedom of speech has shown that judicial review is not an adequate safeguard; and the ambit covered by the Defence of the Realm Act shows that a powerful executive may so sweep a legislature off its feet, that fundamental liberties may become the creatures of executive discretion. We need to avoid the unlimited authority of Parliament, on the one hand, and the unique inaccessibility of the American Constitution to amendment on the other. A written constitution which may be amended by a two-thirds majority of the legislature supplies an adequate *via media*. It secures the electorate against the danger that its liberties may be invaded. It prevents the judiciary from exercising more than a limited control over the political sphere. It leaves room for the making of such necessary changes as have a convinced public opinion on their side. It may be added that an age which, like our own, has seen the classic safeguards of representative government thwarted on every side, needs to reinforce its conviction of their urgency. It ought not, for instance, to be possible for a revolution like that of Mussolini to express itself through constitutional forms. Liberty is, in any case, a sufficiently fragile thing for it to be wise to make its suppression less easy than it has become in recent times. Men who are determined to enforce change of this kind by violence will, doubtless, resort to it if no other means lies open. But it is, it may be urged, better that their effort should be plainly revolutionary than that they should be able to pervert the Constitution to their purposes. Atheism, after all, should not be preached from the pulpit of a cathedral.

The situation in a federal State is somewhat different. There not only are the earlier problems in issue, but also those special problems which relate to a somewhat more rigorous distribution of competence than is the case in a unitary State. I do not, indeed, believe that the problems are qualitatively different; it is as urgent for Manchester to control its special needs as it is for Alberta or Tennessee. But the range of competence in a federal State is likely to be wider than elsewhere, and special provision needs to be made for it. Here, I think, the lesson of experience is tolerably clear. A written constitution is the only method by which the effective control of the powers allotted to the constituent parts of a federation can be guaranteed to them; and the judicial review of the exercise of those powers is the most certain way of securing the maintenance of a reasonable equilibrium. Certainly the Supreme Court of the United States has been remarkably successful in holding the balance even between centrifugal and centripetal tendencies; and decisions like*McCray* v. *United* States,[13] on the one hand, and *Noble State Bank* v. *Haskell*,[14] on the other, show how much elasticity has been provided for in the system.

But it is also obvious that no original distribution of powers will ever be adequate over any long period. While it is possibly too broad a generalisation to urge, with Professor Dicey, that federalism is always a stage on the road to unity, it is certainly true that the interests of a developing nation-State need the continual readjustment of the powers allotted. This, it is clear, has been the experience of the United States. Very notably, the control of labour legislation by the States was much more suited to a pre-industrial epoch than to one, like the present, in which uniform manufacturing conditions are implied by large-scale industry. The same is true of matters like company-law, like bills and notes, and, in a very different sphere, like the rules for admission to such professions as the law and medicine. The uniformity obtainable by negotiation between the different States is too arduous a matter for any subject of urgency. The attempt to secure it by indirect means, the use, to take the example of child labour, of powers like the Commerce clause, is mistaken because it perverts the instrumentalities provided by the Constitution to illegitimate uses. What, once more, emerges as essential is that amendment should be reasonably accessible without being too easy of access.

The American method of amendment is, it should be said at once, far to difficult to be satisfactory. It is built upon the supposition that the areas represented by State-lines are still genuine entities for the purpose of creative administration. That may have been true in 1787; it is no longer true to-day. And to maintain the States as the effective power in the amending process is, accordingly, to deprive the central authority of the instrumental needs to fulfil its ends. Nor is the Canadian technique of federal disallowance of provincial acts much more satisfactory. It raises, in the first place, the very difficult problem of the grounds of disallowance, which are, in each case, problems in policy uniquely susceptible to partisan interpretation, and, secondly, it is a merely negative power, where what is required is a method of positive reorganisation.[15] The Australian system, which provides for the elicitation of public opinion by a referendum,[16] suffers from the fact that it is referring to an indiscriminating and uninformed mass a problem which, from its very nature, requires treatment by expert inquiry. The way out, as I think, lies in allowing the central authority to make the adjustment it requires on three conditions. It must secure a two-thirds majority of the legislature for its proposal; it must be able to pass it by that majority in two successive sessions of the legislature; and, in the event of the legislatures of two-thirds of the constituent States presenting a formal protest against the change, it must be able a third time to secure the assent of a two-thirds vote of the Central Legislature. The advantages of such a method of amendment are clear. It makes the burden of change lie within the control of the body charged with the national interest. It makes the period of change slow enough to prevent any hasty or ill-conceived proposal finding its way immediately to the statute-book, and by providing the constituent States with a means of protest, to which consequences are attached, it offers them the assurance that their insistence will be duly weighed. The method, it will be noted, does not at any point impair the power of judicial review; it would still be competent for the courts to hold either federal or State legislation*ultra vires*. But a court-decision would no longer be able, as it is able in the United States, to hinder the passage of statutes which have behind them the considered opinion of the central legislature.

I said above that the problem of the distribution of powers in a federal State is only quantitatively different from that in a unitary State. In most countries, local government powers lie completely within the control of the central legislature. Outside of Germany, practically every local authority in a unitary State has merely specified powers; and it can only secure an increment of authority by persuading the central legislature to pass a special act conferring the power desired. This is, as a system, unduly distrustful of local experiment. It prevents the local body from exercising initiative in regions where new ideas are not only valuable in themselves, but add both to the responsibility and to the attractiveness of local politics. If the borough of Fulham desires to run a municipal laundry, I see no reason why parliamentary permission should have to be invoked; if Boston wishes to purchase its tram-lines, it should not need to wait upon the will of the Massachusetts legislature. In any distribution of powers in a unitary State, therefore, we seem to need two categories of authority: we need (a) areas to which, at a given standard, the local body must devote its attention; (b) areas the control of which is definitely reserved to the central legislature. In the second, indeed, the control may well be, on occasion, merely the control of inspection, the actual administration, as in education in England, being left to local bodies. But in the residuary area, the larger the volume of initiative left to the local body, the more fruitful is its performance likely to be. The central legislature may still be left to amend the technique of distribution between the central executive and the local bodies. But it ought not, I urge, to be able easily to amend that technique. The majority required for the change proposed ought always to be larger than in the case of ordinary legislation. For in every State, the more opportunity is given for the needs of the community to be satisfied rather at the base than at the apex of the social pyramid, the fuller and richer will be the life of that community. Normally and broadly, central control will be more efficient; but, normally and broadly also, such control will never arouse the degree of interest in the process of law-making that local initiative can secure.

A word here is advisable upon the distribution of powers in the aspect of devolution. It is increasingly assumed in political discussion that we have need, not only of central and local bodies, but also of intermediate bodies which will assume control over areas intermediate between, say, Great Britain, on the one hand, and Liverpool on the other. The case of Great Britain may be taken by way of illustration. Parliament, it is said, is overwhelmed by the pressure of its work because it is continually compelled to deal with questions too narrow to be worthy of its scrutiny. Just as, apart from local government, the United States has forty-nine legislatures to cope with its problems, Australia seven, and Canada eight, so should Great Britain have at least four, in order that the Imperial legislature may be free to devote its time to major issues only. The same would apply to France in terms of one or other of the many regional schemes proliferated there in recent years. The Belgian problem, also, could thereby be solved, since Flemings and Walloons would then become autonomous in local concerns.

It may be admitted that the element of nationalism makes the Belgian problem quite distinct from that of the normal unitary State not keenly divided by bitter feeling between its component parts. But devolution in the latter case has nothing of its *a priori* simplicity when it is analysed in detail. The analogy with a federal State is an unjustified one. America, Australia and Canada are all rather continents than countries;

Germany presents quite special problems of origin and composition; Switzerland is too small a theatre of events to present comparable issues. And, in any case, the pressure on the normal federal legislature is not less than that upon Parliament; what it gains in the limited area to be discussed it loses in intensity within its allotted field. The pressure is, in fact, the natural result of the transformation of a negative State into a positive State. Anyone, moreover, who studies the list of subjects it is proposed to devolve upon local legislatures will be struck by their comparative unimportance.[17] Education, prisons and public health apart, the majority of them do not occupy a twentieth part of parliamentary time; and of the latter, housing and national health insurance raise financial questions of a magnitude that no local legislature could solve without central control (and therefore parliamentary review) of its decisions. Such a division of powers, further, would involve at every point a judicial review of legislation made by the subordinate legislatures, and thereby multiply largely the business of the courts.[18] There will, further, be an immense increase in the size of the civil service, since for the functions now centrally performed, at least a triplicate staff will be necessary. And this is to omit minor questions like the multiplication of elections in which, outside of Parliament, the stimulation of local interest has become so difficult. Certainly that interest is not increased by giving it new issues of mainly a technical kind to disentangle.

It is, I think, a clear general truth in politics that to secure an adequate legislature two things are necessary. There must, first, be the power in the legislature to solve important questions, and, secondly, consideration must be, attached to the position of a private member. Both those conditions are satisfied by the Parliament of the modern State; neither, I think, can be satisfied in the local legislatures suggested. For where, as I have argued, vital questions like education and housing are involved, finance is bound to transfer effective control back to the central legislature; and popular interest in licensing and ecclesiastical measures is not likely to invest the average number with the prestige which comes from the power to handle great questions. The mere multiplication of territorial centres of authority has no contribution to offer to the type of problem we are now seeking to solve. There are, of course, genuine territorial questions; and the problem of area apart, the twofold division into central and local seems fully adequate to their needs. Where other issues arise, it will, I think, be found that the considerations involved are different. We need the central resolution of general principle, as now. But the application of general principle is a matter, not of territorial, but of functional devolution. Our future lies in discovering how to relate genuine industrial units to a central legislature in the same way that we relate territorial units. The distribution of power between those units and the legislature does not raise issues seriously different from those discussed earlier in this chapter. But it is better to postpone discussion of this relationship until we have sought to build our industrial institutions.

## (ii) The Organisation of Citizens

The legislature of a State is chosen by the citizen-body. How is the choice to be made? What are to be the relations between the persons chosen and the electorate which chooses them? I argued earlier in this book that the modern democratic State has no alternative to universal adult suffrage. It lies, as a State, at the disposal of each of its members to enable him to realise the best in himself; and he is entitled, as a matter of logic, to the vote that he may thereby express what his experience seems to warrant him expressing in the push of affairs. I do not argue that universal suffrage has any practical merits which render it inherently superior to other systems. But, theory apart, no tests of exclusion seem available which assist the State to the furtherance of its end. Property as a basis for the franchise merely limits the interests of the State to those of the owners of property. No technique is known whereby an educational qualification can be made synonymous with political fitness. Exclusion on the ground that a man has been in receipt of public relief is merely to stigmatise economic misfortune as a crime. Exclusion on the ground of conviction by the courts is intelligible if it is confined to a small range of offences. But, even here, a time-light ought to operate; for obviously we do not want to exclude men like Jean Valjean from exercising their full part in civic life. Lunacy and mental defect are, of course, different matters. In those cases exclusion is built on the simple ground that attainment of a best self is, in any sense implicit with social meaning, impossible.

But an electorate must be organised to choose. A whole adult population cannot from some vast list select those whom it prefers. It is clear that a local relationship of some kind must develop between the member of the legislature and his constituents. What ought that relationship to be? Broadly, we have a choice between two systems. We may either have equal electoral districts, each returning a single member; or we may have some larger, equal unit area, each returning a number of members upon the basis of proportional representation.

What must be realised at the outset is that the member of a legislature will only be returned as a member of some party or group. The life of the democratic State is built upon the party-system, and it is important at the outset to discuss the part played by party in the arrangement of affairs. Briefly, that part may be best described by saying that parties arrange the issues upon which people are to vote. It is obvious that in the confused welter of the modern State there must be some selection of problems as more urgent than others. It is necessary to select them as urgent and to present solutions of them which may be acceptable to the citizen-body. It is that task of selection the party undertakes. It acts, in Mr. Lowell's phrase, as the broker of ideas. From the mass of opinions, sentiments, beliefs, by which the electorate moves, it chooses out those it judges most likely to meet with general acceptance. It organises persons to advocate its own view of their meaning. It states that view as the issue upon which the voter has to make up his mind. Its power enables it to put forward for election candidates who are willing to identify themselves with its view. Since its opponents will do the same, the electorate, thereby, is enabled to vote as a mass, and decision that would otherwise be chaotic assumes some coherency and direction.

Much time has been spent in the effort to explain the origin of parties. To some they are born of the natural contrast between those who cling to the old and those who embrace the new. To others, they arise from the pugnacious instinct of men. It is, however, clear that no single explanation suffices. There is a conflict of wills in society, and that conflict is decided by the decision of the intermediate mass which is not firmly convinced of the truth of any general cause. To attract its support it is necessary to advertise one's view. Parties are the natural method of effecting that end. Their form is largely dependent upon the conditions of any given time. They may group themselves about religious issues, as in the sixteenth-century France; they may group themselves about economic issues, as in the England of our own day. Naturally, they arouse the pugnacious instinct; naturally, also, there will be a tendency for the radical solution to attract the young. What, at least, is certain, is that without parties there would be no means available to us of enlisting the popular decision in such a way as to secure solutions capable of being interpreted as politically satisfactory.

To say, of course, that parties are natural is not to say that they are perfect. They suffer from all the evils of group separatism which I discussed in an earlier chapter. They distort the issues that they create. They produce divisions in the electorate which very superficially represent the way in which opinion is in fact distributed. They secure, at best, an incomplete and compromising loyalty. They falsify the perspective of the issues they create. They build about persons allegiance which should go to ideas. They build upon the unconscious and they force the judgment of men into the service of their prejudices. Yet, when the last criticism of party has been made, the services they render to a democratic State are inestimable. They prevent popular vagaries from driving their way to the statute-book. They are the most solid obstacle we have against the danger of Caesarism. Above all, they enable the electorate to choose between alternatives which, even though at best an artificial dichotomy, are the only satisfactory method of obtaining a government. For, on practically every issue in the modern State, the serried millions of voters cannot do more than accept or reject the solutions offered. The stage is too vast to permit of the nice shades of quantitative distinction impressing themselves upon the public mind. It has rarely the leisure, and seldom the information, to do more than indicate the general tendency of its will. It is in the process of law-making that the subtler adjustments must be effected.

If this is true, it follows that a political system is the more satisfactory, the more it is able to express itself through the antithesis of two great parties. Each may contain a certain variety of opinion. Both may fail to attract in their ranks much more than that active minority which is willing to devote itself to political affairs. But the superiority of a two-party system over a multiplicity of groups is above all in this, that it is the only method by which the people can at the electoral period directly choose its government. It enables that government to drive its policy to the statute-book. It makes known and intelligible the results of its failure. It brings an alternative government into immediate being. The group-system always means that no government can be formed until after the people has chosen the legislative assembly. It means that the executive will represent, not a general body of opinion, but a patchwork of doctrines which compromise their integrity for the sake of power. It means, also, short-lived administrations, since reshuffling of the groups to overthrow the government is the most interesting exercise in which the legislature can indulge. Short-lived administrations always mean that no coherent policy can be realised. While the group system probably reflects more accurately the way in which the popular mind is actually divided, it is fatal to government as a practical art. For the essential need in administration is the absence of uncertainty. An executive must be able to plan its way continuously to an ordered scheme of policy. That involves a majority, because it involves strong government. A legislature, otherwise, is so much the master of the executive that the latter is unable to attempt great measures, and the time which should be spent upon them is devoted to manoeuvring for positions which are lost almost as soon as they are occupied.

So stated, any electoral system ought to satisfy four general considerations. It ought to enable the legislative assembly to embody the opinions of the majority and the minority on the great issues of public interest. It need not, indeed, if it is to be effective, it cannot, embody the total drift of opinion with any effort after mathematical precision. It must allow all groups of men to make themselves heard; but it is compelled to confine popular selection to predominant groups in order to make the business of government coherent and continuous. The areas, secondly, which return members to the legislature, must be small enough to enable the candidates to be known in a genuine way, and, after election, to be closely related to their constituents so that a personal relation develops between them. There must, thirdly, be a means between elections, of checking the result of a general election by revealing the drift of opinion among the voters; this, it may be added, is admirably secured in England and America by the method of bye-elections. This system, fourthly, must be so organised that the voters are as directly related as possible to the government in power. They must be able to feel that it is their choice and that it is as a government that it will come before them for scrutiny when the term of legislative office expires.[19]

On these grounds we reject the system of proportional representation by which it is sought to obviate the defects caused by the majority-principle. I cannot deal here in detail with the arguments by which it is defended; here it must be sufficient to point out the general grounds of rejection. These are, it may be noted, mainly practical in character. We should be compelled to substitute great multiple member constituencies for the present areas. Thereby, we should intensify the complexity of choice, and increase the power of the professional organiser in politics. We should destroy any prospect of personal relations between the member and his constituents; he would become simply an item in a list, voted for almost entirely on party-grounds. We should get weak government, without that body of support which enables it to operate a great programme. We should multiply the number of vagaries which from time to time, like the supporters of the Tichborne claimant and Mr. Bottomley, obscure the clash of real issues. We should be unable to have bye-elections as a test of changes in opinion; and we should encourage all dissidents within a party to seek that independent structure which, ultimately, means the group-system. Thereby we should transfer the place where governments are made from the country as a whole, to the obscure recesses of the legislative assembly. Not least, we should diminish the responsibility of the private member by increasing his sense that, whatever his personal effort, the party organisers who maintained the list of candidates would be able to ensure his return. Every such complication of electoral machinery is, I believe, bound to result in a decline of civic interest in the political process.

What compensation does the proportional system offer in mitigation of these defects? It will, it is alleged, result in a better representation of national opinion than is now the case. But, in fact, there are few shades of national opinion which do not already find their expression in a legislative assembly; and, at best, the variety is obtained at a sacrifice that is very dubious. It is said, further, that the system makes opportunities for independent persons that are now largely absent. I do not think there is any substance in this view. For, in the large constituency the system involves, what is important is no longer the individual candidate, but the total impression produced by the list to which he belongs. In that aspect, the more independent a candidate the less chance the list will have of conveying a solid impression to the electorate; and the tendency of the party organiser will be to choose as candidates men who can be trusted not to disturb the regular routine. Nor, I would urge, is there any foundation for the view that in the single-member constituency, the minority is unrepresented, while, in the proportional system, this danger is adequately met. "The horizon of a minority", as Dr. Finer well remarks, "is not limited by the boundaries of a constituency". Government is not carried on by presenting to a legislative assembly alternatives which must be fully accepted or rejected. The process of give-and-take which takes place there enables every minority that is organised to give expression to its views, to exercise its "pull" on the total pressure of which a given measure is the result. Political decisions are not made by an arithmetical process of counting votes. More urgent is the weighting of influences that takes place in the law-making process. And minority-views may find adequate institutions therein for the expression of their opinions and desires.

A word should be said upon one aspect of the system to which too little attention is given. In a single-member constituency, it is argued, I may find no candidate I desire to support. But that may equally happen in a multiple-member area, and whereas in the single-member constituency I can give the full weight of my vote to the party I desire to see in power, in the multiple-member area I can give only a fraction of that weight, and the lower preferences I express have no proportionate relation at all to the positive desire I may feel. Something is to be said for the alternative vote in the single-member constituency, where three parties, clearly destined to permanence, exist. But, even there, there is no real relation between the preferences expressed; and the system may result in the choice of the *pis aller* rather than of the man about whom a genuine intensity of opinion has clustered. It involves the danger that the larger the number of candidates who run on special issues, unrelated to the main streams of electoral tendency, the greater the likelihood first that the composition of the legislative assembly will, if they are elected, the atomic, and if they are defeated, that they merely defeat the effort or their supporters to relate themselves to the government of the day.

One final remark in this regard may be made. It is not likely that the difficulties of the modern State are such as to be at all seriously remediable by reforms of electoral machinery. Mainly, those difficulties are moral in character. We shall meet them rather by the elevation of the popular standard of intelligence, and the reform of the economic system, than by making men choose in proportion to the neatly-graded volume of opinion. Proportional representation, where it has been tried, has not noticeably improved the standards of public life. In Belgium it has tended to eliminate independence. In Switzerland, it has so multiplied the tiny groups, that no coherent opinion has been able to emerge. That always implies weak government, and weak government ultimately means irresponsible government. Minorities can always be sure of reasonable representation in the State so long as they are able to make their views articulate and organised to given them driving power. And, in general, the two-party system produces a conflict sufficiently acute to make both of them anxious for ideas likely to attract popular support. The permeation of parties, rather than the creation of groups, is, therefore, the path along which ideas should normally move. There may, of course, come a time when it is evident that assimilation is impossible and that the only way to realisation is through the making of an independent appeal to the voters. That happened, for example, with the Labour Party in England in the years from 1906. But the test of the adequacy of the Labour Party will lie, as it lies with all rebels, in its ability to create a new two-party equilibrium.

### (iii) The Citizen and His Representative

A State divided into equal electoral districts, each returning a single member to the legislative assembly, seems, therefore, the general lesson of historic experience. What ought to be the relation of the member to his constituents? It is necessary, first, to dispose of one view which is fatal to the quality of a legislature. No constituency ought to be limited in choice, as in the United States, to one of its own residents. Nothing is so certain as to make for parochialism. Nothing more tempts a member to lend himself to the service of sinister interests than knowledge that defeat may mean the end of his political career. It is, moreover, a serious waste on another side. The ability at the command of a State does not distribute itself with mathematical accuracy over the electoral divisions. New York is more likely to have a number of men capable of playing a distinguished part in the Senate than Delaware or Nevada. A theory which equates defeat with practically permanent exile does not maximise the advantages of a community. It is all to the good that Mr. Gladstone, defeated in Oxford, should find refuge in South Lancashire, and Mr. Churchill move from Manchester to Dundee. Any other view under-estimates so seriously the importance of experienced leadership in politics as to make it not unlikely that it is at bottom built upon the credulous superstition that, all men being more or less equal in ability, the composition of a legislature is not a very serious matter. That is a mistake so profound that not the least cause, for example, of the declining respect for the Congress, of the United States is its failure to contain the natural leaders of the people. The wider the ambit of electoral choice, the better the operation of political institutions is likely to be.

It is sometimes suggested that a member of the legislative assembly must be either a delegate or a representative, must either vote as he is instructed, or use his best judgment upon the issue he is called upon to decide. That is, in fact, a wholly false antithesis. For no member can state his total views; partly because there is not the time to do so, partly because new issues are bound to arise. And upon those new issues he cannot, item by item, consult his constituents in such a fashion as to elicit from them their considered judgment. Any constituency is entitled to the fullest expression it can get of a member's general attitude. It is entitled to know his views upon the questions of the day. Any elector may reasonably ask him for an explanation of his political actions. But a member is not the servant of a party in the majority in his constituency. He is elected to do the best he can in the light of his intelligence and his conscience. Were he merely a delegate, instructed by a local caucus, he would cease to have either morals or personality. Clearly, he is not entitled to get elected as a free trader and to vote at once for a protective tariff. He is not entitled to get elected and then to decide on a year's voyage round the world. He must be decently consistent in opinion, and reasonably diligent in the performance of his duty. No constituency is justified in expecting more service than these imply, and a constituency which trusts its member will, on the whole, find that he repays it amply. Burke's classical explanation[20] of the relationship is as true to-day as when it was first spoken to the misguided electors of Bristol.

But, as I think, one further safeguard is needed. A constituency that is dissatisfied with the member it has chosen can always reject him at the next election. If, as in the United States, only two years elapse between elections, a mistaken choice is not likely to have serious consequences. But, as I shall argue later, two years is too short a period of office for a legislature; it cannot, in that time, hope to translate a wide policy into statutes. A five year period seems much more adequate to that end, and in five years the electors may feel the desire to register some deliberate dissatisfaction either with the member himself, or with the Government he supports. They should, I think, have the means at their disposal of making that view felt.

I think, therefore, that some form of the device known as the recall would be a valuable addition to our electoral machinery. It ought not, clearly, to be a weapon of easy use. Were that to be the case, the member would at once be transformed into a delegate living under the shadow of a particularly ugly sword of Damocles; and it would be more than likely that the fall of the sword would be arranged by the most undesirable elements in his constituency. But proper safeguards can be had; and they enable the electorate to have some closer check, both upon the member and his party, than the present system permits. Clearly no recall ought to operate before a year has passed from the original election of the member; nor, again, should it be called into play within twelve months of the end of a legislature's term of power. It would therefore be effective for the three years in which a Parliament, for instance, is well under weigh and is dealing with the measures by which it will be later judged. Obviously, there should be no attempt at a recall unless behind the demand for it is the opinion of at least half of the electorate. They would then be entitled to petition for a bye-election in the constituency, but a bye-election in which the voters would decide whether or not they wished to retain the services of their member. He ought not, I think, to be recalled unless some such proportion as two-thirds of those voting desired a change. In this limited form the recall would apply only to extreme cases; and it would have the great merit of calling the attention of the State as a whole to the problem it involved. It would not affect the member who was really performing his task, save where the party he was supporting was deliberately running counter to the general drift of opinion. In that aspect it would serve as a valuable index to the probable fate the party would encounter at the next general election. The recall, so used, is not evidence of a distrust in representative government, but a means of warning the legislature that it needs to make itself trusted.[21]

There is widespread belief that a valuable electoral mechanism is to be found in the referendum and the initiative. These correspond to a desire, negative and positive, to secure a direct expression of public opinion on specific issues as distinct from the general and broad view of policy made in a renewal of legislative power. Both referendum and initiative have now a considerable history, especially in Switzerland and in the United States; and there have even been thinkers enthusiastic enough to find in them the cure for the ills of democratic government. Their rise is probably due to that growing distrust of legislatures which has been one of the great political characteristics of the last half-century. They possess, moreover, a certain superficial plausibility on their side. If the popular will is to prevail, it does not seem unreasonable to build upon the logical basis of allowing that will room for direct expression. Whenever, therefore, a considerable body of electors either desires or opposes some special change, they ought to be able to poll the people in the attempt to secure sanction for their views.

Any discussion of these methods must build rather upon experience of their working than upon first principles. It is clear, first of all, that they have led to no widespread changes; on the contrary they are, as some of their most ardent advocates have noted, more likely to rally the conservative than the progressive forces of society. They rarely enlist much popular interest; on the average, about half as many persons vote in them as will vote for persons in a general election for office. Not seldom, indeed, the number of persons voting is so small, that it is difficult, from the size of the mass abstaining, to know whether there is any public opinion at all upon the question decided. It does not seem that direct government has made much difference, either for improvement or the reverse, to the quality of the legislature. Many of the measures submitted to popular decision bear upon their face the marks of the unpractical enthusiast who has suffered rebuff from the legislature. So far as the actual working of direct government is concerned, there is no reason to suppose that it has any special contribution to make to our problems.

The reasons, I suggest, are not in truth far to seek. The number of specific questions susceptible of popular decision by mass-voting is very small. For what is, as a rule, urgent in the issues they raise is not the simple desirability of affirmative or negative response, but the much more complex question of the desirability of a particular solution stated in all its complex statutory terms. It is not difficult to ask a man whether he is in favour of a protective tariff or no; but the submission of an itemised tariff for acceptance or rejection does not elicit a true public opinion in any sense of the term. A man may say that he favours Dominion Home Rule for Ireland; but the forms in which his desire is embodied are so capable of variation that he may refuse to recognise the particular form submitted as the adequate embodiment of his desires. The difficulty, in fact, which direct government involves is the final difficulty that it is by its nature far too crude an instrument to find room for the nice distinctions inherent in the art of government. You can amend and alter in a legislative assembly; you cannot amend and alter when your legislative assembly consists of millions of members. Most legislation consists of a principle embodied in a mass of administrative detail. The principle may be comparatively simple, but it is rarely capable of appraisal save in terms of the clauses which give it substance. And those clauses will almost always involve a technical knowledge which no undifferentiated electorate can hope to possess.

Nor is that the end. There is a large number of subjects of the first importance upon which, in the nature of things, an opinion can only be formed after long and arduous examination. The public may agree in principle to the national control of the electricity supply; but it will not undertake the research necessary to grasp the methods by which that nation control should be applied. The more satisfactory legislation is to be, the more dependent it is upon its principle in relation to its working technique; and that is inevitably a matter for expert judgment. Two other considerations arise. It will be found, in general, that where the movement for direct government is most widespread, there also the legislative assembly is most distrusted. But, in fact, the remedy for an inadequate legislature never lies in the mere multiplication of machinery. That problem is a moral issue, where mechanical checks are our of place. It is clear, secondly, that the primary assumption of direct government is that administration is a simple matter, upon which each member of the electorate can, fairly effortlessly, possess convictions. Such a view will appear inadequate to anyone who reads the annual volume of statutes in any modern State. And the number of those interested enough to vote upon the technical issues which arise is never large enough to justify the theoretic assumptions of direct government. I do not, indeed, urge the argument that they are likely, when applied, to destroy the sense of responsibility in a legislative assembly; that would involve a far greater frequency of reference to the people than is likely to be the case. But I think that the adherents of direct government belong to that curious group of enthusiasts who have a touching confidence that there exists somewhere a remedy for all political ills which will prove a panacea in use. That is true only as it assumes that the real panacea is the elevation of the moral and intellectual standards of the electorate as a whole.

What, then, can the voters do in the intervals between general elections? We have rejected direct government, and accepted the limited recall as a method that obviously can be called into play only as a remedy of last resort. As individuals, it must, I think, be admitted that they can do little. The world now is too big and complex a world for the activity of the average man to affect its work in any serious way. A distinguished statesman, or an eminent thinker, can doubtless arouse influential discussion; Lord Lansdowne's letter upon the war, Mr. Keynes' *Economic Consequences of the Peace,* worth both of them, in their various ways, historic events. But, for the mass, action that is to entail consequences means organised action; and organised action means the development of relations to particular rather than to general functions. That, at least, with one exception. It is, I think, possible to make the activity of political parties more responsive to the will of their rank and file than is now the case. No one can fail to be impressed by the contrast between the way in which the Liberal and Conservative parties in England respectively adopted Home Rule and Tariff Reform, and the way in which the ideals of the British Labour Party have been formulated. In the former, the will of a leader was practically imposed upon his followers without the latter being able to do much more than accept his policy, or, like Mr. Goschen and Mr. Churchill, leave the party. In the case of the latter, by a complex machinery of advisory committees and conferences, there is a constant flow of ideas between leaders and rank and file which gives every organised opinion an opportunity, if not to get adopted, at least to struggle for adoption. The articulation is, of course, imperfect; and it is always surrounded by that mysterious limitation which is due to the influence of personality. But I do not think there is room for doubt that the British Labour Party has found a method whereby parties may be made much more responsive than in the past to the will of their ordinary members.

Outside of party, the main sphere of the voter will lie in other directions. These are, one imagines, divisible into three main groups. There will, first, be a variety of propaganda associations connected with particular issues. They will press, as now, for the abolition, of vivisection, the proper treatment of aborigines in backward countries, the simplification of spelling, for all, in fact, of the innumerable purposes a society like our own serves to create. There will, secondly, be associations of men in their aspect of producers, engineers, doctors, teachers, miners. These will concern themselves with pressure on the legislative assembly for the remedies which particularly concern the special problems of their profession. But, as I shall show later, the main theatre of their activity is less likely than now to be directly political, and more likely to aim at influencing functional bodies concerned with the government of their professions. Their effort, that is to say, will be concentrated in a narrower field than now; and they will reach the legislative assembly rather through intermediate functional institutions than through a direct appeal. It is in the third group that we may, as I hope, look to the largest growth of activity. Exactly as groups of producers associate to protect their special interests, so is it possible, *mutatis mutandis,* for groups of consumers, locally, and nationally, to associate for similar purposes. Examples will, perhaps, make this clear. There is no reason in the world why the users of the telephone should not, as in France,[22] associate to watch over the operation of the service. They could see that the latest inventions were properly utilised. They could insist upon proper inquiry into complaints. They could watch over the problem of costs. They could employ their own inspectors to test the efficiency of the operating service. They could secure representation upon the advisory telephone committee of the Post Office where, as in England, the telephone was nationalised, or, as in the case of a private telephone system, they could appoint a consultative committee to act with the owning company in the development of the service.

So, too, with a function like that of National Health Insurance. At present, in England, the insurance committees are the only guarantee the insured person has that his interests are properly safeguarded; and it is rare indeed that a complainant is in a position fully to present his case, or to test the adequacy of its investigation. But if we had an association of insured persons, with their own legal staff and their own inspectors, the position would be very different. Complaints could be investigated by persons whose function it was to protect the complainant. They could assure a higher standard of service by a proper surveillance of the medical profession. They could see that no doctor undertook the charge of more patients than he could properly look after. They could act as counsel in the appeals before the Insurance Commissioners. They could see that insured persons had all the benefits to which they were entitled. Or, in a very different sphere, we may take the art service of the modern State. At present, we govern the National Galleries and Museums by trustees who are often eminent, but rarely distinguished in the particular function the institutions seek to fulfil. In England, we usually choose as trustees benevolent noblemen who desire to be known as patrons of the arts; in America it is the custom to select persons who may be expected to endow the institution with new treasures. If, particularly in the case of local galleries and museums, we had associations of persons to whom the incidence of art in life is important, we could prevent the gallery from becoming, as it so often becomes, the mausoleum of official art. In part, the association could itself seek to purchase objects, in part it could criticise what had been purchased, the arrangement of specimens, the uses to which the institution was put. It could nominate its representatives on the governing body of the institution. It could employ distinguished experts, especially, one hopes, from abroad, to report upon the policy of the institution. Should it ever happen that the democratic State is persuaded to realise the importance of national and municipal theatres, it would have an obvious further field of usefulness. So, too, with universities. There is no reason one can see why the alumni of Oxford and Cambridge and Manchester should not be organised to serve them as the alumni of American Universities are organised. Upon the one fundamental condition that they did not attempt criticism of the opinions taught, there are few aspects of university life in which their aid and suggestion would not be helpful; and here again the nomination of their representatives to serve on the governing body of universities would supply a valuable link with the world outside.

There are few services used by the public which are not in some degree susceptible to organisation of this character. Its advantages are threefold. It supplies a means of making opinion flow through channels where it is most likely to prove of service. It enables us to have an external check upon the quality of effort provided by the service involved. It ends that hapless situation where the user of services is left to do the best he can with commodities he is practically unable to control. And, obviously, the general function of these results is an opinion which directly affects the effort of political parties and, through them, of the legislative assembly itself. The latter, indeed, is influenced in two ways. It is influenced from below as the associations make their views felt by the political parties; it is influenced from above as they secure organic connection with the executive. Nor is the latter an impossible task. Already the modern administration sets up consultative committees upon which sit the parties to the work it performs. At the Ministry of Food, during the war period in England, the Consumer's Council rendered valuable service in offering to the officials a body upon which a proposed policy could be tried before being set into general operation.[23] We need to universalise that experiment for every department of administration where it is likely to prove creative. For the more we can convince the body of citizens of their direct interest in the process of politics, the better is likely to be the result of political effort.

On the assumption, however, that such organisation is accompanied by a rise in the standards of public education, it is useless to envisage any widespread increase of interest in political technique unless there is fairly intimate knowledge of what it implies. We cannot make men interested in what they lack the training to understand. At present, to the vast majority of the electorate, the political process is a mass of mysterious occurrences based on rules and ideas which they feel, quite wrongly, to be remote from their daily lives. We have to destroy that feeling. We can only destroy it by making the process intelligible, and that can only come when the educational period is long enough and its standards high enough to make the citizenship of the average man a living reality to him. That will not appear an impossible adventure to anyone acquainted with the history of public education. It will, of course, be difficult; for the last thing men desire is to be persuaded into thought. But so persuaded, they will find, like others who have already made the effort, the fascination of thought. That is the true seed-ground of our hopes.

## (iv) The Legislative Assembly

### (a) *Organisation*

So elected, what is the legislative assembly to be like? It is almost a dogma of political science that it ought to consist of two chambers. Single-chamber government, it is assumed, is the apotheosis of democratic rashness. We need a brake on the wheel. We need a mechanism that enables us to delay the first, rough impulses of a body fresh from its contact with the electorate, and eager, in its inexperience, to embrace every kind of novelty. A second chamber provides exactly this safeguard; and it is regarded as noteworthy that practically every State of importance in the modern world has adopted the two-chamber system.

It should yet be noted that the two-chamber system is largely an historical accident. Bifurcation is, universally, derived from the habits of the English constitution; but there were moments in English history when it seemed likely that we should have at least three, and possibly four, Houses of Parliament. The problem of a second chamber is best approached by considering the forms it may take. We are then in a better position to judge of the need for, and the validity of, its revision. The problem of the central legislative assembly in a federal State is, however, a quite separate one; and I propose to discuss it apart from the general issue.

The second chamber may be elective, and chosen either at the same time as the first, or at some intermediate period; and a chamber of this kind may either have the same powers as the first, or inferior powers. Any such constitution is, I think, clearly unsatisfactory. For equal powers make eventually for deadlock, and a deadlock always involves an unsatisfactory compromise of principle. To elect the chambers simultaneously is merely to duplicate their membership; to elect them at different times is, as American experience has shown, to diminish at every point the efficiency of the executive. Where the second chamber has inferior powers, it can act only as a postponing or revising assembly; and I shall show later that these functions rest upon quite untenable assumptions.

In England, the second chamber is purely hereditary, save for a small infusion of law peers. On the thesis discussed in the earlier part of this book, such a method has nothing to be said for it. Clearly, it involves setting aside permanently a small class in the State and giving to it a special control over policy. That is a denial of equal citizenship, and the basis of the State is its faculty for protecting the equal interest of members in its results. The history of the House of Lords is the history of an assembly that, quite naturally given its constitutive principle, has set its face firmly towards the past. It has been somnolent under conservative administrations, and active under liberal. Save by making its composition numerically ludicrous, it would be impossible to find room in it for an adequate representation of the Labour Party. And even though its powers be limited by some such statute as the Parliament Act, its members cannot be made to represent any but themselves.

It is possible to have a purely nominated second chamber, in which the original membership would be chosen by the executive which replaced vacancies as they occurred. Membership could either be for life, or for a given period, with or without re-eligibility. The field of choice might be unrestricted, or it might be confined to men who have won distinction in specified fields like industry, the professions, and the public services. But such a chamber, it is clear, from the mere fact that it is nominated and not elected, would lack the authority possessed by the popular chamber. At best, again, it could only either revise or postpone. It would tend, from the nature of things, to be a senate which would mistake the experience it had encountered for all relevant social experience. One form of the nominated assembly is the Canadian Senate, which hardly commands even its own confidence. And the Canadian Senate affords the warning that an executive is likely to fill vacancies in a nominated second chamber with its own supporters. With such a body, it is not likely to oppose measures of first-class importance. If it does it either enfeebles the executive, or produces in suitable circumstances a general election in possible defiance of public opinion. It is difficult to see any solid value in a body of this kind.[24]

A second chamber might also be indirectly elected, as the French Senate now is, and as, before 1913, was the Senate of the United States. But, here again, if such a chamber is, at the time of its election, hostile to the Government of the day, it is destructive of the quality of the work, while if it is favourable, it is probably superfluous. Experience, moreover, has lamentably shown that of all methods of maximising corruption, indirect election is the worst. That was why the United States amended the constitution to permit of popular election; it was discovered that the earlier method tended to make the average member the nominee of some great business interest. If indirect election is built not upon inferior legislatures, but as Mr. Graham Wallas has suggested,[25] upon trades and professions, we encounter the insoluble problem of how so to weight each trade and profession relative to another as to have an adequately proportioned assembly. And, even then, there is the further difficulty of seeing why a man elected, say, as a doctor to represent doctors, should have any special virtue in the opinions he expresses on problems of currency and banking. If he does not possess that virtue, he is valueless to the assembly; if he does, it is not by reason of his relation to his profession that he possesses it.

Another method proposed is that in vogue in Norway and recently advocated by Mr. Lees-Smith.[26] The second chamber, in this view, would be a small body elected by the first, and roughly proportionate to the composition of the latter. The will of the party in power would thus be secure of gaining effect; and since the tenure of the second chamber would end with that of its constituting authority, there would be no danger of *a priori* conflict. Its sole functions would be to postpone and to revise; and its value would be found in the fact that, while it could in this way check haste or error, it would be powerless to destroy.

On the general issue, this much may be said. Wherever in a State the legislature has two houses, one or other will always take the lead. One or other will therefore come to be the centre of importance, and to that chamber political talent will invariably gravitate. The second chamber will, as a consequence, either live in a state of suspended animation or else, to secure some degree of attention, it will oppose measures for which it cannot hope to gain the credit. Rather than see itself impotent, it will in Bentham's forcible phrase, "play off the whole artillery of fallacies" against the bills it sought to pass.[27] It will waste time in useless debate; and it will, thereby, keep executive officials from other and more urgent duties. Broadly speaking, any second chamber which agrees with the first is superfluous; and, if it disagrees, it is bound to be obnoxious. For the argument that there must be delay against the rashness of a single, elected assembly mistakes, or ignores, the conditions of modern politics. Legislation is not made *ex nihilo*; it does not suddenly, as out of clean sky, find its way to the statute-book. Almost any measure that is enacted becomes law as the result of a long process of discussion and analysis. The problem of Home Rule for Ireland was debated for thirty years before its essential passage; the reform of the House of Lords has been in the public mind for a generation. The minimum wage, the abolition of the poor law, town-planning, the nationalisation of the mines, all questions of this magnitude are before the public for years before parties adopt them with a view to legislation. Between the Education Act of 1902 and Mr. Fisher's attempt to complete its structure nearly sixteen years elapsed. It took nearly twenty years to accomplish the federation of Australia. What, I think, would most strike the observer who consults the statistics[28] would be the length, and not the shortness, of time which intervenes between the administration and the realisation of ideas.

And, in any case, the kind of check provided by a second chamber is not the most desirable form available. Necessary delay is always secured by the slowness with which a great organisation like a political party is persuaded to the acceptance of a novelty. Necessary revision is best effected by the prior consultation by government of the interests touched by the legislation proposed. Most criticism in a second chamber will merely repeat the arguments already adduced in the first. What it has to say will not, except by accident, possess any special quality of *expertise*. It will tap no sources of knowledge or opinion not already in contact with the first. The true place for such an effort is in the advisory bodies by which the executive departments are surrounded. There, for instance, a minister of the interior can actually frame his Shops Hours Act in consultation with shopkeepers, assistants and consumers. He can learn, far better than in debate, the probable result of his scheme. He can make the necessary adjustments in the light of their special knowledge. The revision of a chamber is either a pure matter of drafting, in which case it is best transferred to an office like that of the Parliamentary Council, or else it is a matter of substance, in which case it can be made equally well in one chamber as in two. The power, in fact, to postpone is a power to defeat the changes regarded as necessary by the party chosen for office by the electorate. That power ought to belong to the electorate only, and at the period when it comes to assess the use made by the party of its authority. The power to revise is either largely verbal, in which case it does not need so substantial an institution as the second chamber, or important, in which case it ought to be a direct challenge to the party in office made on the floor of the elected assembly. I agree that the party in office will make mistakes, and that, in particular, it will assume a desire on the part of the electorate for measures to which the latter is in reality opposed. But a second chamber is no more likely than the first to be correct in its judgment of the electoral will. The necessary checks are always present in the inertia of the mass, and the desire of a government to avoid large changes which may be disastrous. Any other checks will, almost inevitably, be a premium not upon improvement but upon opposition in terms of vested interest.

And this is true even on the supposition that a satisfactory second chamber can be found. I have already argued that this in fact is unlikely. The Norwegian method is the most satisfactory; but it is, after all, but the pale ghost of an effective assembly. The hereditary second chamber is excluded by the first principles of the State-purpose. The elected chamber, if made simultaneously with the first, is merely a reiteration of it; if made at a different time is merely a hindrance to adequate policy making. The nominated second chamber suffers from the fact that if nominated on party-principles it is, as in Canada, entirely noxious, and, if on the principle of eminent service, it does not necessarily relate the service it distinguishes to the political process. Lord Lister was a great surgeon; but that does not qualify him to contribute to a debate on social insurance. Lord Pirrie was a great ship-builder; but his opinions on African slavery are not thereby significant. Every rich man on such a senate would be merely a representative of the interests of prosperity; every great public servant is either, like the retired proconsul from India or Egypt, vaccinated against the democratic habit of thought, or, like the ex-Treasury officials nominated to the House of Lords, valuable rather upon committees of inquiry, than in debate upon bills. It is better, therefore, to have directly single-chamber government, and to throw the burden of control upon the electorate which chooses the chamber, and the executive which directs its activities.[29]

The problem in a Federal State is obviously somewhat different in character. There we have the union of areas different in size, and often enough, different also in interest, which seek in their union some special protection against the danger of being over-weighted by more populous neighbours. In America and Australia the difficulty was met by equal representation in the Senate of those States; in Germany it is met by the Bundesrath. Yet it is worth while to remember that, Germany apart (since the operation, there, of the monarchical principle introduced considerations absent elsewhere), the effect of State equality has been largely overcome by the operation of the party-system. Republicans in the American Senate vote in much the same way as Republicans in the House of Representatives; Liberals in the Australian Senate remember their party as much as their State. Once, in fact, a federal State comes into being there grows up a sense of nationalism which, facilitated by the growth of communications, tends to make largely obsolete the original units of representation. So, for instance, the interests of Massachusetts are hardly distinguishable from the interests of the States of the Atlantic Seaboard; the interests of Minnesota are one with the interests of the Mid-North-Western block of agricultural States. The unreality of State-boundaries was strikingly seen in the way in which West Virginia was carved out of its mother-State. The two Dakotas might perfectly well be one; and they might equally well be linked with Nebraska and Minnesota. America and Australia, indeed, are fortunate in that their federal problems do not possess a racial aspect; that is not the case with Canada, Germany and Switzerland. The French-Canadian has genuine special interests to safeguard, the South German is different from the Prussian, the Swiss must conciliate special religious views. Yet even where such diversities are in issue, I do not see a second chamber is of much assistance.

That is clearly not the case in Canada. "Since the organisation of the Commonwealth", writes Sir J.S. Willison,[30] "the Senate has proceeded on the principle that to question the expediency and justice of conservative legislation is flagrant treason to British Institutions in North America". The Australian Senate has already broken down from any angle of constructive significance. The American Senate, at any rate since the civil war, has been divided, not in terms of States, but in terms of regional economic interests which have equally divided the House of Representatives. I believe myself that no safeguard necessary to the units of a federation requires the protective armour of a second chamber. I suggest that all the requisite protection can be secured (a) by the terms of the original distribution of powers embodied in the constitution and (b) by the right to judicial review possessed by the courts. Amendment of that distribution, if needed, could be secured by demanding a two-thirds majority for its passage in the legislative assembly, and either the assent of a majority, or of two-thirds of the constituent States. These would then possess ample safeguards for their defence. Their representatives in the legislative assembly would be there to protect them with their votes. Their authority could not be altered except by a specially constructed national act. They would lose, doubtless, the right to equal representation in the Senate; but I have already argued that such right is, as a result of the party-system, largely illusory. Even complex racial issues, like the rights of

French-Canadians, admit of adequate protection by such means.

A quite different method of two-chamber government has been outlined with great attractiveness by Mr. and Mrs. Webb.[31] Broadly, they accept the case against a second chamber in its present form. But they are so impressed by the overwhelming burden of the modern legislative assembly that they suggest a division of its business into two parts, each of which is to possess a Parliament for its control. "What we shall call the Political Democracy", they write,[32] "dealing with national defence, international relations, and the administration of justice, needs to be set apart from what we propose to call the Social Democracy, to which is entrusted the national administration of the industries and services by and through which the community lives. The sphere of the one is *Verwaltung, autorité regalienne,* police power; that of the other is *Wirthschaft, gestion,* housekeeping. The Co-operative Commonwealth of To-morrow must accordingly have, not one national assembly only, but two, each with its own sphere; not, of course, without mutual relations, to be hereafter discovered, but co-equal and independent, and neither of them first or last. We regard ... two co-ordinate national assemblies, one dealing with criminal law and political dominion, and the other with economic and social administration, not merely as the only effective way of remedying the present congestion of parliamentary business, but also as an essential condition of the progressive substitution, with any approach to completeness of the community for the private capitalist".

In the scheme set forth by Mr. and Mrs. Webb, the Political Parliament would be elected as now, and its proceedings would be guided by an executive built upon the model of the English cabinet. The Social Parliament would be similarly elected; but it would sit for a fixed term of years with dissolution possible only under special circumstances. It would do its work mainly through committees presided over by chairmen, who would not accept, at least necessarily, each other's views, and would be responsible only for their own committees, the model, in fact, being the structure of the London County Council. To the Social Parliament, it is important to note, will be transferred all the financial powers of the present House of Commons. Admittedly, the two bodies will find it impossible to live absolutely separate lives. Some of the decisions of each will trench on the other's sphere. The Political Parliament, for instance, will have to decide what expenditure it recommends for the subjects is controls, and to present the bill to the Social Parliament. Mr. and Mrs. Webb seem to object to the detailed scrutiny of the bill; they would have only acceptance or rejection. Where disagreement developed, there would be conference, and, if conference proved abortive, there would be a joint session of the two Parliaments in which the aggregate vote would settle the matter. This machinery would also be used for alterations in the constitution. It may also be necessary to have a joint annual session to deal with finance, and a standing joint committee on finance which will prepare the estimates. When deadlock seems incapable of resolution, either a referendum or a double dissolution might provide the means of settlement.[33]

The basic ideas involved in this scheme are, as it seems, two in number. There is, first of all, the notion that only the division of the business to be settled by government into two parts can possibly prevent the legislative assembly from being overwhelmed. There is, secondly, the belief that the balance of power made by this creation of independent assemblies makes for freedom. "It would be open to the Social Parliament", write Mr. and Mrs. Webb,[34] "to organise the public services in whatever way was thought fit ... (but) it would not be within the power of the Social Parliament, without obtaining the concurrence of the Political Parliament ... either to make the use of any public service legally compulsory under penalty, or to make it an offence for the service to be supplied in any other way". Similarly, the Political Parliament ought not to embark upon a policy of increased armaments, or international expansion, without the concurrence of a Social Parliament, guarding the purse-strings of the State for the development of its own schemes.[35]

The plan is, I think, much the most serious so far put forward to deal with the problem of the legislative assembly in the modern State. But it is also, I suggest, despite its great merits, an inherently unworkable plan. It is, first of all, an elementary induction from the experience of history that the Parliament with the taxing-power must, sooner or later, draw essential control to itself; and the Political Parliament would, I believe, quite rapidly develop into a subordinate assembly limited to a partial control over a narrow field. Nor is the division of authority outlined by Mr. and Mrs. Webb a natural one. Foreign policy cannot be separated from economic policy; a tariff-scheme, a State-purchase of raw materials, a part-guarantee of an international loan, all involve areas equally within the competence of either assembly. You cannot ask a Social Parliament to pass measures raising money for a department of foreign affairs and persuade it not to criticise the conduct of foreign affairs, and that the more when such conduct will have profoundly affected matters within its own sphere. For the five years from 1918, the Labour Party in the House of Commons protested that an Anglo-Russian agreement was a partial specific for unemployment; in the plan under discussion, Anglo-Russian affairs belong to one Parliament and unemployment to another. The Political Parliament could not effectively discuss whether refusal to take advantage of a national electricity supply should be made a penal offence without, either avowedly or by implication, discussing the desirability of a national electricity supply. As soon, that is to say, as law-making is seriously envisaged, any attempt at compartmentalising it is purely verbal. Further difficulties, moreover, are involved. If the Social Parliament rejected the Army Estimates of the Political Parliament, it might be upheld in the Joint Session, not by the vote of the Political members, but by the addition of the minority among the latter to its own majority. In that case, the Political Parliament would have to resign; not, be it noted, because its policy was unacceptable to those to whom it was responsible, but because it was disliked by men who could not criticise its details and were not responsible for its application.

Nor is this all. The plan, as I believe, would mean joint committees between the two Parliaments on every subject of importance; and joint committees either imply the acceptance of the report by the two legislations, in which case the joint committees are the true repositories of power, or rejection, in which case the legislatures will find it necessary to sit almost continuously in joint session. But either case reveals the serious defect that the policy ultimately carried would not be a policy at all, but a series of discrete statutes uninformed by any general principles. You cannot actually have a liberal policy in health and a reactionary policy in education at one and the same time. Yet that is the possibility Mr. and Mrs. Webb imply. Nor do they tell us on what issues the Social Parliament is to be elected. Who are to be its leaders will not be known until after it is elected; and, by that fact popular control of its policy is largely denied. If the two Parliaments are not elected simultaneously, their moral complexion may be so different that, other difficulties apart, each may frustrate the purposes of the other; and if they are elected simultaneously, they will largely act as two great wings of a single assembly which never has an opportunity to co-ordinate State-policy. I do not, moreover, believe that merely because one Parliament controlled public services, and the other the mechanisms of justice, personal liberty would be rendered safer thereby. If the postal employees, the miners, and the railway workers went on strike under national ownership, the mere fact that they were responsible to the Social Parliament and not to the Political would not make the latter less involved. It would still have to maintain law and order, and it would have to maintain it under the very difficult circumstances of being unable to end the strike (which would be the business of the Standing Committee of the Social Parliament) and unable to refuse the assistance demanded by the Social Parliament. Where, moreover, does the maintenance of law and order end? May it not, in the instance here taken,[36] involve running the mails, and mines and railways, as all essential to public order? And, in that event, what becomes of the independent powers nicely separated to secure personal liberty?

The making of policy, therefore, seems to involve a single assembly charged with the oversight of the whole field of administration. I agree with Mr. and Mrs. Webb that it is desirable to withdraw much of what is now the concern of that assembly from the field of its competence. I agree, also, that the maximisation of liberty is of the highest importance. But the introduction of rigid categories into administration seems to me attended by the same difficulties as we found to be implied in the doctrine of the separation of powers. Bridges have, in fact, to be built, and those who guard those bridges remain masters of the field. The objects in view can be obtained in a different way, and without the complexities to which this scheme of dyarchy gives rise. Liberty, assuredly, does not arise from the simple mechanical device it would imply. Men have been sent to prison for offences in America that are plainly in the area of the First Amendment to the Constitution; and the courts have refused to question the action of the executive. The real remedy for such outrages is rarely in the forms of constitutions; it is always, ultimately, resident in the spirit of the citizen-body. It may be added that the reason why the procedure of a body like the London Country Council is successful lies in the fact of its limited competence. It is because the area it must traverse is broadly known that it is able to manipulate a committee-system as the operative agency of government. That is not the case with a legislative assembly where the area of authority is broadly undefined. The limits of demarcation must then be fixed by men who survey the boundaries they set up from a broadly similar point of view. They must be able to perform their task in such fashion as to be responsible for each act they do as part of a broad stream of tendency. They must want higher wages because they want better education, better education because they want industrial self-government Mr. and Mrs. Webb give us no access to this coherency. It could, indeed, be obtained under their plan by the chairman of committees meeting together with the cabinet of the Political Parliament; but they would then form a cabinet which would be effective only as it agreed in general outlook, and was able to drive its agreements through the two assemblies. But it is inherent in the plan that there is no assurance of either. Policy would remain, almost certainly, a patchwork of disconnected ideas. But law-making, so conceived, is fatal to good administration, and it is the first business of a legislative assembly to make good administration possible.

### (b) *Membership and Functions*

The single-chamber and magnicompetent legislative assembly seems, therefore, best to answer the needs of the modern State. Who ought to be capable of being chosen for its members? Limitation, if limitation there is to be, must be so safeguarded that it excludes in general terms, and does not weight the scales against any special class of citizens. But there is no reason why we should allow men to be chosen without regard to their experience of affairs. Absence of limitation may give us a younger Pitt, but it gives us also a large number of members who go to the legislative assembly merely for the prestige which membership confers. A rich man persuades a constituency to adopt his son as candidate because he can afford to pay the expenses of election; a retired merchant becomes a candidate to satisfy the social conditions of an aspiring wife; the wife of a member elevated to the House of Lords succeeds him on a wave of sentiment unrelated to the problem of her fitness. It is wiser, surely, to exact a small qualification for membership in order that those seeking election may offer proof of a genuine interest in affairs. Nor is such a qualification difficult to find. If members were, before their candidature was legal, required to serve three years on a local body, they would gain that "feel" of institutions so necessary to success. We should then have some evidence of a real wish on their part to grasp the nature of public business; and we should, I think, do not a little to revivify local life by making it the necessary avenue to a career in the national assembly. We should not, thereby, exclude any serious person from a political career, and it would not be difficult to devise alternative qualifications (such as membership of the civil service) for those to whom membership of a local had been *a priori* impossible.

It is, I think, obvious that, once elected, there should be no limit to the period of re-eligibility a member of the legislative assembly should enjoy. A system which puts an end to his period of service just when he is beginning to gain experience deprives itself of not the least useful instrument he possesses. For in a legislative assembly, few things compensate for the absence of experience. Procedure is inevitably technical; and any limit will merely end a man's term when he is at the height of his utility. It is, moreover, notorious that in assemblies like the American House of Representatives, where what may be termed the legislative turnover is enormous, much of the wastage of time, and not a little of the lack of public esteem, are due to the fact that they are, so to say, almost new assemblies at each epoch of their renewed power. Much of the strength of a chamber like the House of Commons has come from the fact that its leading figures have, over long years, been distinguished actors there. The thirty years' membership of Edmund Burke, the sixty years' service of Mr. Gladstone, the forty years' of Mr. Disraeli, all meant an incomparable insight into the technique of government. Even in the case of the advent of a new party, like the British Labour Party, to power, its leaders had been familiar with the centre of public affairs for twenty years. And only upon the condition of unlimited eligibility can a legislature properly fulfil its selective function. It is not easy for a man to make his mark there. The atmosphere of legislative debate is different from any other atmosphere in the world. A few outstanding persons like Bright may make an immediate reputation; but the majority will need time to impress themselves upon the assembly, and through the assembly, to become known to the public outside as persons to whom the leadership of the State may be entrusted.

The best period of power for a legislature seems to be not less than four, nor more than five years. Not less than four, because a smaller period has two grave defects; it does not give the new member adequate familiarity with the ways of the legislature, and it does not leave time for the passage of an ample programme. Here, it may be suggested, American experience is decisive. The fatality attendant on the two-year term of office is that just when the congressman is learning to grasp his work, he has to devote himself to a re-election he is unlikely to secure; and an executive which, in any case, is at a grave disadvantage has to begin all over again the building of the relationships which secure the realisation of its effort. A period longer than five years is a mistake, above all, because, beyond it, the legislature loses touch with the electorate. A party ought to know that it is not so long protected from popular judgment as to be able to assume that its mistakes will be forgotten. I do not think that fixity of period is desirable. New issues constantly arise upon which a refreshment of legislative authority is desirable. A government which cannot command the confidence of a legislature may feel entitled to consider that a general election will give it a new lease of power. When, for instance, in 1909 the House of Lords threw out the Finance Bill of that year, only a general election could have provided Mr. Asquith with the authority necessary to carry through so great a change in the balance of power in the two chambers; and the same is true of the second general election of 1910 by which a mandate was secured for the Parliament Act of 1911. A legislature that is forced to live out its period of office will always be distinguished by two undesirable features. It will so assert its superiority over the executive as to make the latter its tool; and it will pay the less regard to public opinion from the knowledge that its own attitude has a formidable constitutional protection.

The right of dissolution is an invaluable mechanism for the prevention of those evils. But it is, of course, an exceedingly delicate instrument, about the uses of which there are grave differences of opinion.[37] I believe myself that it is imperative to entrust the exercise of the right to the executive of the day. The safeguards against its abuse are obvious and powerful. No executive will have a causeless dissolution for fear of losing office as a result. It will fear the offence it may cause among its supporters. It will know that every electorate resents the dislocation of private business caused by a general election. It will realise that it is useless to trust the hazards of the unknown unless it has some solid achievement behind it likely to attract widespread popular approval. Mr. Gladstone risked a causeless dissolution in 1874; the result was one of the largest Conservative majorities in recent times. Mr. Baldwin acted similarly in 1923; and the result was the advent of the Labour Party to Office. The right to dissolve cannot be left to the legislature, not only because few legislatures can be trusted to vote for their own extinction, but also because, if the proposal to dissolve were defeated in the assembly, it would, obviously, the equivalent to a demand for a new executive. Nor is there any outside agency which can be trusted, for to give such an agency the powers implied in a dissolution is to make it the master both of the policy and fate of the executive, a position only the electorate can occupy. The absence of a power to dissolve is subversive of all executive morale. It leads it to trim its sails to every legislative wind. It throws it into the kind of helpless position occupied by President Wilson on his return to America after the signature of the Treaty of Versailles. The power of dissolution is the recognition that, ultimately, the electorate is the paramount authority in the State. And no executive ought to occupy the seat of power unless its place is sanctioned by that authority. A coherent representative system would be impossible unless the right to dissolve was always the prerogative of the government of the day.

It is the need of a coherent representative system which gives us the clue both to the organisation of the legislative assembly and to its relations with the executive power. One word may perhaps be said upon the size of a legislature, though it is, in general, a practical matter in which theoretical considerations are out of place. No legislature should be so small that its representatives cannot, from the size of their constituencies, have genuine personal relations with the electorate; no legislature should be so large that effective debate is impossible for its members. A body of more than six hundred members, like the House of Commons, obviously means either such a limitation of debate that no argument can be properly put, or the restriction of debate to a handful of members, while the rest remain silent auditors. But it has been the experience of every system that if the mass of its members are compelled to silence, they will not long remain auditors. They will come to give their votes. But debate will be largely a matter carried on for the edification of the electorate, and it will not normally be able to affect the votes of those who decide. Broadly, I should argue that no legislature ought ever to exceed five hundred members, if it is to perform its function efficiently.

I have already defined the purpose of the legislature as the duty of laying down the general rules. How is that purpose to be fulfilled? All methods to this end turn upon the relationship of the legislature to the executive, and the consequences which follow from that relationship. There seem three possibilities, if modern experience is at all adequate as the basis of a criterion. There may be: (1) A complete absence of any organised relation, as in the United States. (2) There may be a fully organised relation, in which, by various means, the legislature dominates the executive, as in France. (3) There may be a fully organised relation in which the executive directs the legislature, without being able to dominate it with any pretence at completeness.

The American system maximises all the difficulties of law-making. The legislature is organised upon no coherent plan; there is no one to whom genuine initiative responsibility belongs for the passage of legislation. The application of law is entrusted to other hands, with the result that its members are largely legislating in a vacuum. The executive has no reason to expect that ample consideration for its felt needs which is essential to successful administration. It cannot control finance, with the result that members are continually able to devote expenditure to objects which are either remote from, or unrelated to, the needs of the State. Debate ceases to possess reality; for it cannot affect the life of the executive, and it does not, therefore, seriously influence the temper of administration. So rigorous a separation, moreover, means that the two organs may be dominated by different parties, so that the activities of each may be, and often have been, thwarted by the hostility of the other. The chambers, moreover, cannot with any reality exercise selective functions for the simple reason that prominence in them is not seriously connected with the chance of high executive office. The congressional system has the capital defect of failing to dramatise political life. The result is that a deadly inertia settles over its legislature. What it does fails to illuminate the public mind. It does not produce important criticism in the newspapers, because no results of pictorial consequence follow from its working. It destroys the quality of officials, because, from their position, they are unable to influence the executive towards the adoption of a continuous and constructive policy. The legislature is continually tempted to interfere in the executive domain, in order thereby to magnify its office; and much of the latter's time is wasted in the futile effort to frustrate that criticism. The system, in short, makes for the almost complete evasion of responsibility. There is no one body of men who must bear the blame for failure. The executive can always insist that legislation is outside its sphere of competence. The legislature knows that, whatever its attitude, its tenure of office is fixed and certain. The complication which results from the rule of local residence is, of course, merely incidental to these difficulties; but it completes a failure to meet the conditions under which legislative success is possible.

The French system has few of the defects inherent in the American plan. Much, doubtless, of its inadequacy arises from the multiplicity of groups of which the Chamber of Deputies is composed. This makes immediately for uncertainty of governmental tenure. A ministry knows that, however admirable its work, the chances are enormously against its remaining in office for more than two years. The day upon which it assumes power is certain to be the day upon which its fall from power is organised. Nor is it given effective leadership over the business of the assembly. Its projects go into the commissions of the Chamber, exactly as the propositions of any private member. They emerge as fully changed; and even its financial measures are amended out of all recognition with but little regard to the coherency of their plan. The difficulties of the French system are mainly two in number. No French ministry is ever likely to have the time to carry out an ample programme; and behind it there always exists the shadow-ministry of the Commissions which derive their influence very largely from the degree to which they are able to dominate the legal ministry. The result makes the deputy a much more important person than, for instance, the average member of the House of Commons. But it makes him important only by sacrificing to him any genuine responsibility on the part of ministers, and any genuine coherence in legislation. Few tests are simpler in this aspect than that of finance. Only one French minister in the half-century of the Republic has attempted seriously to deal with the incidence of taxation and its results; for to do so brings into view the alternative ministries which are proliferated over the legislative assembly. One other consequence of this system deserves mention though it is rarely brought into view. Because the ministry only bears a partial responsibility for legislation, it does not secure from the French civil service assistance either as loyal or as valuable as that upon which an English minister can count. The French civil servant knows how temporary will be his master's rule, and he is tempted, especially in political affairs, to develop a policy and connections of his own, both in the Chamber of Deputies, and in the press, in order to evade the control of the matters from whom he differs.

The British system, as I shall show, is not free from defects, but its superiority to its alternatives is incontestable. It is built upon three great principles. It is assumed to be the business of the executive to drive a stream of tendency through affairs. It must present a programme to the legislature and stand by the acceptance of that programme; if it is rejected upon any serious point, it must either resign or appeal to the electorate. It is, secondly, the final authority in finance. No private member may either propose a financial measure or attempt the increase (he may attempt the reduction) of estimates considered adequate by the government of the day. As a consequence, thirdly, of these two principles, the initiative of the private member has a much narrower field of activity. He may, as in America and France, present his bills in unlimited numbers; but he knows beforehand that the time table and the procedure of the assembly are under the control of the government, and that there is, broadly, no serious prospect of an important measure finding its way to the statute-book unless it secures the guardianship of the government. The merits of the system are plain. In the first place, it not only provides for a coherent legislative structure, but also that those who have planned it shall, if they can secure its acceptance, put it into operation. It makes responsibility, in the second place, immediate, direct, and decisive. Everyone can see who is to be blamed and praised. Everyone knows where measures must originate. Everyone sees exactly whom to punish. And, in the third place, finance and legislation bear a definite relationship to each other. No one can hope to promote his special nostrum, or to benefit his own constituency. Log-rolling, such as that which takes place in the American legislature, is obviated at the outset.

The plain virtues of this system must not, however, blind us to its demerits. It certainly gives the executive an opportunity for tyranny. It can, if it so please, make the most minor issue a question of confidence, and so proffer the alternative either of a support that is not whole-hearted, or a dissolution which will prove inconvenient. Thereby it undoubtedly tends to make debate unreal; for so much depends upon keeping disciplined the ranks of the party in power, that members are not unlikely to oppose a policy in speech, and support it in the division lobby from fear of the consequences of hostility in the latter place. The initiative of the private member may, further, be so restricted by a strong executive that he is reduced almost to nullity. He can become a person only by revolting, and, by revolting, he may place his opponents in power. The legislature may easily, as a consequence, be reduced to what it was under the administration of Mr. Lloyd George, an organ of registration for decisions it is really powerless either to criticise or to alter. It seems to retain, even in that event, the ability to discharge its selective function; but I believe that careful analysis would show that, at a given point, paralysis of the legislative assembly tends to make the executive look elsewhere for its personnel.[38]

Even with these defects, I believe that the British system provides the model upon which we can build the method of relationship between legislature and executive. We shall need to make the executive responsible for the general making of policy. Its members, therefore, will have to be elected members of the legislative assembly, and stand or fall by the important measures they present. They must have complete responsibility for finance, save that, again, their methods may be rejected. They must control, therefore, the time-table of the legislature; and the power of the private member to steer important legislation to the statute-book must be largely non-existent. In the plan they make of the expenditure of time they must always have adequate room for the three great spheres in which the private member makes his greatest contributions. There must always be full opportunity to gain information from the executive by question and answer; and, obviously, there will be occasions upon which a refusal to answer may properly be made a question of confidence in the executive. There must be time, secondly, for the ventilation of grievance. The opportunity to utter complaint is one of the occasions where a legislature has a special value; and it may generally be said that it is the more effective, the ampler the opportunity. There must, thirdly, be such room for debate as gives to the opposition in the assembly a real chance to make its views known upon the problem under discussion. Granted the pressure of business, it is obvious that a limit to discussion is essential; and, certainly, an executive which cannot control the time-table of the legislature is bound to be a failure as an initiator of policy.

But, in so simple a form, these principles will prove inadequate unless they are supplemented in three ways. It is essential, in the first place, to leave room for diversity of opinion in the legislature upon the details of law-making. The individual member must be encouraged to persuade the assembly that his suggestions are, in fact, improvements. The ideas which prevail must not be wholly ministerial ideas. That means the abrogation of the executive right, now exercised, for example, by the British cabinet, to make any questions it chooses questions of confidence upon which turns the existence of the government of the day. The absurdities to which this leads are well known. Under the Balfour administration of 1900 it actually led to a question of whether pillar-boxes should be green being made a matter of confidence; and the unfortunate critic of the executive (who was actually one of its supporters) found himself compelled to deny his own colour-preferences. No will is ever so completely right as to deserve the power to attach to itself the penalties contingently involved in a vote of confidence. There ought to be an independent authority in the legislative assembly who can impartially settle whether amendments proposed are in truth so fundamental as to require that they be made hanging-matters. In England, the Speaker could perform that function in the same way as he certifies that a bill is a money-bill, in order to preserve it from the control of the House of Lords. A power to act in this fashion would, I believe, be an invaluable protection in a legislative assembly not only to the Opposition, but also to those critics of the executive who are anxious to support it in general, but wish also to retain the right to be independent about the details of Public business. I cannot here attempt a detailed account of the grounds upon which an officer like the Speaker, who is by definition removed from the normal heat of party conflict, is essential to the proper functioning of a legislative assembly. But anyone who considers the history of the Speakership in the American House of Representatives will, I think, understand the grounds for the view here urged.[39]

It is necessary, in the second place, to bring the members of the legislative assembly into some organic connection with the executive departments. There might be set up a series of committees, each of which would deal with a single department. They would, as I conceive them, be a body of some dozen members selected, not so much as representative of parties, though parties would be represented upon them, as of the specialised ability on particular questions which the legislature contains. They would work not as the makers of policy, which is primarily, as I have argued, a ministerial function, but in part as a consultative organ, and in part as a means of bringing to the legislature a definitely competent opinion upon the working of the administrative process. They ought to have access to all papers save those of an especially confidential kind. They should have the power to initiate inquiries in the departments. They should be able to summon public servants before them for the taking of evidence upon particular questions. They should have regular meetings with the minister at which his policy, and especially his legislation, is freely discussed and explained. To them should be submitted those ordinances which every executive is compelled to issue out of its discretion and without immediate legislative sanction. Their function, I would emphasise, would give them no specific duties to the legislature, unless it was deemed desirable to make their approval necessary, as I believe it could usefully be made necessary, before the issue of what is called in England delegated legislation.[40] They could, otherwise, report disagreement with the executive only through the ordinary channels of debate. They would have no power to prevent the introduction of legislation, and no authority to dictate ministerial methods. Their business, like that of the King of England, would be to advise, to encourage, and to warn, with the addition that, in the process, they would also learn.

The advantage of such a system seems to me great. In the first place, it ensures a greater responsiveness on the part of the executive to the opinions of the legislative body. It enables the latter, without displaying overt hostility, to press their views, to make suggestions, to glean knowledge. It ensures the presence in debate of a body of men really equipped to understand, whether in agreement or disagreement, ministerial policy. It provides the minister with a testing-ground where he may learn the kind of view the informed public is likely to take of his schemes. It prevents him from becoming a dictator who, like a god in the machine, makes pronouncements to be received as oracular. Not least in importance, it brings his official staff into contact with the outside world and prevents the growth of that habit, typical everywhere of a bureaucracy, of regarding the legislative assembly as its natural foe. Impersonal institutions are always psychologically inadequate; but when they are transformed into agents of flesh and blood, a co-operative understanding becomes possible. I believe, for example, that such a legislative committee on foreign affairs is much the surest way of maintaining a reasonable continuity in policy, without the necessity of those sporadic outbursts of angry publicity which do so much harm to international relationships.

To suggest the construction of such committees is to meet at once with two great difficulties. Would a given committee interfere with the functions of the minister? The committees of Congress and of the French Chambers interfere, as is well known, to nauseation with the administration of the departments. They try to replace the ministerial will by their own. They waste endless time in investigation. They limit initiative and weaken responsibility. But the root of these difficulties lies, I think, in a fact from which the plan here outlined is free. Both in the United States and France the committees have a duty to the legislature. Their business is frankly to expose the minister. They are set there as a watch-dog upon him. They report systematically upon his actions. They announce their concerted view of his measures. The committees I have in view would have no such opportunities. They would not report to the assembly, except in the single case of delegated legislation, and then only in the event of disagreement with the minister. Their proceedings would be private. They could not introduce any bills of which he disapproved. Antagonism, where it developed, would have its sufficient safeguard in the fact that the executive had a majority in the legislature. It is the division between the two in America, and the group system in France, which make the committees system so noxious in its results.

The real difficulties would depend upon the minister himself. Where he is strong, and really understands the process of administration, the committee would be invaluable to him. He could use it not merely to consult, but also as a pathway through which his policy might pass to enlightened assent in the legislative assembly. He would use it to inform himself of the public view of his policy. He would gain from it suggestions and criticisms likely to be of high value. And his officials, I think, would understand the importance of training up in the legislative assembly a body of members really informed on the functions of a minister. That, it may be added, would improve enormously the selective function the legislature performs; for the committees would serve as the nucleus from which future ministers might be drawn, and there would be absent from the making of ministries much of that difficulty in the choice of office which is now so apparent. With a weak minister, of course, the position would be more difficult. His tendency, undoubtedly, would be to shift the burden of responsibility upon his committee, and that, in the nature of things, would tempt it to using its functions. The remedy against that danger lies largely in the quality of the public service. If they can make the tradition of their department creative, the difficulty will be at its minimum; a man like Sir Robert Morant can always do much to vaccinate a minister against the disease of timidity. But even were it at its maximum, I shall think the experiment is vital. In most matters of administration the lay mind has a fund of common sense to contribute which is unrealised by the expert, absorbed in his daily routine. The mutual impact of minds so different would provide a fund of inventiveness in the details of daily work, and inventiveness in minor detail is the quality by which the official is saved from that dull routine which stifles him in the red-tape of his own traditions. And, lastly, it may be noted that unless some such knowledge as these committees would confer is open to the private member, there is no way in which the legislature can criticise those who lead it from the angle of assured competence. A legislature without access to technical knowledge is always at the mercy of a confident executive. Here, at least, there are the means of mitigating that disparity.[41]

The third supplement to these general principles is more revolutionary. All legislative debate involves at least two stages. There is discussion, first, of general principle, and, second, the dissection of that principle in detail, as it is presented in the clauses of a measure. The mass of business which confronts the modern legislature has made it necessary to delegate the second stage, more and more, to committees of the legislature, which report back their findings to the whole assembly. But these committees largely nullify the value of their work by modelling their organisation and procedure upon that of the legislature as a whole. The methods necessary for the discussion of principle, upon which the life of the executive depends, are not the same as those suited to the discussion of detail. In the latter case, the problems raised are almost always technical, and, as a rule, the normal party conflict is out of place. I believe that, more and more, the committee stage on all bills not of the first magnitude is capable of great improvement. It is clear that there are bills, of which the Treaty with the Irish Free State Act of 1922 is an example, in which amendment by the legislature, save in the form of rejection, is impossible because the executive is, so to say, committed to every comma of the bill as it stands. But that is not true of all save a few measures. The majority are susceptible of change, and the executive itself amend them as they make their way to the statute-book.

Once a bill is sent to a legislative committee of this kind. I believe that the procedure upon it should be transformed into a process akin to that of committees in British municipalities. There, it will be remembered, the permanent official is present at debate; he answers questions, makes suggestions, explains, difficulties, affords information. The whole difference between a good and bad committee on a municipal body is between a committee which really makes use of its officials at its meeting, and one intent on demonstrating the inferiority of the paid servant to the elected councillor. I believe that it would be a great step forward if ministers were to take their permanent officials to the committees of the legislature and give them a full opportunity to be useful to members in the discussion. That would lead, firstly, to the disappearance of much deliberate obstruction. It would give assurance that discussion of questions in their nature wholly, or even mainly, technical were dealt with in a technical way. It would remove the element of partisanship which now tends to permeate problems where it is obviously out of place. It would ensure also that the views of the private member would receive more real consideration than is now possible. For the tendency would be to transform these committees into bodies much more like the Private Bill Committee of the House of Commons, where a bill, however objectionable in principle, is discussed in its details simply with a view to making it an adequate measure. Obviously, of course, the permanent official could only speak when so permitted by the minister in charge of the bill under discussion. But I think it would be discovered in the use of this procedure that much business was in fact non-contentious which is now assumed to be necessarily the fighting-ground of parties. I think legislation thereby would be at once more rapid and more effective. And the great debate would be all the better for being limited to the type of occasion—the analysis of principle—where alone it is likely to be fruitful.

One other problem in the relationship of executive and legislature needs a word. It is always important to prevent the executive from influencing the private member by way of corruption. That influence may take the most diverse forms. It may, as in America, result from a discreet share in the bestowal of patronage; the friends and relatives of the member may be given office, sometimes high judicial office, in return for his vote. A most insidious form is when the size of the political executive is so large that its members have a direct influence upon the size of its majority, and a direct interest, whatever its policy, in keeping it in power. An average British administration to-day, for instance, has at least some fifty members; a French ministry has hardly less. Clearly an upper limit to the size of a ministry is essential when a fifth of the whole party in power may be in office. For similar reasons, no public servants ought to be members of the legislative assembly; for the facilities for influencing them corruptly are too large not to be exercised, and too difficult not to be detected. Another form of influence lies in the right of the executive to confer titles of honour. Man is a vain creature, and the "bit of ribbon to stick in his coat" casts a glamour over official opinion. Either definite legislation against the conference of titles on political grounds, or a self-denying ordinance which makes them impossible of access, would, I think, be of great value. And it should always be illegal for any executive to give paid governmental employment to any member of a legislative assembly.[42] A list of exceptions could easily be made for the type of post where legislative experience is of obvious assistance, a post, for instance, like the governorship of a colony.

It goes without saying that the members of a legislative assembly must enjoy the utmost freedom of debate. They cannot be bound by the limitations which are referable to a court of law. For, obviously, if their statements and suggestions come within the ambit of the law of libel and slander, much would not be said in discussion that is essential to its value. Men must be able then to hint their belief in corruption even when the chain of proof is not legally ample. They must be able to describe the proceedings of, for instance, a colonial governor as tyrannical without having to face an action for damages. Whether they should be so protected outside the legislative assembly is a much more difficult matter to decide. Much of the work of a member is done in letters to the press and in public meeting. He may have views and ideas it is important for him to express, and yet be unable to find occasion for giving them vent in the legislative assembly. He ought not, clearly, to be given an open cheque to slander as he will; but there is some case, to take an English example, for protecting him from the consideration he is likely to receive from a London jury in a political libel action. Certainly it would be difficult for a man who felt strongly about the policy of Governor Eyre to have stigmatised it in adequate terms unless he were able to do so from a point of protected vantage in the House of Commons.

## (v) The Executive

### (a) *Political*

The executive in the modern State has, in general, three aspects. It is, firstly, as I have already sought to show, a committee of the party in power in the legislative assembly, offering proposals to that assembly, and holding office upon the condition of winning assent to those proposals. It is, secondly, an administering body applying legislation. It has to manage the vast body of officials who are necessary if the work of administration is to be efficiently carried out. It is, thirdly, in continuous relationship with the mass of citizens through its function as administrator; and I argued earlier in this book that the quality of its administration depends, in large part, on the way in which those citizens are associated with it in the tasks it performs.

Let us take each of these aspects separately. The executive as a political body has three main functions. It is concerned, first, with the final choice of policy to be submitted for acceptance to the legislative assembly. Its existence, as an executive, will depend upon the fate of that policy. And, since the legislature is generally, and at its most efficient, divided into two parties, it is obvious that the executive is, in this regard, broadly the leaders of the party in power. Its business is to translate the declared will of the party into terms of measures. It derives its knowledge of that will in part from the announcements of the party itself, in part from the reception of its policy from its supporters, in part, above all, from all the complex pressure of opinion that it meets as it moves upon its way. It decides policy; and, once the policy is accepted, it is its business to see to it that the public services apply that policy, in spirit and in detail, in the sense intended by the legislative assembly. For it will have to meet there criticism of the way in which policy is carried out. It will be responsible for what is done. Error will be its error; blame will be blame it has to shoulder. The policy, moreover, cannot be applied in detail from a single centre. It has to be delimited into its various aspects. The man who is responsible for health cannot also be responsible for naval and military defence. The man who deals with foreign policy cannot also charge himself with supervising the details of educational administration. The third function, therefore, of the political executive is first to delimit and then to co-ordinate the activities of the different departments of State.

I shall call the political aspect of the executive the cabinet, since this is the name it has come to possess in the majority of modern States. How shall it be chosen, of whom shall it be composed, what shall be its size? Though these may seem questions of form, they go in fact to the very heart of political theory. Shall, for instance, the formal head of the State, as in America, be the chief member of the cabinet? Are his colleagues to be, as there, his subordinates, or are they to be co-equal with him in a common task. Experience is, I think, clear that every State needs an official head who is not the active head of the cabinet. He may, as in France, be the president of a republic, or, as in England, a constitutional monarch, stripped of all save the ceremonial of power. For the American system is bound to have two results: (1) the tenure of the chief executive is fixed; (2) the nature of his power is such that his colleagues are bound to be subordinate to him in legal as well as actual authority. The method both in England and in France enables the political parties to choose their leader, to permit him to form a cabinet of his colleagues, and, on their defeat as a cabinet, either to give place to their opponents, or to appeal for renewal of power to the electorate.

The leader of a party so chosen becomes Prime Minister. It is, I think, axiomatic that he should be free to select his colleagues, and that his party should not choose those who are to serve with him. The latter method is open to the grave disadvantages that it destroys flexibility of choice, and that it may well mean the triumph of availability rather than merit. Any party will be a collocation of units of varying views, and to leave it to choose the colleagues of the Prime Minister will mean not the representation of those best fitted to make a policy, but of members of each unit who must do the best they can to formulate a unified policy. Such unity is not difficult in opposition, where hostility to a common foe is the law of life. But it is of the highest difficulty when the party has a majority. And, in any case, to give to the Prime Minister legal freedom of choice does not mean that he can pick and choose as he pleases. There will be, in every party, a body of men whose standing in the legislative assembly makes imperative the recognition of their claims. Mr. Gladstone did not like Mr. Chamberlain, but he was compelled to admit him to his cabinet. Lord Salisbury, doubtless, would have been happy not to offer Lord Randolph Churchill the leadership of the House of Commons, but in fact he had no alternative. Where the Prime Minister is really free is in the actual disposition of offices; and here again he is largely limited by the fact that he must induce his colleagues to accept those for which he denominated them. The breakdown of Lord John Russell's attempt to form a government in 1845 through the unwillingness of Grey and Palmerston to accept the offices for which he destined them is evidence that the limitation is real.[43] A further check on error would be obtained if the legislative committees on departments I discussed above were in operation. For their working would tend to allocate members to such office as genuinely interested them. They would act as a sorting-house in which could be separated those members whose interest, like that of John Bright, is in the broad principles of policy, and those who, like Sir James Graham or Cardwell in England, like Gallatin and Roon in other countries, have a positive talent for the specific details of administration.

Outside these limits, the greater flexibility there is, the better for the working of the system; and the concentration of choice in the hands of the Prime Minister seems to be the best guarantee of flexibility. But a cabinet so formed may be of two kinds. It may either, as with the War Cabinet of Mr. Lloyd George, be a body of four or five persons who concern themselves only with general policy, and leave its application to subordinate ministers, or, as with the historic cabinet of Great Britain and the continent, a larger body, the majority of whom are concerned in the active administration of their departments.[44] I do not think there can be any serious question about the superiority of the latter method. Policy cannot really be separated from administration; the essence of measures lies always in their execution. Men who seek to avoid detail will find either that their principles fail because of the neglect of detail, or that, despite their avowed concentration on principle, they are in fact spending their time not merely on detail, but also upon the effort to settle disputes between departments as to whom that detail belongs, without the knowledge which comes from being immersed in the technique of administration. Since, moreover, the departmental ministers will always be subordinate, there will be a tendency on the part of the legislative assembly to disregard them and to appeal beyond to the small policy-making cabinet. That will make for a lack of coherence in administration. For the effort of the cabinet will then be directed to placating the legislature at the expense of its subordinate ministers. The same will be true of the pressure of outside interests; and, sooner or later, those who are the heads of administration in the executive will cease to play a serious part in the disposition of affairs.

The cabinet on the second model therefore seems preferable. It ought not, however, to be a large body. It has to assume collective responsibility for the whole ordering of policy and administration. It needs to develop a unity of outlook, to be able to act quickly and effectively as problems arise for its decision. A body of some ten or twelve members seems the most suitable for this purpose. It is large enough to be able to cover the general field of administration, and small enough to develop a genuine corporate mind about the large issues it confronts. I do not mean that twelve posts exhaust the area of subjects which requires ministers for their administration, but that the division of the field of policy into at most a dozen large categories, each presided over by a minister, leaves room for the best results. That is, I think, borne out by several considerations of recent experience. A smaller number does not enable the great departments to be represented in the making of policy; a larger number inevitably gives rise to a smaller cabinet within the cabinet who will more and more tend to the arrogation of decision. Or, alternatively, the larger number will mean such a volume of cabinet business that the co-ordination of policy will be neglected, and each minister will be left to a largely uncontrolled mastery of his field.

What should be the relationship between the members of such a cabinet? With two exceptions, that is a matter which belongs rather to the art than to the theory of politics. It is plain that a certain primacy belongs to the Prime Minister. He is both the leader of the party and the leader of the legislative assembly. To him, more than to any other person, belongs the responsibility for political strategy. He has to drive the team, to persuade recalcitrant colleagues into harmony, to state the issue to the electorate in their most authoritative form. It will, I think, be found that the most successful cabinets have always been those in which the Prime Minister has been able to impose his will upon his colleagues with an authority to which no other member can pretend. For it must be remembered that in making decisions a cabinet has rather to weigh opinions than to count them; responsibility in its problems does not adequately arise from the simple taking of a vote. The more influence that attaches to the Prime Minister's view, the easier it will be to secure unity of outlook. This does not, it must be emphasised, mean that the Prime Minister should out-distance his colleagues in the fashion of an American President. That leads to a centralisation of authority which always means that decisions are ignorantly taken; it leads to flattery of the chief by his subordinates; to a theory also of indispensability which turns, ultimately, into a doctrine, applied, at least internally, of presidential infallibility. The doctrine of indispensability is impossible for the simple reason that it is the basis of a democratic system that no person is indispensable.

In the second place, a certain primacy belongs to the Minister of Finance. For taxation lies, and is likely increasingly to lie, at the heart of the modern State. The minister who has the power to search the pockets of citizens is entrusted with an authority of peculiar magnitude. With him, also, belongs the control of the national debt, and, through his influence over the banking and currency systems, a power over commerce and industry, which are, from any angle, overwhelming. Inevitably this sphere involves a special attitude to the expenditure of the State; for it must control that expenditure at least to that debatable point where taxation becomes confiscatory in character. It will, indeed, by its relation to the spending-power of other departments involve a certain supervision of their policy. How much supervision it should involve depends upon factors with which I am not here concerned. Certainly, the British system of treasury control has great advantages in that it saw to it that expenditure proposed was not more than adequate for the end desired; but I think most experts outside the British Treasury would agree that it had great defects in compensation. Particularly in the period of the positive state, upon which we have now entered, it needs great courage and determination in a Minister of Finance to resist the pressure of the spending departments. But the principle of a single body of estimates criticised collectively from the angle of what is practically a non-spending department is the key to sound finance; and it obviously makes the minister in charge second only to the Prime Minister himself.

Otherwise, all members of a cabinet are on an equal footing; and the distinctions which appear are the result, not of theory and its needs, but of the interplay of unpredictable personality. A cabinet is likely to be the more successful, the more its basic decisions result from a genuinely corporate discussion. The less respect there is paid to the notion that the minister in each department is omnipotent the better it will be for the spirit of its work. For, otherwise, it meets two dangers that have been strikingly manifest in recent times. The one is that there is really no body of persons effectively charged with the total survey of policy; and the other that what appears as the policy of the minister, and respected as such, is, in fact, merely the policy of his permanent officials. This latter distinction is important. Every bureaucracy, however eager to be liberal, tends to give undue reverence to its own methods and its own traditions; and when it encounters novel suggestions, its habit is to begin by emphasising their impossibility and continue by insisting on their unwisdom. It needs a strong minister to triumph over departmental conservatism; and, outside agencies apart (a point I shall discuss later), there must be means in the cabinet to insist that departmental conservatism is never accepted as final. That will only occur when the cabinet regards itself as free to intervene in the work of the departments, and to insist upon the paramount character of its decisions. It may be wrong; it often will be wrong; but policy is never co-ordinated unless it interprets its function in this way. Otherwise it becomes merely a body whose business is simply the arrangement of work for, and decisions in, the legislative assembly; and, thereby, the half of its value is lost.

I have already pointed out that the Prime Minister occupies a special position of authority among his colleagues. Two corollaries of that position seem implied in the modern history of the office. It is important that he should not be burdened with departmental work. His business is to retain a fresh and open mind upon the general problems of the government. He has to act as the source of general emollience in the ministry. He has to keep himself informed about the broad outline of events in all departments of State. A Prime Minister who endeavours to combine these functions with the pressure, for instance, of an office like that of foreign affairs, is bound to neglect one of other; and each is too important to make neglect admissible. He must be the active leader of the legislative assembly. His presence there has a twofold significance. It co-ordinates, in a way otherwise unattainable, the work of his colleagues in the legislature. If his appearances in the assembly are rare, there will always grow up a tendency to regard him as a court of appeal from the rest of his cabinet. He will become a President instead of a Prime Minister. His absence, secondly, will have the disastrous effect of transferring the centre of decision away from the legislative assembly. The fact that he is not available there will make him sought where he can be found. His office will become a centre of pressure from powerful interests which gain access to him. He will be tempted to make agreements with them, and to present those agreements to the assembly as *faits accomplis* which they can only reject by compelling the resignation of his government. An assembly so placed is bound to decline swiftly in respect of citizens. Its debates will become unreal, because they will be felt not to affect the true source of decision. Policy will not be made in the light of day; and an assembly lives by the policy it can secure. This, it may be added, is another reason for the superiority of the two-party system. For a Prime Minister who presides over a coalition of groups which can always form a new combination is always plagued by an instability that is fatal to the integrity of his work. A policy of ideas becomes a policy of manoeuvres; and the attention which should be given to the large outlines of legislation becomes necessarily devoted to the minor tactics by which the dissolution of the coalition is prevented.

Obviously, this envisages a strong executive forcing a coherent plan of legislation to the statute-book. It is necessary, therefore, to inquire into two aspects of the problems raised by a strong executive. What opportunity, first, is given to the legislative assembly to make its own impact upon the executive? What place, secondly, have the various interests of society in the structure here outlined? The legislative assembly, I think, has three clear safeguards within itself. It can always dismiss the cabinet from office. Though the power to dismiss will rarely be exercised, it always remains as a contingent threat of high value. It cannot, secondly, be forced to pass legislation which affects the constitutional foundations of the State, except under special circumstances, such as a two-thirds vote of the assembly, which are not likely to exist unless there is a situation of grave need. It could not, in the view here taken, be forced to abrogate the Habeas Corpus Act, to pass such a measure as the Espionage Act of the United States, or a bill giving the executive authority to legislate by proclamation. It has, thirdly, its legislative committee for each department which will give it an intimate knowledge of the details of administration. It will thereby know, informally as well as formally, what is in the ministerial mind. It will see what materials lead him to the formation of his judgment. It will be able to criticise and oppose in an atmosphere from which the threat of resignation or dissolution is absent. Here it should be insisted that no such system of committees can possibly be adequate which does not provide for the examination of estimates of expenditure by the departments. We do not need the meticulous control now exercised by the French Commissions, and the Congressional Committees. But we do need to avoid the impasse in which the British House of Commons now finds itself, of being able to criticise national expenditure only after the money has been spent. Committees on estimates, with the requisite staff of experts independent of the executive, and with the right of examination of the departments, are therefore essential, and no criticism so far made of their necessity seems to me to have realised the danger of their absence.[45] One further protection that the legislature requires is the creation, within itself, of what is called in America a legislative reference bureau.[46] Without it, the private member is too often at a disadvantage in his contests with the cabinet. He does not know the materials he ought to use; he is not aware of experiments relevant to his inquiries. The minister, amply protected by the panoply of his experts, evades the issue by a thrust of fact that the proper organisation of the member's interest would always enable him to parry.

A very different relation to the executive exists in the case of the citizen-body. Their problem is to make their will known, in such a way that not only are their needs apparent, but also to demonstrate that the will declared has a strong body of opinion behind it. At present, the citizen-body brings its pressure to bear in a variety of ways. At the electoral period, it awards office to a party with whose general ideas it is, for the time, in sympathy. After the election, the different associations pass resolutions, prepare petitions, canvass the members of the legislature, take deputations to ministers. Sometimes their pressure is strong enough to obtain an inquiry into some special problem; on occasion, as in the Trades Disputes Act of 1906, they are powerful enough to force the executive to act on their behalf. But, in general, public opinion suffers from two grave difficulties. It is rarely organised in a continuous relation with the government; its connections are not institutional, but spasmodic. It can only, moreover, criticise what the government is doing in the light of specific acts which, by being acts, already exist in an atmosphere of prestige which make inquiry no easy matter. The first difficulty I shall deal with later, since its solution depends upon the executive as an administering and not as a political body. The second, I suggest, can be met by a simple expedient for which ample precedent exists in political experience.

That expedient, I suggest, may take two forms. It may either, in the case of public bills, involve what is called in Massachusetts a "public hearing",[47] or, in the case of problems where no bill has been introduced, of organising inquiry with a view to securing definite opinion by its results. Let us take the first form separately. When a bill has been sent to a committee of the legislature, if that committee so decides, it might take evidence, not upon the principle, but upon the details of the measure, from members of the public, either as individuals, or through organised associations. It might, for instance, take evidence from landlords and tenants upon the problems of rent restriction; it might bear from employers and workmen on the clauses of a Trade Boards Act; from dentists and medical men on a bill to prevent untrained persons practising dentistry. And the value of such "hearings" would, I think, be intensified by the presence of permanent officials at that committee stage. The committee would grow into what Mr. Lowell calls a semi-judicial attitude. "It comes to look on itself as sitting in judgment upon the matters presented to it", he writes,[48] "rather than as acting on its own initiative; and this to an extent that is at times surprising. In the best sense, the procedure is extremely democratic, for it gives the whole people a chance to take part in legislation at the formative state. But it is by no means democratic in the false sense that the opinions of all men are given equal importance". The limitations of such evidence to the details of measures follows from the fact that the cabinet has made itself responsible for the principle. The settlement of its wisdom is then a matter for the legislation as a whole. But I see no reason why there should not be a chance for special knowledge to be publicly available at the discussion of details. Matters like the number of witnesses to be heard, the method of their examination, and so forth, are simply questions of detail; and it is suggestive that only 13 per cent of the "hearings" in Massachusetts occupied more than a single day.

The second form of this expedient may suitably take a wider ambit. There is a great variety of problems upon which either little quantitative knowledge exists, or which are not deemed of a nature to involve government action for their solution. Here it seems to me desirable to give wide limits to the discretion of citizens. I have already argued that while the cabinet should generally control the time-table of the legislative assembly, some room should be left for the initiative of private members. It is, for instance, under the scope of that initiative that private members introduce bills into the House of Commons; and it is through the wider use of the private bill that a means may be found for the relationship I am recommending. What I propose is that when any member of the legislature introduces a bill, he may have it sent to a select committee if one hundred (or some other suitable figure) other members support such a reference. That select committee would then examine the bill by public hearings and report back its findings to the legislative assembly. The cabinet could then, as it pleased, help it or not to the statute-book. In any case, there would be left upon record a valuable body of evidence upon the subject matter of the bill; and I have already argued that the increase of knowledge upon public questions is a matter of the gravest urgency. On occasion, doubtless, the findings of such a committee would necessitate immediate executive action; a revelation, for instance, such as that of the condition of the chain-makers at Cradley Heath some fifteen years ago,[49] ought to compel the executive to make decisions. In general, probably, the result will be rather the formation of a general public opinion which opens up an avenue through which, later, government action may make its way. Such an inquiry, for example, into the results of raising the school-leaving age from fourteen to sixteen years, would be invaluable. And the method proposed would avoid the danger of that type of inquiry which, suddenly evolved to meet an unanticipated crisis, conducts its work in an atmosphere of passion that is fatal to scientific results.

Nor is it likely, as may be argued, that such a scheme will make every association with a nostrum to propound seek an inquiry of this kind into its validity. Nothing now prevents a member introducing any bill he pleases; and the fact that a fifth of the legislature have to pledge themselves to the need for inquiry is a safeguard against unnecessary multiplication. For the members themselves will act as the judges of the evidence; and the time at their disposal is always sufficiently limited to make it sure that they will not search after every will-o'-the-wisp that flits before them. I do not think it likely that bills would be promoted to restrict salmon and sturgeon fishing in certain rivers; or to require headlights of certain power on locomotives; or to make special provision for the insurance of goats; or to standardise the amount of alcohol permitted in intoxicating liquors—all of which have been the subjects of the referendum or initiative in America and Switzerland—but if we could, by this means, inquire into the relation of birth control to maternity welfare, or the desirability of abolishing the rule of unanimity in jury-cases, or the unification of social insurance, we should make far easier than it now is the path of social improvement. And we should enable every citizen with special experience to have means of direct contact with the legislative assembly. We have the right to assume that such experience will, by that contact, ultimately bear fruitful results.

I have laid much stress here on legislative processes. That is because the truth emphasised by Sir Henry Maine in regard to judicial work holds also of the legislative process. Social progress is secreted in the interstices of legislative procedure. It is in its flexibility, on the one hand, and its accessibility, on the other, that a legislative assembly is most likely to discover the means of its success. It ought not to be separated from the executive, because, in that event, the latter is deprived of the power to become genuinely creative. It ought not to be dominated by the latter because, where that occurs, the private member ceases to be anything but a unit in a division list. It needs the power effectively to criticise and amend the measures of the government because there is no assurance of infallibility in the latter's work. It needs to associate the general public with its effort, partly because there is therein a fund of common sense and experience which ought not to go unused, partly because its organisation is a sphere where the initiative of the private member has a special place, above all because such organisation provides one of the surest means available both for the education of public opinion and the emphasis of public need. Here, as elsewhere, much obviously depends upon the standard of intelligence in the electorate; but that standard is in a reciprocal relation to the institutions I have outlined. They will not, of themselves, assure the realisation of the purpose the State seeks to embody, but they are likely to make more possible than now the fulfilment of that purpose.

### (b) *Administrative*

When policy has been formulated by the cabinet, and accepted by the legislature, it needs to be applied. Here emerges the second great function of the executive, that of co-ordinating and controlling the administration of the State. Its first great problem is the principle upon which the flow of business is to be distributed between departments. There is, of course, no rigid system of categories into which all business may naturally be placed. But I believe that the broad choice by which any executive is confronted is between distribution by persons and distribution by services. We might have a ministry which dealt with children, one for unemployed persons, one for the aged, one for military and naval pensioners, and so forth, each seeking to supply all the varied needs of the class with which it dealt. Alternatively, we might have, as now, a ministry of defence, a ministry of education, a ministry of health, and so on. The defect of the former is, I think clear. It seeks to provide for each class of persons a variety of services, always specialised in nature, which will be duplicated in every other department. It is better that a Ministry of Education should deal directly with the educational needs of all persons, from the nursery onwards. We then get a fairly specific field of activity which deals with the general needs of the community for each department of the executive. The principle has the great advantages, first, that it enables the members of a department to concentrate their efforts upon a particular subject instead of scattering them over an area too wide to permit of a general level of high quality; and secondly, it enables a better use to be made of specialised knowledge by making it visible upon a plane where its varied aspects have organised relation to one another.[50]

The case, therefore, for departmental organisation by services is plain. But that does not mean that such services can, or will, exist in water-tight compartments. The Ministry of Education may have to concern itself with problems of health in school-children, which it will find directly in relation to conditions of housing and parental wages. It will have to take account of those relations, and connection with other departments will obviously become essential. Each will find that it possesses primary and secondary interests, and that it needs to develop means within itself to deal with them in all their formidable complexity. Each will find on its borders problems which involve co-operation with other departments if they are to be adequately solved. And there will, again and again, be the difficulty of deciding (obviously a cabinet question) whether some particular function belongs to one department or another. Is, for instance, a naval air service to be controlled by a ministry of naval affairs or a ministry of air defence? Much argument has been expended to justify both methods. What I am alone here concerned to insist is that the dubiety is typical of the material we encounter, and to draw therefrom the inference that matters of common interest can be dealt with adequately only by co-operation between the departments involved.

Let us suppose, however, that our departments are defined. Two problems then immediately arise. How is each to be organised and who is to staff it? In the matter of organisation there are, I think, five clear principles which need to be observed. There must, in the first place, always be a minister responsible to the legislative assembly for the work of a department. He must bear the burden of its errors, and, presumably, win the credit for the virtues it can claim. Any other system—the attempt, for instance, to deal with a specific service by means of a board—dissipates responsibility to vanishing point. The legislative assembly must always be able to point to a particular individual and demand from him a justification of departmental policy. It may, of course, through him, be compelled to strike at the cabinet itself; but it is essential, at some given point in departmental structure, to trace decisions to a person who is not corporate, but individual.

There must, secondly, be special provision in each department for adequate financial supervision. That implies, I think, an officer second only in importance to the permanent head of the department who must be responsible (a) for all payments made by the department, and (b) for annotating in terms of cost all the proposals which emanate from it. Obviously he will have special relations with the Ministry of Finance, since it will be his business to explain to its representatives the estimates of the department. Obviously, also, he must supervise the work he performs in such a way that the services of his department may be immediately compared with analogous services in other departments. He must be able to show why the cost per bed in a naval hospital under his charge is higher than a similar bed in an army hospital, and he must make it possible for the Ministry of Finance to know and explain, for instance, the differing expense of dental services in schools and in the army and navy. Wherever there is an attempt to keep the size of a departmental staff at the minimum, the last place for contraction in personnel is in the financial section; for here, ultimately, is the true watchdog of the taxpayer.

Every ministry, thirdly, must possess a committee of members of the legislative assembly with whom it is in organised relationship. I have already dealt with the nature and functions of these committees. Here it may further be pointed out that, as we come clearly to see the nature of administration, these committees will grow in their possible significance.

It is important, fourthly, to make definite arrangement for inter-departmental co-operation. Obviously such co-operation takes many different forms. There is need, for instance, for the development of continuous consultation between departments like the Board of Trade and the Ministry of Labour for the resolution of their joint problems. In part those problems are specific, as where a proposed bill concerns the interests of each, and in part, also, they are general, as where the heads of each department may explore some common issue which touches them both. No one, I think, can survey the methods used by the governments of modern States without the sense that far too little effort is made to pool experience in an organised way. There are, indeed, mechanisms to this end, like the Committee of Imperial Defence in England. But it ought to be a regular habit for the officials of the Department of Overseas Trade to meet the officials of the Foreign Office. Members of the public services must learn to live together and to think together if their *expertise* is to be more than a routine. The same thing, of course, is true intra-departmentally as well. In this aspect, one British ministry[51] has deliberately reorganised itself in order to utilise on a single plane the wide competence that is at its disposal. And even while one need not minimise the value of the doubtless considerable informal discussion that takes place, it is better to know that discussion of this kind has become habitual in administration, and that a definite place has been found for it, than to suppose that men will realise its urgency from the simple facts of experience.

Not less vital than any of these is the importance of making special provision for research and inquiry. One of the great weaknesses in the modern governmental system is the small room we leave for services of this kind. A government needs to think ahead. It needs to work at the problems of peace in the same way as a general staff works at the problems of war. It must plan out the lines of possible policy, collect the facts needed to develop those lines in all their relationships, seek to weigh them duly as they seem to have significance. Little of this work can be taken in their stride by officials already burdened with administrative duties, any more than a general officer in the field can be charged with securing the munitions that he needs. The more, indeed, we leave free the heads of departments to think out the correlation of policy, the higher will be its policy. But we require, also, in each department a group of officials whose main business is research into its problems; and beyond those special investigations of departmental incidence we need a mechanism, always in vivid touch with the departments themselves, for correlating special researches and undertaking inquiries of which the significance is wider than the making of immediate policy would involve. Such a need is implicitly recognised, both in England and the United States, by the existence of committees like that of the Privy Council on Medical Research and of such bodies as the Geological Survey at Washington. But they everywhere lack co-ordination; and they have not, so far, developed that relationship to departmental work which would enable, say, the Board of Trade to call upon the Committee for Medical Research to investigate the health conditions of seamen's quarters in ocean liners; or the Committee on Scientific and Industrial Research to apply its powers to the problem of the degree to which the exposure to heat of stokers may be diminished. Nothing can ever compensate for the absence in a State (a) of systematic and organised research, and (b) the accumulation of material likely to bear on social processes.

What would such arrangements involve? There are, I think, three general ways in which research of importance may be carried on under governmental authority. There may be direct inquiry by departments themselves. Much work of this kind is already undertaken. Each department of the modern State has broadly come to realise that it must have available for its work the body of recorded knowledge upon the matters with which it deals. It must be able, also, to collect at short notice the materials which will enable it to answer the persistent inquiries of members of the legislative assembly upon questions within its competence. It must be able, again, though in a limited way, to undertake inquiries into subjects directly affecting its work. An admirable example of the latter type of work is the volumes of special inquiries of the Board of Education in England.

A second type of research is not less important. There maybe inquiries not directly carried on by any one department, though supervised by it in conjunction with others. Thus, for instance, the Home Office in England may co-operate with the Mine Rescue Apparatus Committee of the Department of Research under the Privy Council in the attempt to develop safety in mines. The Ministry of Agriculture could co-operate with the Food Investigation Board.[52] The difference between the first and second types of research lies not merely in the different personnel by whom it is made, but also in the fact that, in the second case, those who make the report have no responsibility for its application. Their work is done when their conclusions are presented. They do not assist in pressing for their utilisation, nor do they share in administering their results. They act simply and solely as a fact-finding body. How should such research be organised? It needs, I suggest, a body akin in structure to the Committee for Imperial Defence for its direction. To it would be entrusted (1) the co-ordination of research, (2) the development of relations with non-governmental and foreign bodies engaged in work analogous to its own, (3) the communication of its results and knowledge to the departments mainly affected by them. It would, clearly, work largely through advisory committees of experts, both official and non-official. It would cultivate the closest relations possible with the universities and independent research bodies which, like the universities, have a slightly scientific character. It should, I think, be directly under the control of the Prime

Minister, in order both to emphasise the importance of its work, and to secure that its most urgent discoveries are properly represented in the highest quarter. Such a method of organisation has the special advantage of making the Prime Minister responsible to the legislative assembly for the efficient conduct of investigation.

The third type of research is that which, while stimulated into activity by such a body as the Committee outlined above, would be carried out independently of it. There is a great deal of work for which complete independence in investigation is desirable, especially in the social sciences. A government department may announce conclusions on forestry or meteorology without the suspicion of bias being attached to its results. But when we pass to problems in which the personal factor is large, there is much to be said for confining the part of government to assistance in the collection of material, or provision of facilities (including financial facilities) for the independent investigation of problems of which the urgency is obvious. One or two examples will, perhaps, make this clear. There are problems, the most suitable unit of organisation in trade unions, for instance, in which an independent group with full access to the materials would probably do better work than a government department; much the same is true of such questions as the dilution of skilled labour, and the conservation of coal. The more we can persuade bodies like the universities consciously to devote themselves to work of this kind, checking or corroborating, if need be, the work of officials, the better will be the quality of information at our disposal. We rest satisfied a little easily with a government report as the last word upon its problem. Of its integrity as a body of findings there is rarely, at least in England, much room for question. But exactly as the physicist and the biologist will repeat, almost to exhaustion, the experiments of their confréres, so do we need the repetition of social analyses. Once the government has reasonable assurance that the work is undertaken in a scientific spirit, it ought to give all the assistance in its power, without regard to the probable result of the inquiry. In no other way can we obtain the representation of all the varying points of view entitled to their say. At present, the tendency of a government, where it seeks outside expert aid, is to restrict the possession of *expertise* to those who can be relied upon for eminently "safe" conclusions. Yet even in a government department the ferment of a brilliant radical would not be without its advantages. The British Treasury, for instance, may be right in its steadfast adherence to the mystic truth of the gold standard; but it would be comforting to know that it had a research branch in which doubts of that truth could be officially pursued.

It is essential, further, to bring the public into organised relations with the executive as an administrative body. Here, as I believe, is the largest field for experiment that we possess; here, also, governments show themselves perhaps more conservative than in any other area of activity. Their attitude possesses a certain regalian atmosphere of secrecy, which belongs rather to the temper of bureaucracy, than to the democratic state. The theses we lay down are simple enough. The making of policy, we assume, is the more successful, the larger the number of affected interests consulted in its construction. The business of government is to draw upon their experience, not as itself it interprets that experience, but as the interests themselves give expression to it. The administration of policy, in the second place, ought to involve the association with it of all bodies directly influenced by its results, and it should, wherever possible, be decentralised in order to leave room for the largest flexibility in application.

Let us consider, first, the kind of satisfaction afforded to these theses by a modern government, and take the case of England as an example. We have a number of ministries which possess statutory advisory committees, of which the Board of Education and the Scottish Education Department are the most notable examples. We have other committees which are not statutory, but exist at the discretion of the minister concerned, like the business men's committee of the Post Office, and, during the war, the Consumers' Council of the Ministry of Food. We have also certain types of specialised committee, of which good instances are the Adult Education Committee at the Board of Education, and the Prison Education Committee at the Home Office. Now what is notable about these committees is that the minister has exclusive discretion over their personnel, and exclusive discretion over the subject-matter he will submit to them. They are active or passive as he pleases. They have no rights, and their duties are limited to the subjects he thinks it worth while to consult them about. Clearly, it is proper that he should, as he is, be free to accept or reject their advice as he pleases; otherwise his ministerial responsibility to the legislative assembly would be seriously impaired. But the outstanding fact about the committees is their wraith-like character. They are merely concessions to a sense that they are the means of securing public confidence in the work of the department; but there is no evidence that they are in any way substantial.

Secondly, we have ministries in which the administration has a decentralised character. That is true, on the one side, of ministries like the Board of Education which works through the ordinary agencies of local government; of the Ministry of Pensions, on the other, which builds itself upon a hierarchical system of local advisory tribunals with large powers; the ultimate authority being reserved to the ministry itself. But, in general, the striking fact about administration is the power of the central government at Whitehall. The effort is constantly after uniformity of procedure, not less than uniformity of principle. That has not, indeed, gone so far as the amazing centralisation of France which results, as Lamennais said, in apoplexy at the centre, and anaemia at the extremities. But it has gone sufficiently far to have evoked interesting and important protest;[53] and it has thereby evinced the natural tendency of all authority to accrete power to itself, with but little regard to the results of the accretion.

Of the value of advisory bodies there is now no room for doubt. "We think", reported Lord Haldane's Committee on the Machinery of Government,[54] "that the more they are regarded as an integral part of the normal organisation of a department, the more will ministers be enabled to command the confidence of Parliament and the public in their administration of the services which seem likely in an increasing degree to affect the lives of large sections of the community". "Committees", writes Sir Arthur Salter,[55] "are an invaluable instrument for breaking administrative measures on to the back of the public. Modern government often involves action affecting the interests, and requiring the goodwill, either of large sections of the community, or of the community as a whole. The action cannot be made acceptable without detailed explanation of this necessity, for which mere announcements in the press are insufficient. In such cases the prior explanation and the assent of committees of representative men who, if convinced, will carry the assent of the several sections of the community who look to them as leaders, will be of the greatest possible value". "The committees", says Sir Andrew Ogilvie of the advisory committee of business men on public telephones,[56] "... did most excellent work in the provinces ... (They) took a sensible and business-like view of the matters that came before them. A certain competitive feeling between the different public bodies concerned made them select good representatives. Groundless complaints were discouraged. They were satisfied, that the management was intelligent and considerate, and the feeling of mistrust which the British public entertain towards all State officials was largely overcome".

What should be the functions of such committees, and how should they be composed? Let me first emphasise the functions they ought not to fulfil. They are to advise about administration; but they are neither to direct nor to control it. That is in part because the notion of ministerial responsibility to the legislative assembly must be left unimpaired, in part because, as I believe, the root of all effective administration is the devolution of responsibility upon an individual. They are not, secondly, to prepare policy. They may offer suggestions when it has been prepared, or even indicate subjects which require attention; but the definition of measures is essentially a matter for the minister and his subordinates. They cannot, thirdly, commit outside bodies to agreement. They are not bodies of delegates in the sense of carrying a mandate for any particular plans; they are called, not for their authority, but for their counsel. They must never, fourthly, have access to information about the proposed purchase of materials by the government in its capacity as trader; anyone who considers, for instance, the functions of the Treasury in England in such matters as the purchase of foreign exchange, and the issue of Treasury Bills, will realise that secrecy of operations in such matters is essential. Nor ought they in general, I think, to be consulted about negotiations between a government and a foreign power; publicity here seems in place rather in relation to the ratification of results accomplished than of intervention in a delicate process where premature disclosure may be fatal. Above all, they should, as committees, be confidential in character, and without power to disclose collective resolutions to the public at large. But the minister, of course, ought to have the right to authorise the publication of such decisions if he, and the committee, thought publication desirable.

These are elementary limitations. Before we can discuss what such committees can do, it is important to establish the nature of their composition. It must, I think, be first of all postulated that advisory committees which over the whole field of departmental competence are generally a mistake. What is wanted is the power to be consulted on the points which affect special interests; and the opinion of a businessman, say upon technical problems of engineering, is not worth a great deal. Even in an area like that covered by the Board of Education, what we require is rather special, than general, knowledge; we need the experience of teachers in secondary schools, in universities, in elementary schools, rather than to take a number of people eminent in education and to place before them all the various issues with which the ministry is concerned. In the building of such committees, two points are of importance. The committee, in the first place, must be small; otherwise it will inevitably become a small conference in which there will be speeches, but not discussion. It must, in the second place, be representative. Those who attend there must be persons who command the confidence of the interests which are affected by the work of the particular department. Generally a committee of not more than twenty members seems the right size for such a body. It ought to be composed of two parts: (a) a majority chosen by representative associations in the different interests, such as industries, affected by administration; (b) a minority chosen by the minister to represent the public and special bodies sufficiently, though indirectly, concerned to need the protection of representation. Thus, for example, on a Committee of the Board of Education to deal with the elementary schools, there would be representatives of such bodies as the National Union of Teachers, the Assistant Mistresses' Association, of the bodies which represent teachers in secondary schools, and so forth.

A committee of the Home Office to deal with legislation about factories would comprise representatives of the trade unions, of the National Union of Manufacturers, together with specialists in the physiology of industrial fatigue and in industrial law. A committee of the Board of Trade on patents would include representatives of the Institute of Patentees, lawyers specially expert in patent law, and, one may suggest, nominees of such bodies as the Royal Society and the Institute of Electrical Engineers. A committee of the Ministry of Health on the administration of grants-in-aid would comprise representatives of popular bodies like the County Councils' Association, of professional bodies like the Institute of Municipal Treasures, and the National Association of Local Government Officers, and consumers' bodies such as Ratepayers' Associations. Obviously, it is impossible for me here to draw up either a list of the necessary committees or of the bodies which should be represented on them. In any case, such lists would be obsolete before they were made. What, above all, I am concerned to urge, are the two principles of special competence, on the one hand, and of nominated representation on the other.

I urge the first because, exactly as I earlier rejected the idea of a vocational body on the ground that a given vocation has no necessary relevance to general problems, so, similarly, I believe that the general committee would have little relevance. It is essential, if these committees are to function as creative institutions, that they should deal with an area that is a matter of vital interest to their members, and about which the opinion of those members cannot be weighed lightly even by the most sturdy bureaucrat. Wherever problems arose which interested more than one committee it would be a simple matter to submit it to both and, if necessary, to have a joint meeting of them for its consideration. I urge the principle of nominated representation upon two grounds. I believe, first, that a member nominated by a minister never feels himself so free as one who is there as of right. The former is inhibited by complex emotions it is better to minimise at the outset; and, secondly, ministerial choice makes the problem of reappointment and removal difficult. I envisage nominated representation as being for a period of three years, renewal of nomination being within the absolute discretion of the appointing body. The minister ought not to be able to prevent an unpleasant choice. He needs a committee to scrutinise, not merely to approve his policy. The members should, preferably, be elected by the councils of their nominating bodies, miners by the executive of the Miners' Federation, teachers by the council of the National Union of Teachers, and so forth. They should also be paid for their services sufficiently to compensate for lost time, but not enough to make their election sought after on grounds of income. The value, I think, of such method of choice lies in the facts that (1) it makes it easy for the nominating body to express its views to its representative, and (2) that it provides for a continuous interest in his work on the part of the constituency he represents.

What should be the functions of these committees? This is, it must be admitted, a delicate problem; for, just as in the case of the legislative committees discussed above, much will turn upon the personality of each minister and his chief officials. A strong minister, as I think, will know how to use the committees with which he deals as an invaluable repository of suggestion and opinion; a weak minister will be tempted either to evade them through timidity, or to accept their views as the embodiment of public opinion without the effort, where he disagrees, to strike out a strong line of his own and risk the consequences. But I do not believe that the danger is any greater than that which surrounds the relationship of a weak minister to his permanent officials. And, in this latter case, the value of the committee lies in its being an additional check upon the limitations of a bureaucracy which too easily, in any event, evades the categories of public opinion.

The large functions of these committees would be four in number. The committee would be entitled to prior consultation on all proposed bills. When a department contemplated a new statute it would submit it to the committee (of course, in confidence) for criticism. There would be conferences between the minister and his permanent officials, on the one side, and the committee on the other. The bill would be explained; its clauses would be criticised in the light of the committee's experience and knowledge; while the minister would be free either to reject, or to accept, the suggestions he received. There will, of course, be emergency legislation upon which there is no time for the committee to be properly consulted. Here, it would be possible, upon the introduction of the bill, for the minister to be made statutorily responsible for convening the committee on a request from two-thirds (or some such proportion) of its members; and, in that event, the suggestions they choose to make might go to the appropriate legislative committee for introduction as amendments in the committee stage of the bill in the legislative assembly. What, at any rate, would be secured would be that on all matured and fundamental plans the interests involved were able fully to state their attitude before the enacting legislation had become a matter of prestige with the ministry which introduced it.

The committees, secondly, would be consulted upon general administrative policy. Here, once more, the matters for its discussion would clearly depend a good deal upon the minister. If he chose to act without consultation, nothing could prevent him from doing so. But I think most of the difficulties in this regard could be obviated by making it possible for each member to suggest matters for discussion, and entitling him, in the event of ministerial objection, to an explanation of the hostile attitude. Instances of general administrative policy may be taken from various fields. If the Minister of Education, for instance, chose to raise, under statutory powers, the school-leaving age to sixteen, he would consult with the appropriate committee of his department; and, clearly, it would be his duty to acquaint the Minister of Labour with his proposal, and obtain from the advisory committees of the latter department an expression of opinion upon his policy from the peculiar angle of their special interests. If the Minister of Labour proposed to establish a trade board in a sweated industry, he would act similarly. If the Minister of the Colonies proposed to make elementary education compulsory for natives, he would consult his advisory committee on native affairs, in which, in all likelihood, there would be a special sub-committee on the problems of native education. So, too, with housing. The Ministry of Health could present its difficulties to committees of builders, of the building trade unions, of architects, and of medical men. There is, I think, no aspect of policy in which a minister has to make decisions in which he could fail, by a careful use of his committees, to obtain illumination upon his needs.

The committees, thirdly, would be empowered to make suggestions. Here, indeed, is one of the sources of their work in which, by careful exploration, there seems the prospect of high utility. Their suggestions ought to cover the widest possible area. They ought to indicate the need for inquiry to the intelligence branch of the ministry. Where their suggestion covers a field outside the total competence of the department, it ought to be referred to the Government Committee on Research with a recommendation from the minister, the committee being always free to act upon its own views. There are few people who would be chosen for service upon these committees who would not be able to put forward ideas it would be well worth while to explore. Anyone who has talked with a group of miners about their work will have realised how wide is their field of suggestion, over every side of the mining industry, which now goes unused. The same is true of the best teachers. It is, I think, one of the few ways open to us to correct the dangers of professional conservatism. A committee of a Ministry of Justice, for example, upon which the lay mind as well as the legal mind found place, could indicate a score of places in the law where the need for revision and experiment is essential. Legal protection for the poor in civil, no less than criminal, cases,[57] the administration of prisons, the treatment of debtors, the relation between the press and justice in sensational crime, are only a few of the many problems to which such a committee would inevitably draw attention. At present we investigate them not because they are obviously there but because, at some special moment, an ugly instance compels immediate inquiry. It was known in England for years that our law of lunacy was in grave need of revision. The official inquiry merely whitewashed the actual administration; and it was only the dramatic nature of *Harnett* v. *Adam and Bond*[58] which drove the Government to appoint a Royal Commission. We can, if we choose to utilise our experience, be forehanded about these matters. But we shall only be forehanded by creating the institutions to compel forehandedness.

The fourth use to which these committees could be out turns upon a more technical matter which I shall examine below. It is well known that the growing area of state-activity has transformed the major part of legislation from detailed and exhaustive statutes into skeleton acts the details of which are, in various ways, filled in by the departments concerned. This delegated legislation has now grown to dimensions so immense that it easily out-distances the amount of law-making directly due to the legislative assembly. It is, I think, increasingly necessary to protect the public against bureaucratic abuse of these powers. That is a negative function. It is, also, a policy of wisdom to have at hand consultative bodies of competence which can express their views upon the employment of delegated authority. In each case these committees are an instrument which seems naturally designed for these ends. What, generally, I suggest is that no department shall issue orders under its delegated powers without having first consulted the appropriate consultative committee; and that in the event of objection from the latter the order shall not be issued without the specific approval of the legislative assembly.

So far, I have been concerned with these committees in their central aspect, as they bear upon administration at its ultimate source of direction. But there is no reason to confine an instrument of this kind to Whitehall and Washington, to Paris and Berlin. Every State passes a multitude of statutes upon which local comment and suggestion would be invaluable at the centres of their application. I have already quoted Sir Andrew Ogilvie's praise of the work done in England before the war by local committees on the telephone service. Similar testimony exists on a variety of other matters, especially in the organisation of food rationing in England during the war. What I suggest is a large extension of these committees, not by nomination at the discretion of the minister, but, as in the case of the central bodies, by nomination from representative bodies concerned. Thus, for example, there would be in each local education authority a committee of teachers, parents, medical men, and so on, charged with the business of reporting directly upon educational administration. They would point out that the local authority was tending to engage too many uncertificated teachers; that the schools were not being adequately repaired; that there was an insufficient relation between the schools and the public library service. The minister, in his turn, would bring their reports before the local education authority; and there would, as I think, grow up from this network of relationships a genuine interest on the spot in the quality of service supplied.

So, similarly, with measures like the Factory Acts. Everyone knows that no State has a sufficient service of inspection to be able to prevent whole evasion of their provisions. There should, I suggest, be a system of regional committees which would supervise the administration of factory law. They ought to be competent to receive complaints, and, if need be, report them to the local judiciary for the purpose of prosecution. Similarly, agricultural committees could deal with problems like the taxation of a minimum wage in the given area, with rural credits, with the promotion of agricultural co-operation, with conditions of tenancy, and so on. The committees ought always to deal with an area large enough to permit it to undertake genuine administrative functions. I shall give reasons in a later chapter why much of the petty jurisdiction now performed under statute by subordinate magistrates could more usefully be performed by tribunals constituted from committees of this kind; they might inflict fines for the evasion of Factory Acts, Trade Boards Acts and the like. We ought to have local advisory bodies on railway service, on electricity supply, on, in fact, every function where the incidence of administration on persons gives birth to experience which involves suggestiveness. These bodies should always be articulated to the central executive. They should be provided with the official assistance necessary to make them effective. They should have the means and place of regular meeting. They should have the opportunity to publish their comment and suggestion. They will, I think, do much to prevent the atmosphere of administration from degenerating into the issue of orders, on the one hand, and their indifferent acceptance on the other. They will provide means for utilising the services of men who now avoid public life, either because they are unwilling to undergo the process of election, or because their interest is not in the general complex of governmental functions, but in a single aspect of that complex. They popularise the administrative process by widening the area of persons able to scrutinise its substance from an angle of competence. They provide for a constant interchange of opinion and ideas between the centre and the circumference of government. They leave untouched that need in government for simple and intelligible institutions which I discussed earlier in this book. They prevent authority from degenerating into anarchy by the indefinite division of power. They prevent it from becoming autocratic by subjecting it, at each stage, to the pressure of an opinion that is generally informed, on the one hand, and specially competent on the other. They bring the organised interests of men, their churches, their trade unions and the rest, into a definite relation with the central government. They make it possible for the activities of that government to bear throughout the impress of external opinion. They make it live in a constant stream of criticism and inquiry. Not least, they will provide, increasingly, for a growing decentralisation of function. Local officials will find themselves, in their struggles with the central executive, backed by a body of support which ministers will find it difficult to neglect.

What, broadly, these bodies will do is to interpret the law. "The meaning of a statute", writes Professor Cohen,[59] "consists in the system of social consequences to which it leads, or of the solution to all the possible social questions that can arise under it. These solutions or systems of consequences cannot be determined solely from the words used, but require a knowledge of the social conditions to which the law is to be applied as well as of the circumstances which lead to its enactment.... The meaning of a statute, then, is a judicial creation in the light of social demands. It decides not so much what the legislature actually intended, nor what the words of a statute ordinarily mean, but *what the public, taking all the circumstances of the case into account, should act on*". The committees here suggested will explain what are the consequences of a statute. They will build up, consciously, and in the light of experience, a code of tradition which will make a vital impact upon the meaning of law. Its commands will be shot through with the knowledge of those who feel its results. They will be embedded in an experience made articulate through institutions seeking deliberately to give it expression. These bodies will, as I have explained, be advisory; but I do not suppose that it will be easy to neglect their advice. For what they will counsel will bear upon its face the impact of a knowledge to which no others can pretend. They will interpret law, and therefore they will make the law. For they will bring into the light of day the true consequences of law, as those are felt by the men who suffer them. They will determine, therefore, the way in which it is applied. They will indicate, accordingly, necessary change and necessary amendment. They will give each interest in the community organic connection, as an interest with the State. They will infuse its purpose with their own purposes. They will supplement its partial and inadequate glimpse of the total volume of social experience by giving it direct access to the knowledge, emotions, ideas, of which they are the depositories. They cannot paralyse administration by shattering power into fragments; but they can assist administration by building the bridges necessary to its passage to the purpose at which it aims. They preserve the primacy of that civic sphere which, as I have urged, gives the State its special place in society; but they emphasise, by organising the power of dissent, the places where that primacy is inadequately understood or deliberately unrealised. They are at once a warning and encouragement to the executive, and an assistance to the legislature. A warning and encouragement to the one because they indicate openly the limits within which it may work; and to the other an assistance because they give it the body of facts out of which there can grow both the criticism and the enactments that are its functions.

One other word should be said in this connection. I have urged, both in the case of central and of local committees, that their sphere is rather, to use Hamilton's distinction, influence than government. They will rather communicate opinion than actually either administer or legislate. It may be added, first, that the boundary between these categories is one of convenience rather than reality; and, secondly, that it will probably be found in experience that they both, but especially the local committees, will be growingly charged with duties under statutes of minor administration and inspection. They will, I believe, inevitably accrue to themselves a rule-making power. Over and above certain minima laid down at the centre and enforced by it, they will add new demands upon the area they survey as their instructed judgment deems warranted. They will become, in short, centres of power administering it in the light of a direct experience not otherwise available. They will suffuse that administration with the needs that can never be expressed in uniform terms. They will give to government a flexible morphology which has been so far lacking because it has usually meant, as in America before the Federal Constitution, and France before 1789, the absence of the necessary powers of co-ordination. It will have the great merit of shifting the area of the subject administered to meet its special wants. It will revivify that notion of citizenship as the capacity not less to rule than to be ruled, which is the great gift of the city-State to our own times.

## (vi) The Control of the Administrator

I have spoken of administration as the process of applying the law enacted by the legislature. But that is, in fact, to give an incomplete account of its scope and significance. For administration, the world over, involves far more than the scrutiny of statutes for the knowledge of the regulations under which the citizen body lives. Sometimes a government department is entrusted with wide powers. Sometimes these derive from such a prerogative source as the King in Council, or the ordinance-making authority of the President of France. Sometimes they are conferred upon such statutory bodies as the General Medical Council. What is always typical of the modern State is that, over and above the general law-making authority, there will be found a number of subordinate authorities with the power to bind citizens as though they were making statutes.

This position is the inevitable result of the growing pressure of business in the modern legislature. Parliament in England, the Reichstag in

Germany, the Chambers in France, have simply not the time to compile statutes so minutely detailed as to meet every possible situation which may arise. They have not the time, and they have not the competence. For not only is the modern legislative assembly, from its mere size, inapt to the construction of technical details, but also it is impossible to predict the type of problem which will arise under any statute; and many problems will occur which cannot be brought under any foreseen legislative solution. In all such cases it is necessary to entrust powers to the executive, sometimes, though not always, defining to which department of the executive the power is entrusted. The British Post Office will tell the inhabitant of London how much he is to pay for a letter to Mauritius. The Ministry of Labour will tell anyone who proposes to set up a business whether the type of manufacture in which he proposes to engage is governed, and how it is governed, by the Trade Boards Act of 1909. The Foreign Office will tell him whether the city of Hong-Kong, to which he proposes to emigrate, has had the dozen acts applied there which, by the Foreign Judicature Act of 1890, may be applied by Order-in-Council to any foreign territory where the King has jurisdiction. He will learn of court fees not from the Judicature Acts, but from the Rules of the Supreme Court. He will know what he is to do if onion-smut breaks out on his farm in Essex from regulations made by the Board of Agriculture. He will not find a list of official poisons in any statute, but in regulations issued by, and changeable at the instance of, the Home Office and the Pharmaceutical Society. If he has a son at a secondary school whom he would like, if a scholarship is available, to send to Oxford, he must consult the regulations of the Board of Education about scholarships from secondary schools to universities. If he wishes to earn his living by setting up a civil aviation line from London to Amsterdam, he will find that the regulations are not in the Air Navigation Act of 1920, but the many Orders in Council issued thereunder. If he wishes to know the price of a summons for non-payment of debt, he will find it not under the Metropolitan Police Act, as in 1839, but in tables prepared and issued by the Home Office. The situation in which he finds himself may perhaps best be put by saying that the King in Parliament will, on the average, pass some eighty statutes each year, while the number of orders and rules made by the executive will be about thirty times as many.

The result is not merely seen in this virtual creation of many law-making bodies. It is seen also in the limits which develop upon the jurisdiction of the courts. Administrative bodies not only find themselves compelled to undertake judicial duties, but also to perform them in such a way that the courts are excluded from scrutiny of their operations. It has been decided by the highest English tribunal that when a government department assumes quasi-judicial functions the absence of express enactment in the enabling statute means that the department is free to embark upon what procedure seems best to it; nor will the courts inquire whether such procedure results, or could result, in justice.[60] It has been decided by the highest American tribunal that the decisions of the Secretary of Labour in all immigration cases are final,[61] so that, for instance, a Japanese born in America could be excluded from the United States on his return from a visit to Canada on the fiat of an executive department no longer amenable to the rule of law. It has been held there, also, that the findings of an expert commission are final, and will not be discussed again by the courts.[62] The ordinance power of the French President is, similarly, beyond judicial scrutiny. The Insurance Commissioners in England are also, in many ways, beyond the power of the courts. Obviously, a development of this kind needs ample safeguards unless it is to result in a grave invasion of public liberty. That is overwhelmingly apparent when it is remembered that in England, the classic home of the rule of law, a single regulation of the Defence of the Realm Act was held to have nullified a fundamental statute like Habeas Corpus.[63]

Much, indeed, of this development is perfectly intelligible. Where, for example, great problems like those involved in government insurance are concerned, there is undoubtedly a great convenience in leaving their interpretation to the officials who are solving them as a part of their daily routine. They have gained in its application an *expertise* to which no purely judicial body can pretend; and their opinion has a weight which no community can dare to neglect. The business of the State, in fact, is so much like private business that, as Professor Dicey has emphasised, its officials need "that freedom of action necessarily possessed by every private person in the management of his own personal concerns".[64] So much is tolerably clear. But historic experience suggests that the relation of executive justice derived from a rule-working power to the slow infiltration of a bureaucratic régime is dangerously close. The safeguards against abuse of those powers is, therefore, at least as urgent as the need for powers themselves. Where do the remedies lie?

Let us take the problems in their logical order. We need (a) securities against the making of intolerable or unnecessary rules, and (b) adequate protection against undue invasion of the judicial prerogative. The first great need, clearly, is that all delegation of power should be revocable. It may prove to work badly. It may be shown, though good in itself, to have been entrusted to a body which is unsuited to administer it. It may need the addition of special limiting clauses to its exercise. Delegation should, therefore, always be revocable by the legislative assembly. The limits of powers conferred should always be laid down with strictness, and there should never be authority to exclude the courts from judicial definition of that limit. The reason for this second restriction has been stated admirably by Lord Shaw. "The form", he says of the English system,[65] "in modern times of using the Privy Council as the executive channel for statutory power is measured, and must be measured strictly, by the ambit of the legislative pronouncement. That channel itself ... is simply the government of the day.... In so far as the mandate has been exceeded, there lurks the element of a transition to arbitrary government and therein of grave constitutional and public danger. The increasing crush of legislative efforts, and the convenience to the executive of a refuge in the device of Orders in Council would increase that danger tenfold were the judiciary to approach any action of the government in a spirit of compliance rather than of independent scrutiny. That way also would lie public unrest and public peril". In the third place, the department making rules should always consult particular interests affected by the use of its powers before they are issued. Here, as I think, is the place where the advisory committees discussed above would have high value. No department should have the power to issue rules until they have been presented to the appropriate committees for criticism. If they are ratified there, they should then go through their normal forms of publicity and announcement. If the committee rejects them, they should immediately be communicated to the legislative assembly with the announcement that objection has been taken to them; and, in that event, they should not legally come into operation until they have been definitely confirmed by resolution of the legislative assembly. The advantage of this safeguard is that it assures a proper scrutiny of orders by those who are likely to experience their results. It prevents a body of officials from imposing their will upon the community without other sanction than their own necessarily limited experience. There should, fourthly, always be adequate arrangements to ensure full publicity for the orders issued. Though, in theory, all citizens of the modern State know all its laws, there is, in practice, a certain visible hiatus in their knowledge; and it would, I think, be wise to make the departments explain their proposals for publication to the advisory committees. Not all London shopkeepers, for instance, make a habit of reading the *London Gazette*; and their taste for professional literature should be reached so far as possible.

We move to a somewhat different range of problems when we are concerned, not with government departments, but with local and special bodies with the power to make rules. Manchester can make bye-laws; so can the colleges of Oxford and Cambridge, and the Southern Railway. How can we safeguard ourselves against abuse by them of their opportunities? For, unquestionably they will do queer things: a local authority in England has actually prohibited "lounging" on Sunday afternoons, and German municipalities have prohibited boys from playing football in the streets. The difficulty here is to prevent stupid legislation, while at the same time, there is no undue restriction upon the power of the local body to exercise a full initiative. If Oxford University, for instance, legislates against compulsory Greek, there ought not to be anywhere in existence an overriding power; yet few will disagree that such power ought not to extend so far as to allow Cambridge University the right to exclude women from membership. At present, we have, as a rule, two forms of safeguard. The legal character of any bye-law may be tested in the courts, and new bye-laws must be submitted, like those of the railway companies in England to the Ministry of Transport, to some specified government department which may refuse to ratify them. Of the former type of control, there can be no question; it is inherent in the degree of validity we have sought to establish for the doctrine of the separation of powers. The second type is, I think, more questionable. In the case of a commercial body like a railway company, it matters less than in the case of a body which, like a municipal corporation, derives much of its authority from the will of the electorate. In either case, control by officials means the interposition of a departmental will over the will of persons to whom the powers used do in fact belong, and whose initiative, therefore, ought not to lie directly within the discretion of a bureaucracy. The safeguards, I suggest, should be of two kinds. In the case of a commercial body, the disallowance of a rule ought only to be made after the proposed disallowance has been communicated to the legislative committee of the department; it would then be open to any of the latter to raise the question in the legislature. In the case of bodies like municipal corporations, or the universities, disallowance ought never to be exercised save in one of two ways: (1) if the disallowance is on the legal ground that the proposed rule is *ultra vires.* It ought to take the form only of a warning which the public body is authorised to test in the courts; (2) if the disallowance is on the ground that the substance of the proposed rule is undesirable, the department ought directly to report its views to the legislative assembly, leaving the latter body to annul it, if it thinks fit. For if a municipality does think fit to prohibit Sunday "lounging", it is better, I believe, to allow its attitude to be dealt with by the local electorate than to impair its initiative from a platform of superior wisdom. It is surely better that local bodies should have ideas, even if, on occasion, they seem to assume a bizarre form.

The judicial aspect of the problem can, I believe, be met in two ways. I have already suggested that the findings of an expert commission have a validity to which no judicial examination can pretend; the decision, for instance, of the New York Public Service Commission that a gas company ought to provide gas service for a given district is almost inevitably more right than a decision pronounced by the courts in a similar case. And I do not think it is necessary to disturb such findings,. What is essential is that we should have assurance that the methods utilised in reaching such decisions are judicially satisfactory; that, for instance, there is full time for the preparation of a case, proper rules of evidence, and so forth. Every such decision, therefore, ought to be open for scrutiny by the courts, not on the ground of its substance, but on the view that it is wanting in this regard. This, it may be noted, is the attitude taken by the Supreme Court of the United States. "This court", said Clarke, J.,[66] "will ... enter upon such an examination of the record as may be necessary to determine whether the federal constitutional right has been denied, ... whether there was such a want of hearing, or such arbitrary or capricious action on the part of the Commission as to violate the due process clause of the constitution". It is exactly such an assurance that the substance of due process has been observed that we require. It does not, I think, mean stereotyping any special procedure as the only proper method; administrative law, by its nature, demands elasticity. But it does mean that a judge, on examining the record of the case, can satisfy himself that the parties to it have had a full and fair hearing.

This first method is comparatively simple and involves no striking departure from customary effort; indeed, in Anglo-Saxon countries, it might rather be represented as a return to the normal standards of procedure. The second, however, involves quite definite novelty; not, indeed, in parts, but in its breadth of application. What, broadly, I suggest is that the State should be sued for its torts exactly as a private person is sued, that, whenever its officials act *ultra vires,* the public exchequer should be mulcted in damages by the courts exactly as though the offender were John Jones. What is here urged is, after all, the not unreasonable thesis that service in the central functions of government does not release men from their human fallibility. Public enterprise is not less liable to error than private; and its responsibility should, on that account, be none the less strictly enforced. Nor do we sufficiently realise the danger of excluding the State from the categories of legal responsibility. It begins as a legal exclusion, but, sooner or later, that legal category will pass over into the moral sphere. The fact of achievement will become more important than the method by which attainment is reached. Once an end is setup as in itself great enough to set its exponents beyond the reach of law, the real safeguards of liberty are overthrown. Irresponsibility becomes equated with the dubious explanation of public policy, and that, in history, is always the first step to the morally obnoxious ground of *raison d'état*. The release of the State from the trammels of law means in practice the release of its officials from the obligations to which other men are usefully subject. That release breeds the worst evils of bureaucracy. It makes those so released impatient of criticism and resentful of inquiry. The controlling factors of good conduct are thereby loosed; and we discover that men who, in private life, are gentle and tender and kindly, become in their State-aspect different beings. But the inference therefrom is not that we should judge that aspect differently. Rather it implies that we must the more sternly apply the standards of normal justice.

For let us look briefly at the results of the alternative. The British Admiralty may infringe a patent granted to a private citizen by the Board of Trade;[67] though such an infringement by another private person would at once involve damages. The van of the Postmaster-General may run over Miss Bainbridge, but the irresponsibility of the State deprives her of any right to compensation except from the humble wages of the driver.[68] The government may dismiss an official whom it has induced to give up his business by engaging him for a definite term of years, and no action will lie against it.[69] Miss Mighell can obtain no financial balm for breach of promise if the man she believed to be plain Albert Baker turns out to be Sultan of Johore.[70] Nor is the situation in America different. Not only are the constituent States exempt from suit without their own consent, but the federal government occupies a similar position.[71] In France, a category of State-responsibility has, after much hesitation, been evolved. But it remains broadly true in all jurisdictions that if officials choose to cloak themselves in the garb of State-sovereignty, they are, as officials, beyond the reach of the courts. Yet, illogically enough, that is not true of municipal bodies and their servants,[72] even though they are as much a part of the State as the central government; and, when we decline from local bodies to such quasi-public bodies as the trustees of a dock, liability for error and wrong is just as widespread as if a private person were concerned.[73]

What is the ground upon which this doctrine rests? Practically, its whole foundation is the doctrine that the State as the maker of law is beyond the reach of those who receive the law from its hands. The State can do no wrong because it is a sovereign State, and the plain mark of sovereignty is that it cannot be made to answer for its acts. In England the State has, for historic reasons, been personified into the Crown; but what has been said of its position by a strong court would hold of authoritative acts elsewhere. "The maxim that the King can do no wrong", insisted the court,[74] "applies to personal as well as political wrongs, and not only to wrongs done personally by the sovereign (if such a thing could be supposed possible), but to injuries done to one subject by another by authority of the sovereign. For from this maxim that the King can do no wrong it follows as a necessary consequence that the King cannot allow wrong to be done; for to authorise a wrong to be done is to do a wrong; and as the wrongful act done becomes in law the act of those who authorise it to be done, it follows that the petition of right which complains of a tortious or wrongful act done by the Crown or by servants of the Crown discloses no right to redress, for as in law no such wrong can be done, no such right can arise". The subject, that is to say, is left helpless before the State, though it should be noted that in matters of contract the exigencies of a business civilisation have driven the State to admit responsibility.

The simple remedy is to permit the State to be sued in the same way as a private person. That will probably involve the incorporation of government departments in order that the source of liability may be made clear. Officials will not then be able to screen themselves behind the majestic cloak of a non-existent entity without even the ordinary charms of legal fiction. The judges will be able to protect the ordinary citizen from wrong, from whatever quarter that wrong may have proceeded. A single illustration will suffice to make clear the consequence of this doctrine. Where, for instance a man has been wrongly convicted of crime and imprisoned, he will be able to sue the State for damages for wrongful imprisonment. That, as I think, is obvious justice; and the rarity of the occurrence makes it more desirable to throw its results into striking relief. Nor, it may be added, is this doctrine contrary to the development of recent events. The line of evolution in France and Germany is towards a fast-increasing recognition of responsibility; and it is notable that in England a Royal Commission which sought to allay the fears of civil servants in India translated its remedy into the form of a claim against the Secretary of State for the fulfilment of a contract which was to be enforceable in a court of law.[75] It follows, indeed, from the idea of a positive State that the duty of responsibility should be accepted. For no State can permit its officials to dig deep into the lives of men and seek, simultaneously, to evade payment for their blunders.[76]

## (vii) The Position of the Public Official

From all that has here been said, it follows that every State is enormously dependent upon the quality of its public officials. Administration is of its essence; and it is inevitable that those who actually carry out the application of law should hold its virtues in their keeping. How should such officials be chosen? Ought they to be a permanent body, which the political executive cannot, broadly, speaking, change? Or ought they, as in Andrew Jackson's conception, to hold their office at the will of the administration, in order that the latter may be assured of their sympathy and co-operation?

There seems now no reasonable ground for doubt that the less control the political executive possesses over the appointment of permanent officials, the better it is for the State. It is not only that insecurity of tenure depletes the ranks of the public service of experience that is essential to its efficient conduct; that men of ability and character will not be tempted into work where there is no guarantee of a continuous livelihood; and that the absence of a constant tradition will always tempt the political executive to twist the law it applies to its own advantage. It is clear from the experience of every modern State that the power to control appointment to the public service makes certain, where it is possessed by the political executive, an ample corruption of public life. The exclusion of the British Foreign Office from open competition made it for long, in John Bright's phrase, the "out-door relief department of the English aristocracy". The spoils system in America results in periodic crises in which there are revelations of dishonesty perhaps even greater than the most debased commercialism would show. The power of the French-Minister over entrance to his departmental service results in constant scandals, of which the dismissal of a great historian from a lifelong post at the archives to make room for an ignorant political nominee is only a striking example.[77] Unless the public service is, as a body of officials, beyond the reach of the executive, it is inevitable that the mind of the minister should be devoted not to the problems of his office, but to the need of rewarding his followers; and the assassination of President Garfield is only the climax of what that need will involve. There will grow up in every State a race of men who live by giving service to one or other of the parties in the State in return for a brief period as an official, a career for which they have neither training nor competence. And it is further clear that they will use the posts they fill not for the performance of their duties, but for lining their own pockets at the public expense. Anyone who studies in detail the history of this system as reflected in the administration of President Harding in America will realise the implications it makes possible.[78]

The public service of a State must, therefore, live under the aegis of two definite rules. It must be appointed by persons other than those in the cabinet, or its subordinate political posts; and it must be appointed under rules which reduce to a minimum the chance of personal favouritism. There is, I think, no question but that the principle of open competition alone satisfies these rules. That means, for all except such purely technical posts as, for example, that of a veterinary surgeon in a department of agriculture, that admission to the service is on the sole basis of being able to satisfy suitable tests for the type of appointment vacant. Experience seems to show that those tests are the more satisfactory the more they are adapted to the selection of good, general intelligence than to an attempt to measure, say, suitability to a particular post like that of an assistant in the department of foreign affairs. The habits of a special function not involving the kind of special competence required by medicine or mathematics can always be obtained in the actual manipulation of the material. Entrance, therefore, to the public service should normally be at the age when, in a similar position in ordinary life, a young man or woman expects to earn a living. And they should be chosen by a commission the members of whom can only be removed under circumstances similar to those of a judge. What powers the executive should possess will, therefore, begin only after the official has been appointed to his department. Selection is, *a priori,* entirely outside its competence.

But here certain important considerations emerge. Every public service may be roughly divided into two great categories. There will be a large number of persons whose work mainly consists in purely manipulative functions. They copy letters, fill out forms, enter items in accounts. There will be a much smaller number who are engaged in genuinely creative work, who think out policy, undertake investigations, make decisions. The majority of this latter class will be persons who by education have been trained for this type of effort; and the cost of such training will, in the contemporary State, on the whole confine the sources from which they are drawn to the middle and upper classes of the community. It is well known, for instance, that, until quite recently, the administrative class of the British civil service was drawn almost entirely from Oxford and Cambridge; and the average working-man cannot hope, even if he has a really able son, to send him there. Broadly speaking, therefore, unless the educational system of a State is democratic enough to correct this kind of limitation, the effective public service will be confined to the comfortable classes of the community. That means two things. First, the experience upon which its members will draw is not representative of the community as a whole; and even the new facts they encounter will be envisaged in terms of that special experience. Secondly, the advice they will offer to the political executive will be fairly narrow in range, unless they contain among them, what is, in any case, rare, men of great imaginative insight. How are we to correct deficiencies of this kind?

To some extent, clearly, the problem is one of time: the more rapidly we recognise that right to an adequate training I discussed earlier in this book, the wider will be the provenance from which the administrator is drawn, the more representative, therefore, of the different aspects of social life. But, predominantly, I believe that the corrective is most largely to be supplied by the system of advisory committees discussed above. For there the official will be compelled to measure his knowledge and experience against a much wider range of variety than is now the case. He will less and less draw his conclusions from the reading of reports, the arguments he can think of in an office; he will more and more tend to build them out of personal contact with business men, trade unionists, doctors, school teachers. He will be far less protected than he now is by the armour of an office routine into which he can always withdraw from external contacts. He will have to meet a more direct and personal criticism, informed as his own views can rarely be informed, by what William James happily termed the "pungent sense of effective reality". It is one thing to construct a dietary for a dock labourer in the cool seclusion of a department; it is quite another thing, and it is a liberal education, to defend that dietary before a committee where he may be examined by dock-labourers.[79] The official may be, as Sir William Beveridge has urged, bound, like the Franciscan, to "the triple vow of poverty, anonymity, and obedience",[80] but he must not forget that the influence and value of the brotherhood came from the fact that it mingled with the world, and particularly with the disinherited of the world. I believe that he will learn much, also, as he seeks to adjust himself to the arrival of new classes to the leadership of the State. For these will bring with them new views and new experience, and in the attempt to serve their wants he will gain new insights of his own. That has rarely been his fortune in the past. Anyone, for example, who looks at a list of British cabinet ministers in the century before, 1914 will be impressed, I think, by the fairly uniform experience they represent. Eton and Oxford, the law and the ownership of land, great family and great business enterprise, find uniform place there, whatever the party in power.[81] Much the same was true, until 1906, of the House of Commons. *Mutatis mutandis,* the hypothesis admits of illustration from France and Germany, and if there has been a greater variety in American institutions it has not, for a number of reasons inherent in their character, affected the experience of officials. But the tradition has been broken, and we are clearly upon the threshold of experiment. The public services will need, in this background, the mechanisms through which the temper that welcomes innovation is in every possible way encouraged.

Something also can be done in another way. No one who studies the literature of politics can fail to be impressed at the dearth of studies which aim at the deliberate improvement of public administration. "The civil service", writes Sir William Beveridge,[82] "is a profession, and I should like it to become and realise itself as a *learned* profession". That involves, I think, a good deal more experiment with the technique of public administration than has, so far, been found suitable. It means, in part, collective thinking about the problems of administration, the attempt, ever more wide, to relate them to the largest volume of available experience; but it means, also, the effort to make thought on the work of the official a scientific discipline which can be taught and explored. We must, that is to say, be able to formulate the rules of public administration as a system of working hypotheses constantly modified by an experience conscious of itself. To that end, I believe, two things are necessary. We must, first of all, associate the official with the government of his profession.

We must make his thought about the standards under which he works articulate and organised in the same way as those standards are articulate and organised in the law and medicine. We must, also, allow the official, under suitable circumstances, to write and publish about governmental organisation. Obviously, we cannot allow, say a treasury clerk, to criticise the budget of his department, but there is no adequate reason why he should not indicate what he considers desirable changes in the structure of treasury organisation. Sir Ian Hamilton[83] has recently pointed out the stupidity of that censorship in England which prevents the army officer from making his technical criticism of the War Office public until his retirement has made it obsolete. Scientific public administration cannot be developed by leaving its formulation either to unconscious tradition or to the formulation of principles by even the wisest of outsiders. It can come only when the speculations of experts upon their problems are checked by the criticism of the public. It is unhealthy for any body of men to be in a position where they are sheltered from organised analysis. Yet we seem, under modern governments, to take the most special pains to prevent such analysis being made. Administrative methods are so largely a body of secret and unexplored habits that criticism of them must inevitably be, in some degree, ignorant. That is bad for the public official because his detection and exposure of the criticism tends to make him a little complacent of those habits. He stands by them because he knows them, and instead of being encouraged to initiate, he develops the habit of infallibility. That is a dangerous frame of mind, especially in a world, like our world, where the need of change is so wide and instant. We must develop a habit of breaking habits in the official if we are to use him to full advantage.

There are, I think, three important expedients of which we shall have to make increasing use if that full advantage is to be realised. The first, and not the least important, is the idea of a sabbatical year for public officials. For what he needs, above all, is freshness of mind, the ability to make new contacts and to assimilate new experience. To be immersed year after year in an office where, inevitably, problems come to him very largely as issues on paper, is fatal to that freshness in all save a few remarkable men. Change of work and scene is fundamental to him. He must be able to free his mind from the embarrassment of detail, to put his travellers' pack, so to say, on the mountain peak from which the vast panorama of life unfolds itself as a whole, and not in the compartments that are his daily round. One aspect of this is particularly urgent. The man who is to write despatches to Canada from Whitehall must see Canada; he cannot really know the mind with which he has to deal from an annual visitation in London with Canadian officials and public men. The man who is to take charge of problems concerning the League of

Nations needs to be seconded for a year to service in Geneva. He will the better serve the State by an intimate sense of the international mind at work there than by trying to guess its meaning from exchange of correspondence and an occasional visit to the Assembly of the League. The official who is to advise the Minister of Agriculture on the marketing of farm products will much more creatively grasp his function if his knowledge of other methods has been gained by direct observation instead of from the reading of reports embodying the observation of others. All this, of course, has an especially urgent emphasis when we move from the problems of civilised States to those involved in the guardianship of more primitive peoples. But I shall deal with this latter system in a later chapter.

There should, secondly, be a much more organic connection than there is now between the public service and the universities. Its value lies in two directions. The university is, first of all, the place where the problems of administration can be considered, probably more effectively than elsewhere, upon the plane of political science. They are freed there from the harassing penumbra of their immediate psychological environment. They can be rationalised into their abstract form in a way that is impossible in the market-place, on the one hand, and the department itself upon the other. They can be given their adequate historical background. And, secondly, I believe that the university has much to contribute to the training of officials. For it can set the issues they have to solve in a perspective richer than is possible in the department troubled by the intervention of immediacy. It can remove from their consideration the prejudices due to persons and special interests. That is, to some extent, already clear from the experience we have. Bodies like the Institute of Public Administration in England, the Institute of Government Research in America, the École des Sciences Politiques in France, have provided a meeting-ground between the official mind and the academic mind, from which there has emerged, in even a brief space of time, work of considerable value; and a great Secretary of War has borne striking testimony to the value of university instruction, even in the period of practical work, for public officials.[84]

In the third place, I believe that it is profoundly important to shorten the average period of official life. One of the great dangers to a public service lies in the permanence that is its characteristic; for this tends to make at least the upper layer of officials a caste whose habits are, from the inevitable rigidity due to long experience, hardened against the intrusion of novelty. This can, as I have argued, be largely counteracted by such devices as advisory committees and a sabbatical year. But the dangers still remain (a) that some men will be retained in the service far too long, either because they are too old, or because they are obviously unsuited to its special atmosphere; and (b) that men come to work of creative responsibility at too late a stage in life, when their mental faculties have acquired a certain hardness, and their habits have made them eager rather for the routine than from the departure from the routine. The latter danger, it may be added, is intensified by the doctrine of ministerial responsibility and the loyalty it will engender from the official to his political chief. For since the latter must bear the burden of all mistakes, the official is tempted to choose the decision which will occasion the least controversy. He seeks correctness. He shrinks from sowing intellectual wild oats, with the result that at the height of his career he has rarely intellectual wild oats to sow. A skilful minister can, doubtless, remedy this passion for the orthodox by insisting on experiment and defending his department even when it has obviously blundered; but not all ministers are skilful.

The minister apart, we can, I think, do much to obviate these difficulties in three ways. We can, first of all, make it much easier than it now is for a man to leave the service who finds, after eight or ten years, that he is either unsuited to or dissatisfied by it. Instead of fixing his pension rights at the end of his career, we can build up a proportional system of accruing rights which will enable him to risk a new career without financial sacrifice. We can, secondly, develop the habit of special appointments to a small number of technical posts, so that the department is constantly invigorated by new blood, free from its traditions, and with experience largely gained in a very different world. We must not, of course, so organise such posts that they become merely a reservoir of ministerial patronage; appointment ought always to be, at the least, a matter in which the Minister selects from a short list of names provided by the Public Service Commission, and chosen by the latter from whoever, granted the requisite qualifications, chooses to apply. But if, for instance, a government sets up a system of labour exchanges, and has at hand a man who has specialised in the knowledge of their function and working, it ought to be able, if it thinks fit, to secure his services. If it has a department of animal husbandry, it ought not to be compelled to recruit its head necessarily from the promotion of subordinates. The safeguard is that the minister should be made to satisfy the body normally filling vacancies in the public service; and a distinction, quite clearly, must be made between general administration and the administration of specialised subjects. But within those safeguards the principle, I think, is clear.

In the third place, we need to lower the age-limit for retirement. It is, perhaps, dangerous here to be too specific; but I should suggest that except in the quite special case of an extraordinary man, no person ought to stay in the public service, especially in a responsible position, after the age of fifty-five. He will then, it must be remembered, have been normally engaged on administrative work for over thirty years. If he is young, when originally appointed to a premier position, he blocks the way for younger men; if he is near to the retiring age, the chances are that his appointment is a tribute rather to his seniority than to his quality. It is urgent in any public service to develop the notion of giving men clearly responsible work before, at the least, the age of thirty-five. For, otherwise, they grow rapidly into the habit of looking to a superior for orders. They are lost and helpless when time gives them the duty of making important decisions. They have grown mature not in creative thought for themselves, but in providing the material for other people's thought. Some, of course, like Austin Dobson, may evade this danger by making the true centre of their lives outside the department; a man may be in reality a great golfer masking his powers in the guise of an official. But such exceptions will be rare; and if we desire the type of public servant to whom his work appeals so as to evoke all the qualities of mind and heart at his command, we cannot too early offer him functions he can fulfil with complete satisfaction to his self-respect. Either there must be a sense of creativeness once the technical aptitude has been acquired, or there will be a failure to secure the best results from the sources we use.[85]

A kindred problem which needs discussion is the relation of the lower grades of the public service to the administrative class. How are we to ensure that the former are given adequate opportunity to prove their fitness for more responsible work? There is, I think, little doubt that it has so far been too much the assumption of modern governments that the minor official is permanently destined to be a hewer of wood and drawer of water to his superiors; and little or no effort has been made either to discover or to evoke what talent he possesses. The tendency is, indeed, to give the ranks and classes of a public service a somewhat rigidly hierarchical character; with the result that it often reproduces for the subordinate officials many of the problems, both financially and intellectually, of the modern proletariat. The problem, indeed, is a complex one. The officials who determine promotion naturally make their contacts for the most part with the officials who expect promotion; and the later are already in the administrative class. And this situation is further intensified by the narrowness of the sources from which that administrative class is taken. It consists, as I have already pointed out, quite largely of people of the same social class and the habits of that class; and it is neither difficult nor unnatural for them to assume that their habits are essential to the proper performance of the public business. That is not in fact more likely to be true than the assumption that only an hereditary aristocracy is fitted to govern, or that only well-born people can fulfil the functions of the diplomatic service. In a body of men who, in the non-administrative classes of the English civil service are, the Post

Office and the Defence Services apart, nearly two hundred thousand in number, it would be remarkable indeed if there were not a body of men who would amply repay the conference of an opportunity to do work of first-class magnitude. How are we to organise their discovery?

As in every large-scale enterprise, it is unlikely that any system will do more than very partially fulfil its purposes; and it is certainly undesirable to adopt any such mechanical device of allotting some percentage of vacancies to the lower grades. Nor ought we to be impressed by seniority; that is, most emphatically, to mistake antiquity for experience. The qualities we want to discover are energy and originality of mind, the power to manage men, the ability to handle large subjects, rather than the mere knowledge of departmental routine. A variety of expedients suggest themselves. Something can undoubtedly be done by the zealous insight of higher officials. If they are genuinely anxious to discover talent, they will find that talent lies there to be discovered. But I am not inclines unduly to trust to the experience of a large degree of this kind of discrimination in officials who have heavy work to get done, and are naturally more anxious to get it done than to be interested in the question of who has done it. More help, I think, can be obtained by the careful organisation, especially for the younger members of the lower classes of officials, of opportunities for further education. Those who take advantage of those opportunities at once discriminate themselves as persons of energy and initiative; and if they give proof in the use of them of talent, channels for their advancement should be open. A man, for instance, who takes a high university degree while in the public service ought to be entitled to credit for his achievement; and this might reasonably take the form, either of being seconded on probation for more responsible work, with permanence if he is a success, or of permission to attempt entrance into the administrative class some years later than is normally the case. So, also, the publication of a competent book on problems of governmental interest ought always to lead to investigation by the department. A man who can do an inquiry as able as the investigation into the results of boy labour at the Liverpool Docks ought obviously never again to be left to perform any routine work; his competence for skilled research is immediately beyond question.[86] A man in government service who publishes, say, a competent book on public health administration ought to be selected for promotion in the same way as a young university lecturer who analyses the problems of his subject. Much, also, may be accomplished as self-government within the public services becomes a realised ideal. A second-division representative on a Whitley Council, for instance, ought to be able, by proof given of his capacity there, to ensure himself a period of probation on administrative work. And the plea that the department is fully staffed ought never to be a hindrance to his opportunity. For it is not the nature of any government department to feel itself fully staffed unless it wishes to do so.

I cannot here proceed to multiply indefinitely such types of possibility at our command. But one further suggestion needs to be explored because it seems to involve opportunities of which a skilled administrator might make good use. I have already urged the importance of the departmental conference in the making of policy. Inevitably, that will, almost entirely, be a conference of the chief officials. But I see no reason why we should not develop the idea of conferences of minor officials on departmental problems, of which the presidency was entrusted to the heads of departments who would go there, not merely to cultivate good relations with their staff, but also find out the range of their minds when at ease, in a fashion open to them rarely in the hours of public business. Foreigners have often been bewildered by the habit of the political week-end in England; but that wise invention was based on the profound truth that men come to know each other better when they are away from the convention of full-dress uniform. The decency of English political life, not a little, also, of its creativeness, is built on the fact that men who face one another over the benches of the House of Commons have enough social intimacy to join their minds in making a common solution of difficult problems before the breaking-point is reached. What I suggest is, so to say, the administrative week-end, in which the permanent secretary deliberately sets out to feel the minds of men whom he will, otherwise, hardly know save as persons who put papers upon his table. Just as the minister best learns to know his officials by dining with them, and smoking with them, so the official best learns to know his minor subordinates by seeing them outside the routine of office-hours. And unless he is capable, to that point of breaking the hierarchy in which he is involved, he will never be able fully to elicit the qualities he might secure.

I do not discuss here the question of the official in a nationalised industry; that is a problem in economic institutions which is treated in a later chapter. But it is of high importance to insist with emphasis that what is said here of the central departments applies also, in all its implications, to the public service in local government institutions as well. First of all, because they are, not less than the central department, the public service; and they require standards not less high, devotion not less exacting, than work in Whitehall or Washington or Paris. Every great municipality, therefore, needs its civil service commission not less than the central government. In England we have such a body in London and Manchester; in America it exists, though with but partial efficiency, in New York. But it is in Germany, above all, that the importance of a high standard in the service of local government has been most closely taken to heart. There is, undoubtedly, too much of the spirit of bureaucracy in their routine; many of them complain themselves of the needless formalities through which they have to work their way. But the standard of their work is better than elsewhere because the conditions of entrance to the service are much more rigorously controlled, and far more free from partisan nomination, as in the United States, and favouritism, as in Great Britain.

It is, of course, clear that any local service is subject to the limitation that, except for its higher appointments, where the necessary qualifications are usually fixed by the central government, the personnel of the service must largely be drawn from the locality itself. But that ought not to mean that local residents can be taken into municipal employment merely because they happen to be local residents. At the minimum an educational test ought to be applied; certainly no entrance ought ever to be possible for persons who are not eligible for admission to a university. Here, once more, Germany has much to teach the rest of modern States. Her schools of local government, as at Dusseldorf and Cologne before 1914, as at Eisenach and Nerchau even since that time, are notable achievements. At Eisenach a communal official can, in a two years' course, study problems like those of local finance and taxation, education, town planning and poor relief; instruction for which the hapless official elsewhere would, I think, be genuinely grateful. There is no reason available why, as in Berlin, the continuation schools of other States should not provide training to young people who wished to enter the service of local government, or why the authorities should not ask the schools to nominate probationers who shall, say at the end of a three-year period in which general education is combined with practical work, be engaged permanently if their work is satisfactory. It will be difficult, on any other plan, to get officials of the requisite quality; and it will be impossible properly to carry out the policy of a central government, which leans much, inevitably, upon local co-operation, unless local officials can grasp the aims and methods of the central power. Otherwise, there develop that friction and jealousy which prevent a proper combination of their joint endeavours; and the result is either an excessive centralisation or an inertia at the seat of central authority about local problems which is fatal to their adequate solution.

### (viii) The Principles of Local Government

In strict theory, there is no reason why all the necessary functions of government should not be carried on by a single body. It could maintain its local officials, who would report directly to it, and apply the necessary solutions in accordance with its directions. In a real sense, indeed, this is not an inadequate description of local government in France. There, at least, few outside the pettiest details fail to come within the province of the Perfect, himself an appointed official delegated by, and reporting to, the Minister of the Interior; and it is fair to say that all serious changes in local government policy originate from, and are sanctioned by, officials in Paris. Occasionally, indeed, an outstanding person may be able to make innovations, as in the famous administration of M. Herriot at Lyons. But, in general, a vivid local life in France is not lived in political terms; and it seems to be felt that the existing centralisation is necessary to preserve an adequately uniform system. Not, indeed, that protest against its results has been lacking. The literature of French regionalism is in a high degree the literature of revolt against a decay enforced by Paris upon the provinces; and it is there urged that unless the resumption of active powers by local authorities is made possible, the central authority will not merely stifle all local initiative, but destroy also that well-spring of local knowledge and local interest without which it cannot possibly exercise its functions.[87]

The case, indeed, for a strong system of local government in any State is clear almost beyond the needs of discussion. We cannot realise the full benefit of democratic government unless we begin by the admission that all problems are not central problems, and that the results of problems not central in their incidence require decision at the place, and by the persons, where and by whom the incidence is most deeply felt. Among the inhabitants of some given area, that is to say, there is a consciousness of common purposes and common needs by which they are differentiated from the inhabitants of other areas. I am, as a citizen of London, deeply interested in the water-supply and public libraries of London; I share that interest with six million fairly similar citizens. But neither I nor the six million would feel at all deeply involved if we heard that the water-supply of Manchester was unduly expensive, or that the citizens of Sussex could not get the latest books. Neighbourhood, in other words, makes us automatically aware of interests which impinge upon us more directly than upon others. We find that those interests differ in quantity and character from the interests of other neighbourhoods. We find that by common counsel we can seek to give those interests a quality of satisfaction which contents us more than we should be contented if that quality of satisfaction were contributed by others from without. For administration from without lacks the vitalising ability to be responsive to local opinion. It is bound, in the nature of things, to miss shades and expressions of thought and sentiment the perception of which are in a real degree urgent to the success of administration. And such government is bound, almost inevitably, to aim, not at variety, but at uniformity. It will seek to meet, not the special wants of Liverpool, but those wants which are similar to wants just met in Hereford or Leicester. It cannot grasp, in other words, the genius of place. Because, further, it is government from without, it fails to evoke either interest or responsibility from the neighbourhood it controls. It may well evoke indignation; but it does not succeed in eliciting the creative support of citizens. Its solutions may be well meant in conception, and efficient in application. But they fail to arouse in the neighbourhood a desire actively to participate in the realisation of their best result.

There are, moreover, other reasons why strong local government is an advantage. If a service is exclusively applied to the benefit of a particular district, it is obviously only fair that the inhabitants of the district should pay for it; and to raise from them the funds for payment means the certainty that they will demand control of the service, and the probability that they will manage it efficiently in order to keep their bill of costs as low as possible. Clearly, further, we cannot make an average man realise his citizenship in any creative way if his only relation to government is obtained by voting once every four or five years in a national election. Its relevance to him must be brought more directly home, otherwise his interest in the political process will wane to vanishing process; and it is elementary that the more inert the citizen-body, the more likely is there to be corruption and sinister privilege in the State. A man who realise that his street is badly paved because a body of persons directly under his view and influence are inefficient begins to have a sense of the network of interest in which he is involved. Local government, in other words, is educative in perhaps a higher degree, at least contingently, than any other part of government. And it must be remembered that there is no other way of bringing the mass of citizens into intimate contact with the persons responsible for decisions. It is clear that any great degree of centralisation must mean, and can only mean, a bureaucratic system. No legislative assembly in the world will be able, however greedy of power, to make decisions upon more than the largest outlines of local problems. The application of their details will be left to the departments. Appointed officials will therefore dominate them, and they will never be genuinely accessible to public opinion. For complaint against them can only be investigated in general terms; and it will only produce a revised decision, again in general terms, which the same officials will proceed again to apply, with, doubtless, the same results.

There are, of course, dangers in the conference of powers upon local territorial groups. Uniformity is usually cheaper, because it is almost always easier to make a single solution and apply it wholesale than to make a variety of solutions and have them applied piecemeal. It involves, also, some sacrifice of the greater knowledge and greater capacity that are almost bound to be at the command of a central, compared with a local, authority. Localism, also, lends itself a little easily to the sinister influence of powerful persons or bodies within a given neighbourhood; the record of American cities, and even of American States, is a plain lesson in this regard. Nor must we omit the results of the truism that the conference of power is in fact the conference of power. You may not be able to persuade a local body adequately to utilise its powers. A backward corporation may resist every stimulus except the passion for reducing the cost of its services to itself. It may refuse, for example, to take advantage, like some English counties, of the Public Libraries Act; it may remain, like Georgia in the United States, adamant against the abolition of child labour. Everyone knows the difficulties we encounter in persuading a rural community adequately to endow the education of its children. It must be admitted that in many respects the creation of a local government system is the offering of hostages to fortune. For a backward community may be hostile to every species of improvement, and it is rarely indeed that its forced conversion to novelty is at all satisfactory. It neglects, as a rule, that care for the gradual education of opinion which, ultimately, seems to lie at the base of all genuine freedom, and to be more important than any given statute, however urgent it may seem to the advocates of its enforcement.

No problem in local government is more difficult than the delimitation of the areas of local government. Every principle that has been recommended seems, almost inevitably, at some point to betray us. Scientific discovery makes obsolete the boundaries of historic tradition; the needs of things like drainage and water-supply overpass the urgency of tradition. Geographical considerations are rarely of any final importance; for a bridge can span a river, and a tunnel may make a mountain governmentally irrelevant. The idea of transport zones was suggestive in the days when the means of communication hardly differentiated our civilisation from that of the Romans; but with the advent of the railway and the aeroplane transport zones may well make Brighton a suburb of London and New Haven merely an outlying district of New York. The most convenient practical means lies, I think, in the indication given by density of population. The inhabitants of the modern city, for instance, need more special provision for services like water, lighting, and drainage than the dwellers in a rural area. For that reason, convenience indicates the city as a fairly natural unit of local government. But the lines of its boundaries are inevitably arbitrary, since, to take an obvious case, a tramway system will often link a city with its surrounding country districts. Nor is this all. It is clear that a service like the provision of electric power requires for economy a much larger area of distribution than a service like paving, and the combination of areas suited to their particular functions into an adequate unit of government is a matter of grave difficulty. All,

I think, that we can say is that each area, whether urban or rural, needs to be planned as a complex of functions, and that the method of administration must always leave room for co-operation between areas in the resolution of their joint interests.

Area, that is to say, must correspond to function, while, at the same time, we provide the opportunity for maintaining the special interest of each group of neighbours in the needs and possibilities of their special environment. That clearly involves two things. It means, first of all, that the persons responsible for the general principles upon which the different local circumstances are administered must be elected by the body of citizens and not appointed; and it means, secondly, that those so elected must oversee the general complex of services which relate to each local area. That will enable the same body of men to sit on bodies which deal with any given function by which their electorate is served. They will probably, for instance, completely control such services as paving and cleaning the streets, or providing public baths, where the area of provision can be small and yet efficient and economical; they will, probably, only partly control such services as lighting, university education, and provision of facilities for recreation and town-planning where the function needs to be organised over an area which transcends the principles of neighbourhood. But the interest of the elector in the person chosen will be protected by the fact that his nominee will sit on whatever body deals with the subject involved; and he will, accordingly, have the means directly at his disposal for the expression of his opinion. Cities could then be divided into electoral districts of a size small enough to permit adequate contact between the elector and his representative, and yet not so small as to make the governing municipal body too large for the efficient conduct of business. In rural districts it would, in this view, be necessary to combine smaller villages into units similar in character, though necessarily smaller in population, than the urban electoral districts, which would, in combination, provide an area large enough to cope with the problems to which, in the aspect of local government, rural life gives rise. The representative of each electoral district thus determined would automatically sit as member for that district upon the body governing any function of local import. He might be, for instance, a member of the city council of Manchester for all the services in which Manchester is a natural and normal unit of government; and a member of a council for, say, the north of England in relation to its electricity supply.

What is involved in such a scheme? Firstly, I think, elected service in local government will become, exactly like service in the modern representative assembly, full-time and paid work. For any member who desires seriously to grasp the issues which come before him for judgment, many of them technical and all of them intricate, cannot adequately do so if he is merely to deal with them in the intervals of his business. They require a fresh mind and a full mind. If we maintain the principle of unpaid work, we shall always find that membership of these local bodies will be predominantly representative of the richer classes in the community; and the standards of their performance will accordingly be set, not by the needs of the area, but by the desire of those classes to make local government as cheap as possible. They will provide excellent drainage but inadequate education, good roads but poor libraries. They will not grasp the psychological issues by which, for instance, the mind of the poor is moved. Anyone who watches the endeavour of the average English Board of Poor Law Guardians to understand the hatred of the poor for indoor relief will see why it is only final and abject destitution which is willing to take refuge there. And local government based on the unpaid member has, the world over, somehow seemed to accrete to itself a variety of persons—small contractors, publicans, shopkeepers and the like—whose disinterested zeal for the public welfare has been less apparent in the quality of work done than in their pronouncement of intention. Even in England, the home of the unpaid representative, we have seen the need for remunerating the mayor of many boroughs; and we have begun to pay expenses incurred in the performance of their duties by members of committees on Insurance and War Pensions. To refuse to extend the principle is to narrow dangerously the services of membership; and it is bound to be merely temporary as the class so largely excluded makes its way to power.

The elected member, secondly, will have what may be called magnicompetence; he will oversee the administration of a general range of functions rather than be chosen, generally speaking, to attend to a special subject. The case for magnicompetence against specialism is, I think, a clear one. Functions dovetail into one another. Education and health, transport and housing, cannot, without the danger of Lilliputian administration, be viewed separately. The system of *ad hoc* bodies has been constantly tried, especially in English experience, and it has always ultimately broken down. It prevents any total view of local finance; the elector cannot be expected to construct for himself a systematic view of the budget in which he is involved. It multiplies elections to the point of nauseation; and that is a position which, as American experience shows, always leads to indifference on the part of the elector. He knows that Jones is generally competent, but he cannot seriously measure competence in relation to burial boards, libraries, highways, schools. And such a system seems to lead always to candidatures which seek to represent not a general concern for the quality of administration, but a special interest in some aspect of it. The school-board system in London, for instance, led to the selection not so much of members interested in education, as in members interested in preserving Church schools or Roman Catholic schools, in keeping scripture teaching in the curriculum or keeping it out of it. And when the school board grew into concern with larger interests, it found at once that the field involved was outside its sphere of competence. The suggestion that this difficulty can be met by joint meetings of *ad hoc* bodies is open to precisely the same objections as the scheme for two Parliaments outlined by Mr. and Mrs. Webb. For either, say in the case of commissions dealing with health and education, there will be a permanent joint committee, in which real power will lie, or the two commissions will, on all large matters of principle, function as a single unit.

The persons chosen to sit upon these magnicompetent bodies should, thirdly, be directly and not indirectly elected. This principle is as much a matter of solid experience as of abstract theory. The only way in which we can secure anything approaching a continuous democratic control of policy-making bodies is by preserving direct contact between the elector and his representative; for, otherwise, an inevitable remoteness supervenes, and public interest in the making of policy declines through that remoteness. The result, that is to say, is a diminution in the educative value of a representative system. People are less likely to be informed of the significance of what is being done because their access to its achievement is not straightforward. They miss the simplicity of being able immediately to affix responsibility for what they dislike. There are, moreover, two further dangers in an indirectly elected body. Almost inevitably it seems to tend to bureaucracy. Because it is not checked by public opinion, it fails to appreciate the importance of public opinion. Because it is removed from public control, it tends to be impatient of public control. It is, further, clear that an indirect system will exaggerate all the weaknesses of majority-rule. It will reflect not the total opinion of the bodies from which it is chosen, but merely the dominant opinion; and where, as so often in America and Canada, that dominant opinion has a special religious complexion, the making of policy is distorted in a peculiarly vicious way. It is, finally, much more difficult in this system to secure adequate publicity for the proceedings of the body. We hear much of the work of borough and county councils in England; we hear little of their joint committees for managing schools. And even when such management is efficient, that is because the policy of management lies outside the committee; nor is the gain, if there is a gain, in efficiency superior to the loss involved in a full public interest in what is being done.

It is obvious that the central government must retain a power generally to control the work of local authorities. How far is that power to extend? It is clear, first of all, that there are many subjects in which at least a uniform standard of minimum attainment must be enforced. In education, in health, in housing, whatever the local will, it is impossible for the State to allow their standards to fall below a level consistent with the fulfilment of the rights of citizens. Such standards, therefore, require to be defined by the legislative assembly; and though their administration may be organised in concert with local bodies, the power to inspect, and, if need be, to control, cannot be surrendered to them. It is clear, also, that changes in social need involve continuous alteration both in the sources from which power is exercised and the area over which powers extend; and it is necessary to make the legislative assembly the ultimate reserve authority for the enactment of necessary changes. There are, thirdly, certain subjects over which local bodies ought not to exercise any control at all. They ought not, of course, to be able to mitigate the purposes of State legislation, save in so far as there is provision deliberately made for it. They should not be permitted to make regulations upon subjects like railways and the postal service, which are clearly central in character. Their powers of taxation ought, I think, to be defined with some rigidity, though the experience of France and Germany in the possibilities of local taxation ought to make us a little careful in the boundaries we erect for this power. It is, moreover, always advisable to reserve what may be termed a right of entry for report and inspection to the central government, even where the full control of some given subject is local in character. For, clearly, the central government cannot abandon the general duty of investigation. It will always be able to survey experience, to compare methods, to suggest experiments, from an ampler view than the vast majority of local bodies. It will, as a rule, be more discriminating and less partisan in its interpretation of the results it encounters. I do not think there is need, as in England, of a special ministry charged with the specific duty of supervising local government; it is better that the control of each function should reside in the department to which it naturally belongs. For there is an inevitable temptation to such a ministry with general powers to extend the amplitude of its jurisdiction. It will make itself a tutor over subjects in reality beyond its control. It will be worried over departures from the uniformity which makes its task an easy one. It will be dubious about experiments it has not itself initiated. The less we have of such central interference, above a general minimum level of competence, the better it is likely to be for the quality of local effort.

This, I believe, involves the transference of much greater powers to local bodies than it has been customary to give them in Anglo-Saxon countries. There it has been the rule that no power can be exercised for which there does not exist a specific warranty in statute. Every local experiment, therefore, outside the range of statutes has always involved a fresh application to the legislature. Such application is not only slow of result, but it is also exceedingly expensive; an average act of Parliament cost the city of Leeds, in the years from 1897 to 1913, nearly seven thousand pounds. In the five years from 1901, the twenty-eight London boroughs spent over seventy thousand pounds on legislation; and in the three years from 1903, the London County Council itself spent, in promoting and opposing bills, more than one hundred thousand pounds. Legislation, clearly, is an expensive amusement; and it would hardly have been possible for a device more deterrent of innovation to have been invented. If Leeds, for instance, is to spend seven thousand pounds in discovering whether it may have a municipal theatre, the probability is that it will not have a theatre at all.

It seems to me, therefore, the better theory to build the relationship between local and central government on the model of the relation between the States and Washington in the American union. There the reserved powers belong to the Federal authorities, and the residuary powers are within the ambit of State-control. So, in similar fashion, powers not specifically forbidden to a local authority might be exercised by them. It would, I think, be easy to devise quite adequate safeguards against abuse of these powers. There might be a provision for a local referendum; the citizens of Manchester, for instance, might prevent the building of a municipal theatre by plebiscite. All schemes might well assume the character of provisional orders which have to be submitted to the legislative assembly, and become inoperative if the latter, by resolution, indicates its disapproval of the scheme proposed; and it might well be made the duty of the appropriate department to accompany the laying of the provisional order upon the table of the legislature by a memorandum in which the proposal, especially on its financial side, is critically explained. Such sanction, it may be added, ought not to be required where legislation already permits the use of powers. If Manchester, for instance, decided to raise the school-leaving age to sixteen, what would seem to be required is congratulation rather than permission. And, within the limits of discretion, it ought to be possible for such experiment to be accompanied by financial novelties. A locality ought to be permitted, if its inhabitants agree, to raise a special rate in aid of an object it desires, and to attempt, for instance, to pay for some special purpose by such an expedient as the taxation of local ground values. The value also of legislation like the Communal Taxation Law of 1893 in Konigsburg, which permits special contributions to be levied on the owners of property who enjoy economic advantages owing to the execution of such public works as street-widening, slum clearance, and the provision of parks and open spaces, seems to be beyond discussion.

The notion that residual powers might, within the limits indicated, belong to local authorities is by no means a leap in the dark. It has been for the last fifty years the secret of the success which has attended municipal effort in Germany. Persons accustomed only to the limits of the Anglo-Saxon system would be amazed at the extent of local powers in Germany. "The urban commune", says a decision of the Supreme Administrative Court of Prussia,[88] "using its own resources, may claim as falling within its powers everything that promotes the welfare of the whole community, and the material interests and intellectual progress of the individual citizens. It may, of its own will, establish any institutions and arrangements for the common welfare which serve this purpose. It has a general right to promote the moral and economic interests of its citizens, and to use the resources available for the purpose. But it is always—and this is the boundary beyond which its acts are *ultra vires*—subject to the limitation that itself and its organs must restrict themselves to the care of local interests". It is under these powers that German towns have, without recourse to any legislative authority, set up their theatres, built their tramways, embarked upon municipal trading, established school medical services, and the provision of meals for school children; have promoted music, the drama, learning, dispensaries for the tubercular, municipal savings banks, house building, the guardianship of illegitimate children, bureaus of legal advice, and unemployment and fire insurance. "The German town of today", says a well-known authority upon them,[89] "is the standard-bearer in intellectual, economic, and social progress".

The special value of this system lies in three directions. It provides the means for important experiment in social matters, while restricting the necessary area of the experiment, and, therefore, what danger may be inherent in its failure. It contains, therefore, the great advantage that is offered by a federal system of encouraging local initiative and, at the same time, minimising the cost of that initiative to the community as a whole. It lessens, secondly, the pressure of local affairs upon the central legislative assembly. I myself believe that practically all the advantages claimed for the system of devolving authority upon subordinate Parliaments can be more easily attained by this method; and its greater institutional simplicity is a further recommendation. It is, further, a means not otherwise available of stimulating local pride in civic achievement, and, inferentially, of associating local effort with the task of government in a much more creative fashion than is now possible. For many to whom gas and water politics are permanently unattractive will be drawn into interest in municipal functions once their contingent area is dependent so largely upon the local will. When it is possible, for example, to make the drama a natural branch of local activity, it will be found that there exists in each area a largely untapped source of public energy waiting to be used; and the energy which begins by confining itself to the drama will quickly find that the proper use of a local theatre sends it into the schools, and from the schools to the homes of the people.

So far I have discussed the problem of local government predominantly from the angle of the central departments of the State. But it is, I think, clear that such a structure as that here outlined offers room for large possibilities from two angles. An attempt can be made to relate its organs to the consumer, regarded as a citizen, on the one hand, and to the producer, regarded as a technical expert, upon the other. There is no reason why every activity of a local council should not be surrounded by its advisory committee. Upon it there would sit, as upon a national body, representatives of the different interests involved. An education committee of this kind, for example, would naturally include representatives of teachers, of parents, and of former students of the schools. For one day it will be realised as obvious that the English or American elementary school has as much need, and as distinct a title, to its old students' associations as Eton or Girton: and the members of them will be as anxious to create and preserve a tradition as the alumni of more narrow foundations. So also, I imagine, the modern school will find it more and more useful to group the parents with whom it has to deal into some kind of organisation, and to elicit their support and encouragement in developing itself. The interaction of the teacher's mind with that of the parent cannot but result in a deeper perception on the latter's part of what an educational system might imply; and those who represent these bodies on an advisory committee on local educational policy will do much to strengthen the energy and stir the ambition of their elected representatives. So also an advisory committee to the Health Committee of the Council, upon which there sit doctors and dentists, nurses and sanitary inspectors, welfare workers and architects, will easily develop functions of genuine importance if it lends itself to the task of watching step by step the policy of the governing body. They would be empowered to make suggestions to the elected council, to initiate inquiries, to issue announcements on the larger issues of local importance. A municipal body which understood its function would never fail to associate with, for instance, its library work, the local associations of teachers; and, if it happened to be a university town, to ask the university for assistance in its work. Nor ought it ever to neglect the importance of advice from the local press. To secure proper publicity for its activities is a really urgent function. Public apathy is in a large degree the result of public ignorance, and the proper use of the press is one of the straightest roads to the remedy.

What would be the form of government to be utilised by these elected representatives? There are here several quite distinct problems. No small part of local government is quite definitely expert administration in which general opinion is only valid upon large outlines of policy, on the one hand, and finance upon the other. It is this consideration which has made the German municipal system so largely government by experts, and relegated the elected representative to little more than an advisory person of special importance. The ideal has been to make it certain that every branch of local administration is in the hands of men who are definitely specialists, and can take the necessary steps to secure efficiency without waiting upon the consent of the elected council, or the pressure of public opinion. Practically, their relationship to the elected council is not unlike the relationship of the British Government to Parliament. The latter may criticise, demand explanation, and, in the last resort, reject; but it is essentially the business of the cabinet to tell their superiors what to do, and how they ought to do it. The Anglo-American system, on the other hand, has retained omnipotence in policy for the elected amateur; and the expert official has been like the King in the English constitution, a person who may advise and encourage and warn, but cannot pass beyond counsel into the self-determined exercise of power. The American system of commission government, in which a small elected body, usually of some half-dozen persons, devote their whole time to oversight of the expert administrator seems to be a compromise between the English and the German methods.[90]

On the whole, and granted a right relation between the elected representative and the expert, I think it probable that the classic model of Anglo-American has the largest advantage on its side. It ensures a direct and continuous relation between government and public opinion. It brings a constantly fresh mind to the problems of administration. It breaks the rigidity of outlook to which the professional mind is too often prone. It prevents the assumption, not uncommon with the expert, that he possesses a technical competence about which amateur opinion is simply irrelevant. And most of the dangers implicit in control by the untrained amateur can, I think, be obviated by proper use of the expert and by the fact that as service on local government bodies becomes more and more a full-time, paid service, there will be greater opportunity for the disappearance of the amateur who remains incompetent. Largely, of course, the relationship between the elected member and the expert is not susceptible of definition; it is a habit of mind, a tradition, which can be recognised when seen, but eludes the printed word: We know that it is not the relation between Mr. Nupkins and his clerk; and it is not the relation of overwhelming dominance which, on occasion, has been the characteristic of an English town-clerk near the age of retirement. But anyone who has seen an English municipal body at work will have realised that the whole difference between efficient and inefficient administration lies in the creative use of officials by elected persons.

We can, fairly easily, organise room for this creativeness in the structure here envisaged. Local administration is largely government by committee; there, above all, is found the centre where policy is finally determined. We can, I think transform the composition of these committees so as to ensure that expert opinion carries its full weight. Each committee should be compelled to co-opt to membership representatives of the vocations allied to their work. The latter could not, of course, vote; but they would speak, and they would see to it that the officials were allowed a full opportunity to develop their plans. We should then have teachers on the education committee; doctors and dentists and nurses on the health committee; architects, surveyors, building operatives on the housing committee; accountants on the finance committee; representatives of the local Trades Council and the Chamber of Commerce on the establishment committee; these would, I think, bend the energies of the council to the proper appreciation of technical competence. They would also provide a link between the elected body and its advisory committees of great value, for they would be able to trace, as the public cannot now trace, the real responsibility for lack of constructive thought in administration. An official, so bulwarked, who could not get adequate consideration for his ideas would either be a genius so far ahead of his time as to invite misapprehension, or a man not competent for his task. For it is not the least part of the expert's function to be able to make plain the importance of his conclusions. It is no part of his duty to play the Cassandra in local government.

With the relationship between employers and employed in local government I shall deal later, since that is an economic, rather than a political, matter. Here it is sufficient to say that there must be room for much greater vocational self-determination than now exists, and that, as urged earlier in this chapter, all the considerations which govern the problems of appointment in the service of the central government apply with not less force to local government also. A different but an urgent issue is the sphere of trading enterprise by these local bodies. The lines of demarcation are, I suggest, fixed by two considerations. There are types of industry, of which railways and electricity supply are obvious examples, the scope of which is national in character; and much is lost, and nothing gained, by attempting a multiplex provision of what needs unified supply There are types of industry, secondly, like milk-supply, bread, the distribution of coal, which can better be undertaken by consumers' co-operation; and in that form present the important advantage that the quality of service offered is then open to independent scrutiny, for instance, by the health inspectors of a municipal body. In between the two there is a great range of service where local provision has obvious advantage. Tramways, for instance, gas and housing, the provision of medical service both of a remedial and preventive character, are all examples of service in which the local body has shown itself able to excel. I do not see, either, why municipal bodies should not co-operate to produce many of the commodities they now jointly use on a vast scale, either securing them by direct manufacture or through such agencies as the Co-operative Wholesale Society in England. It is the peculiar value of this form of enterprise that it permits, if properly organised, either the elimination of profit, or, as in the case of many municipal tramway systems, the devotion of profit to public purposes. The degree to which development of this kind can be carried is obviously great, but it depends very largely on making the initiative of local bodies a real and living thing. There must not fall across their path the suspicious shadow of a government department, distrustful of its endeavours. Once they are free to exploit the genius of their neighbourhood, there is no reason not to expect such a flowering of local patriotism as marked, for instance, the Italian cities of the Middle Ages or the Hansa towns.

For the main difficulty, heretofore, in local government is that it has been rare to attempt the evocation of a community spirit. It has meant a little, but not too much, to be a citizen of some city; but the power has not been there to make citizenship creative, and the general mass has not been related to the process of government. Its art gallery has been a matter for its curator and his committee; it has not been a matter for every citizen possessed of a love of art. Its infant death-rate has been a matter for the medical officer of health; he has not been allowed effectively to appeal to a civic conscience, alert and armed. We must strive to create a local pride in achievement and a local sense of shame in failure. It must matter, for instance, to the resident of a rich borough like Kensington that its infant mortality rate is higher than that of a poor borough like Poplar. It must be brought home to the citizens, say, of Liverpool that their neighbour, Manchester, has a municipal repertory theatre, while their council remains content with the normal supply of commercial dramatic art. We need to set local authorities striving against each other in ceaseless rivalry, to produce in men that urgent local patriotism which Mr. Chesterton depicted in the *Napoleon of Notting Hill*. That, I think, can be achieved if the local authorities are free to think out great policies and to apply them in freedom. And it will not be unimportant to the standards of central politics that we are able thus to revivify the quality of local life.

Such emulation, it should be added, means an immense growth in two aspects of government of which we are only beginning to perceive the significance. We shall need, if emulation is to be creative, a great increase in the volume of investigation in local affairs, and we shall need, also, a great increase in co-operation and the pooling of knowledge between local authorities. The first aspect is one in which the central government could be of immense assistance. Its power of investigation is always greater than that of any local body, and its right of inspection gives it access to material not otherwise likely to be accessible. If we could know annually in each measurable department of the national life the comparative achievement of each local authority, we should go far towards stimulating competition in achievement and in providing ourselves with an index to what should be the standard of minimum service exacted from local bodies by the State. We could compare library systems and the degree to which their use was organised; the number of children in each area who passed from primary to secondary schools and from secondary schools to the university; we could see what service was made available for the sick in Durham and compare it with the kindred service in Winchester; we could measure the reduction in cost to the consumer of tramway services in Cincinnati and Cleveland; we could get reports upon the local museums of Boston and Glasgow. What Mr. and Mrs. Webb have called "the impartial qualitative assessment of each town as a whole"[91] seems to me a really urgent task if its governance is to approach adequacy.

We need, secondly, the co-operation of local authorities. There is a number of directions in which such co-operation can usefully develop. Not only can the local authorities jointly undertake certain obvious services for themselves, of which insurance against fire is the most obvious, but they can also—sometimes by direct co-operative production, sometimes by centralised purchase of goods on a larger scale than is open to a single authority—largely reduce to themselves and their constituencies the cost of the services they provide. They could co-operate to provide, region by region, a common rate in support of the universities. They could jointly undertake the provision of far more complete vital statistics than are now available in any existing State. They could form the habit of holding conferences—sometimes of elected persons, sometimes of officials—for the discussion of specific and common problems, and see to it that the conclusions reached were emphasised in the proper quarters. They could unite to secure the proper town-planning of a region and the proper provision of services, like tramways, which now suffer so seriously from "dead-ends" through the artificiality of boundaries. It is to be hoped that they will grow into the habit of interchanging their chief officials for limited periods to prevent their methods from becoming stereo-typed and rigid. They might unite to provide a costings service, in which each item of municipal expenditure will be carefully compared throughout the State. It is clear, as Mr. and Mrs. Webb point out, that there are many ways of developing the advantages of a centralisation without its dangers, of which the self-imposed standard is not the least beneficial. The wider the field of such co-operation, it may be added, the better the service they are likely to obtain from their officials; for nothing so contributes to pride in work as the knowledge of possible alternative achievement. Ultimately, moreover, there is no reason why such mutuality should not become international, and the common basis of experience from which ideas are drawn admits the general knowledge of civilisation as a whole. Certainly there is no habit we need so urgently to acquire as the recognition that the parish needs to build its methods on the ideas of the world. So far such effort has been rare, though the systematic endeavour of Japan and the bureaus of municipal research in America are evidence that its importance is being realised increasingly. Certainly there is no field of social activity in which the deliberate co-ordination of knowledge is more likely to bear fruitful results.

## (ix) Conclusion

Such a scheme of political institutions represents, of course, only a small part of the area in which the activity of the State will necessarily go deep; it represents, however, that part in which its influence is most likely to be direct. Its advantages, as I see them, are, above all, that while it maintains as simple the organs of legal registration, it provides for the admission that law affects only a small part of social life; and it therefore surrounds each organ of legal competence with bodies entitled to advise and so made that their advice is fully weighed. Those bodies are so constituted that they bring into the ambit of State decision the views and ideas of all the various interests affected by its results. The underlying theory, that is to say, upon which the scheme is built is a recognition that the sources of decision are multiple, and that therefore the result enacted in statute should be a function of the many variables which enter into its making. It gives the voluntary body, therefore, a definite position in the making of law; and it thereby ensures that its experience and its desires shall be counted by those who have the ultimate decision in their hands. It does not assume for that ultimate decision any quality superior to its substance. It admits that it will make mistakes; it agrees that, on occasion, it will commit deliberate wrong. But it argues that the checks and balances with which it is here surrounded reduce the likelihood of error and minimise the possibility of wrong. It is, as I think, a prescription of value against serious disorder in society; but it is not, and it does not pretend to be, a final prescription. The only way to make the State a subject of passionate loyalty is to make it deserve passionate loyalty, and the degree of its desert will depend upon what it achieves for the happiness of ordinary men and women. Here, at the least, those ordinary men and women are given the opportunity to make fully known that upon which they believe their happiness to depend. It will be open to the State to deny their will, but it will be the nature of this system to make that denial a much more difficult, sometimes even a more perilous, adventure than it is to-day. As a system, also, it strives at every angle of its compass to make its working a mechanism of education to those who encounter it. For it is built on the conviction that the Greek notion of citizenship—the capacity to rule and be ruled in turn—contains a truth the importance of which we are in danger of forgetting. We cannot go back to the simplicity of the city-State, but there is no reason why we should not profit by their wisdom.

It seeks also, as a scheme of institutions, to concentrate attention less on the problems of power than on the problems of administration. It is its argument that much more time has been spent than is necessary upon what may be termed the abstract metaphysics of politics. For so long as we deal with the concept of an intangible State, so long we shall miss the central fact that what is truly important is the relationships of those who act as its agents. It is the things they do and fail to do, the process in which their actions are embodied, that constitute the reality of political discussion. The sovereign State of philosophic theory never existed except in the imagination of philosophers. The true State of everyday life is, I have here argued, a body of men issuing orders, and what must be considered is the range of subjects to which their orders should refer, and the methods by which abuse of power must be adequately prevented. I have not urged that prevention is always possible—men who are determined on the commission of wrong will always find the safeguards of justice frail enough for the ends they have in view—but I have urged that they may be more firmly welded in the heart of the communal life than they now are, and, consequently, that their neglect may be made more dangerous than it has been in the past.

Much of the theory here defended has turned upon a denial that the rulers of society, as such, are entitled to any special prestige. That has been the reason, for instance, on the insistence that their agents are, at every point, subject to the rule of law. That is why, also, it has been made a matter of grave difficulty for the legislative assembly of the State to invade such basic rights as freedom of speech. I have not denied that the government of a State ought to be the just guardian of general social interests; but I have built my hypotheses upon the view that the performance of this function cannot, without careful examination of its results, be admitted as in any way adequate. That is why, again, the mere enactment of law does not seem to me impressive. What is important is its substance; and the quality of that substance will depend upon the degree to which the makers of law are compelled to take account of the varied, and often opposite, social interests which dispute for the mastery of the State.

One last word may fitly be said. There will be many to whom the idea of organised consultation seems a pale ghost alongside more complex arrangements for the division of legal power into a multiplicity of unrelated groups. Of this criticism two things are, I think, fair comment. The separate functioning of groups always involves some system of interlocking relationships at the boundaries of their function; and the harmony thereby attained seems to me both more artificial and less responsible than that attainable by the method here outlined; and, secondly, organised consultation seems to me a weapon of which the quality and strength depend entirely upon the spirit and the intelligence of the citizen-body. In a society divided, like our own, into rich and poor, where, because of that division, the avenues of intelligence are largely under the control of a small class of wealthy persons, it is not possible to realise the full implications of the system, because those full implications are fatal to a society divided into rich and poor. But in a society built upon principles of justice such organised consultation would, as I think, be as powerful a safeguard as we require for the protection of the rights men possess in virtue of their humanity. Public opinion will then be the organised utterance of the community's instructed conscience; and they who seek to prevent its purposes or to frustrate its desires will lack the chief weapons they have at their disposal. A society, in fact, in which there are freedom and equality has already divided power. Its difficulty is the long road it has to travel before freedom and equality may be attained.

## REFERENCES

1. *Ut supra.*
2. (1916) A.C. 120.
3. Cf. J. Holmes in *Jensen* v. *Southern Pacific*, 244 U.S. 205.
4. Cf. Duguit, *Les transformations du Droit Public*, chap. vii, and my *Foundations of Sovereignty*, chap. iii.
5. *Federalist*, No. 46 (ed. Ford), p. 319.
6. *Esprit des Lois*, Bk. xi. chap. vi.
7. See the separate report by Orr.
8. *La Separation des Pouvoirs*, p. 1.
9. Duguit, *Separation des Pouvoirs*, p. 99.
10. *Hansard*, 4th series, vol. 160, p. 370; 5th series, vol. 22, p. 366.
11. Cf. the citations in Chaffee, *Freedom of Speech, passim*.
12. In the case of Kitchloo and Satya Pal, cf, the evidence in*O'Dwyer* v. *Nair*, May 1924.
13. 195 U.S. 27.
14. 219 U.S. 104.
15. Keith, *Responsible Government in Dominions*, 725-49.
16. Moore, *The Commonwealth of Australia*, 597-606.
17. *Conference on Devolution* (Cmd. 692), 1920, Appendix III, pp. 16-17. See Henderson and Laski in *Economica*, March 1925; and Chiao, *Devolution in Great Britain* (1922).

18. Even if the Murray MacDonald's scheme (*ibid.*, p. 13) of reference to the judicial committee is adopted; and he does not prevent recourse to the courts of law by private persons.
19. See all this excellently put in Dr. H. Finer's pamphlet, *The Case against Proportional Representation* (Fabian Society, 1924).
20. *Speech to the Electors of Bristol Works* (ed. of. 1815), vol. iii, pp. 11 f.
21. For adverse comment on the recall see Lowell, *Public Opinion and Popular Government*, p. 147.
22. There is, I believe, an analogous association formed recently (1924) in Great Britain.
23. Cf. Beveridge, *The Public Service in War and Peace.*
24. I do not here discuss the complicated second chamber recommended by Lord Bryce for this country. It seems to me at once fantastic, and to combine all the worst features of all existing second chambers. For a discussion of its proposals see Mr. H.B. Lees-Smith's *Second Chambers in Theory and Practice*, pp. 216 f.
25. *The Great Society* (1914), p. 288.
26. *Second Chambers in Theory and Practice*, pp. 249 f.
27. *Constitutional Code*, Bk. I, ch. xvi.
28. Cf. the table in *Systems of Government within the British Empire*, p. li.
29. On the whole question see the remarks of Mr. J. Ramsay MacDonald, *Socialism and Government*, vol. ii, pp. 50 f.
30. *Sir Wilfrid Laurier and the Liberal Party*, i. 412, quoted in Macdonald, *op. cit.*
31. *A Constitution for the Socialist Commonwealth of Great Britain*, Part II, Chap. i, pp. 108 ff.
32. *Op. cit.*, p. 111.
33. *Op. cit.*, pp. 110-28.
34. *Op. cit.*, p. 129.
35. *Op. cit.*, pp. 136 f., and especially the importance note on parties in the Socialist State on p. 144.
36. It is Mr. and Mrs. Webb's own instance, *op. cit.*, p. 142.
37. Cf. my *State of Parties and the Right of Dissolution* (Fabian Society 1924) for a full discussion of the whole question.
38. Cf. my analysis in the *Nation*, October-December 1920.
39. Cf. M.P. Follett, *The Speaker of the House of Representatives.*
40. Cf. C.T. Carr, *Delegated Legislation*, and my paper on *Administrative Discretion* in *Journal of Public Administration*, April 1923. See also *Parliamentary Debates*, 5th series, vol. 144, col. 429, where some interesting statistics are given. Mr. W.A. Robson's *Justice and Administrative Law* (1928) and Lord Hewart's *The New Despotism* (1929) bring out, in their very different ways, the urgency of this need.
41. Cf. my lecture in *The Development of the Civil Service*, from which I have borrowed some sentences in these paragraphs.
42. For some useful remarks on this general question see Sidgwick, *Elements of Politics*, pp. 462-3.
43. Trevelyan, *Life and Letters of Lord Macaulay* (Nelson edition), ii. 142.
44. On the system of Mr. Lloyd George see the *Report of the War Cabinet for 1917* (Cd. 9005) and Lord Curzon's speech in the House of Lords on June 19, 1918.
45. See the Ninth Report (H.C. 121 of 1918) of the Select Committee on National Expenditure, especially the appendices of evidence. I note that its conclusions are in the main approved by the *Report* of the Machinery of Government Committee (Cd. 9230 of 1918), pp. 14-15.

46. Cf. McCarthy in P.S. Reinsch, *Readings in American State Government*, pp. 63 ff.
47. Cf. Lowell, *Public Opinion and Popular Government*, pp. 250 f., for some interesting details.
48. *Op. cit.*, p. 252.
49. Cf. R.H. Tawney, *Minimum Rates in Chain-making Industry*.
50. See this worked out in detail in the *Machinery of Government Report*, pp. 8 f.
51. The Board of Trade, Cf. Cd. 8912 of 1918.
52. Cf. *Report of the Machinery of Government Committee*, p. 32. Since this was written, the Committee on Civil Research, largely, planned, I believe, by the late Lord Haldane, has come into being on almost exactly the model here outlined (1929).
53. *Reports of Commissions on Industrial Unrest* (1917), Bulletin 237 of the U.S. Bureau of Labour, p. 49.
54. *Report*, p. 12.
55. *The Development of the Civil Service*, p. 220.
56. *Ibid.*, p. 108.
57. Cf. R. Heber Smith, *Justice and the Poor* (New York, 1919), is a mine of information on this question; the nearest English equivalent I know is Judge Parry's *The Law and the Poor*.
58. Though I believe a departmental committee has previously sat. On the whole problem see M. Lomax, *Experiences of an Asylum Doctor*.
59. *The Process of Judicial Legislation*, in 48 *American Law Review* (1914), pp. 161. 183. The italics are Professor Cohen's. I should like here to emphasise the debt I owe to this brilliant paper.
60. *Arlidge* v. *Local Government Board* (1915), A.C. 120.
61. *U.S.* v. *Ju Toy*, 198 U.S. 253.
62. *Baltimore & Ohio, R.R. Co.* v. *Pitcairn Coal Co., 215* U.S. 481; *I.C.C.* v. *Union Pacific R.R. Co.*, 222 U.S. 541.
63. *R.* v. *Halliday* (1917), A.C. 226. But note the dissenting opinion of Lord Shaw.
64. 31 *Law Quarterly Review* (1915), p. 150.
65. *R.* v. *Halliday, ut supra*, at p. 287.
66. *New York, etc.* v. *McCall*, 38 Sup. Ct. Rep. 122, 124.
67. *Feather* v. *Regina*, 6 B. & S. 257.
68. *Bainbridge* v. *Postmaster-General* (1906), 1 K.B. 178.
69. *Dunn* v. *Regina* (1896), 1 Q.B.C.A. 116.
70. *Mighell* v. *Sultan of Johore* (1894), 1 Q.B. 149.
71. *U.S.* v. *Lee*, 106 U.S. 196, where at p. 206, it is admitted that the exemption from suit rests on no "solid foundation of principle".
72. Cf. R.D. Maguire, *State Liability for Tort*, 30 *Harvard Law Review*, p. 20.
73. *Mersey Docks* v. *Gibbs*, 11 H.C.L.C. 686.
74. *Feather* v. *Regina*, 6 B. & S. 257.
75. See Report of the Lee Commission on the Public Services in India (1924).
76. On the whole subject cf. the paper on the *Responsibility of the State in England* in my *Foundations of Sovereignty* and Mr. E. Borchard's *State Liability for Tort* in the *Yale Law Journal* for 1926-7. The report of the Hewart Committee in 1924 is, at least, a programme for Great Britain.
77. On this general problem cf. my *Authority in the Modern State*, chap. v.
78. Cf. *The New Republic*, 1923-4, *passim*, for details of the oil scandal, the war hospitals' scandal and their ramifications.
79. Evidence before Lord Shaw's Commission on Transport Labour, vol. i, pp. 185 f.
80. *The Development of the Civil Service*, pp. 231, 244.

81. Cf. my *Personnel of the British Cabinet* (Fabian Society, 1928).
82. *The Development of the Civil Service*, p. 242. The word "learned" is italicised by Sir William Beveridge.
83. *The Soul and Body of an Army*, pp. 21 f.
84. See the evidence of Lord Haldane before the Royal Commission on the Coal Industry, 1919, reprinted in the *Problem of Nationalisation*, p. 18.
85. On all this, Sir William Beveridge's *The Public Service in War and Peace* is a mine of informative comment; see especially pp. 39-47.
86. *Boy Labour at the Liverpool Docks*, 1919 (Ministry of Labour).
87. Cf. Charles Brun, *Le Regionalisme*.
88. Decision of September 21, 1886; and see the comment thereon of H. Kappelmann, *Verfassung und Verwaltungsorganisation der Stadte*, vol. i. p. 55.
89. Most, *Die Deutsche Stadt und ihre Verwaltung*, vol. i. p. 51.
90. For government by commission, cf. Professor W.B. Munro's excellent *Government of American Cities* and his *Principles and Methods of Municipal Administration*.
91. *A Constitution for the Socialist Commonwealth of Great Britain*, p. 240. My obligation to this brilliant chapter will be clear from the degree to which I have adopted Mr. and Mrs. Webb's conclusions on local government.

# 9. Economic Institutions

## (i) The Purpose of Industrial Organisation

From the standpoint of politics, the problems of industry have two aspects of importance. There is, first of all, the problem of safeguarding, throughout its operations, what I have called the natural rights of men. An industrial system must satisfy the principles of justice; it must give to the worker a secure and adequate livelihood, reasonable conditions of work, and a full opportunity to share in the making of the conditions upon which his happiness in work will depend. He must not feel that his life is at the hazard of another man's will. He must be able, by his effort, to purchase for himself the means to self-realisation, so far, at least, as these are dependent upon material factors. The authority which presides over his destiny must be an authority that is explicable in terms of moral principle. Obviously enough, none of these conditions is fulfilled under the present system. It involves, as a system, the abstraction of labour-power from the labourer, so that the price paid for the former is only partially determined by the needs of the latter. That price, moreover, is paid only when there is need of the particular kind of labour which the worker is able to do; if his employment does not involve the making of profit, he is not entitled, whatever his needs, to the engagement of his services. Nor has he, in return for his labour, any effective share in the organisation of production even when he is employed. The broad characteristic of modern industry is the almost absolute separation of management from labour. The area of consultation is narrowed down to the conditions attaching to the price to be paid for labour and the physical conditions of its employment. The worker has no right to express his ideas upon methods of production. He has no organised opportunity for suggestion. Even when he has demands to make, or grievances to put forward, their formulation usually involves a test of power in which the thing of import is not the moral quality of the demand or the grievance, but the strategic condition of the parties to the industrial relation. Nor, finally, has the worker any claim upon the product of his work. Once his price has been paid he is insignificant in relation to it. He is, in a full sense, that animate tool which to Aristotle was the essence of the slave.

Nothing of all this is qualitatively altered by the fact that exceptions to it can be shown. There are employers who make it a custom always to pay adequate wages; who give to their workers a full share in the determination of labour conditions; who have invented machinery for the co-operative investigation of demand and grievance; who regard the welfare of their employees as a matter of urgent moral importance to themselves. There are many employers of whom this would be true, some of whom it would even be an inadequate account; but any survey of industry as a whole would make their numbers irrelevant to the general character of the industrial relation. It is significant that every great advance in industrial welfare has had to be fought for as though it represented an attack on the very citadel of industrial prosperity; and that every attack, always supported by the emphatic argument that it represents the experience of men peculiarly fitted to estimate the future, has within a short time of being made disappointed the prophecies of its protagonists. It is significant, also, that the moral relations of industrial enterprise are avowedly distinct from those of private life. Every investigation made reveals corruption and waste as its necessary and inevitable accompaniments. It should be added that this is not less true of the worker than of the employer. The latter is not less tempted, by the conditions under which he lives, to evade the right. He fails to give his best work, he does not realise himself, simply because the system does not permit its emergence and its restoration. The Mr. Bounderbys of the modern Coketown mean perfectly well, but in the circumstances of their environment their intentions are *a priori* frustrated.

From this angle the interest of the State in an industrial system is the protection of the producer, whatever his position in the industrial hierarchy. It is called to his protection because he is a citizen, and cannot, upon the plane of civic life, function as a citizen unless certain qualities are inherent in the process of production. But the State is bound also to the protection of the consumer. He lives because certain services are available to him. He needs continuous access to certain commodities without which life is impossible. These are urgencies which cannot, in the nature of things, be withheld. He needs also other commodities, the absence of which does not, indeed, destroy life, but may well destroy that which gives to life the flavour of beauty and comfort. Finally, and at a further distance from the interest of the State, there are commodities the need for and want of which is in no sense universal, but which supply a genuine quality to a portion of mankind. In such an analysis it is, I think, plain that the interest of the State in the first group of wants is immediate, direct, and comprehensive. It must ensure such a supply of them as will serve the total need of the community. It must see to it that their quality is adequate; the maxim *caveat emptor* cannot apply in regard to primary qualities in a civilisation so complex as our own. The failure to secure these services being fatal, it is obvious that the State cannot risk their production by private enterprise. Nor can it risk even their distribution save under such safeguards as will ensure that no section of its citizens is deprived of access to them. The second group of wants does not involve such vigorous supervision by the State. It is desirable that they should be satisfied; it is not fundamental that they should be satisfied. The interest, consequently, of the State in their production is an interest in the results of production, on the one hand, and in the effect of the methods of production on the producer, on the other. With the third group of wants—the production of cosmetics, for example—the interest of the State in the fact of production is negligible; where alone it is concerned is to protect the producer in such enterprise in order that the process in which he is involved shall accept the standards essential to the quality of citizenship.

It follows from this analysis that the government of industry can generally be resolved into three large categories. There are industries urgently affected by a public character which are monopolistic in their nature. Their operation is essential to the welfare of the community. They have to be operated for use and not for profit. There must be the maximum of continuity in the service they afford. There must be stringent public regulation, not only of the conditions of production, but also of the selling price of the commodity produced; and it may even be necessary to maintain the production of such commodities when there is little prospect—as in research, for instance—of a measurable economic return. In this first category the only possible method of government is the nationalisation of the service involved. By nationalisation I do not mean a specific form, such as that taken in modern States by the Post Office. There is room, and to spare, for experiment in the method of government in nationalised industry. The one consideration it excludes is the notion of private profit. In the second category, we are given the production of urgent commodities which are not naturally monopolistic, in which, indeed, as in agriculture, there may be clearly a large place for the individual producer, but in which, also, the interest of the State is paramount; and, secondly, commodities which are definitely desirable, but not necessarily urgent, in the former sense. Here, I believe, the forms of government admit of a much larger range of variation. But in the first group of this category—as, for instance, in the supply of milk and bread—the less room there is for private profit the better; and I shall argue that these services, as they mainly affect the householder, are the natural and proper sphere of the consumer's co-operative movement. The second group of this character may be organised privately, whether like the modern company, or by such a producer's guild as those which seem likely to revive under modern pressure for the democratisation of industrial control. They will be characterised by a considerable degree of government intervention, under forms, and through standards, I shall discuss later. There will, thirdly, be the category in which the commodities produced are not invested with a public character. Here, as I think, the forms of industrial government may be as various as human ingenuity can suggest. All that the State will exact is conformity with certain standards, in wages, in hours of labour and the like, and in the erection of institutions to ensure that the will of labour has a full opportunity to impress itself on the making of those standards. But in the third category, the problem of the amount of profit will not directly concern the State. If a firm, for instance, invents a toy so appealing as to enlist the universal allegiance of children, the State will not seek to limit the profits of its manufacture; or if it publishes a book which has an immense sale, it will regard the publisher as entitled, once the interests of its writer are safeguarded, to what he can make from his enterprise.

I do not, therefore, envisage anything like the disappearance of private enterprise. Its province, indeed, will be smaller than is now the case. It will, wherever it operates, be subject to a much more rigorous control than in the past; and, especially in the basic industries, initiative will have to display itself under different forms than it assumes under the present system. But I do not assume that any special formulae, whether State socialism, guild socialism, or syndicalism, represent a universal truth applicable to all industry under all conditions. I believe that there will still be a place for industrial adventure, but I do not expect that place to be within the area upon which public welfare depends. I believe, further, that many occupations, especially on the distributive side of industry, will have no natural place in the system. Advertising, for instance, and the middlemen of trade who neither manufacture nor consume, can, as I shall seek to show, be largely eliminated in their present form by a less wasteful organisation of the channel between producer and consumer. But I am not envisaging a world in which the enormous economic disparities of the present system have any place. Men will still be able to make fortunes; but, especially in the period of transition, they will be subject to heavy taxation upon income, and still heavier duties upon their estates at death. For it must be emphasised that to establish a system of rights involves expenditure by the State; and, particularly in the epoch of change, the wealth devoted to that purpose must largely be derived from the taxation of wealthy men. That is one of the unavoidable privileges of the rich. It will, I do not doubt, be deeply resented at the outset. Changes in the habits of society are always deeply resented by those whom they affect. But as men grow into the new conditions, I believe that the result will be increasingly to transfer social significance from wealth to service; and men will prefer to be known for what they do rather than for what they possess. Indeed, as I argued earlier, I think it probable that such a society will, in the result, be totally richer than at present, even though its appearance does not show the great peaks of fortune now possible. For because it is generally informed by justice, because, generally, it reflects the desires of those associated with its effort, it is more likely to secure from all save a few an effort more commensurate with their powers than the present order can win from them. It will be able to draw upon a larger area of inventiveness. It will have fewer disastrous casualties than now. It will have a higher standard of honour than a society built, like ours, upon the motive of profit-making. It will have found the means to make men share not less in the gain than in the toil of living.

## (ii) Socialised Industries

Any discussion of the process of nationalisation must begin by insisting upon three things. It is not, first of all, a question of catastrophic nationalisation. So far as we can see, the process will be a piecemeal one, the character of which will change as it learns by experience. Nor, secondly, need it be assumed that each nationalised industry needs an identical form of government; it needs a constitutional form of government in which certain principles and elements will, in different guises, always be found. Nor, thirdly, is it possible for me, even if I had the knowledge, to draw up a catalogue of the industries which may naturally be grouped under each of the three categories outlined above. There could not, in any case, be agreement upon such a list. I think myself, for example, that the service of banking ought definitely to be a nationalised service; but powerful reasons can be adduced for leaving it a private industry, under some substantial, but still not final, public control. There are industries, like the mining and oil industry, in which the case for nationalisation seems to me clear beyond discussion. There are others, like shipping, in which the predominant part seems to me an obvious case for a nationalised service, but in which, also, there is no reason why auxiliary aspects, a steamer-service, for instance, between Margate and Ramsgate, should not be either private or municipal in character. It is not, indeed, improbable that many nationalised industries will continue to be surrounded by a residuum of private enterprise, sometimes for the purpose of making special commodities, sometimes for the purpose of export, sometimes to make articles the demand for which is not large enough to justify the devotion of national factories to their production. Nor will the list of nationalised industries ever remain permanent over a long period. Invention and discovery will always imply additions to, and subtractions from, the list. We have, therefore, to concern ourselves with leading principles rather than with details, to set out the foundations rather than to build the superstructure.

It is essential, in any national plan of industry, that the ownership of the means of production should be vested in the State. That is necessary for two reasons. It emphasises where the ultimate incidence of control must rest. It enables us to insist that the producers in the industry are not entitled to regard it as existing solely for their benefit; they cannot, therefore, claim such a level of prices as will give them a wage disproportionate either to need or to the result of effort. It emphasises, also, that the surplus value created by the industry, over and above cost of production and the distribution of the product to the ultimate consumer, belongs to the community as a whole. We reject, that is to say, any purely syndicalist plan of industrial organisation. It is not less objectionable in principle than any other plan of private ownership. There is no reason to suppose that the ownership of the American mines by the United Mine Workers of America would be more careful of the public interest in coal than has been the case under their ownership by corporations like the present interests. The fact is that all exclusive control of this kind is morally vicious. It confers a title to special privilege which is corrupting in its essence, even if its possessors believe that they will devote it to the noblest ends. That has been the case with churches, and even with bodies within churches, like the Franciscans, who have started out from the principle that private possessions are morally dangerous. It has been seen, in the case of working-class, both in the treatment often accorded to trade-union officials by their constituents, and in the inability of the Co-operative Movement to adopt a satisfactory policy towards its employees. A statement like that of Mr. Cole, that "the control of actual production ... is the business of the producer, and not of the consumer",[1] altogether omits consideration of the intricate relationship between the aspects of the productive process. It is only by making ownership from the outset a matter in which the community has the ultimate power that we can build adequate relations beyond.

But while the community, through the State, must own the instruments of production, the producers are entitled to participate in management. What does such participation imply? Clearly, it must include a share in the making of the conditions under which the members of the given vocation, whether they be lawyers or miners, chemists or carpenters, exercise their function. They must assist in settling their pay and their hours of work, the sanitation of their factories, the character of the particular job they do, the men with whom and, to no small degree, under whom, they are to work. They must be free, in a word, to make their vocation an effective function in the same way as the doctor and the lawyer. There can, I think, be no doubt that the standard of these professions is in no small degree built upon the autonomy of the members of the craft. They accept a discipline to live under because it self-imposed. It is creative because it is derived from their own experience of what will make them conscious of a great tradition which they must not only preserve, but also develop. Their code of honour is born of self-determination. There must similarly be room in factory and office for a kindred freedom. And this self-determination is not a generalised right of a few workers chosen to represent an indifferentiated mass of their fellows. It is a right for each class and grade of workers who feel themselves as distinct from one another as the dentist from the doctor. Their control will be worthless unless it is specialised control. There will be the need to protect themselves against the invasion of their special sphere. There will be the demand that their peculiar technique secures its apposite qualification before anyone can be permitted to practise it. This specialism, moreover, is essential the more technical the work becomes; for then the worker is a member of a small group to whom protection that is general will become purely illusory in character. Nor do I believe, as Professor Graham Wallas[2] has argued, that these safeguards merely intensify professional conservation. There is a sense in which professional conservation is the best safeguard we have of the tradition of experience; and, broadly speaking, it is only in vocational self-determination that a particular group of workers can grow conscious of themselves. I believe that consciousness is more truly the root from which freedom grows than we are inclined to admit.

Participation, further, must mean the right to be consulted in the making of policy for the industry. But, here, certain differentials are important. The making of policy is not daily administration. The former is the long plan, the general direction of events over a period. Here, assuredly, the workers in a given industry have a right to be heard, to explain their point of view, to emphasise doubts, and, at the margin, to resist decision. But they cannot make the policy; that is a matter which must rest with those who speak in the name of the community. Thus, for instance, it would not be for the miners to say how much coal should be produced in a given year. They might urge on the deciding body that the number of tons was too large for the number of hewers in the pits, or too small to produce a wage-fund consistent with an adequate standard of life. But though they would thus share in the decision made, its making depends upon considerations of which their interests are only part. Administration is a different matter. Once a policy has been decided upon, its application is a matter of technique where each grade involved in the technique has the right to help. But help must be proportionate to qualification. The hewer of coal cannot settle problems which belong to the mining engineer simply because he lacks the knowledge to do so. He ought to be able to make representations, whether of grievance or suggestion. But as soon as administration passes beyond the technique of a given grade of worker, whatever the advisory capacity in which he may attend to settlement, he cannot expect to control it. That would be as absurd as to allow the patient to control the doctor in the choice of the medicine he requires.

The classical method in a nationalised industry has been a system like that of the British Post Office in which a minister responsible to Parliament is supposed to make the policy which directs its operations. It is clear that such a simple method is altogether inadequate to our needs. In the first place, the system does not permit any real knowledge of the work of the Post Office. An annual examination of estimates, an occasional question, and, quite rarely, a special debate, makes the supposed control of Parliament very largely a myth; and the assumption that the methods of the Post Office are a matter of cabinet policy is irrelevant to the proper character of industrial enterprise. The doctrine, moreover, of ministerial responsibility cannot work in a realm such as this. It is resented by the government of the day; it is disliked by the official, who realises the ignorant character of most of the criticisms he has to meet; it is a source of irritation to the private member who finds that his inquiries are met by the skilful evasion of their substance. The nationalised industries we are discussing will inevitably be the subject of discussion in the legislative assembly. But their relation to the government of the day will, I think, have to assume a different form.

I have already argued that the distribution of government business should be by functions and not by persons. One of those functions is the control over the production of commodities in its varying forms. The more unified the nature of that control, in its large outlines, the better is the national policy likely to be. We ought not to have a separate minister of mines, of agriculture, of the postal service. We need a single minister of production co-ordinating the policies of a number of subordinate ministers, and presenting, for the cabinet, a co-ordinated body of ideas to the legislative assembly. These subordinate ministers will not, in the case of a nationalised industry, be directly responsible for its operation. They will communicate to those who administer it the general ideas upon which the legislative assembly insists. They will receive from those administrators their report upon the methods they propose to use in giving those ideas practical application; that will lead, on his part, to criticism, suggestion, and, on occasion, to definite objection. They will be supported, as I pointed out earlier, by a legislative committee each of which will enable them to advise the legislature upon problems connected with the industry. They will, in a word, exercise, not administration, but control; and the latter will be derived from the policy sanctioned by the legislative assembly itself. Their knowledge of the way in which the stream of tendency they direct through affairs flows to its appointed end they will derive from a body of experts in their departments who will spend their time in providing them with statistics of cost and output, with audits of accounts, with the result of inspections, and with, perhaps above all, the record of research into new possibilities which they can bring to the notice of the service of administration. Their part will have been played in satisfying the legislative assembly that the policy it has sanctioned has been put into operation. They will not be responsible if, for instance, a local chamber of commerce is dissatisfied with its telephone service, or an angry clergyman dislikes the extra stop on a train from London to Eastbourne. Those will be recognised as technical problems about which the ideas of the administrative personnel are the real factor in government.

Two questions arise here of the first importance. Does such control offer an adequate guarantee that the interests of the State will be safeguarded in the administration of the service? I see no reason why this should not be the case. There is preserved in all its fullness the ultimate power of the legislative assembly to make the policy of the industry. It will be able to control the principles which underlie its direction far more fully than is now possible. It will be able to criticise the operation of those principles from a basis of much fuller knowledge than is now available, say, to the average member of Congress or the House of Commons. It will have its group of members in touch with every item of importance in the working of the assembly. It will learn from the advisory committees the impact that working on the persons affected by it. The publicity secured by the minister's department will throw a flood of light on the technical efficiency of its operation. The system here outlined surely adds to, rather than subtracts from, the safeguards of national ownership.

The second question is more complex in character. If final control, as here suggested, is placed outside the nationalised industry, can the self-government of the producer therein, the democratic nature of the process in which he is involved, be made effective? It must be said at once that if by self-government in industry is meant the total and absolute control of all operations and the policy upon which those operations depends by the producers, it is impossible, in any real way. We can allow a postal guild to tell the State what ought to be charged for the delivery of letters; we cannot allow it finally to determine the price of delivery. We can give it the opportunity to make its case an overwhelming one; but an external view is essential to the protection of others interested in the delivery of letters. We can allow miners to develop what they consider adequate tests for entrance to a mining guild; but we must retain for the State the right to revise those tests. In the vast majority of cases, I believe that the administration of a nationalised industry will be almost entirely left, in every question of practical importance, to those engaged in working it. But the safeguard must always exist that the producers do not seek to exploit the community for their own interest. The criteria which Mr. Cole regards[3] as sufficient proof that a society will never be exploited by the guild do not seem to me in any way adequate. The guild, he thinks, is prevented from exploitation because it is charged a "substitute for economic rent" in return for the use of the instruments of production. But, obviously, that substitute must be fixed in terms of the cost of production, and those costs may be charged with a wages bill, for example, for which there is no justification. Such a doubt Mr. Cole thinks a betrayal of faith in human nature; to which I think the simple answer is that we have been betrayed by human nature so often that it is elementary wisdom to safeguard ourselves against it. To urge, as he urges, that the taxation of guilds will solve the matter because the competent authority will fix the burden in terms of the productivity of the industry, and that since productivity depends on price, "the heaviest burdens will be laid on the broadest backs", is to omit the fact that those "broadest backs" will dominate the competent authority. Nor do I believe we can secure the necessary mechanisms of industrial change, and the necessary degree of industrial audit, unless control remains outside. Freedom in industry seems to me to mean the chance to make one's personality creative in the vocation pursued; and it will appear later that there is a full opportunity for that creativeness in the administrative institutions of a nationalised industry.

Let me turn, then, to the institutions of administration. At the apex of each national industry will be a governing board in which there will be vested the full power to carry out the policy approved by the legislative assembly. What will be its constitution and functions? It should, like the cabinet, be essentially a small body; any committee charged with executive duties cannot be large if it is in any real degree to be efficient. It will need to represent three different types of interest in the industry. There will be members who represent the side of management, in which the technical side is included; others, again, will represent the different vocations, both manual and clerical; others, finally, will represent the public, and especially those industries which are allied to the service concerned. How the membership is to be chosen is not a matter upon which anything final can be said; much, obviously, will depend upon the character of the industry and the variety of the vocations of which it is composed. But certain principles, I think, are clear. The representatives of the vocations should always be chosen by the vocations themselves. That does not necessarily mean election at large, by all the members of the vocation; personally, I think it probable that their choice, either by the executive committee of the vocation or by an *ad hoc* delegate meeting, will give better results than those available from an indiscriminate mass vote in which it is difficult for the merits of the candidates to be nicely judged. The members who represent management should be elected by the managers and technicians jointly; and it will be advisable to ensure that each group shall be able to have their own members on the board. The representatives of the public should be nominated by the subordinate minister in charge of the department under which the industry is grouped; but he should, I think, submit his proposed list to the legislative committee of his department for endorsement, and there should always be included in his list one representative nominated by the consumers' Co-operative Movement. The members should be appointed for a term of years, and they should be re-eligible without limit. The board needs to embody the maximum it can secure; it is not a method of training apprentices. The members should, of course, be paid for their services, and they should meet as often as their business requires.

The functions of the Governing Board define themselves, at least in principle, with some simplicity. It is charged with carrying out the general policy of the legislative assembly. It must interpret its meaning in large outline, and think out the implications it contains. It will co-ordinate the work of the districts into which it will be necessary to divide the industry as a whole. It will act, therefore, as an advisory body to those districts, consider their problems criticise their operations, remit to them suggestions, ask them to carry out experiments either sectionally or upon a national scale. Clearly, also, it must be charged with three essential functions if an adequate unification of its work is to be achieved. It must maintain the control of the statistical side of the industry, its estimates, its accountancy, its audit. That is urgent, both for the purpose of proper estimates of cost, of, therefore, the fixation of price, and for the making of decisions upon such financial problems as the maintenance of an adequate reserve, the raising of new capital and so forth. It is by the Governing Board that relations with other industries will be determined; not, indeed, the details of those relationships, but such systematic principles as will secure a just uniformity of treatment. It must, secondly, maintain a district service of inspection. Where, for instance, there is a fall in total output it must be able to have its independent explanation of the fall. Where the industrial relations of management and men are bad, it must have an independent survey of the conditions which surround that badness. It must, thirdly, maintain an independent research organisation communicating to the district novelties in method, the results of foreign experiment, the possibilities of new machinery and so forth. Its meetings, clearly, will not be public; but its account ought to be accessible in the same way as the national accounts and its proceedings published in the large outline of their results. It ought annually, at least, and, possibly, more often, to summon conferences of the District Boards, of which the powers will be outlined below, and of the vocational bodies in the industry; there, criticisms, recommendations, ideas, should be freely exchanged, and the meeting should bear something of the relationship to the industry that the annual conference of the trade unions in England bears to the movement as a whole. It does not, that is to say, control, but it gives the directing force of the movement a sense of the wider influences at work there. It should be the duty, also, of the Governing Board to report annually to the minister in charge of the department concerned with its work.

Two other aspects of the work are also important. It will have, clearly, certain powers of appointment. It will select, as will be seen in detail later, the public representatives of the District Boards; and it will need to appoint its own staff. For the latter purpose it must maintain an establishment section whose business it will be to see that no person is appointed to any post who does not possess the requisite qualifications. These will be, clearly, largely vocational in character; and that is, in itself, some safeguard against favouritism in its various forms. But it is, I think, important to prevent even the Governing Board making the establishment section the creature of its own will; and, to that end, I suggest that the members of the section, some five or seven in number, shall be chosen by the vocations in the industry as permanent nominees and shall be dismissible only by action of the minister in charge of the department. They would then be as independent in tenure and character as the members of such a body as the Civil Service Commission in England. To them, also, ought to be submitted not merely the national appointments, but also such local positions as the managership of a factory or a mine. They can, in each case, only require proof of qualification: but the power to require such proof is essential to the proper working of the industry.

The Governing Board, secondly, must obviously have powers in relation to strikes or lock-outs. It ought, I believe, to be made a local condition in such a relationship as a national industry implies, that no national stoppage should take place until the Governing Board has sought the means of settlement. District stoppages are, in the first instance, a district matter; but the Governing Board ought to have the right to demand an immediate report of the issues in dispute, to explain to the District Board the principles of settlement it proposes, and, if it is dissatisfied with the handling of the case by the District Board, to be able to revoke it into its own hands. In all such disputes it is essential that there should be maintained uniform rates of wages, and uniform hours of labour throughout the industry; and the Governing Board must admit no settlement that violates this principle. There is no case for admitting variation on any other ground than the character of the work done or the amount of output over a minimum which admits of a full wage for the purposes of citizenship.

The Governing Board will act rather as a co-ordinating factor in administration than as itself the directly administering factor. For a centralised service in which complete uniformity prevailed would leave no room for flexibility, or for the display of initiative outside the Governing

Body. The inevitable result of such a policy would be bureaucracy at its worst. The mine and the factory would be hampered by a network of regulations which would make it difficult for them to meet the special conditions they are bound to confront. Each industry, therefore, must be divided into regions of which the number will depend upon the character of the industry and the principles upon which it is organised. The coal industry, for instance, is in England divided into six Districts by the Mines Department, and in the scheme devised for its governance by Mr. Justice Sankey it was divided into fourteen. Each of these Regional or District Boards should be composed of representatives of each of the interests which find place in the Governing Body. The representatives of management and the vocations would be similarly elected; those of the public being appointed by the Governing Body. The persons chosen to represent the public would include a district representative of the Co-operative Movement.

The functions of the Regional Boards will be similar in character, though narrower in the area with which they deal, to those of the Governing Body. They will be responsible for the administration of the industry in their district. They will apply on the spot the national policy with the flexibility demanded by the special district conditions they confront. Over two problems, basic wages and basic hours of labour, they ought not, I think, to exercise control; these are essentially national matters because they require, from their nature, uniformity of principle. There is no reason why a miner in Northumberland should work longer hours than a miner in Yorkshire; nor can rational grounds be alleged why he should be paid less for the same basic effort. The Regional Board, also, will appoint the managers of the different mines or factories in their areas. In each case, their choice should be surrounded by two safeguards. They should, I think, select only after opportunity has been given for all qualified men to compete for the appointment; and they should be compelled to report their choice to the Establishment Section of the Governing Body. The latter ought not to be able to refuse the nomination made, except upon the ground of inadequate qualification; it is, I think, of the first importance that each Regional Board should be fully responsible for problems of personnel within its area. It should act as the primary authority in all industrial disputes within its area; with the two limitations that the Governing Body should have the right to revoke a dispute into its own jurisdiction, and that the workers should be able to appeal thereto from its decision. Under it, also, there would be departments to deal with the purchase of materials and the marketing of the product in the given area, linked, obviously, to each mine or factory by the necessary channels. For it is clear that centralised purchase of materials is an obvious economy; and organised marketing is the only way in which we can eliminate the host of middlemen who, without performing any genuine service that is indispensable, now infest the ranks of industry. The more direct the highroad from producer to consumer, the more efficient is their relationship likely to be.

Below the Regional Boards will be the individual mines and factories of the industry. Two things in the constitution of each are, I think, quite clear. The factory or mine must at the source be under the control of a manager who is directly responsible for its working; and his relationship with his workers there must be arranged through the medium of a Works Committee. There is no substitute possible for the individual responsibility which control by a person represents in each unit of production. There must be a single mind planning the application of decisions and responsible for their result. Committees are much more effective either in vetoing action it is proposed to take, or in outlining a policy, than in actually attempting operation. The mainspring of the latter is an actual person free to plan his way to the end he is instructed to reach. He may be surrounded with restrictions, those are the material to which the effort of his hand is subdued. But it is quite certain that the individual factory will be a failure unless the responsibility for its management is single and personal.

But this does not mean that the manager should be an autocrat, free to hew his way as he pleases to his appointed goal. The average worker is much more intimately affected by his policy than he is likely to be by the decisions either of the Governing Body or the Regional Board. His freedom at his work is undoubtedly increased by the sense that he ultimately contributes, through his representatives, to the making of policy. But what mainly touches him and influences his sense of happiness in life depends most largely upon the circumstances of his daily life. It is the order of the foreman, the decision of the works manager, that he feels most intimately; and it is to this end urgent that he should participate in, and vitally help to make, those orders and those decisions. Clearly the character of such Works Committees cannot be uniform. Anyone who looks at the already existing variety of structure will realise that uniformity is neither attainable nor desirable.[4] There will be cases in which a mixed committee of management and workers is desirable. There will be others in which the representation is confined to the workers alone. There will be others, again, in which the committee will more suitably represent a special grade of workers than a heterogeneous collection of them. Some factories will be so large as to need all three types; others, again, will probably be small enough to need a single form only. The one essential limitation of power to which they will be submitted is that they will not be able to alter the principles of national or regional agreements made with the Governing Body or the Regional Board respectively; that must always be a matter for the vocational associations as a whole, though suitable adaptations of principle to local conditions may be made with the assent of all concerned.

The functions of the Works Committees would lie mainly in two directions. They would discuss with the management the day-to-day grievances which inevitably arise in all administration—cases of unfair treatment, of unusually heavy work, of inadequate routing of work throughout the factory; the delays, for instance, from which miners suffer through the failure to supply sufficient tubs for coal; and they would contribute suggestions to the management for the improvement or organisation in the factory. Anyone who studies the functions now performed by existing Works Committees will gain at least a general notion of the place they will come to occupy in the industrial structure. And it is worth while to set these out in some detail, because a realisation of their scope will provide a means of measuring the extent to which the worker's life will be planned by a process of which he is largely the creator. I add that they must always have, as a matter of constitutional right, the power of access to the manager; that service upon them must count as working time; and that where their functions are of large enough volume they should have their paid officials. We cannot, beyond this, define with any precision their actual relationship with the management. But two things may be said. The more freely the manager seeks to avail himself of their services, to consult them, to try and grasp the point of view they urge, the more likely is he to stimulate the quality of effort we require in industry. Much, of course, will depend upon managerial temperament; there are some men to whom consultation is the most difficult of all habits. But such men are fitted rather to be experts in some special sphere than to seek to drive a team of men. We cannot have autocracy, and where it is sought, an appeal to the Regional Board ought always to be in order.

In this background, I suggest, that our experience already indicates that the problems dealt with by Works Committees will comprise at least the following range of subjects.[5] (1) Works rules. (2) Distribution of hours or work; time-keeping; breaks in working hours. (3) Payment of wages. (4) Settlement of grievances. (5) Holiday arrangements. (6) Physical welfare in mine and factory; such problems, for instance, as baths at the pit-head, safety appliances, heating and sanitation. (7) Factory and mine discipline. (8) Training of apprentices. (9) Education in the factory—the provision of a technical library, organisation of lectures and so forth. (10) Reception of suggestions for improvement in method and organisation of work; facilitation of tests for such suggestions. (11) Organisation of social side of factory life, e.g. sports, dramatic group, etc. (12) Investigation of factors, e.g. housing conditions, inadequate provision of schools, which may affect the proper working of the factory. I do not, of course, pretend that this list is adequate, much less complete; but it at least serves to indicate how much of the worker's life can be ruled by institutions in which he has a share.

Nor can it be doubted that these Works Committees are a powerful creative force. There is a large body of evidence in proof of their value. They have secured better time-keeping. They have aided in the maintenance of a greater volume of output. They have prevented the wastage of material in manufacture. They have prevented the violation of safety rules. There are cases where petty theft has almost entirely disappeared through the action of such a committee. There are others where their investigation into the machinery used has brought about substantial technical improvements. There are others, again, where the committee has maintained output while securing a decrease in the number of hours worked weekly by the staff. Another committee had a chart of output placed on each machine in order that the workers might see for themselves the variations in their efficiency. "It has been found", says a report of the British Government,[6] "not only that they serve as an effective substitute in the individual establishment for the no longer direct relations between employers and work-people, but that they provide also, in many case, a means of meeting the demand of work-people for an insight into the economic conditions of the industry, and of the particular establishment with which they are connected. Difficult as in many cases such questions are, Works Committee at least ensure the confidence between employers and work-people without which discussion of the problem involved is impossible".

It should be emphasised that these Works Committees are the root of freedom in the factory. The individual worker is himself helpless before the size of modern organisation. He can only make himself felt by the evolution of institutions through which his will has a full opportunity of expression. In committees such as these there is, I think, a reasonable guarantee that this will be the case. They will work on the spot. They will be composed of men who know each other in the intimacy of kindred effort. They will be elective; and the period of office can, without serious difficulty, be made much shorter than in the case either of the Governing Body or the Regional Board. They will have real value for the latter institutions, since it will be generally true that a manager who is in continual difficulty with his Works Committees is at some important point unfit for his post. That is why it is important to give the committee not merely functions of the range indicated, but also the right to protest against the manager to the Regional Board. There cannot, I think, be the right to carry a proposal against him in the factory itself, simply because he is the person responsible for its operation, and he cannot responsibly apply a policy built from below with which he is in disagreement. Nor do I believe that this right of protest will impair discipline in the factory, for it is general experience that discussion on the plane of comradeship and equality almost always leads to a satisfactory compromise. The occasion for protest will be rare; and, were it absent, acute disagreement would have no alternative save unconditional surrender or a strike. It is, I think, a mistake to create alternatives of this character. They are bound to lead to that psychological *malaise* so evident in European industrial conditions since 1918 and so fatal to the proper working of the industrial machine. The right of protest secures a determination from a disinterested body upon which both management and men find their place; and I believe that in all save a few instances the determination of that body will be accepted without difficulty. Where, indeed, it meets with refusal it will probably reflect a problem so large as to need decision in principle by the legislative assembly.

There remains the problem of the recruitment of staff, and of the methods of appointment and dismissal, of discipline, indeed, in general, in the nationalised industry. Here, the basic principles have the merit of simplicity, even if it is impossible to determine the varied forms they will assume. It is clear that vacancies must be filled by advertisement; and that the persons selected to fill them must be qualified for the post, as the vocation to which they belong determines qualification. There can be no question of a right to a position, in the way, for instance, in which the son of a present-day employer enters his father's business as a matter of course. We shall need in each factory and pit, or in such a grouping of them as is found most satisfactory, an appointments section working in close connection with the management. It will be connected with the local schools and colleges in an organic way, and people will enter it at the age of work through such means. Where it is not the apprentice, but adult manual labour, that is required, the appointments section will furnish particulars of its vacancies to the local branch of the vocational organisation which will act as the employment exchange for the area. In the case of clerical labour, the experience of the modern civil service suggests that, at the base, competitive examination is much the best method of recruitment. Once we pass from first appointments to promotion and selection for technical posts, other and more complex considerations arise.

All minor posts in each factory are, broadly, of four kinds. (1) There is the position of foremen. They should, I suggest, be appointed by the manager after consultation with the Works Committee. (2) There are positions like those of managerial assistants where the work involved is not technical in nature, but involves general planning and oversight. They should be chosen by a special selection committee, presided over by the manager, with representatives on it of the management side, and the

Works Committee. This selection committee should, preferably, be a standing committee of the factory, for experience suggests that the judging of men is a quality which can be acquired by experience. (3) There are, thirdly, positions of a technical nature like that of an accountant or a chemist. These should, I think, be similarly appointed to the second group, save that the selection committee should in these cases be fortified by the addition of a member of the technical vocation involved. (4) The final class is that of manager. I have already suggested that he should be appointed by the Regional Board. The latter can make all inquiries it needs to satisfy itself that its selection is likely to be approved in the factory concerned, but the chief problem is that of capacity. Mr. Cole's suggestion[7] that he should be chosen by the Works Committee in a factory is, I think, open to all the usual objections that such self-election involves. It maximises intrigue, and it sails to do justice to ability. Anyone who studies the results of the system as it worked in the old self-governing workshop, or, even more, in the colleges of Oxford and Cambridge, will not be inclined to trust to its working. It is a simple illustration to compare the record of Masters of Trinity College, Cambridge, who are appointed by the Crown, with those of any other Cambridge college, to see the advantage of external device. There can be ample consultation, but the final power ought to scrutinise the problem from the angle of the industry as a whole.

All this, of course, is simply an indication of technique. What, generally, it seeks to avoid is the placing of the power to make appointment in the hands of those from amongst whom the choice must be made. There can be, and there ought to be, the most ample consultation of them; and, other things being equal, no views ought to weigh more than theirs. But there is, in our experience, little reason to doubt that the absence of an external appointing authority either leads to availability in the American sense, or to seniority, as the criterion of fitness; and neither is adequate for industrial functions. I do not suppose that any technique adopted will precisely resemble that here outlines; but the principle upon which it rests is, I am fairly certain, at the heart of successful enterprise.

Promotion is a different matter. Everyone who works has, I think, a right to the satisfaction of two expectations. He has a right to have his period of service count, up to a certain point; and he has the right to be considered for promotion. In academic work, it is not unusual for each year of service, after a period of probation, to be recognised by a small increment of pay, the total of these increments not being greater than the salary affixed to the grade next above that to which the recipient belongs. The same principle characterises the public service of the modern State. It is, of course, dependent on satisfactory work. It is, I think, the simplest system of recognition there is, and its general adoption is in accordance with justice. It enables us to reward the man who works hard, even while his capacity does not justify us in giving him more responsible function. For where capacity must above all count is in the promotion of men. The method I would suggest is twofold. In the case of all subordinate appointments, the Works Committee might nominate a candidate to the committee of selection. In most cases, their choice will be unexceptionable and, with the consent of the latter, he should be promoted to the vacant post. But beyond this level, promotion should follow the path now usual, for example, in the higher posts of the municipal service. The committee of selection would fill it from within if it was convinced of the suitability of some person in the factory itself; but if it was doubtful of his fitness, or if it thought definitely that it could do better outside, it would throw open the post to competition and leave the man on the spot to be weighed against those who chose to apply. That is, I suggest, an important guarantee against what may be called industrial inbreeding. It will weight the scale somewhat in favour of the known candidate, but not sufficiently to risk his choice merely on the ground that he is known. So, similarly, the average permanent secretary to a British department of State will be chosen from inside; but instances do not fail to occur when it is considered advisable to transfer an official from another department.

The problem of discipline in a nationalised factory seems to me likely to be much simpler than it is under the present system. Most of the present difficulties are inherent in the autocracy of the system. Men can be appointed by the employer without regard to the will of those they control, and they are, similarly, subject to dismissal. The strategic dispositions of the parties to industry, the fear of unemployment, the desire to stand in well with the management, tend only too often to make the foreman a bully and each problem of discipline a matter of prestige which may engage, as in the famous Knox Strike of 1912, on the North-Eastern Railway in England,[8] all the forces of combat on either side. Much of all this is removed in a nationalised industry on the one hand by the removal of the profit-motive, and on the other by the existence of the Works Committee, which will enable most problems to be confronted long before the difficulties of prestige are involved. But friction will, of course, occur; and the best way to deal with its incidents has been shown to be a Board of Discipline in which management and men equally participate under the chairmanship of an impartial person, preferably drawn from outside the industry. In each case there can then be a formal hearing, with evidence from witnesses and a punishment which, in the majority of cases, seems to be accepted as representing substantial justice. It is overwhelmingly important that the whole process of industrial administration should avoid the existing habit of condemning men, almost always without even a hearing, to penalties as serious as dismissal. Often enough the offence does not merit more than a warning, and the absence of such instant severity, or the sense that it has been visited upon the offender only after deliberation which his fellows share is vital to the sense of dignity modern industrial methods too often fail to recognise in the worker.[9]

So far, I have not discussed the methods by which the rates of pay, the number of hours to be worked, the period of apprenticeship to be served, in each vocation, are settled for a national industry. That is because I do not believe that any of the institutions so far proposed are likely to be adequate to this end. For no industry will include all the members of any given vocation; the mining industry will have doctors and engineers, clerks and accountants, chemists and lawyers as part of its normal staff. There will be grades within each vocation, and their varying numbers will mean a very different bargaining power in such matters if they were left to their own devices; for on the Governing Body, and even on the Regional Board, the less numerous workers are not likely to be represented. Similar work, moreover, must be performed under similar conditions, no matter what be the industry in which it is performed. It seems clear, therefore, that, the basic pay of the worker in his capacity as citizen apart, the conditions of each vocation must be settled by the trade union of that vocation by mutual discussion with the Governing Body of the industry. Over and above the minimum, the rates of pay conceded will obviously depend upon the productivity of the industry concerned. There will, I imagine, be provision made for increase of pay where there is increase of effort; and special considerations will attach to work of a particularly dangerous kind. I add that I do not believe that the settlement of these issues will be free from difficulty; nor do I doubt that, on occasion, such difficulty may lead to a strike. It is, however, probable that certainly the extent and largely the bitterness of these disputes will be mitigated by the important fact that a refusal to increase pay on the part of the Governing Body will not mean an increase in profit for the shareholder who contributes nothing to the well-being of the industry, or the financier who is concerned, not with its service, but merely the return it can make. The Governing Body, also, will have to decide the amount to be set annually apart to cover such fixed charges as depreciation, and replacement, of plant. Prices will, as nearly as possible, be fixed so as to cover cost of production; and where there is a reduction in cost below what is produced by sale, there should be a special return to management and labour as the reward for their efficiency. There must, of course, be a limit to this reward, and when, in any year, the surplus realised passes a certain percentage of affixed revenue, it ought to go to the reduction of price, so that the public as a whole participates in the accruing benefit.

I have already discussed, in another connection, the part that may be played in the constant stimulus to improved service by the creation of advisory committees of those by whom the service is utilised. In the consumers' Co-operative Movement, for example, such methods as the District Meeting undoubtedly do much to prevent the purchaser from falling into an apathetic dullness about things which vitally concern him. There are, I think, great possibilities in bodies of this kind. There are few users of motor-cars who cannot contribute ideas to their manufacture. The telephone, the postal service, the railway, are all immediately susceptible to institutions of this kind. Obviously enough, there are services so technical in nature that it is impossible to organise a serious consumers' opinion about them; but in the building of ships, for example, I do not think we can doubt that the Seamen's Union could contribute an experience of great importance; and the engine-driver and fireman might well be asked for their views upon the construction of locomotives. There is everything to gain by the multiplication, in every department of industrial life, of voluntary advisory bodies which give results of their experience to the particular trade they use. They may even come, like the *Société des Abonnés au Telephone* in Paris, to employ their own experts to check the work, and stimulate the inventiveness, of those by whom they are served. Such advisory bodies point also, especially where the nationalised industry produces commodities of universal use, to the need for research associations, in which, outside the official categories, ideas may be exchanged and developed. Bodies like the Institute of Naval Architects, like the Teachers' Guild, are rather remarkable for their rarity than for their frequency, though in Germany they seem to have attained a much greater importance than elsewhere.[10] We have, indeed, vast bodies like the Chambers of Commerce in England and the National Association of Manufacturers in America; but these seem to have developed into trade-protecting societies concerned with little else than the prevention of any growth of government enterprise. What we need is bodies which, by unofficial research and inquiry, will deliberately seek to improve the standards of service in the different trades.

Partly, one hopes, these might develop as definite branches of the vocational bodies. There is room and to spare in the trade-union movement for independent investigation of this kind. No reason exists, for instance, why the Miners' Federation of Great Britain should not independently study the problem of safety in mines, the more particularly when it is remembered that on certain phases—the fighting of "gob" fires, for example—their members have a vast and unequalled body of experience upon which to draw. Similarly, one would like to see suggestions for the improvement of the legal profession from solicitors' and barristers' clerks, a body of men with more practical knowledge, and less recognition, than any kindred group in the vocational world. A federation might, in addition to the improvement of their status, throw a flood of light upon the administration of the law. It is, of course, important to prevent critical inquiry of this kind from being regarded as a breach of discipline; we cannot permit such an attempt, unfortunately an unsuccessful one, as that of the Postal and Telegraph Clerks' Association in England to study the working of the postal cheque system in Europe to be hindered by the Post Office on the ground that it implied a criticism of the apathy of official methods. Medical men and engineers have shown in a notable way what can be done by organised research of this kind. There is no reason why their achievement should not be copied by the rest of the vocational world. The greater the stream of criticism and suggestion that flows through the working of each nationalised industry, the richer will be the results it can obtain.

And it is here, as I think, that we find the answer to the problem of authority in the world of industry. A system such as that which I have outlined has the merit of transferring the questions which arise to what may be termed the plane of measurable discussion. Orders will be issued in terms of a need that is always verifiable. Demands will be judged in an atmosphere of co-operation. The will of each person engaged on industrial work will find a channel through which it can seek to realise itself. There is initiative where initiative is required; but that initiative will operate always in an environment of general consent. The producer will be safeguarded by the fact that he makes the essential conditions of his effort; the consumer is protected, first, by the ultimate control of policy by the legislative assembly, and, secondly, by the advisory committees through which his wants will be made directly known to the leaders of the given industry. We marshal, that is to say, the searchlight of all informed opinion upon the function each industry seeks to fulfil. We cease to enshroud its operations, as now, in a secrecy that withholds at every point the essential facts which make judgment upon its efficiency impossible. We shall be able to test all cases of supposed inefficiency by the reports of experts who have no other duty than the impartial discovery of those facts. We offer to the humblest worker in the lowest grade of any mine or factory the opportunity to co-operate with its management in the improvement of its operations. We permit every substantial grievance he feels to be judged, not by an authority alien from his interests, but by an authority he shares in making. We need not deny the complexity of the means by which these ends are achieved. A service which aims at supplying the wants of States of the modern size cannot, in the nature of things, avoid complexity. We do not avoid it now; and it is, to-day, more dangerous because it is autocratic and secretive. Admittedly, the worker in the new era, as in the old, will find the need imperative to submit his will to the will of others. But he will be able to formulate his will; he will secure consideration for his wants, and if he fails to win regard, it is by the facts that he will have been defeated. That situation, I believe, may with justice be defined as the status of a freeman. For by it he is made the servant, not of other men, but of the logic inherent in social organisation. He, in fact, helps to make that logic, and his service is thus a function which he masters as he fulfils it.

### (iii) The Sphere of Consumer's Co-operation

I have already pointed out that nationalised industries, in the form above discussed, will occupy a part only of the industrial field. Mainly they will be confined to services like those of mining, railways, shipping, where an element of natural monopoly enters into the service offered. A second great area in the industrial field belongs, as I think naturally, to the province of consumers' co-operation. I am not here concerned with those forms of consumers' co-operation which, like the gas supply of a municipality, are essentially compulsory in character. There, so to say, the nature of the service requires oneness and indivisibility. The consumer is offered no alternative; he has a standard product which he can only have from one authority and in a single form. I am concerned with the place and prospects in the democratic State of the form of consumers' co-operation of which the foundations were laid by Robert Owen and the model created by the famous Rochdale store in 1844. That movement now includes within its ambit not less than one-third of all the families of Great Britain; and both on the continent of Europe and in America it has shown that it represents a permanent form of industrial enterprise.[11]

Practically speaking, the character of the Co-operative Movement may be described by saying that it is a democratic movement for the production of any article required by its members, the method of production and distribution eliminating the idea of profit. The range of the commodities it produces is very striking. It has its own banks, and its own insurance service; it runs its own farms and its own tea-gardens; it manufactures its own boots and shoes; it bakes its own bread; it sells milk and meat and furniture. Broadly, it has concentrated its operations on what may be called the general wants, and largely the standardised wants, of the householder. It has, of course, quite definite limitations. It does not seem to have appealed either to the comfortable classes, on the one hand, or to the very poor, upon the other. It has been essentially a movement of the solid working class, and its productions have the quality that influence would lead us to expect. A man could furnish his house from the co-operative store, but he would not satisfy the taste of a skilful interior decorator. He could clothe himself in garments of co-operative manufacture, but he would appear rather serviceably than attractively clad, and if his wife bought at the co-operative store the whole range of her wardrobe, she would not, unless she was an exceptional person, acquire that note of distinction in dress which appears to be an unchanging object of human desire. There is, moreover, a considerable area of service in which direct co-operative production would not pay, because the demand from the membership of the movement is not large enough, or consistent enough, to justify direct manufacturing. It appears, moreover, fairly clear that the technique of consumers' co-operation is not generally applicable to agriculture. It might succeed where what is required, as in the production of wheat, is essentially large-scale operations; but where a peasantry makes the personal element in landholding fundamental, consumers' co-operation does not seem suitable.[12] The argument, so often made, that the co-operator cannot engage in the export trade, has been, I think, clearly contradicted by the experience of recent years; and as the movement becomes universal in character, the difficulty of the problem of profit can, I think, be automatically solved. For either goods can be exchanged against goods, as in the relationship of the German and Danish movements, or the profit made can be devoted to such communal purposes as education.

What, I think, emerges from any systematic analysis of consumers' co-operation is, broadly speaking, that it is eminently suited to carry on that body of industrial operations requisite for the supply of household needs, without differentiation of class in the community. For the problem of quality in the Co-operative Movement is simply a question of demand. It can supply the needs of Whitechapel not less than those of Mayfair. Granted a fair approximation to economic equality, the divisions of taste and standards which now divide the various classes of society will be absent. The community will meet upon a level of kindred want, and its absorption into the Co-operative Movement will transform the latter into an agency able to meet the wants it encounters. I do not, of course, suppose that in each department of household need consumers' co-operation will be the sole source of supply. There is no reason why the independent craftsman should not survive to supply peculiar wants. In dress, in articles of household decoration, in design, in the arts, I assume the likelihood that men and women will earn their living by ministering to the taste of a small number of clients, and that in such a realm there will be a sphere for the small guild of producers who will market productions which are above, or different from, the fairly standardised commodities in which consumers' co-operation will seek to specialise. Normally, for example, I shall have my house decorated on some fairly simple plan thought out in the proper department of the local co-operative branch; but if I desire in a room, or a garden, features of uniqueness, I shall go to a group of craftsmen such as those whom William Morris gathered about him.

The relation of the Co-operative Movement to the central State and local authority admit, I think, of fairly simple definition. An industry like mining seems to me essentially fitted for such a scheme of nationalisation as I outlined in the previous section; the co-operative store then becomes, at least in the sphere of domestic consumption, the natural distributing agency. It will thus enable us to cut out at a stroke the vast horde of middlemen who at present increase price by their intervention between producer and consumer; and the absence of profit in its own operations is a further fact in its favour. It is not necessary, I think, to assume any sharp-cut cleavage between co-operative production and production by the State. The one may be the purchaser of the other's commodities, where the State is the predominant producer, and it will then distribute them as its members demand. It may well itself attempt manufacture; and there will be some advantage in this rivalry of two forms of production from which alike the motive of profit-making is absent. It is, indeed, clear that there are subjects of production unsuited to the movement, which must be left to operation by the State; and the case for the national ownership of coal and oil seems to me final in view of the State interest in their conservation being paramount over the wishes of a constituency whose interest, like that of a body of members in the Co-operative Movement, is in immediate consumption. On the other hand, I think the controversy between those who desire a co-operative milk supply, as against those to whom municipalisation is the ideal, should be resolved, as a general rule, in favour of the former. The latter can then preserve the all-important function of safeguarding quality by constant inspection and control. It becomes an independent and impartial authority testing the level of service in the interests of consumers. The fact that the municipality distributes free milk in large quantities is easily met by arrangements with the co-operative agencies. The same is true, *mutatis mutandis*, of other services like coal.

What, then, will be the institutions by which the Co-operative Movement is governed, and, particularly, by what means will it ensure its members a full opportunity to control in a continuous way its operations, while, at the same time, there is an adequate self-government for its employees? Save in scale and detail, the basic institutions of the movement seem to me fully adequate to its need. Each district will have, as now, its local system of stores each governed by a district executive elected by the membership of the district. It will be necessary to make that executive a full-time body, choosing its own chairman; and its members will, for the first time in the history of the movement, have to be fully remunerated for their services. There will be, moreover, a special accounting staff at each branch with, as I hope, independent powers to report the result of their findings directly to the members as a whole. The branch executive will be small; but I think that one-third of its membership should always be composed of representatives of the branch employees. This is, of course, a matter upon which there have been grave differences of opinion in the Co-operative Movement;[13] but if there is to be genuine democracy in the movement, the orders issued must be subject not less to the scrutiny of those who receive them than of those for whose benefit they are intended. Membership of the executive committee ought to imply continuous re-eligibility; and the present safeguard against error or corruption, that a member may be recalled by a two-thirds vote of a special general meeting of the members, is well worth retention. There should always be, as in many branches there already is, a labour advisory committee, empowered on behalf of the employees to discuss the problems of labour with the management in similar fashion to that of a factory in a nationalised industry. There should, of course, be retained the quarterly meeting of the branch; and its activities should be increased and intensified by a system of advisory committees on which, it may be suggested, women ought to find a consistently larger place. Much, also, could be done to maintain the interest of the member in the work of the society by adopting the useful German expedient of the group-agent.[14] Those co-operative societies are bound to be the most successful which aim most carefully in making their store not merely a magazine of retail articles, but the embodiment of a great social philosophy of which the spirit is the more active in the degree that the average member is alive to its problems.

There are, indeed, many questions in which the advisory committees and the general meeting might be asked to share. The former might well report on the quarterly progress of the branch to its members; it might organise social activities; it might attempt inquiry, through the group agents, into sources not fully explored; it might investigate the activities of other societies with a view to the improvement of its own service; they might receive complaint from the members about inadequate supply of, or defective quality in, commodities. The success of the experiment made by the Leeds Co-operative Society, which embodies many of these ideas, is a decisive proof of both its need and its value. The members of the advisory committees should, of course, be elected by the members of the branch year by year, and, beyond the repayment of their expenses, their services should be voluntary. No one who knows the Co-operative Movement at all intimately can, I think, doubt that a little effort will secure invaluable knowledge from this service. And when, again as in Leeds, these branches meet together each quarter to survey the problems of the whole area, we have at once an invaluable mechanism of general discussion.

There is an experiment of great interest in the selection by these voluntary advisers of an unofficial executive of their own to act, so to say, as their cabinet. It provides a means of forcing upon the executive of the society problems they might either be indifferent to, or neglect, and it provides, not less significantly, an invaluable training-ground from which the future direction of the society may be chosen. The meetings, in short, of these advisory committees can perform for the Co-operative Movement the service performed for the cabinet in the selective function of the legislative assembly.

What the branch meeting can do will, I think, depend most largely on the zeal of the branch committee and the group agents. To the degree that they are able to make the mass of the members conscious of the fact that the movement is what they make it, and that to make it effective they must offer the criticism and suggestion indicated by their experience, it will be a full expression of what they conceive themselves to need. Here also, as I believe, is the field in which the body called the Co-operative Union can be most valuable. So far, it has remained much too much a congress passing pious resolutions, much too little a body seeking to instil a coherent body of principle into every nook and cranny of its immense constituency. It must realise that educational effort is at the centre of co-operative effort; and, as a collateral problem, that merely because a man is an ardent co-operator he is not necessarily the person best fitted to make the union's literary appeal effective. Here, it is certainly impressive that much the most fruitful work should have been done by the women's organisation; though even the Co-operative Guild has not 5 per cent of the members in its ranks. Upon the work of these educational bodies will depend the amount of interest that can be created in the rank and file of membership; and it may be added that much of its quality will depend not so much on consciously direct propaganda as on the way in which it uses its potentially immense powers to raise the general level of citizenship.

On the local side, the problems of a co-operative society are comparatively simple in principle. So long as they create the institutions necessary, as in a nationalised service, to guarantee adequate self-government to their employees; so long as they create a directorate well paid enough to attract the ability their functions need; so long, finally, as they check their efficiency by expert audit, on the one hand, and popular control on the other, the field of their activities is almost as wide as they may choose. It is on the federal side of their relationships that they raise, as might be expected, more complex problems. As is well known, practically all the retail societies are linked together in a great Wholesale Society by a federal constitution. It is from the Wholesale that the local societies buy the goods they are to retail to their members; and the profits gained by the

Wholesale are returned to its constituent members as a dividend on purchase exactly as in a local society. The government of the Wholesale is similar. Each local society has one vote as a society, and additional votes in terms of a certain unit amount of purchases. The societies elect the directors, thirty-two in number, of the Wholesale, and the latter present their policy before a quarterly delegate meeting of the local societies. The latter being the ultimate authority, they can clearly control the productive methods of the Wholesale at every important point in their operation.

As a trading corporation, the general efficiency of the Wholesale compares favourably, I believe, with that of any private enterprise in the world. But the problems it has to solve for itself are of a different nature from those connected with the mere increase of its volume of business. That, at least ultimately, is a matter in which the constituent societies have the real control of its future. Rather, the issues it has to learn to confront are connected with (1) the organisation, within itself, of a democratic relationship with its employees; (2) a much more co-ordinated effort to foresee the growth of new needs; and (3) a much better system of internal criticism and suggestion than it now possesses. Let me try to deal separately with each of these issues. First: it is, I think, clear that whatever holds for the employees in a nationalised industry holds also for the employees of the Wholesale. They are therefore entitled to membership, elected from within their own ranks, of the Board of Directors. As in the Governing Body of a nationalised industry, these should represent the interests of the vocations, on the one hand, and the management on the other; together they should choose at least one-third, and possibly one-half, of the Board. There is no other way in which their interests in so vast an organisation can be properly safeguarded. The constituent societies will still be paramount; but they will meet on equal terms those who, in the experience of the Co-operative Movement, have clearly been regarded as its step-children. To this representation other structures must be added. The Works Committee at each factory, the Discipline Board for the employee who has offended the rules, must exist in the co-operative world not less fully than elsewhere. Appointments are a different problem in structure, though not in principle. I see no reason why the local co-operative society should not, through the schools, have its organised relation with the boy or girl who wishes to enter its service, and organise a systematic plan of entrance with the requisite trade unions. On the side of clerical labour, they should recruit in the first instance by competitive examination; with the restriction, if they so desire, that only the children of co-operators in good standing shall be eligible. Minor promotions should be made, factory by factory, with the assent, either of the general Works Committee or the special body which may deal with a special department. Major promotions should be a matter for the Board; but there should always be (a) advertisement of the post, (b) proof of special qualifications where that is desired, and (c) consultation of those over whom the person promoted will exercise authority. If this is done, the interest of the staff in appointments will be properly safeguarded by the presence of its staff representatives on the Board of Directors. It is perhaps relevant here to remark that the Wholesale will have to free itself, at any rate over the next few generations, from its limited view of adequate financial reward in the highest posts, if it is to attract the ability it needs. It will always, undoubtedly, be able to get better men for a lower rate of pay than private industry, at any rate upon its Board of Directors; but that is less true of its technical and managerial appointments. It must learn the danger, and guard against it, of staff in-breeding. It ought, to use a concrete illustration, to be as natural for the Co-operative Bank to want the services of an economist like Mr. Keynes for its directorate, as it is for a profit-making bank to seek the services of retired statesmen. And, *mutatis mutandis,* that holds for every aspect of its activities. It must draw its personnel, especially at the top, from the whole range of the industrial field.

It needs, secondly, I have said, much more co-ordinated effort to plan the response to the growth of new needs. That is particularly evident on the side of publicity. The weakness of the Wholesale has lain in its failure to utilise competent and disciplined minds in the production of its propaganda literature and the advertisement of its commodities. Its literature must be of a quality as high as the service of its ideal seems to warrant. So far, the tendency has been in all of its educational activities to subordinate them to the development of trading. But no one can study the Co-operative Movement without seeing that these educational activities are the real key to the development of trading. New needs can be answered adequately only as the body of members are aware of their presence, and that awareness will come only as the co-operator is trained to think out continuously their significance and to press them, in organised fashion, upon the directors of the Wholesale. That implies a staff for the purpose of education and propaganda, not recruited merely by election, but built as a body of experts for no other purpose. It would, indeed, be an admirable thing if two of the directors were specifically appointed to this end; and they might oversee the literary activities of the movement. These will not be satisfactory until they are read, not as a matter of duty by the co-operator, but as a matter of interest by the outsider, much as he compelled, by their sheer quality, to read the technical publications of Mr. George Russell. That will have the important effect of disturbing the complacency of co-operators by bringing to bear upon them a steady fire of criticism and comment from those outside the mainstream of the movement. They must get into the habit of employing the expert from outside to explain and survey their efforts. They impinge much more upon the unconverted through a study by Mr. and Mrs. Webb than by a hundred pamphlets by their own zealous members. But this service must be organised to be successful; and it is the only way of building a highroad through what are at present desert places.

They need, thirdly, I have suggested, much better mechanisms of internal criticism. That is the more important as the area of the movement widens, and absorbs, as it ought to absorb, the private trader in household commodities. To that end, the Wholesale needs to develop a much bigger relationship to the local societies than it now occupies. Just as I have argued that the Central Government of the modern State must help the local authorities by inspection, by criticism, by suggestion, so must the Wholesale assist its constituent members. It has at its command immeasurably more information to establish a disinterested comparison of their working in every department of their effort. It must show not merely the growth of their trading, the amount of their balance, the number of their members; it must compare society with society over a period of years in every item of work. It must set up what is called in the United States an industrial audit in which the merit and defect of every method in use is analysed and revealed. It goes without saying that such audits would be made by men who had no authority to apply the lessons they taught; they would be communicated to the society and used by the society for its own improvement. They would be published as a means of stimulating each society to surpass the achievement of its fellows. I am not suggesting any impairment of the federalism of the Co-operative Movement; the independence of the local society in its own concerns is a feature to be touched only at one's peril. I am rather suggesting that the Wholesale is in a position which cannot be otherwise occupied to survey and make known the implications of co-operative effort; and, therefore, that as it makes them known, so will there be the knowledge, and so only, by which progress is possible. That would mean the establishment in the Wholesale of a department of research from which there would issue reports on every aspect of the movement. It would report all new advances and new methods. It would explain what was being done abroad. It would offer to Leeds an itemised study of its work in terms of a similar study of Glasgow or Woolwich. It would be there for every local society to seek assistance from as it desired. "Every group of men", writes Mr. Webb,[15] "can be incited to strive voluntarily to excel other groups of men in any undertaking whatsoever, if only there are commonly accepted and widely published tests of success". Certainly it is only by their establishment that the Co-operative Movement can hope to make itself commensurate with the general body of citizens.

It is, I think, obvious in such an analysis, that it is difficult to set limits to the part consumers' co-operation may play in the State of the future. It is worth while to insist again on the importance of the two vital facts that it provides a mechanism for (a) the abolition of the profit-making motive over a vast area, and (b) that it cheapens the whole cost of production by the abolition of the chain of middlemen who now intervene between producer and consumer in the distributive process. Nor must we neglect the fact that it is a direct and democratic method of enabling the objects of production to be determined by the consumers themselves in a manner that obviates no small part of the wastage inherent in the present system. A simple illustration will serve to make this clear. Let us take the manufacture of cups and saucers. In private enterprise the sole question which determines their production is the question of whether they can be made at a profit. The public does not know that there is a scheme for their production; it learns of it only by a vast system of advertisement the cost of which becomes a part of the price it eventually pays. Demand is not ascertainable except by experiment, and the history of business enterprise is the proof that this experiment is both costly and wasteful. The consumer may buy the cups and saucers; but he knows nothing about them except what the manufacturer may choose to tell him, and the price he pays has no necessary relation to the cost of production. Nor is the position, I suggest, much better if we substitute a producers' guild in the place of the private manufacturer. Here, again, there is no volume of ascertained demand; there is no indication of consumers' desires; there is no direct relation between producer and consumer. Under the system of consumers' co-operation all these difficulties are eliminated. When the Wholesale decides to manufacture, it is upon the basis of an ascertained demand. It does not have to search for its market, and it hears directly and in detail of the way in which its commodity satisfies the public which has asked for it. The ideal of production for use seems to me more largely capable of fulfilment within the ambit of the Co-operative Movement than in any other system of industrial organisation.

There remain two questions upon which a word is necessary. If, it may be said, the boundaries of the Co-operative Movement are so ample, why may not consumers' co-operation be the ideal form of production for industry as a whole? Why is it necessary to cumber social theory with the study of alternative forms? The answer, I think, lies in the fact that consumers' co-operation is successful just because it is restricted to the production and control of commodities upon which the judgment of the general body of consumers is as good a judgment as we can have. It is ministering, not to a body of expert needs, as in the manufacture, for instance, of tools and machinery, but to a body of general needs. It has an obvious constituency immediately capable of concentration upon the processes directly interesting them. That is, I suggest, less obvious immediately we pass from articles of general to articles of special consumption. There the constituency is of a different nature. I do not see why those who utilise, for instance, particular types of machinery should govern those who make the machinery on their behalf. They are not interested in anything but the finished machine, and its relation in price and quality and volume of supply, to their needs. The producer ought, therefore, broadly to control the process which supervenes between demand, on the one side, and the completion of the finished product on the other. Nor, in practice, do I think such trades as engineering will offer, under the form of consumers' co-operation, the most efficient unit of production. In theory, undoubtedly, Mr. Woolf is right in his contention[16] that it is as easy to envisage the co-operative control of the railways as to think of them in terms of nationalisation; in practice I believe that all the advantages offered by co-operation can be secured by advisory committees of consumers, and that a nationalised form will offer greater scope to the producer from every angle. Nor, secondly, is there any gain in making the forms of industrial organisation correspond to any one type. There is a positive advantage in variety, because of the experiment it permits; and inadequacy can always be controlled by its transformation to another form under the aegis of the legislative assembly.

That raises the question of the relationship of the Co-operative Movement to the State. What powers will the latter possess over the movement in its expanded form? Clearly enough, the Co-operative Movement must satisfy all the requirements of that civic minimum of rights I have urged it is the peculiar province of the State to enforce. Whatever rates of pay it offers, it must at least offer the rate required as minimal by the State. It must, also, submit to control in the details of manufacture. If it is discovered, for instance, that boric acid is an undesirable form of preservative, and its use is forbidden by legislation, the co-operative dairy must submit to State inspection in the same way as any other enterprise. Its factories must conform to State requirements of sanitation and safety. It ought to possess, in the future, something of the relation to a Ministry of Production which it now occupies to the Board of Trade; and there would, I suggest, be real advantage in the annual analysis and criticism of its work by the appropriate authorities in the Ministry of Research. If it supplied milk to the City of Manchester of which the quality was deemed defective, it would have to submit to inspection; and its refusal to accept competent findings, and to alter its methods in conformity therewith, would, I think, necessarily involve penalties. Here, of course, lies one of the supreme advantages of the co-operative system; for a complaint by the Medical Officer of Manchester to its citizens would also be a complaint to its co-operators, and the latter would immediately have the means of remedy in their hands. But, outside these necessary limitations, the non-official character of the Co-operative Movement is one of its greatest gains. It means greater responsiveness to expressed need, greater flexibility, and a greater power of control in the ordinary man and woman. It is for these an additional and important lesson in the art of government, where what they do reacts directly upon the quality of their own lives. Anyone who has seen the work of the Women's Co-operative Guild will know the hopefulness of this aspect of the co-operative effort. It makes creative citizenship as few other factors in the community. The more it is encouraged, the greater will be its accomplishment.

### (iv) Private Enterprise

The forms of private enterprise are so various that it is impossible within the compass of this book to do more than indicate the basic principles of its control. They follow, as I think, upon the earlier discussion of the rights inherent in men as citizens, upon the one hand, and the nature of property in its relation to those rights upon the other. But anyone who reflects for a moment upon the range of differences between the one-man motor repair shop on a country road, the guild of peasant weavers producing their hand-woven fabrics for a small number of customers, the great co-partnership enterprise like the Zeiss works at Jena, cotton mills upon the scale of Horrockses at Preston, will realise that each form is a matter for the separate application of general principles, and that the application will vary as the nature of the industry varies. In some, it is probable, individual production will be permitted; but the product will be marketed by co-operative methods, as in Danish agriculture, or brought collectively through the State, or the Co-operative Wholesale Society, as in the case of the purchase by the British Government of the Australian wool-crop during the war. In other trades, as in jewellery, for instance, it is possible that it will be found most advantageous to have State ownership of gold and silver mines, and of more specialised products like precious stones, while their manufacture and sale as finished products are most largely left to private hands. In other hands, again, as in building, there is, I believe, great room for the small guild of producers who will work either for the private householder or the municipality much as those who built the cathedral and the dwelling-house of the Middle Ages were accustomed to do. There will be industries also in which the State will hardly concern itself at any stage, as, for example, the manufacture and sale of cosmetics. What alone I can here attempt, in the presence of such complexity, is an indication of general theory; and I can only emphasise my full admission that the changes suggested are not likely to take place in the precise form I suggest, or even with precisely the same ends in view.

Generally speaking, State regulation of private industry will have three general interests to protect. It needs, in the first place, to safeguard the welfare of the producer in industry. It must secure to him an adequate return for his labour and such minimum conditions of effort as assure to him the full opportunity to exercise his functions as a citizen; in a word, to be himself at his best. It must prevent his degeneration into that animate tool which is to-day the position occupied by innumerable workers in every branch of industrial activity. It must assure them the same consideration for their personality as human beings that is, in the scheme here outlined, offered to the worker in the industries operated by itself. It must prevent that domination of management and technique by the speculative financier which has in recent years—to take two famous examples—done so much to impair the prosperity and destroy the service of the cotton industry in Lancashire and the railroads in the United States. It must, secondly, protect the consumer against extortionate prices, on the one hand, and defective quality of product upon the other. Anyone who reads, for instance, the history of the trust in American industry will have little difficulty in admitting that its rigorous control is not merely urgent in the consumers' behalf, but even in the protection of political freedom itself; the president of a great American corporation has frankly admitted that he himself, and every business man similarly placed, attempts the deliberate domination of parties in their own interest by corrupt methods.[17] "Franchises to the use of streets and highways", says a distinguished American publicist,[18] "the grant of rights of way, concessions of charter privileges, legislative sanctions to corporate undertakings, lucrative usufructs of various species of public wealth, real estate development in connection with municipal improvements, etc., are fields of investment for many millions of private capital, an obvious policy with whose representatives is to confederate their interests with political influence". We have seen the results of such a "confederation of interest" in the history of President Harding's administration. Nor is the power of the trust confined to the United States. English combines, like the Imperial Tobacco Company and the Coats Sewing Cotton Trust, literally hold the consumer in their grip; and the range of their activities is only partially explored by government research.[19] The cartellisation of the German industry is probably the most scientific in the world; and our own generation has seen the activity of a single man thwart the foreign policy of the government, settle the hours of labour of thousands of workers, dictate the price of coal and steel products to the body of consumers, and then, as a final wrench to the screw, bend their minds to his support by owning the newspapers they must read.

The State, thirdly, must protect the investing public. That will, it may be added, be a wider duty under the scheme here outlined than it is at the present time. Under the modern company laws, any body of men may secure capital from its owners, with no sufficient guarantee either of a genuine service to be rendered or of a possible return on the investment. The company may be dishonest in its operation, or inefficient, without the public being able at any point to have knowledge. Its proceedings are wrapped in secrecy throughout. Its balance-sheet is, often enough, unintelligible except to a skilful accountant; and even he can only tell its true meaning by comparison with the actual physical assets it is supposed to represent. Modern financial manipulation, moreover, has reduced both management and technique to mere creatures of a body of directors who, like the boards of an American railroad, may know nothing at all of the actual operations of industry. Increase of capitalisation may be determined upon without any regard to the welfare of the investor. Output may be limited in accordance with arrangements of which he is kept completely ignorant. Ownership and control are almost wholly divorced and, generally speaking, management and control are divorced also. So long as the investor receives his due return, he is supposed to be content; and if that due return fails, either he confronts liquidation of the company, in which case he is helpless, or else he must be content to trust those already unsuccessful in the hope of a return to prosperity. The resultant wastage of capital under the system is enormous;[20] and the system, of course, has no means at its disposal of securing the loyalty of those who labour under it. For their interest ceases when their wages have been paid, and its prosperity does not affect them; nor, in past times, does it assume that it has any responsibility for their well-being. Under it, they are chattels to be purchased or thrown aside according to the prospect of profitable employment.

Practically speaking, the plans here laid down must confine themselves to the corporate aspect of business enterprise. In the one-man business, or the small partnership, considerations arise which can hardly be met by any general scheme; and, in any case, the company practically covers the larger part of the industrial field. We assume, therefore, a body of persons who desire to form a company under such rules as may constitute company law in the given State. What principles ought to underlie that law? Each company will consist, basically, of investors, management and labour, since the Board of Directors will represent, in part at least, the first of these classes. The process, I suggest, through which a company will pass in its working life will be built upon two general principles. To the investor there will be issued capital stock of a par value equivalent to his investment; and the total issue will be secured by an exclusive title to the property of the company. It follows, therefore, that as additions are made to the plant, or as capital is paid out, the original investment will be of less value than the actual physical assets of the company; and the security to the investor will be, accordingly, strengthened. Such stock, will, of course, be assignable in the ordinary way, and it will carry with it voting rights. But it is, I think, important to surround such voting rights with two safeguards. Voting, first, should always be in person and not by proxy. The investor, that is to say, must be more than a person blindly confiding his powers to directors of whom he knows little or nothing. His responsibility must be called into being by the sense that the ultimate responsibility is emphatically his own. And, secondly, upon the admirable example of the Co-operative Movement, whatever his holding, he should exercise only one vote. The control, therefore, of the general meeting of the company will be governed by persons and not by amounts of stock. This would, I think, transform the general meeting of the company from a formality into a genuine legislative assembly; it would end the autocracy of the directorate. The shares would carry with them a limited and preferred rate of dividend like the preference share in the ordinary company.

But there is a class of investors who search only, as in trustee securities, for an assured and unchanging return. They do not desire to share in industrial risk; they are uninterested in a part responsibility for management. Ideally, they would invest in State or municipal bonds; but we may assume that, with some greater risk, they desire a proportionately higher return. To them would be issues debentures, equal in par value to their investment and charged with a fixed rate of interest, necessarily lower than that of the first class of shares; that fixed rate would be the primary liability of the company, to be satisfied, apart from the earnings of labour and management, before the claims of any other investors. They would have no voting power in the company. As their interest was met, their concern in it would cease; and they could be active only if the company failed to meet its obligations to them.

When the operating costs of the company have been met, the holder of stock will have the first claim upon the remaining net revenue. He will be paid, that is, the preferred rate of dividend, his 5 or 6 or 7 per cent allocated at the formation of the company as its basic dividend. The remaining surplus will be divided into three equal parts; one will be devoted to the investors, one to labour and management, and one to the public. Each will thereby possess a definite claim on the results of efficient operation. The public surplus should, I suggest, be divided also into two parts. The one would be definite State revenue, of the nature, clearly, of the modern corporation tax; the other would be devoted to the improvement of the company, whether by the extension of its plant, the retirement of debentures, or the development of new enterprise as is best thought fit by the company directorate and the government department concerned.

But it is not enough to secure to labour and management a share in the surplus earnings of which they are most essentially the creators. It is necessary, also, to associate them with the direction of the industry. To that end, on any company's Board of Directors, one-half of the seats should be reserved for the elected representatives of management and labour, in equal proportion. They should have equal power with the representatives of invested capital. Thereby we assure not only the proper protection of their interest in the company, an interest, it may be added, far more real than that of the investor, but also we have a safeguard against the manipulation of the company by the financial side of its direction. We get a means of appealing to the investor against such methods of reorganisation as have been, for example, so largely responsible for unemployment in the cotton industry since 1920.[21] Here also, it may be pointed out, the association of investors' voting power with persons instead of amount of investment is another protection against manipulation.

But it is necessary, also, to prevent the possibility that the power of the company may be used, as has been the habit of corporate enterprise in the past, to the detriment of the public interest. That makes the public regulation of the industry essential. Every company, therefore, must be compelled to keep its accounts in a prescribed manner; it must be made, year by year, to set apart for maintenance and depreciation such a proportion of its annual gross revenue as is deemed necessary to conserve the integrity of the original investment in it. It should be required annually to submit to the central government a report upon its working, together with a full balance-sheet which displays both its total assets and its total liabilities and does not serve as a screen for secret reserves. If its net surplus is, after payment of interest on the invested capital, beyond a certain amount, power should be had, either to utilise that surplus for public purposes, or to enforce a lower rate of price to the consumer, as the circumstances of the industry as a whole may seem to warrant. The government, moreover, must retain at all times the right, so to say, to inspect the company, to audit its accounts and to measure its efficiency; and on the appeal of the representatives of labour and management on the board of the company it ought to have the power to initiate a thorough inquiry into its working.

In such a perspective, the life-history of a company would be, in the nature of things, a public adventure. Its profits would be known; its costs would be published; its wages and salaries could be scrutinised as though they were the wages and salaries of a minister and his officials; its efficiency would be measurable by any person who took the pains to grasp the processes by which it lived. We cannot, I would urge, sufficiently emphasise the importance of such publicity. We know, better than ever before, to what passions and suspicions the ignorance and secretiveness of business relations give rise. We cannot have either clear thought about them, or harmony of feeling in them, unless we disperse that miasma. We cannot ask for co-operation between capital and labour when the indispensable facts about the process of production are deliberately concealed from view. Anyone who analyses the modern industrial dispute will see at a glance that often its inception and always its acerbity are due to the ignorance on either side of the fundamental conditions in the industry. We can never secure a genuine public opinion about the issues of business, because the facts upon which such a public opinion can be formed are never offered to us. We hear of sweating, on the one side, and ca' canny on the other. We are told that a group of employers is profiteering, or that a body of workers is abusing a privileged industrial position. These characterisations are, at present, largely without meaning because they are not definitely measurable. They hearten either side for the conflict, but they do not assist, they rather prevent, the victory of justice.

But if we insisted that each company must reveal its true assets and its real profits, if we had a cost analysis of each industrial process, much of this ignorance would disappear. A charge of profiteering could immediately be referred to the facts. The exact situation could be presented impartially as though it were the chemical analysis of a dye or the report of an engineer on the load a bridge may safely bear. I do not say that the general public would grasp the precise import of all the results; but their expert sifting would imply general conclusions explicable to the public, and we should be able, as we are now rarely able, to use the impact of opinion as a safeguard of industrial abuse. We should also, I believe, improve the general level of business efficiency, in part by the disappearance of feebler economic units, in part by the improvement in them which knowledge would bring. We should discover, probably, that there are few industries to-day in which the existing unit represents the most efficient unit of production; and we could press for the necessary reorganisation. Nor does that imply, in the system here outlined, danger to the consumer; for it is the virtue of such publicity as is here assumed that it makes possible, almost by its mere existence, efficient public control. It is the only way, moreover, to meet properly the various incentives which fuse together in the industrial process, to apportion to each its due place in the structure of the whole. It is the only way by which the State can be enabled to play its proper part in the national economy. For as it then acts the meaning of its act will be measurably known. If it secures, for instance, a settlement in an industrial dispute, it will be able at once to set out the precise meaning of its solution; if it decides upon a change in the basic hours of labour, it can at once measure the effects of its action upon productivity. Publicity, in a word, is the necessary condition of science; and until there is the organised knowledge such publicity affords, there cannot be satisfactory conditions in industry.

It is perhaps worth while to summarise briefly the advantages inherent in this method of organising private enterprise before we discuss the governmental institutions it involves. It secures, first of all, effective co-operation in each industry. It gives to worker, to management, and to finance a full share in the direction of the enterprise. It protects the owner of capital not only by maximising the integrity of his investment, but also by assuring to him safeguards against financial manipulation of his due rights by other owners. It protects the interest of labour and of management by giving them their place in the direction of the industry, and assuring them their due share of the reward of increased efficiency. It no longer regards capital as the natural residuary legatee of profit. It offers to it a fixed return upon its investment; but it insists that any return beyond that limit must be duly divided between all the parties to the industrial relation. It protects the consumer, first by providing for the proper public oversight of the industry, and second by returning to him, in the shape either of reduced prices or of a contribution to State revenue, surpluses beyond a fair rate of profit. It prevents thereby the undue curtailment of purchasing power, in itself a cause of unemployment by the restriction of production it entails. It is, of course, based frankly upon the assumption of a much more even distribution of wealth than now exists. I have already explained the grounds for that need. It involves the picture of an investing public drawn from a much wider area than at present. It ought also, I think, to involve a much more organic relation than now between the investor and the working of his capital. The smaller the class we have who live by owning, the better it will be for the quality of life we have in the community. The device here adopted of the personal and equal vote among shareholders will, it is urged, contribute to that end. It will prevent the individual enterprise from being dominated by the large owners of capital, a domination, it may be added, that is particularly dangerous in the case of the press. There is full room in it for initiative, and a return to the special effort which initiative involves. But it is avowedly, a system built upon the principle that the controlling factor in industry must be the will of the community and the standards imposed by that will; and it is mainly concerned with findings due place for them, on the one hand, and, in the other, of offering to the incentive of the normal business man a fair field for his activity.

It is perhaps advisable to meet at once one criticism which will be made of these principles before I proceed to discuss the way in which they may be related to the part played by the State in their operation. They are, it will be said, the apotheosis of officialism. Yet we know that the official is hostile to the introduction of new methods, while private enterprise is continually awake and alert to the prospects of experiment.

Unless we leave unlimited room for the great business man, who is by temperament as individual and as little capable of control as the great artist, the community will lose the great advantage of his services. But is such a criticism true? Is it, indeed, even a fair description of the system under which we now live? No one, I think, can seriously pretend that the average investor in modern business enterprise takes the slightest interest in the working of the concern from which he draws his profit. He is not searching for new methods. He does not keep himself abreast of technical discoveries and seek to force their use upon the management. He rarely attempts criticism of the company's operations except when he is deprived of his expected dividend; and the case is rare for him to attempt opposition to any person nominated as a director of the company. As a definite factor, indeed, he is practically obsolete; and his position has hardly changed since Adam Smith wrote that "the greater part of the proprietors seldom pretend to understand anything of the business of the company, … they give themselves no trouble about it, but receive contentedly each half-yearly or yearly dividend as the directors think proper to make to them".[22]

Nor is the position very different in the directorate of those industries where the economic unit is of any considerable size. No one pretends that the miscellaneous collection of men who govern our railways have in general any real knowledge of their problems, or that they contribute any real improvements to their operation. The same is true, perhaps in an even greater degree, of the directors of mines. It is, as is well known, a habit of the English company to attract the investor by advertising upon his prospectus the presence of a stray peer upon its Governing Board; and their value, and the part actually played by them has been revealed in more than one instance in proceedings before the courts.[23] The ignorance, indeed, of boards of directors has been revealed wherever careful inquiry has been made into business conditions. It was shown strikingly, for example, in the report of the Coal Conservation Commission on the supply of electric power.[24] It was revealed in the inquiry into the iron and steel industry by the Industrial Fatigue Research Board. "It seems probable", says the latter,[25] "that if all the iron and steel works in this country adopted the most efficient methods, they could, on an average, improve their output by something between 50 and 100 per cent". Similar criticisms could be multiplied indefinitely. Practically every report of the Interstate Commerce Commission of the United States is an implied condemnation of American railway methods. Sometimes the defect revealed is the lack of cars, sometimes insufficient tracks; in other cases the freight cars are inadequate, in others, again, the terminal facilities.[26] The whole import of the conservation movement in America is a similar criticism of the wastefulness and inefficiency of those by whom industry is controlled.

When we move to responsible management, the situation, though on a different plane, is not immensely different. The three great qualities upon which the largest aspect of business success depends, the willingness to use the results of science, the desire to stimulate the careful measurement of their own methods, the quick sense of the importance of psychological factors in industry—none of these is conspicuously general. Nor is there any general evidence of the training necessary for the management of modern business enterprise—knowledge of economics, of finance, of psychology. "The very notion of the need of such training", writes Mr. J.A. Hobson,[27] "appears to almost all of them a ridiculous pandering to an intellectualism which unfits men for a real business life". They are content with that they call practical experience. But practical experience is always acting upon assumptions awareness of which is essential; and the easy maxims of tradition with which the business man contents himself seem to act rather as barriers to initiative than as a stimulus to its development. Men who live, like Mr. Sinclair Lewis' Babbit, in the atmosphere of Main Street, are not likely to be injured by the injection into their world of scientific habit instead of rules of thumb. Lack of initiative is largely the outcome of provincialism, and nothing is so likely to destroy provincialism as the introduction into business of standards of qualification and measurement of processes.

The case, I think, of the really great business adventurer—men like Lord Rhondda in England and Mr. J.J. Hill in America—is quite different. But an analysis of their careers will, as a rule, reveal that the thing they seek is not a response to the incentive of profit, but a response to the incentive of power. They are eager to feel that they have their hands on a big machine. They are anxious to satisfy the creative impulse. They have the big conceptions, the restless temperament, the unwearying experimentalism, of the great scientist and the great explorer. Of them two things may be said. There is ample room for their talent in the nationalised industry. Their brains can find there an outlet of which the scope is infinitely bigger than private enterprise can offer, in which, also, they can satisfy the motive which, as Lord Haldane pointed out to the British Coal Commission, "is equally potent with the best class of men, namely the desire to distinguish himself in the service of the State".[28] It is, indeed, dangerous to allow full play to minds such as these except under such safeguards as I have discussed. There are few societies able to afford the services of men like Mr. Rockefeller or Mr. Carnegie; the price we have to pay for them is too high. That, I believe, has been clearly shown in the case of a man like Stinnes in Germany. We cannot hand over whole populations to satisfy the Moloch-like lust for power in these men. And if they refuse, as I think will rarely be the case, the devotion of their talents to public industry, there is still left for them the sphere of private enterprise. Only, it is left on the condition that they cannot use what is vital to social life—food, credit, transportation, coal—as their playthings. If the prize they want is not the power of doing a big job, with public esteem as the chief reward, but the prize of monetary reward, they must make it in fields where they do not impinge upon social security. And, even there, they must make it only under the safeguards which protect the rights of every other citizen. Profit made by the methods revealed to the Industrial Commission of the United States is made at a price we must refuse to pay.[29] If that means that the modern Napoleon will not enter industry, it follows that we must do without his talents.

Finally, in this regard, it is worth while to point out that much of the criticism directed against government control, even against government methods, cannot be rightly estimated unless it is seen in its proper perspective. Two things here may be noted. The criticism usually starts from the assumption that *laissez-faire* is the ideal condition, and that each departure from it is an assault upon liberty. But what Matthew Arnold called "doing as one likes" is exactly the reason why government control became necessary. Factory Acts, Trade Boards, and the like were all the logical outcome of *laissez-faire*; it is because without them the community would have found a civic life impossible to the vast majority of its citizens. The notion, secondly, that government methods are destructive of initiative is largely a mythology built upon the fact that business men are accustomed to take rapid decisions without reference to other wills, that they rely upon personal influence, and that faith in their judgment is, in their own world, one of the chief causes of their success. But all these qualities are essentially the roots of that industrial autocracy which is, as I have argued, without moral justification. It assumes that there is virtue in placing the will of the many in subordination to the will of the few, without it being incumbent upon those few to offer rational ground for their actions. Nor, I may add, is the supposed inferiority of government methods so patent as the business man tends to assume. I quote the testimony of one who is, in general, hostile to the State as trader. "I do not myself find", says Sir Lawrence Weaver,[30] "the methods of correspondence, of filing, and other elements of government routine at all difficult or irksome, and I think on the whole its methods of handling business are far more efficient than many of the much-vaunted business systems". It is, of course, obvious that a business man would find the duty of keeping records, and the necessity of explaining his policy, a strange and irritating adventure. He lives upon an almost intuitive sense which he can rarely hope to translate into words. He issues orders which he expects to have obeyed without protest. But it is precisely because he has sought neither to keep the record of what policy involves, nor to make his orders a function of common counsel, that we have to move to a new basis of industrial organisation.

## (v) The Regulation of Private Enterprise

How, then, is the State-relation to private industry to express itself in institutions? Let us first note the purposes that such relation must have in view. It aims, on the side of production, in securing the worker in industry, whether he be a manager at one end of the scale or a machine-tender at the other, that civic minimum of rights essential to him as a human being. It aims, on the side of consumption, at protecting the ordinary citizen in his purchase of necessary commodities, so far as organisation can secure him protection. It seeks, therefore, three things: (a) continuity of supply; (b) reasonable price; (c) the safeguard of quality. Nothing in all this, it may be noted, implies the admission of any revolutionary principles into the structure of industry. The idea of unregulated competition does not exist outside of economic theory; even the maxim *Caveat emptor* holds only within the margins of statutes like the Pure Food Acts. Regulation, indeed, has become the rule rather than the exception; and an economist who would paint a portrait of the industrial process must deal rather with the friction by which his hypotheses are frustrated than with the hypotheses themselves. *Laissez-faire* as a systematic principle ended with the outbreak of war in 1914; and the effort it implied has become impossible of achievement in the background of the great society. The problem. In fact, is not whether government intervention is desirable. The truth is that government intervention is essential, and the problem is simply of methods whereby it can bear its maximum fruit. For to leave to the unfettered play of economic forces the supply of those needs by the satisfaction of which we live is to maintain a society empty of all moral principles; and such a society more surely moves to disaster than at any period in history.

I can attempt here only the bare outline of what, as I think, the government regulation of private industry will imply. We are not, I may add, without experience of its meaning, particularly of its meaning in relation to a specific purpose. Anyone who studies the record of war-control of industry in the period from 1914 to 1918, will be amazed at the mass of material we possess upon the necessary mechanisms of regulation. It may in general be argued that this material is divisible into five great categories. We know much, firstly, about the stabilisation of prices, of profits and of wages. We are beginning to realise that the trade-cycle is not, like a comet, a vast natural force shot into earthly phenomena from without, and therefore beyond human control. We can attempt, bit by bit, the estimate of supply and demand, on one side, and the stabilisation of currency on the other, so as to repair the evils of gross fluctuation. We can, secondly, control the issue of capital. We can establish priorities according to degree of social importance. We can, not less urgently, check the export of capital, particularly where it searches for undesirable channels. We can attempt, thirdly, the centralised control and distribution of raw materials; the purchase, on government account, of the wool-supply of Australia, of manila hemp, of Russian flax, were experiments which were the more hopeful and the more significant, the more closely they are scrutinised. We can control each industry, fourthly, by means of councils representative of the industries concerned, which can be entrusted, as I shall explain, with quite large functions of self-government. We can, finally, in the realm of food and essential raw materials, greatly reduce costs by an efficient system of zonal distribution.

At the centre of any such control will clearly lie the Ministry of Production. Its officials will be charged, above all, with maintenance of two basic services: they will keep a census of production for each industry, and a costings department. These will be united under what may be termed an economic general staff whose function it will be to co-ordinate the multifarious activities which arise from government control. I do not conceive that it will be necessary for them, in any really organised trade, directly to undertake the work of actual administration. They will, one may hope, rather co-operate with business men than drive them; though their control of price in the interest of the consumer will involve, clearly, that they be entrusted, subject to the ultimate control of the legislative assembly, with regulating prices. But they will be able, through the statistical information at their command, to even out the fluctuations of supply and demand into something like an even adjustment, and, through their knowledge of the cost of production, to establish the nature of a fair price. They will attempt, where it seems advisable, to buy directly at the source, and thus minimise speculation and the chaos of the middleman. They will attempt, especially in food supplies, the standardisation of quality. They will act, in times of scarcity, as the natural organ for the control of demand. They will, if experience indicates anything, definitely encourage production by the policy of buying over a period of years at a stable price, instead of leaving innumerable dealers, as in agriculture, to make innumerable separate bargains with innumerable producers.

I do not, of course, suggest that a single formula applies to the whole intricate mechanism of business. Even, for example, in a fairly straightforward matter like centralised purchase of raw materials great variety of methods is possible. The government might itself import the total needs of the community and sell the stock to the manufacturers; in the woollen trade, for instance, it was found advisable in England to replace the machinery of private trade completely. Or the government might act through private agents who would be paid a fixed commission on their work, as in the case of the purchase of Russian flax. Or, again, the trade itself might be organised as a single purchasing agency, subject only to a general control audit by the government. The decentralisation possible under this last method, the wider scope, therefore, that it permits, seems to offer, on the whole, the possibilities of maximum advantage. Whatever the form, it is, I think, clear that centralised marketing of staple commodities is the only way both to assure stability of supply, on the one hand, and to minimise the cost of distribution, on the other. In general, it is obvious that each trade will require its own special methods, and that they will be the better the more they are self-evolved.

What, broadly, seems to be required in all industries of importance that are to remain private in character is the creation in each industry of an association of manufacturers similar in character to a trust. There are, indeed, few industries of any size to-day in which combination on a large scale has not taken place;[31] but their object has, of course, been unconcerned with public advantage. And precisely as the interests of owners become fully organised, so, also, must the interests of workers by hand and by brain. We can obtain from the parties to any form of industry a council for its government which would consist of four parties. There is the interest of owners; there is the vocational interest; there is the interest of direct users of the products of the industry; there is the interest, finally, of government as the body concerned with the general public well-being. Each of the parties would be equally represented on the council. It would be necessary to make membership of the associations representing both ownership and vocations compulsory upon all companies engaged in trading; and the council would possess the power to issue orders which, upon approval by the Ministry of Production, and subject to the control of the legislative assembly, would be binding upon the industry as a whole. I think, further, that each council should possess a judicial department with the right to inflict penalties for the evasion of its orders; such penalties, of course, being subject to the ordinary right of approval of the courts. It is an experiment of great importance to attempt, as in the legal and medical professions, to make responsibility for what may be called the morale of industry, a matter in which those engaged therein have an interest that is not only direct, but also explicit.

What would be the functions of such a council? Here, once more, it must be emphasised that we have to deal in general terms. It is natural that they should vary from industry to industry, and no single council, probably, will reproduce all the features here indicated, or any of them in quite the same way. Nothing can be identical where the material itself is different, and a different body of persons manipulate that material. But, subject to such limitations, the following scheme is, I think, a fair outline of the jurisdiction it would exercise. It would discuss and issue orders upon (1) the wages, working conditions, and hours of labour, in the industry as a whole; (2) the stabilisation of employment and production; (3) the creation of machinery for the settlement of disputes. It would, obviously, be a great advantage if each council possessed a permanent court of conciliation to which all disputes could, where necessary, be referred; (4) the collection of information upon all matters pertaining to the industry. This would include (a) statistics of cost, (b) statistics of output, (c) methods of manufacture, (d) research into all matters. All such information would be published; and it would, of course, be of first importance in the establishment of prices. (5) Facilities for the consideration of inventions in machinery and method, with the provision of safeguards for their devisers. (6) Investigation of special problems in the industry and, particularly, the study of foreign methods. The results of such investigations would, again, be published to all the members of the industry. (7) Research into the health conditions of the industry, particularly with a view to reducing the use of noxious materials, e.g. white lead in paint. (8) Supervision of apprenticeship in the industry in conjunction with the vocational bodies concerned. (9) Organisation of education of a technical nature after the period of apprenticeship, again in conjunction with the proper vocational bodies. (10) The provision of necessary publicity for the industry, this to include an annual report to the Ministry of Production upon the work of the council. (11) To serve as the link between the industry and the government. (12) To co-operate, where necessary, with the councils of other industries on matters of joint interest.[32]

What I am proposing is, practically, a parliament for each industry, with the power to lay down binding conditions upon each of its members. But before I discuss the personnel and officials to which such a parliament gives rise, it will be useful to emphasise generally the characters of the powers it will exercise. There is involved, firstly, the idea of publicity in the industry. The output, the costs of manufacture, the gross and net profits of each member-firm in the industry will be a public matter. It is, indeed, largely upon such publicity that the Ministry of Production will base the scale of prices to which it gives assent. And, in order that such publicity may be effective, it is clear that the Ministry certainly, and possibly, the audit and costings department, must possess such powers as appertained to the Food Controller in England during the war, under Regulation 2G. That regulation involved three things. It meant, first, the right to exact information considered necessary, whether of manufacture, purchase, sale, distribution and such like; it meant, second, the power of access to the books of the firm for the purpose of verification; and it meant, thirdly, that refusal of such information or access should be treated as a summary offence. Clearly, also, such publicity involves also standard forms of book-keeping and the rest. It is only upon the basis of such knowledge that legislation in regard to the industry can partake of a scientific character.

There is involved, secondly, the idea of standardisation. That has two aspects. It will mean, on the one side, common rates of wages, of hours of labour, of physical conditions in the industry; and, on the other, a relatively common technique in manufacture and, not seldom, in distribution. This is, of course, the general history of combination. It involves, as a rule, an increasing tendency to common purchase of material, as, for instance, in the great soap combine of Great Britain.

It involves, increasingly, the standardisation of all processes where the article produced is made by repetition of manufacture; the work, in this aspect, of such a body as the Engineering Standards' Association, is a model of what I am trying to urge. It involves, also increasingly, a growing specialisation within the trade, companies tending more and more to devote themselves to one or two types of work, and becoming more and more expert in its development. It permits also such obvious and important economies as centralised distribution and collective advertising, and, if the system of district councils, to be outlined presently, be adequately worked, it permits also of great economies in the cost of transport. We can eliminate such waste as experienced by the Ministry of Food when it found that milk going from South Wales to London used to cross milk going from Gloucester to South Wales.[33] It will tend to transfer competition from price to quality, with a public guarantee that each commodity made represents a standard and identifiable specification. There is involved, also, the fact that the whole body of new knowledge is placed at the disposal of the industry. The temptation to suppress inventions will be obviated by the public character the industry has acquired.

Such a form of organisation as is here outlined offers, I suggest, the maximum safeguards obtainable from any industry left in private hands. The procedure of each firm is controlled in such fashion that it has to share all additional profit with the public beyond a certain level. Its prices are controlled from without. What have been termed the "circumstantial safeguards" against the evils of trustification[34] are increased in value by the fact that the ultimate control of the industry does not lie in the hands of its owners, or even of the workers, whether by hand and brain, in combination with those owners. The government retains the power to fix price and the right of entry. It can check at any point failure in quality or output. The industry is made to function as a whole, and it acquires, through its council, a common mind and a common conscience. The device, moreover, of a fixed price is a mechanism of great value in the enforcement of industrial efficiency upon the more backward firms.

For while it operates to leave a margin of greater profit to the best, that profit, as I have already shown, will be shared in by the State and the consumer; and the less efficient are definitely and, I think, necessarily driven out much more rapidly than is now the case. The modern spectacle of the small and incompetent manufacturer who lives year by year on the edge of financial abyss and seeks to keep alive by economy on wages and the quality of his product is not an attractive one. It is to him, as a rule, that there gravitate the individual labourer who undercuts the general wages standard, the clerk who is beyond his best, the untrained who know nothing of the hours of labour or the proper physical conditions which should attach to their work. The modern trust either crushes him bit by bit, or pensions him off. At any rate, the more rapid the process of elimination the better it is for the health of the industry.

The national council in each industry need not, and in general will not, be the sole authority in its sphere. In most industries, it will be found essential to supplement its work by the creation of district councils which, *mutatis mutandis,* will perform similar functions for the area they cover. For, obviously, there are certain local differentiae which cannot be adjusted from a single centre. Problems like variation in the wage rate to meet special conditions of rent, problems of overtime, peculiar conditions of a local market are much better adjusted within the area where they occur than by reference to a central body the majority of whose members will be unacquainted with the problems involved. Quite clearly, no district council can attempt national solutions; quite clearly, also, its major results, if they are of a far-reaching character, ought to be confirmed by the central council before they become operative. In general, too, it would be unwise for these district councils to undertake research. That is essentially a matter for the industry as a whole, and for communication to the industry as a whole; for a district to obtain results is to raise the question, which ought never to be raised, of the area of their availability. Nor is it, I think, necessary to make the composition of a district council quite so complex as that of the central body. The representatives of the government may well be reduced to a liaison officer; and the representatives of allied industries will, in all probability, need to be present only where problems arise of special interest to themselves. But the judicial work of the district council should, I think, be a fundamental feature of its activity. It will not be difficult so to separate the area of large and small problems as to make the petty fine one inflicted at the source, while the graver offence is judged by the industry as a whole.

The district council, moreover, can, I think, be made of great use in another way. I assume, as a matter of course, that there will be reproduced in the structure of private industry the same system of works committee that I have already outlined in nationalised and co-operative industry.

And there must be, I suggest, a kindred power in the works committee of a private factory to appeal, in suitable cases, beyond its management to the district council for redress. Cases, for example, like the evasion of national agreements, like the refusal to reinstate in case of wrongful dismissal, things which are, and will remain, the groundwork of strikes, are a territory in which the intervention of an authority representative of the industry can be greatly valuable. We need to build up the tradition of an industrial ethic evolved by the men who actually operate the industry from their own experience of it. We cannot, I believe, make their solutions legally binding in many of these cases. But we can use them in two valuable ways. They are, first of all, authoritative publicity. They enable the body of citizens to know what is felt about some definite grievance by those best qualified to judge it. We can, secondly, use it as expert evidence in such legal proceedings as may follow from action by an industrial district council. It follows, therefore, that it must have the right to compel the attendance of witnesses, in its inquiries, and to take evidence upon oath; and it must develop a procedure which will be accepted by the courts as judicially valid in the same way as they now accept, for instance, the findings of Public Service Commissions in the United States. Under the conditions to which, in the plan here outlined, private industry will be subjected, we can, I believe, look forward to the development of an industrial jurisprudence as valid for its special sphere as the jurisprudence of the courts themselves. And it will be a jurisprudence the more valuable in that it will represent, not the experience of a single party to the process, but of the total experience within the industry. Little by little, also, there are many minor aspects of law enforcement which these district councils might well take over, of which obvious examples are violations of the Factory Acts, of hours of labour laws, and of such statutes as those concerned with pure food and the prevention of traffic in noxious drugs.

What would be the size and composition of these councils? They need to be large enough to admit a genuinely full representation of the interests concerned, and, at the same time, to be small enough to permit a fairly complete and intimate discussion of the details of policy within each industry. Some such figure as a hundred members is, I suggest, a reasonable size. The representative associations of employers and workers would be the obvious electoral units of two of the four parties concerned; the representatives of the government would be appointed by the Ministry of Production; and those of allied industries by their representative bodies in turn. I do not pretend to know how often they should meet. Clearly, however, they will need at least four general meetings a year; and details, as opposed to the large outlines of policy, would be worked out in committees much upon the lines of a municipal body in England. They will need provision, of course, to enable a special meeting to be called at any time, where urgent problems arise. They would vote in the usual way, save that, where they recommend the passage of an order binding upon the whole industry, there should be a two-thirds or similar majority in its favour. They should have the power to mend their own constitution by a similar vote. They should have direct and continuous access to the government departments dealing with their work, a connection, it may be noted, that will be facilitated by the presence on them of government representatives. They would be, also, the normal vehicle of communication between the industry and the government. The latter would, of course, consult it, as in duty bound, upon all matters of legislative policy. It would go to it for negotiation and discussion in such matters as the fixation of prices, the settlement of national minima of wages and hours of labour, the attitude to be adopted by the State to proposed international conventions in industrial matters. In none of these things could it, or should it, tie the hands of the government; that is a matter where the control of the legislative assembly is fundamental. But, from the very character of its composition, its opinion will carry weight; and the higher the ethical and technical standard it sets itself, the greater the authority that will attach to its decision.

Each council will need a permanent staff; and it is a mater of some interest to work out the type of staff it will probably evolve. Here we may note the difference between the conception which underlies the present scheme, and that which seems inherent in the structure of the Whitley Councils. Those who built the latter seemed to imagine that with a secretary and a clerical staff the council would be able without difficulty to perform its functions.[35] That is not, I think, likely to be the case; though it is perhaps the inevitable result of a theory built upon the co-operation of capital and labour on the present basis of industrial relationships. I have already argued that this is generally impossible, and that the more powerful the organisation of labour in a given industry, the less likely such co-operation is. For the greater the degree of labour organisation, the more widespread will be the perception of the absence of moral principle in the structure of industry; and it is only as that condition is remedied that co-operation will become creatively possible.

There will be, I suggest, at least six general departments attached to the permanent secretariat of the council. There will be, of necessity, an audit department engaged in formulating the necessary inquiries into the financial side of the industry. There will be, secondly, a costings department upon which will fall the important burden of providing the material whereby the council can make its recommendations upon price-fixing to the Ministry of Production. There will be, thirdly, a research department, which will, I believe, become of growing importance, especially in the heavy industries; and already, indeed, the better firms, both in England and America, have come to see the importance of making proper provision for scientific investigations. Such a department ought not, of course, to confine itself to the purely technical side of the industry; its psychological problems, its methods of sale, its organisation in the factory, are not less important. Nor should it neglect the special problem of industrial disease. Miners' nystagmus, plombosis, Sheffield grinders' disease—it is incumbent upon the trades where maladies such as these mean a special mortality-rate to bestir themselves for their prevention. There will also be a legal department charged in part with the task of drafting, in part with the quasi-judicial work which, as I have argued, could well be made a function of the councils. Probably, also, there will develop a department to deal with education in the industry, and such general problems of its welfare as insurance and superannuation. I do not myself think that the problem of the workers' leisure is in any way a concern of these bodies, or of the district councils. For in an industrial society dominated, as our own must be, by a machine-technology, the less the life of the working-day is projected beyond its boundaries, the better it will be for the average citizen. He must find his own means to make that leisure fruitful; and the key to its utilisation must be sought, originally in the schools, and, later, in the general civic life about him.

If such a pattern of organisation is at all correct, it is clear that we are envisaging the growth of an industrial civil service the opportunities and, ultimately, the powers of which will not be less important than those of the government departments. They, we have seen, must be removed, if they are to function adequately, from the atmosphere of patronage. The same is true of this industrial civil service. It will be not less necessary to devise qualifications for its officers than for judges in the courts, or doctors in the operating-rooms. They will need a quite special training for many of their functions; their lawyers, for instance, will not be the genial young men who have ambled delicately through dinners at an English Inn of Court. Exactly as we require a diploma of public health from the doctor who seeks a post as a medical officer, so I suggest, we shall require a special competence in industrial law for admission to the legal department of a council. There will be, one imagines, in such a body a small establishment committee which will select its officials in terms of qualifications. And exactly as in law and medicine, we are developing special training for special work, so also shall we need such training for business enterprise. It is more than time that the study of business enterprise became, as it is slowly becoming, a subject for university study. It is more and more evident that the problems of business, like marketing, like costing and the like, are all of them subjects in which an academic habit of mind has much of value to contribute. Work like that of the Harvard Business School or the School or Rural Economy at Oxford is laying the foundations of a revolution in the discipline and habits of business life.

I have written of private industry as through the limited liability company would be the normal unit in its operations. That is not, of course, necessarily the case. There is likely to be a future of importance for at least two other forms of organisation. In industries where, as in building, a large fixed capital is relatively unimportant, there is, I think, a great future for the guild idea. I see no reason why independent bodies of craftsmen should not provide houses in the same way as the ordinary master builder of the present time. The problem for them is almost entirely a problem of credit, on the one hand, and of discipline on the other. Each of these is, in its turn, largely a matter of experience and tradition. They will need to devise with great care the technique of their government. They will have to subject themselves to the general rule of their industry in the same way as a private company. They will have to make their way by the proof of quality inherent in their work, and their ability to produce something different from the machine-made article. But the governing body of such a guild cannot, of course, be the workers themselves. That would be to repeat again the tragic and fatal history of the self-governing workshop.[36] The control must lie in a committee representative of the vocational bodies concerned; and the men working on a particular job will be related to that committee exactly as though they were in, say, a nationalised industry. Much, of course, of the future of such guilds depends upon the ability of the rank and file to submit to conditions of organisation probably even more stringent than those required in private business. That can be without question where there is a proper appreciation of the importance of management in industrial success. And the problem of the provision of credit is, I believe, likely to be solved if such efforts as the trade-union banks, now multiplying rapidly in the united States, prove successful. The history, for example, of the part played by labour in the reorganisation of the Philadelphia Rapid Transit Company is highly significant in this regard.[37] If labour can develop superior productive efficiency, and prove able to finance it, the extension of its democratic control is likely to be a permanent factor in the making of a new industrial order.

There is, I think, a place of importance also for what has come to be called the collective contract. There is no reason why the workers in a particular factory should not take over from the employers the total performance of a given body of work. They could negotiate with them for the partial or complete production of certain definite commodities at a fixed price. They could then themselves arrange for the hiring and firing of labour, the appointment of foreman, the determination of the hours of labour. Arrangements could easily be made for the period over which the work was to be completed, the rates of pay upon which the price was to be fixed, the penalties to be involved in non-performance. In industries like cotton and engineering, where it is the custom for groups of workers to perform collectively an allotted range of functions, there is ample room for what may perhaps be termed controlled democracy in the workshop. The employer would supply material and specifications; he would fix the time within which he expected the contract to be fulfilled; he would bargain for the price; but he would, on the one hand, be relieved of responsibility for the myriad difficulties of workshop discipline, from the irritation that comes from doubt whether the working force is doing its job, from the resentment which so often develops when a foreman is unpopular. The workers, on the other hand, would have a sense of freedom and responsibility in their effort. Time lost, poor work, bad discipline, would fall upon their shoulders. A mistaken appointment would be their error, and not his. The problem of engagement and dismissal would not lead to the perpetual challenge which now seems inherent in the industrial relation. "The fundamental significance of this plan of action", writes Mr. Cole,[38] "lies in the fact that it is directed, not to the admission of the workers to the conjoint exercise of a common control with the employer, but to the transference of certain functions *completely* from the employer to the workers". Such a collective contract is an alternative and limited form of the guild production I have just discussed. It must, of course, satisfy in rates of wages and hours of labour the normal standards of the industry; and it will involve subjection of the wage-rate to the normal cost of production fixed by the council of the industry upon the basis of the price of its product as defined by the Ministry of Production. Clearly, therefore, it builds greatly upon the efficiency of the workers to whom the contract is entrusted. But where they know one another, and have what may be called a body of corporate habits, it is, I believe, an invaluable method of procedure. For it combines the mechanical routine with the intellectual effort. It gives the worker a real say in the disposal of his labour. It is experimental and elastic. It could be applied to a single stage of manufacture, and extended or contracted as it proved successful. It might be used on the riveting of steel plates on a ship, on the sale of some portion of a company's output in an allotted territory, on the spinning or weaving of certain types of cotton goods. Nothing is of greater industrial importance than the building of habits in the workers such as the collective contract makes possible. For it ends, where it is properly utilised, their position as tenders of a machine. It makes them the authors of a process instead of the servants of a routine. It is built upon a trust in their ability to think and plan. It regards them as more than the blind tools of forces they can neither understand nor control.

Such a system of institutions fulfils, I think, the purpose I outlined earlier of industrial organisation. It leaves room, and to spare, for the industrial magnate who searches not merely for power but also for fortune. It gives the individual worker a full opportunity to make his experience felt in the working of the process of which he is a part. He is no longer simply a commodity to be used or tossed aside as the market demands. His vocation is protected alike by its compulsory recognition and by the places allotted to him in the governance of his industry; and he can himself look forward to a place on the body charged with that governance. We do not abolish the profit due to efficiency, but we compel it to build itself on the attainment of standards, and we prevent capital from functioning, as in the past, as the residuary legatee of industry. Nor do we leave the consumer, as now, at the mercy of powerful combinations. He is protected at once by the share in the industrial government that is played by his representatives, and by the power of the Ministry of Production to fix prices. I do not, of course, deny that in such a scheme as this the business man can no longer conduct his business in his own way. He will pay standard rates of wages. He will be subject to rigorous control in the conditions of his factory. His profits will be limited to a reasonable rate; and where he makes more than that rate, he will return a due share of it both to his workers and to the public. Nor will he be able, as now, to surround himself with the fantastic barrage of secrecy that he protests is essential to his work. He will have to depend much less on personal influence, much more on the efficiency of his organisation and the quality of his business. He will be scrutinised in the large outlines of his work by men who are charged with the duty of enforcing the public interest in his effort. The region within which his own unrestricted will may operate is professedly narrowed and rigorously defined.

He has, it may be remarked, compensations of importance in return. His business is made the servant of moral principle; and there are thereby enlisted in his service instincts and emotions he could not otherwise hope to call into play. Where he has been compelled to rely upon fear, he is able to depend on co-operation. Where his working force has tended to be slack and incompetent, it is given incentives, in no other way accessible, to effort and efficiency. He can secure, if he so pleases, all that there is of inventiveness and energy in labour. He has the assurance that if he is defeated by his rivals, their victory will be due not to competition, or undercutting, but to the superior quality of their effort. He will have at his disposal an organisation, in the research department of the council, which will keep him in touch with all the facts of his industry. If his costs are unduly high, he can have them investigated; if his commodities do not, say, retain their previous market abroad, he will learn just what is attractive in the product of his competitors. I do not claim that he will be free from strikes; a strikeless industry is not, I believe, attainable in an imperfect world. But he is far less likely to meet industrial dislocation than under the present system. He will not encounter the suspicions by which he is surrounded to-day, belief in hidden reserves, conviction that he is profiteering, faith in a vast market he does not in fact control. If he is met by a demand for increased wages, the justice of the demand will be susceptible to exact quantitative measurement. If he requires an increase in the hours of labour, he will be able to show with precision its relation to output, thereby, to profit. Industry, in the phrase of Mr. Justice Brandeis, will have been transformed into a profession; and its relation to the public will be one of service by the very law of its being. The economic difference between employer and worker will not be as vast as it is to-day; but, where it exists, it will be referable to causes analysable and intelligible.

There is, moreover, one other aspect of this new synthesis which deserves a word. It is, of course, a frankly collectivist system. It attempts a wholesale planning of the methods whereby the purpose of industry is achieved. Is it likely, in a régime which, confessedly, implies much greater equality than now, that adequate provision can be made for new capital when the rewards of risk are on a smaller scale? We are here in the realm of prophecy, and gambling in the realm of economic futures is a dangerous, if agreeable, adventure. But it is permissible to point out certain contemporary facts from which important inferences may be drawn. Production in war-time, in the first place, taught us two great lessons. It showed that a fuller and more scientific use of the available factors of production could lead to a greatly increased volume of output, and that the chief cause of that increase lay in the new incentives injected into industry by the universal will to victory. It showed, secondly, that this increased volume of output was accompanied by a greatly increased demand for commodities as a result of the change in the distribution of income. From that experience, I think, two inductions may be drawn. If we could keep the industrial system working in terms of war-time incentive, if, that is, organisation could assure the full and continuous employment of capital and labour, and, second, if we could draw the necessary saving from a wider area, even if we did not, as now, draw largely upon the mechanical accumulations of a small number of rich persons, we could in publicly owned industries partly provide for new capital by the automatic accumulation of reserves, and in industry as a whole from the fact that a comfortable income for the body of workers would implant habits of saving not possible under existing conditions.[39] Men cannot save when their income is hardly adequate to the burden of life, even more, where it is rarely secure. But once a regular minimum is established which makes possible a standard of fair comfort, the cost of saving is not too great to make immediate consumption more attractive. And it may be added that the larger the field of safe investment offered, the greater will be the incentive to save. A higher level of consumption will mean an increased demand for articles of general comfort; and this institution will act, almost automatically, to replace what Mr. Hobson calls "an irregular, unreliable, and insufficient demand for luxuries on the part of the rich" into channels that assure continuity. And, as I shall show later, the development of social insurance will offer possibilities in this regard of which the present methods are unable to take advantage.

One last remark may be made. It need not be denied that there are two groups of thinkers to whom such plans as these are finally unpalatable. On the one hand, to those who conceive of the reorganisation of society in rigorously communistic terms, they will appear timid and conservative. They lack the logic of inevitable catastrophe. They do not envisage either the rapid or the complete disappearance of the capitalist system in its present phase; rather they imply the development of a new society within the shell of the old. They are even bold enough to envisage the disappearance of that class-war which now lies at the root of social structure, for they conceive it possible to harmonise the interests of those who are parties to the industrial relation. The answer to such a criticism is, I believe, a final one. Revolutions do not achieve the direct end at which they aim; and the weapons of which they are driven to make use destroy by their character the prospects they have in view. An English social revolution, for instance, could, even if it were successful, be achieved at a cost few will be prepared to pay; and that cost would, as I think, prevent the consummation of the ideals at which the revolution aimed. It is probable, moreover, that an English social revolution must, to be successful, be a phase in a general European revolutionary movement; for the experience of Russia makes it obvious that a communist State cannot maintain the rigour of its outline in the midst of capitalist States. The conditions of a successful revolution, in other words, seem to me so improbable of fulfilment that the adventure could only be justified, first, as a weapon of last resort, and second, when the chances of victory were very great. For the failure of an economic revolution would, under modern circumstances, entail penalties more fatal than at any previous time.[40]

Yet I do not believe that such communist pessimism is either half so unjustified or so disastrous as the naive faith that *laissez-faire* is still the major solution of the problems before us. The history of industry all over the world has been the record of the necessary abandonment of *laissez-faire* for reasons that have, at every point, been overwhelming. The hours of labour a man may work, the level of wages he may receive, the materials to be used in the commodities he makes, the conditions of sanitation and safety in the factory or mine where he has to labour, it has been found necessary unceasingly to control these if we are to have even the prospect of decent living for the majority of the people. Countless investigations have shown what is meant by their absence. Pictures like that drawn by Engels of England in the 'forties, like Charles Booth's magistral survey of Victorian London, like Rowntree's description of York in the first years of the twentieth century, above all the relentless and accurate analysis of capitalism at its apogee of Karl Marx,[41] are of all of them explanations of why *laissez-faire* involved as its inevitable consequence the attempt by the State to enforce standards of minimum welfare upon industry. Statesmen, therefore, who can still proclaim, like Sir Robert Horne,[42] that "State interference with industry was never an advantage", are either completely ignorant of the course of industrial history, or else prepared to face with equanimity the maintenance of the present system.

For this latter view it is difficult to see any tenable grounds. The working-classes of the world have no longer any faith in capitalism. They give to it no service they can avoid. It involves industrial dislocation as the law of its being. It implies a distribution of property at no point referable to moral principle. It means waste and corruption and inefficiency. Nor, historically, can it avoid the difficulty that political power has now been conferred upon those who least share in the benefits it secures; there is not, I think, any evidence of men coming to the possession of political power without trying, as a consequence, to control economic power also. They may, of course, be resisted. But the result of such resistance on any large scale will inevitably be revolution, and there will then be precipitated exactly the situation predicted in the communist analysis. I do not say the revolution will be successful. I do, however, urge that even its defeat will destroy the prosperity of capitalism, on the one hand, and imply such an iron dictatorship of the capitalist, on the other, as to usher in a period of guerilla warfare almost certain to ruin the prospects of civilisation. It is to the avoidance of such a dilemma that the view here urged is directed. It is an attempt to make possible the triumph of reason in a vital department of human affairs. Frankly, it demands from the economic rulers of society a sacrifice greater than they have ever been called upon to make. Frankly, also, it admits that their refusal of such sacrifice involves unthinkable disaster. We have reached a moment when institutional change is bound to be rapid, in either a backward, or a forward, direction. The one, as I think, implies the end of coherent civilisation; the other offers, at the least, the prospect of an ordered society built upon justice. That is why men who oppose the drift towards change will seem like those whom Burke described when he wrote of men who persisting in "opposing the mighty current, will appear rather to resist the decrees of Providence itself than the mere designs of men".

## (vi) Vocational Organisation

I have argued here that vocational bodies will have a place of primary importance in the new State. What will be the character of vocational bodies? How are the lines of demarcation to be drawn? What will be their purposes? Of what nature will be their powers? This must, I think, be said at the outset that the position they will occupy differs qualitatively from the position occupied by the trade union in the modern State. For the purpose of the latter is, above all, a fighting purpose. It is built upon the notion of class-consciousness. It involves breaking down the separation of vocations and fighting, where possible, along the most extended front. That is why, in the contemporary situation, industrial unionism is superior to craft unionism, why amalgamation is better than federation. That is why, as Mr. and Mrs. Webb have pointed out,[43] "what is desirable for the battle with capitalism, whether fought on the industrial or on the political field, may well be 'the one big Union', so organised and so directed that the whole of the manual working class, and the whole of the allied brain-workers may move as one with one will, and for one purpose. The more homogeneous and the more highly disciplined the force, the quicker and more complete may well be the victory".

I am concerned with a different position. It is with a society into which the idea of equality has already been injected that we must deal. It is upon the assumption that we have moved through the class struggle to a free commonwealth that we must build our vocational structure. What, in such a society, is a vocation? It may, I think, be defined as a permanent and continuous association of persons who are separated from others by the possession of a special competence secured by a definite training. Where we have such a body of persons, they will always insist, so far as they can, on the practice of their craft under conditions that they determine for themselves. They will feel themselves members of what the mediaeval world finely called a "mystery" alien from other "mysteries". They will desire to settle how they are to work, the standards of their performance, the ethics of their profession, the admission to their ranks. They come to develop, like the modern nation-State, a body of traditions peculiarly their own, a corporate personality that feels itself violated when it is ruled by others who do not share in those traditions. The characteristic of a vocation is that it operates within a given function where it is, relatively speaking, expert, and that it has no collective view outside the ambit of that given function. It is concerned to protect its differences from other vocations, not its identity with them. The vocation of a doctor has no interests in common with that of a lawyer; that of an engineer has nothing in common with the vocation of a typist. The tie which binds the members of a vocation together, the thing which gives them their common outlook, is not their general function of producers, but their special function as producers of a limited and fairly definite service.

It seems, therefore, to follow that the type of vocational organisation with which we have to deal is built, not upon the general range of a given industry, but upon the categories of function within that industry. In a nationalised railway service, for instance, the State would be concerned, not with a single trade union of railwaymen, but with a variety of craft-bodies, of engine-drivers, firemen, platelayers, porters and the like, combined, it may be, for the defence of common interests, but essentially recognising inherently different purposes in their function. The porter of the Examination Schools at Oxford is a necessary part of the university staff, but he has no proper place in a body concerned with the interests of university teachers. A hospital cannot do without its doctors; but they are out of place in a body seeking to protect the interest of nurses. I do not doubt the need of common organisation for common interests; but it seems to me that the essence of vocational self-government lies in the emphasis laid upon distinctions and not upon identities. It is, of course, impossible to say *a priori* when a vocation becomes so distinct from an existing body as to need separate protection of this kind; or, conversely, when two vocations have become so genuinely merged as to be in fact performing a single function. New bodies grow up, like accountants and secretaries, who, a half-century ago, had no recognisable technique of their own; older separations, like that between the solicitor and the barrister, or between the physician and the surgeon, break down in the light of changing conditions.

What is, I think, certain is that the making of demarcations can never be entrusted to the body itself. It ought to share, and share largely, in the decision; but its interest in self-protection is too great to make it possible for complete self-determination ever to be its prerogative. Nor, further, can it solely decide the conditions of entrance to the vocation. Anyone who considers, for example, the way in which doctors and lawyers resisted the admission of women to their professions will realise why it is essential to retain an ultimate right of external control. An analysis, moreover, of the conditions of entrance to the profession of solicitor in England will make it clear to any disinterested observer that the regulations have been so framed as to assure, as far as possible, the hereditary character of the vocation. There is everything, I think, to be said for making a period of qualification and a proof of competence a necessary condition of entrance to the vocation; with, of course, the corollary of a proper register of qualified persons, whether in the vocation of a domestic servant, or of a doctor, or of an engineer. But if the profession is left with a free hand to settle the conditions of entrance, it will always seek to protect existing practitioners, sometimes by limitation of numbers, sometimes by the requirement of unnecessarily high standards of qualification, and so forth. There begins, then, to emerge, I suggest, a twofold conception at this point. The recognition of new vocations is a matter to be settled by the government and (a) those in the allied vocations, (b) those seeking recognition for what they claim to be a new vocation, (c) relevant subject bodies like, for example, the Royal Society or the Engineering Standards Committee, whose opinion is entitled to weight. The determination of the conditions of entrance to the vocation would, in similar fashion, be determined by a body equally composed of (a) those already practising the particular vocation, (b) those who would teach persons who would desire to enter it, and (c) representatives of allied vocations. It would be possible, also, in many cases to associate with such a body representatives who would put the point of view of those who, later, would be the employers of the entrant to the vocation. Often enough, the presence of the latter would be a valuable protection against that professional conservatism which insists upon uniqueness where none in fact exists.

Qualification, of course, does not imply the guarantee of employment; there are said to be lawyers and doctors who do not pay their way. But it is, I think, clear that under the scheme here outlined we shall have the means at our disposal of establishing much more closely an adequate relation between size in the profession and its annual recruitment than is now the case. A model from which such a relation may develop is offered by the practice of the Civil Service Commission in Great Britain. There, year by year, the number of vacancies to be filled by examination is notified; and it is possible, by that means, to limit fairly effectively the number of applicants for positions. If such a practice became general, and if there were established under each education authority a committee of teachers and parents who worked in conjunction with appropriate bodies in the different services, it would be possible to know within reasonable margins the number of posts likely to be filled. That need not, of course, operate to limit the number of those who desire to qualify in a particular profession, even when they either cannot, or choose not to, practise in it. The more we can encourage the habit of alternative qualification, the better .it will be for the standards of our democracy. That is not only because there are many posts which need a dual qualification; it is also because it is, particularly in a civilisation dominated by machine-technology, important to have people who can be shifted from one special form of labour to another; for the study of the physiology of industry makes increasingly evident the importance of change in work. Not the least of our present difficulties lies in the fact that once a man has adopted a particular profession, he is condemned to practise it for life, save in the most exceptional cases. The growing interest in adult education, moreover, makes it increasingly possible that after the period of compulsory training is over, we may be able to persuade larger numbers (we must dwell here only in the realm of persuasion) to fit themselves for a wider sphere of work than seemed possible or attractive to them at the period of their entrance into industrial or professional life. That is important not only from the standpoint of a man's usefulness to himself, but, industrially, in relation to the problem of unemployment, and, intellectually, from his value as a citizen. The ampler we can make his experience, the greater the contribution he will make to social effort.

How will each vocation be governed? Here, obviously, I can only indicate some leading principles; details are a matter in which discussion would need to take account of the thousand varying problems the pattern of vocational structure affords. But certain things are clear. The vocation will be governed by an executive council elected by its members. It will need therein, as with the Miners' Federation of Great Britain, to take account of regional interests, not less than of the general number of members. It will choose such permanent officers as it requires, remembering, one hopes, that administration is a specialised art, in which continuous opportunity of practice, as opposed to constant change, is of the first importance. Beyond its executive council, it will have need of local bodies; and it will be a matter of the first importance to select proper units of local organisation. It is, for instance, clear in the majority of occupations that the true local unit is not the place where the member resides, but the place in which the vocation is actually practised. Much of the efficiency of vocational life depends upon the opportunity to consult, as in the Miners' Lodge, the men who are actually working together.[44] The difficulty, sometimes urged, of finding a suitable time for meeting can, with a little inventiveness, always be overcome. Two engineers who live at Clapham have less interest in common, or, perhaps less effective means of articulating their experience, than two engineers who work in the same factory in Clapham, but live respectively in Poplar and Battersea. They meet on a plane uniquely devised to bring out what is common in their experience. It is error of a serious kind to lose the opportunity to use it. I think, further, that experience points to the vesting of certain powers in the executive council that are now, especially in the trade-union movement, relegated to the rank and file. The council, for instance, should always choose the officials of the vocation; no large body of men can appreciate the technical qualities which go to the making, say, of an efficient secretary. So, also, the council should choose the representatives of the vocation who are to sit upon such bodies as the governing body of a nationalised industry. Anyone who studies the statistics of trade-union voting[45] will realise how small is the interest of the rank and file in such questions; how little, also, in such interest related to genuinely competent appreciation. It is clear, on the other hand, that where the questions to be decided relate definitely to the personal experience of members, as in the number of hours it is proposed to work, or the necessity of a strike, it is desirable that the decision shall be based on the votes of the total membership. It is, further, important that there should develop in the vocational world bodies which correspond to the quarterly meeting of the consumers' Co-operative Movement. For, often enough, the grave danger exists that the official at a central or regional headquarters will lose touch with the rank and file. He needs to know, not only what individual members are thinking, as he makes contact with such members, but what emerges as points of grievance and suggestion when discussion is corporate and organised. And it is through such institutions of continuous consultation that there will develop the proper type of voluntary body within a given vocation. Medical men, for instance, who are impressed by the importance of birth-control could then form a society which would use the quarterly meeting to impress their views upon the profession as a whole; and where it was desired to represent the medical profession upon a public inquiry into that question, that society would form a national unit to choose a doctor to express its point of view.

One fact of importance should, however, be noted here. I have assumed that it will be obligatory on all members of the vocation to join the association concerned with its governance. That association, nevertheless, cannot, under the assumptions I have made, be the ultimate governing body in the industry any more than, for instance, the Miners' Federation or the British Medical Association is the ultimate governing body in each respective vocation. The rules, the observance of which are binding upon the members of an association in the sense of involving a legal penalty—expulsion from the vocation, for instance—must, I think, be framed, not by the association itself, but by the association in conjunction with an external authority who, in the instance taken, would be the Minister of Justice. Wherever, that is to say, the rules of the association involve by their nature deprivation of the right to practise the craft, the power of the association should never be final. It should always be a power of which the substance should be approved by the State, though its enforcement is best left to the vocation itself. Exactly as the General Medical Council and the Bar Council have the right to strike practitioners from their rolls, but are limited as to the causes for such expulsion, so, I suggest, each vocation should be limited. Nor do I see any reason why it should not be open to private persons to delate to such bodies for alleged unprofessional conduct meriting expulsion. The larger the degree of self-government we can develop in this direction, the better it will be for the *esprit de corps* of a vocation. Responsibility is more certainly born from powers of this kind than in any other way; and I believe that, as a general rule, the average professional court will be a better medium of justice than a body of lawyers to whom the professional ethic of the given vocation has to be explained as a thing of strangeness. Appeal to the ordinary courts must, of course, be preserved in order to see (a) that a proper procedure has been followed, and (b) that the action taken is not *ultra vires,* but if these conditions are met, the power of the vocation could usefully be left as final.

We begin now to see the purposes at which a vocational body should aim, and the powers it requires to fulfil those purposes. It is the vocational body, whether in the region, or in the nation-State as a whole, that will choose those who are to represent it in governing bodies in industries, in advisory committees of government department and the like. They will go there frankly to protect the interests of their vocation, to bargain about its hours of labour, its rates of pay and the general conditions upon which its effort depends. They will not, of course, be plenipotentiaries, but ambassadors; in the last resort it is the vocation itself which must determine whether it will accept the terms offered to it. The right to accept involves, also, the right to reject, and there will clearly be cases, even in a nationalised industry, in which men will withhold their labour rather than submit to the conditions offered. I do not think the right to strike can be denied to any vocation. In a State such as we have been here considering, it will, I believe, be a rare thing for a strike to occur. But if a body of men believes with any intensity that to continue work under the conditions proposed is impossible, they will, as I have already argued, strike, whatever be their legal situation. The real safeguard against such a position lies in two directions. It is secured, first of all, by making the conditions of the vocation materially and spiritually adequate. When men know that the economic order is permeated by just principles, the will to strike is largely absent; and it is secured, secondly, by the conference of a large degree of self-government upon the vocation. That is, I may perhaps point out, the value of the Whitley system in the British civil service. Its present weakness lies in two directions also. It is a mistake to make civil servants act as the employers' side in a Whitley Council; that function is much better entrusted to the legislative committee of the department. It is a mistake, also, not to allow the councils to deal with such matters as promotion. It would be wise, further, to relate the work of the Civil Service Commission to the vocational bodies in the public services. The standards of entrance, the method of testing efficiency, the relation of grades one to another, are all of them questions upon which the views and experience of those bodies is of the first importance. One would like to be certain that they are utilised.

The vocation, further, must take up, as a matter naturally within its scope, the study and advancement of its own technique. Partly, of course, that is a matter in which, as in medicine and the law, there will always exist within the vocation voluntary associations working at the problems of the craft. But that is not adequate to its needs. It is always urgent that there should be recognised officially by the vocation itself the need of organised improvement in the standards of the profession. One would like to see the miners employing their own medical men, their engineers, their lawyers. The teaching profession might well maintain in every country a great institution like Teachers' College in New York to act as a definite centre for the making of new knowledge in educational technique and its communication to the profession as a whole. The medical profession might well set out to discover men like Banting and Lister, and set them to solve the difficulties of medicine and surgery. The actuary, the engine-driver, the boilermaker can all add to the quality of their effort by making it part of their business deliberately to search for the means of improvement. That is important not only as an item in professional self-respect; it is important also because discoveries so made become the common possession of the vocation, and not simply a source of profit. And it enables us to avoid the difficulty met, for instance, in what is called scientific management when an efficiency engineer like Mr. F.W. Taylor seeks to impose a routine upon a body of workers to whom he does not belong. Improvement made from within, as made by co-operation with the vocation itself, has a quality of responsibility in no other way obtainable. And it is, particularly in routine-work, an immense factor in giving to the vocation an avenue to self-importance. If, for example, the fatigue of say shop-assistants was studied under the aegis of shop-assistants themselves, the conclusions arrived at would have the quite special value of immediately electing a volume of support that would not attach, for instance, to an inquiry by a government department or an employers' association. If miners would study scientifically the problem of safety in mines, I believe that the reduction of accidents in mining would be much more rapid than in the past. If, even, the Miners' Federation of Great Britain or the United Mine Workers' of America were to survey the equipment of coal-mines in order to determine its adequacy, the change they could produce would be enormous. For such an effort wins for its support a driving force obtainable because its translation into effective terms involves the dignity of the profession as a whole.

The vocation, further, must develop its professional standards. What, exactly, does that imply? Professional standards may be defined as rules intended to prevent the victory of self-interest over service in the working of the vocation. It is to that end, for instance, that doctors and lawyers in England are forbidden to advertise. It is for that reason that a solicitor's bill of costs is subject to the scrutiny of the courts. No doctor is supposed to take a commission from another doctor to whom he introduces a client; though business men think nothing of asking, for instance, a commission from a stockbroker to whom they have introduced a friend who desires to float his business as a limited company. Nor may a professional man use the knowledge he obtains in the practice of his vocation to the detriment of his client. I do not doubt or deny that many vocations now carry the code intended to embody such safeguards to a point where, in reality, they involve grave dangers. It is, for example, probable that medical etiquette often prevents the criticism of a method of treatment where the purpose is, quite rightly, to prevent the criticisms of a fellow-practitioner. It is practically certain that the ethic of lawyers as a profession is much the largest obstacle in the way of reasonable law reform. Nevertheless, I believe that the creation of standards of conduct which the profession can enforce upon the members is essential to its function, and if, as suggested, research is recognised as inherent in that risk, the charge that professional interest will oppose originality can quite largely be broken down. We cannot allow the British Medical Association to prevent the wider use of midwives, district nurses and health visitors upon the ground that "any salaried hierarchy of the professionals is inconsistent with the personal dignity and individual freedom of the practitioners, that the creation of any specialism whatever inevitably diminishes by so much the sphere of the general practitioner".[46] But the fact of danger is rather a ground for having the ultimate control outside the profession than a ground for assuring to it the power to determine its own standards. And when the last word has been said against the professional habits of doctors, it remains, I think, true that their standards of conduct still easily outdistance those of any other vocation we know. The power to revise is not a power to interfere day by day. One would like, nevertheless, to see the habit grow up of a small commission to inquire, every decade or so, into the professional habits of a vocation. It would be a commission, not of experts, but of public-minded and disinterested men who would take evidence upon the working of the professional code, and try to invent ways for its improvement. It would prevent much of the rigidity against which so much complaint is now made. It would check the habit of repeating customs in parrot-fashion as though they represented eternal truth. It would enable the interested outsider to offer suggestions to the craft in an atmosphere likely to ensure a more fitting reception than they now receive. Granted, for example, that a bonesetter ought to be a qualified practitioner, it would be a comfort to the general public to know that qualified practitioners were efficient bonesetters. At present, indubitably, criticism is received with impatience unless it comes from sources within the profession. Such a commission could voice authoritatively the criticisms often felt without, but which lack the means to reach their proper goal.

Finally, it is, I think, important that the vocation should grow into the habit of voicing deliberately the sense it has of national need. To some extent, this has already been provided for by the system of advisory committees I have already outlined. But these, in any case, cannot speak for the vocation as a whole, and much of their work will necessarily be done under conditions of official secrecy. It is important to break down that monopolisation of access to the ministerial mind which any body of permanent officials naturally seeks, for its own conveniences, to possess. It would be a great step forward if the General Medical Council were able to speak for the profession on the minimum policy required to decrease infant mortality; or the Teachers' Registration Council to have a united policy on the number of cubic feet per child in a school necessary as a minimum to educational efficiency; or the council of a united legal profession to speak with vigour on the question of prison reform. Such a function would have the further merit of persuading the practitioner in each vocation to follow out the public implications of his experience. And, obviously, the State has a right to that experience, though it too rarely receives it. No one knows so much about the desirability of birth-control as the medical profession; but we probably know less of the views of the medical profession upon that question than we do of almost any other group in the community. No one knows as much about the desirability of a public defender as the legal profession; but our ignorance of its views is similar to our ignorance of the views of the medical profession upon birth-control. This is a sphere, it may well be, in which the quarterly meetings of vocations in different regions would have a special value. It would be possible there to collect the professional opinion of the locality; and a little ingenuity upon the method of eliciting opinion, and the majority necessary to enable a view to be presented as the prevailing view, is not very difficult. Otherwise, we are left to accept policies which may well represent the apogee of unwisdom. Take, for example, the question of vaccination. What is the predominant medical opinion upon the conscientious exemption clause? Many in England to-day believe that the medical profession is fairly divided upon the subject; and few will either study or understand the quite final statistics of Doctor MacDonnell.[47] But if the doctors spoke in a general way, we could avoid the laxity which now surrounds the law. Nothing is so integral to the proper fulfilment of professional purpose as the prevention of the wastage of its experience. We can hardly attempt too quickly the use of means to prevent the continuance of the present chaos in this regard.

### (vii) The Principle of Social Insurance

At the basis of any reconstruction of economic institutions must lie the conception of social insurance. Exactly as an individual seeks to safeguard his dependents against the consequences of death by life assurance, so must society protect itself against the avoidable risks of modern life by insurance against them. A non-insured class is always a burden upon society; an insured class is not merely a burden, but the wise administration of insurance is actually a definite gain in benefit to the society as a whole. For every scheme of insurance that is built upon the contributory principle is in fact built upon saving; and proper actuarial methods might make such savings a source not merely of individual security, but also of social prosperity.

I do not need to point out that in matters like health and unemployment the principle of social insurance has already been accepted in the two chief countries of Western Europe; and no one seriously proposes to abandon what is, quite frankly, the main security we have against revolution. But the substance of social insurance need not be limited to that narrow field. There is no reason in the world why every citizen should not, as a matter of course, be safeguarded against disablement from accident or disease, from old age (even when non-contributory pensions operate at sixty-five), against unemployment; and there would, equally, be State-endowment, on the same principle, of the widow and the orphan, of maternity, and of the education of children through at least that period we distinguish as secondary education.

Here we are in the realm of what may be termed compulsory social insurance. Each type of benefit is one that the State must directly undertake as a matter of elementary precaution. Such insurance should be compulsory, not only because the financial burden on the State becomes, otherwise, too heavy, but also because, properly administered, it inculcates the habit of thrift, and the sense in the citizen of a common interest with other citizens. I add that it is essential to the adequate working of these forms of social insurance that they should be unified into a nationalised industry.[48] There is no room in what is quite obviously a natural monopoly for the private company competing against other private companies. That way lies a wastefulness of which the price is unnecessarily paid by the insured person. The investigation of the working of private industrial assurance shows that, in England, only 48 per cent of the premiums collected are returned to the insured, and that the profits are excessively high.[49] So many policies lapse, moreover, that the annual loss to the holders reaches an enormous sum. The expenses of administration, the payment of directors, commissions to agents, the cost of collecting premiums, the expense of advertising, the enormous and unnecessary multiplication of offices—all these represent a waste that can at once be eliminated by State management.

That does not, of course, mean centralised management. There is no reason why, while the general control of finance is directed from a single office, there should not be a large measure of local autonomy in administration. I think myself that, once the idea of a national minimum of insurance is accepted, the most simple form of its administration would be its transference to the ordinary units of local government. That would have the great merit of enabling the local authority to experiment with schemes beyond the national minimum, and thereby to develop initiative in an urgent department of social welfare. It would permit the coordination of insurance policy with the health measures, the housing effort of, for instance, a municipal council; if the claims for sickness benefit in Manchester were unduly high, it would then be possible to ask questions of the medical officer of health. I assume, of course, the abolition of the right to contract out of the insurance minimum on the part of any area or vocation. The whole point of such a scheme as this is that it should be universal, and removed from the sphere of private profit-making. It is, I think, also clear that no local authority ought to be permitted to embark upon experiments in insurance without the approval of the central authority. The actuarial and investment risks in matters of this kind must be safeguarded by the maximum of knowledge.

The sphere of compulsory insurance is one, I submit, in which the profit-making motive is out of place. It is the protection of the community against inevitable social loss, and the corollary of such protection is the maximum possible return to the insured person within the area that it covers. Beyond that sphere, as experience may define its boundaries, the problem is a different one. Protection against fire, or burglary, or accidents inflicted by a motor-car, the desire to secure to one's children the certainty of the highest form of educational training, are all of them methods of insurance which are rightly left to the will of the individual citizen. He may feel that the chance of his house being robbed is so small that it is not worth paying against the risk. He may decide that if his son is capable of benefiting by a university education, the normal means of access thereto are adequate. Yet in all the normal forms of private insurance which remain after the needs of the State have been met, the case for making it a government monopoly is, I think, a final one. At every point in its administration economy of charges would be effected; and there would, as a result, be the means of increasing the return to the insured person. The experience of the United States in insuring the lives of its soldiers is evidence of the ease and efficiency with which a nationalised system could be administered. I see no reason why the State should not make reasonable profits out of the Post Office; and it could apply those profits to whatever purpose was deemed most wise at the given moment in each year when the Minister of Finance introduced his programme. Nationalised insurance, moreover, would place at the disposal of the government a great reserve for investment which it could use with great effectiveness is industrial development. There is no reason, either, to expect laxity of service or inadequate experiment with new forms. Such a department could be surrounded with bodies of organised critics in precisely the same way as any other industry. Insured persons could utilise every method they now adopt for their own protection, and they would enjoy the disappearance of enormous charges for services which such a unification would immediately make superfluous.

It is not, I think, possible to exaggerate the importance to the community of an adequate system of social insurance. Whatever the character of the State, whether it retain its present form, or whether it become practically communist, it will need to secure itself against the inevitable costs of life. There will always be sick persons; old age is an inescapable burden; not even the wisest social scheme can prevent the maladjustments which will occur through a bad harvest in Russia for a poor monsoon in India. Every parent with children to educate will find the cost of that education a growing burden upon themselves. It is, therefore, the obvious part of wisdom to meet these problems with the least possible cost to the community as a whole. Nor can we offer immunity to any from the obligations they entail. State insurance then becomes as obvious as a State post office, or a State police force. And the higher the minimum of the service is set, the richer, in the end, the community will be. We shall not need the vast relief-services of the modern State, its poor-law system, for instance, once we are able to put the problems which make the poor law necessary upon the footing of insurance. We shall not compel the hospital to rely upon the casual donation, to face, as it continually faces, the danger of inadequate equipment, or impossibility of experiment, when it has the right to call upon the medical insurance fund for the services that it offers; when, also, the citizen can go to the hospital as of right, in the knowledge that the charge of his treatment is borne by the insurance he has paid. We can, in brief, immensely multiply the certainties of life by this means; and we can do it in such a way that the individual citizen is himself the means of their manufacture. The last twenty-five years have made the principle an elementary one in the life of the State. Our business is so to enlarge the sphere of its operation that we may realise the full implications of its promise.

## (viii) Property and Inheritance

I have throughout this book insisted on the importance of equality in the political relationships of any community. I have argued, further, that in the concept of equality in politics the key will be found to lie in the property-system of any given State. The manner in which property is distributed will always, in a system so largely individualist as our own, determine also the distribution of economic power. And it is inevitable that economic power should, in its turn, chiefly determine the distribution of political power also. For those who can decide not only what is to be produced but, also, the manner of its production clearly command the working lives of other men. Their decisions, doubtless, will be quite largely influenced by considerations in which economic motives have only a partial place. They will make concessions to the demands of humanitarianism, as in the Factory Acts. They will yield, as in the establishment of the checkweighman in a colliery, to the power of combination among the workers. But, at the base, the political system will practically reflect their interests to the degree that they are united in their consciousness of them. And in an age, like our own, of vast concentration of industrial capital it is unlikely that such consciousness will be lacking. Unless, therefore, the power of property is to dominate the rights of personality in a community, it is necessary to limit the opportunities of which it may seek to take advantage.

In part, at least, we have already provided for such limitation in the plan of industrial organisation here outlined. For in a nationalised industry, by definition, private profit making is excluded, and though there will doubtless be among its members those to whom, relatively speaking, a large salary will be paid, their power will arise not from the salary they receive, but from the service they perform; and it will be inherent in the method of performance that the possibility of autocratic control is removed from them. So, also, in that sphere of industry which I have argued is the natural sphere of consumers' co-operation. Here, again, the accumulation of property by the medium of profit is, *a priori*, ruled out of our discussion. The special expert may be well paid; but he will not be able to tax industry in the enormous way now characteristic of the captains of trade.

When private industry is concerned, it is not unlikely that some men will make large fortunes. Short of confiscation, I see no way in which, for instance, a man with the talents of Mr. Bernard Shaw can be prevented from earning a large fortune. Where industry is concerned, I believe myself that the methods of control here urged permit such fortunes to be earned with justice. The consumer and the producer alike are thereby enabled to share in the results of enterprise returning more than that share to which capital is entitled by the price it can command in the market. Where men choose to save, and to profit by the results of postponed consumption, I see no reason why they should not be permitted to do so; on the condition always that the investment of their savings does not carry with it a power of exclusive industrial control. Where the income so obtained is unduly large, it is not difficult to correct its dangers by means of a graduated income-tax; and I believe that it will be possible in such a community as we here are envisaging to lighten the burden of taxation upon small incomes by its transference to the swollen revenues so characteristic, in our own time, of the millionaire class in the United States.

The real problems, I believe, lie in two directions. There is, in the first place, the question of the terms upon which industries now in private hands are to be transferred to public or quasi-public ownership; and there is, secondly, the question of inheritance. It is best to deal with the second question first, since the results reached in its analysis will be found, I think, quite largely to determine the other question. I have already argued that the only principle upon which the possession of private property can be justified is the performance of function. I own because I serve; I cannot own because someone else has served. And, ideally at least, what I own ought to have measurable relevance to what I do. A writer, for instance, of great poetry ought to be able to secure for himself that solitude without which great poetry cannot be written; for though Robert Burns might sing in the peace of exacting rural labour, it is not probable that he could have sung in the crowded misery of a Glasgow slum. A Prime Minister cannot adequately perform his work except under conditions which necessitate a somewhat larger income than would suffice for the comfortable maintenance of a policeman. I do not argue that the high-road to measurable relevance is either direct or easy; but, ultimately at least, it is a road we must seek to discover.

If, then, I can own only because I have served, it follows that there cannot exist an exclusive right of bequest. That will, accordingly, be limited in two ways. There will be limitation upon the amount of property I can bestow, and there will be limitation upon the persons entitled to receive it. The limitation of amount may, also, be regarded from two points of view. There will, firstly, be an absolute limitation upon a total fortune; the State will assume the position of universal heir to all estates over a certain sum. There will, secondly, be a limitation upon the amount of property any single person can receive as an inheritance.

Such a view is, of course, met by those who defend the existing order with the argument that it attacks the rights of property. The answer to that argument has been well put by John Stuart Mill. "The idea of property", he wrote,[50] "is not some one thing identical throughout history and incapable of alteration ... at any given time it is a brief expression denoting the rights over things conferred by the law or custom of some given society at that time; but neither on this point, nor on any other, has the law and custom of a given time and place, a claim to be stereotyped for ever. A proposed reform in laws or customs is not necessarily objectionable because its adoption would imply, not the adaptation of all human affairs to the existing idea of property, but the adaptation of the existing idea of property, to the growth and improvement of human affairs". Certainly no other method of approach to the problem has the right even to pretend to be scientific. Our views of the right to inheritance or bequest are utterly different from what they were even a generation ago. They change with time and place. They are not the outcome of any considered philosophic principle; and they have been continually adjusted to the pressure of new wants and new ideas.

Broadly speaking, we may consider inheritance, under the limitations noted above, from three special angles. There is (a) inheritance to a wife and children; there is (b) inheritance to collateral relatives or friends; there is (c) the special problem of the charitable bequest. Inheritance to a wife and children, obviously, has two distinct sides. The children may be immature or adult; the wife may, and, in the modern world increasingly will, be earning her own living. Let us take as the simplest instance, the case where the wife has been dependent upon her husband and the children are all in the early years of school. If property is to be related to function, to what are they entitled? The wife, I suggest, ought to receive by inheritance an income adequate to maintain that system of established habits which she has pursued in the life-time of her husband, the average standard of living, broadly speaking, to which she was accustomed in the last ten years of his life. We then enable her to avoid the break with the past which continuous expectation so often, and so naturally, makes painful and difficult. But she is entitled to it only in her own lifetime, or until remarriage. With her own death, her interest in it ceases, and it should revert to the State as the universal residuary legatee. Its purpose is then fulfilled, and can have no moral right to bestow what she has not earned. In the event of remarriage, equity suggests that she is entitled to such a share of that income as will, with the earnings of her second husband, bring their joint income up to the standard she enjoyed before remarriage; with, of course, the corollary that if the income of her second husband is larger than her income as a widow, the latter should revert to the State.

What is the position of the children in such an instance as I have assumed? Clearly, they are entitled to such maintenance during the period of immaturity as will give them the best education by which they can profit. They ought to be able to enter the battle of life without in any degree suffering from the premature death of their father. But they cannot, I think, be regarded as having such a title in his estate as will permit them, when the period of youth is over, to live by owning. They have no right to what, for them, would be the enjoyment of unearned increment. No children have the right to demand from their parents that they be left in circumstance which preclude them from exertion; for that is, in fact, a demand that they be left parasitic upon society. Society, may of course, agree that, in the period of maturity, they enjoy some small income which, while never sufficient to preclude the necessity of work, is yet the means of increased comfort; and I think myself that this is the method by which we shall transform the present mode of inheritance into one more capable of moral defence. But they will enjoy it only as income and not as capital. Upon their death, it will lapse again to the State. Their provision for their own children must be a matter for their own exertions. They ought not to be permitted to provide unless they have made the effort to provide. We cannot regard an estate as a permanent organism to which living people are functionless appendages.

What again, of inheritance where, on the death of the father, the children are already of mature age? They are then either earning their own livelihood, in which case they are receiving what society adjudges them to be worth, or parasitic upon their father, as in the case of an unmarried daughter who serves as an ornament in the parental home. In the first case, I suggest, equity is amply served by such an addition to income as will represent a modicum of increased comfort, without ever being large enough to permit the children to live by owning. In the second, it is ground either, where possible, for such an income as will, over a period, train the daughter to maintain herself, or, where that is impossible, offer her reasonable comfort in her own lifetime. The case for this view is the simple one put concisely by Mill in the remark that "it is really no grievance to any man that for the means of marrying and of supporting a family he has to depend on his own exertions."[51]

I assume these principles to be just whatever the testamentary disposition of the father. I assume, that if he dies intestate the children have an equal right to that share in his fortune herein implied; that, if he makes a will, he cannot unreasonably exclude either wife or children from participating in its benefits, if the latter are below legal age, though he may so exclude them if they are already dependent upon their own exertions. I admit, of course, that, short of revolution, it is unlikely that we shall attempt their practical application at a single stroke. More probably, we shall pass through a series of progressive stages in the diminution of inheritance. We shall increase the Death Duties and Inheritance Taxes. We shall permit estates up to, say, five hundred pounds, to be left undivided, and we shall compel the division of larger states until, for instance, the proportion of a millionaire's estate heritable by a single person may be only 1 per cent. I speak only of direct inheritance by a wife or children; and I am seeking to prevent the situation that has been well described by Professor Clay. "When a millionaire dies", he writes,[52] "his place is taken by another millionaire; the object of this type of proposal is to secure the dispersal of each generation's accumulation at the end of the generation, to enforce a continual redistribution of property, and to substitute a large number of small fortunes, for a small number of large fortunes. The rate of change would be set by the scale adopted, and the steepness of the scale would depend on the strength of society's desire for equality".

With collateral inheritance the problem is a different one. A man may be presumed to have a direct and immediate interest in the economic welfare of his children; there is no special reason to suppose that he has similar feelings, beyond a general sense of good-will, about his cousins or nephews. In the case, therefore, where there are no children at death, and the man dies intestate, there is no ground that I can see for allowing the estate to pass to indirect heirs. It is not to be assumed that the fortune was accumulated on their behalf; evidence that this was the case ought always to be the conclusive evidence built upon the production of a will. There is no right on the part of collaterals to expect to inherit; except, indeed, in the case of entailed estates, such inheritance is, in most cases, probably a surprise. On general principles, therefore, I suggest that intestacy should, where the dead man has left no children, leave the State free to take the estate to itself. It will be easy to make special provision for family heirlooms and the like; indeed, contingently upon their not being sold, I see no reason why they should nor pass free of legacy duty. What is mainly involved is the prevention of the endowment by accident of persons whose protection cannot, by the fact of intestacy, be assumed to have been the purpose by which the deceased was moved.

The case, is, I think, slightly different where a will is actually made. Here the motive of a legacy may be entirely admirable. A man may desire to recognise service from a friend, or to recompense the devotion of a relative. In general, the principle upon which such cases should be decided is, it may be suggested, twofold. In the case of simple gifts which do not involve a serious addition to income, which do not, that is to say, permit the legatee to live by owning, equity is not outraged by leaving them untouched. They even have a real value, quite apart from the sentiment they embody; a teacher, for instance, who receives a legacy of two hundred pounds may well find that the travel upon which she decides to spend it makes all the difference to her life. In such cases as this, interference by the State does not appear to be necessary; for gifts of this kind do not involve a power seriously to affect the life of the community. Nor, *mutatis mutandis,* is there serious ground for interference where a man endows a sister or niece who has shared his house with him over a period of years. Here it is entirely reasonable that he should recognise the devotion of such service by leaving them a moderate income the capital by which shall pass to the State upon her decease. But immediately large sums are in question, the case for limitation is a final one, especially when, as in Anglo-Saxon communities, it is not seldom the case, the bequest is accompanied by limiting conditions which seriously impair the legatee's freedom of action. Bequests, for instance, contingent upon marriage within a certain time, or upon the condition that the legatee does not change his religion, ought always to be regarded as illegal on grounds of public policy; for such a binding of the will of one who lives to the purpose of one who is dead is a mental slavery of a peculiarly obnoxious kind. In general, then, I urge that all bequests, either to friends or collateral relatives, should be void of such limiting conditions as I have noted, and should never be of such amount as will make it unnecessary for the legatee to live by his own exertions.

Much more complex questions are raised by what are termed charitable bequests. To leave property for public uses is, in general principle, a meritorious act; it is a good instance of that quality called by Aristotle munificence.[53] But an examination of the problem makes it appear less simple. It is, for example, unjust that a man should found a place of education and dictate in perpetuity what doctrines should be taught there. It is, as Mill pointed out,[54] "impossible that anyone should know what doctrines will be fit to be taught after he has been dead for centuries". Clearly each generation has its own ideas; and while there is good reason why a man who endows, for instance, a Roman Catholic college in his own lifetime should not see it turned while he lives into a Jewish seminary, there is no reason why, after a suitable period, he should be able to control its developments. The right, therefore, of each endowed institution to alter its purpose, say once in fifty years, is, I think, clear; and if protection were needed against wanton perversion, as in the classic case of Serjeant's Inn,[55] it could easily be found by requiring reference to a body like the Charity Commissioners in England. There is, indeed, good ground for making it proper for such a body to receive applications for the alternative use of a bequest, or the waiving of any conditions attached to it, immediately it has been paid over. The testator, for instance, who founded a school of economics in a great American university on condition that the virtues of a protective tariff were taught there, will be felt by most to have gone beyond the bounds of reasonableness. Experience has shown that few institutions are strong enough to avoid the desire to please their rich friends; American education has notably suffered by its sacrifice of academic freedom to the search for endowment.[56] It is only by insisting that the power to endow shall at no point involve even the power to make use of endowment specific and permanent that we shall avoid not merely being ruled by the dead, but also the effort to please the living at the expense of conviction.

But to permit bequests to be generally applied in this fashion without some power of social control would be disastrous. There is no limit to the eccentricity of testators. The good lady who, three-quarters of a century ago, left the whole of her considerable fortune to propagate the sacred writings of Joanna Southcote only illustrates the imagination of which a testator may be capable. I think, therefore, that in all cases it should be necessary to establish that the purpose endowed is rational and not contrary to a public policy interpreted in a liberal way, and that in all cases where the bequest amounts to a considerable sum, those endowed should be required to submit schemes for its use to the body charged with the supervision of charitable bequests. For, otherwise, there will always be the danger, first, that the bequest will, like the endowment of much English education, be quite wantonly perverted,[57] and, secondly, that the money will be frittered away upon objects that cannot be expected to secure a reasonable return upon the outlay. The present habit, for instance, of American millionaires of establishing by bequest large general funds held absolutely at the discretion of a small number of trustees confers upon the latter an immense power and prestige of which the consequences might easily be sinister. Society is entitled to protect itself against possibilities of this kind. For either such funds are controlled by voluntary trustees, in which case their supervision is almost inevitably inadequate, or they are controlled by a permanent staff to which there then accrues a power of interference which has often, in modern experience, reached dangerous dimensions. It is a power analogous to that of a proprietor of a great newspaper. It makes them able, unless there are countervailing conditions, to control the actions, and the ideas, of those who grow to rely upon them for assistance.

It is said that such safeguards as are here suggested will diminish the incentive to enterprise, and that society will suffer from such diminution. That the motive to effort in many is the desire to benefit their children I do not deny; but it is a motive traversed by the social interest of safeguarding the community against the growth of a class that is not required to exert itself to live. I believe myself that, outside a man's children, the desire to endow others is not a motive of real importance; and of the former it still remains true, as Mill remarked,[58] that, "in a majority of instances the good, not only of society, but of the individuals, would be better consulted by the bequeathing to them a moderate rather than a large provision". Every child, as he said, has a claim to a successful start in life, but it is socially disastrous to render him independent of his own effort. Indeed, it may in general be argued that, apart from the parental impulse to safeguard one's children, the real purpose of monetary accumulation is power; and I have already argued that such power is, by its very nature, illegitimate, since it can so rarely be referred to moral principle. And, surely, that would be inevitably a better and a richer society in which no one could assume that the means of life were at his disposal unless he earned them. We should, thereby, avoid what poisons so much of our effort to-day: the conspicuous waste of a few, with the feverish exertion of many to emulate and copy that conspicuous waste. To make the irrational luxury of a few the source of social prestige is to multiply in society every avenue of meaningless waste that it can exploit. We must set our canons of conduct by other standards.

If this analysis be justified, we have a method of approach to the problem of what should be the mechanisms to be used in transforming a private into a public industry. Broadly speaking, there are three avenues of transformation. It is possible to confiscate, as in revolutionary Russia. It is possible to compensate by purchasing the industry at a valuation, and giving to the former owners either money or bonds in return. It is possible, finally, to attempt partial compensation by taking over the industry and paying to the owners a limited sum either in the shape of a capital sum or of annuities. I shall argue that the third of these methods is probably the best at our disposal.

Confiscation, of course, makes a dramatic appeal to those who are impatient of the present system. They see the injustices upon which it has been built. They cannot discover any defence for those injustices; and they realise that attempts at defence—those made, for instance, by the owners of mining royalties before the British Coal Commission in 1919[59]—are too absurd to stand analysis. They point out that the United States of America, in which private property is more firmly entrenched than anywhere else in the world, suppressed the liquor industry without a penny of compensation. They insist that most landowners, for instance, in Great Britain, have acquired their possessions without service of any obvious kind. They do not think that the State can afford to assume the burden which full compensation would involve. But the answer to this view is, I think, a final answer. The first result of so drastic a step as confiscation is the evolution of ill-will. That ill-will has two consequences, as in Russia, of a disastrous character. It leads to sabotage by the directive ranks of an industry at a time when we can least afford it; and, if it is confiscation on any large scale, it leads to an attempt, which may be a successful attempt, at fascism. It is, I think, a practical truth of the first importance that it is always wise for statesmen to avoid the disappointment of established expectations so long as they can be abridged to reasonable dimensions. The community may pay a higher price in money; but the gain in the good-will that accrues is always, I think, more than compensation for that price. And the amelioration of the transaction for many who would otherwise find the task of adjustment hard is no light boon. A case like that of prohibition in America is not really in point, since there the industry was not continued but suppressed. And, in any case, there is the precedent on the other side of the payment to West

Indian slave-owners in 1833. Morally, doubtless, it would be most difficult to justify that payment; but on the ground of a wise expediency it is difficult to question it. I do not deny that in many cases the logical ground for confiscation is irrefutable; but it is, I think, an instance where to follow the strict path of logic is to fall into grave error. For in politics the best means always the best possible; and prudence in the measurement of possibilities is the first virtue in a statesman.

Compensation, on the other hand, is a relative item. No community could afford to give a body of owners the price they would demand for their possessions. That is clear for two reasons. In the first place, to arrive at a true valuation of most industries has become an almost impossible research. They do not represent a genuine value. Many of them, notably, for instance, the railways, have been built most wastefully;[60] most of them are founded upon a basis of capitalisation which represents no genuine assets of any kind. The Lancashire cotton mills, for example, changed hands in the boom of 1919 at fantastic prices; and their valuation, to be in any way sane, would at least have to go back to 1913, and in many case farther. That artificial element, moreover, known as good-will, is, as the history of liquor licences bears witness, a morass from which a community will make its way out only after the gravest difficulties. In most industries, national purchase on any terms acceptable to the owners would saddle the State with a burden of debt which would either mean low wages to the producer or high prices to the consumer. And, secondly, it would have the further danger of offering to the owner property rights which would perpetuate rather than diminish the existing differences between classes. Just as the owners of the national debt are the most solidly entrenched of all proprietors to-day, so the owners of bonds upon national industries would be similarly entrenched. The thing for which we are concerned is to obviate a situation where a class of owners can remain parasitic upon the community. The ordinary formulae of compensation are powerless to help us in this regard.

We are left, therefore, with the third of our three avenues of transformation. That would consist, as I have already briefly suggested, in the payment of annuities to the actual holder of property rights in the given industry during his lifetime; with, of course, the corollary that those rights would pass absolutely to the State at his death. The owner of mineral royalties in coal, for instance, would continue to receive year by year what he was accustomed to receive in, say, a five year period before the transformation was accepted, but on his death no further royalties would be paid. Similarly with the owners of railway shares, or shipping shares, or bank shares. We should then have the assurance that within a measurable period the maintenance of functionless ownership would cease to be a charge upon any nationalised industry. We should disappoint no reasonable expectations. We would even make special provision for hard cases, like those of the widow and the orphan. We could offer the alternative of a lump sum in compensation to those who preferred it, though in this case it would, I think, be necessary to pay a lower rate of compensation than was represented by the annuity system. The great point, as I see it, of this method is that it enables us at once to meet established expectations, and at the same time to see a definite period within which there will be no class that lives only by reason of idle ownership. If it be said that cases will occur in which the sudden death of a proprietor will practically make the extinction of his ownership amount to confiscation, the answer is, I think, that provision would easily be made for making the minimum term of the annuity at least ten years, though the limitation would be important that the death before that period of the proprietor could create rights for his children only. The community can rarely afford not to be generous in its dealings with property. It cannot, indeed, afford to mortgage the prospects of prosperity to existing owners at any given time; but it need not seek to make the transition more difficult for them than the total economic interests of the community seem to require.

There is one argument usually urged against views such as I have here advocated upon which a word is necessary. If, it is said, men are prevented from leaving their property to their children after death, the only result will be that they will divide it in their own lifetime; and, thereby, the whole purpose of this scheme will be vitiated at the outset. I believe myself that the effects of *donationes inter vivos* can easily be exaggerated. If the gift is small—a donation, for instance, of a few hundred pounds—it hardly becomes relevant to the problem we are discussing. If it is large, it will normally be discovered and so reached by means of income-tax. It is likely that such taxes will, where unearned income is concerned, be larger in the future than in the past, and the benefits of such gifts will, accordingly, be lessened. They may also, moreover, be met by an extension of the present law of inheritance in England whereby *donations inter vivos* are taxable as part of the testator's estate, if they are made within three years of his death. It would be possible, further, for all inherited wealth to be placed under the control of official trustees, in which case the testator would be able to divert out of income only. Nor is that all. Anyone who studies day by day the habits of wealthy men, as their wills reveal those habits, will realise that they do not, in general, desire to distribute their possessions in their lifetime. Their acquisitive faculty is satisfied only by the contemplation of their riches. To distribute them before death is no diminish their power, and the vanity which is met by the exercise of that power. That is notable, for example, in the case of charitable bequests. Men endow institutions after their death rather than during their lifetime, even if such endowment involves the taxation of the benefit the institution will receive. These habits will probably always govern those in whom the instinct to accumulate is strong. Where, finally, an attempt is made to evade the law by a contract of sale which is in fact fictitious, the courts have already—for instance, under the bankruptcy laws, and in, America, in the famous case of *In re Gould*—shown themselves willing to go behind the fictitious contact to the real substance it seeks to conceal.[61]

### (ix) Conclusion

So far I have discussed economic institutions as though each nation-State was a self-contained unit, independent of world conditions. That is not, of course, the case. It has become finally clear that international relations are the governing factor to which all economic change must ultimately be referred. Russia cannot exist as a communist State when she is surrounded by capitalist communities. England cannot be prosperous except upon the condition that the countries to which she is accustomed to export are prosperous also. We are learning, moreover, that it is increasingly urgent to establish international standards in certain spheres of economic life. The English cotton industry cannot survive against Indian and Japanese competitors if the wage-standards of the latter are infinitely below those which obtain in Lancashire. The American worker in the steel industry of Pittsburg cannot maintain his wage-standard unimpaired if cheap labour from Poland and Ruthenia is to swamp his market. The English miner is bound to be unemployed if his time-unit of labour, upon which the setting cost of coal will depend, is a seven-hour day, compared with a ten-hour day in German mines. And wage-standards in general are bound to mean little unless there exist (a) a general assurance of a continuous and adequate food-supply for the world and (b) international control of those basic raw materials upon which the industrial life of any community depends. We need, also, the maintenance of free and equal access to the means of communication. For it is obvious that if Great Britain, for instance, were able to impose discriminatory tolls upon foreign vessels using the Suez Canal, or America upon foreign vessels using the Panama route, equitable commercial relations would be impossible. Clearly, further, the colonies of the world, and especially the colonies mainly peopled by subject races, must offer equal commercial privileges to all communities. For, as Sir Arthur Salter has said, "a large proportion of the world's wars have obviously resulted from the abuse of the power of government in order to secure an undue commercial economic profit by means of the political force and the military force which it commands".[62]

I shall deal in a subsequent chapter, though necessarily in the most tentative way, with the institutions implied in these hypotheses. Here it will be sufficient to point out the broad considerations they involve. They mean that our conception of the nature and functions of a League of Nations must be at least as much economic as purely political. They mean, further, that such a body as the International Labour Office must grow into an organ of effective government, setting minimum standards of labour all over the world, and limiting, by insistence upon those standards, the power of national governments to be the final arbiter of their level of economic civilisation. I do not think they necessarily imply a single body, an executive or a legislature, seeking to deal with such vast problems. Almost inevitably, as I shall seek to show, each function will need its separate organ of authority and control. We shall need a commission to deal with oil, a commission to deal with coal, a commission to deal with the wheat supply, and so on. Behind these conceptions there obviously lie two general conceptions of the first importance. We shall have to ration our resources in the interest of international conservation, exactly as, during the war, the allies were compelled to ration the use of essential commodities. We shall, further, have to utilise the principle of priority. First things first is an obvious necessity in international economics. We cannot allow petrol to be used for pleasure-cars if there is a lack of petrol for ocean-going cargo ships. We shall have to develop, as the basis of social organisation, a statistical service which will provide the fullest possible knowledge of the production, the stocks, and the consumption of each commodity of which the use has international significance. Admittedly, there is no region of life in which progress is likely to be so slow as here; but, also, there is no region in which the fact of progress will produce more assured results.

Half a century has passed since Matthew Arnold warned the English people to choose equality and abjure greed.[63] The warning has a universal significance. No nation can hope to survive, no civilisation has ever survived, in which there is a permanent division of its people into rich and poor. That has been finally impossible since the invention of printing made access to knowledge universal, and the invention of mechanical transport made a unified economic system inevitable. We live under a system of which the moral assumptions are rejected by the majority of those affected by them. It is unable to retain their loyalty or their affection. It arouses in many a desire for its active overthrow which, given their possession of political power, must lead either to concessions or to revolution. The latter, as I have argued, is probably incompatible with the maintenance of civilised life; for, if it is attempted on any large scale, its destructiveness will reduce the standard of living for vast populations to the level of the Indian ryot. But if we are to avoid revolution, the concessions must be large enough to assure a world-order in which the average man is assured of the opportunity to realise his best self. That means, as Arnold said, equality; and equality means, undoubtedly, great sacrifice on the part of those who now enjoy the gain of living while bearing very partially the cost of that gain. The system of institutions here outlined is, in the economic sphere, an effort to depict what those concessions will involve. They do not meet the time-problem involved. Probably they will be most effective as they grow gradually into acceptance; for new habits need a period in which to realise their fruition. But it is important to remember that the time-problem is not determined solely by the classes in the possession of power. They are required by the conditions of our age to offer proof that within the categories of the existing order great improvements are possible. They have to prove their good-will to the disinherited. Only as that proof is rapid and substantial shall we be able to maintain the best prospects of the human race.

## REFERENCES

1. *Self-Government in Industry* (ed. of 1919), p. 151.
2. *Our Social Heritage*, chap. vi.
3. *Self-Government in Industry*, p. 237.
4. Cf. for details in Great Britain the Report on *Works Committees* of the Ministry for Labour, and, for America, the similar report published by the Bureau of Industrial Research in New York. For Germany, see the Report of the International Labour Office of January 1921 on *Works Councils in Germany*.
5. Cf. *Report on the Establishment and Progress of Joint Industrial Council*, H.M. Stationary Office, 1923, pp. 70-1.
6. *Ibid.*, p. 83.
7. *Self-Government in Industry*, p. 217. But all Mr. Cole's suggestions in this matter seem to me to show less than his usual insight.
8. On the Knox Strike, G.D.H. Cole and R.P. Arnot, *Trade Unionism and the Railways*, p. 33.
9. On the working of such Discipline Boards see Cole and Arnot, *op. cit.*, chaps. vii and ix. The court-martial system in the army in time of peace is an approach to a similar idea.
10. Cf. H. Finer, *Representative Government and a Parliament of Industry*, p. 54, and especially the survey noted in note 4 on that page. Mr. and Mrs. Webb undertook a survey of professional associations in the *New Statesman* for October 2, 1915, and April 21-28, 1917; but the situation has much changed since then.
11. On the movement as a whole see Sidney and Beatrice Webb, *The Consumers' Co-operative Movement*; Percy Redfern, *The History of the C.W.S.* L.S. Woolf, *Co-operation and the Future of Industry*. For the statistics of the movement the *People's Year Book*, published by the Co-operative Union, and the *Annual Report of the International Co-operative Alliance* should be consulted. See also L.S. Gordon and C.O'Brien, *Co-operation in Many Lands*.
12. Woolf, *op. cit.*, pp. 104-5.
13. See, for instance, the *Report of the General Co-operative Survey Committee*, p. 194, (1919).

14. Cf. Sidney Webb, *The Constitutional Problems of a Co-operative Society* (Fabian Tract No. 202), pp. 16-17.
15. *The Need for Federal Reorganisation in the Co-operative Movement* (Fabian Tract No. 203), p. 25.
16. L.S. Woolf, *Socialism and Co-operation*, chap. iv, especially p. 103.
17. Senate Report No. 606, 53rd Congress, 2nd Season.
18. Testimony of the President of the American Sugar Refining Company, especially at pp. 351-2, quoted by H.J. Ford, *The Rise and the Growth of American Politics*, p. 318.
19. Report of the Committee on Trusts (1919) p. 3.
20. See the estimates of Lord Russell of Killowen, quoted in Webb, *Decay of Capitalist Civilisation*, p. 67.
21. See *The Times* of August 25, 1924, for comment on this situation.
22. *Wealth of Nations* (Everyman's Edition), ii, 229.
23. As in the case of G.L. Bevan and his companies.
24. Cmd. 8880, p. 5.
25. *Fifth Report* of the Industrial Fatigue Research Board, p. 95.
26. See, for instance, its Report for 1916.
27. See his admirable *Incentives in the New Industrial Order*, especially chap. iv.
28. *The Problem of Nationalisation*, p. 17.
29. *Final Report* (1916), *passim*.
30. *Development of the Civil Service*, p. 73.
31. Cf. *Report of the Committee on Trusts*, Cd. 9236 of 1919, p. 2.
32. It will be obvious how much this analysis of functions owes to "the model form" issued by the Ministry of Labour in England. See their report on *Joint Industrial Councils*, 1923, pp. 204-5.
33. E.M.H. Lloyd, *Experiments in State Control*, p. 381.
34. *Report of Committee on Trusts*, p. 25.
35. *Report on the Progress of Joint Industrial Councils* (1923), p. 206.
36. Cf. B. Jones, *Co-operative Production*, and C.E. Raven, *Christian Socialism*, chaps. vi and x.
37. But their future must be regarded as in the highest degree experimental and dubious. Co-operative banking, which might perform a similar function, is a different matter.
38. *Chaos and Order in Industry*, p. 156. The italics are Mr. Cole's.
39. See on all this the excellent remarks of Mr. J.A. Hobson, *Incentives in the New Industrial Order*, pp. 50 f.
40. On the problem of revolution in general see L. Trotsky, *The Defence of Terrorism*; B. Russell, *Practice and Theory of Bolshevism*, Part II, chaps. ii, vi, vii; and my *Communism* (1927), *passim*.
41. Engels, *Condition of the Working Classes in England in* 1844; Charles Booth, *London*; B.S. Rowntree, *Poverty*; Karl Marx, *Capital*, vol. i, especially chaps, x, xv, xxv.
42. London, *Times*, September 8, 1924.
43. *Constitution for a Socialist Commonwealth*, p. 276.
44. On this see the conclusive argument of Mr. J.T. Murphy in his paper *The Unit of Organisation*, published in the fifth number of the Re-organisation of Industry Series by Ruskin College.
45. As given, for instance, by Mr. Murphy in the essay just referred to on p. 15.
46. See Wallas, *Our Social Heritage*, p. 130, where the quotation is given in full with a characteristic comment.
47. *Biometrika*, vol. i. p. 375, and vol. ii, p. 135.
48. Cf. Sir W. Beveridge, *Insurance for All, passim*. His figures are based on the existing

English scheme, but there is no reason why they should not be largely increased upon the basis of increased premiums.

49. Cf. the Holman Gregory Report, 1922, Cond. 816, and Sir W. Beveridge's remarks, *op. cit.*, p. 10.
50. Quoted from Mill's posthumous essays on Socialism in the *Fortnightly Review* for 1879 by Sir W.J. Ashley in note K to his edition of Mill's *Principles of Political Economy*, p. 989. For Mill's own earlier views on inheritance cf. *ibid.*, pp. 221 ff.
51. *Principles of Political Economy* (ed. Ashley), p. 225.
52. *Property and Inheritance*, p. 29.
53. *Politics*, ii, 5, 1263a.
54. *Principles of Political Economy* (ed. Ashley), 228.
55. *The Times*, April 10, 1902.
56. Cf. Upton Sinclair, *The Goose-step*, and the earlier warning of Mr. J.A. Hobson, *The Crisis of Liberalism*, pp. 218 f. See also my article *Research, Foundations, and the Universities*, in *The Dangers of Obedience, and Other Essays*, (1930).
57. Cf. H.T. Wilkins and J.A. Fallows, *English Educational Endowments, passim.*
58. *Op. cit.*, p. 224.
59. *Minutes of Evidence*. Evidence of the Duke of Northumberland, Lord Dynevor, the Earl of Durham.
60. L.C. Money, *The Triumph of Nationalisation*, pp. 10-15.
61. Cf. Dalton, *The Inequality of Incomes*, pp. 325 f., for a discussion of this question.
62. *Allied Shipping Control*, p. 268.
63. *Mixed Essays*, p. 49.

# 10. The Judicial Process

## (i) The Importance of the Judiciary

"The importance of the judiciary in political construction", Henry Sidgwick has written,[1] "is rather profound than prominent. On the one hand, in popular discussion of forms and changes of Government, the judicial organ often drops out of sight; on the other hand, in determining a nation's rank in political civilisation, no test is more decisive than the degree in which justice, as defined by the law, is actually realised in its judicial administration, both as between one private citizen and another, and as between private citizens and members of the government". Certainly no man can over-estimate the importance of the mechanisms of justice. There have been few greater avenues to freedom than that beaten out by the writ of *Habeas Corpus*. There have been few guarantees of equity more solid than that clause in the Act of Settlement[2] which declares that the judges of England shall hold office *quam diu se bene gesserint*. What seem, on the surface, insignificant procedural changes—as when a man becomes entitled before trial to a copy of the indictment upon which he is charged, or is able, in the witness-box, to testify upon his own behalf, or may appeal from the verdict of a jury and the sentence of a judge to a body of legal experts beyond them—these, for all their forbiddingly technical character, are more nearly related to freedom than the splendid sentences in which Rousseau depicts the conditions of its attainment. Obviously, therefore, the men who are to make justice in the courts, the way in which they are to perform their function, the methods by which they are to be chosen, the terms upon which they shall hold power, these, and their related problems, lie at the heart of political philosophy. When we know how a nation-State dispenses justice, we know with some exactness the moral character to which it can pretend.

I have already argued that the independence of the judiciary from the executive is essential to freedom. In that sense, the doctrine of the separation of powers enshrines a permanent truth. For it is obvious that if the executive could shape judicial decision in accordance with its own desires, it would be the unlimited master of the State. The interpretation of the law must, therefore, be entrusted always to a body of persons whose will cannot be bound by the will of the executive. They must be able to call the executive to account. They must be able to resolve disputes between private citizens in such fashion as to make their decision an equitable precedent for cases of a similar kind. They are seeking, as judges, to evolve from the competing social interests which appear before them a solution which maximises the public advantage. They are making from a given and particular instance a universal rule by which the conduct of other men will be shaped and determined. It is clear that the more independent their position, the more likely they will be to realise the purpose of their institution.

What is the general nature of the proceedings which take place in a court of law? Its business is the resolution of a complaint. A states that he has been wronged by B, whether A is a public or a private person. It is necessary, first, to investigate the facts. Did B truly wrong A? Does what B has done truly constitute a wrong? If it does, what is the penalty for the wrong committed? Certain difficulties in this process must be borne in mind. The court finds the law, but in finding it the court also makes it. No statute has ever been drawn that has covered or can cover the infinite variety of acts of which human ingenuity is capable. Some will be covered by a statute, as when a man forges banknotes and meets the penalty involved. Others may be included by what the court will deem the intent of the legislature, as when the court holds that a particular statute was intended to cover a class of cases not hitherto included within its ambit. Others, again, will be settled by the judge evolving a principle to meet them from what he deems the implications of social experience. Others, once more, will be settled by reference to a judicial precedent which was, in its day, an induction from what an earlier judge believed to be the lesson of an earlier experience, his view being, for sufficient or insufficient reasons, held to control the actual case in dispute. Each case may be a species of a larger genus; but the observer will note always its uniqueness, and that effort is required to bring it within the ambit of the factors by which decision is controlled.

The fact of that effort is of the first importance. The judge who makes it moves one way, rather than another way. What are the sources of information by which his motion is decided? Certainly, they are larger than most will be concerned to admit. Statute and precedent are relatively simple; but when, for instance, the Supreme Court of the United States held that a New York statute prohibiting night work in bakeries was unconstitutional under the Fourteenth Amendment, whatever moved their effort, it was neither statute nor precedent.[3] So, also, when the House of Lords handed down the Osborne judgment,[4] the moving cause of their decision lay outside the simpler sources of law; what the majority of them said, a body of trade unionists trained in the law would not have said. When, again, the *Conseil d'Etat,* in the Pluchard case,[5] held that the French State was responsible for the negligence of its agents, it was making new law, outside of statute and of precedent. Whereby was it so moved? There are judges whose sentences in sexual cases are notoriously light, there are others who, in similar cases, inflict punishment of the utmost rigour. There are benches of magistrates in England where conviction for violation of the Factory Acts is punished severely; there are others where the penalty inflicted is almost always nominal. What have we to take into account in our effort to grasp the working of the judicial mind?

The only possible answer, I think, is that the judge will decide, where he is not, as in the cases I have noted, obviously bound down by statute and precedent, by his conception of what ought to be the law; and that conception will be determined by what William James called his sense of the "total push and pressure of the cosmos". To that test all issues before him are ultimately brought. "We may try", writes a distinguished American judge,[6] "to see things as objectively as we please. None the less, we can never see them with any eyes except our own". That is the answer to Mr. Justice Holmes' plea that law and morals live their lives upon different planes. For as soon as the judge is free to make law, the guide he follows, the test he applies, is the experience of life that he knows. No one can read the summing up of Braxfield in the trial of Muir for high treason without seeing that his interpretation of life was the simple one that all political reformers are *a priori* guilty of high treason.[7] The decision of the House of Lords in the *Taff Vale Case*[8] was an obvious decision from men who had no experience of the conditions under which trade unions must work. The majority of the Supreme Court in *Coppage* v. *Kansas*[9] had never been driven to learn why the open shop is the controlling factor in low standards of labour. Law, therefore, is always made in terms of what life has meant to those who make the law. Nor is that conclusion invalidated by the fact that great judges, like Mr. Justice Holmes, are able in rare instances to transcend the limitations of experience and see the issue in a wider perspective.

Obviously, therefore, of law as made by the courts this must first be said, that it can never be a final source of State-decision. It represents only what its makers represent. It is limited by the narrow experience the average judge will possess, the certainty, in the field especially of industrial relations, that he will find it usually difficult, and often impossible, to grasp a point of view usually alien from what he himself has known. The larger, therefore, the field in which the legislative assembly can lay down rules of general guidance, the more will the courts be able to respond to the popular sense of justice. And no legislative assembly ought ever to be hampered by so complex a constitutional procedure as that which makes the Supreme Court of the United States the effective master of social change. Nothing is more likely to engender disrespect for law than the perception that experiments which have behind them a vast body of experience, and have proved acceptable to a legislative assembly, can be prohibited by a court on purely technical grounds which will almost always be found to conceal a dislike for the substance of the experiment prohibited. No constitution ever enacts a static philosophy; and those responsible for its judicial interpretation must always be careful lest they mistake their private prejudice for eternal truth.

A position of this kind gives, of course, special importance to two aspects of the judiciary. It makes the method of choosing judges one to be analysed with special care, and it makes the mechanism for the discovery of necessary legal change one that cannot be discrete and casual, but organised and continuous in character. I take first, the question of judicial appointment. Practically, we have a choice between two methods—election and nomination. The former is, the federal judiciary apart, the typical method in the United States; the latter is the English system, practically all judicial appointments being under the control of the Lord Chancellor. In France, Italy and Germany all judges are appointed by nomination; but in Switzerland the fourteen members of the Federal Court are elected by the legislative assembly. This method is followed by two American States; in six, the governor of the State recommends, and either the Council or the Senate confirms. In the remaining States, popular election for a term of years which may, as in New York, be as many as seventeen, is the rule.

Of all methods of appointment, that of election by the people at large is without exception the worst. For either the candidate is chosen for purely political reasons, which is the last ground upon which he should be made a judge, or those who vote for him are not in a position to weigh the qualities upon which his choice ought to depend. An electorate which had to choose, say, between Eldon and Erskine for judicial position would almost certainly choose the latter; and, almost certainly also, Lord Eldon had most of the equipment of a great judge, and Erskine none. Most of the great judges in recent English history, men like Blackburn, Bowen, Watson, Macnaghten, were entirely unknown to the public outside. The latter judges legal eminence largely by its political relations, on the one hand, and its position in the *causes célèbres* of crime upon the other. Candidates for judicial office cannot possibly but before an electorate either a programme, on the one hand, or a personal plea, on the other, which can have the slightest relevance to their future conduct. American experience, moreover, is, I think, clear, that the method of election hinders the independence of the judges, and, in general, attracts an inferior type of lawyer to the bench. That is particularly the case when the period of election is for only a short term of years. The position may perhaps best be put by saying that if the election is for life, probably the wrong type of man will be chosen, while if it is for a short term, the judge's conduct in office will be determined, at least partly, by considerations which should never be in his mind. The desire to court popularity is a temptation few will be able to resist when their re-election is dependent on their popularity. And, in America, it is notable that the highest tradition in judicial affairs among the States belongs to Massachusetts, where appointment is by nomination; while, in general, the federal judges, who are nominated by the President with the consent of the Senate, enjoy far greater esteem among the public than the judges of State courts. The judicial office, in brief, requires a technique competence for which is not a matter upon which public judgment is of much value. And dependence upon public judgment introduces elements into the decision which are better absent.

Election by the legislature is less open to objection; but it is still, I think, an undesirable form of appointment. For, once more, if the choice is to be made on grounds of legal fitness, the average member of a legislature has no special qualifications for judging, and he is therefore likely to be swayed by political considerations irrelevant to the problem. It is notable, for instance, that Republican Presidents of the United States have usually submitted Republican names to the Senate; and the one case, in recent years, where the Senate has stoutly fought appointment was a case in which the lawyer nominated had rendered distinguished service to organised labour.[10] The Swiss system of legislative election, on the other hand, has undoubtedly worked well; though it has been assisted therein, first, by the comparatively small size of the legislature, and secondly, by the fact that political appointments are virtually excluded from consideration by statute. The inability, moreover, of the court to declare federal legislation unconstitutional operates to diminish the likelihood that there will be deep antagonism to any candidate of real legal eminence. The temper of Swiss politics, indeed, makes legislative intervention in the judicial sphere much less noxious than it would be elsewhere.

For consider what would occur in the House of Commons, for instance, if the members were entitled to elect the judiciary. Obviously, there would have to be a small committee to sift the nominations made, and to report thereon to the House. If the report of the committee were accepted, and its nomination adopted as a matter of course, it would be possible, on one condition, to hope for reasonable results. That condition is that no member of the House itself should be eligible for appointment. But such a condition immediately excludes men of great eminence from the field of selection; and it practically compels a lawyer to choose between a legal and a political career in a most unfair way. If, on the other hand, the House rejected the report, the position would be an intolerable one. A sensitive person might well shrink from the ordeal involved. And even with the committee, the opportunities of wire-pulling, the attempt to gain illegitimate influence, the use of political prestige, would do much to lower the quality of appointment. And in any period of acute partisan temper, it would be difficult to suppress the tendency to make the judicial office the reward of party loyalty.

We are therefore thrown back upon nomination as the best available method of choice. But simple nomination, as in England by the Lord Chancellor, is not, I think, an adequate system. It leaves the door too wide open for measurement of fitness in terms of political eminence rather than judicial quality. It is notorious that Lord Halsbury used his power of nomination to elevate members of his own party, whenever possible. The position of the Lord Chancellor as a party leader makes him peculiarly liable to the pressure of men who feel that a place on the bench is a fair reward for party service; and there have been notorious cases in which a Lord Chancellor has not been strong enough to resist that pressure. It is, then, necessary to surround the power of nomination with safeguards. I do not myself think that a legislative committee is a satisfactory channel for that end. In America, it has always proved a means of reserving appointments to the party in office; and, even if the English judicial tradition is different, more satisfactory ways lie open to us. It would be possible, for instance, to make appointments on the recommendation of the Minister of Justice, with the consent of a standing committee of the judges, which would represent all sides of their work. They, after all, know the bar as few others can know it. They are not likely to be moved by political prestige. They are in the best possible position to assess the probable fitness of the men likely to prove successful on the bench. They would represent the best guarantee we could have that appointments were made only with the needs of the office in view.

I speak here, of first appointments. The question of promotion raises further problems. In most judicial systems, it is necessary to have a graded series of courts, ending in a supreme tribunal of which the decisions can only be reversed by the legislature. In England, appointments to these superior posts are technically made by the Prime Minister, though the Lord Chancellor is usually the effective source of choice;[11] in America they are made by the President with the concurrence of the Senate. No one can study the history of appointments to these higher posts, especially in the United States, without the sense that there is too little relation between them and membership of the inferior courts. A man who accepts a federal district judgeship in America practically excludes himself from the Supreme Court, and, in England, men distinguished in politics who decide upon a judicial career, usually go straight to such a position as the Mastership of the Rolls, or the House of Lords. To gain a reputation in America for a liberalising attitude in economic matters, is for a judge to rule himself out when promotion is in question. That has not been the case in England, but it is notable that the office of Chief Justice has, for almost half a century, been the reward of political service. Yet it is, I believe, not less important in the judiciary than elsewhere that the man whose services in a lower court are really distinguished should have a reasonable assurance of promotion in recognition of them. We do not want, of course, promotion on the ground of seniority; but we do not want an able judge to feel that he will not be passed over for some clever political hack who has known how to press his claims at the right time. I suggest, therefore, that when a vacancy occurs in a superior court (as in the Court of Appeal or the House of Lords in England) the committee of the judges should present to the responsible minister (whom I have here called the Minister of Justice) a list of, say, three names from the judges of the lower court from whom he shall select one for promotion. The danger that a political protege will be too rapidly advanced can easily be met by requiring that no judge shall be advanced who has not already served for five years in his present position; and the danger of merely promoting senior judges could be met by the proviso that no judge who is less than five years from the age of retirement shall be recommended for promotion.

Once appointed, a judge should obviously hold office during good behaviour; otherwise he cannot acquire that habit of independence inherent in his position. Good behaviour is sufficiently defined by the classic method of requiring a vote of the legislative assembly for his removal, and since we are visualising single-chamber government, such a vote, to be effective, should be supported by two-thirds of the members who take part in the division. That type of stringency is important, for a case in which high feeling is aroused in the public, or where the judge, with the best intentions, makes some observation which creates deep party resentment, might easily, in the absence of proper safeguards, either actually involve his removal or so damage his prestige as to make his continuance on the bench a matter of difficulty. There should, further, be a retiring age which might reasonably be fixed at seventy years. There are, of course, judges who, even at eighty, are capable of doing magnificent work. But, in general, after seventy, the average judge is less and less able to meet demands, particularly those of a new era, made upon him. "Judges", Mr. Justice Holmes has written,[12] "commonly are elderly men, and are more likely to hate at sight any analysis to which they are not accustomed, and which disturbs repose of mind, than to fall in love with novelties". That perception is important because, as I have already argued, it is the judge's experience of life that determines his attitude to the problems of law. Most people's philosophy, both in its conscious assumptions and its much more significant unconscious prejudices, is fairly fixed at forty; and thirty years later the average judge will belong to a generation of which the general outlook is very different from his own. Nor is that all. A judge, I imagine, is, in the first five years of his service, fairly convinced that most of his opinions are wrong in critical cases; in the second five years he will be equally convinced that they are right, and afterwards he will bear himself with serenity whether they be right or wrong. When that serenity becomes habitual, it is time for him to retire.

### (ii) The Judiciary and the Executive

That the judicial function requires removal from the sphere of executive influence I pointed out in an earlier chapter. But that removal needs to be discussed in the light of certain mechanisms and problems which are integral to its understanding. What, essentially, is here in issue is the problem of making the executive subordinate to the judiciary in all points which concern the interpretation of the law, where the judgment of the executive is questioned by a private citizen. I have already dealt partly with this question. I have argued that the State must be liable for the acts of its agents as an ordinary citizen is liable. I have argued, also, that even where, for purposes of convenience, judicial powers are conferred upon a department, the methods it utilises, the procedure it employs, shall be open to scrutiny by the courts, with the power to upset a decision which, in their view, has not been reached by adequate inquiry; the latter having reference, not to the finding of facts, but to the mode of investigating them. Unless this type of judicial supremacy is maintained, the executive will always have an overwhelming advantage against the private citizen; and the latter will be unable to invoke his rights against those who shelter themselves beneath the cloak of official acts.[13]

But there are certain other safeguards that are important. It follows, I think, from the method of judicial appointment here urged, that no member of a government in office should be appointed to a judicial position. Such appointment diminishes, I think, the chance that he can bring a really judicial mind to the range of legal questions in which the interests of the executive are involved. A man, for instance, who as Attorney-General, was responsible for such a statute as the *Restoration of Ireland* Act of 1920[14] is quite definitely not a suitable person to decide cases like *Ex parte O'Brien*; for there surrounds his mind a penumbra fatal to genuinely disinterested opinion. I would even go further and urge that persons who have acted as legal officers of the executive power ought to be disqualified from judicial office for a period of seven years. A man, for example, who, as Attorney-General of the United States, is responsible for the incredible prosecutions under the Espionage Act, cannot really recover in a short period that judicial frame of mind which will enable him to decide them reasonably upon the bench. The converse is, I think, also true. Once a man has attained judicial rank, he ought to be ineligible for political office. If candidates for the Presidency of the United States can be selected from the Supreme Court, a prize so glittering will not fail to sway the minds of some judges at least who sit there; and their decisions will follow the path to their ambition. If an English judge may hope to be Lord Chancellor, he can hardly avoid, in all cases where the authority of the executive is in question, remembering that ministration to its comfort will not be unlikely to bear its fruit. A judge may do his utmost to embody the pure spirit of reason; but that is not less cause for us, on our side, doing what we can to aid him in the process. A self-denying ordinance of this kind is here an assistance we may not neglect.

It follows from this that executive and judiciary must, so far as possible, abstain from mutual criticism of each other's work. There will, undoubtedly, be occasions when this is impossible; cases inevitably arise in which criticism is implied in the task of judgment. But two instances may be selected to illustrate what I mean. In *O'Dwyer* v. *Nair* it became necessary to review the riot at Amritsar in 1919.[15] In his summing-up to the jury, Mr. Justice McCardie, speaking, as he said, "with full deliberation", expressed the opinion that General Dyer, who had suppressed the outbreak, was unjustly condemned by the government for the part he had played. That was a view which, however important, was not strictly relevant to the case; and since the government had refused the evidence upon which General Dyer, rightly or wrongly, was condemned, he was not in possession of all the facts when he uttered his criticism of the executive. No one can doubt that he acted from the highest motives; but no one, I think, can doubt also that a judge .ought not to advise a jury, and through the jury the public at large, upon highly controversial questions of a non-legal character upon which the jury itself has to make no finding.[16] His actions led to vehement discussion in the House of Commons, and a notion was actually tabled for his removal from the bench. Most people will feel that the remedy proposed was unduly drastic, since the fault was, at the worst, an error of judgment made in all sincerity; but most people, also, will feel that such errors are bound to result in the effects to which Mr. Justice McCardie's action gave rise unless the judge is almost over-careful not to speak on any issue which does not fall directly and obviously within his province. So, also, when, in *United States* v. *O'Hara,* a member of the Socialist Party was on trial, it was a mistaken conception of the judge's function for the court to say that the Socialist Party, if it held the defendant's views, had "no place on the American soil either in times of war or times of peace".[17] That is a direct incitement to the executive, especially in a period of inflamed opinion, to use the courts generally, and one judge in particular, to silence opinion which it happens to find inconvenient.

Conversely, it is important for the judge that he should not be hampered in the performance of his duties by attack on the part of the executive power. Much of this danger is obviated by making his position secure against wanton dismissal; no judge, either in England or America, has been dismissed for two centuries and more in the manner of Sir Edward Coke.[18] But an Attorney-General of the United States has complained that the construction placed by certain courts on a clause in the Espionage Act of 1917 was so narrow that "most of the teeth which we tried to put in were taken out"—a remark that is little less than the assertion that some judges destroyed the effectiveness of urgent legislation; and the criticism was the more lamentable in that it was easy to discover to what judges he was referring. Even more remarkable was the attack of Daniel Webster, when Secretary of State, upon the opinion of the court (now generally held to be mistaken) in *The People* v. *McLeod*.[19] He denounced it, writes a distinguished lawyer, "probably in stronger terms than have been used in modern times by any responsible officer in regard to any judicial decision".[20] The denunciation was quite unnecessary; and the way in which the judge is hampered by an attack of that kind is too obvious to need comment.

A range of questions is relevant in this connection where the judicial function essentially consists in critical inquiry into government acts. Cases occur in which, for a variety of reasons, endeavour is made to control the situation by executive fiat, to the exclusion of judiciary inquiry. In some of those cases, as, for instance, whether a given State is at war with another State, it is obvious that the opinion of the executive authority must be final.[21] The same is broadly true where problems arise in relation to the recognition of a *de facto* government, though here it is probable that, in the future, recognition will be dependent upon the act of an international authority rather than of a temporary executive, since the problems involved, say in Mexico, where one set of powers do not recognise a government recognised by other powers gives rise to impossible situations. I have already discussed the problem of tortious acts committed in the name of the State. Anyone who remembers the purely historical reasons which govern the absence of liability will recognise the need here for change. The impossibility of the present position can best be illustrated by saying that while in England an action for trespass lies against the servants of the Crown, an action for ejectment will not lie;[22] though ejectment is the clear purpose of an action for trespass.

The real nature of the problems involved, however, appears in the relation of the courts to a situation of martial law. No one can doubt that there is a point in the suppression of disorder where it becomes a matter of duty on the part of the executive to take all necessary means for its suppression, and those means will involve the use of military force and the punitive measures such a force will adopt to secure the end for which it is used. How far ought the fact of martial law to operate so as to exclude the courts from inquiry into the offence alleged, and punishment where it is proved? With the technical nature of martial law I am not here concerned. The problems, from the standpoint of general political theory, with which the judicial authority is concerned are two in number. How far, firstly, can the courts allow their jurisdiction to be ousted on the ground of military necessity? How far, secondly, can the court accept as a defence to an action the plea that the action taken was done in the course of his duty by a person acting as a martial law official?

The answer to the first question can, I conceive, only be given in a general way. It is that so far as is humanly practicable it is the business of the judge to insist that no jurisdiction shall supersede his jurisdiction, that so long as his court can effectively function, no other courts can be permitted to function. For unless there is the utmost rigour in the maintenance of this view, it is certain, on the experience of history that there will be excesses in the administration of martial law. The temper I am urging as essential was, of course, nobly demonstrated by Chief Justice Fitzgibbon in the *Case of Wolfe Tone*.[23] Unless it is established that a military tribunal can punish, unless the civil courts literally cannot sit, abuses of authority are inevitable. We have ample experience of such abuses. Anyone who reads the evidence in, for example, *Ex parte Milligan*,[24] or *R.V. Nelson and Brand*[25] will be able to realise the way in which, as counsel for the petitioner put it in the Milligan case, "the executive department of government ... becomes absolute master of our liberties and lives".[26] I do not doubt that in the suppression, for instance, of rebellion it is necessary to punish both instantly and severely. But I think all the evidence goes to show the necessity of certain restrictions on the executive power, in a period of disorder, if the paramountcy of civil justice is to be maintained. (1) All trials under martial law, except for trivial offences, should be carried out by civil officials nominated by the judges for this purpose from a standing panel of barristers. (2) These tribunals should not have the power to inflict sentences of more than one year's imprisonment. (3) All trials for serious offences, involving a longer sentence than one year, should be held in the ordinary civil courts, and the accused should have the right to counsel. At these trials the ordinary procedure of criminal justice should obtain. (4) No person, when arrested under martial law, should be detained for more than twenty-four hours without a charge being formulated against him; nor should he be detained for longer than one week without being brought to trial. Where the circumstances necessitate a remand, the accused should be entitled to such treatment as will afford him full facilities to prepare his defence. (5) Every martial-law officer who proposes to create a new offence should be compelled to secure the assent to his proposal of two of the civil officials acting in the judicial capacity described above. In the event of their objection, his proposal should not become operative until the central government has confirmed it.

These may seem drastic proposals; but their justification will be apparent to anyone who considers the alternative to them. I take as an example a series of occurrences in the suppression of disorder in the Punjab during April and May of 1919.[27] Two men were arrested in Amritsar prior to the declaration of martial law and deported to an extreme part of the province; on the declaration of martial law, they were brought back to Lahore, which was in the martial-law area, and tried and sentenced by a special martial-law tribunal.[28] A number of pleaders were arrested at Gurdaspur, taken, under revolting conditions, to Lahore, and confined there in the common jail for a period lasting up to a month. They were then released, without any charges having been preferred against them; on the evidence, indeed, it seems difficult to know of what they could have been charged. In the trial, again, of Harkishan Lal and others, for treason and waging war against the King-Emperor at Lahore, the accused were not allowed to have a lawyer of their own choosing; a full record of the case was not taken; and the notes taken by counsel for the defence had to be surrendered by him to the court at the end of each day. Under such conditions it is difficult to see how any adequate defence was possible. A punitive detachment, under a Colonel Jacob, flogged a man who refused, seemingly with some truculence, to say who had destroyed some telegraph wires; it later appeared that the man, as he had asserted, had in fact no knowledge of who had destroyed them. In Lahore—to take a final instance—the military officer in command prohibited more than a few persons to congregate in the streets; a group did so congregate, and its chief members were flogged. On investigation, it turned out that the group was a wedding-party whose purpose was as innocent as that of any persons engaged in a similar function.[29] I do not, of course, suggest that there is anything especially cruel or remarkable in these instances. Whether the instance selected is repression in Ireland, in Bavaria, in Hungary or Russia, what always emerges is that once the operation of justice is transferred from the ordinary courts and handed over to the executive, excesses of this kind are bound to occur. It is, therefore, urgent so to organise the power of the courts that only with the disappearance of the power to govern do they abdicate from their functions and their procedure.

The second problem arises in relation to pleas of defence against actions brought against officials for their conduct in a period of martial law. Here, at least, we have, under the common law, one invaluable safeguard. It is established that no act is justified that cannot be proved to have been necessary to the maintenance of order. "It is the emergency that creates the right", says an American court,[30] "and the emergency must be shown to exist before the taking can be justified". No executive officer, that is to say, can urge in defence of his action that he thought it necessary;

he must prove to the satisfaction of the court that not he only, but an average jury, can be made to agree with his judgment. It will, I think, be admitted that no other satisfactory criterion is available. Granted all that can be said of the difficulties of judging in cold blood responsibilities that have to be taken in hot blood, those difficulties constitute ground for mitigation of penalty, if the judgment goes against the defendant, and not ground for exonerating him from conviction. The position is not dissimilar from that of a man who commits murder under grave provocation; the murder then becomes intelligible, but it is none the less murder. The provocation is ground for a mitigation of penalty; it is not a ground for acquittal. In every case, therefore, the business of the judge is to measure with scrupulous care the relation between the act done and the situation it was considered by the doer important to resolve. And that doer is not entitled to escape the control of the courts because he is acting in a special executive position.

This, of course, raises the question of Acts of Indemnity. In the modern State, the occurrence of disturbance has, practically invariably, been followed by legislation exonerating those concerned in its suppression from any responsibilities they might otherwise have incurred. Nor is that true merely of disturbance; for the arrest in and deportation from England of persons suspected of complicity with crime in Ireland was also followed by an Act of Indemnity.[31] The broad result of such a process is to prevent all judicial inquiry into acts which might, conceivably, have serious consequences for their perpetrators. It is to leave those who believe themselves to have suffered unjustly from such acts dependent upon the charity of the executive power. It enables the executive fairly effectively to protect itself from any ample inquiry into its conduct such as might follow from a series of cases in which that conduct was found to be unjustified by the circumstances it was intended to meet. All cases where martial law is applied are cases where judicial inquiry is peculiarly necessary; and Acts of Indemnity almost always make judicial inquiry difficult and unsatisfactory. If, then, at a point in the relationships between executive and judiciary the work of the latter is to be properly performed, the ordinary Act of Indemnity seems to me a most improper form of procedure. It should always be open, in such cases, for the citizen who believes himself to be wronged to prove his right to remedy in the courts within a suitable time. There is, I think, ground for insisting that such wrongs shall be proved within a short period after they are said to have occurred, that the writ, for instance, shall be sought within not more than one month; an Act of Indemnity might then be reasonable. But an executive which can always be sure of legislative protection will be careless of judicial scrutiny because it knows that it has the means of evading judicial scrutiny; and that evasion will influence its agents at the circumference even more than at the centre. All Acts of Indemnity, therefore, ought to require a special majority for their passage by the standing orders of the legislative assembly; and that majority ought to be at least two thirds of its membership.

### (iii) The Judiciary and the Layman

Every legal system involves, in its working, an unprofessional element, of which the jury is the most notable example. The right, indeed, to trial by jury has been, at one period or another, the object of most political systems as a safeguard against the bias of a judiciary often at the mercy of the executive power. The jury was then at least a partial guarantee that the opinion of a fairly disinterested body of persons was taken into account. Anyone who reads, for example, the records of the treason trials of 1794[32] can see that without the presence of the jury the results of those cases would have been built simply on the equation of liberal opinion with high treason. Anyone, further, who studies the habits of the English judges in criminal cases half a century ago will realise that, whatever the presumptions of English justice, the judge did in fact assume that the persons charged were probably guilty; and the jury served the invaluable purpose of being a means of appeal from the fixed prejudices on the bench. On the other hand, of course, the jury system has grave disadvantages. It will tend, in all cases where political opinion is involved, simply to reflect the prevailing current of opinion about it. Juries in the Southern States of America, for instance, are notably prejudiced when cases involving a Negro are concerned; and an average London jury looks upon a libel very differently when the defendant is a conservative magnate from its views when he is a radical trade unionist. In all cases that are not definitely criminal cases, the average juryman lives in a world of which the standards of opinion are rarely investigated by him. He lives by the views of his neighbour, and he applies those views, outside that field controlled by the judge, to facts upon which he has to pass. To read, for instance, the charge of Cockburn, C.J., to the grand jury in*R.* v. *Nelson* and Brand[33] would make it impossible to understand why no true bill was found except upon the assumption that most Englishmen felt, like Carlyle, that whatever put down the Jamaica rebellion was good, irrespective of the manner of doing it.

Nevertheless, I believe that the jury system is an important safeguard in all criminal cases, and in such civil trials as involve a personal, as distinct from an impersonal interest; a libel, for instance, as distinct from a breach of contract. It is important that jury service, like the franchise, should involve no property qualification; if it is to be an average mind, that is the only way to make it genuinely average. It is important, also, that the juror should be adequately remunerated. Anyone who has sat on a jury for any length of time will have realised that, after a period, what concerns the jurymen is neither the evidence nor the result of the case, but the very different question of when they will be able to return to their usual routine. That results in the introduction of curiously irrelevant matters into their mind. They become prejudiced in favour of the counsel who is brief, without much regard to the importance of what he is saying. Their minds wander from the matter in hand to reflection upon whether the judge will begin early or late after the week-end adjournment. Difficulties of this kind have suggested to some the need for a standing panel of jurors who shall find a career in that service. But the whole point of the system would be lost by such a method. For what we require in these cases is not a specially trained opinion, but the opinion of the man in the street; and that is, on the whole, not ineffectively reached under the present régime, so long as the right to appeal from its decisions, especially in criminal cases, is retained.[34]

The position is, however, different where the problem concerned in a case is hardly personal, but, broadly speaking, technical in character. It may be a matter of trade practice in a matter of contract, of trade union customs, of violation of a trade-mark, of the law of agency, and so forth. In technical issues of this kind a jury, I suggest, is out of place unless it is a special kind constructed to suit the problem in dispute. The simplest way, I think, to meet this need is to have a standing panel of jurors from representative associations who will serve when necessary. That has the additional value of enabling the opinion of the expert witness to be tested by men who are able to assess from genuine knowledge the value of the testimony he offers. It offers to the judge the assurance that this view will be examined by a body of men to whom the import of his words will matter seriously. Each of these is a benefit of no small kind.

The unprofessional element in the judicial process has also a notable body of representatives in unpaid justices of the peace whose record, especially in England, has been a noteworthy one, if the range of their functions is borne in mind. I believe myself quite definitely that it is a final mistake to entrust a general jurisdiction to persons of whom no experience in the law is required. There are several elements in the problem which require discussion. The ground of appointment is, in the first place, unsatisfactory. Almost always, that ground is political. The office becomes what Mr. H.G. Wells has aptly termed a "knighthood of the underlings". It is used to recognise inferior political service of which the quality is not sufficient for greater recompense. It becomes a minor note like the Order of the British Empire; and an important Member of Parliament will secure it for his useful henchman much in the way that the dead fox is given to the hounds after the day's run. That is, surely, an inadequate way of filling an important judicial office. But, in the second place, the methods of fulfilling the function leave much to be desired. If the case involves a point of law, the ignorance of the magistrates leaves their court clerk the master of the decision. If the case is a matter of discretion, the compelling motives are what is supplied by the experience of a man whose actual knowledge of his work is limited, as a rule, to a fortnight's sitting in the year. The results are of a serious nature. There are magistrates who cannot be restrained from expressing their views on every conceivable subject. There are others who are unnecessarily severe in some cases, and unnecessarily lax in others. A study of the variations of sentence in particular offences would reveal the hazards to which a prisoner is exposed when he is judged by the unpaid, as against the paid, magistrate. I do not doubt that much invaluable service is performed by a small section of the justices of the peace. But the average justice has neither the knowledge nor the training for the position that he fills. He is the man in the street on the bench instead of on the jury. And when he is a country justice dealing, for instance, with a poacher, he does not possess the frame of mind or the experience to enable him to do justice. It is, therefore, a matter of importance in any judicial system to confer powers of general jurisdiction only upon persons of trained competence in the law.

The matter is different where special problems are concerned. There are certain infractions of the law, on the one hand, and civil cases, on the other, where I believe that the conference of original jurisdiction, the right of appeal being always reserved, would bring with it great good. There are cases in which a given trade has a special interest in the result; as, for instance, food shops in the legislation intended to protect the public against the sale of bad food. There are cases, again, like those which come under the Factory Acts, in which it is desirable to develop a general sense of responsibility to the acts among employers of labour. In such cases, I believe, the constitution of regional tribunals composed of persons nominated by representative institutions would be a useful means of offering to those most directly affected by the law a means of applying it. The danger of partial administration could always be met by a right of appeal. If, for instance, we had the scale of wages made by a trade board enforced by a court composed of representatives of the board, we should develop a proper sense in the given industry of the importance of such legislation. There would grow up a genuine *esprit de corps* in the industry, the desire to compare favourably with other industries in the infrequency of court cases. The same is true in the case of the use of prohibited materials. And, under such a system as I have described in the previous chapter, it would be possible, I think, to develop within each Industrial Council a legal tribunal which would deal with infractions of the law as they affected the standing of the given industry. There is no reason why we should not evolve a moral discipline in the industrial field comparable to the standards of professional conduct in medicine or the law. A man then who persistently evaded the Pure Food Acts might be expelled from the trade, or a company dissolved, for the preservation of its standards of honour in the same way as a doctor is struck off the medical register. Decentralised jurisdiction of this kind, so long as it is confined to certain special offences, and is carried out by tribunals which grow out of the proper authority involved, have little of the amateur character which belongs to the unpaid judges of the present time. And it has the merit of making the industry itself a genuine unit for other purposes. It could then advise the Ministry of Justice upon the administration of law, as it is thereby affected, in a way that is bound to improve its quality. We have already found great value in the powers of arbitration which belong to chambers of commerce. That is because the jurisdiction there exercised is confined to problems the chambers are peculiarly fitted to solve; and the extension of such powers is bound to result in benefit.

A third and, at present, unutilised aspect of the unprofessional element in the judicial function relates to the problem of crime and its punishment. In most States, to-day, the law simply fixes the upper limit of sentence, and leaves its actual nature to the unfettered discretion of the judge. Any revision of the sentence then becomes a matter for the executive power. When the judge makes his decision he has before him a report from the police upon what is known of the prisoner, and such evidence as may have been produced in the case itself. That is, I think, an inadequate method of procedure. In the first place, there are types of offence the penalty for which was settled long before any real knowledge of their nature was possible, of which sexual offences are the best example. In cases of this kind, no judge ought to be able to sentence until he has considered competent medical opinion upon the case. It ought to be as natural for a medical assessor to be consulted in such cases as it is for a naval assessor to be consulted in admiralty cases.[35] It ought, secondly, to be possible to devote much more attention to the use to which the sentence ought to be put than now occurs. A judge who sentences a burglar to seven years' penal servitude is, as most modern research goes to show, sentencing him to a prison discipline which is almost certain to send him back to burglary on his release. It seems to me clear, on all the evidence, that we need to assist the judge by providing him not merely with the police record of the defendant, but with all that can be discovered of his mental and social history by a trained body of investigators. We should then be in a position to offer the judge material upon which he could act in the light of a much more real knowledge than he now possesses. And I believe that the system in which the judge's interest in a prisoner ends with his conviction is a mistake. If means were devised to associate the judge with the administration of prisons, he would have what, as a rule, he now lacks, a much more intimate realisation of his responsibilities. There is, indeed, good reason for making such an association the means of obtaining year by year a commentary upon the character of prison administration. If the State were divided into regions, and a judge of the High Court made responsible for the inspection of each district, with the duty of visitation and report, we should end much of the ignorance which now surrounds the whole character of our prison system; and we should have the means of utilising a body of expert suggestion as the avenue to continuous reform. At present it is a notable fact that world over that all penal reforms of a serious character originate outside prison officials; and they are rarely adopted without a long struggle. To acquaint the judge with the effect of his decisions is to call into being a lever of great value in a region where it is urgently required.[36]

### (iv) Equality Before the Law

Equality in justice is a primary condition of attaining justice; yet no one could even pretend to believe that it is obtained under the present system. That is true not only of criminal, but in civil cases also. The modern State maintains a vast organisation for the prosecution of alleged offenders; there is no such organisation to ensure their adequate defence. There is one law for the rich and another for the poor whenever the preparation of a defence is an item of importance in the case. Nor is that all. In the personal relations of life, as in divorce, for instance, lack of means generally implies lack of access to the courts. Often, also, in civil cases the inability of a poor person to employ a counsel, still more to employ really skilful counsel, is a fatal bar to their obtaining justice. Another region of inequality is notable. If a poor person steals, conviction follows rapidly; if a rich person steals, she is usually bound over on the plea of nervous trouble. If a taxi-driver is proved to have been drunk in charge of a car, he pays the penalty; but it is notorious that magistrates do not like to convict the rich young man in a similar position, since he will usually appeal and often get his case reversed on appeal. What is disorderly conduct in resisting the police in White-chapel is not seldom regarded as an ebullience of high spirits in Mayfair. If directors of a company in high social position pay no attention to the affairs of the company, they are not held responsible when it is compulsorily liquidated; but if a petty official is confused in his accounts, charges of embezzlement are difficult to avoid. Clearly, we need to remedy such a state of affairs.

In part, of course, we cannot remedy it by legislation, since, in part, the temper which is responsible for the position will change only as the social atmosphere changes. A magistrate who sees guilt in a poor thief, but nervous disease in a rich one, will continue to make the distinction until differences of economic status are negligible; a judge who does not believe that distinguished directors of public companies ought to be responsible for a negligence they are paid to prevent, will only find them responsible when there is a genuine relation between income and service. Wherever, in this aspect, differences in the administration of law are dependent, not upon the law itself, but upon the social results of the inequality of wealth, only a movement towards the equality of wealth can obliterate those differences. The situation here is only a particular of a much more generic problem. Things seem wicked in the poor which are not wicked in the rich; the rulers of civilisation were horrified when Bolsheviks murdered aristocrats, but they were not horrified when aristocrats murdered Bolsheviks. The atmosphere I am seeking to describe was perhaps best shown in the Franks murder trial in Chicago when it seemed to be assumed by the public opinion of America that the sons of millionaires would not, despite their guilt, be sentenced to death by the courts.[37] The temper, in fact, which permits the English peer a special trial by the House of Lords will only disappear with the abolition of the privileges typified by the House of Lords.

Yet all this is no reason why we should not seek to deal with that aspect of the problem which admits of direct remedy. Two aspects are here involved. In the case of crime, exactly as we have a Director of Public Prosecutions, as in England, a District Attorney, as in the United States, so do we need a Director of Defences whose business it will be to see that no prisoner, accused of a serious charge,[38] shall be tried without a proper defence being prepared. Where it is possible to make a reasonable charge for his services, there is no ground for their being given free; but where the defendant is too poor to pay, the costs ought to be regarded as part of the normal expenses of justice. It is only by such means that the average prisoner can be assured that his case will be properly presented to the court. The judge, doubtless, will do everything he can to present the full bearing of the evidence to the jury; but there are matters of investigation, production of witnesses, and so forth, that depend very largely now upon the prisoner's financial position. In a great murder trial, I am told, it is customary for a newspaper to bear part of the cost in return for a sensational article from the prisoner. That is obviously an indefensible method of procedure. It panders to the lowest taste of the human mind. It tends to make the criminal into something of a hero. It adds a glamour to crime instead of showing it for the mean and sordid thing it usually is. If the institution of a public defender resulted only in the suppression of this traffic, it would be largely justified. But its main justification is that it will put the prisoner upon an equality with the State which prosecutes him.

A Public Defence Office is essentially centralised by its nature; in the case of civil justice, what is wanted is a mechanism for assisting poor persons on the spot with competent legal advice. The need for such a mechanism is already largely recognised in theory; and, in practice, the poor man's lawyer is usually part of the welfare agencies of the modern city.[39] But voluntary agencies cannot even pretend to cover the ground. Not only do they lack the means to cover the whole range of law, but they are rarely able to do more than give the applicant advice, without pursuing that advice into the courts; and, not seldom, they depend upon the young and inexperienced lawyer for the advice they can offer. In Germany, indeed, the system exists upon a much vaster scale; and the 110 bureaus of legal advice supported in part by the municipalities dealt in 1912 with over a quarter of a million cases.[40]

But something much wider is needed. We need a public office of legal advice attached to every court in the State. The office should be attached to the local authority which is served by the court, and should be staffed by officials appointed by the local authority, since experience serves to show that a large number of its cases will be concerned with problems which arise out of questions within the competence of the local authority. It should, broadly, have three divisions: (1) a division of advice; (2) a division of mediation; and (3) a division for the preparation of cases for the courts. Any danger of it becoming bureaucratic and formal could be obviated by providing it with an advisory council of lawyers whose business it would be to watch over, and report upon its working. It would also, I think, tend to raise its status in the estimation of the Bar if appointment to legal positions that were not positions on the High Court, or quasi-political in nature, like that of the Attorney-General, were made dependent upon a period of service in such an office. Certainly a borough stipendiary, for example, who had watched at first hand work such as I shall outline could not fail to be a more valuable public servant as a consequence.

I take separately each of the divisions I have suggested in this office. Advice and information should be given on all questions relating to public and private law with two exceptions. No advice should be given where the applicant had already consulted a lawyer; nor should it be available where the suspicion arises that the applicant is seeking advice in order to evade the law. It is not the business, for instance, of such an office to assist in the evasion of income-tax or to arrange a collusive divorce. But an applicant who desired information or counsel upon such matters as those of the Insurance Act, or Workmen's Compensation, or the law of landlord and tenant, ought to receive it. A man who had received a summons could be advised upon the position involved. A creditor who could not obtain repayment of a small loan, a debtor in the hands of an extortionate money-lender, a person who had suffered damage from the negligence of a motor-driver, could come to such an office in the same way as the rich man goes to his private lawyer.

In the second place, the office would have a division of mediation. Year by Year there come into the courts hundreds of cases which a little tact and ingenuity could preserve from judicial settlement. There are cases of slander and libel; there are cases where husband and wife have quarrelled and resort is had to judicial separation; there are cases where breach of promise is alleged to have occurred; and cases where some sudden quarrel between a debtor and creditor makes the latter go to court in a burst of ill-temper. I need not suggest the great range of questions which will occur to anyone who studies at all carefully the working of the average police court on an average day. If such an office as this were given the power to attempt private settlements a good deal of unnecessary suffering could be avoided. It would be necessary, I think, to give the office the power to summon parties to a private hearing; and where mediation was accepted, and the solution agreed to by both parties, it would be necessary to make the result a bar to future action. On these conditions, if the environment of the office had something of the dignity of a court of law, and if, secondly, the officials appointed had the infinite patience of a good London magistrate, there is no doubt that we could add enormously to the sum of human happiness.

There would, thirdly, be a division concerned with actual cases in the courts. Here the office would do all that a lawyer is accustomed to do, but would do it at a fee that was within the means of the applicant. It would, I think, have to work upon the basis that, where the applicant had in legal fact no case at all, it would not minister to mere litigiousness. There is a section of the poor, as there is a section of the rich, to whom the opportunity of legal proceedings is a method of response to the combined impulses of vanity and pugnacity. We may admit that the determined litigant has not seldom been the guardian of public liberty, but that is not a reason for providing him with a public office for his assistance. In general, the officials must satisfy themselves that the applicant has a real claim to be met or a real defence to urge. They must, of course, make real inquiries, and where the applicant feels that he has not been fairly treated by them, he should have the right of complaint to the advisory council of the office. I do not, of course, deny that an institution of this kind will deprive the lawyers of much business which would otherwise fall to them. But it has certain merits of great importance once it establishes itself in public confidence. It is likely to end the régime of that class of lawyers who now live on the misfortunes of the poor. It will do much, also, a humanise justice. The poor litigant who is defended by a public authority will not receive the cavalier treatment not seldom meted out to him to-day. And in humanising the law it will strengthen the law by increasing the respect in which it is held in the hearts of the people.

Such a system, I would urge, has value also in that it offers a medium, of which lawyers may avail themselves, to serve the public. We have at the present time a small number of men who devote themselves to such service; and there must be many a poor litigant in Boston to whom the legal-aid bureau of the Harvard Law School has stood as the embodiment of justice.[41] It would, I think, be possible, by co-operation between the lawyers of each district to arrange for a panel of voluntary service in such an office as would result in a greatly diminished expenditure upon its functions. In general, it may be, it would be difficult for the average barrister to give up his day to acting as counsel in a court case. But the conditions of modern economic life will make much of the work of these offices evening work; it is when the working man comes home in the evening that he will resort there in his need. I see no reason why the lawyers should not arrange that, night by night, they supply a panel of helpers who will advise and mediate. Such a plan has manifest advantages for themselves; it would be for the younger lawyer what resident hospital work is to the young surgeon. To the older lawyer, doubtless, it would present less attraction. But both sides of the legal profession have to remember that they are a profession; and I have argued in this book that it is the main characteristic of a profession not to be motivated merely by considerations of profit. And an analogous experience suggests that, even for the expert practitioner there are rich rewards in such an effort. Certainly every university teacher who has served in the movement of adult education would agree that the enthusiasm and devotion he can inspire is out of all proportion to the time and trouble he is called upon to expend. He learns there far more than he can ever hope to teach.

The same would, I believe, be true of the lawyer, particularly on the advocate's side of the profession. He would learn a good deal about human nature of which he is now ignorant. It would be an advantage to him to adjust his mind to an atmosphere in which he was seeking human solutions and not legal solutions. He would see the raw facts of law, not as points in a case, but as problems to be adjusted to the wants of human beings. He would need less legal insight into the law than moral insight into the law. I believe myself that an experience of this kind would do much to increase the value of the lawyer in his ordinary work. He would multiply his chances of becoming what the best type of family solicitor has been—a trusted friend of those whom he professionally advises. His own view of the law would broaden. He would be more likely to grasp what is meant by saying that justice is the end of law. He would see justice, in fact, simply as a method of response to human desire, away from the formalism in which, in certain aspects, it has to clothe itself. There might develop from such an effort what may be termed a preventive justice which would bear the same relation to the justice of the courts as preventive medicine to hospital treatment. And, as I shall point out later, the experience he might gain from such effort has a value of high importance in relation to the reform of the law.

There is one other aspect of equality in law which demands a word of comment. That is the problem involved for the poor in the infliction either of prison sentences, or of heavy fines; and the rather special problem coated by the costs of law proceedings as distinct from the cost of lawyers. The family of a wealthy man is not seriously disturbed by these things; for the poor they may make all the difference between sufficiency and want. It seems clear, therefore, that in all save really serious offences the business of the magistrate is to use his discretion against a prison sentence. He must, therefore, relate the payment of fines to the wages of the defendant fined; for there are few cases in which such a penalty is not rather a punishment inflicted upon the family than a punishment inflicted upon the individual. Indeed, there is ground for the argument that all fines of a pound and upwards should be paid in instalments, rather than in a lump sum, when the means of the defendant are small; and the relief would be greater if a system like that of the family-wage advocated by Miss Rathbone[42] operated to protect his wife and children. Because, in fact, guilt is personal, we should do all we can to narrow the number of those injured by its consequences. So, also, I suggest, much is to be said for enabling the judge, in appropriate cases, to remit court fees where the defendant or plaintiff ought not to have been brought to court; and, where possible, means could be devised to surcharge those responsible for unnecessary and unjustified litigation. A similar problem is raised by the cases in which poor debtors are imprisoned. Here, certainly, unless failure to pay arises, as in maintenance cases, out of deliberate effort to evade responsibility, the penalty inflicted has consequences which go far beyond the nature of the offence.

I do not, of course, urge that such methods as these will do more than mitigate the grosser evils of legal inequality. Wider problems exist, especially in such branches of the law as Employers' Liability and Workmen's Compensation. The remedies the law here offers are obviously grossly inadequate compared to the miseries involved. But no merely administrative mechanisms will meet such cases. Their cure depends upon legislative effort, especially in the direction of social insurance. All that we can do within the categories of the existing system is to ensure three things. We can make certain of an adequate defence for all accused persons, whether rich or poor. We can offer legal advice of the highest quality to all, regardless of their means. We can see to it that no one with a grievance to be remedied, or a good answer to a complaint, is without the opportunity to prosecute his grievance or to make his answer. In doing these things we could also, as I have urged, develop a preventive jurisprudence which would solve by prudence what is now too often answered unnecessarily in terms of law. I believe that changes such as these are of high importance. For, in the end, systems of justice are measured by the degree to which they respond to the wants and needs of humble men.

### (v) The Reform of the Law

It is almost an inevitable characteristic of the legal mind that it should tend to conservatism. It is largely engaged in the study of precedent. What it can do is most often set by the statutes of a preceding generation. Its chief exponents are, as a rule, men already well past middle age who come to positions of authority just when new wants they have not known are coming to be expressed. Lawyers, in fact, are more definitely the servants of tradition than any other class in the community; for the demonstration that novelty is desirable is, with them, more difficult, because more impalpable, than with any other aspect of social life. The great changes in medicine, as with aseptic treatment, in industry, as with the development of mechanical transport, in education, as with the Workers' Educational Association, can, all of them, be proved rapidly by experiment, and the weapons to overcome the habitual conservatism of the average man lie, accordingly, ready to hand. That is much less the case in the law; and yet for law to lag behind the needs of its generation has consequences of profound seriousness. We need, therefore, to devise means whereby the study of necessary legal change can be made definite and continuous, in order that the adaptation of the processes of law to changing wants in such generation may be as rapid as possible.

This conclusion will not, I think, appear doubtful to anyone who studies, for instance, the history of the legal profession in England. It is not insignificant that every great period of social change in England has been accompanied by a temper of antagonism to lawyers. The hatred of the peasants in 1381 was chiefly directed against the attorneys whom they regarded as the makers of their chains; Jack Cade's first desire was to hang all the lawyers; and not the least notable mood of the Puritan rebellion was the demand for a complete reform of the law. It is not insignificant, also, that it was forty years before the common sense of Bentham attracted to his service that little band of zealots who changed the character of English social history in the nineteenth century; and it is remarkable that, amongst them, only two lawyers, Romilly and

Brougham, were prominent in any consistent way. Lawyers have contributed little or nothing to the amelioration of penal systems. They have been consistently reactionary about the education of their own profession; and even when, as in the case of Lord Westbury,[43] urgent effort has been made for improvement, it has languished after a brief enthusiasm. Anyone who reads the record of the effort of Fitzjames Stephen to secure proper attention to the problems of codification will realise how accidental is the possibility of improvement.[44] English lawyers have made great contributions to legal history; they have written, in particular branches of the law, textbooks of high value. But, since Austin, if Austin is to be accounted a great jurist,[45] they have done little or nothing for the science of law; and until law becomes a matter of genuine and widespread scientific investigation, its continuous improvement is unlikely to be secured.

I do not, of course, argue that the English situation is lamentable when other countries are brought into comparison. The administration of law in England, and especially of the criminal law, is probably better than in any other civilised community; and in France, where legal science has reached a high degree of excellence, the Code Napoléon still hangs like a millstone round the neck of a generation for which it has largely ceased to have validity.[46] But in Germany it will be obvious to anyone who studies, for instance, the history of the adoption of the great Civil Code, deliberate and creative legal reform has been made possible by the devotion to legal science which exists there; and a survey of American effort in legal science would, I think, suggest the likelihood that the successor of Bentham will be born in the Western Hemisphere, so far, at least, as the future of the common law is concerned.

There are, generally, five conditions precedent to the possibility of an attempt at the continuous improvement of the law. In part, it is a matter of the way in which lawyers are trained. If their education as lawyers is a genuine human and philosophic discipline, it is much more likely to engender the temper which adopts a sceptical attitude to legal principles than if it is merely the absorption of that minimum of information considered sufficient for admission to practice. In part, secondly, it is a matter of the way in which the legal profession is organised. If it is made a definite purpose of the associations within the profession to attempt improvement, if it has, that is to say, subject associations attempting the advance of legal knowledge, like the Institute of Mechanical Engineers, or the Royal Society of Medicine, there will at least be within it a meeting-ground for those lawyers conscious of defect in the law, and public-spirited enough to search for its remedy. In part, thirdly, there is need, within the national Ministry of Justice, of a permanent commission of lawyers whose business it is to research into the means of legal improvement, in part by the investigation of complaint, in part by absorbing the lessons of international experience, in part also, by the development in the profession through their stimulus of deliberate inventiveness about the law. Not less important, fourthly, is the proper consideration of lay experience of the law; especially where, as with doctors and business men, there quite obviously exists a great reservoir of creativeness which largely goes unused. Certainly, to take an obvious example, if I desired to know the real effect of the Workmen's Compensation Act it is from doctors and trade union officials rather than from lawyers that I should seek to learn it. Of great importance, finally, is the utilisation of judicial experience in the amendment of the law. For the most part, all that we have now are occasional dicta, as in Lord Russell of Killowen's praise of juries, or the special knowledge that is contributed to a recondite inquiry as that which resulted in England in the amendment of the law of real property.

Let us take each of these points separately. The method by which lawyers are trained is, I have argued, at the root of the attitude they will take in their profession to legal reform. Legal education, that is to say, must be more than the acquisition of a merely practical technique. It must seek to convey an interest in the law as a science, the sense of it as a vital tract in human experience which is continually charted more adequately for those who use its paths. Legal education, therefore, must be not less a general intellectual discipline than a reception of information. It must wrestle with problems as well as offer statements. It must not assume that the judicial decisions which are its substance are right because they are judicial decisions. It must be so organised as to induce the critical temper in the student. I should myself argue that, if this be true, the study of law is in its nature a subject to be taught by the methods, and in the atmosphere, of a university, and that, preferably, it should be regarded as more suitably embraced as a specialised and higher training, in the same way, for example, as legal study in Harvard University, where, as Maitland pointed out[47] the true inheritors of the great traditions of Padua and Bologna are to be found.

What does this involve? It is, I think, simplest for my purpose to consider as an example the typical English barrister and to suggest the changes which are, in this view, important. It is, broadly speaking, a training which does not have in view a philosophic grasp of its subject. Its aim is to enable the aspirant to the profession to pass a certain number of relatively simple examinations which do not call so much for an insight into law as a science, and the relations of law to the neighbouring subjects which determine its character, as they demand the memorising of a number of cases, and the ability to apply to similar cases rules that can be forgotten once the examination is over. The barrister's training, indeed, is nothing like so serious an intellectual effort as that of the solicitor. He has the future of the law in his hands. Yet he rarely knows anything of the history of the law, and even more rarely of its basis in jurisprudence. There are, of course, some who gain such insight in the universities. But it is, I think, significant that the Inns of Court have not taken the teaching of law very seriously, and not less interesting that men like Maitland—perhaps the greatest legal genius in England since Bentham—were never able to gather about them disciples eager to carry on their work. In general, moreover, the teaching of English law, especially in the Inns themselves, is the teaching of dogma rather than of inquiry. There is no real effort to stimulate curiosity about the law. It is, for the average lawyer, simply a system of doctrines made by the courts and to be learned as the courts shape the system. I do not, of course, deny that the method produces lawyers of great learning and distinction. But I do deny that it produces a race of lawyers who are concerned to reshape the law to fit the needs of a changing environment.

Here, I believe, a great example has been set by the tradition and methods of the great continental law schools, on the one hand, and the great American law schools on the other. They train successful lawyers. But the method by which they are trained has results different from those in England. In America, for example, the student learns from the outset what Mr. Wells has happily termed a scepticism of the instrument. He learns that legal cases are legal problems, and that the judicial answer to the problem is to be proved as much as any other answer. His teachers are usually engaged, as in the great law school of Harvard University, in remaking the foundations of the law. I mention only the dead; but I know of no teaching tradition among English lawyers to compare with the great teaching tradition of Langdell, Ames, and Gray.[48] And any great teaching tradition, as Maitland showed in England by his work on trusts and corporations,[49] inevitably becomes a great reforming tradition. The students of such men go out not merely to practise, but also to improve. They become missionaries for new ideas. They attempt experiment. No one who studies the history of recent law, for example, can fail to see the influence of men like Saleilles and Duguit in France, of Gierke and Kohler in Germany. With them, consciously, law has been an expression of life, adapted to meet the changing needs of life.

I argue, therefore, that a conscious effort to make legal training an insistence upon the possibility of experiment would, upon experience already in our possession, attune the mind of lawyers to the implicit needs of their subject. But a training in positive law alone is, I believe, inadequate. The study of jurisprudence is integral to the intellectual discipline I am advocating because without a knowledge of jurisprudence, especially in its comparative aspect, no lawyer, however practically eminent, can really measure the meaning of the assumptions upon which his subject rests. Jurisprudence is the eye of the law. It gives the law its insight into the environment of which it is the expression. It relates the law to the spirit of the time, and the richer the jurisprudence of a given system in a given age, the nearer will be the law of that system to the needs of its time. The poverty of English jurisprudence since Austin is the measure of the inadequacy of our law to meet the swift changes of our social situation. We should not have had reactionary decisions like those in the Free Church of Scotland case, or the Osborne case, if our lawyers had been trained to watch the juristic significance of the judgments they make.

Nor is that all. Because law is a part of life it must enter into relations with those parts of life by which it is largely determined. No man, for instance, can adequately study law unless he has an intimate acquaintance with political economy. "The present divorce between the schools of political economy and law", writes Mr. Justice Holmes,[50] "seems to me evidence of how much progress in philosophic study still remains to be made". No one, certainly, can study the decisions of the Supreme Court of the United States in the last twenty-five years without the sense that they are in general a patient attempt to apply the apriorism of the 'sixties to a situation that period could not, in the nature of things, contemplate. To study the judgments of that court in such cases as *Lochner* v. *New York*,[51] and *Adair* v. *United States*,[52] as *Coppage* v. *Kansas*[53] and *Hammer* v. *Dagenhart*,[54] is to realise that to the degree that lawyers are left to obtain their economic ideas from business men, they will be ignorant of the general results of an economic science which continuously enlarges the boundaries of its knowledge. That is not true merely of the United States, where the power of judicial review makes political economy particularly important. English judges who had been trained to grasp the meaning of trade union organisation, who had been taught to realise, for instance, that in the issues of *Osborne* v. *Amalgamated Society of Railway Servants*,[55] Mr. and Mrs. Webb's *History of Trade Unionism* was as important as any number of cases in the law of unincorporated associations, would not have gone so wildly astray. Contract, tort, property, all these are legal categories which are inexplicable in any save their economic context. Nor is constitutional law intelligible except as the expression of an economic system of which it is designed to serve as a rampart. It was Maitland who pointed out that Magna Carta is a feudal document; and the rights it conveys are meaningless without reference to the good syndicalists who extracted them from their unwilling suzerain.

Not less urgent than the training of lawyers, as a condition of law reforms, is the organisation of lawyers. At present they are well organised for the protection of their interests. They control the conditions of entrance to their profession. They determine almost completely their own standards of professional ethic. No other body of workers possesses quite so completely the Indicia of self-government; and their natural aptitude for a political career gives them an over-whelming position in the legislative assembly. Yet it cannot be said that lawyers have shown any special desire to balance these advantages by a measure of service to the community which would justify them. In England, a few small societies like the Society for Comparative Legislation, manage to secure the interest of a few; in America and the major Dominions, bodies like the Bar Associations meet annually for a brief period to eat and drink and hear solemn orations on the great traditions of the law. But there is no organised effort, place by place and month by month, to study the problems of law and to suggest the means of their solution.

It would, I think, be possible to take a great step to this end if each unit of legal organisation were not merely a trade union but also a research association. If the Bar, say, of Manchester, recognised its obligations not merely to conviviality, but also to progress, it ought not to be difficult to produce from the accumulated experience of Manchester lawyers ideas for legal change. They would have their published transactions. They would seek to answer, not merely general legal problems, but also the special legal problems of their own city. A single instance may suffice to illustrate my meaning. A few years ago, the city of Cleveland was shocked by the discovery of a grave judicial scandal which threw into high relief the bad administration of justice there. A committee was formed to investigate the whole position of criminal law and its administration in Cleveland. Two distinguished lawyers from Harvard were employed to analyse in detail the existing situation, and to make suggestions for its improvement. They produced a masterly report,[56] but what was even more important than their report was the formation of a permanent body, partly of lawyers, partly of interested laymen, to watch over and report upon the administration of the law in the future. There is no reason that I can see why such bodies should not be formed elsewhere. Probably, indeed, they are best confined, so far as they are general and permanent, to the legal profession only, meeting similar bodies in other professions for the exchange of mutual knowledge and suggestion. But no one can read the history of what has been done in Cleveland without the sense that it opens immense possibilities in any effort to make legal reformation a habit of the legal mind. For the mere publication of judicial statistics does not give us more than the bare anatomy of legal administration; and to confine research to a few lawyers who, for one reason or another, do not enjoy an ample practice is to leave unused experience of precious import.

But voluntary investigation of this kind, valuable though it is, is not sufficient. It is necessary not merely that conclusions should be arrived at, but, also, that they should be sure of adequate consideration by the executive power. To that end, I believe, there should be in the Ministry of Justice a small but permanent Commission of which the purpose would be the study of law reform. It would have, as I see it, three types of function. It would amass information, both domestic and foreign, upon all the problems of legal doctrine and legal administration. It would investigate, from time to time, and by the creation of such agencies as it deemed proper, particular branches of the law. It would receive from every relevant source criticism, inquiry, suggestion, upon the working of the law. It would hear, for instance, from the bodies organising legal aid for the poor that the law in relation to bastardy cases seemed, in their experience, to need amendment; and it would organise inquiry into the possibilities of change. It would discover that a penal reform had been attempted with success abroad, and it would send out a representative to discover the value of the new method and the degree to which it was applicable to its own situation. It would endeavour to collect the results of all that might indicate avenues of improvement and to bring them to the attention of the Minister of Justice. Gradually, as I believe, it would make possible the possession by the latter of quite wide rule-making powers which, subject to the ultimate approval of the legislative assembly, would make possible many more legal changes, and much more widespread legal experiments. We cannot, of course, develop an instrument such as this if the legal offices of the executive remain what they are in the majority of States a combination of judge, advocate, and, so to say, consulting legal physician. But their transformation into a genuine Minister of Justice would give, for the first time, the occasion for significant innovation.

We need, further, to utilise much more creatively than we now do the knowledge and experience of the judiciary. Here, indeed, we must proceed with caution; for our effort must never involve such a connection between the judiciary and the executive as will break that independence in the former which, I have urged, lies at the root of civilised justice. But it would be possible, and would not, in this respect, be harmful to require from the judges an annual report upon the working of the courts. They could indicate there at least reforms that the lesson of their work has taught them to be desirable. They would say, for instance, that no judge sits in the English Divorce Court without the sense that what he is compelled to do there is an insult to his self-respect. They could point out how often the procedure of appeals protracts litigation to a point that is intolerable. They could suggest their sense that the punishment inflicted in certain classes of crime, as of sexual violence, for instance, are not genuinely relevant to the offence they are intended to meet. I do not think their report should be anything more than a published document. But it would offer important suggestions to the Ministry of Justice which the latter could then proceed to explore.

For the results of its exploration, of course, the judges would not be responsible. Their part would be done when they had indicated needs their experience had encountered. We get something of this indication now, as when a judge makes a remark *obiter,* or in a speech expresses his sense of the answer to some general problem. So, for example, Mr. Justice Holmes has told us that he does not see any harm in abolishing the power of the American Supreme Court to declare congressional legislation unconstitutional, though we do not know the views of his eight colleagues.[57] So, also, the Chief Justice of England has commented upon the method of appointment to the judicial bench.[58] But the difficulty of such methods lies in their occasional character; they do not relate an experience, however deeply felt, to the channel of action through which it ought to flow. It is only by organising judicial experience into coherent and continuous suggestion that we can best utilise the wisdom it embodies.

### (vi) Quasi-Judicial Powers in the Executive

One final problem remains. There is quasi-judicial power in certain executive officials which, quite apart from the area of administrative law, raises questions of importance. The judiciary makes law by giving its judgment upon issues submitted to it by private persons or by the executive. How is submission by the executive to be organised? In all States there is a Minister of Justice, or an authority equivalent to that office, who acts as the legal advisor to the government of the day and, on the criminal side, organises the prosecution of offenders. What should be the limit and character of his powers?

Broadly speaking, the real problem involved is that which occurs on the side of prosecution, especially in relation to political offences. Every government has a power to decide not to prosecute or, prosecution having been commenced, to decide upon its discontinuance. Is that power political, or judicial, in its nature? Ought it to be, in the latter case, exercised by a politician who, like the Minister of Justice, is by the character of his office necessarily in continuous contact with the government of the day? Can he, in the light of such contact, possibly separate the judicial from the political aspect of his duty? Is it, then, preferable to entrust the power to undertake, or to discontinue prosecutions, to a permanent official safeguarded, for example, as the Controller and Auditor-General is safeguarded in Great Britain?

The political solution is, I think, alone possible for the simple reason that there are types of offences, sedition, for example, and blasphemy, the decisions about which can be settled only upon expediency and not upon principle. A permanent Prosecutor-General could not distinguish between, say, sedition as practised by Lord Birkenhead and Lord Carson, and sedition as practised by an unimportant group of revolutionary Communists.

He could not proceed in the second case without proceeding in the first, and to proceed in the first might have involved consequences which no government was prepared to face. To entrust such a power, therefore, to a permanent official is, at the margin, to give him power of life and death over the executive. It is surely obvious that such a power can only be exercised by a minister responsible to the legislative assembly. It is clear that the basis upon which he must, if he is wise, proceed is that of general policy; and this necessarily involves consultation with his colleagues wherever the issue raised appears to involve considerations of gravity. It may be wise to prosecute to prevent a feared disturbance from gathering volume. It may be unwise to prosecute because political convictions make martyrdoms, and causes prosper by the martyrs they create. These are all of them problems for executive consideration, for they depend upon a nice balance of consequences the nature of which affects at every point the life of government. If a Communist is prosecuted for sedition, the government will inevitably be challenged by those who doubt the wisdom of such effort; and if the government agrees with the challenge, its only remedy is either a pardon, which stultifies the prosecution, or else some underground communication to a permanent official the judicial nature of whose function is thereby invaded from the angle of politics. And it is inevitable that the mind of the official should, in such an atmosphere, be biased by the opinion he encounters. It is therefore better that all such cases should be frankly admitted to be within the scope of the executive power. For then the cabinet is definitely responsible for what occurs, and we do not surround the problem with a miasma of obscurity and prejudice. We obviate the very real difficulty that, in undertaking such prosecutions, the mind of a permanent official may be seriously affected by his own opinions.

I do not, of course, deny the difficulties inherent in this view. It may lead to the inception or withdrawal of prosecutions from motives which have in view something other than the mere fulfilment of the law. Pressure may be brought to assure the escape of influential persons from punishment, and that for offences which cannot possibly be regarded as political. But the answer to that danger is a twofold one. Pressure will be brought in any case, whoever may be the person charged with the duty of prosecution; and by making questions connected therewith questions of ministerial responsibility, we at least assure that they are amenable to the will of the legislative assembly. And, secondly, we bring the political aspect of prosecution into the light of day. It is inconceivable, for example, that the Liberal Government of 1913-14 should not have discussed the desirability of prosecuting Lord Carson and his friends for tampering with the loyalty of the army. In the method here proposed, the decision taken is clearly traceable to a definite source. The responsibility for it is a plain one, and the government of the day is called upon to justify the action that it takes.

What is to occur when action is taken to initiate to prosecution which it is subsequently decided to abandon? Here again the cases of importance are nearly always political in character. No one would have objected to the abandonment of the case against Adolf Beck on the ground that careful research in the police archives has established (as it would have established) the fact of mistaken identity. But what of a case like that in which the prosecution of Mr. J.R. Campbell was abandoned? Certain formulae would, I think, be observed. (1) There should be no communication with the judge or magistrate except the formal announcement of a proposed abandonment. (2) There should be an official announcement of the grounds upon which the abandonment has been made. (3) It should be understood that abandonment, especially in political cases, involves the responsibility of the government of the day. (4) The judge or magistrate should not be entitled to refuse withdrawal; for, otherwise, he becomes at once prosecutor and, at least in the first instance, judge, in the given case. (5) All such cases should be officially notified to the legislative assembly, and to the advisory legislative committee of the Ministry of Justice. We then have, I think, ample safeguards against the abuse of this power. We have definite responsibility on the part of the government. We have certain publicity, and an authoritative pronouncement of the grounds upon which the government takes its stand. Where error or injustice has been committed we have the means of challenge in the one place where it is fitting that such challenge should be made. Such an atmosphere, I suggest, is infinitely preferable to the half-lights of the present régime.[59]

No one, of course, denies the vital importance of keeping the administration of law as free as possible from political influence. But that is not the same thing as saying that, in England, for example, the Attorney-General "in forming his opinion on matters of prosecution, is entirely free from any political influences whatsoever".[60] Whenever the case is, in its nature, political, political influence is inevitable. For the whole business of such prosecutions is expediency, and no government, immediately expediency affects matters of policy, can submit to the dictation of its Attorney-General. If that is not the case, Acts of Indemnity are clearly unjustified, since all such acts are a plain interference with the course of law on precisely the ground of expediency. They take away from wronged persons rights possessed by the latter in the ordinary course of justice because the executive deems their abolition desirable. The only way to enable the administration of justice to be free from "any political influence whatsoever" is to place the whole process of prosecution in the hands of a permanent official who is not answerable to the government of the day. I have already discussed that view. It is, I have argued, impossible of application once it is realised that the function involved raises questions of policy. For the only place where the latter can be ultimately decided is upon the floor of the legislative assembly. A permanent official who prosecuted a political figure under a statute of Edward III[61] directed against robbers from over the sea would obviously give rise to debates in Parliament, and if Parliament thought his action impolitic it would obviously censure his action. But immediately that occurred, a function supposedly judicial in character would clearly be merged into one of which the emphatic political incidence was beyond all question. The effect of such an incidence would be fatal to any non-political official. He would hesitate to act in the next similar case. He would judge it not by its merits but by its consequences in difficulty to himself. He would have no real protection against the difficulty, since no ministerial cloak could be thrown about his acts. His position would be an intolerable one. He would be attacked without adequate power of defence, and it would be necessary rapidly to abandon the fiction that his office was judicial in character. For immediately he began to explain himself, it would be found that he was acting upon grounds of policy, and he would be revealed as a branch of the executive whose relation to it was inadequately organised. The purity of judicial administration is not to be found in Sir Robert Horne's theory. For its result would merely cancel the consultation which must take place, the suggestions that are inevitable in any system, from the public view. And no one will be persuaded that their concealment is proof that they have disappeared when the most elementary analysis reveals their urgent importance.

## REFERENCES

1. *Elements of Politics*, p. 481.
2. 12 and 13 W. III, c. 2. III.
3. 198 U.S. 45.
4. See the verbatim report published by the National Union of Railwaymen in 1910.
5. *Ut supra*.
6. B.N. Cardozo, *The Nature of the Judicial Process*, p. 13.
7. *Rex* v. *Muir, S.T.* xxiii, 237-382.
8. *Taff Vale Ry. Co.* v. *A.S.R.S.* (1901), A.C. 426.
9. 236 U.S. 27.
10. The case of Mr. Justice Brandeis. See the extraordinary volume of evidence before the Senate Judiciary Committee on his nomination in 1916.
11. *Report of the Machinery of Government Committee*, p. 66. On the character of judicial appointment in England see my paper in the *Michigan Law Review* for 1926-7, where a statistical analysis of the last hundred years is given.
12. *Collected Papers*, p. 230.
13. Cf. my *Foundations of Sovereignty*, chap. iii.

14. 10 and 11 Geo. V. c. 31.
15. See the daily reports in the London *Times*, May 1-June 6, 1924.
16. For Mr. Justice McCardie's summing-up see *The Times*, June 6, 1924; for criticism in Parliament, see *Parliamentary Debates*, June 9, 1924; on the trial generally, see the London *Nation*, June 13, 1924.
17. Nelles, *Espionage Act Cases*, p. 47.
18. Holdsworth, *Hist. of English Law*, vol. v. p. 440.
19. 1841, N.Y. *Hill*, 377.
20. W.H. Moore, *Act of State in English Law*, p. 44.
21. Cf. *The Pelican. I. Edwards*, Adm. Reports, App. D.
22. *Cawthorn* v. *Campbell* (1790), 1 Anstr. 205.
23. *Ut supra*.
24. (1866) 4 Wall 2.
25. See separate reports by Cockburn.
26. *Loc. cit.*, p. 22.
27. I am not, it must be noted, discussing whether martial law was or was not necessary at this time and place. My criticism is limited to a series of occurrences which are the inevitable result of military administration unchecked by full judicial control.
28. The case of Kitchlew and Satya Pal.
29. These cases, and many others, will be found in the evidence given before the Hunter Commission in 1919, and are supplemented in the evidence given in the case of *O'Dwyer* v. *Nair* in the spring of 1924.
30. *Mitchell* v. *Harmony*, 13 Howard, 115, 134.
31. The deportations were declared illegal in *Ex parte O'Brien* (1923), 2 K.B. 61; the Act of Indemnity is 13 and 14 George V. c. 12. See the debates in Parliament (fifth series), vol. 164, pp. 859, 1682 f., 1703 ff.
32. A good summary of theme is in P.A. Brown, *The French Revolution and English History*.
33. *Ut supra*.
34. I do not, of course, mean that the prosecution should have a right of appeal in criminal cases.
35. Cf. Graham Wallas, *Our Social Heritage*, p. 192.
36. On this whole question see especially R. Saleilles, *The Individualisation of Punishment*; Stephen Hobhouse and A. Fenner Brockway, *The Prison System*; Sidney and Beatrice Webb. *English Prisons under Local Government*; T. Mott Osborne, *Society and Prisons*; James Devon, *The Criminal and the Community*.
37. See an article entitled "The Franks Case" in *New Republic*, September 24, 1924.
38. By which I mean an offence for which the penalty is six months or more.
39. Cf. R.H. Smith, *Justice and the Poor,* for a wealth of information upon this whole subject.
40. Cf. W.H. Dawson, *Municipal Life and Government in Germany*, p. 308.
41. Cf. Smith, *op. cit*.
42. Eleanor Rathbone, *The Disinherited Family*.
43. See his speech in *Hansard*, March 1, 1854.
44. Leslie Stephen, *Life of Fitzjames Stephen*, pp. 351 f.
45. On which see the remark of Professor Maitland in Fisher, *F.W. Maitland*, p. 117.
46. Cf. G. Moran, *La Révolte des faits contre le Code*.
47. *English Law and the Renaissance*, p. 35.
48. Cf. the *Centennial History of the Harvard Law School*.
49. See the papers on legal personality in vol. iii. of his *Collected Papers*.
50. *Collected Papers*, p. 195.

51. *Ut supra*.
52. 208 U.S. 161.
53. *Ut supra*
54. 247 U.S. 251.
55. *Ut supra*
56. *Criminal Justice in Cleveland*.
57. *Collected Papers*, p. 296.
58. Speech to the Hardwicke Society, London *Times*, November 1, 1924.
59. On all this see debate on the Campbell case in the House of Commons, *Parliamentary Debates*, fifth series, vol. 177, No. 128, October 8, 1924, pp. 381 ff.
60. Cf. the remarks of Sir R. Horne in the debate cited in the note above, pp. 581-2.
61. The case of Mr. George Lansbury in 1913.

# 11. International Organisation

## (i) The Basis of International Organisation

I argued in an earlier chapter of this book that the scale of modern civilisation has made the national and sovereign State an institutional expedient of which the political unwisdom and moral danger are both manifest. We are committed to international experiment by the facts about us. We have been driven to recognise the economic interdependence of States. We have come to see that outside purely domestic concerns settlement in terms of common rules is the only method likely to make possible satisfactory international arrangements. The experience of what world-conflict has involved seems to have convinced the best of this generation that the effective outlawry of war is the only reasonable alternative to suicide. We have realised, moreover, that politics includes economics, and that the consequences of a world-market are the settlement in common of those matters of common concern which arise from the fact of a world-market. Since, that is to say, matters like the supply of raw materials, or tariffs, or emigration, affect the world as a whole, no State can be a law unto itself in laying down the rules which obtain in relation to them. International control of some kind and degree is postulated wherever a given State-function directly impinges upon the common life of States.

It was, of course, this perception which led to the inclusion, in the Peace of Versailles, of the Covenant of the League of Nations. I have not here to deal with the grave defects of that instrument in its original form. I do not need to argue—since conviction upon the point is general—that the effectiveness of the League depends very largely upon the degree of its inclusiveness; that, consequently, the absence of States like Russia and America is fatal to the proper fulfilment of its purposes. Nor need I dwell upon the purely technical issue of whether the League is juristically a super-state or merely an association of sovereign nations. I believe myself that it is inevitably destined to become the former and that this character will become increasingly obvious as its functioning becomes more adequate. For it has, in fact, the power to bind its members; and there are already spheres of activity within its ambit of authority in which evasion of the obligations it creates are, if not theoretically impossible, at least sufficiently difficult to be impossible in practice. But the notion that State-sovereignty in international affairs is in truth obsolete still troubles a generation inflamed by the fever of national prejudice; and it is both wiser, and more fruitful, to approach the problems of international organisation from a different angle.

That angle is the discussion of the functions it has to perform and the organs necessary to the performance of those functions. By the analysis of their nature we are much more likely to grasp the character of that which reconciles nationalism with civilisation than if we commit ourselves to the dissection of purely abstract ideas. Broadly speaking, matters of common concern in modern civilisation can be divided into three general categories. There are political problems, there are economic problems, there are social problems. I do not, of course, suggest either that these categories are exhaustive, or that they do not often enough shade off into one another. But, as a rule, the great majority of the questions we have to solve fall fairly reasonably within one or another of them. I shall try to list the main subjects which fall within each, and to say something about their significance as matters of common concern. One general observation may, however, be made. There are many problems of which the incidence concerns mainly two or three States, in which the general international interest is both small and remote; of which a good instance is the work of the International Commission which controls the traffic of the Danube. The solution of such problems can always be confided to the parties predominantly concerned upon two conditions: it must be reached in a public manner, and its substance and the administration of that substance must be approved by, and open to the inspection of, the general international authority. The League of Nations, that is to say, is not likely to become a State in the normal sense of the word. It will concern itself less with direct administration than with propounding, or accepting, solutions which will be administered by others. It will, therefore, be a source of principle rather than an agent of action; though it will, as I shall show later, have to be regarded as the ultimate reserve force in society from which, in the last resort, definite action originates.

## (ii) The Functions of International Organisation

### (a) *Political*

I take first of all the political functions of the League of Nations; and we may first discuss those among its political functions of which the international significance is unquestionable. It is clear—

#### (1) *All Treaties must be Registered*

All treaties must be registered with the League, whatever their extent and nature. This is necessary, not only because of their possible effect upon other States, which, by the fact of registration, are able to raise the question of their substance before the League, but also because secrecy in international arrangements is fatal to the atmosphere of peace. There are, moreover, certain types of treaty which are, *a priori,* obnoxious, which must, therefore, be rendered invalid by the action of the League. Treaties, for instance, in which one State binds itself to joint military action with another, as France practically bound herself to joint military action with Russia before 1914, are indefensible. I do not, of course, .argue that to make registration compulsory will ensure that secret arrangements are obviated. But if only publicly registered and internationally approved treaties are sanctioned by the League, the revelation of arrangements which their makers had attempted to conceal is likely to make those arrangements less effective than they would otherwise be. Had the precise terms of the Anglo-French *entente* of 1904 been revealed when they were made it, would have been much more difficult to secure the atmosphere of war in 1914. Secrecy breeds suspicion, and suspicion is the nurse of fear. The result of compelling publicity is to throw the onus of a grave offence upon powers which, even in the existing atmosphere, do not like to brave the hostile opinion of the world. And such publicity makes possible the necessary provision that no treaty should be regarded as valid until within three months from its publication by the League. For we then have a period in which States affected by the new arrangements may protest against them if they are adversely affected. That is, I think, a legitimate matter for appeal to the Council of the League.

(2) *Boundaries*

The authority of the League should always be invoked in fixing boundaries. Where the States concerned are in agreement upon the line to be drawn, the League may be no more than a source of approval. Where the problem, as with Poland and Germany, is a debatable one, the authority of the League is the only source of a reasonably impartial solution. It is, moreover, through the League only that there can adequately be worked out that system of neutral zones through which we may hope to avoid the difficulties which arise from considerations of strategy. Take, for example, a definitely German territory like the Rhineland. It is unquestionably a source of danger to French security through the opportunities it offers for invasion. If it could be neutralised in a military sense, neither the political nor the economic interests of Germany need suffer. But such demilitarisation can only be effected through the agency of an impartial authority. And, as a rule, the making of boundaries, as in the Balkans, involves the weighing of social and national considerations which are interpreted differently according to the State which makes the interpretation. The League of Nations is the best assurance we have that the changes effected will be reasonable. The assurance, indeed, is not complete; for the plebiscite in Silesia was flagrantly violated by the solution of the League itself. In general, it is probable, the League must make for itself a self-denying ordinance that all boundaries which seek to settle problems of racial affinity must go by majority-rule, and the actual voting must be carried out with safeguards of secrecy as complete as those of an English general election.

(3) *Disarmament*

Ideally, the solution of the disarmament question is a position where no State possesses more armed forces than are necessary for the problems of internal police; as a matter of practice, that solution is Utopian at the present time. But our experience of national competition in the scale of armaments has already taught us some obvious lessons. It has shown that preparation against war is no safeguard against war; that, on the contrary, preparation is the inevitable prelude to war. The history of Anglo-German naval rivalry is in this regard final. And it is clear that unless there is some agreed and proportionate method of defence, under the auspices of the League, observance of which is a condition of continued membership, there is no proper protection against the atmosphere of suspicion which arises out of the uncontrolled power to arm. What principles, then, of control may be said to emerge from our recent experience? They are, I suggest, five in number. (1) No State should be permitted to maintain a conscript army. The training of the adult population to arms is tantamount to an invitation to the powerful State to use its forces for the extension of its influence. It is clear that the relation between the numbers of French and German citizens was, in the atmosphere of conscription, one of the contributory causes in the war of 1914. The maintenance of a purely professional army operates to demilitarise the habits of the general population. It follows, of course that such unpaid troops as the British Territorial Army should likewise be prohibited. (2) The manufacture of armaments, whether naval or military in nature, should be confined to governments. Anyone at all intimately acquainted with the history of the armaments "ring" before 1914 will have realised the disastrous results of allowing private enterprise to live by the belligerent habits they can induce in governments; and it is clear, even after the war, that the new States created by the Peace of Versailles are dragged by the inherent vices of the system into a kindred atmosphere. The manufacture of munitions in Austria was forbidden by the Treaty of Trianon; but there seems no doubt that armaments have been made there for the use of the now independent succession-States. (3) It is necessary, further, to prohibit the manufacture of certain types of armament, of which an obvious illustration is poison gas. There is, doubtless, an irony almost as savage as that of Swift in the notion of civilising warfare. But no one who has seen the effects, say, of poison gas, or of the bombardment of unfortified towns, especially from the air, can doubt that they release barbarisms fatal to the elementary decencies of human nature. And the greater the advance of science, the more disastrous are the consequences of such usage. The matter has become serious enough to affect the whole future of the human race; for if this inventiveness is unchecked, and the chemist, for example, has a period of thirty years in which to perfect his discoveries, the effects of war will be to reduce civilisation to a shambles in which decency will have become a legend. (4) There must be agreed scales of armament between States on the basis partly of population, and, partly, of the volume and area of trade to be defended. Such a rationing of permissible armament does not, of course, seriously diminish the possibility of war; at the best it merely decreases the cost of war in time of peace. But it has the very great value of making the scale of defence public; and the result of that publicity is to lower the dangerous suspicions out of which and upon which the atmosphere of war emerges. It releases public funds, moreover, for pacific purposes; and that is a consequence which, particularly in the sphere of education, has contingently unlimited importance. (5) It is vital that no naval or military bases should be built without the specific approval of the League. It is clear that such efforts as the fortification of Heligoland by Germany or of Singapore by Great Britain, raise questions of far more than merely domestic significance. Had Lord Salisbury foreseen the future of Heligoland, he would never have exchanged it for Zanzibar; and a fortified Singapore is inevitably regarded by Japan as a menace to her safety. If States with outlying possessions are to proliferate fortifications over the world, it is obvious that their neighbours will be compelled to retort in kind, and we shall be threatened with a new form of competition in armaments not less menacing than those of the past. If there is a good case for a naval dock at Singapore, Great Britain ought to be able to make out that case before an independent tribunal. To leave her with the final power to decide is to violate, *ab initio,* every principle of international organisation.

Once it is conceded that disarmament is a matter for the League, the method of securing the observance of these principles becomes important. Clearly, no ordinary executive could expect to cope with the problems to which they give rise. They involve the existence of a standing body of experts who shall report from time to time to the League upon their application. To report, they must have the right to inspect; and to inspect, they must have the right of entry. The League, therefore, must have beneath its executive body a Disarmament Commission charged with the supervision of these functions. It will, of course, be a commission of inquiry and not of action; it will do only what it is authorised to do by its superiors. And such a functional body within the League serves as a type of administrative authority which will doubtless have to be created for not a few purposes. It will act as an eye for the League. It will render its observations independent of the material supplied to it by the States which might, conceivably, be interested in evading their obligations. I do not imply that such a Commission will prevent evasion, any more than the criminal law prevents murders from being committed. But at least it will serve as a safeguard against them.[2]

(4) *Treatment of Minorities, Racial and Religious*

Not the least urgent problem raised in an acute form in the nineteenth century, and accentuated by the provisions of the Peace of Versailles, is that which is raised by the fact that no geographical boundaries, however drawn, can possibly give territorial autonomy to each group of persons claiming distinctive characteristics; nor, on economic grounds, would such separation be desirable. It is, accordingly, important that minorities should be guaranteed in the possession of those rights without which, as I have sought to show above, a creative life is impossible. They are not attained merely by the insertion of a Bill of Rights in a constitution. In Poland and Roumania, in Hungary and Jugo-Slavia, equality before the law has neither existed nor has effort been made to ensure its existence. The only way in which it can be made real is to offer to these minorities the protection of the League. What rights that protection should safeguard varies, naturally, from State to State. In some countries, it involves linguistic protection; Germans do not desire to be coerced into speaking Czech or Polish. In others it is religious protection which is important; Roumanian Jews do not wish to be excluded from universities because their faith is different from that of the general population. What seems necessary, in general, is the establishment of a minority's right to protest to the League against its treatment, with a consequent duty on the part of the League to investigate complaints which seem substantial. Such an investigation ought to involve recommendations after hearings, and it should be an obligation inherent in membership of the League that any State to which such recommendations have to be sent undertakes to carry them out in principle and in detail.

Can the League enforce its recommendations upon an unwilling State? To the point of making war to that end, obviously such enforcement is likely to be, for some time, impossible. But it could, I think, insist that any State which failed to carry them out as a matter of deliberate policy could be subjected to economic boycott. It could be prevented from raising loans abroad; its securities could be removed from the lists quoted in the Bourses of foreign powers; and in extremely bad cases it might be prohibited from trade with those powers. Suspension from membership of the League is also a penalty of a useful kind; for that would be an announcement that the recalcitrant power had defied the public opinion of the world.

It is a question of much interest as to when the treatment of subject-minorities moves over from being a domestic issue to being one of which the League must take account. Suppose, for example, that Egypt or India appealed to the League, as Ireland appealed to the Peace Conference in 1919. Suppose that the Philippines, or Haiti, or San Domingo asked the League for assistance against what, rightly or wrongly, they believed to be maltreatment by the United States. What, in instances such as these, is the duty of the League? A prior question must here be asked. What is to be taken as an appeal from Egypt or Ireland or India? Obviously some discontented minority association has not the right to be heard; its business is, as it best may, to become a majority in the community it seeks to represent. An official appeal must, I think, be taken to mean an appeal from a majority of members representing the minority concerned in the elected assembly of the given State. If they complain of oppression, it should, I think, be the duty of the League to investigate their alleged grievances. The only case against that view is that which rests upon prestige. England did not, in 1919, like the idea of its relations with Ireland being investigated by foreigners; the United States wants independence to come to the Philippines at a time of her own choosing. But a case built only upon prestige is, I think, one that is impossible to maintain. No people, as Sir Henry Campbell-Bannerman said, is ever good enough to govern another people; and if the latter's elected representatives combine to protest against their suzerainty there is at least a *prima facie* case for investigation.

In such cases it should, I suggest, be the function of the League to make independent inquiry. Clearly, all such investigations must be *ad hoc* investigations; and they must take the form of general recommendations which are not binding in character. No League of Nations which ordered England to withdraw from India or Japan to surrender Korea could hope to enforce its views; the most it can attempt is the publication of conclusions and suggestions. And if that work is effectively done, it will be difficult for any government to resist the accretion of public opinion about such a report. It will, moreover, serve another important purpose. Half the difficulties which face the modern world come from our ignorance of foreign affairs; and much of what knowledge we believe ourselves to possess is in fact a system of inductions from tendencious reports. Englishmen actually believe that India is well governed because they govern it themselves; Indians, equally naturally, believe that their exclusion from supreme control is a cause of misgovernance. Only genuinely independent inquiry can awaken either to the other's point of view. But it is important that the inquiry should be genuinely independent. It is no use sending a Roman Catholic to inquire into Hungary's treatment of its minorities to an Anglo-Indian civilian to report upon the future of the Philippines. Bias and error we shall doubtless always have; but the League must take pains to see that they are at their minimum.

(5) *The Treatment of Backward Peoples*

Closely connected with the problem of minorities is that of subject races. Here the League has already acknowledged a measure of responsibility by insistence upon the mandate system for colonies and territories which, as a result of the war of 1914, have been handed over to the victors in that conflict. By Article XXII of the Covenant of the League certain principles of government have been laid down. These territories are divided into three general groups. In the first, of which Iraq and Palestine are examples, the community is recognised as "having reached a stage of development where their existence as independent nations can be provisionally recognised", but they must receive the advice and assistance of the Mandatory Power in matters of administration. The latter, broadly speaking, may regard them as a temporary protectorate. In the second group, the territory becomes what is, in the British Empire, a Crown Colony without representative institutions. The Mandatory Power guarantees religious freedom. It agrees to enforce the prohibition of slavery and the slave trade, of the liquor traffic and the sale of arms, and to protect the interest of the natives in all transactions about land. It agrees not to establish fortifications, or naval and military bases; and to train the natives in arms no further than is necessary for police and defence. Freedom of trade is also secured. Togoland and the Cameroons are examples of this type of mandate. The third class is of territories which, either because of their small size, like Naurn, or their thin population, like South-West Africa, are integrally absorbed into the territory of the Mandatory Power, and become subject to such laws as it chooses to make. In all three classes the Mandatory Power must make an annual report on its work to the League; and the latter has established a Permanent Mandates Commission of nine members, five of whom belong to non-mandatory, and four to mandatory States, to watch in detail over the operation of the system. None of these members, moreover, who sit for the Mandatory States, must be in the employ of the governments concerned.

No one can deny that these principles represent, in general, a great advance upon methods so far suggested for the government of native races. Anyone who compares them, for example, with the principles actually involved in the penetration of the African continent[3] will realise that the possibility of a new atmosphere has been created. But, it may be suggested, there is still a great gulf fixed between the principles adumbrated and the measures taken to ensure their application. The annual report is made by the Mandatory Power; the State to be scrutinised, that is to say, reports from time to time that its conduct has been good; and the attitude of South Africa over the Bondelwarts rebellion will make most independent observers a little dubious whether such reports are the best way to the goal in view. There are, in fact, two quite obvious ways in which they can be supplemented. There should, in the first place, be accredited to each mandated territory of the League a commissioner who will act as its ambassador upon the spot. He should belong always to a different State from that of the Mandatory Power. It should be his business to keep watch upon its work, and independently to report upon it to the League. All regulations made by the Mandatory Power should be referred to him for approval, and, in the event of his disagreement, they should be confirmed or denied by the Permanent Mandates Commission. Where trouble occurs, as in the Bondelwarts rebellion, it should be his function to make an independent judicial inquiry and to report directly to the League as early as possible after the outbreak. He should himself always speak the most usual language of the territory, and have an independent staff speaking the languages of the different peoples. Thereby the League would possess an independent and continuous check upon the work of the Mandatory Powers; its discussion of their work would not be based mainly, as now, upon what the latter had chosen to tell them. It could really investigate trouble; whereas, at present, if it chose to make investigation, most of the relevant evidence would already have perished. Dead natives do not differ from other men in being able to tell no tales. It may be added that there is no reason why the mandate system should not be extended to all territories in which the native races predominate. Every reason for League control of Togoland is a reason for League control of Kenya; and there is already provision in the Covenant whereby this extension might without difficulty be made.[4]

Such a system of inspection, I believe, is of the first importance; but it will not by itself guarantee adequacy. Not less important is the quality of the personnel engaged in the administration of mandates. The League cannot, of course, control appointments to the colonial service of a Mandatory Power; but it can, if necessary, and after appropriate investigation, demand disciplinary measures, including dismissal from the service, of persons so appointed. It can, further, insist that no person shall be appointed to the service without an adequate training in ethnology and anthropology, and ability to speak the language of the territory he is to administer. It is the clear lesson of research that ability to understand native customs is essential to wise administration in these matters; and only a genius can hope to learn them by rule of thumb on the spot.[5] It is important, further, to see that no white settlers engaged in commerce should possess judicial powers. They are there for profit, and it is obvious from the history of commerce in such territories that the trader cannot be trusted to do justice to the native. Nor, so far as possible, should forced labour be permitted; certainly the native should never be hired out over a period in which specific performance is enforced to private persons. The matter is different where public works, like the making of roads, are concerned. But the general rule that labour employed should be normal wage-labour is a principle of great importance.

### (6) *Aggression, Wars and Disputes*

The value of the League of Nations depends clearly upon its power to prevent war. Let us examine the provisions already made in the Covenant for the peaceful settlement of disputes. Each member, in the first place, guarantees both the territory and the existing independence of all other members of the League against external aggression; and it is the function of the Council of the League to advise upon the methods of fulfilling this obligation.[6] War, or the threat of war, is, secondly, a matter of concern to the League, whether its members are affected or not; and when such emergency arises, the Council of the League is to be summoned forthwith. Every member of the League has "the friendly right" to bring to the attention either of the Assembly or the Council circumstances tending to disturb international peace.[7] In the event of dispute between members of the League, they agree, if the dispute seems suitable to arbitration or judicial settlement, to submit the problem to such settlement if the ordinary diplomatic channels fail; and they agree not to resort to war until three months after the award under such a settlement has been made, the period of that award being six months, at a maximum from the submission of the dispute to the council.[8] The members of the League agree to carry out the terms of an award in good faith, and failure involves action against the recalcitrant member by the Council.[9] For the purpose of such arbitration a permanent International Court of Justice has been created.[10]

But, obviously, the root of the matter lies in disputes which members of the League are not prepared to submit to arbitration. In that event, the members agree to submit the matter to the Council, and submission is effected by one of the parties to the dispute giving notice thereof to the Secretary-General of the League. Preparations are then made for full inquiry, and the Council seeks the means of settlement. If it fails, it makes, either unanimously or by a majority, a report of conclusions and recommendations; and dissenting members are entitled to publish a minority report. If the report of the Council is unanimous, and one part to the dispute agrees with it, the members of the League pledge themselves not to make war upon that party. If no unanimous report is issued, the parties remain free to take individual action. The Council does not act when the subject of a dispute is found to be of a domestic and not of an international nature; and it may, if it think fit, refer the dispute to the Assembly of the League which then acts in the place, and with the powers of the Council, so long as the member-States on the Council and a majority of the Assembly concur in the report. In all such decisions, of course, the parties concerned in the dispute do not take a voting part.[11]

So much is already League-law, binding upon its members; and, before we discuss the method of its enforcement, it is perhaps well to see how far it takes us. The Covenant provides machinery for the settlement of disputes which do not raise the difficult problems of prestige; particularly, it makes permanently justiciable problems which arise out of treaties or international law. It compels settlement in non-justifiable disputes where the Council is unanimous, but it still leaves open the door to war where there is disagreement on the council. No one, I think, can deny that work of some significance has already been done under these provisions. Certainly the issues between Finland and Sweden over the Aaland Islands, and between Jugo-Slavia and Albania, over the northern frontier of the latter States, were settled promptly and fairly by these means. That, however, which arose between Greece and Italy in the summer of 1923, and resulted in the bombardment by Italy of Corfu, is evidence that the utilisation of these provisions is no easy matter. Sanctions apart, it is clear that they need supplement, especially in the direction of a definition of what disputes are justiciable, and how an aggressor in the case of conflict is to be defined. The provisions, moreover, do not bind non-members of the League, and the provision of two of these powers, America and Russia, may be decisive in the future of civilisation.

Let me take these points separately. It is, I think, urgent in the interests of peace that it be emphasised in the regulations of the League that there is no such thing as a dispute not capable of settlement either by an international court of justice or by arbitration. For immediately a nation-State assumes that a given issue touches its honour, and it cannot, therefore, submit itself to an international jurisdiction, it is, in fact, adopting the same mental attitude as the protagonist in a private duel. Austrian "honour" was not vindicated in 1914 by making war upon Servia; Italian "honour" was not vindicated in 1923 by bombarding Corfu. In each case real issues were evaded by being enveloped in a miasma of prestige which prevented their exploration in terms of the facts they involved. The conception that a nation-State which either commits wrong, or believes itself to be wrong, can make its own law, represents a faith as outworn as, and infinitely more dangerous than, the creed which assumed that an insulted aristocrat of the eighteenth century could only vindicate himself by blood. "The national honour", as Mr. Veblen has well said,[12] "moves in the realm of magic, and touches the frontiers of religion". For no one seriously believes that an outraged corporate personality is made whole again by any of the ways involved in the code of diplomatic procedure. The common man does not, as a rule, even know that it has been outraged until his patriotism is appealed to by methods which frequently lose sight of the facts which are said to constitute outrage. And if honour, being dissatisfied in terms of punctilio, then proceeds to war, the common man may pay the penalty in terms which go far beyond any price commensurate with the original sin.

I believe, therefore, that it is necessary to define the jurisdiction of the League over disputes much more broadly than is now the case. (1) It must not only have jurisdiction, as now, over disputes susceptible of legal decision, or by agreed arbitration, or by settlement in terms of unanimous decision by the Council of the League. It must assume (2) that all disputes are within its competence and that any decision reached by even a bare majority must be accepted by the parties to the dispute because such a decision, even when regarded as unfair by either or both, is, in the light of historic experience, preferable to decision by war. The latter type of decision is either no decision at all, or, at best, merely involves the welfare of a small group in the victorious nation-State to the detriment of the vast majority of its citizens. The universal jurisdiction of the League is, therefore, elementary. The problem then becomes one of organising the administration of its powers, rather than of inquiring into those powers themselves.

One point of importance may here be noted. If, it is argued, compulsory settlement is to be the rule, two vast areas of dispute immediately come into view. (1) There are problems connected with the Treaty of Versailles the present settlement of which is bound to be a temporary one. The present constitution of the League, especially by canonising, in Article X, the present frontiers of nation-States stereotypes obvious injustice; and many nation-States, rather than submit to justice, will defy the League and risk war. (2) There are also problems, like the admission of Japanese to Australia, or of Indians to Kenya, which may be settled on paper by arbitration; but the white races, in either case, will fight, whatever the risk, against a settlement imposed from without that is contrary to their own view. Neither of these views is, I think, a tenable one. No one who reads the Treaty of Versailles can doubt that it is instinct, at many points, with grave injustice. But no one also, as I think, can deny that those injustices are susceptible of remedy in such a system as is here outlined, and that, alternatively, the making of war is not in the least likely to remedy them. There are injustices in relation to the boundaries of States. These can, it may be suggested, be met in a variety of ways. If the difficulties involved, are economic in nature, as when a State becomes landlocked by the revision of boundaries, it is possible to arrange for utilisation, on agreed terms, of the nearest available seaport. If the difficulties are strategic in character, the way out lies through the building of neutral zones. If they relate to the treatment of a national or religious minority, the principles already urged above become germane. It will, of course, become essential eventually to amend Article X by permitting of its revision upon agreed principles; as it stands, it represents the passion of a war-time period. But, as those passions die away, there is room for its amendment within the confines of the Covenant of the League; and such a method is clearly preferable to the use of a force which cannot, in its employment, be possibly confined to any precise or limited objective.

Nor, I believe, do the problems of which the admission of Japanese to Australia is an example offer final difficulties. The issue is not, of course, a simple one. Ultimately, it is inevitable, I think, that problems of international migration should come within the ambit of the League. But it is obvious that to decide such problems in principle is a very different matter from deciding upon their administrative technique. Australians, clearly, cannot claim to exclude Japanese altogether, without agreeing to their own exclusion from Japan. That is, probably, an impossible position in view of the economic relationships involved. But, in admitting Japanese, Australia might well be regarded as entitled to settle (1) the annual number of immigrants she is prepared to receive; (2) the conditions they shall observe after entrance into Australian territory; (3) their possible segregation to specific belts of territory. The ideal of a "white Australia" is a perfectly intelligible one; and no League of Nations which strove to be realistic could fail to demand of those who proposed to emigrate the observance of those conditions upon which the standard of a "white Australia" depends. But the converse is also the case; and white people who emigrate, say, to the hinterlands of Africa cannot demand that the mandatory powers use their authority to safeguard the type of civilisation to which they are accustomed against conditions to which it is unrelated.

If, then, all disputes are to be within the province of the League, how is aggression involving League action to be defined? There are, I think, three categories of acts which make possible the naming of an aggressor. (1) A power which refuses to accept the jurisdiction of the League is an aggressor. (2) A power which, having accepted jurisdiction, refuses to accept a settlement made by the League is an aggressor. (3) A power which, under (1) or (2) uses the intervals before League action to prepare itself for war by increasing its armaments or its effectives becomes thereby an aggressor. In all these cases the League must exercise against States which put themselves in any of these categories all the authority at its command.

A general question here arises with which it is necessary to deal before the methods of enforcing League authority are discussed. The question has two sides. There is the issue, first, of dealing with non-members of the League. For some period, at any rate, America will not join the League. What will occur if she becomes involved with Japan in a crisis which seems likely to result in war? The answer is, I think, plain. America, like any other power, must be offered arbitration by the League. Her refusal to accept such arbitration must be recognised as not less definitively an act of aggression than if it were made by England or France or Italy. For the consequences of an American-Japanese war cannot be limited to the original combatants; and the State which fights must be made relentlessly aware that it fights at its peril. If it is argued that Canada or Australia would, in such a conflict, refuse to accept the orders of the League, would, indeed, possibly fight on the side of America, the only possible answer is that if this should occur, as it might well occur, it would, of course, destroy the League. Upon the consequences of that destruction I do not need to dilate. But it is, I think, obvious that with the breakdown of the League there would be an end to international experiment. We Should then revert to the pre-1914 situation, which is, as we have learned, the inevitable source of war.

The other aspect of the general question is the possibility that member-States may refuse to accept either the jurisdiction or the recommendations of the League, in defiance of their plain obligations. I do not deny such a possibility; it is inherent in all that has here been urged about the general nature of legal obligation. All that can be said to the contrary is this: The degree of allegiance the League commands will depend (a) upon the confidence it commands by the work it does and (b) by the sanctions at its disposal. The League, clearly, if it can prove its good-will to its members, is, to the degree of its success, unlikely to forfeit its authority; and if it can make the position of a recalcitrant member impossible, the motive of fear may prove adequate. But there is, frankly, no guarantee in either position. Anyone, whether in the State or in the League of Nations, who is determined to resist authority whatever the consequences will naturally resist it; no law is immune from the wilful lawbreaker. All, accordingly, we can do is to minimise by organisation the chance that such infractions will occur.

If, then, such be the jurisdiction of the League, we have to inquire into the powers that it needs to carry out its functions. The existing sanctions are defined in Article XVI of the Covenant of the League. These, broadly speaking, are three in number. (1) Any nation-State which resorts to war under the conditions outlined above is penalised by the severance of all economic relations with members of the League, and all other intercourse of a financial, commercial or personal kind. (2) The Council is to recommend what effective naval, military or air force the members of the League are severally to contribute for the protection of the Covenant. (3) Passage through its territory is to be afforded by all members of the League to any State co-operating with the League by a unanimous vote of the Council to expel from membership any State which has violated the Covenant.

In principle, at least, these sanctions are powerful enough to satisfy anyone of their theoretical effectiveness. In part, clearly, the machinery of sanctions must always be left vague; it would be ridiculous to call into being the same scale of attack against a recalcitrant Great Britain as against a recalcitrant Albania. But, assuming the nature of such sanctions, the question of whether they can be called into being is obviously a question of the first importance. Obviously, in the first place, the military obligations of each power concerned must be defined. The League must know what forces—naval, military, aerial—it can count upon in applying sanctions. It must, obviously also, publish these facts, in order that members of the League may realise the striking force of the League. But would the States so obliged fulfil their obligations? Here, of course, we dwell in the realm of conjecture. If they did not, obviously the League would come to an end amid derision. If it is necessary to apply force, and it found that it could not depend upon its members, it would be useless. Yet that failure is unlikely, for the reason that the League, in deciding upon military sanctions, is, after all, the States which have to supply the means of sanction; and they will not cover themselves with ridicule. They may default; but if the problem involved in serious enough to necessitate the use of armed force, their default seems unlikely.

The use of economic, sanctions is in another, and less difficult, atmosphere. This is probably the most effective weapon at the disposal of the League; for in the midst of an economic world-order it is improbable that any State can afford to pay the penalty such sanctions would involve. Its credit-structure would be ruined. It would be shut out from all sources of export. It would not be able to import necessary food commodities and raw materials. Italy, for example, would lack coal, copper, and iron; and, all else apart, without these the conduct of war is impossible. Experience of the blockade in the years from 1914 has taught most European nations that the power to control the flow of goods and services is a fundamental power. It is a weapon which can be brought into play without great effort, and it is rapid in its results. Save in the case of self-sufficient

States like Russia and America, it is doubtful whether any member of the League could long withstand its rigorous application. Its silent character, moreover, the fact that it does not involve the contingent expenditure of life on the part of the States co-operating in its use, makes it likely that this will be the most general type of sanction applied by the League in cases of importance. Nor do I think it is a sanction in which States will refuse to co-operate.[13]

### (b) *Social*

Under Articles XXIII to XXV of the Covenant of the League of Nations certain matters of general social welfare are placed under its supervision. They possess, I believe, an importance which far surpasses the attention they have commanded in popular interest. For, in part, they constitute a body of functions in relation to which the League already encountered either existing international agreements, on the one hand, or a body of fairly coherent international opinion on the other; and they represent a field of activity success in which is likely to result in the transference of faith in international organisation to the more striking functions of the League. As at present defined, and omitting matters already discussed above, these social functions may be divided into six general groups. The League (1) is to secure and maintain fair and humane conditions of labour for men, women and children both in the territories of League members and of those with whom these have dealings, and to create appropriate international institutions for the purpose. (2) It is to supervise and execute agreements relating to the traffic in women and children, and such noxious drugs was opium. (3) It is to secure and maintain (a) freedom of communication and transit, and (b) equitable commercial treatment for the members of the League. (4) Where disease has an international incidence, the League is to take steps for its control and prevention. (5) It is, by consent, to extend its supervision to existing international bureaus, such as the Institute of Agriculture at Rome, and, where such as the Institute of Agriculture at Rome, and, where such supervision is not exercised, it is to assist in whatever way is thought desirable by the Council; and all future international organisations are to be placed under its direction. (6) It is to promote and assist Red Cross Organisations which aim at "the improvement of health, the prevention of disease, and the mitigation of suffering throughout the world".

This is, clearly, an ambitious programme; but, with some hesitation, as in the case of Russia, not unconnected with the partisan atmosphere of war, the League may fairly be said to have genuinely attempted to give it concrete substance. I shall deal below with the economic activities of the League. But it is useful here to note the type of effort which illustrates this branch of international function. Much has been done to repatriate prisoners of war, and, analogously, to relieve refugees from Russia and the Near East. Something has been achieved in mitigating the horrors of the White Slave Traffic and of the deportation of women and children to Turkey and Asia Minor. Conferences have met in the effort to control the traffic in opium and cocaine; and though what has here been revealed is perhaps rather the degree of homage paid by commercial hypocrisy to the international conscience, there are greater signs of good-will in the matter than at any previous time. A real effort, further, has been made to check the spread of typhus in Eastern Europe, and it is likely that only the League could have been effective in this regard. The financial reconstructions of Austria and Hungary are very definite achievements. Less, perhaps, has been accomplished for the maintenance of the common intellectual life of European civilisation, though instances of assistance in a small way are not lacking. In sum total, I think, it is fair to say that a real start in beneficent organisation has been made. The problem is the intensification of effort rather than the realisation of its importance.

What direction should that intensification take? Certain obvious possibilities suggest themselves. There are needed, in the first place, under the aegis of the League, permanent Commissions, parallel to the existing Commissions on Mandates and on Intellectual Co-operation, of which the importance would, over a period, be very great. (1) There is needed a Commission on Educational Work in Backward Countries. This applies not merely to mandated territories, where special technical problems are involved, but also to areas like the Balkans, where education is still at an unreasonably primitive level. We need to develop a common minimum of educational effort among all members of the League if the full impact of its work is to be made plain to the common people. We have to organise interchange of teachers and pupils among different States if our educational systems are to transcend their present provincialism. We have to be able to offer advice to States which realise their lack of adequate staff and methods, and, where possible, to provide access to a supply of teachers. There is, of course, some cultural interchange now; but its organisation is directed rather to the enhancement of specific national influence than to building a medium of international advantage. (2) There is needed, secondly, a Permanent Medical Commission dealing primarily with the organisation of medical work in backward areas, with sub-commissions under its control actually doing medical work in those areas. The work now done on a small scale by such bodies as the Yale Medical College in China needs to be co-ordinated with the deliberate end of relating it in a coherent way to world needs. Such a commission could cultivate relations with foundations like that of

Mr. Rockefeller in New York. It could advise and report upon current medical organisation. It could organise expert inquiries into particular medical problems. It could bring to the knowledge of medical men in Jugo-Slavia the importance, for instance, of recent American work on the prevention of rickets among children.[14] A series of carefully prepared bulletins on medical progress in different branches would be of the highest value in regions which, at present, are for practical purposes entirely ignorant of the advances which have been made. (3) There is needed, thirdly, an International Commission on Official Statistics. I have already urged the great importance of quantitative knowledge upon social questions; and such knowledge is the more valuable, the wider the area of comparison upon which it is built. At present that area is narrow because it is practically impossible to compare the statistics of one country with those of another, through differences in form and method. We can compare the infantile death-rate of English and American cities, but we cannot compare, in any realistic way, the wage-rates in similar industries. We need, therefore, an international body charged with two functions: (a) The adoption of increasingly uniform methods in the collection and presentation of statistics, and (b) the preparation of reports upon the results of comparing State with State upon this basis. This does not require any large organisation. It involves a small permanent staff at Geneva, and the association therewith of government officials and other experts in an organised and continuous way. Such an effort, it may be added, is really urgent if we are to tackle in a hopeful way the problems of economic co-operation by which the world is confronted. (4) There is needed, fourthly, an International Commission on Law. Such a body would, of course, sit under the ultimate control of the International Court of Justice. It would seek to effect three things. (a) It would assist in the codification of international law, both public and private. (b) It would attempt to develop uniformity in branches of the law, as, for example, that of bills and notes, or the incorporation of public companies, where incorporation is obviously desirable. (c) It would act as an advisory body on questions of law where, though the paramountcy of the individual State must be preserved, it is desirable to have an expression of expert international opinion. Examples of this type of question are legislation relating to aliens; to the legal position of women who marry foreigners; to the position of political offenders who have fled from the State, where their offence was committed, and so forth. Such a commission, once more, does not need any formidable panoply of organisation. It requires a small permanent staff, together with the power to initiate sub-commissions of special inquiry. And, in general, it would be advisable that these sub-commissions should be composed not only of government representatives, but also of persons delegated thereto by legal organisations for their special competence in particular problems.

### (c) *Economic*

Obviously, no international organisation would be effective which failed to take account of economic questions. I argued in an earlier chapter that the relation of nationalism to industrialism is now so complex and so interwoven that the problems raised by the one can only be solved by meeting the problems specifically raised by the other. That has been, at least in part, recognised by the labour section in the Treaty of Versailles, and by the creation, under the Covenant of the League of Nations, of the International Labour Office. Indeed, it does not need discussion to demonstrate that a tariff may be not less a cause of economic conflict than a frontier; and in modern diplomacy the objects of discussion tend more and more to be concerned with economic questions. Anglo-Russian relations, for instance, are poisoned by the problem of the debts incurred by Russia before the Revolution of 1917. The boundary of Mesopotamia is connected, as is the status of Mexico, with its oil-wells. The relation of the Great Powers to China is set by its immense and unused natural resources. The prospects of Italy in a world-system are built upon her access to a supply of electric power; and the absence from her territories of a coal-deposit makes the problem of fuel for industrial purposes one of immense political significance for her. So, also, with the large issues of foreign investment and of a mercantile marine. It is clear that an ability to invest abroad may bring one State under the political dominion of another, as Egypt became a protectorate of Great Britain. It is clear also that if the mercantile marine of one nation-State has lower freight-costs than that of another, by reason, for instance, of differential advantages such as America could grant by her control of the Panama Canal, grave international complications might result. It is clear, finally, that only with reasonably uniform labour conditions can industrial competition approximate to fairness. The price of English coal is bound, broadly speaking, to be higher than that of German coal, if the standard-day of the English miner is seven hours and that of the German miner eight; even more, for similar goods, the English cotton-operative cannot maintain his market if his price is to meet that, for instance, paid by the millowners of Bombay and Osaka.

I take, of course, only a few instances amid the great variety that exist. They imply, I think, that the League must undertake far wider economic control than is provided for under its existing organisation. I can only attempt here the broadest kind of indication of the economic categories over which, as I believe, the influence of the League should become paramount. I do not argue that it is likely to become paramount in any short space of time. No nation-State is likely to part with sovereignty over its economic concerns until, in the area of political affairs; the competence and good-will of the League has been proved beyond a doubt. It is, indeed, possible that in some of these categories the power of the League will develop less into thoroughgoing control than into the authority to make recommendations, or to find conclusions, which the good-will of individual States is left to translate into substance. But a brief discussion of one or two categories of this kind will serve the purpose of at least indicating the region into which the League must make its way.

(1) *International Investment*

I do not need to dwell in any detail over the power of international investment. English dealings with South Africa and Egypt, American dealings with Haiti, with San Domingo and with Mexico, French dealings with Russia, are merely instances of a traffic of which the consequences have been incalculable.[15] What, I think, emerges from any consideration of their meaning is the need of a twofold system of control. (1) Where the loan involved is made to a State, its terms should be approved by the League, whether it is made by the investors of a single State or on some apportioned system of contribution, as in the loan made to Germany under the Dawes scheme in the autumn of 1924. (2) The method of repayment should never include a power which may threaten the political independence of a State, as the independence of Egypt was destroyed under the British occupation. (3) It should never carry with it the grant of economic concessions to the citizens of any special State; there develops, otherwise, the type of problem which is illustrated by the history of concessions in Morocco and Persia. (4) Where the money loaned is to be spent outside the debtor-State, as in the purchase, for instance, of rolling-stock for a railway, the purchase should be made by the decision of the debtor-State in concert with an *ad hoc* advisory committee appointed by the League. (5) No State should be entitled to act on behalf of any investors who have participated in a loan without the sanction of the League. (6) No State should permit its citizens to invest in any loan to a State which is not a member of the League fully performing its functions as a member, and, in especial, the obligations involved in the conventions of the International Labour Office.

But loans to a State, even when so safeguarded, do not exhaust the problems of international investment. It is important, also, to organise methods of supervising the operations of business men abroad, especially in backward territories. Anyone who reads the history of the Congo, or of Putumayo, will realise without difficulty why such supervision is required. But these are only the last terms in a series the consequences of which demand at every point scrutiny. The grounds of this control have been succinctly stated by Mr. Brailsford. "If a man or a company wishes to trade or lend money abroad under cover of our flag", he writes,[16] "it is obvious that if we intend in any degree to protect or recognise his business, it must be open to investigation, and it must conform to such rules as the present standards of international morality may lay down". Mr. Brailsford was writing in 1914, when a League of Nations did not seem practical; the requirement in our own day must be conformity, not to a State-made basis of obligation, but to one arrived at under the aegis of the League. It would, I think, involve some such system of conditions as the following: (1) Each State should keep a register of undertakings engaged in business abroad. The register should be divided into enterprises receiving recognition and those to which, for reasons set out below, recognition was refused; the cost of registration being met by an annual fee like that now charged for the registration of companies. (2) The register should be revised annually, and should be open to inspection by the public. A copy of it, brought up to date, should be kept at the headquarters of the League. (3) Recognition should be refused to any person or company which (a) does not observe the labour conditions established by the International Labour Office; (b) the obligations, especially under the Mandates, established by the League of Nations; (c) which attempts to trade with countries in which slavery persists; (d) which attempts either financial or military intervention in a State which is either engaged in civil or foreign war. (4) Where a company asks for recognition and it is refused, an appeal should be permissible to the courts. (5) Where appeal against a recognition already made is lodged with the League of Nations, it should be competent for the International Court of Justice to hear the appeal, the costs, on failure, to be borne by the appellant. If the appeal is successful, the State in which the company is registered should pay the costs. (6) No company to which recognition has been refused should have the right (a) to have its securities quoted on the stock exchanges of any member of the League; (b) the right to sue in any court of law, except for the purpose of appealing against any refusal of recognition; (c) the right to the services of any embassy or consulate of any member of the League; (d) the right of entry into any mandated territories. An infraction of this latter rule should be punished by the imprisonment or heavy fine of the agent attempting entry.

It is not pretended here that such a system as this is exhaustive, for, clearly, experience will suggest a variety of other expedients. But at least a register of this kind would put grave difficulties in the way of the undesirable trader who, like Don Pacifico, or the Mannesmann brothers, is really exploiting the national prestige for his own personal benefit. It would not, I think, in any way hinder legitimate trading. Practically every firm which does business with the normal civilised State would be recognised as a matter of course; those excluded would be firms dealing, for the most part, with backward areas upon conditions which seemed inequitable. To deprive the latter of commercial status in international affairs is to recognise the reputability of recognised firms; and that is to introduce a much-needed element of ethics into business enterprise. I do not, of course, deny that, upon occasion, the possible gains from unauthorised adventure will be high enough to persuade men to the risk; and some of them, at least, will be able to evade the safeguards here suggested. But at least we shall discourage hereby the majority of adventurers of this type; and the advantage of so doing will, I think, appear unquestionable to anyone who surveys impartially the history of foreign investment.

(2) *Tariffs*

For reasons into which I cannot here enter, a tariff for revenue only, as opposed to tariffs which attempt to protect the domestic industries of a given State, seems to me a clear path to international peace.[17] But it is fairly clear that, outside Great Britain and Holland, the majority of the members of the League are likely, over a long period, to remain fully persuaded that what may briefly be described as economic Colbertism is to their advantage. The business of the League, therefore, reduces itself to the function of preventing a tariff being used as a method of economic discrimination against its members, or of using a tariff as a means of penalising those of its members who do not observe the economic obligations which arise under the Covenant. The League, therefore, should aim at equality of treatment for all its members under any tariff .adopted by one of them; it should prohibit those "most-favoured nation" clauses in commercial systems which operate to the disadvantage of other States. Inferentially, therefore, it should, I think, prevent the granting of preferences by the Dominions to Great Britain, and vice versa. For these operate to erect a closed economic system between the States concerned; and that has, historically, a pernicious effect on international relations.

(3) *Other Economic Functions*

But a temporary inability to deal with tariffs beyond this point does not, I think, debar the League from considering ways and means of dealing with two other matters of grave economic importance. There are countries in which the standard of life, whether measured in wages, hours of labour, or factory conditions, are so low that its commodities can be purchased at a cost far below that of other countries where better standards obtain. Factory labour in India, for example, has still to learn the meaning, in any vigorous way, of trade unions; and, while its standard of wages is intolerable, its hours of labour are reminiscent of the conditions in England before the Ten Hours Act of 1844.[18] What is to be done in cases where the products of such labour undersell that produced under equitable conditions? There should, I suggest, be a power inherent in the Council of the League, upon recommendation from the International Labour Office, to demand from such a State the creation, within a specified time, of a system analogous to the Trade-Board system in Great Britain, but with powers extended to cover the whole range of industrial conditions. These Trade Boards should apply standards agreed upon as adequate by the International Labour Office, and certified to be such by the latter within twelve months of their establishment. If the Council is informed that the required improvement has not been effected, it should be empowered to demand from member-States an embargo upon the imports from the recalcitrant power. Such a policy, I believe, follows logically from the pledge in the Covenant to secure and maintain fair and humane conditions of labour.

The second problem is much more far-reaching in immediate, though not, I believe, in ultimate character. It is concerned with the utilisation of raw materials in mandated territories or unexploited areas. There is no reason why, unless we regard profit-making as a final reason, we should allow the wastage of natural resources in such areas as has taken place in civilised countries. In all such cases exploitation should take place only upon conditions approved by the League; and the working of those conditions should, from time to time, be inspected by the League in order to make certain that the conditions are observed. If, for example, oil is discovered in large quantities in Mesopotamia, the technical circumstances of its production ought not to be determined by the company which secures the concession, but by an *ad hoc* commission of the League, assisted by independent expert testimony. If gold is discovered in Tropical Africa, its production ought to be organised in similar fashion. There is every reason why the League should, in this sense, come to regard itself as a trustee for the future; and to the degree that it insists upon such trusteeship it will remove a source of grave friction in international relations.

This problem of the control of natural resources in unorganised areas raises, of course, the much more complicated question of their control in normal States. Here, at the least, we have some small, but important, experience, to go upon. We learned in the years of war that it was possible (a) to organise service in terms of need, and (b) to establish international[20] mechanisms for the determination of that need. No one can have read Sir Arthur Salter's history of the control of allied shipping or the record of the British Government in the purchase in bulk of necessary raw materials, without the sense that such methods look towards a system in which there is a permanent replacement of the middleman by a combination of States purchasing, through the League, the stock of raw materials over a series of years, at an agreed price, and distributing the stock on a principle of prior need.[21] The investigation, at least, of such a possibility appears important for two reasons. It makes possible, in the first place, the maintenance of a stable world price-level for essential commodities; and it brings, secondly, into the field of possibility, the removal of unnecessary and expensive competition in the commodity so controlled.

Before I attempt to explore the implications of this principle, it is worth while to note that certain indirect steps to this end of an interesting kind are already in existence. When, in 1904, Mr. Lubin founded the International Institute of Agriculture, one of the purposes he had in mind was the reduction of speculative dealings in the food supplies of the world, and he proposed international organisation against rings and monopolies which acted to that end. Here, as elsewhere, international business has been in advance of international government. Bodies like the White Sea and Baltic Conference, like the International Rail Syndicate, like the Continental Commercial Union in the Glass Industry, have for years conducted their operations on the basis of an agreed sales area, an agreed output, and an agreed price.[22] Their object, of course, was the maximum of profit with the minimum of risk. There does not seem to be any *a priori* reason why the governments of States should not utilise the machinery of the League in suitable regions to assist their peoples to a full supply of necessary commodities at a reasonable price.

The method, indeed, by which such operations are effected is not likely to be of any uniform pattern, nor is it likely to be entrusted to an *ad hoc* body with plenary powers, like the Reparations Commission. It is much more likely to be a series of consultative bodies, appointed through, and reporting to, the League, but working through the executive of each member of the League. The latter will, as Sir Arthur Salter has pointed out[23] be influenced by and co-ordinated in their operations by these bodies; but they will be jointly moved less by direct control than by reciprocal influence. It may be, for example, that the English Government will purchase that proportion of the world's wheat supply needed by its people separately from France; but it will purchase it in the light of a full knowledge of what France is doing and a sense of the impact upon France of its separate action. So, also, Italy may contract with Great Britain for the purchase of coal; and the settlement of that purchase will be made by a body which realises its influence upon the policy of the South American Republics. Thereby is established the vital principle of international organisation that governments would deliberately and continuously negotiate upon the joint settlement of large economic issues.

Certain inferential principles which here emerge may be noted in passing, since their results bear upon a later stage of the argument. It is possible, I have urged, for governments to co-operate in settling large economic questions. That settlement will probably be best effected, not by an executive body, but by the co-ordianted consultation of those in the separate States who are responsible for the political action involved. In general, it is best that such consultation should take place, not, as in the older diplomacy, through the medium of Foreign Offices, but through direct connection between the specialised department. The British Board of Trade should deal directly with the French Ministry of Commerce; the Italian Minister of Agriculture should concert measures with the German Minister of Agriculture. Direct connection entails permanent institutions of contact. It is not enough to have occasional meetings of heads of departments. The responsible permanent personal must learn to know each other intimately, to feel out each other's minds, to gather from these continuous relations the ability to apply a sense of international need to the work of their own States. That involves, as Sir Arthur Salter has rightly insisted,[24] the growth between officials of a confidence great enough to enable them "to discuss policy frankly in its earlier stages, and before it has been formed and formulated in their respective countries". For, thereby, we avoid the danger of implicating in discussion the prestige of an administration; we prevent it from having to give way in the public view. We get the basis of a common decision reached before governments have committed themselves to one view or another. No officials, of course, can, or should, commit their respective countries; but when the margins of agreement are known, it becomes a far easier matter to settle the powers to be conferred upon officials who make the solutions in terms of principles of which the limits are fairly well defined. Meetings of governments then become official occasions sanctioning plans of which the outlines are already organised. And the plans so made may become instinct with a spirit of internationalism simply by the way in which officials, through their personal contact, have learned to realise and weigh other points of view.

I emphasise the importance of contact outside the Foreign Offices of State. I believe it is of real urgency in building up such a method of international administration to multiply the sources of contact between States. The more we can localise action, the more it can be dealt with in terms, not of prestige, but of technique, the greater is the opportunity for the growth of technique. The normal channels of diplomacy centralise issues in a way of which the consequences may come to possess far more significance than is warranted. A problem of oil in Downing Street may easily loom larger than it looms in Whitehall. Technique keeps the trivial in its right perspective. If a Foreign Office is brought in to grapple with a dispute about railways, almost inevitably a hinterland of discussion beyond railways begins to pervade the atmosphere. And to keep discussion technical has the great additional advantage of keeping it undramatic. It cannot easily be made a journalistic sensation. It cannot be surrounded with that miasma of report and scandal which have poisoned so many international conferences in the last few years. It makes the notion of a triumph much less accessible when, *a priori,* the nature of the triumph is not intelligible enough to be news. Anyone who has studied the working of things like the London Conference of 1924 will have realised that their best work was done when two or three men gathered together in a quiet room, not to bargain with each other, but to find solutions satisfactory to them both; and it is not difficult to understand why a habit of gathering together over a long period of time should build bridges of mutual confidence over which success may be reached.

(4) *Migration*

Certain special problems occur in relation to the movement of peoples of which the consequences may be momentous. In part, the issue is illustrated by the colour-bar upon immigration into certain States of which I have already spoken. But, in part, also it involves discussing what is to be the general protection offered to the emigrant who leaves his native State, the organisation, for his advantage, of the full knowledge of what he will encounter; and it involves the prevention of such movement as that of the Chinese immigrants to South Africa except upon terms that are adequate in a general way. The sooner the League turns its attention to these issues, the better it will be for the League. It needs to set up, under the aegis of the Council, a permanent Commission on migration with very definite functions. (1) It should have the power to prevent emigration from backward or mandated areas unless the wages and conditions of labour offered are the same as those obtaining for similar work in the country to which the emigrants are going. (2) It should organise the inspection of vessels carrying emigrants and insist upon the maintenance of a minimum standard of accommodation. (3) It should be given the right to inspect (a) the work of emigrant bureaus in different countries, and (b) the power to license them to perform that work; the licence being withdrawn in the event of abuse. (4) It should be given the right to inspect the accommodation for emigrants at ports of landing, and to make suggestions for their improvement to the proper authority; failure to improve being followed by publicity about the facts involved. (5) It should receive at the beginning of each year a statement of the total number of immigrants each State is prepared to absorb, the occupations in which there is room, the conditions upon which such occupations can be followed; and it should, through sub-commissions in each State, publish the information available. Each emigration bureau should be compelled to give this information to each person who proposes to emigrate. (6) It should, by agreement with members of the League, work in concert with the consular authorities in different States and act as a clearing-house to check the numbers of emigrants so that no more set out upon their voyage than are likely to be received. It is difficult not to believe that there is here a region of activity in which the League can do incalculable good. The powers I have suggested do not reach a long way; but, wisely used, they may become the nucleus of wider authority from which there may one day emerge that attempt at an organised distribution of population in terms of area upon which ultimately much may come to depend.

### (5) *Labour Conditions*

Under the Treaty of Versailles there has already been set up an International Labour Office, the general purpose of which is to maintain and improve the standard of life of the working-classes throughout the world. I shall discuss later in this chapter the methods adopted by that office and the institutions through which it does its work. Here it is sufficient to note why it is necessary for the League to undertake functions of this kind. I have already pointed out that there is a world-market, and that the pressure of competition tends to produce a common level of industrial conditions in that market. But, obviously, it is of the first importance to determine what that level ought to be. In the long run, depressed wages in Germany mean depressed wages in England; long hours in Japanese cotton-mills mean long hours in Lancashire cotton-mills. Italy will not supply proper accommodation for its seamen, if French sailors live under bad conditions. A world-market, in fact, ultimately implies that the conditions of the State where the lowest cost of production prevails will determine the conditions of production in other States. It is, therefore, urgent to obtain a minimum standard throughout the world below which no State may permit its workers to all. This involves a common minimum of sanitary conditions, of hours of labour, of wage-rates. It means a universal prohibition of child labour, a universal enforcement of a weekly rest in industry. It means that when certain materials, like white phosphorus, are discovered to be dangerous, they may not be used anywhere in industrial processes. It means that such safeguards of the working-classes, as the right to associate for the joint sale of their labour and for collective bargaining about the conditions of their labour must be assured to them. I take only obvious examples; in the first three sessions of the Annual Conference of the International Labour Office, seventeen conventions were passed.[25] It may be said in general that no more valuable work has been accomplished by the League than that for which the International Labour Office has been responsible. It has quite definitely, in the five difficult years since its origin, marked an epoch in the history of the working-class.

A word must be said about the character of international legislation upon these issues. There are certain areas of activity upon which the International Labour Office is bound to commit its members to a definite policy, and to no other policy than its minimal substance. But that policy will inevitably be minimal in character. It cannot legislate directly in the sense of itself administering its laws. It must seek their enforcement through the legislatures and public services of its member-States. It can, indeed, as it does, adopt not only binding conventions, but also recommendations, that particular conditions are desirable, even when the time has not yet arrived for their universal enforcement; and such recommendations will be valuable for the stimulus they provide to public opinion in the member-States to press for their realisation. Yet it must be understood that the problem of international labour legislation raises issues at once delicate and complex. We can impress upon a State a minimum below which its standards must not fall. We have to take care, first, that minimum standards do not become maximum standards, and that, secondly, enough account is taken of the great variety of conditions to make the legislation proposed capable of effective administration.

The latter problem is at least partly met by making the parties to the contract of legislation not merely the representatives of governments, and partly by making it possible, as in the Seamen's Conference at Genoa in 1920, to have special expert assemblies to deal with issues of a peculiarly complex kind. The first expedient is an invaluable one. It not only makes possible the expression of industrial opinion from the most divergent angles, and that in an authoritative way; but it also, in particular, makes possible the expression of emphatic dissent from the official view of government. It is invaluable, for instance, when the Japanese government delegate paints an idyllic picture of labour conditions in Japan, to have his interpretation promptly denied by the representative of the Japanese workers.[26] Much, further, is gained by encouraging, through international contact, the sense that these problems are common world-problems, and that only genuinely corporate action can resolve them. If the Conference were purely governmental in character, it would be much less authoritative. But when an official, say a Minister of Labour, argues that some given legislation is impossible in his own State, the possibility that his argument will be overthrown by a workers' delegate from his own State not merely adds piquancy to the debate, but also genuinely leads to care in the formulation of objections to that legislation. I shall, indeed, argue later that this procedure could be very usefully adapted to the Assembly of the League itself.

It is, finally, of urgent importance within the League that every type of economic inquiry be undertaken. Legislative action, the world over, is built upon knowledge; and it is amazing how little knowledge we have about the issues with which we have to deal. Problems of currency, of investment, of the effect of tariffs, of productivity, of labour conditions—upon all of these what little information we possess is surrounded by an ocean of ignorance. The League has already shown in a variety of spheres its capacity for this type of work. Not only can it survey conditions, it can invite the expert to make a special report; it can summon a special commission to discuss the meaning of knowledge in its possession. The Treaty of Versailles[27] made it one of the two main purposes of the International Labour Office to "collect and distribute information on all subjects relating to international conditions of industrial life and labour". There is no reason why that power should not be extended to every aspect of economic life. Wherever its incidence or substance affects international relationships, there is a fitting subject for investigation by the League. And such research has the additional value that it is much more likely, from the source of its origin, to be exhaustive and impartial than research taken under the auspices of separate States. Its facts are, from that character, more likely to be antiseptic in character. Few people would regard without suspicion an inquiry into the working of the Silesian coal-mines by a Pole or a German; but few people would be disinclined to believe a report made thereon by an independent commission of the League upon which neither Pole nor German had served. I do not argue that the mere finding of facts is itself a guarantee of wisdom. But I do argue that wisdom is impossible without an expert fact-finding agency, and that the League is by its nature the best fact-finding agency at its disposal. The more widely it is used to that end, the wiser will be the foundations of international policy.

## (iii) The Institutions of International Organisation

Such an outline of the functions of international organisation at least serves to indicate the necessary organs of action. Clearly the League of Nations has need of four definite institutions. It requires a legislature or assembly to formulate the general principles of international policy; it needs an executive or council to direct a stream of tendency into the legislature and to act as a maker of solutions in the intervals of legislative action; it needs a permanent civil service, or secretariat, charged with the preparation of business and the conduct of necessary inquiries; it needs, finally, a judiciary to interpret the legal implications of its activities.

But to use, in this fashion, the terminology of democratic government does not imply that these institutions will be analogous to the internal institutions of the modern State. Two considerations rule out that possibility. The League, in the first place, is an association of nation-States which are politically unequal while they are ,juridically equal; their representatives are, therefore, necessarily the representatives of governments. However each State may decide to choose its delegates, they cannot act, like a member of the House of Commons, as their instructed judgment deems best warranted; they must act upon the orders given to them by those from whom their authority is derived. The actions of the League, in the second place, cannot follow from the normal process of majority-rule. In most of what it does, its business is to win the consent of each nation-State to policy; and the attempt to bind these to acceptance of policy by the mere counting of votes would be fatal to the existence of the League. It constitutes much more a channel of continuous consultation than a law-making body enforcing rules upon an opposition. It rather weights opinions than counts them. It is not a super-State in any administrative sense of the word. Much more, it is a permanent congress of ambassadors who seek the means of equitable compromise where disagreement occurs. It is a recognition that common problems involve organs of common decision, and that common decision is best reached as statesmen seek to pool their minds in an effort to find solutions. Upon occasion, doubtless, the League will have to insist upon the acceptance of its views by those who dissent from their substance. But, in general, its effort must, from the nature of the interest it comprises, seek a path alien in nature from the division-lobby of a legislative assembly. Where its problem admit of a direct “yes” or “no”, it will, in the main, require at least an approach to unanimous agreement; and, in other regions, most of its issues will involve solutions of a quantitative kind. It may, for instance, absolutely prohibit child labour among its member-States; but in fixing rules of wages for international labour it will not attempt, because it cannot attain, legislative simplicity of a qualitative kind.

I may make one other remark before I attempt to deal separately with these institutions. The solutions made by the organs of the League must be regarded, I think, as law in the full sense of that term. They are, that is to say, decisions which will be binding upon the parties. But, clearly, they are not binding in the sense that a decision, say, of a police-magistrate is binding upon a defendant whom he imprisons. There will not be, in general, a court which can move to the execution of decisions. That does not, I believe, deprive its decisions of legal competence. It means only that their execution is effected through a different process than that which obtains for the internal life of a State. We may grant that Italy, for instance, may refuse to accept the findings of the Permanent Court of International Justice upon some issue to which she is a party. We may grant, further, that the process of bringing her to acceptance is much more intricate than any we have previously known. It is yet clear that League decisions must, in the last resort, be enforceable, and that there is, of necessity, arrayed behind them the corporate power of its members. To say that such corporate power cannot be called into action does not mean ultimately more than to say that certain Acts of Parliament cannot be enforced. Law, whether national or international, is built upon the presumption of good-will. It has to assume that what it does will be accepted by those whom it affects. Marginal cases of refusal will, of course, occur; and the secret of successful law-making is so to shape its substance as to reduce those cases to a minimum. That problem, admittedly, is much more intricate in the relations of States than in the relations within some given State; the interests touched are wider, the sanctions to which appeal is in the last resort made are more complex and more remote. But the intricacy still involves quantitative and not qualitative difference. The root of what is being done is the same. Wrong is being punished, disputes are being settled, standards are being created. We are finding in the one, as in the other, behaviour patterns that make possible the life of civilisation. In the one, therefore, as in the other, we give to those behaviour patterns the name of law. They are norms of conduct established by the analysis of experience.

### (1) *The Assembly*

The League must have an organ in which each member-State is entitled to its say. The Assembly, therefore, consists of delegates from each State who are to be not more than three in number, and to exercise between them a single vote. Upon the floor of the Assembly, as a consequence, all member-States are equal; and its competence as a body extends to every subject within the power of the League itself. It is to meet at stated intervals which, in practice, has come to mean an annual session, and at such other times as may be required. All questions before it must be settled unanimously, except those concerned with the admission of new members of the League, which require a two-thirds majority; those which concern the election of non-permanent members of the Council, which require also a two-thirds majority; and those which concern questions of procedure, which require a simple majority only. The Assembly, with the Council, elects the judges of the Permanent Council of International Justice; it amends the Covenant, where amendment is deemed necessary;

it considers disputes referred to it by the Council, or by the parties concerned; it adopts the annual budget of the League, and apportions expenses among the member-States; and it considers both the annual report of the League's work and the measures taken to execute its decisions. Any member-State may withdraw from the League upon giving two years' notice, provided that at the time of withdrawal it has fulfilled all its obligations under the Covenant, and it ceases to be a member either by breaking its undertaking or by rejecting a duly passed amendment to the Covenant.[28]

Most of these powers and forms are implied in the logic of what the League is by its original nature. But certain grave problems arise, both of form and substance, which must be discussed in some detail. What States, in the first place, ought to be admitted to membership? The only conceivable answer, I think, is that every State must be admitted which is willing to accept the obligations thereby incurred; and this must apply not less to States like Russia whose philosophy of government differs so widely from that of most members, than to States like Mexico which finds difficulty in achieving a settled government of any kind. For an objection to the first on the ground of its character is, ultimately, an objection also to the membership of States like Spain and Italy, where governments not built upon popular consent also hold power; and objections to Mexico would apply also to some of the South American States where stability is often more apparent than real. The admission of Mexico, indeed, possesses a quite special importance, since its entrance into the League is an assurance of protection to it against the danger, possibly remote but still existent, of American aggression. Nor is the permission of withdrawal a difficulty. The period of notice is, firstly, a period of warning; and a State which seeks to play a lone hand is always hampered by the fact that action against one member of the League is action against all. It will never, in other words, pay any State to withdraw from the League unless events prove that the League itself cannot be made a reality.

These are, broadly, simple matters. Much more difficult are the rules which demand unanimity on all save a small number of relatively unimportant questions. It is elementary in the history of States that a demand for unanimous consent is fatal to effective government; the *liberum veto* in Poland, for example, was not the least cause of its decay. Even a requirement like the two-thirds rule of the American Senate has, on occasion, been fatal to decisive action at points where decisive action was sorely wanted. But there are, it may be suggested, two important considerations which mitigate the force of this apparent weakness. (1) From the nature of its membership, the Assembly can only be effective on grave questions by convincing its constituent States, and no conviction will be genuine which does not arise from consent freely given. The State must be made to feel that its own will finds place in the decisions made, if it is to accept them as moral obligations. (2) There is, secondly, a way in which action may be taken by the Assembly which binds the members of the League without ultimate unanimity being required. The Protocol for the Pacific Settlement of International Disputes,[29] for instance, had, as a draft before ratification, to be passed unanimously, but, assuming the success of the Disarmament Conference that it calls for, it becomes binding on members of the League when a majority only of the permanent members of the Council and ten other member States have ratified it.[30] Under these circumstances, for instance, Great Britain might dissent from the Protocol and yet be compelled to accept its obligations. Clearly, therefore, the rule of unanimity is less onerous than it appears.

The constitution of the Assembly has been vehemently criticised on the ground that it is undemocratic in character. Only governments, it is said, are there represented; and it is suggested that the personnel of a State-delegation should be elected by the legislative assembly, or some similar body which can protect it from being the creature of a temporary administration. But the answer to such criticism is, I think, a final one. There is nothing to prevent any State from making its own arrangements about the character of its representatives; and South Africa has already selected as one of its delegates the citizen of another State. And, in the second place, since the government of the day is responsible for the making of foreign policy in a State, it is inevitable that it should decide by whom its commitments should be made. It could not continue to act as a government if one policy were to be presented to its own legislature and another, possibly quite different, to the Assembly at Geneva. Yet there is, I believe, this much of reality in the criticism. One of the consequences of the League is to make continuity in foreign policy important; and that can only be achieved by making its substance largely an agreed matter between the government of the day and the opposition. That can, it may be suggested, be achieved by making one of the members of each State-delegation a member of the opposition nominated by the latter for that post. The working of the International Labour Office has shown the great value of a kindred procedure. It affords a valuable opportunity of ventilating points of difference before the body most likely to be affected by them. It will tend to take foreign affairs out of the field of normal partisanship, since any final divergence of view in a national delegation will deprive the State in which it occurs of much of its authority. And where it does exist, it is of high utility that it should be declared before the bar of international opinion, and not screened from view by the facade of governmental unity. It is, of course, evident that, in all such cases, the voting power must be exercised by the government representative.

The members of the Assembly have, almost uniformly, been statesmen, and not officials, and it is clear, I think, that this must necessarily be the case. In all matters of high policy the statesman can criticise and argue, where it is, in public, difficult for the official to do more than announce. The statesman, further, has a power to commit which reaches beyond what can be confided to an official; the latter cannot speak beyond his precise terms of reference, and debate would be stifled if a delegate had to wait upon telegram or telephone for additional instructions. But it is a matter of some importance to decide by what political personage a State should be represented. I think myself that on occasions of really vital importance the Prime Minister himself should be the head of his delegation; and on normal occasions his place should be taken by the Foreign Secretary. Obviously, where the business of the Assembly is largely routine business, it ought not to occupy the time of the former. But when great matters are on hand, the greater the authority lent to the Assembly by the character of its personnel, the better will be the quality of its work. Alternatively, the Foreign Secretary should be in his place; for to attach a separate department in the national governments to the work of the League is to suggest a difference between that work and normal foreign policy. That is, in fact, not the case. Normal foreign policy has to become League policy; and it will only come to be so if both permanent officials and Foreign Ministers come by experience of the League to permeate their daily work with the spirit of the Assembly. Separation of personnel, is, in this regard, dangerously, liable to become separation of function; and even in the brief history of the League the absence of the Foreign Minister of State from Geneva has tended to make his policy different both in texture and approach from that of the member-minister of the Assembly. There is even something to be said for making the permanent head of the Foreign Office the third member of the delegation for this purpose. For, ultimately, his impact upon policy is so much deeper and more continuous than that of his temporary chief, that lack of personal contact with the Assembly may easily, especially in its formative years, mean the development of half-conscious antagonism to it.

Any Assembly, of course, is bound to be different from what its formal constitution makes it; it lives, not by its inaugurating clauses, but from the habits engendered by its experience. It is, it may be suggested, already legitimate to hazard certain inferences about the nature of the Assembly of the League. It is able to overcome the barrier made by differences of languages. It can genuinely debate proposals, and genuinely ventilate grievance. It can draw to itself a public opinion capable of transcending parochial loyalties. It provides an invaluable sounding-board for the better impulses of mankind. It offers the opportunity for great personalities, whether they come from the large State or from the small

State, to win attention for views which would otherwise go unheard amid the pressure of events; for it makes those views events by the circumstances of their utterance. It enables the small State to meet the larger power upon the footing of equal discussion. It permits the reference of problems to bodies more likely than any other to be free from immediate interest or inherited prejudice. It adds to the stature of justice by persuading reasonable men that those who evade its authority are afraid of the judgment of reason. An observer who scrutinised the record of the Assembly would, doubtless, find room for serious blame. But he would, I think above all, conclude that, if it had no other value, it would be invaluable because it is a brake upon the power of the great State. It forces it into the public view, and compels it to submit to analysis and criticism. These, in the end, are the real remedies against the dangers that confront us. For the States, at long last, which fail are those that, defying them, have sought to be a law unto themselves.

(2) *The Council*

To dissect the Council of the League is inevitably a more difficult task than to analyse the Assembly; for the structure of the Council is admittedly incomplete, and it cannot pretend to finality until Russia, Germany and the United States are represented there.

But, if we assume their ultimate representation, a simple but essential principle lies at the basis of the Council. It is naturally divisible into a permanent part, composed of representatives of the Greater Powers and a temporary part composed of representatives of the Lesser. That is, I think, an inevitable division. The world must be taken as it is, and decisions made, say, for Great Britain by Chile and Belgium would not possess effective validity. The balance of advantage lies in recognising the significance of the great State, while refusing to it ultimate power upon the Council. This is done by making the number of States permanently represented less by two than the number of temporary members.[31] The competence of the Council, like that of the Assembly, is limited only by the range of the Covenant itself; and, as with the Assembly also, its decisions, except upon questions of procedure, and one or two other, but minor, matters, must be unanimous. The rule of unanimity is, on the whole, less of a stumbling-block than might appear. For, in the first place, it is undoubtedly a safeguard against the very real danger of coalitions within the Council, and, on the assumption proved by the experience of the British Empire, unanimity seems attainable so long as there exists a will to agree. The Council is bound to meet annually; though, in point of fact, it has met at least six times each year since the foundation of the League. Its special authority in disputes is notable. (1) If contending

States do not agree either to arbitration or judicial settlement, they must submit their dispute to the Council. If the latter cannot effect an agreement, it may, either by a unanimous or a majority vote, publish a report of the facts, with recommendations; if the report is unanimous, apart from the parties concerned, and one of these carries out the recommendations, the other cannot make war upon it. If unanimity is not attained, war may be embarked upon after three months from the publication of the Council's decision. If one party claims that the dispute is domestic in nature, and the Council agrees, its jurisdiction ceases; it cannot, therefore, interfere in the internal affairs of a State. It may also, either of its own motion or at the request of one of the parties, refer a dispute to the Assembly, in which case, the latter assumes the same powers of settlement as the Council itself. Where such reference is made, the member-States on the Council must be unanimous, and a majority of the delegates of other States must occur in the report and recommendations. New member-States may be invited to temporary membership for the settlement of disputes with a member-State. If the invitation is accepted, the normal procedure applies; if it is refused, and war breaks out, the whole League becomes involved.[32]

Obviously, the Council is the real pivot of the League. It is the real source of executive decision. It is the primary factor in the settlement of disputes. Upon its activity depends the creativeness of the Assembly as a whole. How far is its structure satisfactory for the purposes it has in view? Let us note, first of all, some deficiencies. The rule of unanimity is, I have urged, necessary in the major work of the Council; it is not, it may be suggested, necessary also in its minor work. Unanimity ought not to be necessary for undertaking those social activities—the suppression of the traffic in harmful drugs, for example—in which, as I have already argued, there lies the opportunity of much fruitful work. In these instances, the obligation to accept a two-thirds majority ought to be regarded as sufficient. Nor, secondly, ought the Council itself to consider whether a dispute is or is not domestic; for it England regards, for example, conflict in Egypt as a domestic matter, the view of France is likely to be coloured by her own special position in Morocco. It is better, therefore, that such questions should be referred to the Permanent Court, and that the Council should act upon its decision. Non-members of the League, thirdly, should have the right to appeal to the Council for arbitration even when their dispute is with a State which is also not a member; for if, to take an obvious example, the United States were to make war upon Mexico, the annexation of the latter would so profoundly alter the position of the South American Republics as to make their interest in the decision one that needs all the emphasis the combined authority of the League can give.[33]

Certain other questions of importance present themselves. By whom shall States be represented at meetings of the Council? So far as possible, for reasons I have already explained in dealing with the Assembly, it is important that the delegates should be the Foreign Secretary of each State. There are, of course, necessary exceptions to this rule; distance, for instance, makes the presence of the Japanese Foreign Minister at present impossible. But representation, either by ambassadors or subordinate ministers, is not, in general, satisfactory. Their instructions are necessarily less flexible. They do not enable the minister to learn the meaning of international relations by direct contact with their substance. They tend to become separated from that common mind which grows from continuity of intercourse at meetings of the Council; and it is, in general, a bad thing for any government to have its international policy in different hands from those which conduct its foreign affairs. Certainly it has been possible to recognise in the Foreign Office of Great Britain difference of outlook from that which prevailed in the department presided over by Lord Cecil, a difference not less important in method of approach than in the object desired.

More complex is the question of publicity. Here, it is obvious, the considerations which apply to the Assembly are out of place. Publicity is the life of the Assembly; in the Council, publicity before decision may not seldom, especially in the settlement of a dispute, do more harm than good. But it is also important that the Council should not degenerate into a body debating behind closed doors, and uttering *ex cathedra* pronouncements which it does not condescend to explain. It is, therefore, important that all decisions arrived at should be published with an official explanation of the results achieved; for, as M. Branting has said,[34] "reasons are quite the best way by which the decisions of the Council can be defended from criticism". It is, I think, further clear that the Council could well hear in public (1) all statements by parties to a dispute; (2) all questions submitted to it about the conduct of Mandatory Powers; (3) all questions which relate to the activities of the League under Article XXIII. No one who heard Lord Balfour's denunciation of General Zeligowski at the Fourteenth Meeting of the Council can doubt the salutary effect of publicity; and it is a general rule that secrecy should be resorted to only when negotiations of a delicate nature, as the financial reconstruction of Austria, are under discussion.

A matter of great importance is the relation of the Council to the Assembly. Here it is necessary at the outset to put on one side the tempting analogies of parliamentary government. The Council is a cabinet, but it is also a legislature; and in its combined nature it corresponds to no previously existing institution. It dominates the Assembly, since the latter cannot act without it; yet, in certain fields, it is amenable to the control of the assembly. A report upon its work is annually submitted by the Secretary-General of the League; and its discussion by the Assembly corresponds to the discussion of the Annual Estimates by the House of Commons. But discussion in the Assembly, while it may influence the Council, need not do so; the latter may stand by its decisions, and, if it does so, it will not fall upon account of them. It is, therefore, clear that the Assembly is, at every point, a body inferior, both in power and authority, to the Council, and, apart from its normal meetings, its extraordinary sessions depend, for practical purposes, either upon the will of the Council or upon reference to it of a dispute by one of the parties concerned. Generally, therefore, some nine members of the League are settling the essence of world-policy in its name.

Is this an adequate relationship? We have to remember the conditions under which the League must work. A body so diverse as the Assembly, so subject, also, to the difficulties of distance, cannot be summoned often in the nature of things. Its members must, as a rule, be given reasonable notice of matters to be discussed if their judgment is to be arrived at after mature consideration. Inevitably, therefore, the Council is bound to be the root of decision in interim periods; and its power needs to be elastic in character if it is to meet with success the problems that will arise. It must have, in short, what in England is called a prerogative power; and the limits of that power can be settled, as occasion serves, by the Assembly. But it would in general be impossible to allow, for instance, disputes once settled to be reopened by the Assembly. If it was known that such revision was possible, every party to a dispute which felt itself aggrieved by the decision would appeal to the Assembly for a rehearing. *Stare decisis* is an inevitable principle of the situation we confront. The Assembly is bound, therefore, to be a means of criticism rather than a means of control. The differences of jurisdiction inhere in the character of the problem. It is, moreover, to be remembered that the situation will gradually be modified by two factors of experience. The Council will accumulate precedents, and these will gradually, even if half-consciously, limit its power of innovation; and, as the work of the Permanent Court proceeds, a volume of legal decisions will be collected within which the Council will have to act. But it is important that the Covenant of the League should bind the Council to accept the determination of the Court upon questions of law. For unless that is done, the decisions of the Court will be no more than expressions of opinion, weighty perhaps, but entitled to be rejected if they are inconvenient. That will deprive the Court of what is essential to its authority, since it will transform it into a body of legal advisers, instead of a body of judges. To make the Council bound by law is, one may urge, the surest way to make its findings instinct with justice.

One other power over the Council, I suggest, the Assembly might reasonably exercise. Even if we grant that in major matters decisions of the Council must be regarded as *choses jugées,* that character need not extend to matters which, though important in themselves, are relatively of minor significance. The Council, for instance, has dealt with the problems of transit, health; registration of treaties, the liquor traffic in Africa, none of which is likely to lead to serious differences of opinion. Decisions on questions of this character might, it may be suggested, be subject to revision by the Assembly. They will come before it year by year in the annual report of the Secretary-General; and it would be a useful addition to the powers of the Assembly if it was given authority, by a two-thirds vote, to revise the decision of the Council. A case in point is the question of famine-relief in Russia which was rejected through the opposition of the Great Powers, despite the eloquent advocacy of the smaller States. To override the former in such cases will not seldom be to replace the political or economic considerations of a great State by the humanitarian considerations of a smaller. We cannot expect Great Britain to surrender India at the behest of Holland; but it would be good for her soul, or for that of Japan, to surrender, even at grave economic loss, a traffic like that of opium, say, at the demand of Norway or Denmark. Anyone who looks over the range of functions comprised in Article XXIII of the Covenant will not find it difficult to believe that for these, at least, the Assembly might well retain supremacy. How far beyond such matters its competence as a revising body should extend will depend, quite clearly, on the success of the League in building habits of international co-operation. Partially, at least, the problem is one of prestige; and it is only as habits of co-operation grow that prestige will give way to justice.

Anyone who examines the record of the Council since its origin will, I think, be driven to two conclusions. It has been, for the first five years of its history, still greatly permeated by the legacy of the war-spirit. In obedience to that spirit, as in problems like the Saar Valley and Silesia, it has been guilty of grave errors; in obedience, also, to that spirit, it has failed to take account of questions like the invasion of the Ruhr Valley by France, which cried aloud for its intervention. It has, secondly, shown a serious lack of courage in dealing with the great issues upon which its influence must be built. It was successful in small things, like the settlement of the Aaland Islands difficulty,[35] and the frontier of Albania;[36] it was not successful in greater things like the Graeco-Italian dispute of 1923, the Franco-German issue in the Ruhr, the Anglo-Egyptian dispute of 1924. This last difficulty, it may be urged, showed all the weaknesses of the Council in their clearest perspective. For a penumbra of uncertainty surrounded both the international status of Egypt and her part in the governance of the Sudan; both of these were questions which required at once legal and impartial handling, yet both of them were questions England settled by herself, without reference to the League. Egypt, moreover, was not a member of the League; and her appeal to it, though made with unanimity by the legislative assembly, was not concurred in by an executive which had hardly assumed office at the time when the appeal was made; yet the Secretariat of the League did not accept the appeal as official, on the ground that it did not emanate from a "government" in the technical and administrative sense of that term. The League, in other words, allowed great issues to be decided without intervention upon the most narrowly legal grounds. The misfortune of that action lies in the fact that it was submission by the League to the will of a great State, when the party affected was a small State, and at a time when the great State was acting in the name of its prestige. But it is exactly to prevent action in the name of prestige that the Council of the League has been given its authority to intervene. Refusals like that in the Anglo-Egyptian case, silence, as in the case of the Ruhr, weakness, as in the case of Greece and Italy, do not encourage a belief in the *bona-fides* of the Council. It is necessary, Mr. Ramsay MacDonald has said, "to empty our minds of those revolutionary, futile ideas that one nation by its strength of will and determination, can simply ride roughshod over the rest of the world".[37] But our minds will be emptied of such ideas only as the Council firmly decides upon intervention whenever such aggression is attempted. Granted, as we may grant, that such a policy may break the League, it is also not less likely to make it; and until the Council attains the authority such intervention implies, the Great Powers will look to it, not as an arbitrator, but as a contingent convenience.

(3) *The Secretariat*

By Article VI of the Covenant the administrative staff of the League comprises a Secretary-General and such assistance as he may require. The first Secretary-General was appointed by the Peace Conference at Versailles in 1919; his successor will be appointed by the Council with the approval of a majority in the Assembly. His duties, roughly, fall into ten large categories. (1) He acts as recorder of the decisions of the Council and the Assembly. (2) He co-ordinates the general work of the League Secretariat. (3) He prepares an annual report upon the work of the Council for presentation to the Assembly. (4) On the request of any member of the League, he summons, under Article XI of the Covenant, a meeting of the Council to deal with any emergency situation which foreshadows conflict. (5) He receives, under Article XV, notice of submission by a party to any dispute, and makes the necessary arrangements for its investigation and discussion. (6) He receives and, on registration, publishes, all treaties made by any member of the League.[38] (7) He informs members of the League when amendments to the Covenant have taken effect.[39] (8) He arranges for carrying out the decisions of the League through the offices of the permanent Secretariat.[40] (9) With the approval of the Council, he appoints members of the Secretariat and its staff.[41] (10) He prepares the agenda for all bodies meeting under the auspices of the League.

It is obviously difficult to over-estimate the significance of the Secretariat.[42] Its functions are both large and complex; it oils the wheels of the League machinery; and not a little of the adequacy of the League depends upon the competence of its work. But it functions, also, within certain well-defined limits. It is an international civil service, and, as such, it comprises citizens of every member-State within the League. It has not, therefore, a single tradition of *expertise* upon which to build; it has to mould its routine out of cosmopolitan habits which are not seldom at variance with one another. While, moreover, it is an administrative body, it does not itself execute; it can only organise the process of execution which must be carried out by the members of the League individually. It cannot embark upon such effort as it thinks fit. Its work is limited, firstly, by the budget granted to it by the Assembly, and, secondly, by the degree to which member-States effectively co-operate with it in its work. Yet, even with these limitations, it is bound to play a growing part in the League; and much of what it does will involve a skill in negotiation and a delicacy in statement probably greater than the civil service of an individual State has so far known.

How is this Secretariat to perform its duties? I shall not discuss here the purely technical problem of its internal organisation; rather I shall seek to discover what methods are involved in its work, and the significance of those methods. The outstanding fact in the function is clearly the business of inquiry. In almost every avenue of social and political life, the Secretariat of the League is collecting information upon which the decisions of the League will eventually be based. How is that to be done? There will be problems, firstly, which it must itself directly answer. There will be others where what is required is less direct investigation than the co-ordination of existing knowledge. There will be others, again, where what is required is investigation by a body of outside experts organised *ad hoc* for their analysis. There will be others, once more, where what is needed is less any of these than the presentation of recommendations by a body of experts to be acted upon or not as the League thinks fit.

It is only necessary to outline the implications of such a function to realise that it needs to be organised by men of the highest ability. The Secretariat of the League, clearly, cannot be composed of men who were just not quite good enough to reach the highest posts in the civil service of their respective States. It follows that the League must build its Secretariat upon foundations which attract the ablest men of each member-State into its ranks. Its pay, its security of tenure, its condition of work, must be not less adequate than those of the best national civil service in the League. It must, of course, find room for every member-State citizens in its ranks; but, at the top, it must regard competence as more important than nationality. It is clear, further, that much of the success of the Secretariat in this regard will depend upon its connections with research bodies, the world over, and with individual experts in the fields with which it is concerned. Partly, of course, it can obtain such connection by means of the Permanent Advisory Commissions of which I spoke earlier in this chapter; partly, also, it can, as the International Labour Office does, establish correspondents all over the world who keep the Secretariat in touch with developments of importance to it; partly, also, by special conferences, like the Brussels Finance Conference, it can create an avenue through which expert opinion will be directed towards it.

I do not myself believe that these methods will prove adequate by themselves. If the League is to be effective, it must have an observer in each State with the powers and privileges of an ambassador in that State. He must be a centre of knowledge, and a liaison between the national life, on the one hand, and Geneva upon the other. He must be able to organise for the League inquiries on the spot. He must have the authority to insist, for instance, that some convention of the International Labour Office is not being observed. He must serve as the medium of negotiation between the State to which he is accredited and the League itself. He must, so to say, represent the visible existence of the League among its members. Nor need we belittle the ceremonial importance of such observers. To collect about themselves men and women in each State upon the basis of an interest in internationalism would be a service of high importance. Such observers, of course, would never be citizens of the country to which they were sent. They would, like the ordinary ambassador, be seconded from Geneva to such work; and on their return there they would bring to its activities a knowledge and a freshness of high importance to their quality. They would prevent the League, again and again, from acting on biased information or seeking assistance from mistaken sources. Their confidential reports would greatly aid in enabling the Secretariat to make the results of inquiry of maximum advantage to the League.

But the Secretariat has not merely to investigate. It is charged also, as I have noted, with the task of negotiation. Part of this duty is what may be termed statutory in nature, as when the Secretary-General summons a meeting of the Council on the occasion of a dispute; part of it is routine work undertaken in the fulfilment of League decisions. In both types, it may be remarked, observers such as I have spoken of could play a part of high value. Certain other considerations, moreover, emerge. It is clear, firstly, that the Covenant of the League cannot cover all the emergencies that will arise; it visualised, for instance, appeal to the League by a member against a non-member, but it did not visualise an appeal by a non-member against a member of the League. Yet no difficulty ought ever to escape the notice of the League merely upon technical grounds. In these cases of emergency, therefore, apart from summons of the Council at the request of a member, it ought to be the duty of the Secretary-General, with the approval of the President of the Council, to summon the latter body when any appeal, though not legally substantial, seems to him from its character one it would be unwise to neglect. There is not, I think, any undue risk in the conference of these powers. It would still be open to the Council, on its meeting, to decide that no action should be taken; and a decision by the Secretary-General not to summon the Council would provide the Assembly with a possible lever for debate in its next meeting. Gradually, in fact, there would accumulate a body of precedents which would guide the Secretary-General in his decision; and the existence of such a reserve power, in independent hands, would protect the League from itself. For there is always a danger that the Council will leave a dispute untouched, not because it is outside the scope of its authority, but because each member-State is anxious not to wound the susceptibilities of others. We must guard against any punctilio of that kind.

Another consideration of importance emerges. While the authority of the League will, of course, depend upon the relationship it is able to establish with the Foreign Offices of member-States, it will have not only to win what may be called an external confidence from them, it must be able, also, to persuade them to look at their own problems from the angle of their impact on world-relations as a whole. I do not need to emphasise the difficulty of that effort. What, as I think, it clearly involves is developing the Secretariat of the League as a place to which the officials of member-States may be seconded for temporary service as part of their normal duties. If we could be certain, for instance, that no man served as a permanent head of a Foreign Office unless he had spent two years in the service of the League, we could also, I suggest, be certain that he would look upon the assumptions of national policy from a larger and more creative point of view. He would have learned much from the international outlook which continuous residence at Geneva unconsciously enforces. He would learn to trust the League by helping to work it; he would cease to regard it as simply one more instrument with which he has to negotiate. He would come to know in the intimacy of continuous colleagueship men who do not accept the assumptions which, in London or Paris or Tokio, go without question. He would learn how national policy appears, not as it affects the interests of his own State merely, but as it affects the total interest of the League. Such service, in fact, would be a liberal education in that cosmopolitan outlook which the needs of humanity have made so essential. For until the international mind is rooted in the civil services of member-States not less than in Geneva itself, it will be difficult to make the League grow into the consciousness of diplomacy as a thing inherent in its nature and not alien to it.

Upon one problem it is worth while to say a special word. The Secretariat of the League is drawn from different States, and there are some who deny that an official who is, say, an Englishman or a Frenchman who comes to Geneva only after he has reached the age of manhood, can divest himself of national bias. If by this is meant that a League official who is an Englishman will tend to look at League questions through English spectacles, it is, I think, completely untrue. For where an issue is dealt with by the League, especially if it be critical in its nature, there is no simple English view" to be *a priori* laid down. No one can say, for example, that Lord Morley of Blackburn ceased to take an English point of view because he opposed the Boer War; no one, I believe, would now argue that it is un-American to favour the entrance of the United States into the League. It is not *a priori* more difficult for a League official to be impartial than it is for an English civil servant to be neutral between the contending parties it is his duty to serve. The latter is not a passionless expert who merely does what he is told. He has, often enough, strong political views in a marked degree hostile to those of the minister he is serving. But he is able, by the compelling force of the tradition of which he is a part, to put his own opinions on one side. He is told the goal in view and he seeks, with uncompromising loyalty, the direct highroad to that goal. It is, of course, true that the tradition of such loyalty is not so strong in some countries as it is in Great Britain, and that national prejudice may be a deeper passion than party prejudice. Yet even when all this is remembered, I do not think it militates against the probability that an official of the League can remain a good Frenchman and, at the same time, learn to regard its problems from an angle where French interests are not unduly weighed. And the fact that his views are being subject to the unconscious pressure of opinions formed from other traditions is, on any rational hypothesis, bound to round the edges of bias in a marked degree. The first Secretary-General of the League has been an Englishman; but a scrutiny of what he has done, in particular of his annual reports to the Assembly, does not suggest that the record would have been different, above all that the decisions would have been different, had he been a Frenchman or a Swede.

One final remark about the Secretariat may be made. Among its functions, as I have noted, is the preparation of agenda for the meetings of the Assembly. Such agenda contain three groups of items. There are matters decided upon by the Assembly at a previous meeting; there are matters introduced by the Council; and there are matters introduced on the initiative of a member-State. The Secretariat circulates to the delegates all documents relative to the work of the Assembly. Here, it may be suggested, there is a realm in which the initiative of the Secretariat may be of quite primary importance. There are two kinds of initiative in relation to the agenda of the Assembly about which the work of the Secretariat may well be decisive. (1) It may indicate to delegates subjects that it believes are worthy of consideration by the member-States, together with the grounds upon which their consideration is proposed. By so doing it will secure either actual discussion at the Assembly or an international publicity which will ultimately lead to discussion. Such suggestions will have the further importance that, while they may not be ripe for immediate resolution by the League, their indication as important may prevent them from passing unnoticed in the pressure of affairs. (2) The Secretariat might also, in sending relevant documents to the delegates, inquire further if other information is desired upon the subjects to which they refer. It ought, in fact, to play the part that the legislative Reference Bureau of Wisconsin was able to play at the height of its prestige.[43] Few things are more necessary in the working of the Assembly than the assurance that its delegates have at their command all the information necessary to the making of adequate decisions, and it is, also, of importance that there should be available for the Assembly not merely governmental facts, but the expression of views opposed to government opinion. This suggests the possibility of organising within the Assembly a procedure for the reception of petitions akin to that of the Parliament of the modern State. The reception of those could be notified to members when the agenda for an Assembly is sent out; and States interested in one or more of them could then either ask the Secretariat for information upon them or, if they thought fit, raise the questions to which they give rise in the Assembly itself. That would, I believe, supplement in a valuable way a procedure which, otherwise, compels minority-movements in a State to be unheard by the body dealing with world-opinion. By such means, minorities could at least make their views accessible to members of the League; and we should have some safeguard against the natural tendency of governments to insist that their view has the overwhelming support of those over whom they rule.

(4) *The International Court of Justice*

No League of Nations could pretend to completeness of structure which lacked a permanent judicial organ. "The League", writes Sir Frederick Pollock,[44] "has to rebuild and extend the law of nations, and a rule-making, or even a legislative, authority will not suffice for this. Formal definition and enactment must be kept alive by constructive interpretation, to the end of producing a continuous tradition of doctrine, a 'jurisprudence' in the French sense of that word. Isolated decisions of different and independent authorities, however respectable, will never make such a doctrine". But it is not merely for this important reason that a Permanent International Court is essential. Where the problems involved are judicial in nature, it is important that the body giving judgment should be independent of the governments of member-States. Every reason, in fact, which makes for the independence of the judiciary in municipal causes, makes, with even added force, for its independence in international causes. Settlement of judicial matters by either a body of statesmen or by judges nominated *ad hoc* by governments can never have either the freedom or impartiality of a court independent of transitory situations. What is required is, as Sir Frederick Pollock has aptly pointed out, a body which, like the Judicial Committee of the Privy Council in the British Empire, exercises its authority by consent, before which member-States of the empire can be summoned, but which is yet independent in constitution of executive purpose or desire.

The Permanent Court of International Justice was created under Article XIV of the Covenant. It is competent to hear and decide any international dispute which the parties therein concerned agree to submit to it; and it may give an advisory opinion upon any question referred to it by the Council or the Assembly. The judges of the Court are appointed by a somewhat complicated process. There is, in the first place, limited nomination by the judicial members of The Hague Tribunal formed into national groups, or by similar groups from States not represented there, certain legal qualifications being required for nomination. From the list so formed, fifteen judges, of whom four are deputy-judges, are chosen by the concurrent votes of the Council and the Assembly, an absolute majority in both being required for election.[45] The judges are elected for nine years, and no State may have more than one of its citizens upon the Court; though any State which is a litigant is entitled, for the purposes of its case, to a seat thereon. The Court sits at The Hague; and it is required to hold at least one session annually. To secure continuity of jurisdiction, it is also provided that its President and Registrar, with their staffs, must reside at The Hague, just as the High Court organises the presence of a judge in London during vacations.

The competence of the Court has not been settled in an entirely satisfactory way. Under Article XIV of the Covenant it can only deal with disputes referred to it by both parties, though it is clear (1) that the Council will refer to it for opinions upon legal questions which arise out of disputes, and (2) members of the League may, at their option, recognise the jurisdiction of the Court as compulsory by signing a clause to this effect.[46] In general, then, the Court seems likely to deal with five types of question: (1) It will interpret treaties; (2) it will settle questions of international law; (3) it will determine, subject to the limitations noted above, the reparation to be made where there has been a breach of international obligations; (4) it will determine the existence of any situation which, if it does exist, constitutes a breach of such an obligation; (5) it will advise the League upon any question referred to it by the Council or the Assembly, though its advice is not binding unless it is endorsed by the body concerned. A typical case under (5) was the question referred to it in 1922 of whether the workers' delegate from Holland to the Third Conference of the International Labour Office had been appointed in conformity with the provisions laid down in Article III of the Labour Covenant of the League, which lays it down that the non-government delegates must be chosen from the most representative industrial organisations.[47] Finally it may be noted that the law to be applied by the Court is built out of four sources. (1) The rules recognised in international conventions made by contesting States; (2) international custom so general as to be accepted as law; (3) such general principles of law as are recognised by the civilised world, and (4) judicial decisions and the doctrines of recognised publicists as guides to the making of legal rules.

The main comment upon the Court that an observer would be tempted to make is, I think, that it has been unduly restricted in its competence by the powers conferred on the Council and the Assembly. If it is to be genuinely and continually authoritative, it needs to be certain that its advisory opinions will be treated as binding; otherwise, inevitably, its members will be tempted to find what is likely to prove acceptable lest it suffer by the rejection. It should, secondly, be given a compulsory right to adjudicate all questions which give rise to a dispute as to whether the matter involved is or is not domestic in nature. For to leave to the Council matters of this kind is to make the States giving the decision concern themselves less with the facts involved than with the effect of a precedent made upon their own situation. It should, thirdly, be the normal method of settling disputes, and the signing of what is now an optional clause of acceptance should clearly be obligatory on all members of the League; otherwise the tendency will unquestionably be to make the Court the source of judgment for small States, while the Council remains the body to which the larger States refer. That will, it may be suggested, very seriously diminish the prestige of the Court. It is only the knowledge that Great Britain no less than Brazil is answerable to the tribunal that will make its activity a settled part of the habits of mankind.

It should be noted, further, that the jurisdiction of the Court is, apart from the interpretation of the Labour clauses of the Treaty of Versailles, original only; and it is obvious that, in general, this must remain the case. But there are, I believe, several directions in which the Court could provide material of great value for municipal jurisdictions. Under Article III of the Covenant it would, as Sir F. Pollock has suggested,[48] be empowered by the Council with the task of consolidating international law, and revising its substance from time to time in the light of experience. No one would suggest that this is a simple task, or one to be performed in any brief space of time. But its successful achievement would not only be an immense international service, but it would confer great credit upon the Court; and it would give desirable uniformity to much that at present is divergent in substance and application. There is, moreover, a range of questions where the conference upon it of appellate jurisdiction could hardly fail to do good. It is, for example, the law that if a foreign sovereign claims property as the public property of his State, his declaration cannot be investigated and is exempt from the consequence of jurisdiction.[49] There seems no good reason why, if such a declaration is challenged, the facts should not be determined in the ordinary way by the Permanent Court, and that the more since the present doctrine is only, as I pointed out earlier, a regrettable result of the classic doctrine of sovereignty. So, also, in cases of the detention of an immigrant alien in alleged violation of a treaty, the national decision might well be appealed from to the Permanent Court.[50] So, again, if, under municipal law, alien property is destroyed outside the municipal jurisdiction, an appeal ought to lie even from the highest tribunal of a State on grounds of justice;[51] for the property destroyed might have easily been lawfully used under the laws of the plaintiff's State. What generally emerges, I think, from cases of this kind is that where act of State, in one of its various forms, is urged as a bar to jurisdiction, a plaintiff should be able to cite the State concerned from the Municipal Court into the Permanent Court. Only in that way can the individual be protected from the irresponsibility of sovereign powers.

What, in fact, I am here pleading for is that the rules of international law should be made universally binding through the power to have them definitely interpreted by a recognised tribunal. It is only in that way that we shall escape from the tradition started by Hobbes of regarding the law of nations as merely the law of nature disguised.[52] Obviously we should have to limit with some stringency the occasions of appeal; obviously, also, we would have to make the decisions of the International Court binding upon all Municipal Courts and enforceable by their authority. There is good reason for this plea. The famous epigram that international law is not law at all has had a serious effect historically, both upon its prestige and its range of influence. Because it has had no domicile of permanent pronouncement, its practical effect has been weakened because it seemed to lack the certainty and the sanctions of municipal law. It is, I think, possible for the International Court to do for law in general what the Praetor's Edict did for Roman jurisprudence in its golden age. But, to that end, it will be necessary to admit that the supreme tribunal of a national State cannot have the last word if the decision it makes involves the clash of principles derived from more than a single source of law. There is no reason to suppose that such uniformity as would be involved would destroy the elasticity of the present régime, since most ultimate jurisdictions already depart with difficulty from their own precedents. And there is, it may be urged, great value in making it possible to prevent the denial of justice by allowing the plea of sovereignty to bar process. If sovereigns, personal or corporate, are different from other beings, personal or corporate, the best way to deal with them is to constitute a special court to deal with them. By so doing we can end the notion that conduct by or in the name of government is clothed with a special sanctity. If the International Court did no more than contribute to that end, it would have achieved results of the highest importance.

One further question remains. I have already spoken of the need, under the League, of a Permanent Commission of Law; and it is clear that such a body must work in the closest relationship with the International Court. The latter would, clearly, be the best possible body for the appointment of its members. It would be the vehicle for transmitting the finding of the Commission to the League itself. It could use it as its own organ of inquiry into problems where investigation is, in its opinion, desirable. The Court, in fact, may be visualised not merely as a body recording findings as cases come before it for decision, but also, at least equally, as a body concerned to stimulate the general development of the law. In this respect it has a great weapon in its hands. Legal inquiry, properly undertaken, is one of the great sources of future progress. And it may be suggested that there is a number of kindred organisations which might well be shepherd under the wing of the International Court. A good example of this is the International Prisons Conference. One of the more regrettable features of criminal administration is the small part played in its improvement by judges. If the International Court would organise such a conference, and bring its findings, and their bearings, to the attention of national judiciaries, it would possibly do good, and, at least, could do no harm. It might, further, inaugurate international conferences of judges for the discussion of matters where the interchange of opinion—as, for instance, the protection of judicial independence—has great importance. There is, briefly, a great field for the International Court not merely as a judicial organ, but as an institution concerned to make law the response to need. And the more urgently it works to that end, the more likely it is to assist the League towards the increasing fulfilment of its purpose.

### (5) *The International Labour Office*

I have already suggested that the League; if it is to be successful, must increasingly undertake economic functions. That aspect of its activity is provided for, in part by the Economic Section of the Secretariat, in part also, and most importantly, by the International Labour office.[53] The latter consists of two parts: it has a General Conference of representatives of its member-States, and a permanent organisation at Geneva. Membership of the office is not confined to members of the League, though all members of the latter are also members of the former; but under the provisions of the Labour Office, States like Russia and America could accept the obligations of membership without being, at the same time, committed to the larger obligations of the League. Under these terms, Germany was for some years a member of the Labour Office, though not in the League itself.

The International Labour Office will, if the Draft Amendment of 1922 is, as seems likely, ratified,[54] governed by a body composed of thirty-two persons. Of these sixteen represent governments; eight of them are nominated by States of chief industrial importance,[55] and eight by the government delegates, excluding those from States so nominated, of the remaining members. It is provided, also, that six of these sixteen members shall come from non-European States. Of the remaining sixteen persons, eight, representing the employers, and eight, representing the workers, are elected by the delegates of these classes at the Conference, it being, again, provided that two of each come from non-European States. The Governing Body holds office for three years; it fixes its own time of meeting and procedure; and it may be especially summoned when any twelve or more of its members so desire. Vacancies and substitutes are provided for by its own vote, subject to its methods being accepted by the Conference. It receives annually from each member of the office a report upon what the member has done in the fulfilment of its obligations as a member; and it has the right to prescribe the form in which the report shall be made. It receives complaints from industrial associations about the non-fulfilment by members of their obligations, and it communicates such complaints to the State concerned; if the answer is deemed unsatisfactory, it has the right to publish complaint and reply. It can also receive a complaint on similar lines from one member about another, and, if it thinks fit, can appoint a commission of inquiry into the complaint;[56] and each member is pledged to offer all facilities to the Commission. The latter body then reports, and makes recommendations for dealing with the complaint; if these are not accepted, the case is referred to the Permanent Court, which has then the duty of "affirming, varying, or reversing the findings" of the Commission, and suggesting appropriate economic methods of carrying out its recommendations. Any member may then apply these methods to the defaulting State. The Governing Body directs also the general activities, and controls the finances of the Labour Office, the executive management being confided to a Director.

The Director is responsible for the general management of the Office, and the appointment of its staff, which, by statute, must include women. The functions of the Office fall broadly into three large categories. (1) It collects and distributes information upon all aspects of international economic life, it examines particularly questions to be brought before the Conference, it conducts inquiries into problems within the range of its interests and publishes the results; (2) it prepares the agenda for meetings of the Conference; (3) it receives complaints upon the non-fulfilment of obligations by members. For the purpose of its work, the Office is divided into three divisions. The Diplomatic Division carries on correspondence with governments, and prepares the groundwork of the Conferences; the Intelligence and Liaison Division undertakes the collection and distribution of information; the Research Division is in charge of general scientific investigation. Connected with the last section are the Advisory Commissions of which there are two types: (1) Consultative Commissions, of which the International Maritime Commission of 1920 is an example. These are composed of equal representation of the interests concerned, and they make recommendations to the Governing Body within the terms of reference decided upon by the latter. (2) Technical Commissions, like that on the problem of care and employment of disabled soldiers and sailors, upon which sit only experts chosen by, and responsible to, the Director of the Office.[57] There are also correspondence offices in various countries, and special representatives in others. These serve to keep the Office at Geneva in touch with events through knowledge on the spot. Conversely, many of the members of the office have appointed attachés to it, so that contact is maintained from the centre to the circumference also. The staff, it should be added, consists of the most diverse nationalities;[58] it is recruited, where possible, by a combination of examination and selection, except in the case of the higher posts;

and it seems to have been extraordinarily successful in overcoming the difficulties of language.

The Conference is, of course, the apex and crown of the work of the Office. It meets at least once each year. Each member-State sends four delegates, who are nominated by its government, two of them representing the government itself, one representing the workers, and one the employers; and it is stipulated of each of the two last that they shall be representative of the most important organisations in their respective States.[59] Each delegate is entitled to be accompanied by two advisers for each item on the agenda of the Conference, though advisers may not vote; it is thus possible for any particular problem to be treated by an expert from one of the three angles involved. The Conference has a President, and three Vice-Presidents, who must be of different nationalities and belong to the three classes of the Conference. The President, who neither debates nor votes, organises the working of the Conference and enforces its standing orders. Any delegate can move resolutions, providing that at least two days' notice of his intention is given; but proposals relating to expenditure are first referred to the Governing Body which examines and reports upon its financial implications to the Conference. Voting is normally by show of hands, and no vote is valid unless it totals one-half the delegates present. Methods also exist for the enforcement of the closure, and for the introduction of emergency resolutions. The order of proceedings in the Conference is determined by a Committee of Selection composed of twenty-four members; twelve of these represent governments, and six each employers and workers respectively, no State having more than one member. These are chosen by the groups of delegates in the respective categories. There is a committee on credentials of delegates; a committee, which need not consist of delegates, on drafting, to which is entrusted the drawing up of recommendations or conventions out of the decisions of the Conference; and the groups into which delegates are classified choose, with the Selection Committee, such other committees as are necessary for the work of the Conference. All the committees have a chairman, and the minority, if there is one, has the right to present and explain its dissent in a separate report. All the secretarial work of the Conference is performed by the staff of the Labour Office.

The decisions of the Conference take two forms; they may be either draft conventions or recommendations, and either, to be accepted, must be adopted by a two-thirds majority of those voting at the Conference. A convention is so drafted that it may practically be written into the legislation of each member-State without important alterations. It has all the details of substance and exception of a normal English statute. Conventions, when ratified, must be accepted in their complete form, and remain in force for at least ten years. But though every State is bound to submit draft conventions to its appropriate legislative tribunal, it is not bound to ratify them, its sovereign power, thereby, remaining unimpaired. Recommendations differ from conventions in being mainly statements of general principle which States are advised to adopt as best they can; but their ratification may be either partial or complete, and there is no period within which they cannot be repealed. They also must be submitted within a year, at most eighteen months, to the appropriate ratifying authority in each State, just as in the case of a draft convention. It is, however, notable that no method seems to exist of compelling the submission of Conference decisions to these authorities; and it is notable that the Draft Convention for a forty-eight hour week, probably the most important single decision of the Conference, has not yet been presented for ratification by any member-States which are permanent members of the Council of the League.[60]

Such a bare outline of anatomy does much less than justice to what is not merely an important, but, so far, by all odds the most successful, part of the machinery of the League of Nations. Any discussion of it involves two related groups of questions. We have to inquire, in the first place, into the significance of what the Labour Office has actually done; and we have to examine, in the second place, into the value of the powers at its disposal for the end it has in view. Its actual achievement is divisible into two parts. There is, first of all, the legislation, as it may not unfitly be termed, of its Conferences; and there is, secondly, the vast body of information and research it has, often for the first time, made available. Its legislation covers a wide field, though one may note that, whereas its first three Conferences were prolific in Draft Conventions, at the fourth and fifth only recommendations were adopted. It has legislated upon such subjects as the hours of labour, the employment of children, the right of association for agricultural workers, the use of white lead, a weekly rest in industry, night work for women, the medical examination of young persons at sea; in the first three Conferences, apart from recommendations, seventeen draft conventions were adopted. Of these, Esthonia, among members, has the place of honour, since its legislature has ratified fifteen of them; Great Britain has ratified eleven; Japan, seven; Italy, five; and France, one; some of the smaller States, like Finland, Holland and Sweden, have also proportionately good records in ratification. Certain of the members—Chile, for example, and Germany, Italy, and Holland—have also introduced various measures involving ratification. What, in hard, material fact, is the value of these draft conventions? They serve, broadly speaking, three large general purposes. They are, in the first place, an announcement of the irreducible minimum standard of industrial life, as that standard is acceptable to the common consciousness of modern States. They are, secondly, a very real weapon in the hands of the labour movement in each State concerned; for they constitute an index to policy which has real value for the purpose of securing social advance. They are, thirdly, a means of forcing upon backward States standards of legislation which are essential to the welfare of the poorer classes throughout the world.

As at present organised, however, there are obvious lacunae in the mechanism of draft conventions. The duty of submission for ratification ought to be peremptory; and the government of each State ought, on failure to submit, to be called upon to give a satisfactory explanation to the Governing Body of the Labour Office. But, also, when ratification has been completed, we need a process of inspection far more complete than now exists. There is, of course, a machinery for the formulation of complaints against States which have failed to carry out covenants they have ratified; but that is, clearly, machinery of the last instance, and it omits provision for the more subtle form of evasion. It would be a great advantage if, year by year, both the government, on the one hand, and representative industrial associations, on the other, were asked annually to report to the Labour Office on the operation of such conventions as were supposed to be working; and the Labour Office itself should, every three or five years, inspect the administrative methods used to enforce their operation. It should, further, be realised that many of them, if they are to be satisfactory, depend entirely upon the presence in each State of strong trade unions; and in Japan and Hungary, for example, the law itself, or the administration of the law, practically prohibits the very existence of trade unions. The sooner, moreover, ratification is made to follow upon the adoption by the Conference of a convention, the more likely are they to be treated seriously by those who support them. The wide divergence between adoption and ratification suggests that, so far, States have not been inclined to view conventions as much more than urgent recommendations. And since that purpose is already served by the recommendation itself, the greater obligation of the convention needs to be thrown into more striking relief.

Another point in relation to the Conference is important. At present the Government of each State not only has twice the number of non-official delegates, but it also, though in agreement with representative organisations, nominates the latter as well. That is probably unexceptionable in cases where, like England and Germany, the labour organisation is powerful enough to secure that its view of who represents it is fairly certain to prevail; but that will not always, as the difficulty with Holland has shown, be the case. It is probably, therefore, more satisfactory to allow industrial associations, whether of employers or of workers, directly to appoint their own representatives. Otherwise, there is a real danger, especially in those States where trade unions are weak, that the government will be tempted to choose worker-delegates whose vote it can rely on for its own purposes. The difficulty in relation to employer-representatives is a different one. The need of the Conference is, undoubtedly, for the attendance of men actually engaged in industry rather than the permanent officials of business organisations. "The latter", says Mr. Behrens,[61] "are apt to endeavour to get quick party "scores" which will gain the recognition of superiors, rather than take the longer and more statesmanlike point of view". Of government delegates this, above all, should be said, that, so far as the problem of distance permits, they should always be the Minister of Labour and his chief official adviser. There is literally no other way of bringing home the significance of the Conference to the government of the day in each State. By that means, above all, the proper bridges of contact can be built, and an international official responsibility can be created without which draft conventions are not likely to be effective.

Much the most interesting type of work performed by the Labour Office is in the direction of research. Here, certainly, the basis upon which its effort has been built represents a diplomatic departure of the first importance. For its principle is the right to communicate directly with the persons of parties interested in its problems without going through the channels of government offices in the various States. That represents a recognition that the information upon which its conclusions will be based are not likely to be adequate if they are built solely upon the knowledge that official sources are prepared to supply. There are, consequently, many problems upon which the information collected by the Labour Office is the only real source of adequate judgment; and its headquarters are bound, increasingly, to become the most important centre in the world for any industrial research which seeks for a broad basis in its inductions. The fact, moreover, that its publications are the product of minds of the most diverse types has the advantage of making them largely free from the danger that any special emphasis is accorded to a particular national view. The important question here arises of what research the Labour Office is to undertake. "There is always a danger", says the Director in his Report,[62] "of the protagonists of certain opinions and certain causes making the International Labour Office an instrument for the collection and compiling of statistics to support their interest and to help them in attaining their particular ends". That is undoubtedly the case; and it involves, I think, organising with some care the organs entitled to demand that researches should be undertaken, where these are of a special kind. One can easily conceive, for instance, that comparative statistics of output in a given trade might be used to promote longer hours, or dilution of skilled labour, unless there are careful safeguards.

In general, I think, the methods adopted might be upon the following lines: (1) All investigation must be undertaken that is asked for by the Conference; (2) all investigation must be undertaken that is asked for by the Governing Body; (3) all investigation must be undertaken that is demanded by a majority of one of the three groups in the Conference, subject to the approval, by a majority, of the Governing Body. Other investigations, where they are of a minor kind, will clearly depend upon the Director's views. If they are important, and objection to them is taken, the Director should submit them to the Governing Body with his own recommendations as to action. It is, I suggest, clear that the bulk of the normal work of the Office must be what may be termed continuous in character, like the Annual Reports, in Great Britain, of the Chief Inspector of Factories; and that investigations of magnitude should be undertaken in response to specific demand. The more, of course, such large-scale inquiries permit of transformation in annual reports upon their substance, the better it will be for the work of the Office. So far as possible, moreover, it must be less a conclusion-making body than a fact-finding body; for its influence and reputation will depend almost entirely on the confidence it can inspire. In general, it is for the Conference to make conclusions, and for the Office to supply the material out of which they can be made. Or, alternatively, conclusions should be reached by the advisory Commissions of experts of which I have already spoken.

But it is of the first importance that the Office should take no narrow view of the boundaries of its research. Labour is not an abstract entity which can be divorced from the total social environment in which it is placed. The Office deals, for instance, with vocational education; but it cannot usefully collect facts upon that subject without also explaining their relevance to education as a whole. It cannot explain the nature and functions of works councils without, simultaneously, discussing also their impact upon trade-union organisation. America, for instance, is the home of the "company union", with, often enough, institutions for discussion of considerable magnitude; but a discussion of their incidence would be worthless which did not also take account of the degree to which they are deliberately intended, as in the ironworks of Colorado, to act as a barrier against the development of industrial unionism of the normal form. So also, if in a wider sphere, with unemployment. The Office could not, to-day, usefully investigate its causes without examining the relationship of currency methods to its incidence. This implies, of course, a close co-operation with the Economic Section of the League itself; but, beyond such co-operation, it implies a duty also on the part of the Labour Office to follow out the ramifications of its problems into whatever direction the facts may lead them.

One final remark may be made. An organisation with over fifty members, speaking the most varied and dissimilar tongues, is obviously concerned very greatly with the question of how to make its work known in an effective and enduring way. In part, of course, that is accomplished by the translation into the languages of member-States of the more important publications of the Office; in part, also, it is attempted by making the Director and his chief colleagues representatives on mission in an effort, by speech and interview, to explain the functions and achievement of the Office; in part, again, it is effected by the publicity in the press for the work of the League, especially of its conferences. All this, no doubt, is to the good. But it may be suggested that, even collectively, these methods are not finally adequate. It is above all important that the Conferences of the Office should be held not merely in Geneva, but, occasionally, in every region where it deserves to have influence. In Japan, in South America, in the Balkans, it is more likely to make its way by showing itself as a living thing than by all the publications it can ever issue; in particular, I believe, it is much more important that it should meet in States where Labour conditions are bad than, as in Geneva or Washington, where they are in the van of development. Much, further, could be done, by organising, on the same basis as the full Conference itself, special regional conferences where local difficulties could be discussed, and resolutions, perhaps, passed in the shape of recommendations to the Conference proper. And it is vital to the Labour Office that its main regular publications should be available in every language in which they are likely to be read. That may mean, of course, the publication of special journals rather than the translation of existing ones; the problem is one of adapting means to ends. Certainly it is urgent that not the Office only, but the League also, should acquire the habit of thinking of language, not as a barrier to impede, but as one to transcend. There is every reason for limiting the languages of official use; there is no ground for limiting the languages of possible utility. The Labour Office is not likely to meet, for a long time, with difficulties of a grave kind in the more advanced industrial countries. That is all the more reason for making itself influential in those regions where its influence is more greatly needed.

## (iv) Conclusion

International government as far-reaching as that here outlined is, of course, a new experiment in the history of the world. Men have for centuries sought the means of peace without a desert as the condition of peace; those whose names bear an honourable place in that tradition—Postel, Penn, the Abbé Saint-Pierre—have seemed even to our own generation to belong to the category of Utopian thinkers. Yet, after all, the Utopia of one century is the reality of its successor; and if the hypotheses we have here laid down are dismissed as Utopian, that does not mean that they are unnecessary or impractical. For we are so often the prisoners of our old traditions that we do not recognise our presence in a new world.

Every claim, of a certainty, that has been made against the principles of international government can be shown to be false as it has been applied. The national interest of the States concerned has not suffered diminution; their administrative independence has remained secure. The love of men for their kith and kin can be not less real in its atmosphere than it was in the days of Napoleon. The right of a State to retain a monarchy or to become a republic has not altered. The decisions in which it has become involved are made by itself not less than by others, as it is affected by those decisions; and those which concern itself alone are, not less than before, matters about which it retains a full autonomy. We have learned, indeed, that through international organisation we can transcend the narrow limits of geographical boundaries. We can unify interests which, like those of the wage-earners of the world, were hampered and frustrated by frontiers. We have learned, also, that whenever protests are made against international government in the name of national prestige those who make the protests, as England in the case of Egypt, have always something to conceal. We have realised, in brief, that the territory between States which seemed to the last generation a permanently uncharted hinterland is, in fact, not less susceptible of organised government than that which has already been mapped and surveyed.

But two great problems remain to trouble the lawyer and the sceptic. The lawyer can understand sovereignty. He can grasp the concept of a State wrapped in the majestic garments of irresponsibility, declaring its own will, and being subject to no other will save its own. This mysterious realm of obligations, half-legal, half-moral, in which the State may obey itself, but is yet constrained to reliance upon others, has nothing of the simplicity in which juristic concepts have moved since the beginning of the seventeenth century. Sovereignty in international law gave him definite sources of reference. He knew by whom the State was bound. What Hegel called the "indwelling unity" of things was reduced thereby to measurable proportions. The State which was the guardian of the world, but not itself a factor in an organised moral world,[63] had behind all the sanction of traditions of which he was the guardian and interpreter. To move from these concrete and hard realities to an international society where the State was but a One in a Many without definition being conferred upon its manyness was to leave the brightness of day for a twilight world where all things were vague and obscure.

Yet, after all, it is the facts which compel this movement. The sovereignty of States is seen to be a fiction as soon as they attempt the exertion of their sovereignty. Their wills meet with one another; they cannot cut a clear and direct route to their goal. Their wills meet, because their relations grow ever more intimate, and the institutions of the sovereign State fail to express the moral wants of those intimate relations. We have therefore required institutions to embody the *sittlichkeit* which arises from their interaction. We find them in building a vehicle of spiritual unities and giving to its decisions the power to bind the separate wills related to them. We discover, in short, that the sovereignty of the State is a power only to fulfil certain purposes and obligations; and with the emergence of the great society those purposes and obligations are, in their largest outline, capable of definition only by an organ in which the single State has influence but not ultimate power. The lawyer is witnessing, in fact, the transformation of the sovereign State into a unity of local importance in a vaster community of which it is a part. That vaster community will, as it grows into the common consciousness of men, take to itself the power and authority that it needs to fulfil its end. It will, of course, move slowly and obscurely in its beginnings; and the lawyer who is troubled by this transaction will do well to remember that the modern State did not spring full-born from the Reformation. Men did not at once take Bodin for gospel; and, when they did, they discovered that his was a gospel which remained true only by not being applied. That has been the history also of States in their international context. But because there is danger that, as with France under Napoleon, or Germany under the Hohenzollern, States may seek to give substance to their sovereignty, what we have done is to arm against them the moral consciousness of an organised world. But the lawyer finds moral consciousness inadequate as a source of legal reference.

For he argues with Hobbes that "covenants without the sword are but words, and of no strength to secure a man at all". But the sword is in the Covenant; only the method of organising its use is different from in the past. At this point the sceptic intervenes. The thing, he argues, cannot be done. Englishmen will not, in the last resort, fight at the bidding of Frenchmen and Germans, of Serbians and Italians. They will be masters in their own house; and if their own house is the world, then they will be masters of that world. For to rely upon other States for justice is to really upon broken reeds. Their interests are not the same as English interests; their wants are not English wants. Human nature does not possess the ingredients from which may be hammered out the solutions of right reason. The world is on the side of the big battalions, and to write fine words on paper is not to win victories.

The poison of Machiavelli is in our blood; and certainly he who read the record of history would be entitled to his pessimism. "Most successful men", wrote Lord Acton,[64] "deprecate what Sir Henry Taylor calls much weak sensibility of conscience", and he quotes the famous remark of Lord Grey that the intercourse of nations cannot be strictly regulated by the rules of morality. If by this is meant that men will often enough care so passionately for the end they seek as to be negligently about the means by which they attain it, no one, I suppose, will deny its truth. But for all men there exists what Tocqueville called a *patrie intellectuelle,* and the history of mankind is the history of their allegiance to it. The purpose served by States is the purpose served by the fragmentary communities of the Middle Ages; they serve, by the barriers they create. To secure self-government against the absorptiveness of power. But exactly as those communities could be embraced, without moral loss, in a larger system, so, it may be urged, can the States of our own time yield to the pressure of needs greater than, and beyond, themselves. Either they must abandon their right, or we must surrender the scale on which we seek to live. For that scale involves, by the inherent logic of its nature, the pursuit of purposes to which private interests must be sacrificed or, rather, its purpose is such that only by its realisation can private interests themselves be realised. If there is any lesson in the results of history, it is above all the lesson that we cannot attain ends in carelessness of means; for the means enter into the end and transform it. To make private success the goal is impossible to any State which seeks survival in a world of States. For reckless pursuit of that undefined chimera is, in the end, fatal to existence. It destroyed Louis XIV; it destroyed Napoleon; it destroyed Germany. It destroyed them because they exalted private interest over public well-being. They saw good only in terms of their own desires; and that blindness has, in the end, brought with it its own penalty.

We need not deny that evil is real, and that the pain men have suffered is something for which there can be no compensation. We need not, either, insist that there is an unfolding purpose in the world which, whatever we do, will realise itself. What there is of purpose in the world, what soul of goodness also, is there by the deliberate effort of men. That, after all, is the groundwork of hope. Amid passion and differences, amid, also, the passion of differences, we are able dimly and yet securely to discern interests of mankind that make them one and indivisible. For the interests of men are less and less set by the geographical frontiers of the nation-State. Social organisation has transcended those limited boundaries. The working-classes of the world are beginning to see that a quarrel between the rulers of Serbia and Austria is not their quarrel; the scientists of the world know that the increase of their wisdom is a matter of international co-operation; the consumer realises that he is a world-citizen whether he likes it or not. States as the ultimate units of mankind cannot express those group-consciousness in any real or enduring way. They can, doubtless, exploit the instinct of man to love his own herd and delude him into a belief that obedience to their orders is identical with right conduct. But a term is being set to that power of exploitation by experience.

We are being driven, in fact, to see the position of the nation-State in new proportions, as one only in the varied groupings of mankind. We can see developing beneath the older structure new organs expressive of needs thus far only half-conscious of themselves, but increasingly anxious for a larger development. They can attain their maturity only as the nation-State combines with others in an order at once more integrated and more various than we have thus far known. But combination means the sacrifice of primacy and its replacement by co-operation. Co-operation means principle, and principle in its turn means standards. We are evolving instruments which greatly add to our power of avoiding the delusions through which, in the past, we marched to war. Humble men are being led by education to dream of a life in which they realise beauty and the joy of living. An East that was once unchanging has become conscious of newer and larger destinies. In Africa we ourselves are seeking to avoid the bitter wrongs of earlier experiments with the simpler peoples. It is too early to say that we shall succeed; it is even too early to claim that we ought to succeed. But, at the least, there is in the world a growing impatience at the exploitation of man by man. There is a fuller sense, more widespread and more deeply felt, that the inheritance of the world is not the possession of a few, and that for the others life is merely an endless toil. We have discovered the significance of equality; and its demands upon us are not likely to be less than the demands we have known in the name of freedom.

The sovereignty of the State, then, is in process of disappearance in international affairs because it has served its purpose there. It no longer enfolds and absorbs the allegiance of the individual; his loyalties are as diverse as his experience of life. As he grows into the consciousness of the world; so does he reduce that world to the service of his personality. He is coming to see that the categories utilised by the State when it sought freedom from religious bondage are no longer valid. What he requires is not the concepts of imperialism, but the concepts of federalism. What he has come to see is the futility of independence in a world which is interdependent. There are concerns where he will allow intervention from none. There are matters where with those about him of his own kindred he claims the right to self-determination. Beyond, there are the greater issues which he sees are the common concern of mankind. It is the paradox of self-government that, to be free, he must share with others in making the rules of fellowship among men. But life has taught us in the sternest fashion that without those rules there will be no fellowship, and without fellowship there will be no freedom. Either we have to make a world by deliberate plan, or we court disaster. It is a grim alternative. It makes men feel how near their feet lie to the abyss. But it is also an alternative that may prove the pathway to their salvation.

## REFERENCES

1. Cf. H.N. Brailsford, *The War of Steel and Gold*, chap. ii, pp. 88 f. The revelations of Mr. Shearer's activities at Geneva in 1927 illustrate the permanent character of this evil. See the London *Times* for October 1929.
2. This is, of course, provided for by Article IX of the Covenant of the League.
3. Cf. L.S. Woolf, *Empire and Commerce in Africa*; Norman Leys, *Kenya*.
4. Article XXIII, Clause (b), "... the Members of the League ... undertake to secure just treatment of the native inhabitants of territories under this control".
5. Cf. the remarks of W.H.R. Rivers in *The Depopulation of Melanesia*, and the remarks, *passim*, of Sir F. Lugard in his great work, *The Dual Mandate in Tropical Africa*.
6. Article X of the Covenant.
7. Article XI of the Covenant.
8. Article XII of the Covenant.
9. Article XIII of the Covenant.
10. *Ibid*., Article XIV.
11. Article XV of the Covenant.
12. Veblen, *The Nature of Peace*, p. 29.
13. Cf. D. Mitrany, *The Problem of International Sanctions* (1926).
14. See J.B.S. Haldane in the *Nation* for November 7, 1924.
15. Cf. Mr. H.N. Brailsford's *War of Steel and Gold*, chaps. ii, iii and viii, for a full discussion of these matters.
16. *Op. cit*., p. 241.
17. The best general statement against tariffs that I know will be found in Professor E. Cannan's *Wealth* (1914), chap. xiv.
18. The reader should compare Engels' *Condition of the Working Class in England* in 1844 with Miss Gladys Broughton's *Labour in Indian Industry*.
19. Article XXIII (a) of the Covenant of the League.
20. To be accurate, inter-allied.
21. Cf. J.A. Salter, *Allied Shipping Control*; and E.M.H. Lloyd, *Experiments in State Control*.
22. Cf. L.S. Woolf, *International Government*, chap. vi, for a wealth of material upon this subject.
23. *Op. cit*., p. 254.
24. *Op. cit*., p. 258.
25. Cf. E.B. Behrens, *The International Labour Office*, Appendix VII, for a full list of these up to April 1924.
26. Behrens, *Op. cit*., p. 121.
27. In Article 396.

28. Covenant, Articles I, III, V, XV, XIX.
29. Passed unanimously at the Fifth Assembly on October 2, 1924.
30. Article 21 of the Protocol.
31. At present the numbers are four and six respectively; if Russia, Germany and the United States were to join, the Council would, I assume, be increased by the addition of three other lesser States.
32. Covenant of the League, Articles, IV, XII, XIII, XV, XVI, XVII.
33. By Article XVII the League may invite non-members to submit to its authority. I am anxious that the invitation may be made merely upon request from one of the parties to the dispute.
34. Proceedings of the Second Assembly, September 1921.
35. Geneva, June 1921.
36. Paris, November 16, 1921.
37. Speech at Port Talbot, in *The Times*, November 29, 1924.
38. Article XVIII.
39. Article XXVI.
40. Article II.
41. Article V.
42. It comprises at the present time (1924) some three hundred persons.
43. See an article by Mr. C. McCarthy in P.S. Reinsch, *Readings on American State Government*, pp. 63-73.
44. *The League of Nations* (2nd edition), p. 252. I have here to record my great obligations to this invaluable book. On the Court, the best technical description is Mr. A. Fachiri's, *The Permanent Court*, (1926).
45. If, after a third ballot, there are still vacancies, a much more elaborate mechanism of choice comes into play. This has not yet been necessary. For details cf. Fachiri, *op. cit*.
46. The chief states signed this Optional Clause, sometimes with minor reservations, at the Assembly of 1929.
47. Cf. Behrens, *op. cit.*, pp. 124-5. The International Court is also, under clauses 415-20, and 423 of the Treaty of Versailles, the source of appeal for Complaints about the fulfilment of matters relating to the organisation of labour.
48. *Op. cit.*, p. 173.
49. *The Parliament Belge* (1880), 5 P.D. 197.
50. As in the *Chinese Exclusion Case*, 130 U.S. 581.
51. *Zuron* v. *Denman* (1848), 2 EX, 167; and compare *Carr* v. *Fracis Times & Co.* (1902), A.C. 176.
52. *Leviathan*, Part II, chap. xxx.
53. Part XIII of the Treaty of Versailles deals with the principles of its organisation; its standing orders were adopted at the Washington Conference on November 3, 1922. They are conveniently reprinted as Appendix V and VI of Mr. E. Behrens' *International Labour Office*.
54. Cf. Behrens, *op. cit.*, 184 n.
55. The question of what States are "of chief industrial importance" is to be settled by the Council of the League.
56. For the construction of the Commission see Article 412 of the Treaty of Versailles.
57. On the Commissions see Mr. Behrens' very interesting account, *op. cit.*, chap. vii.
58. In 1923 it had twenty-eight different nationalities among its members.
59. In the event of objection being taken to any nomination the Conference as a whole is, by decision of the Permanent Court, competent to decide on eligibility.

60. Though Belgium claims—on what grounds I do not know—to have applied the substance of this Convention without formal ratification. See the table in Behrens, *op. cit.*, Appendix VII.
61. *Op. cit.*, p. 118.
62. *Report* of the Director to the Third Conference (1921), p. 236.
63. Bosanquet, *Philosophical Theory of the State*, pp. 324-5.
64. *History of Freedom*, p. 219.

# Index